www.wadsworth.com

wadsworth.com is the World Wide Web site for Wadsworth Publishing Company and is your direct source to dozens of online resources.

At *wadsworth.com* you can find out about supplements, demonstration software, and student resources. You can also send e-mail to many of our authors and preview new publications and exciting new technologies.

wadsworth.com
Changing the way the world learns®

AMERICAN DELINQUENCY
Its Meaning & Construction

4TH EDITION

LaMar T. Empey
EMERITUS, UNIVERSITY OF SOUTHERN CALIFORNIA

Mark C. Stafford
THE UNIVERSITY OF TEXAS AT AUSTIN

Carter H. Hay
WASHINGTON STATE UNIVERSITY

Wadsworth Publishing Company

I T P® An International Thomson Publishing Company

BELMONT, CA · ALBANY, NY · BOSTON · CINCINNATI · JOHANNESBURG · LONDON · MADRID · MELBOURNE
MEXICO CITY · NEW YORK · PACIFIC GROVE, CA · SCOTTSDALE, AZ · SINGAPORE · TOKYO · TORONTO

Executive Editor: Sabra Horne
Assistant Editor: Shannon Ryan
Editorial Assistant: Cherie Hackleberg
Marketing Manager: Christine Henry
Project Editors: Debby Kramer/Jerry Holloway
Print Buyer: Karen Hunt
Permissions Editor: Robert Kauser
Production: Vicki Moran, Publishing Support Services
Text and Cover Design: Paul Uhl/Design Associates
Copy Editor: Tom Briggs
Cover Image: Danielle Epstein/Graphistock
Cover Printer: Phoenix Color Corporation
Compositor: Thompson Type
Printer: R. R. Donnelley & Sons

Printed in the United States of America
1 2 3 4 5 6 7 8 9 10

For more information, contact Wadsworth Publishing Company, 10 Davis Drive, Belmont, CA 94002, or electronically at http://www.wadsworth.com

International Thomson Publishing Europe
Berkshire House
168-173 High Holborn
London, WC1V 7AA, United Kingdom

Nelson ITP, Australia
102 Dodds Street
South Melbourne
Victoria 3205 Australia

Nelson Canada
1120 Birchmount Road
Scarborough, Ontario
Canada M1K 5G4

International Thomson Publishing Southern Africa
Building 18, Constantia Square
138 Sixteenth Road, P.O. Box 2459
Halfway House, 1685 South Africa

International Thomson Editores
Seneca, 53
Colonia Polanco
11560 México D.F. México

International Thomson Publishing Asia
60 Albert Street
#15-01 Albert Complex
Singapore 189969

International Thomson Publishing Japan
Hirakawa-cho Kyowa Building, 3F
2-2-1 Hirakawa-cho, Chiyoda-ku
Tokyo 102 Japan

 This book is printed on acid-free, recycled paper.

Library of Congress Cataloging-in-Publication Data

Empey, LaMar Taylor, 1923–
    American delinquency : its meaning & construction / LaMar T.
Empey, Mark C. Stafford, Carter H. Hay. — 4th ed.
        p.   cm.
    Includes bibliographical references and indexes.
    ISBN 0-534-50707-7
    1. Juvenile delinquency—United States.   2. Juvenile justice,
Administration of—United States.   I. Stafford, Mark C.   II. Title.
HV9104.E56   1999
364.36'0973—dc21   98-8084

Brief Contents

CONTENTS

CHAPTER THREE
The Invention of Delinquency   35

CHAPTER EIGHT
Cultural Deviance Theory   141

CHAPTER NINE
Differential Association Theory and Social Learning Theory   165

CHAPTER FIFTEEN
Integrated Theories and Some Conclusions About Theories of Delinquent Behavior   303

CHAPTER SEVENTEEN
Juvenile Court   341

CHAPTER EIGHTEEN
Rehabilitating Delinquents   373

CHAPTER NINETEEN
Conclusions: Childhood and Delinquency   397

PREFACE

1999 celebrates the centennial of the creation of the juvenile court system in America. The past two decades have witnessed remarkable changes in the American concepts of delinquency and juvenile justice: The reputation of the juvenile court has been badly tarnished; the rules that define delinquency have been altered; the philosophical foundations, the accuracy, and the policy implications of scientific theories of delinquency have been challenged; faith in the concept of rehabilitation has been seriously eroded; and current efforts at "reform" are being threatened by a resurgent, neoclassical philosophy of retributive justice. In short, we are witnessing changes in our treatment of the young that are every bit as revolutionary as was the invention of the juvenile court in 1899 or the construction of prisons and reformatories almost a century before that.

In writing this book it seemed to me that any attempt to make sense out of these remarkable changes would require more than attention to current concerns over juvenile crime rates or to contemporary debates, theories, and policy changes. Indeed, the scholarly work of the past two decades had indicated all too clearly that "delinquency" should not be conceived merely as the illegal acts of children but as a changing social construction in which rules for behavior, and society's organized reactions to it, as well as the behavior itself, should be the elements of which "delinquency" is comprised. When conceived in these terms, therefore, it became obvious that any full understanding of the phenomenon would require that it be analyzed in terms of the larger cultural and historical contexts out of which it has arisen.

As a part of culture, "delinquency" may be said to include a profoundly complex set of elements:
- An evolving body of beliefs about the nature of childhood.
- A changing set of rules designed to reinforce prevailing beliefs about childhood.
- A social phenomenon in which children not only engage in various forms of illegal behavior but, more often than adults, are the victims of that behavior.
- Elaborate bodies of social thought which we call scientific theories.
- A welfare-oriented system of justice that is applied only to children.

Each of these products of culture merits considerable attention if we are to put the total mosaic of delinquency together. Hence, each of them is treated in detail and comprises a major segment of this book.

Second, it seemed clear that much would be missed if attention was restricted solely to the impact of contemporary culture for the origins of delinquency. Many of the traditions and practices which have given delinquency its particular character in the United States derive their meaning not merely from the relatively short span of American history but from the much longer history of Western civilization. Hence, even a modest understanding of the delinquency "problem" requires a context which only history can provide. Indeed, when the various elements of delinquency—beliefs, rules, behavior, theories, and legal practices—are analyzed in historical terms, that analysis not only illuminates the past but raises provocative questions about the future. Consider but a few of those that will be examined in this book:

The nature of childhood. The juvenile court was not invented until 1899. This implies a concept of childhood that is relatively recent in the history of Western civilization. How were children perceived and treated in prior centuries? Why were attempts not made until the dawn of the 20th century to provide elaborate legal protections for them, and to circumscribe their moral as well as their criminal behavior? Even more important, how has our concept of childhood changed in recent years so that we now question the assumptions upon which the juvenile court was originally constructed?

Rules that define delinquency. Delinquent behavior can only be understood as departure from some set of desirable, conformist standards. What are those standards? How did they evolve? Why did they remain relatively unchanged for most of this century? Why are they now changing?

Delinquent behavior. Since the rules that define "delinquent" behavior are of recent origin, does that mean that such behavior did not exist in prior centuries? Since it obviously did, how was it perceived? How did society deal with it? Equally important, in what segments of our youth population does it occur today? Who are its perpetrators and its victims?

Theories of delinquency. Theories of delinquency are more than pristine guides for research. They are influential and evolving bodies of social thought. To what degree, then, do they reflect traditional as well as contemporary values and beliefs, and how might they have altered those beliefs in return? Upon what assumptions about human nature and social order are they based? How have they influenced social policy? In what way have they contributed to the current revolution in juvenile justice?

The juvenile justice system. The juvenile court was hailed as a triumph of American jurisprudence and benevolence for two thirds of this century. Why, then, has it suddenly been subjected to scathing attacks from almost every quarter? What have been the sources of those attacks? How is justice for children likely to be organized in the future? May current "reforms" be viewed as undeniable steps forward in the progress of humanity?

In short, this book attempts to tell a story. As each element in the mosaic of delinquency is unfolded, its historical evolution, as well as its contemporary state, is analyzed. Attention is paid not only to the content and adequacy of various theories, to the debate over the extent and implications of juvenile crime, or to the way in which the juvenile justice system is run, but to the place of all of these in the larger context and history of American life.

LaMar T. Empey

CHANGES IN THE FOURTH EDITION

Like the first three editions, this book tells a story about the changing construction of American delinquency. Since the publication of the previous edition, however, much has changed to affect the content of the story. Each of the chapters has been revised to reflect such changes, incorporating the latest data and research. Hence, *American Delinquency* has been revised as follows:

Part I, *The Discovery of Childhood and the Invention of Delinquency,* describes the historical interdependence of our concepts of childhood, delinquency, and juvenile justice. It is wrong to assume that historical accounts, once put forth, are forever fixed, and we have made many changes to reflect what historians continue to discover about the treatment of children in earlier times.

Part II attempts to improve our understanding of the *Extent and Distribution of Delinquent Behavior* by including the latest data from official accounts of lawbreaking as well as from self-reported and victim accounts. The "facts" about delinquency and our interpretation of them frequently change, forcing reappraisals of what it is that criminologists need to explain.

Part III deals with *Explanations of Delinquent Behavior.* During the 1980s, criminologists produced a host of studies to test these explanations, and while it has not been possible to incorporate all of them, readers will find that many new studies, including coverage of social disorganization, have been included to further our assessment of the causes of delinquency. Part III outlines and assesses the ways that labeling, radical, and neoclassical theories have contributed to a new concept of juvenile justice, one that deemphasizes rehabilitation and, in its place, stresses punishment and deterrence. This *Revolution in Juvenile Justice* began in the 1960s, and we show how it has persisted through the 1990s.

Part IV focuses on *Juvenile Justice.* As before, we present and evaluate the traditional concept of juvenile justice. However, the previous edition examined the impact of this traditional concept on the actions of the police, the juvenile court, and corrections only through the late 1960s. We now extend the discussion to include juvenile justice practices through the 1990s which includes community policing, crime prevention, and recent changes in juvenile justice such as determinate sentencing.

We would like to thank the following people for their reviews: David Brotherton, John Jay College of Criminal Justice; Judith Caron, Albertus Magnus College; William Mathias, University of South Carolina; Greg Pierce, Blue Mountain Community College; and Larry Salinger, Arkansas State University. We would like to especially thank Carter Hay for his contribution to this edition.

THE MEANING OF DELINQUENCY INCLUDES NOT JUST THE LAW-VIOLATING BEHAVIOR OF JUVENILES BUT ALSO THE REACTIONS TO THAT BEHAVIOR.

CHAPTER ONE

HOW DELINQUENCY IS CONSTRUCTED

This book is about smoking marijuana, stealing cars, skipping school, fighting in gangs, committing robbery, getting arrested, going to court, being put on probation, and getting locked up—all the different things we call **delinquency.**

People have many questions about delinquency: Why do kids violate laws? Why don't they do the things that parents, teachers, ministers, legislators, police officers, and judges consider best for them? What can people do to protect themselves from young law violators? Those are important questions that we will consider in this book. But they are not the only questions we need to consider. If we limit ourselves to those questions, we will be guilty of tunnel vision.

Few people know that *delinquency* is a relatively new word. It was seldom employed prior to the 1800s, and juvenile courts were not created until the late 1800s. Viewed historically, then, juvenile delinquency is a relatively recent phenomenon. This does not mean that youths did not violate laws before the 1800s. Behavior that we now define as delinquent has been common throughout history; but it has not always been illegal, nor has it always been called delinquency.

In the 1500s and early 1600s, young people enjoyed considerable sexual freedom. Schoolboys, said Montaigne, "practiced more vices by the age of 16 than anyone else would have by 60" (Aries, 1962: 324).

Similarly, young persons were heavy drinkers. Schoolmasters first tried to moderate student drinking and then forbade it entirely. However, students reacted by simply going to nearby taverns, where drinking was allowed.

As late as the 1600s and 1700s, European children continued the medieval practice of carrying and using weapons (Aries, 1962:315–321). Boys as young as age 5 wore swords. In the 1600s in France, schools were marked by so much violence that students eventually were forbidden to keep firearms, swords, or clubs in their rooms or bring them to class. But, even then, such weapons were merely stored in a central place for use outside of school.

There was little concern over drugs until recently, even though opium use dates back at least to the ancient Greeks (Inciardi, 1992:1). Although people did not fully understand opium's chemical properties, they clearly grasped its effects; and they used it both recreationally and medicinally. In 1805, a London youth named Thomas De Quincey (1907:179) bought some laudanum (an opium derivative) for a toothache, reported in ecstasy that he had discovered the secret to happiness, and continued to use and write about it throughout his life. Opium was introduced into the United States in the second half of the 19th century. By the end of the century, probably more Americans were addicted to it than before or since. Opium could even be purchased legally at neighborhood stores until 1914. In contrast to the present, however, the addict was typically a middle-aged white female, not a young person (Ray, 1983: 334).

It was not until the 1800s that much of the behavior that had been acceptable in the Middle Ages and only partially lamented in the 1600s and 1700s became cause for great alarm. Writing on the evils of promiscuous sex, an anonymous London author decried the extent to which novels pictured "the dissipated rake, who glories in his debaucheries . . . as humane, generous and benevolent; whilst the heedless female . . . forgets his want of principle, his diseased body, and his rotten heart" (Sanders, 1970:93). And, during an age of considerable optimism, 19th-century Americans expressed concern and fright over the behavior of youths. It was said that no decent person could safely walk the streets of San Francisco (Bell, 1962:172), and the term *hoodlum* was coined to describe members of teenage gangs (Bruce, 1959:13). Young girls, many of them under age 12, were described as "brutalized . . . by premature vice, . . . with harsh laughter and foulness on their lips, . . . with thief written in their cunning eyes and whore on their depraved faces" (Nevins and Thomas, 1952, 2:56). It was reported that New York City police officers would enter the central Manhattan area near Broadway only if they were armed and in pairs (Bell, 1962:171).

How should such past events be interpreted? What should we make of our current concern with delinquency? Two interpretations are possible: (1) Either the behavior of young people has somehow grown worse over the centuries, or (2) changes have occurred in the way we now define and react to such behavior. Many historians conclude that the latter interpretation is probably more accurate. Delinquency is a relatively recent social creation. It is a concept that focuses our attention on forms of youthful behavior that, although common throughout history, have caused increasing concern in recent centuries.

That conclusion is very important. Members of a particular society tend to take that society for granted, as if its beliefs and practices were universal. For example, modern Americans tend to believe that children always have been treated as they are now. Most believe that children are born fragile and innocent. To ensure their proper development, children must be safeguarded by their parents. They must receive a long and carefully directed education, and only after many years of moral and physical "quarantine" can they be allowed to move into adulthood. It is the failure of this quarantine from the adult world that causes delinquency. Thus, it surprises those who unquestioningly accept these beliefs to discover that such beliefs have not always prevailed—that children have not always been perceived as delicate and innocent and that their departure from innocence has not always been defined as delinquent.

All societies have strongly held beliefs about children, but the content of these beliefs may differ greatly (Jenks, 1996:7). Something like delinquency, which is seen as a problem in one society or at one point in time in several societies, may not be seen that way in other societies or at other times. One cannot understand delinquency, therefore, merely by looking at the illegal behavior of children or by focusing mindlessly on current issues, such as whether working mothers ought to stay home with their children, whether marijuana ought to be legalized, whether more police officers and judges are needed, or whether everything would be all right if there were more child psychologists. A broader perspective is needed, one that not only looks at the undesirable behavior of children but also questions why that behavior is now of overriding concern. Without revealing the whole story, the remaining sections in this introductory chapter provide a preview of the issues we will be examining in this book by helping to spell out the broader meaning of delinquency.

CREATION OF CHILDHOOD AND DELINQUENCY

The modern juvenile court exists as a result of widespread beliefs that children are different from adults and therefore require special legal protection and special care. In the United States and many other countries, legal codes specify that a child can be brought under the jurisdiction of a juvenile court for one of three kinds of problems: (1) **dependence, neglect,** exploitation, or cruelty; (2) **criminal offenses** for which adults can be punished, such as robbery, assault, or auto theft; or (3) juvenile **status offenses** that apply only to children because of their age, such as drinking, truancy, or running away. Children can be processed legally for any of those problems, but they are not treated the same as adults.

With regard to the first set of problems, if children are dependent or neglected, steps may be taken to ensure that they have adequate food, clothing, and shelter. They may be removed from their homes and placed in the care of others, or their parents may be required under the threat of legal punishment to change the way they treat them.

Second, if children are charged with criminal offenses, there are special procedures for dealing with them. Furthermore, the laws stipulate that officials should help to solve their problems rather than simply punish them.

Finally, children's status offenses not only incorporate special treatment for alleged offenders but are unique in themselves. They include such things as "incorrigibility," "truancy," "waywardness," "growing up in idleness," "being in danger of lewd and immoral conduct," and "being beyond reasonable control." Children can be charged with such things, but adults cannot. And in many states, status offenses are so broadly defined and so subjective that almost any child can be referred to the courts if some parent or official believes court action is warranted.

Why is this? Why are children singled out and treated differently from adults? The answer is that **childhood,** like adulthood or old age, is a social status—a phase in the life cycle to which a special set of beliefs and expectations is attached. In most modern cultures, the implication is that children are different from adults: more innocent, less guilty of criminal intent, and more in need of both protection and discipline. The term *status offense,* in fact, implies acceptance of those beliefs, indicating that children are to be treated in a special way because of their age. This means that if we are to understand what delinquency means, why special laws apply to children, and why the juvenile court was invented, we must first explore the meaning of childhood. We cannot understand why children are singled out for special treatment until we determine how and why their special status developed.

What Is a Child?

Webster's Dictionary defines a **child** as "a young person of either sex between infancy and youth." This definition implies that there are at least three periods in the life of a young person: (1) *infancy*—the first few years of life; (2) *childhood*—the period between infancy and youth or adolescence; and (3) *youth*— the period after childhood and before adulthood. *Webster's* also agrees with most states' laws in noting that a child is "a person not yet of age," that is, someone who has not yet reached the legal age of adulthood. This means that most young people under a particular age will be treated as delinquents rather than criminals for committing a crime, and they cannot be held fully accountable as an adult until they reach that age, which is 18 in most states.

Childhood, in short, is not a clearly defined status in our society. In one sense, it is defined as ending at youth, while in another, it continues until adulthood. Although such a definition is ambiguous, its meaning is clearer when we consider several assumptions about the development of children (Jenks, 1996:123; Skolnick, 1973:316–321):

1. Children go through several stages of development. The stages broadly coincide with those described in *Webster's,* with full entrance into adulthood not occurring until the twenties or even later (Coleman, 1974). The developmental process takes that long to complete.
2. Throughout the stages of development, children are qualitatively different from adults: "Adults work and are responsible, children play and are irresponsible; adults are controlled and rational, children are emotional and irrational; adults think abstractly, children think concretely; adults are sexual, children are asexual; and so on" (Skolnick, 1973:316).
3. Until children's full emotional, moral, physical, and rational skills have been cultivated, they should be at home, in school with their peers, or in places of constructive recreation. Until they mature fully and are well educated, they should be quarantined from adult vices, activities, and responsibilities. Although the quarantine may be reduced gradually as children proceed through the developmental process, it should not be lifted entirely until adulthood.

In a very real sense, then, we view young people from birth to adulthood as children in different stages of development. Although we do not react to a 6-foot, 200-pound 16-year-old in the same way we react to a 5-foot, 85-pound 10-year-old, we do not view either of them as fully responsible. Instead, we see them at different stages in the growing-up process. That is why our society is ambivalent about granting full rights to young people, even those attending college. Although we have lowered the age at which people can vote, we are reluctant to grant 18-year-olds full recognition as adults until they have completed school and found regular employment. And even then, parents, employers, professional sports coaches, and politicians tend to call them "kids"—young people who are not quite mature or experienced enough to merit full acceptance as adults.

How Old Is the Concept of Childhood?

Many historians suggest that our current concept of childhood is largely a product of the past few centuries. Before that time, much less attention was paid to the development of children. The young people we call children today were regarded more as small or inadequate versions of their parents than as special beings in need of protection and nurturing. Many unwanted children, particularly girls, were put to death at birth, deliberately abandoned, sold into prostitution, or, at best, left to be raised by others. Even when the children were wanted, many parents were not greatly involved with these children except to help preserve the family line or serve some economic purpose.

For parents who could afford it, the preferred method of caring for babies was to send them out to be **wet-nursed** by women who rented out their breast milk and services. If the wet-nursed baby survived the first few years of life, it was soon apprenticed to another family to learn skills appropriate to its station in life, whether noble or commoner. Children were not spared, as they are now, from full participation in hard work, lewd jokes, sexual acts, or adult greed and manipulation. All of these became a routine part of their lives at very young ages.

The modern notion that growing up requires careful guidance through a series of physical, moral, and intellectual stages was alien to most societies throughout Western history. Not until Europe began to awaken from the intellectual hibernation and so-

THE "JOE CAMEL" CONTROVERSY

Antismoking groups have attacked "Joe Camel," alleging that the advertising cartoon character encourages smoking among children. Such an attack reflects a belief among many Americans that children should be protected from adult vices, such as smoking, because they are not mature enough to understand the consequences of such behaviors. Although all states currently restrict the sale of tobacco products to youths, it was not too long ago that children were allowed to smoke, drink, and engage in sexual acts with few restrictions. It is a modern concept that children are different from adults and need to be safeguarded.

them fully accountable for their acts and to pardon those found guilty of crimes. But, as mentioned previously, it was not until the late 1800s that the first juvenile court was created and not until almost 1950 that every U.S. state had one. The view of delinquency as something uniquely applicable to children had been gaining increased acceptance for many years. However, only when Americans had prepared special machinery for dealing with delinquency was its full impact as a unique social creation actually felt.

Our first task in assessing the meaning of delinquency will be to consider this fascinating history in greater detail. In doing so, we will seek to identify factors that led to the discovery of the modern concept of childhood and the goals of the social reformers who invented delinquency.

Are the social creations of childhood and delinquency living up to the high expectations associated with them? Many critics today are not sure. Though they may not want to return to the child-raising practices of the Middle Ages, neither do they sweepingly endorse our current treatment of children. They suggest instituting new reforms.

cial stagnation of the Middle Ages did a few moral philosophers begin to question the customary treatment of children. Over the next two or three centuries, age-old tendencies either to exploit or to ignore children were replaced with a concern for their welfare. Parental care for children replaced the **apprenticeship system;** and childhood became a transitional period in which protection from, rather than participation in, adult activities became the norm. Out of this process grew the **modern concept of childhood,** which stressed that children have value in their own right and, because of their sweetness and simplicity, require careful preparation for the harshness and sinfulness of the adult world.

It was only after childhood became a special phase in the life cycle that the perceived need for a special court for juveniles began to emerge. Along with the changing concept of childhood, there was an increasing tendency to be less harsh with children charged with crimes. Though children were still subject to the same laws and courts as adults, officials were increasingly inclined to refrain from holding

RULES THAT DEFINE DELINQUENCY

The process of discovering childhood and inventing delinquency involved the gradual evolution of an elaborate set of social rules or norms to govern the lives of children. First came a set of informal rules that, before they ever were written into law, helped to create an ideal image of childhood toward which parents were expected to strive in raising their children. That image is now changing, but the social rules that helped to shape it are very familiar to us: Children should be protected from the evils of drinking, sex, and other adult vices; they should be self-controlled, modest, hardworking, and diligent in their educational and other pursuits; and they should be submissive to the authorities who guide them in those pursuits. It goes without saying that they should not commit the dishonest acts and predatory crimes of adults.

Several characteristics of rules like these are central to the meaning of delinquency. First, such rules define and distinguish between desirable and undesirable behavior. Not only do they indicate how the ideal child ought to behave, but they become the standard for indicating when he or she is misbehaving. Thus, where there are rules, there is rule breaking. For the young, rule breaking may be relatively minor, like talking back to one's parents or failing to do the dishes; or it may be more serious, like getting kicked out of school or using heroin. Because rules are the standards by which behavior is judged as good or bad, attention must be paid to the nature and character of those rules. It is not very productive to be concerned only with delinquency without looking at the rules that define it. It is like trying to eat soup with a fork.

Second, as reformers sought to moralize the young, protect them from exploitation, and safeguard their premature induction into a corrupt adult world, they looked at the age-old acts in which the young customarily had engaged and discovered immorality. In seeking to make children more virtuous, they defined more of their acts as deviant and narrowed the range of acceptable conduct.

It was out of the long evolutionary process of developing new rules to govern childhood that delinquency was invented. Eventually, the informal controls of families, schools, and neighborhoods no longer seemed adequate for ensuring conformity to the rules. Therefore, formal legal rules were adopted, and a juvenile justice system was created to enforce them. From the seeds of vague and informal changes beginning in the 1500s, formal legal structures were created in the 1800s and 1900s.

Third, many historians suggest that it was a white, middle-class image of childhood that led to these legal changes. Such an image overlooked the fact that in Western societies, including American society, all people are not cast in the same mold. American society is pluralistic, with a variety of racial, ethnic, and social class differences. All young people are not taught to conform to the social and legal rules by which delinquency is judged. Moreover, opportunities to conform and thereby escape censure are not distributed equally.

It is for all these reasons and many more that a review of the rules by which delinquency is judged will constitute our second main focus. On the one hand, organized human societies imply the existence of social rules; without them, people cannot coexist. On the other hand, existing rules are not necessarily sacred and need not prevent us from asking some important questions: To what extent is there agreement or conflict about existing rules? Under what circumstances may rules, perhaps more than rule breakers, be at fault? To what degree do existing rules fail to achieve the goals for which they were created?

It is rare for everyone to adhere willingly to existing rules. Is this due to an innate perversity, or does it signal the need for even greater attention to the rules by which conduct is governed? Conversely, rule violations may become so extensive that human predators threaten both the physical and psychological well-being of the many. What should be done?

There was a time when rules seemed immutable because they were products of a relatively unchanging world, but that time has passed. Today, change is rapid and ubiquitous. For this and many other reasons, we will be exploring the rules that determine what delinquency is, the degree to which the rules are violated, and the way the rules are enforced.

BEHAVIOR THAT VIOLATES RULES

If media accounts about delinquency are to be believed, the nation is under siege from an army of kids gone berserk. For example, we hear reports of juveniles involved in drive-by shootings and killings in schools over athletic jackets and shoes. To be sure, many neighborhoods are infested with gangs, and students are searched routinely for weapons in some schools. If our attempt to discover the meaning of delinquency is to be successful, however, we must go beyond sensational accounts. Not only do they fail to paint an accurate picture of the serious offenses committed by children, they also fail to acquaint us with the less serious kinds of delinquency, such as the status offenses with which adults cannot be charged. In pursuit of a more accurate picture, we will be looking at delinquency from three perspectives: official, self-report, and victim.

For the first perspective, we will use accounts of delinquency from official sources, particularly the police and juvenile courts.

For our second perspective, we will turn to surveys in which young people are asked how many and what kinds of delinquent acts they have committed. Social scientists began collecting such **self-reports** because they suspected that (1) many children commit delinquent acts without ever being caught by legal officials and (2) official records are often a better indicator of the behavior of legal officials than the behavior of young people. That is, they reveal whom officials were lucky enough to catch, on what segments of the youth population they concentrate their attention, with what kinds of illegal acts they are most concerned, and so on. When young people self-report what they have done, their accounts do not always conform to many traditional beliefs about who is most delinquent. Thus, they provide us with a different perspective on delinquency.

For our third perspective, we will turn to the victims of delinquency and crime. President Lyndon Johnson appointed a special commission in 1967 to study crime and delinquency and make recommendations. As part of that effort, the commission initiated the first national survey of crime victimization (President's Commission, 1967). The survey found that there were far more victimizations than there were crimes reported to law enforcement officials. After that, the U.S. Department of Justice, in collaboration with the Bureau of the Census, began to conduct annual **victimization surveys.** These more recent surveys indicate that the results of the first survey were no fluke: The large gap between victim and official accounts continues to appear.

EXPLANATIONS OF DELINQUENT BEHAVIOR

Explanations of delinquent behavior—theories about why juveniles commit delinquent acts—constitute the next major set of issues that will be reviewed. Some explanations emphasize irresponsible parents and psychological abnormalities. Others stress poverty and the lack of opportunity. Still others focus on the way delinquency may result from associations with the wrong kinds of peers. To fully understand such theoretical explanations, we will look not only at their more obvious aspects—factors such as family conditions, social class membership,

or delinquent friends—but also at the assumptions about **human nature** and **social order** on which they are based.

Theories of delinquency have changed markedly over the past several centuries, not because they were always given a thorough test, but because of the changes in the way children (and adults) are viewed. As the basic ideas of influential philosophers, religious leaders, and other reformers have changed, so have their theories. Indeed, only in recent times have we stressed the word *theory* and applied scientific methods in attempts to understand delinquency. In earlier times, few attempts were made to empirically test influential ideas. It is important, therefore, to pay attention to the many ideas that predate empirical scientific inquiry and to determine how they affect our current thinking.

Thomas Hobbes (1957), a 17th-century English philosopher, assumed that humans are predatory by nature. According to this view, if there is no enforcement of rules, people are governed by such passions as the desire for power, self-preservation, and personal gain. If one seeks to explain delinquency, one need look no further than the inborn tendencies of young persons. And because they are naturally delinquent, there is nothing to be explained. The real task thus is to find ways to control their naturally brutish tendencies and to train them to be law-abiding citizens.

By contrast, some 18th-century philosophers, such as Cesare Beccaria (1963), an Italian, and Jeremy Bentham (1948), an Englishman, emphasized the doctrine of free will and assumed that individuals are governed by reason, not passion. In pursuit of their own interests, people seek to maximize pleasure and minimize pain. According to this view, delinquency results from the exercise of a rationally directed free will and a desire to maximize personal satisfaction. If young people believe they can gain more pleasure than pain by committing delinquent acts, they will do so. If not, they will refrain from committing them.

The ideas of Beccaria and Bentham were so influential that long before they could be tested systematically, they found their way into the laws that govern crime and punishment. They became the foundation for what is now called the **classical school of criminology.** Because rule breaking was believed to result from the exercise of free will, much less attention was paid to why people commit illegal acts than to how punishment could be used to convince them that crime does not pay.

Yet a third set of theories reflects the same forces that produced the modern concept of childhood and the idea that children must be nurtured. These theories reject the notion that people are completely free to choose how they will behave. Instead, they suggest that behavior is determined by factors over which an individual has little control. Theories of this type range from the commonsense idea that children's family, friends, and neighbors strongly influence their behavior to highly sophisticated ideas advanced by biologists, psychologists, and sociologists. Ultimately, however, all imply that human behavior is determined, not free. Whether people become thieves, carpenters, professional athletes, or lawyers, their careers will reflect how they were raised and with whom they have associated.

The implications of that type of theory are profoundly different from Hobbes's idea that people are naturally inclined toward evil or Beccaria's idea that they are free to choose between good and evil. Such differences might be unimportant were it not for the fact that elements of all three types of theory underlie our modern juvenile justice system. Hence, we must be aware of this and seek to determine how much they and other traditional ideas affect our current explanations of delinquent behavior.

SOCIETY'S REACTIONS TO DELINQUENT BEHAVIOR

American society is organized to react to delinquent behavior in certain ways. The reactions both reflect and influence what form our explanations of delinquency take, how serious it is assumed to be, and whether children are treated differently from adults. Before the creation of a separate juvenile justice system, legal officials were supposed to react to youthful lawbreakers ages 7 and older in the same way they reacted to adult offenders. After the "discovery" of childhood, however, pressures for change eventually resulted in a new system. That system currently is made up of police officers, prosecutors, defense at-

torneys, courts, probation officers, correctional institutions and their personnel, and a host of other public and private personnel and agencies charged with addressing the problems of difficult children. Most of those problems involve **law-violating behavior,** but the law is written so that the problems might be of almost any conceivable type—emotional, educational, economic, or social. As originally conceived, the juvenile justice system was to become society's *superparent.*

Whenever there was a breakdown in another social institution, such as the family, school, or neighborhood, the juvenile justice system was supposed to solve it. How did all this come about? The criminal justice system is designed primarily to deal with adult crime. Why was the juvenile justice system expected to become a superparent? The answer lies in the evolution of Western culture and its changing treatment of children.

There was a time in American history when children helped to colonize the nation and extend the frontier. Later, they worked on farms and in factories, contributing inexpensive and much needed labor. The consequences, at least according to current standards, were both good and bad. On the one hand, youths were seen as economic assets, and their separation from the world of adult work was not so great as now. On the other hand, children did not always realize much direct benefit from their labors. In our terms, they were exploited largely because vestiges of the medieval apprenticeship system were present in pre-20th-century America and because the economic system relied on cheap labor. In the colonial era, they were indentured to farmers and artisans. Later, they were employed in sweatshops, mines, and factories and forced to work up to twelve hours a day for a pittance, sometimes under the most miserable conditions. The children of the poor, in particular, were little more than slaves. Indeed, children had virtually no protection under the law. They were expected to be obedient and to accept the subservient roles assigned to them. If they got into trouble or disobeyed authority, the right to punish them rested with their masters, not the state.

Today, by contrast, child labor laws, designed to prevent the exploitation of children, also prevent meaningful employment for many who would like to work. Several factors have contributed to this state of affairs, including (1) the belief that children are harmed by premature toil and responsibility, (2) technological developments that have reduced the demand for unskilled labor, and (3) a level of affluence that permits the nation to support its children without them having to contribute much economically. As a result, meaningful participation in economic affairs by young persons has dwindled. Apprenticeship, which until the 1900s was the main method by which children learned their future societal roles and thus gained their educations, is virtually nonexistent. Instead, families and schools have become increasingly important.

In part, it is because families and schools often failed that the juvenile justice system was created. Although it was clearly expected to get children out of adult jails, courts, and prisons, the system also was designed to enforce society's view of children. With regard to education, for example, many delinquency laws stipulate that a child can be defined as delinquent for defying school authority, truancy, or dropping out. Likewise, instead of requiring that children obey their apprenticeship masters, laws require that they obey their parents.

After attempting to fulfill the role of superparent for much of this century, the juvenile justice system has been undergoing changes every bit as revolutionary as those that led to its initial creation. Modern reformers have grown disillusioned with the notion that the system can be an effective superparent and are seeking to limit its power and influence. It is difficult to predict whether these reforms will lead to desirable outcomes. The desirability and acceptability of social change depends more on the emergence of new values and beliefs than on some immutable standard of goodness.

The best we can do to determine whether we approve of current changes or want the juvenile justice system to operate as it has in the past is to examine such questions as the following: How and why is childhood organized the way it is? What special institutions, particularly legal ones, have been set up to govern children's lives? What kinds of people, with what kinds of values, provide leadership in those institutions? What kinds of changes are now being introduced? And how will such changes likely affect the future?

SUMMARY AND CONCLUSIONS

This introduction has suggested that delinquency is a social construction comprising not only the illegal acts of children but many other social phenomena as well. Hence, the remainder of this book is organized to take them into account:

- *Part One* is concerned with the creation of childhood and delinquency—the discovery of childhood, the invention of delinquency, and the ways childhood and delinquency are defined according to American norms.
- *Part Two* is concerned with the extent and distribution of delinquency as indicated by official accounts, young people themselves, and victims of law-violating behavior.
- *Part Three* is concerned with explanations of delinquency, the assumptions on which they are based, and their implications for the way delinquents are viewed and treated.
- *Part Four* is concerned with the legal institutions that society has created to enforce its beliefs about children. Part Four also considers revolutionary changes of recent years: the growing disillusionment with the concept of rehabilitation, the emergence of a new concept of childhood, and transformations in the juvenile justice system and the treatment of children.

DISCUSSION QUESTIONS

1. What is childhood, and how is it a social status?
2. In anticipating the study of delinquency, why do you think juveniles commit delinquent acts?
3. How are status offenses different from criminal offenses, and how do status offenses reflect the modern concept of childhood?
4. For what kinds of problems can a child be brought under the jurisdiction of the legal system?
5. How is delinquency a recent social creation?

REFERENCES

Aries, Philippe. 1962. *Centuries of Childhood: A Social History of Family Life.* Translated by Robert Baldick. New York: Random House.

Beccaria, Cesare. 1963. *On Crimes and Punishments.* Translated by Henry Paolucci. Indianapolis, Ind.: Bobbs-Merrill.

Bell, Daniel. 1962. *The End of Ideology,* 2nd ed. New York: Collier Books.

Bentham, Jeremy. 1948. *An Introduction to the Principles of Morals and Legislation.* Edited by Laurence J. Lafleur. New York: Hafner.

Bruce, Robert V. 1959. *1877: Year of Violence.* New York: Bobbs-Merrill.

Coleman, James S. 1974. *Youth: Transition to Adulthood.* Chicago: University of Chicago Press.

De Quincey, Thomas. 1907. *Confessions of an English Opium Eater.* New York: Dutton.

Hobbes, Thomas. 1957. *Leviathan.* London: Oxford University Press.

Inciardi, James A. 1992. *The War on Drugs II: The Continuing Epic of Heroin, Cocaine, Crack, Crime, AIDS, and Public Policy.* Mountain View, Calif.: Mayfield.

Jenks, Chris. 1996. *Childhood.* London: Routledge.

Nevins, Allan, and Milton H. Thomas. 1952. *The Diary of George Templeton Strong.* 4 vols. New York: Macmillan.

President's Commission on Law Enforcement and Administration of Justice. 1967. *Task Force Report: Crime and Its Impact—An Assessment.* Washington, D.C.: U.S. Government Printing Office.

Ray, Oakley. 1983. *Drugs, Society, and Human Behavior.* St. Louis: Mosby.

Sanders, Wiley B., ed. 1970. *Juvenile Offenders for a Thousand Years: Selected Readings from Anglo-Saxon Times to 1900.* Chapel Hill: University of North Carolina Press.

Skolnick, Arlene. 1973. *The Intimate Environment: Exploring Marriage and the Family.* Boston: Little, Brown.

THE DISCOVERY OF CHILDHOOD AND THE INVENTION OF DELINQUENCY

Many historians have concluded that the modern concept of childhood in Western civilization is largely a product of the past few centuries (e.g., Aries, 1962; Jenks, 1996; Stone, 1974, 1981). They do not agree on all the important facts about childhood and the way those facts should be interpreted, but they do tend to agree that childhood has not always been a stage in life to which much importance has been attached. Indeed, the opposite often has been true. Stone (1974:29), for example, has described the historical treatment of children as a "catalogue of atrocities." How, then, did our modern concern with children come about? Why, today, do we pay so much attention to them? To adequately address such questions, we must understand two basic concepts: childhood and ethnocentrism.

CHILDHOOD

In Chapter 1, we pointed out that childhood in the United States and most Western societies has become a phase in the life cycle, separate from adulthood. There are prevailing beliefs that compared to adults, children are more innocent, less capable of evil, and more in need of protection, direction, and training. They should be allowed to confront the harsh realities of adulthood only after many years of moral and physical "quarantine" in home and school.

Childhood, however, is not something tangible, like a rock or a tree. Instead, childhood is a social construction. To be sure, young *homo sapiens*, like other young animals, are less well developed physically and intellectually than adults of the species. But it does not necessarily follow that children should sleep in a bassinet rather than in a cradleboard, be sent to school rather than farmed out as servants or apprentices, or require treatment rather than punishment for their rule breaking.

Young people exist in every society, but there is enormous variation in the values, beliefs, and social institutions that organize their lives. Childhood, as we know it, has not been universal throughout history, nor is it universal today. Instead, it is peculiar to some times and places. That is why we should be concerned with the historical factors that have given rise to our particular construction of it. Because our construction of childhood determines the way we view and organize the lives of young people, it leads us to define certain acts as delinquent, write laws to control those acts, and organize a juvenile justice system to administer the laws.

ETHNOCENTRISM

One reason it is important for us to be aware of our construction of childhood is that many people tend to be ethnocentric, that is, to use their own way of life—in this case, their concept of childhood—as a standard for judging other ways of life. Having been raised according to the dictates of their own culture, they tend to assume that those dictates are, and should be, universal. Any departure from them by another group or person is perceived as a sign of inferiority. Such perceptions, however, are serious impediments to a full understanding of the range and potential of human existence.

In the first place, ethnocentrism inhibits a full appreciation and understanding of one's own culture. Our culture has been anything but unchanging; and, if we ignore the changes, we will not have the perspective to ask important questions, seek out injustices, or recognize that alternative ways of life are possible.

Ethnocentrism also inhibits an appreciation and understanding of other cultures. An inclination to perceive others as inferior because their way of life is different overlooks the fact that their behavior cannot be judged meaningfully outside the cultural context of which they are a part. Although we may choose eventually to disagree with them and prefer our ways of doing things, it is important to recognize that behavior that they regard as truthful, right, and moral is dependent on the particular values and beliefs of their culture. Just as our construction of reality tells us we are right, their construction of it tells them they are right.

Our ethnocentrism will soon become apparent when we delve into the history of childhood and encounter practices so different from our own that they tend to shock us. But while shock may be warranted according to our standards, we will miss much that is important if that is all we experience. Childhood has been constructed differently in other times and places, not just because other people were somehow less sensitive to children than we are, but because of the unique circumstances to which they had to adapt. What we seek from our review, therefore, is some understanding of those circumstances in Western civilization so that we can place our own construction of childhood and delinquency into a larger context. Should we be successful in that endeavor, we may be better prepared to understand our own beliefs as well as those of others.

To determine how our own concept of childhood came about and how delinquency was invented, this part of the book is divided into two chapters:

- In *Chapter 2* we examine the period in Western history when children were treated with indifference and even cruelty, and we trace the gradual discovery of childhood and the development of the beliefs that make it what it is today.
- In *Chapter 3* we assess the transformation that the discovery of childhood brought to modern society, including the invention of delinquency and the creation of a juvenile court.

REFERENCES

Aries, Philippe. 1962. *Centuries of Childhood: A Social History of Family Life.* Translated by Robert Baldick. New York: Random House.

Jenks, Chris. 1996. *Childhood.* London: Routledge.

Stone, Lawrence. 1974. "The Massacre of Innocents." *New York Review of Books,* November 14, pp. 25–31.
1981. "Family History in the 1980s." *Journal of Interdisciplinary History* 12 (Summer): 51–86.

CHILDREN HAVE NOT ALWAYS BEEN EXCLUDED FROM ADULT ACTIVITIES, INCLUDING ADULT LABOR.

CHAPTER TWO

FROM INDIFFERENCE TO CHILDREN TO THE DISCOVERY OF CHILDHOOD

We are shocked today by child abuse; but according to many historians, practices now defined as abusive have been common for much of recorded history. If these historians are correct, children in premodern times often were treated with indifference and even cruelly exploited. Modern Americans, in contrast, have been described as child-centered to an extreme (Skolnick, 1973:314). We need to consider events over the past two millennia to understand just how this marked change came about.

INFANTICIDE

To begin with, **infanticide**—the deliberate killing of infants—appears to have been a regular practice in many ancient civilizations and, some argue, was fairly common as late as the 1700s. In the civilizations of the ancient Middle East, in Greece and Rome, and among the Gauls, the Celts, and the Scandinavians in

Europe, infants sometimes were thrown into rivers, flung into dung heaps, left to be eaten by birds and other animals of prey, or sacrificed to gods in religious rites. Ancient Roman children, for example, "whose natural parents were unwilling or unable to raise them might be exposed (i.e., put out in a public place—doorsteps, temples, crossroads, rubbish heaps) either to die or to be claimed by their finder" (Rawson, 1986:172).

DeMause (1974:25) claims that the practice of killing legitimate children diminished only slightly during the Middle Ages (roughly from A.D. 500 to 1400) while the practice of killing illegitimate children continued into the 1800s. He cites historical references suggesting that infanticide may have been punished only sporadically before the 1500s and that during the Middle Ages children were still being suffocated deliberately by their mothers or abandoned in the streets. He quotes a priest in 1527 who said that "the latrines resound with the cries of children who have been plunged into them" (deMause, 1974:29).

Likewise, Marvick (1974:282) notes that the criminal law of 17th-century France specified the conditions under which a father had the right to kill an adult son or daughter and indicates that the right to kill an infant may not even have needed official license. In England during the same period, midwives had to pledge that they would "not destroy the child born of any woman, nor cut, nor pull off the head thereof, or otherwise dismember or hurt the same, or suffer it to be so hurt or dismembered" (Illick, 1974:306). The need for such a pledge can be taken as evidence that child killings still were occurring.

Infanticide apparently was rooted in norms that defined which children should not survive (Garnsey, 1991:56). In antiquity, any child who was imperfect or cried too much might be killed. As the Roman statesman Seneca (1963:145) put it in Christ's time: "Mad dogs we knock on the head, the fierce ox we slay; sickly sheep we put to the knife to keep them from infecting the flock; unnatural progeny we destroy . . . yet, it is not anger, but reason that separates the harmful from the sound."

Historically, boys have been valued much more than girls. DeMause (1974:26) notes that the few statistics available from antiquity "show large surpluses of boys over girls; for instance, in 79 families who gained Milesian citizenship about 228–220 B.C., there were 118 sons and 28 daughters." He is implying that more girls than boys were put to death (an implication supported by Golden, 1981, and Harris, 1982, for ancient Greece and Rome, and by Atkinson, 1991:83–84, for medieval Europe). The firstborn of any family was usually permitted to live, particularly if it was a boy. Girls, however, were less desirable, as the following advice to parents reveals: "If, as may well happen, you give birth to a child, if it is a boy let it live; if it is a girl expose it [leave it outside to die]" (deMause, 1974:26). And the same pattern continued for centuries. Seventeenth-century French writers, for example, noted that there had been a surplus of boys over girls for three centuries, suggesting that greater efforts were expended on saving boys (Marvick, 1974:283–284).

ABANDONMENT

Abandonment is a practice similar to infanticide (Kertzer, 1993:18). In some cases, mothers abandoned their children for profit. In antiquity, for example, both boys and girls were sold into slavery or prostitution or used as security to pay debts (deMause, 1974:33). In other cases, babies were abandoned because their parents could not afford to care for them or simply because all of a couple's children were not prized equally. Infanticide and abandonment, rather than contraception, were methods of controlling family size (Stone, 1981:59).

In European towns of the Middle Ages, many destitute mothers or mothers of illegitimate children brought their offspring to monasteries to be raised by monks (Boswell, 1984:17). As late as the 1800s, mothers sometimes left their children on the steps of a hospital or a foundling home, if one was available; but the children were usually filthy and starving, and most died (Fuchs, 1992:12; Gottlieb, 1993: 146; Kertzer, 1993:17, 138–139; Marvick, 1974:286; Wrightson, 1983:14).

In trying to place these practices in some kind of time frame, deMause (1974:51) states that infanticide was most common prior to the 300s and that abandonment was more frequent from the 300s to the 1200s. During those periods, few questioned such practices. Boswell (1984:28), for example, has observed that early Christian moralists' concern about abandonment involved incest rather than parental dereliction of duty: "In the relatively few places where early Christian literature touched on the practice . . . , authors complained of the possibility that parents might unknowingly use as prostitutes children they once abandoned."

THE CARE OF INFANTS

Abandonment did not always take the form of leaving a child to die or selling it into slavery, nor were such practices confined to the poor and uneducated. The wealthier classes also followed child-raising practices that would constitute abandonment by modern standards.

Wet-Nursing

The first such practice was the **wet-nursing** of young children. Prior to the 1700s, most young children of affluent parents were cared for by a wet nurse. Rather than feed and care for their own children, these mothers would hire other women to perform those tasks (deMause, 1974:32–34; Gottlieb, 1993:145–151; Hunt, 1970:100–117; Illick, 1974:308; Robertson, 1974:410–411; Ross, 1974:195; Sommerville, 1982:80). Soon after birth, a baby would be placed in the home of a wet nurse until it was weaned, which could take anywhere from a few months to a few years.

Wet-nursing apparently was denounced by some for both medical and ethical reasons from the time of the ancient Greeks and Romans, but the practice continued. Infants sent to wet nurses died at a higher rate than those who remained in their own homes (Johansson, 1987:356; Sommerville, 1982:154–158; Stone, 1981:59; Wrightson, 1983:11–12). Wet nurses were often malnourished and disinterested women who had their own children to tend. Some wet nurses accepted too many babies for their supply of milk (Stone, 1974:29). Furthermore, wet nurses frequently used other commonly accepted child-raising practices that may have contributed to a higher death rate, one of which was swaddling.

Swaddling

As described by a 19th-century physician, **swaddling**

> consists in entirely depriving the child of the use of its limbs, by endlessly enveloping them in an endless length bandage . . . by which the skin is sometimes excoriated; the flesh compressed, almost to gangrene; the circulation arrested; and the child without the slightest power of motion. (deMause, 1974:37)

Swaddling was believed to serve many functions. Air, sunlight, and soap were thought to be dangerous for a child (Robertson, 1974:410–412), so the baby could be protected by keeping it wrapped tightly. A 17th-century account noted that "when the child is seven months old you may (if you please) wash the body of it twice a week with warm water" (Tucker, 1974:242). The account also advised that the bandages should be shifted often so that the "piss" and the "dung" could be managed. The accumulation of excrement and filth on a baby can only be imagined, and it is no wonder that infant mortality rates were so high.

Although swaddling was thought to be a means of protecting the child from hurting itself and ensuring that it would grow straight, it also must have been an enormous convenience to mothers and wet nurses preoccupied with other tasks (Sommerville, 1982:80). Lacking modern labor-saving devices, they had to devote most of their attention to activities other than caring for babies. While the baby was swaddled, it could be left like a parcel in a convenient corner or hung on a wall.

DISEASE AND DEATH

To put some of these historical practices in perspective, remember that premodern life was more difficult and brutal than it is today. In his novel *Shogun,* James Clavell (1975:697) presents the reflections of an English sea pilot, John Blackthorne, on the premature aging of his wife, Felicity, and on the filth in which they lived in 16th-century England:

> *Felicity*. Dear *Felicity*. A bath once a month perhaps . . . always hidden to the neck and wrists, swathed in layers of heavy woolens all year long that were unwashed for months or years, reeking like everyone, lice-infested like everyone. . . .
>
> Sleeping most of the time in your dayclothes and scratching like a contented sea dog, always scratching. Old so young and ugly so young and dying so young. *Felicity*. Now twenty-nine, gray, few teeth left, old, and dried up.

Captain Blackthorne's lament was accurate. As late as the 1600s, the average life expectancy was approximately age 30, and between one-half and two-thirds of all children died before reaching age 20 (Bremner, 1970, I:3–4; Gillis, 1974:10–11; Gottlieb, 1993:133). Living in filth, in societies lacking knowledge even of such simple (to us) diseases as measles and pneumonia or the consequences of poor hygiene and malnutrition, few children survived even among the privileged classes. For example, in colonial America, only two of Cotton Mather's fifteen children survived childhood. In one measles epidemic in 1713, he lost his wife and three children in a two-week period (Bremner, 1970, I:46). "Before they [children] are old enough to bother you," a Frenchman said, "you will have lost half of them, or perhaps all of them" (Aries, 1962:38).

Thus, the premodern child-raising situation has been described as a "melancholy procession of cradles and coffins" (Queen and Adams, 1952:211). In light of that melancholy procession, some historians have argued that high mortality rates among the young led to indifference toward them. Stone (1974:30), for example, argues that parents could not afford to invest much emotion in their children when so many of them were likely to die.

Garnsey (1991:53) believes that parental attitudes toward children were more nearly "stern realism" stemming from "high . . . fetal, perinatal, and infant mortality" than it was indifference (also see Fuchs, 1992:13; Kertzer, 1993:176–178). Yet, whatever the attitudes toward children may have been, they were very different from those of today (Atkinson, 1991:135–136). Aries (1962:28–29) notes that

in earlier times, some languages did not even include words to describe childhood and the meaning of age:

> In its attempts to talk about little children, the French language of the 17th century was hampered by a lack of words to distinguish them from bigger ones. The same was true of English, where the word "baby" was also applied to big children. . . . People had no idea of what we call adolescence, and the idea was a long time taking shape.

What, then, was the nature of family and social life for children? What role in the scheme of things did they play?

THE LIVES OF CHILDREN

Today we live much of our lives in households where contact with people from other social classes or even our own extended family is often infrequent and sporadic. In the past, by contrast, households could be far less private. The well-to-do and their servants sometimes lived together in large, barnlike dwellings, and a child returning from the home of a wet nurse might have to compete for the attention of his or her mother with as many as twenty-five other people (Aries, 1962:390–398; Bremner, 1970, I:5; Ross, 1974:195–196). Mixed together under one roof might be parents, servants, apprentices, other children, possibly slaves, and a host of visitors flowing in and out. No rooms were set aside specifically for dining or sleeping or meeting with guests or clients.

The one major exception to this kind of household involved a large lower-class population whose lives, if less communal, were spent in shacks and on the streets or in the fields. However, many poor adults and children lived and worked in the large homes of wealthier people as servants and apprentices. Hence, many were familiar with the communal living and lifestyles of the well-to-do.

Moral Rules

Prevailing conditions also meant that the **moral rules** of the time were vastly different from our own. Throughout the 1800s and 1900s, we have been very

PROTECTING CHILDREN ON THE INTERNET

Many consumer and parent groups have expressed concern about how easily children can access sexually explicit Web sites and chat rooms on the Internet, and these groups have asked Congress to impose stricter regulations on Internet use. Today, we believe that children should be shielded from information about sex and prevented from engaging in sexual behavior until they are adults. It is hard for us to imagine that it was not that long ago—only a few centuries that most people saw little reason for sexual restrictions on children.

concerned with protecting the moral innocence of children. Contrast that concern with the moral rules that prevailed in the 1500s and 1600s:

> It is easy to imagine the promiscuity which reigned in these rooms where nobody could be alone, which one had to cross to reach any of the communicating rooms, where several couples and several groups of boys or girls slept together (not to speak of the servants, of whom at least some must have slept beside their masters, setting up beds which were still collapsible in the room, or just outside the door), in which people foregathered to have their meals, to receive friends or clients, and sometimes to give alms to beggars. (Aries, 1962:395)

Consider the treatment of young Louis XIII, who was the son of King Henry IV of France (Aries, 1962: 100–103). According to the diary of Heroard, the king's physician, Louis was seen as an amusing little figure by adults. "He laughed uproariously when his nanny waggled his cock with her fingers. An amusing trick which the child soon copied. Calling a page, he shouted, 'Hey there!' and pulled up his robe, show-

ing him his cock" (p. 100). Jokes like this were repeated over and over by members of the household.

By contemporary standards, the queen played immodestly with her son. Grasping his penis at one time, she said, "Son, I am holding your spout" (p. 101). Not to be outdone, the king got into the act. While playing in bed with Louis and his sister, the king asked Louis: "Son, where is the Infanta's bundle [Louis' penis]?" Louis showed it to his father, saying, "There is no bone in it, Papa." Then, as it did distend slightly, he said, "There is now, there is sometimes" (p. 101).

Louis was married at age 14 and was put into his wife's bed almost by force by his mother. Young men who also were present told Louis some ribald stories to encourage him. After making love to his wife twice and sleeping for a while, he reported back to the group that his penis was red. That kind of behavior and familiarity between males and females of all ages was due not merely to communal living arrangements, but to a set of norms very different from contemporary norms.

The Training of Children

The methods for training children in the past also were different. The current emphasis on formal education has been confined largely to modern times. Previously, however, children received training for adulthood by working in the homes of other people as apprentices (Gottlieb, 1993:163–164; Hareven, 1985:11). The day of **apprenticeship** was a major turning point in children's lives. "Ready for semi-independence, they were dressed as miniature adults and permitted to use the manners and language of adult society" (Gillis, 1974:8). This was true, says Aries (1962:365), not only of the poor but also of the rich, "for everyone, however rich he may be, sends away his children into the houses of others, whilst he, in return, receives those of strangers into his own."

This European orientation to childhood carried over into the settling of America. Although there were changes in the concept of childhood during colonial times, older traditions still carried a great deal of weight. For example, Bremner (1970, I:5) notes that the English settled the Middle Atlantic colonies in the 1600s as individuals, not in families. And just as colonial officials sought older artisans or farmers to help in the task, they also sought young children to serve as apprentices.

In some cases, children were signed to **indenturing contracts** by *spirits,* or agents, who found workers for merchants, shipowners, farmers, tradesmen, and other settlers. Many young people wished to go to the New World and signed up voluntarily; others were kidnapped.

Because indentured persons could not pay for their passage, they were bound to serve their new masters for at least four years. The masters, in turn, could sell or reassign the contracts of indentured persons to anyone they pleased. Dependent children from the streets and asylums of England were indentured for even longer periods and were shipped to the colonies in large lots.

The treatment of dependent English children was not unlike the treatment of black children who were kidnapped in Africa and shipped to the colonies. Although there was little chance that black children would ultimately receive their freedom, as would most of their white counterparts, they were considered valuable. For example, the "exchange rate" was 3,000 pounds of tobacco for a black child between the ages of 7 and 11, 4,000 pounds for a child between 11 and 15, and 5,000 pounds for a young man over 15 (Bremner, 1970, I:16).

Although slave children and the children of the poor were the most likely to be exploited, children of affluent parents sometimes were sold on indenturing contracts as well. The important point is that children helped to settle the colonies and were viewed as sources of labor and service, not as fragile, undeveloped beings requiring long periods of special care and freedom from responsibility.

Social Control of Children

Severe punishments were used throughout the ages to control children and secure their obedience. The evidence, says deMause (1974:40–42), warrants the conclusion that by present standards, a large percentage of the children born before the 1700s could be considered *battered children.* Even supposedly enlightened persons approved of beating children. The wife of the poet John Milton, for example, complained because she did not like to hear the cries of his nephews as he was beating them, and Beethoven

used a knitting needle to whip his pupils and sometimes bit them.

There were efforts to temper the violence of child beating during the Renaissance—the transitional period between the 1300s and 1600s (deMause, 1974: 42). But rather than attempting to eliminate the practice, reformers urged adults to use instruments lighter than cudgels and to strike children about their bodies rather than on their heads. It was not until the 1700s and 1800s that child beating decreased noticeably, probably due to the emergence of the **modern concept of childhood.** Until that concept emerged, however, children were not protected.

GLIMMERINGS OF CHANGE

As Western civilization began to awaken from the intellectual and social stagnation of the Middle Ages, the glimmerings of a new concept of childhood began to emerge, albeit slowly. In Italy in the 1300s, for example, people started to exhibit ambivalence over wet-nursing. A fashionable 14th- or 15th-century mother may not have wanted to nurse her baby because it stretched her breasts too much, but at least she took greater interest in the selection of the woman who would care for the infant (Atkinson, 1991:24). The new rule was that a wet nurse "should be prudent, well-mannered, honest, not a drinker or a drunkard, because very often children draw from and resemble the nature of the milk they suck" (Ross, 1974:185). Today, of course, we reject such reasoning, but Michelangelo attributed his calling as a sculptor to the fact that his wet nurse was a stonecutter's wife (Gottlieb, 1993:146).

In 15th- and 16th-century England, the color white was increasingly used to suggest children's innocence (Tucker, 1974:232). When they died, children were dressed in white, their coffins were white, and the funeral attendants wore white. Similarly, children became symbols of godly qualities or good luck. Their images in the form of little angels were placed on gravestones or used to decorate frescoes.

In the 1500s and 1600s, artists and writers also began to attribute special qualities to children. Portraits of well-to-do families began to include children garbed in special costumes rather than in the dress of adults (Aries, 1962:33–49). It was as though adults were now seeing children through different lenses. Furthermore, wealthy women began to cuddle children somewhat more often, to be more solicitous toward them when they were hurt, and to take pleasure from them as we do from kittens or puppies today (Aries, 1962:129).

Finally, in the late 1500s and 1600s, reformers increasingly criticized the traditional treatment of children. Stressing the innocence and dependence of children, they argued that children required discipline and guidance, not exploitation or indulgence (Aries, 1962:130; Illick, 1974; Marvick, 1974; Robertson, 1974; Sommerville, 1982:108–119).

THE MODERN CONCEPT OF CHILDHOOD

Although it had taken many centuries, the modern concept of childhood was beginning to emerge. But as it did, children were perceived as odd creatures who were fragile, innocent, and sacred on the one hand, but as corruptible, trying, and arrogant on the other. "Unless you give children all they ask for, they are peevish and cry, aye, and strike their parents sometimes; and all this they have from nature. Yet are they free from guilt, neither may we properly call them wicked . . . because wanting the free use of reason they are exempted from all duty" (Hobbes, 1972: 100). Children needed to be safeguarded and receive a carefully structured education in order to ensure their proper development. The groundwork had been laid for the belief that a child "had to be subjected to a special treatment, a sort of quarantine, before he was allowed to join the adults" (Aries, 1962:412).

Sources of Change

Many factors contributed to the emergence and growth of these ideas: the Renaissance, the Protestant Reformation, the colonization of the New World, and, eventually, the Industrial Revolution. But the original impetus was from a small band of moralists, schoolmasters, and church persons who became concerned about young people and the corrupting influences on them (Aries, 1962:329–415; Atkinson, 1991:194–217; Illick, 1974:316–317; Marvick, 1974: 261; Sommerville, 1982:88–97).

John Winthrop, the first governor of the Massachusetts Bay Colony, justified the Puritan migration to America as a method for permitting young persons to escape the corruption of the Old World. The fountains of learning and religion had been destroyed, he said, such that "most children, even the best wits and of fairest hopes, are perverted, corrupted, and utterly overthrown" (Bremner, 1970, I: 18–19).

Reformers stressed the importance of formal education (Sommerville, 1982:115–116). In medieval Europe, by contrast, there was little or no interest in education. The few existing schools were not intended specifically for children, but rather resembled technical schools that prepared people, young and old, for the clergy (Aries, 1962:330). Hence, the revival of interest in education, beginning in about the 1400s, was a watershed.

Reformers also stressed the importance of parents in raising their children, seeing to it that their children were educated, and reducing the chances that they would be subjected to undue influence from nonfamily members. John Eliot, a 17th-century American churchman, phrased it well (Bremner, 1970, I:33):

> It is a very false and pernicious principle that many people and parents are trained with, viz., that youth must be suffered awhile to take their swing, and sow their wild oats, to travail into the world, to follow the fashions, company, and manner of the time, hoping they will be wiser hereafter. Oh false principle; God speaks fully to the contrary. Prov. 19:18. *Chasten thy son while there is hope, and let not thy soul spare for his crying.* Prov. 13:24. *He that spareth the rod, hateth his son, but he that loveth him, chasteneth him betimes.*

Besides advocating harsh methods of control, such injunctions spoke of love for children and the importance of attending to their moral welfare. Thus, a slow transformation in the status of children took place over two or three centuries. The lone voices of the first reformers in the 1400s became a veritable chorus by the 1600s, all attesting to the dependence of children and demanding the enforcement of newer standards of morality for them. Older practices had not disappeared, but important changes were taking place (Hessinger, 1996:135).

The Ideal Child

Based on the precepts of the new morality, many treatises and manuals were written in the 1600s and 1700s to guide parents. They set forth important principles, implicit in which was an emerging image of the ideal child. When Americans became very concerned with delinquency in the 1800s, that image still retained a great deal of currency. It was the standard by which undesirable conduct by children and failure by unworthy parents were evaluated. Indeed, there is much about the image that is still familiar today (Aries, 1962:114–119; Bremner, 1970, I:passim; Sommerville, 1982:108–119).

These principles centered on five areas:

1. *Supervision.* The first principle emphasized the importance of keeping a close watch over children. Benjamin Wadsworth, a Boston clergyman, put it this way: "Children should not be left to themselves, to a loose end, to do as they please; but should be under tutors and governors, not being fit to govern themselves" (Bremner, 1970, I:35).

2. *Discipline.* The second principle stressed the importance of disciplining rather than pampering or coddling children. It was seen as cruel to allow children to do as they pleased, to forbid them nothing, to let them laugh when they ought to cry, or to permit them to remain silent when adults spoke to them. They had to learn self-control and appropriate manners (Sommerville, 1982:110–111).

3. *Modesty.* The third principle stressed the importance of modesty. Children should *not* be permitted to go to bed in the presence of a person of the opposite sex. Young girls should be covered completely and not lie in an immodest position. Songs expressing "dissolute passions" should not be sung or even heard. Language should be pure and wholesome, and only the most chaste books should be read. Noneducational games should be avoided.

"Ordinary entertainments provided by jugglers, mountebanks, and tightrope walkers [were] forbidden" (Aries, 1962:117). Even puppet shows were considered unfit.

4. *Diligence.* The fourth principle admonished parents to bring up their children to be "diligent in some lawful business" (Bremner, 1970, I:110). Work for children was not only important economically but morally desirable. Throughout the 1700s and 1800s and well into the 1900s, adoption of the work ethic was considered a cardinal virtue.

5. *Obedience.* The fifth principle stressed a virtue that encompassed all others—respect for and obedience to authority. Children had to honor not only their parents but any authority figure because disobedience inevitably led to destruction (Bremner, 1970, I:32; Gillis, 1974:21).

Such principles may have been softened somewhat during the 1800s, but not markedly. Throughout the 1800s, in fact, key opinion makers felt that children who were not being raised by these principles should be taken from their parents and placed in institutions where they could be raised properly. Thus, not being able to govern themselves, children had to be trained to be self-controlled, modest, hardworking, and obedient.

THE ORGANIZATION OF CHILD RAISING

The new concept of childhood was accompanied by changes in the way society was organized to raise children. This does not necessarily mean that the discovery of childhood caused these changes. More likely, the various changes were both causes and effects of one another.

The Family

As we have seen, part of the change was an increasing emphasis on the importance of the family, and particularly the role of parents, in raising their children. The Puritans in colonial America were so committed to that idea that the Massachusetts Bay Colony

YOUTH EMPLOYMENT

Child labor laws substantially limit labor force participation by youths. However, child stars like Macaulay Culkin and LeAnn Rimes have earned millions of dollars. There also are young persons with lucrative sports careers, such as Olympic gold medalists Tara Lipinski and Dominique Morceanu, to name just two. What does this say about the modern concept of childhood? Do you believe that all young persons should be prohibited from pursuing *adult* careers until they are *adults*?

passed a law in the 1640s to broaden and enforce the educational and socialization responsibilities of the family and to ensure that parents carried them out. The new law required that each family teach its children a trade and how to read. Parents who failed were brought before authorities, while children who disobeyed their parents could be dealt with severely. The law also decreed that no single person, especially a young one, could live outside some family. The family was to be a guardian of the public as well as the private good (Demos, 1970:100–106; Farber, 1972:passim).

Despite such innovations, the Puritans did not discard entirely the practices of the apprenticeship system. Rather, the rules were changed. Everyone had to work if the new settlements were to survive, but instead of working for others, young children worked for their parents. Apprentices had to be age 14 or 15 before they could leave home. Furthermore, parents were warned that when they did apprentice their children, it should be to a lawful calling in a religious home (Bremner, 1970, I:110–111).

At the same time, beliefs in the innate depravity of children continued to legitimize severe physical punishment (Gottlieb, 1993:170). People took very

seriously the notion that to spare the rod was to spoil the child. Consequently, the debate was not whether children should be whipped, but at what age the whipping should begin (infancy, age 3, age 5?), how it should be administered (a birch or leather thong?), where it should be administered (bare bottom or covered?), and at what age it should cease (15 or older?). Most people preferred such methods to isolating offenders, putting them on bread-and-water rations, or tying them up; but even those methods were sometimes used (Robertson, 1974:414–420).

The School

Possibly the greatest consequence of the Renaissance and the moralists' efforts to reform child-raising practices was the emphasis placed on formal schooling for children. Though the colonial schools in America were eventually organized differently from European schools, the emphasis on education was an Old World derivative (Cremin, 1977:12).

Virtually all European schools in the 1500s and 1600s were run privately, not publicly (Aries, 1962: 269–285). Because not every town or hamlet had a school, students were recruited not only from the towns in which schools were located but from other towns and the countryside as well. As a result, students who lived too far from the school to return home each night were forced to reside in town, either as boarders, as servants on school premises, or, most commonly, as lodgers in private dwellings.

The practices surrounding the school reflect the transition of society from medieval to modern. There is evidence, for example, that boys of all classes and ages were housed together in many of the lodgings. Furthermore, the principal source of discipline and control, when it existed, was the boys themselves (Sommerville, 1982:181). As a consequence, their lives scarcely could be distinguished from those of unfettered adults. Plumb (1972:83) notes that students "lived like hippies and wandered like gypsies, begging, stealing, fighting; yet they were always hungry for books." And Aries (1962:254) observes, "There remained a great deal of the free and easy attitude of the preceding centuries."

Reformers in the New World, meanwhile, stressed the importance of schooling, but there were important differences in the way they implemented it

(Bremner, 1970, I:72–102; Cremin, 1977:19–21, 36). In the English colonies, the responsibility for education initially was divided among parents, the masters to whom older children were apprenticed, and clergy. As the education movement gained momentum, however, increasing emphasis was placed on the family and its new ally, the school. Because parents were often ill-equipped to teach their children, special provisions had to be made for educating them. Hence, along with discipline, education became an important means by which the world was to be shaped into a new and more moral pattern.

Social Stratification

The factors that helped to produce the modern concept of childhood also contributed to broad changes in the class structure. During the Middle Ages, the nobility and the commoners were the only principal groups. However, Western nations increasingly engaged in trade and commerce with other parts of the world. This trade was associated first with the commercial revolution of the 1600s and 1700s and later with the Industrial Revolution of the 1800s. In response to both revolutions, a whole new middle stratum of entrepreneurs, merchants, traders, and professionals emerged. Many historians (for example, Hareven, 1985:17) maintain that it was this middle class to whom the modern concept of childhood appealed most, at least originally.

Bremner (1970, I:343) and Platt (1969:passim) describe an American scene in which class, ethnic, and religious differences abounded and had profound effects on children. "What," asks Bremner (1970, I:343), "did . . . immigrant children in city slums, children of a doctor or minister, and children of a proud aristocrat on a plantation, or those of a wealthy New England merchant really have in common?" They had little in common; America was very diverse. The significance of that diversity lay in the likelihood that children in different social classes were being socialized in different ways. If the emerging concept of childhood was held largely by middle-class people, its influence on lower-class children would be lessened. Even more important, if the norms associated with that concept were those of the rule makers of society, then the children of the poor

likely would be penalized. Without proper induction into the world of the successful, they could not compete on an equal footing. Worse, they might be defined as deviant or unworthy to the extent that they departed from the expectations of teachers, employers, and community leaders. There is considerable evidence, in fact, that this kind of situation developed.

Aries (1962:272) reports that in 16th- and 17th-century Europe, some private scholarships and special schools were organized for the poor but that more affluent students soon co-opted such opportunities. Early American schools also favored well-to-do over poor children. But Americans were confronted with racial as well as class differences that Europeans did not face. Racial discrimination was far more widespread than class discrimination. Although dominant white groups in the colonies increasingly stressed the importance of education for their children, they did not do so for minority groups, mainly Native Americans and blacks. Some religious groups and some individuals attempted to see to it that both white and minority children were educated, but those attempts produced few results (Bremner, 1970, I:72, 335–339).

Regarding Native Americans and blacks, colonists were more concerned with their religious conversion than with their secular education. This view is captured by the remarks of a Virginia clergyman in 1724 (Bremner, 1970, I:98):

> As for the Children of Negroes and Indians, that are to live among Christians, undoubtedly they ought all to be baptized; since it is not out of the power of their masters to take care that they have a Christian education, learn their prayers and catechism, and go to church, and not accustom themselves to lie, swear, and steal, though such (as the poorer sort in England) be not taught to read and write; which as yet has been found to be dangerous upon several political accounts, especially self-preservation.

In other words, Native American and black children, like the poorer classes in Europe, were to learn and adhere to the social rules that would make them willing to accept their subordinate status. But they were not to arm themselves with the kinds of educational skills that would make them politically or socially dangerous.

In the next chapter, we will discover that the consequences of such attitudes grew even more troublesome in the 1800s as ever-increasing numbers of different ethnic groups emigrated to America— ethnic groups whose lifestyles and images of childhood differed from those of the Anglo-Saxon middle and upper classes. Although some groups were assimilated into the American culture more easily than others and the class structure of the United States did not become as rigid as that of many European countries, there were still many conflicts over the appropriate image of childhood. In fact, many contemporary theories of delinquency, as well as the operation of the juvenile justice system, are directly traceable to traditional beliefs about social class differences.

Gender Stratification

Another issue of great interest today is the effect of the modern concept of childhood on the treatment of girls. After the "discovery" of childhood, girls were spared some of the neglect and cruelty to which they had been subjected formerly, but this generally improved treatment did not eliminate the sexism of previous centuries. For example, females often could not attend 17th-century European schools, and the situation remained that way for a long time. Despite the emerging belief in the necessity to improve the intellects as well as the morals of children, it apparently was felt that the needs of girls could be fulfilled without using schools (Aries, 1962:331–333).

One French writer of the 17th century describes and criticizes the results (Aries, 1962:332):

> How many masters and colleges there are! ... This shows the high opinion people have of the education of boys. But the girls! It is considered perfectly permissible to abandon girls willy-nilly to the guidance of ignorant or indiscreet mothers. ... It is shameful but common to see women of wit and manners unable to pronounce what they read. ... They are even more at fault in their spelling.

If virtual illiteracy was characteristic of "women of wit and manners" (upper-class women), imagine what it was for other women. Aries (1962:334) maintains that "girls of good family were no better educated than girls of the lower classes." The situation was much the same in America. By the end of the colonial period, almost 90 percent of men but only about 50 percent of women could sign their names (Degler, 1980:308; Moran and Vinovskis, 1985:33). Efforts to improve boys' skills through formal education were not extended to girls until much later. In fact, the thought that girls should receive extensive formal education was largely a product of the 1800s (Degler, 1980:74, 307–309).

Age Stratification

The "discovery" of childhood also resulted in an increasing tendency to stratify people by age— to divide the life cycle into such major segments as infancy, childhood, adolescence, adulthood, and old age, and then to further subdivide those segments by year of birth or grade in school. In antiquity and during the Middle Ages, such age grading, especially where young people were concerned, seemed to be relatively unimportant (although some age grading certainly existed) (Stone, 1981:68–70; Strauss, 1976: 75–77). As the modern concept of childhood continued to grow, however, grading by age was extended further and further. Today, kindergarteners are segregated from first- and second-graders, and so on. We are very conscious of the ages of childhood, and our social institutions, our beliefs, and even our scientific theories reflect that consciousness.

It may be surprising to discover that such a consciousness is mainly a function of the last century or two. Kett (1973:97), for example, notes that "the word 'adolescence' appeared only rarely outside of scientific literature prior to the 20th century." Instead, it was given prominence in 1904 by G. Stanley Hall, whose two-volume work, entitled *Adolescence*, described adolescence as "a second birth, marked by a sudden rise of moral idealism, chivalry, and religious enthusiasm" (Kett, 1973:95). Yet in less than a century, consider how extensively adolescence has been defined as the last stage of childhood and how adolescents are relegated to a childlike status:

1. Following Hall's original work, a parade of works emerged describing adolescence as the "awkward age" and noting its relationship to school problems and delinquency.
2. Adolescents largely have been eliminated from the job market.
3. The period of formal education has been extended to the late teens and early twenties.
4. Adolescents increasingly have been segregated from adults and expected to confine their primary relationships to their peers.
5. Adolescents have become a burden on the family, rather than contributing economically to its welfare. Moreover, parents have become less and less capable of imparting specific work skills to their children, because parents and children no longer work together (Coleman, 1974; Kett, 1973, 1977).

Our society, in other words, is organized to separate children from adults and to provide ways for taking the presumed developmental stages of childhood into account (Hareven, 1985:18). The invention of delinquency, the creation of the juvenile court, the drafting of child labor laws, the legal requirements regulating the age for compulsory school attendance, the emergence of pediatrics and child psychiatry, and the development of elementary and secondary schools—all are reflections of our modern construction of childhood.

SUMMARY AND CONCLUSIONS

Childhood has not always been viewed as a special and highly protected phase of the life cycle. In other words, *littlehood* is not the same thing as *childhood*. The deliberate killing or abandonment of children was common until the 1100s or 1200s. Between the 1300s and 1600s, infanticide and abandonment did not disappear, but they became less common, particularly for legitimate children. Nonetheless, newborn babies still were farmed out to wet nurses, and young children still were sent to the homes of others to serve as apprentices and servants.

Infants were thought to exist "in a sort of limbo, hanging between life and death, more as a kind of animal than a human being, without mental activities or recognizable bodily shape" (Skolnick, 1973: 333). Many languages lacked words to distinguish babies from those we now call adolescents or young adults, and young persons were not shielded from depravity, work, sex, or death. "The cruel truth . . . may be that most parents in history have not been much involved with their children, and have not cared much about them" (Stone, 1974:29).

In contrast to the premodern view, the modern concept of childhood suggests that children must be safeguarded stringently and receive a carefully structured education. Only after many years of moral, physical, and intellectual quarantine can they be allowed to join the adult world. It took many centuries, however, for this concept to develop and become a part of the institutional fabric of American society.

Small children became symbols of innocence and purity in the 1400s and 1500s when people began to take increasing pleasure in them. New moral standards for the young began to appear in the 1500s and 1600s, as did a new emphasis on parental responsibility for the welfare of children. Schools solely for young people became common. Finally, stratification of society by age became an accomplished fact in the late 1800s and 1900s.

The consequences of this extended process were significant. By the mid-1900s, childhood had become a long transitional period in the life cycle. Community solidarity across generational and social class lines was virtually nonexistent. Families, schools, and peer groups had replaced apprenticeship and interaction with nonfamilial adults as the primary sources of socialization, and the new morality for children had stripped them of adult pleasures and responsibilities.

The costs of those changes in economic terms would have been unbearable had it not been for the labor-saving technology introduced by the Industrial Revolution. For the first time in Western history, society eliminated a huge segment of its population—its children—from productive work in the labor force. Nonetheless, for social as well as economic reasons, the presumed benefits of the changes were not distributed evenly.

Lower-class and minority children not only were kept in the labor force and denied educational opportunities for a much longer period of time but were socialized at home in ways that hindered their chances of adapting to the new concept of childhood. In a similar but less obvious way, gender differences persisted. Although girls undoubtedly were affected by the altered child-raising practices of the family, they remained locked into traditional roles.

As a result, the institutionalization of childhood clearly has had mixed consequences. Infanticide is now rare, most babies are raised and loved by their parents, and most children are not exploited. But there is a darker side to the picture. In seeking to moralize the lives of children, reformers looked at age-old behaviors and discovered immorality. In seeking to foster conformity, they defined more of the acts of children as deviant. And in encouraging greater discipline and control, they narrowed the range of acceptable childhood conduct.

In the next chapter, we will inquire further into this side of childhood. Rather than looking only at the ideal image of childhood, we will be examining its counterpart, delinquency. We will focus on how delinquency was invented, why it was invented, and who invented it. Specifically, we will examine how, after discovering childhood, reformers were forced to decide not only how the ideal child might be produced but also how to deal with children who appeared to depart from the ideal.

DISCUSSION QUESTIONS

1. What does it mean to say that "*littlehood* is not the same thing as *childhood*"?
2. Suppose you are a child and a time machine has transported you to Europe during the Middle Ages. How would you behave, and how would this differ from your behavior as a modern child?
3. Suppose you are a child and a time machine has transported you to the 22nd century (the 2100s). Would the 22nd-century concept of childhood differ from that of today, and if so, how?

4. What was the image of the ideal child in the 1600s and 1700s? Is there anything about that image that is still familiar today?
5. How has the modern concept of childhood affected the treatment of girls?

REFERENCES

Aries, Philippe. 1962. *Centuries of Childhood: A Social History of Family Life.* Translated by Robert Baldick. New York: Random House.

Atkinson, Clarissa W. 1991. *The Oldest Vocation: Christian Motherhood in the Middle Ages.* Ithaca, N.Y.: Cornell University Press.

Boswell, John E. 1984. "*Expositio* and *Oblatio*: The Abandonment of Children and the Ancient and Medieval Family." *American Historical Review* 89 (February):10–33.

Bremner, Robert H., ed. 1970. *Children and Youth in America: A Documentary History.* 3 vols. Cambridge, Mass.: Harvard University Press.

Clavell, James. 1975. *Shogun: A Novel of Japan.* New York: Dell.

Coleman, James S. 1974. *Youth: Transition to Adulthood.* Chicago: University of Chicago Press.

Cremin, Lawrence A. 1977. *Traditions of American Education.* New York: Basic Books.

Degler, Carl N. 1980. *At Odds: Women and the Family in America from the Revolution to the Present.* New York: Oxford University Press.

deMause, Lloyd. 1974. "The Evolution of Childhood." Pp. 1–73 in Lloyd deMause, ed., *The History of Childhood.* New York: Psychohistory Press.

Demos, John. 1970. *A Little Commonwealth: Family Life in Plymouth Colony.* New York: Oxford University Press.

Farber, Bernard. 1972. *Guardians of Virtue: Salem Families in 1800.* New York: Basic Books.

Fuchs, Rachel G. 1992. "Child Abandonment in European History: A Symposium." *Journal of Family History* 17:7–13.

Garnsey, Peter. 1991. "Child Rearing in Ancient Italy." Pp. 48–65 in David I. Kertzer and Richard P. Saller, eds., *The Family in Italy: From Antiquity to the Present*. New Haven, Conn.: Yale University Press.

Gillis, John R. 1974. *Youth and History*. New York: Academic Press.

Golden, Mark. 1981. "Demography and the Exposure of Girls at Athens." *Phoenix* 35 (Winter): 316–331.

Gottlieb, Beatrice. 1993. *The Family in the Western World from the Black Death to the Industrial Age*. New York: Oxford University Press.

Hall, G. Stanley. 1904. *Adolescence: Its Psychology and Its Relations to Physiology, Anthropology, Sociology, Sex, Crime, Religion, and Education*. 2 vols. New York: Appleton.

Hareven, Tamara. 1985. "Historical Changes in the Family and the Life Course: Implications for Child Development." Pp. 8–23 in Alice Boardman Smuts and John W. Hagen, eds., *Monographs of the Society for Research in Child Development* 50 (4–5, Serial no. 211).

Harris, William V. 1982. "The Theoretical Possibility of Extensive Infanticide in the Graeco-Roman World." *Classical Quarterly* 32:114–116.

Hessinger, Rodney. 1996. "Problems and Promises: Colonial American Child Rearing and Modernization Theory." *Journal of Family History* 21 (April):125–143.

Hobbes, Thomas. 1972. *Man and Citizen*. Edited by Bernard Gert. Garden City, N.Y.: Anchor Books.

Hunt, David. 1970. *Parents and Children in History: The Psychology of Family Life in Early Modern France*. New York: Basic Books.

Illick, Joseph E. 1974. "Child-Rearing in Seventeenth Century England and America." Pp. 303–350 in Lloyd deMause, ed., *The History of Childhood*. New York: Psychohistory Press.

Johansson, S. Ryan. 1987. "Centuries of Childhood/Centuries of Parenting: Philippe Aries and the Modernization of Privileged Infancy." *Journal of Family History* 12:343–365.

Kertzer, David I. 1993. *Sacrificed for Honor: Italian Infant Abandonment and the Politics of Reproductive Control*. Boston: Beacon Press.

Kett, Joseph F. 1973. "Adolescence and Youth in Nineteenth Century America." Pp. 95–110 in Theodore K. Rabb and Robert I. Rotberg, eds., *The Family in History*. New York: Harper & Row. 1977. *Rites of Passage: Adolescence in America, 1790 to the Present*. New York: Basic Books.

Marvick, Elizabeth W. 1974. "Nature Versus Nurture: Patterns and Trends in Seventeenth-Century French Child-Rearing." Pp. 259–301 in Lloyd deMause, ed., *The History of Childhood*. New York: Psychohistory Press.

Moran, Gerald F., and Maris A. Vinovskis. 1985. "The Great Care of Godly Parents: Early Childhood in Puritan New England." Pp. 24–37 in Alice Boardman Smuts and John W. Hagen, eds., *Monographs of the Society for Research in Child Development* 50 (4–5, Serial no. 211).

Platt, Anthony M. 1969. *The Child Savers: The Invention of Delinquency*. Chicago: University of Chicago Press.

Plumb, J. H. 1972. "The Great Change in Children." *Intellectual Digest* 2:82–84.

Queen, Stuart A., and John B. Adams. 1955. *The Family in Various Cultures*. New York: Lippincott.

Rawson, Beryl. 1986. "Children in the Roman *Familia*." Pp. 170–200 in Beryl Rawson, ed., *The Family in Ancient Rome: New Perspectives*. Ithaca, N.Y.: Cornell University Press.

Robertson, Priscilla. 1974. "Home as a Nest: Middle Class Childhood in Nineteenth-Century Europe." Pp. 407–431 in Lloyd deMause, ed., *The History of Childhood*. New York: Psychohistory Press.

Ross, James B. 1974. "The Middle-Class Child in Urban Italy, Fourteenth to Early Sixteenth Century." Pp. 183–228 in Lloyd deMause, ed., *The History of Childhood*. New York: Psychohistory Press.

Seneca. 1963. *Moral Essays*. Translated by John W. Basone. Cambridge, Mass.: Harvard University Press.

Skolnick, Arlene. 1973. *The Intimate Environment: Exploring Marriage and the Family.* Boston: Little, Brown.

Sommerville, C. John. 1982. *The Rise and Fall of Childhood.* Beverly Hills, Calif.: Sage.

Stone, Lawrence. 1974. "The Massacre of Innocents." *New York Review of Books,* November 14, pp. 25–31.
1981. "Family History in the 1980s." *Journal of Interdisciplinary History* 12 (Summer):51–86.

Strauss, Gerald. 1976. "The State of Pedagogical Theory c. 1530: What Protestant Reformers Knew About Education." Pp. 69–94 in Lawrence Stone, ed., *Schooling and Society: Studies in the History of Education.* Baltimore: Johns Hopkins University Press.

Tucker, M. J. 1974. "The Child as Beginning and End: Fifteenth and Sixteenth Century English Childhood." Pp. 229–257 in Lloyd deMause, ed., *The History of Childhood.* New York: Psychohistory Press.

Wrightson, Keith. 1983. "Infanticide in European History." Pp. 1–20 in Henry Cohen, ed., *Criminal Justice History: An International Annual,* Vol. 3. Westport, Conn.: Meckler.

EARLY JUVENILE COURT JUDGES WERE TO ACT AS WISE FATHERS BY RESPONDING TO THE PROBLEMS OF CHILDREN AND CORRECTING THEM.

CHAPTER THREE

THE INVENTION OF DELINQUENCY

Throughout history, children have committed acts that today not only would be defined as delinquent but could require that parents and other adults be charged with contributing to their delinquency. During the Middle Ages, and even as recently as the 1600s, most children learned and used obscene language and gestures, and many engaged in sex at very young ages. They drank freely in taverns. Few of them ever attended school; and when they did, they sometimes wore sidearms, instigated brawls, and fought duels (Aries, 1962; Sanders, 1970).

Today, these same acts occur, but they are illegal, and officials are charged with curbing them. How did that change come about? How should the modern response be interpreted? Two interpretations are possible: (1) Either the undesirable behavior of children has increased over the centuries and become more serious, or (2) marked changes have occurred in the way the behavior is defined. The latter is probably the more accurate interpretation. As the concept of **childhood** grew and expanded, the meanings attached to it were altered considerably. Children's actions that in earlier times had not been seen as particularly troublesome now became sources of concern. New norms and expectations developed as childhood became a special phase in the life cycle.

Although it was not until the 1800s that most laws applicable only to children were written and a juvenile court was created, we must begin our analysis in the 1700s. Delinquency did not come about suddenly, but was the product of considerable cultural change, demographic upheaval, and institutional experimentation (Schlossman, 1977:55).

EIGHTEENTH-CENTURY CHILDHOOD AND ORGANIZATION[1]

Although Puritan child-raising practices were by no means universal throughout the colonies, the moralist principles they espoused—self-control, modesty, hard work, and obedience—had considerable impact on 19th-century reformers. Furthermore, small colonial towns were well suited to implementing those principles.

Few individuals or families in colonial times commanded the resources to free themselves from dependence on their neighbors. Life was dominated by a subsistence existence in which cooperation was vital: "Common goals demanded community action" (Rothman, 1971:12). Most people were Protestant and worshiped at the same church. Marriages turned many neighbors into relatives, and daily contacts with a limited number of people fostered a reliance on strong, informal social control. In short, community interdependence and insularity encouraged local control, an emphasis on individual responsibility, and a distrust of outside influence. There were exceptions, of course, especially toward the end of the 1700s. But even then, people still had

to band together to build water lines, protect themselves, and care for the old, the sick, and the poor.

Family, Church, and Community

Life in the 18th century was dominated by three major social institutions: family, church, and community. "Families were to raise their children to respect law and authority, the church was to oversee not only family discipline but adult behavior, and the members of the community were to supervise one another to detect and correct the first signs of deviancy" (Rothman, 1971:16). The values and beliefs surrounding those institutions provided whatever explanations or solutions were needed to deal with the behavior of children and adults.

The tracts and sermons of the day identified the functions of the family and the rules for fulfilling them (Moody, 1970; Wadsworth, 1970). Parents were to love their children and provide for them. As the Bible states: "He that provides not for his own, especially those of his own house, hath denied the faith, and is worse than an infidel" (1 Tim. 5:8). Conversely, as the following catechism indicates, children were expected to reciprocate with obedience and respect (Bremner, 1970, I:32):

> *Question:* What is the fifth commandment?
> *Answer:* Honor thy father and thy mother, that thy days may be long in the land which the Lord thy God giveth thee.
> *Question:* Who are here meant by father and mother?
> *Answer:* All our superiors, whether in family, school, church, and commonwealth.
> *Question:* What is the honor due to them?
> *Answer:* Reverence, obedience, and (when I am able) recompense.

Disobedience to authority could only lead to destruction.

Such admonitions revealed strong religious influences. The church tended to provide the core values around which community life was organized. The assumption was that the existing social order was divinely inspired. The church, as a consequence, set strict standards, stressed the need to observe

---

[1]The framework for this analysis relies heavily on David J. Rothman's *The Discovery of the Asylum*. Readers are invited to consult it for detailed discussion and extended documentation of many of the points made here.

them, and linked obedience to eternal rewards and punishments.

Crime and Sin

The colonists were concerned about crime and adopted harsh methods for dealing with it. But they did not see it as a serious social problem in the sense that they blamed themselves or their communities for it, nor did they expect to eliminate it. Crime and evil, they believed, were inherent in people, and therefore endemic to society (Hessinger, 1996:139; Rothman, 1971:115). To some Americans later in the 1800s, this was a pessimistic and unenlightened view that they rejected. To the colonists, however, it made sense. They equated crime with sin; hence, their criminal codes defined a wide range of behaviors as criminal—witchcraft, sexual misconduct, disrespect for parents, property crimes, blasphemy, and murder—and drew few distinctions between adults and children or between serious and minor offenses. Any offense signaled "that the offender was destined to be a public menace and a damned sinner" (Rothman, 1971:15–17).

At first glance, such thinking might seem contrary to colonists' emphasis on family life. If the seeds of crime and sin were present in everyone, why the heavy emphasis on training children? The answer is that the colonists did not share the modern belief that people can be shaped easily into some desirable form. By nature, they felt, people were inclined continually to the temptations of the flesh. The purpose of training, therefore, was to secure the strict obedience of children to rules, not to eradicate evil impulses which could never be eliminated totally. The colonists did not have a strong impulse to rehabilitate sinners; rather, their transgressions demanded **retribution.** If offenders were allowed to escape, God would be displeased.

The most common punishments were fines and whippings, but wide use also was made of the stocks, the pillory, and occasionally branding. Both the **stocks** and the **pillory** were located in a public place. The stocks held the offender while sitting down, with head and hands locked in the frame. The pillory held the offender while standing. In some instances, offenders also might be whipped. In others, they might

have their ears nailed to the pillory. Offenders also might be branded with a *T* for thief, a *B* for blasphemy, or an *A* for adultery (Barnes, 1972:56–67).

Capital punishment served a protective as well as a retributive function. The criminal codes identified a long list of capital offenses, including arson, horse theft, robbery, burglary, sodomy, and murder. The execution of offenders was a way of ridding the community of them forever. The small jails found in most towns were used primarily to hold offenders awaiting trial or debtors who had not met their obligations. The American invention of the prison was yet to come (Rothman, 1971:48–53).

The Child Offender

What was the status of the child offender in the 1700s? There was no distinct legal category called **juvenile delinquency.** Americans still relied on ancient common law that children under the age of 7 could not be guilty of a serious crime. From ages 7 through 14, they might be presumed innocent unless proven otherwise. Juries were expected to pay close attention to children; and if they deemed the children capable of discerning the nature of their sins, they could be convicted and even sentenced to death. Anyone over the age of 14 could be judged as an adult, although some colonies made exceptions. For example, in Pennsylvania, only youths over the age of 16 could receive such severe punishments for non-capital offenses as public whipping (Bremner, 1970, I:307–308; Platt, 1969:187–188).

Although a long list of criminal offenses applied to everyone, some applied only to children: rebelliousness, disobedience, sledding on the sabbath, and playing ball on public streets. In some colonies, the penalty for rebelliousness against parents was death: "If a man have a stubborn or rebellious son of sufficient years of understanding, viz. 16, . . . such a son shall be put to death" (Bremner, 1970, I:38). In other places, whipping was prescribed. In actual practice, however, courts and juries were often lenient toward the young. Children frequently were acquitted after a nominal trial or pardoned if found guilty (Platt, 1969:183).

In many ways, elaborate legal machinery for children was unnecessary in the small-town colonial environment because the family, neighborhood, school, and **apprenticeship** system served so well as methods of social control. Thus, although town members may have shrunk from punishing children as criminals, they did not shrink from treating them as subservient beings. Moreover, if a family was unable to control or educate its children, town officials could remove the children from their homes and place them in other homes where they would "receive a decent and Christian education" (Rothman, 1971:14).

The Treatment of Poverty

In the 1800s, Americans came to view poverty, along with unstable families, as a cause of juvenile misconduct and crime. Eighteenth-century Americans, however, accepted the long-standing Christian belief that the poor would always be with them (Rothman, 1971:7–14). They did not view poverty as evidence of a tragic breakdown in social organization; rather, they "serenely asserted that the presence of the poor was a God-given opportunity for men to do good" (Rothman, 1971:7).

People did not fear and distrust the poor as they would later. The more common reactions to poverty were pity and sympathy. The one major exception was the idle "ne'er-do-well" who might be told to move on to another town. But the sick, the elderly, the widow with children, or the family down on its luck received help in one of two forms: (1) *outdoor relief,* whereby they received food and care in their homes, or (2) *indoor relief,* whereby they went to live or board in the homes of others. As a result, poor adults did not live in constant dread of the poorhouse; and children did not face the prospect of confinement in an institution simply because they were destitute. Such institutions, with rare exceptions, did not even exist. It was the duty of townspeople to care for the children.

NINETEENTH-CENTURY ENLIGHTENMENT

Colonial social organization did not survive in the 1800s as Americans were subjected to changes that irrevocably altered the tightly knit communities to which they had become accustomed.

Changes in Belief

Framers of the Declaration of Independence and the Constitution relied heavily on the Enlightenment for many of their ideas (Becker, 1932). Whereas the moralists and religious reformers of the prior two centuries had suggested that people were inherently depraved and foreordained to a particular destiny, Enlightenment philosophy stressed individuality and the possibility of unlimited human progress. Through reason and application of democratic principles, people could reach unimagined heights. Optimism, not pessimism, was the cornerstone of Enlightenment thinking.

Just as they began to cast off some of their former religious beliefs, Americans began to regard aspects of 18th-century methods of social control as obsolete (Rothman, 1971:57–59). They were influenced by such Enlightenment philosophers as François Voltaire (1694–1778) and Charles de Montesquieu (1689–1755), and particularly by the Italian economist and jurist Cesare Beccaria (1738–1794). Inspired by Voltaire's and Montesquieu's attacks on the notorious abuses and cruelties of the criminal law system, Beccaria (1963) proposed a series of reforms in 1764 to make the treatment of lawbreakers more equitable, rational, and humane.

The administration of justice, Beccaria argued, should not be left to the nobility or its judicial minions. Instead, the only hope for a just and equitable system involved laws reflecting the will of the people and constraints on the officials who enforced the laws. Furthermore, laws and legal procedures would take precedence over self-serving, secretive, and arbitrary officials, and the severity of punishment would be reduced. Moderate punishments, equitably and swiftly administered, would accomplish what severe punishments could not.

Such a message squared well with the revolutionary experience. The British legal system, with its severe punishments, often had seemed arbitrary, vengeful, and ineffective to Americans. Hence, criminal codes were rewritten in the early 1800s, and steps were taken to make due process a larger part of the administration of justice. Punishments for such acts as petty larceny were reduced, and such corporal punishments as burning offenders' hands, or cutting off their ears were abolished. In some states, whipping also was prohibited, and only murder was left punishable by death (Rothman, 1971:59–61). No longer, said a number of influential reformers, could Americans abide the use of barbarous punishments, particularly for children.

Altered Explanations for Crime and Sin

New explanations for crime emerged in the late 1700s and early 1800s. More and more, Americans began to reject traditional notions that crime and sin were synonymous and that lawbreaking resulted from inborn tendencies. Instead, criminal tendencies were traced to early childhood, particularly a breakdown in family discipline. Orphaned children or the children of drunk and licentious parents were those most likely to fall prey to temptation and vice. The typical road to crime was paved first by a lack of discipline and then by drinking and intemperance. Criminals had been inadequately prepared early in life to be respectable community members (Mennel, 1973:13–15).

Another social evil—community corruption—soon was added to that of unstable families as an explanation for crime (Rothman, 1971:57–59). Between 1750 and 1850, the population increased from about 1.25 million to 23 million (Bureau of the Census, 1955). Simultaneously, as manufacturing and commerce continued to develop, the simple economic and social organization of the colonies was no longer adequate. Again, there was pressure to reconsider existing methods of social control.

The memory of small, well-ordered communities was still fresh in the minds of many Americans. Thus, when they looked around and saw hordes of new immigrants, economic change, and social instability, they concluded that those factors also promoted crime. Community disorder went hand in hand with unstable families (Schlossman, 1977: 19–20).

Such ideas demanded a major turnabout in thinking. If criminals were not innately depraved, then they could be redeemed. If young children were in danger of becoming criminals, then their misconduct could be prevented. However, such thinking did

little to alter 18th-century child-raising principles. Indeed, if families and communities were at fault, then even greater attention to childhood was required. Parents were warned of the dire consequences of a lack of discipline and admonished to take stern measures against any loss of family control.

Rothman (1971:76) states that 19th-century Americans were so sensitive to childhood and so concerned with moral matters that "they stripped away the years from adults and made everyone into a child." Yet they also were faced with serious questions: How was **social order** to be maintained? What were the best ways to reduce the harmful effects on children of inadequate family discipline and community disorder?

THE INSTITUTION AS A PANACEA

In seeking answers to those questions, Americans took a step that impacted the future treatment of both children and adults in trouble—a step that was to alter dramatically the search for community solutions to crime that had characterized colonial society. Of the many possible methods for rehabilitating offenders and preventing crime, the reformers chose **confinement.** They built prisons for adults and houses of refuge for children. Asylums for abandoned children had been used in England and elsewhere in Europe for some time. However, it was a new idea to use places of confinement to punish and correct criminals *and* to substitute for the family and community. Confinement also was viewed as an enlightened alternative to the traditional brutal methods of control and punishment (Bremner, 1970, I: 122; Schlossman, 1977). Through the mercies of incarceration, rather than physical torment, stigma in the stocks, or death on the scaffold, criminals would learn the errors of their ways.

Pennsylvania led the way in 1790 by converting the Walnut Street Jail in Philadelphia into a state prison and in 1829 by erecting the huge Eastern State Penitentiary. Not to be outdone, New York City erected Newgate Prison in 1796 and built a rival to

Pennsylvania's huge edifice around 1820 at Auburn. Other states soon followed suit (McKelvey, 1968: 6–11).

The first **houses of refuge,** designed to separate children from hardened adult criminals, were built by private philanthropists in New York in 1825, in Boston in 1826, and in Philadelphia in 1828 (Mennel, 1973:3–4). Several assumptions led to their construction. First, they were designed to house not just young criminals but all problem children, including runaways, rebels, and vagrants who were presumed to be in danger of falling prey to the sorts of evils found in taverns, gambling halls, and theaters. Reformers were not bothered that they might be infringing on the rights or wishes of those children. "A good dose of institutionalization could only work to the child's benefit" (Rothman, 1971:209).

Second, the sponsors and managers of the first houses of refuge took the public school, not the family, as the model to be emulated. Children would be saved through education, hard work, and discipline rather than through the loving care of parental surrogates.

Those who managed houses of refuge, says Schlossman (1977:24), were very frank in describing them "as an instrument for compelling lower-class children to conform to middle-class standards of behavior." They would deter crime and "would reinforce the crumbling authority of impoverished parents . . . , giving them a potent symbol of fear with which to scare 'ungracious and disobedient' children into humility and quiescence."

In short, the purpose of houses of refuge was to produce ideal children. It caused considerable shock, therefore, when they were branded as failures by a new generation of reformers.

Failures of the Panacea

By 1850, criticisms of houses of refuge had begun to mount, and by 1870, there was an overwhelming demand for change. Rather than models of care, the houses of refuge had become prisonlike warehouses for large numbers of children from the margins of society. Furthermore, said Elijah Devoe, assistant superintendent of the New York City House of Refuge, corporal punishment was "liable to be used everywhere at all times of the day" (Schlossman, 1977:35).

Joseph Curtis, superintendent of the New York City House of Refuge, "put one boy in leg irons for forty-three days and another in cloth handcuffs which the boy ate off in order to escape" (Mennel, 1973:19). Rather than turning out ideal children, houses of refuge were producing young people who either marched, thought, and acted like robots or were more criminal than ever (Bremner, 1970, I:696–697; Rothman, 1971:258–260).

In response, one group argued that the exemplar for saving troubled children should not be the large institution, but the family; a rural home was considered the best reformatory (Mennel, 1973:35–42, 48; Schlossman, 1977:45). Beginning in the 1850s, therefore, thousands of children were sent each year away from large cities to live and work on farms—a practice known as **placing out** (Mennel, 1973:35). Indeed, that practice exemplified the colonial belief that "the place for the poor in a Christian community is the home of those who are not poor" (Schlossman, 1977:46). But in the face of momentous social change and a large population of children, the practice was destined to fail.

In addition to the Civil War, the second half of the 1800s was marked by more urban growth and social instability. Immigrants, moreover, were seen as contributing disproportionately to this mess (Mennel, 1973:15–16). As early as 1850, children of foreign-born parents composed almost three-quarters of the population of the New York City House of Refuge, more than half the population of the Cincinnati Refuge, and two-thirds that of the Philadelphia Refuge (Rothman, 1971:261–262). Furthermore, immigrants alarmed native-born Americans with their unfamiliar customs—different religions, strange sexual habits, and new ways of talking and behaving. And because those customs were disapproved, they further contributed to the belief that immigrants were inferior and a threat to the social order.

The tendency to deprecate immigrants, the poor, and criminals was also reinforced by new scientific theories in the second half of the 1800s. Americans heard about Charles Darwin's notion that life is a competitive struggle for existence and that only the fittest survive. One interpretation was that some people are biologically predetermined to succeed, and others to fail. Destitution, poverty, and crime were believed to result from innate inferiority (Hofstader, 1959:31–50).

The Italian physician Cesare Lombroso (1836–1909) lent further credence to such notions when he proposed that many criminals are born, not made. According to Lombroso, many criminals were throwbacks to a more primitive level of human development. Other criminals, he believed, were mentally defective (Gould, 1981:123–143; Mennel, 1973:83–84; Vold and Bernard, 1986:37–40).

Such notions were reflected in the thinking of leading reformers. Enoch Wines, one of the most prominent American reformers of the 1870s, believed that criminals had three great "hindrances": depravity, physical degeneracy, and bad environment (Henderson, 1910:12, 19). Peter Caldwell, a reformatory superintendent, said that the typical delinquent was "cradled in infamy, imbibing with its earliest natural nourishment the germs of depraved appetite, and reared in the midst of people whose lives are an atrocious crime against natural and divine law and the rights of society" (Platt, 1969:52).

Institutionalization Reaffirmed

Such thinking most likely led a new generation of reformers after the Civil War to reaffirm the utility of children's institutions, despite their initial failure. The task of saving children, if anything, had taken on more monumental proportions:

> This whole mass of pestilent and pestiferous juvenility is already supported at your expense. . . . They all have mouths to feed and bodies to be clothed . . . not only at the expense of your purses, but at the far more extravagant and alarming expense of your public and private morals. (Report of Joint Special Committee, Hartford, 1863:2–7, in Sanders, 1970:401)

Reformers believed that the fault with institutions lay in their methods, not in their goals.

In the Cincinnati Prison Congress of 1870, delegates framed a **Declaration of Principles** that incorporated a new philosophy for children and adults. The new philosophy was less punitive than that which prevailed when the first prisons and houses of refuge were built. An institution governed by force and fear, the declaration stated, is mismanaged. Punishment that degrades is a mistake. Why not use rewards on inmates? Why not cultivate their self-respect, educate them, provide them with honorable labor, and teach them self-control? These were now seen as the principles that should govern institutions (Henderson, 1910:39–63).

Symbolic of those principles, new names were found for places of confinement—**industrial schools** for destitute, disobedient, and neglected children, and **reformatories** for young criminals. Moreover, new guidelines stressed the importance of locating those institutions in rural areas and seeing to it that industrial schools, if not reformatories, emulated the character of the well-disciplined family. "Add to [them] the holy and softening influence of a quiet, moral, and Christian home and family, and we are complete" (Sanders, 1970:404).

Reformers were prepared to keep marginal children for as long as it took to save them. For example, consider what was prescribed for one "giddy" and "restless" girl (Hart, 1910:72):

> When she reaches the age of 14 or 15, she becomes restless, uneasy, discontented. She chafes under restraint, desires more liberty, wants to choose her own associations and recreations. She wants to go out at night. She craves pretty clothes and admiration. Perhaps she is the recipient of flattering and dangerous attentions from some young man. . . . The girl is not vicious, she does not want to do anything wrong, but she is in a critical and dangerous situation. She is giddy, headstrong, easily influenced. She needs to be kept safe for a few years or two, until she comes to herself, and in the meantime she ought to receive such training as will either enable her to support herself or will make a more efficient housewife and mother. It is for this class of girls that [industrial] schools are now demanded.

The new reformatory would maintain a stern regimen, but it would make use of enlightened principles. Indeed, when the nation's model reformatory opened in Elmira, New York, it resembled a military school (Mennel, 1973:102–103). Zebulon Brockway (1910), its first superintendent, stressed that offenders' lives should be regulated carefully according to scientific principles. He devised a marking system for

IS CHILDHOOD STILL GOOD FOR AMERICA?

Perhaps the modern concept of childhood should be reevaluated. Ellen Goodman (1996) has suggested, albeit satirically, that childhood should be eliminated because it is too costly:

> Childhood has become far too burdensome for the American public to bear: It isn't good for the country. . . . Adolescence . . . wasn't invented until the early 20th century. Nor was the concept of juvenile as in delinquency, nor the notion of teen-age as in pregnancy. . . . Now we are stuck with this useless thing called childhood, a drain on the private and public exchequers. . . . There are still a handful of people troubled with the fact that America has the highest child poverty rates of any industrialized country and that when this [recent welfare] "reform" clicks in, a million more children are expected to become poor. . . . Why not apply the same principles of "personal responsibility" and "work opportunity" to our youngest citizens [as we do to adults]? . . . If we eliminated the entire notion of childhood we wouldn't have to worry about children having children. Or about child care. Or after school care. Or school. Child labor would become another "work opportunity."

classifying offenders; an **indeterminate sentence** that would allow officials to keep offenders until they were reformed; a strict regimen of education, work, military drill, and hard physical exercise; and supervision upon release to the community. Nothing would be left to chance or to well-meaning but misguided people who did not understand the need for systematic controls.

There were a few dissenters from this renewed faith in institutions, and most Southern states did not bother to create them at all until the late 1800s (Bremner, 1970, I:672; Platt, 1969:61–62; Shelden, 1992:96). Otherwise, the movement once again swept the nation. But by 1900, it had come full circle, just like the house of refuge movement before it. Institutions were still not a panacea.

In hindsight, it is not surprising that institutions failed. Not only were they poor devices for socializing people, but even if they had been built on every street corner, they could not have counteracted the effects of immigration, urban growth, industrialization, and ideological change. Nor could they have served as a surrogate parent capable of producing the same kind of offspring as a family located in a small rural community. The means were totally inappropriate to the ends. But there were other reasons for a search for alternatives. By the end of the 1800s, child savers were concerned not only with controlling "pestiferous" juveniles but with doing more to protect all children.

THE "RIGHTS" OF CHILDREN

Over several centuries, the values and beliefs associated with the **modern concept of childhood** had resulted in a series of **children's rights.** But those rights were not of the constitutional variety—free speech, free assembly, or freedom of religion. Rather, they were more fundamental.

Nurturance Rights

In contrast to the attitudes toward children in the Middle Ages, the discovery of childhood gradually led to acceptance of several *nurturance rights* for them: the rights to life, food, clothing, shelter, and proper moral standards to follow. Both the provision of outdoor and indoor relief for them in the 1700s and the construction of houses of refuge and industrial schools in the 1800s were evidence of the commitment to those rights.

Because it was impossible to institutionalize all children whose nurturance rights were being violated, even more dramatic reforms were required to protect them from economic exploitation and ensure that their parents cared for them properly and that they were educated. Hence, the late 1800s and early 1900s were marked by efforts to make such reforms a part of the institutional fabric of society.

Educational Rights

Before the Civil War, many states required that children attend school. Although those requirements were supposed to benefit the young, they proved largely unworkable. Employers ignored them, and many children worked rather than attend school. Some parents even joined in circumventing the law. However, lower-class children were the most likely to be exploited. Although hard work was considered morally desirable by most people, the employment of children was an economic necessity for the poor (Bremner, 1970, I:559).

Employment of children increased as the nation industrialized. In contrast to prior centuries, however, it generated references to "cannibalism," "child slavery," and the "slaughter of innocents" and led to a crusade against it by lawyers, social workers, various charitable groups, and even some industrialists (Bremner, 1970, I:601–604; Sommerville, 1982:160–178; Zelizer, 1985:56–72). By the early 1900s, therefore, most states regulated child labor and required that children attend school. "Educate the rising generation mentally, morally, physically," a U.S. senator told his colleagues, "and this nation and this world would reach the millennium within 100 years" (Welter, 1962:151).

Distinctive Legal Rights

Before education and other nurturance rights for children could be enforced, some legal teeth were required. Experience had indicated that children's rights would not come easily. Hence, a new set of principles, solely for children, gradually evolved—

principles that differed greatly from those that governed the constitutional rights of adults.

Any adult charged with committing a crime was assured of due process: a clear statement of charges, protection from hearsay and other questionable evidence, and a jury trial. In short, carefully prescribed procedures, not the arbitrary discretion of authorities, were to govern the adult criminal justice system.

Because the modern concept of childhood suggested that children were immature, it was assumed that they were incapable of appreciating the consequences of their behavior. Thus, due-process principles did not apply to them. Rather, officials required broad discretionary powers to act on their behalf, not only to protect them but to inquire into the most private of family and personal matters.

In tracing the origins of those powers, legal scholars like to cite the English doctrine of *parens patriae,* which emerged in medieval times and gave the crown the right to intervene in family affairs as a means of protecting the property rights of juveniles (Mnookin, 1978:84–85). They also point out that ancient common law tended to protect young children from the full penalties of the criminal law (Mnookin, 1978:759). But it was not until the 1800s, in both England and America, that a unique system of justice for juveniles began to take shape. And even that system took a century to complete.

Throughout much of the 1800s, the laws and legal procedures that granted power to authorities to place children in houses of refuge without the benefits of due process were constitutionally questionable and far from clear. Thus, not surprisingly, they were legally challenged. Perhaps the most noteworthy case was that of **The People v. Turner** in 1870 (Schlossman, 1977:11–13). A boy named Daniel O'Connell had been institutionalized in the Chicago Reform School under an Illinois law that specified that children under age 16 who were found to be "vagrant . . . destitute of proper parental care . . . growing up in mendicancy, ignorance, or vice" could be confined until they were reformed or reached the age of 21. Daniel's father sought to have him released. Illinois Justice Thornton, writing the majority opinion, ordered Daniel discharged from custody. "The disability of minors," he concluded, "does not make slaves or criminals of them.... Even criminals cannot be convicted and imprisoned without due process of law.... Destitution of proper parental care, ignorance, idleness, and vice are misfortunes, not crimes" (Bremner, 1970, II:485–487). The logic of Justice Thornton's opinion notwithstanding, the O'Connell case made hardly a ripple. Instead, virtually every other higher-court decision affirmed the right of states to intervene in the lives of children without having to ensure that their constitutional rights were protected (Schlossman, 1977:11–14). A conflict over which set of rights should dominate was set in motion—a debate that even today continues to bedevil us (Stafford, 1995).

At the same time, reformers grew increasingly uncomfortable with the practice of adjudicating children's cases in criminal courts. It was not that they doubted the wisdom of discarding due-process protections for children. Indeed, their concerns were just the opposite; that is, they were convinced that the formal legal procedures of the criminal courts were too mechanistic for and too insensitive to children. Therefore, beginning in 1869, Massachusetts required agents of the State Board of Charities to attend the trials of children to protect their interests and make recommendations to the judges. The city of Boston went even further. In 1870, it began holding separate hearings for juveniles under age 16; the state of New York followed suit in 1892 (Bremner, 1970, II:485–501).

Many reformers in the late 1800s also became increasingly concerned over the continued confinement of young lawbreakers in jails and prisons (Colomy and Kretzmann, 1995:198). In 1883, for example, members of the Chicago Women's Club attempted to improve jail conditions for adult criminals. But when they began to visit local lockups, they were horrified to find that the jails held a sizable number of young children, despite all the talk about special institutions for them. Consequently, their focus changed. Rather than saving criminals, they would save children (Lathrop, 1925). The women ultimately asked these questions: Why not go further than Boston and New York? Why not create a **juvenile court**? Indeed, why not legislate an entirely separate system of justice for juveniles?

CREATION OF THE JUVENILE COURT

The Chicago Women's Club drafted a bill in 1895 to present to the Illinois legislature; but when they submitted it to their legal advisor for his approval, he indicated that it was too broad and lacked procedural safeguards. As Justice Thornton had done twenty-five years before, he questioned whether the state had the right to intervene in the lives of children for non-criminal offenses or to deprive them of their liberty without the protections of due process (Lathrop, 1925).

The club members took the advice to heart and moved to drop the project. But when some other influential people learned about it—including clergy, lawyers, judges, and prison wardens—they believed it should be continued. Consequently, in 1898, the Illinois Conference of Charities reviewed the proposal and drafted a new bill. The Chicago Bar Association threw its support behind the bill, and the Illinois legislature passed it.

This new legislation was broad and sweeping, giving the juvenile court jurisdiction over all children under the age of 16 who were in some kind of trouble. It provided for a special judge, a separate courtroom, and separate records; and it specified that court sessions were to be informal rather than formal. Indeed, the new law was to "be liberally construed to the end that ... the care, custody and discipline of a child shall approximate ... that which should be given by its parents" (Bremner, 1970, II: 511). What family could operate effectively if the resolution of its difficulties required indictments, prosecutors, defense attorneys, strict rules of evidence, and a jury? Those features of the adult criminal justice system would only aggravate the problems of children.

In addition to a justice system tailored to families, new **detention homes** would house children awaiting a hearing; no longer would they be jailed. Also, probation officers would be appointed to investigate and diagnose each child's problems, assist the judge, and supervise children in their own homes. In short, the new **juvenile justice system** was to be nothing less than society's new superparent, charged with protecting the nurturance rights of all

children—be they delinquent, dependent, or neglected—and rehabilitating those who needed it.

Delinquent Children

The way this new system was to be applied to juvenile
lawbreakers was described in idealistic terms before
the American Bar Association in 1909 by Julian W.
Mack (1910:296–297), one of the first judges of the
juvenile court in Chicago:

> Why isn't it just and proper to treat these juvenile
> offenders as we deal with the neglected children,
> as a wise and merciful father handles his own
> child whose errors are not discovered by the au-
> thorities? Why isn't it the duty of the State instead
> of asking merely whether a boy or a girl has com-
> mitted the specific offense, to find out what he is,
> physically, mentally, morally, and then, if it learns
> that he is treading the path that leads to crimi-
> nality, to take him in charge, not so much to
> punish as to reform, not to degrade but to uplift,
> not to crush but to develop, not to make him a
> criminal but a worthy citizen.

As Judge Mack's remarks indicate, those who
invented the juvenile court saw themselves as decriminalizing the misconduct of children, not criminalizing it. First, **delinquent children** would not be
treated the same as adult criminals. Second, the court
would not intervene as a harsh, punitive monitor of
evil conduct, but as a thoughtful, kindly superparent.
Juveniles would be lent a helpful hand rather than
punished into conformity. The purpose of the court
was to discover a child's problems and correct them,
not to respond to the acts he or she had committed
as a criminal court would.

Within ten years, twenty states and the District
of Columbia had enacted similar laws, and within
twenty years, all but three states had done so. By
mid-century, all states and territories, as well as many
foreign countries, had adopted similar laws (Caldwell, 1961:496).

Most of these laws were modeled after the original Illinois statute, and relatively few changes were
made in them until recently. For example, a South
Dakota statute, which was not revised until 1968,
defined a delinquent as

any child who, while under the age of 18 years,
violates any law of this state or any ordinance of
any city or town of this state; who is incorrigible,
or intractable by parents, guardian, or custodian;
who knowingly associates with thieves, vicious,
or immoral persons; who, without cause and
without the consent of its parents, guardian or
custodian, absents itself from its home or place
of abode; who is growing up in idleness or crime;
who fails to attend school regularly without
proper reasons therefor, if of compulsory school
age; who repeatedly plays truant from school;
who does not regularly attend school and is not
otherwise engaged in any regular occupation or
employment but loiters and idles away its time;
who knowingly frequents or visits a house of ill
repute; who knowingly frequents or visits any
policy shop or place where any gaming device is
operated; who patronizes, visits, or frequents any
saloon or dram shop where intoxicating liquors
are sold; who patronizes or visits any public
poolroom where the game of billiards or pool is
being carried on for pay or hire; who frequents
or patronizes any wineroom or dance hall run in
connection with or adjacent to any house of ill
fame or saloon; who visits, frequents, or patronizes, with one of the opposite sex, any restaurant
or other place where liquors may be purchased
at night after the hours of nine o'clock; who is
found alone with one of the opposite sex in a
private apartment or room of any restaurant,
lodging house, hotel, or other place at nighttime
or who goes to any secluded place or is found
alone in such place with one of the opposite sex
at nighttime with the evident purpose of con-
cealing their acts; who wanders about the streets
in the nighttime without being on any lawful
business or lawful occupation, or habitually wanders about any railroad yards or tracks, or jumps
or attempts to jump onto any moving train, or
enters any car or engine without lawful authority; who writes or uses vile, obscene, vulgar, or
indecent language, or smokes cigarettes or uses
tobacco in any form; who drinks intoxicating
liquors on any street, in any public place, or
about any school house, or at any place other
than its own home; or who is guilty of indecent,

immoral, or lascivious conduct. (Rubin, 1974: 1–2)

Few laws could be more inclusive and still be enforceable. Only two or three lines in the South Dakota law were devoted to prohibiting the kinds of criminal acts for which adults could be charged— those stating that a child should not violate "any law of this state or any ordinance of any city or town of this state." All the remaining lines were devoted to describing **status offenses**—offenses that apply only to children.

This way of defining delinquent behavior indicates why, even now, such behavior cannot be equated with criminal behavior. The definition covers much more ground than that. In virtually every case, state laws embodied in formal language the modern concept of childhood. They emphasized the dependent status of children and stressed the need to quarantine them from many activities in which adults are free to engage. Though these laws have concentrated on what children should *not* be, by turning them around one can get a good picture of what legislators and other child savers have thought they *should* be. The list of behaviors covered by the South Dakota statute is amazingly similar to those drawn up in the child-raising manuals of the 1700s and 1800s. Specifically, the ideal child should be submissive to authority, obedient, hardworking, studious, sober, chaste, and circumspect in habit, language, and associates; and the ideal child should avoid even the appearance of such evils as staying out late, wandering the streets, being alone with a person of the opposite sex, or playing in dangerous places like railroad yards. Children who acted that way and stayed within the limits of their quarantine were appropriately playing the role of child.

The goal of modern child savers was to legislate the morality of children so that the rules for their conduct would be broader than the rules for adult behavior. Otherwise, children might not develop properly. And because the announced goal of the court was assistance, not punishment, benevolence would triumph over any shortcomings in procedure:

The fundamental function of a juvenile court is to put each child who comes before it in a normal relation to society as promptly and as perma-

ABOLISH THE JUVENILE COURT?

In stark contrast to the optimism that surrounded its invention, there is considerable pessimism about the juvenile court today, with many people denouncing it as ineffective and calling for its abolition. Recent increases in juvenile violence have made it difficult for many Americans to continue to justify separate criminal and juvenile justice systems. We will consider recent trends in juvenile violence and other types of delinquency in the next several chapters, and we will consider current issues in the juvenile court and its future at the end of this book.

nently as possible, and that while punishment is not by any means to be dispensed with, it is to be made subsidiary and subordinate to that function. . . . As far as practicable [children] shall be treated, not as criminals, but as children in need of aid, encouragement, and guidance. Proceedings against children . . . shall not be deemed to be criminal proceedings. (Baker, 1910:321)

Dependent and Neglected Children

Attitudes toward and the rules for **dependent and neglected children** were very much like those for delinquent children. This is illustrated by the original Illinois statute. "The words dependent and neglected child," it said,

shall mean any child who for any reason is destitute or homeless or abandoned; or dependent upon the public for support; or has not proper parental care or guardianship; or who habitually begs or receives alms; or who is found living in any house of ill fame or with any vicious or disreputable person; or whose home, by reason of neglect, cruelty, or depravity on the part of its parents, guardian, or other person in whose care it may be, is an unfit place for such a child; and any child under the age of eight years who is found peddling or selling any article, or singing or playing any musical instrument upon the street, or giving any public entertainment. (Bremner, 1970, II:507)

Besides noting that a dependent or neglected child might be homeless or destitute, the law described this child in much the same way that it and other laws described delinquents. For example, it noted that a *dependent* child is one who begs for alms, lives in a house of ill fame, or lives with some vicious person. Yet any difference between that child and a child who frequents saloons, loiters away his or her time, or stays out too late at night is purely academic. For most of the 1900s, there has been a tendency to equate the two types of children, probably because of the persistence of the 19th-century belief that poverty and neglect cause delinquency.

Juvenile court practices have been criticized because they seem contrary to the classical concept of justice: If people are not really criminal, they should not be in court. Yet such criticisms often have missed the point. According to the fundamental premises on which legal rules for children were drawn, the court has not failed because it has not distinguished between dependent/neglected and delinquent children. In principle, the juvenile court was created to serve a different and much broader set of functions than the criminal court. Specifically, it was devised (1) to elevate the standards of child raising for society as a whole; (2) to act as a monitor over other societal institutions to ensure that children are not exploited or maltreated, but are fed, loved, and educated; (3) to apply scientific knowledge to diagnose and cure the physical or emotional ills of children; and (4) even to prevent crime by serving as a catch basin for the children of poor, uncaring, or licentious parents (Schlossman, 1977:57–63).

Given this sweeping but benevolent mandate, society's new superparent enjoyed widespread support for about two-thirds of the 20th century (Rosenheim, 1962). Although the juvenile court could be harsh at times, the popular opinion was that its desirable aspects outweighed its undesirable ones. Law-

yers remained ignorant of, or at least shied away from, the procedural dilemmas it posed; and when on occasion these dilemmas were raised, the constitutionality of the juvenile court was sustained by various appellate and supreme courts (Paulsen and Whitebread, 1974:4).

In recent years, by contrast, dissatisfaction with this concept of juvenile justice has mounted, and revolutionary changes have been made (Ferdinand, 1991). However, because those changes are products of recent events and ideologies, they will be discussed in later chapters.

SUMMARY AND CONCLUSIONS

Throughout this and the previous chapters, we have seen that childhood and delinquency are social constructions, the products of an ongoing process of cultural change and institutional experimentation that spanned many centuries. By the 1800s, steps had been taken to solidify the rights of children and make them a part of the legal and bureaucratic structures of society:

1. By the early 1800s, the values associated with the concept of childhood had resulted in a series of nurturance rights for *all* children, even those of the poor: the right to life, food, clothing, and shelter, and moral standards to follow.

2. In the 1800s, problems associated with rapid immigration, industrialization, and urbanization led to the construction of houses of refuge and reformatories to control the children of poor and inadequate parents and to act as surrogate families and schools for them.

3. In the late 1800s, the continued exploitation of children resulted in laws to regulate child labor and make some education mandatory for the children of lower- as well as middle- and upper-class families.

4. In the early 1900s, a unique legal system—the juvenile court—was established to enforce those laws and see to it that children (and their parents) conformed to the standards that defined the ideal child.

5. By 1950, the status of children was unmistakably and officially defined as different from that of

adults. Childhood had become a long and powerless phase in the life cycle. The rights of children reflected their dependent and unequal status. Legal as well as moral rules defined what was expected of them. The family and the school, not the larger adult community, were charged with socializing children; and, in the event that either failed or that some children departed from the ideal, the juvenile court would assume the parental role. Thus, by defining childhood in that way, society also defined and invented delinquency. And although delinquency was viewed as undesirable, it was not to be equated with adult crime. Rather, it represented a form of childish behavior from which both its perpetrator and society would be rescued.

As might be expected, the ideals associated with these constructions of reality often have been at odds with actual events and feelings. Ambivalence toward children persists. The juvenile court, to say nothing of families and schools, has been unable to rescue all dependent and neglected children; and delinquency continues to be a serious social problem.

In part two, we will inquire further into those issues and review the extent to which delinquent children continue to slip through the institutional cracks of society, despite its avowed concern for them.

Discussion Questions

1. How did 18th- and 19th-century Americans differ in their explanations of crime?
2. If you had been a reformer in the first part of the 1800s, what kinds of reforms would you have proposed for dealing with pestiferous juveniles?
3. Why was the juvenile court invented? What were its purposes?
4. Why was the juvenile court invented when it was, and not at some other point in history?
5. Based on what you have read so far, do you believe the juvenile court was a useful invention?

References

Aries, Philippe. 1962. *Centuries of Childhood: A Social History of Family Life.* Translated by Robert Baldick. New York: Random House.

Baker, Harvey H. 1910. "Procedure of the Boston Juvenile Court." Pp. 318–327 in Hastings H. Hart, ed., *Preventive Treatment of Neglected Children.* New York: Russell Sage.

Barnes, Harry Elmer. 1972. *The Story of Punishment,* 2nd ed. Montclair, N.J.: Patterson Smith.

Beccaria, Cesare. 1963. *On Crimes and Punishments.* Translated by Henry Paolucci. Indianapolis, Ind.: Bobbs-Merrill.

Becker, Carl. 1932. *The Heavenly City of the 18th Century Philosophers.* New Haven, Conn.: Yale University Press.

Bremner, Robert H., ed. 1970. *Children and Youth in America: A Documentary History.* 3 vols. Cambridge, Mass.: Harvard University Press.

Brockway, Zebulon. 1910. "The American Reformatory Prison System." Pp. 88–107 in Charles R. Henderson, ed., *Prison Reform and Criminal Law.* New York: Charities Publication Committee.

Bureau of the Census. 1955. *Current Population Reports.* Series P-25, no. 123. Washington, D.C.: U.S. Government Printing Office.

Caldwell, Robert G. 1961. "The Juvenile Court: Its Development and Some Major Problems." *Journal of Criminal Law, Criminology and Police Science* 51 (January–February):493–511.

Colomy, Paul, and Martin Kretzmann. 1995. "Projects and Institution Building: Judge Ben B. Lindsey and the Juvenile Court Movement." *Social Problems* 42 (May):191–215.

Ferdinand, Theodore N. 1991. "History Overtakes the Juvenile Justice System." *Crime and Delinquency* 37 (April):204–224.

Goodman, Ellen. 1996. "Childhood Isn't Good for America." *Austin American-Statesman,* August 29, p. A15.

Gould, Stephen J. 1981. *The Mismeasure of Man.* New York: Norton.

Hart, Hastings H. 1910. *Preventive Treatment of Neglected Children.* New York: Russell Sage.

Henderson, Charles R., ed. 1910. *Prison Reform and Criminal Law.* New York: Charities Publication Committee.

Hessinger, Rodney. 1996. "Problems and Promises: Colonial American Child Rearing and Modernization Theory." *Journal of Family History* 21 (April):125–143.

Hofstader, Richard. 1959. *Social Darwinism in American Thought.* New York: Braziller.

Lathrop, Julia C. 1925. "The Background of the Juvenile Court in Illinois." Pp. 290–297, 320–330 in Julia Adams, ed., *The Child, the Clinic, and the Court.* New York: New Republic.

Mack, Julian. 1910. "The Juvenile Court as a Legal Institution." Pp. 293–317 in Hastings H. Hart, ed., *Preventive Treatment of Neglected Children.* New York: Russell Sage.

McKelvey, Blake. 1968. *American Prisons.* Montclair, N.J.: Patterson Smith.

Mennel, Robert M. 1973. *Thorns and Thistles: Juvenile Delinquents in the United States, 1825–1940.* Hanover, N.H.: University Press of New England.

Mnookin, Robert H. 1978. *Child, Family and State: Problems and Materials on Children and the Law.* Boston: Little, Brown.

Moody, Eleazar. 1970. "The School of Good Manners." Pp. 33–34 in Robert H. Bremner, ed., *Children and Youth in America: A Documentary History,* Vol. I. Cambridge, Mass.: Harvard University Press. (First published 1772.)

Paulsen, Monrad G., and Charles H. Whitebread. 1974. *Juvenile Law and Procedure.* Reno, Nev.: National Council of Juvenile Court Judges.

Platt, Anthony M. 1969. *The Child Savers: The Invention of Delinquency.* Chicago: University of Chicago Press.

Rosenheim, Margaret K., ed. 1962. *Justice for the Child: The Juvenile Court in Transition.* New York: Free Press.

Rothman, David J. 1971. *The Discovery of the Asylum.* Boston: Little, Brown.

Rubin, Ted. 1974. "Transferring Responsibility for Juvenile Noncriminal Misconduct from Juvenile Courts to Nonauthoritarian Community Agencies." Mimeographed. Phoenix: Arizona Conference on Delinquency Intervention.

Sanders, Wiley B., ed. 1970. *Juvenile Offenders for a Thousand Years: Selected Readings from Anglo-Saxon Times to 1900.* Chapel Hill: University of North Carolina Press.

Schlossman, Steven L. 1977. *Love and the American Delinquent.* Chicago: University of Chicago Press.

Shelden, Randall G. 1992. "A History of the Shelby County Industrial and Training School." *Tennessee Historical Quarterly* 51 (Summer): 96–106.

Sommerville, C. John. 1982. *The Rise and Fall of Childhood.* Beverly Hills, Calif.: Sage.

Stafford, Mark C. 1995. "Children's Legal Rights in the U.S." *Marriage and Family Review* 21 (3/4): 121–140.

Vold, George B., and Thomas J. Bernard. 1986. *Theoretical Criminology,* 3rd ed. New York: Oxford University Press.

Wadsworth, Benjamin. 1970. "The Well-Ordered Family." Pp. 34–36 in Robert H. Bremner, ed., *Children and Youth in America: A Documentary History,* Vol. I. Cambridge, Mass.: Harvard University Press. (First published 1719.)

Welter, Rush. 1962. *Popular Education and Democratic Thought in America.* New York: Columbia University Press.

Zelizer, Viviana A. 1985. *Pricing the Priceless Child: The Changing Social Value of Children.* New York: Basic Books.

PART TWO

EXTENT AND DISTRIBUTION OF DELINQUENT BEHAVIOR

Although occasional questions were raised about the juvenile court before the mid-20th century, it was not seriously challenged until the 1960s. When those challenges arose, they were probably due to an increase in delinquency rates rather than radical changes in the concepts of delinquency and juvenile justice. Reports of further increases in delinquency rates in the 1980s and 1990s intensified the challenges even more.

Recent increases in delinquency rates have suggested, to some people at least, that the traditional juvenile court philosophy has failed. Perhaps delinquents should be treated like adult criminals, with a greater emphasis on punishment than on rehabilitation.

Given the importance of such issues, it is obvious that we must pay attention to the extent of delinquent behavior—the amount of delinquency—at present, as well as in the recent past. Do large portions of American children violate the law? Have they been committing more and more delinquency over the past several decades?

We also must pay attention to any clues that delinquency statistics might provide us about the distribution of delinquency—about who is most likely to commit delinquent acts. Do certain segments of the youth population commit more delinquency than others? Do boys, for example, commit more delinquent acts than girls? Are there any notable differences among the races? What factors stand out that must be explained by theory?

Such questions are not answered easily. Valid information on delinquency has been difficult to obtain because much of it has gone officially undetected. Moreover, official police and juvenile court statistics are as much a reflection of what legal officials do as what delinquents do. In the recent past, however, important alternative sources of information have been developed and added to official statistics. In this part of the book, we will review these alternative sources of information as well as official statistics:

- In Chapter 4, we examine official accounts of delinquent behavior derived from the records of the police and juvenile courts.
- In Chapter 5, we consider self-reports of delinquent behavior from young people themselves.
- In Chapter 6, we examine reports from the victims of crime and delinquency to obtain yet a third estimate of the extent and distribution of delinquency.

Those three accounts sometimes differ. But by triangulating on delinquent behavior, we should be able to get a reasonably good fix on it, just as surveyors do when they attempt to locate a particular position by viewing it from different angles. Once this is done, we will be able to draw some conclusions about what the recent trends in delinquent behavior are, where in society it is most heavily concentrated, and what "facts" are in need of explanation.

A JUVENILE LAWBREAKER DOES NOT BECOME AN OFFICIAL DELINQUENT UNTIL CAUGHT AND HIS OR HER ACTS ARE RECORDED.

CHAPTER FOUR

OFFICIAL ACCOUNTS OF DELINQUENT BEHAVIOR

T here are two major sources of official data on delinquent behavior: (1) the number of juvenile arrests reported by the police each year to the **Federal Bureau of Investigation** (FBI) and (2) the number of cases reported annually by juvenile courts to the National Center for Juvenile Justice, the research arm of the National Council of Juvenile and Family Court Judges. Of the two, police data are more accurate. The **juvenile justice system** is like a funnel, in which estimates of delinquency are increasingly less accurate the farther down the funnel those estimates occur. A delinquent act does not always result in an arrest, and an arrest does not always result in a referral to juvenile court. At each stage in the system, therefore, some accuracy is lost in estimating the extent or amount of delinquency. In addition, different juveniles may have different chances of being arrested or referred to juvenile court even if they commit the same delinquent act. If an 11-year-old and a 16-year-old are caught shoplifting, for example, a police officer might not arrest both of them. The officer may believe that the 11-year-old is too young to be arrested and should be released to his or her parents but that the 16-year-old is more nearly an adult and should be held responsible. Age bias also may exist farther down the funnel of the juvenile justice system, with older juveniles having a greater likelihood of referral to juvenile court. Furthermore, there may be biases at both the arrest and juvenile court stages involving gender, race, and social class. As with estimating the extent or amount of delinquency, therefore, some accuracy may be lost at each stage of the juvenile justice system in estimating the distribution of delinquency or the individuals most likely to commit delinquent acts.

POLICE ESTIMATES OF DELINQUENT BEHAVIOR

Police estimates of crime and delinquency appear yearly in the **Uniform Crime Reports** issued by the FBI. Today, over 16,000 law enforcement agencies, representing 95 percent of the U.S. population, voluntarily submit information to the Uniform Crime Reporting Program (FBI, 1997:1). The latest figures indicate that in 1996, approximately 13.5 million serious crimes were reported to the police, and ap-

proximately 15.2 million arrests were made (FBI, 1997:5, 214).

FBI data on arrests are examined more closely in figure 4.1, which plots the relationship between age and the arrest rate per 100,000 population for all nontraffic offenses. The reason arrest *rates* are compared rather than *number* of arrests is simple: Unless arrest figures are standardized by population size, the larger age groups may have a greater number of arrests because there are more people to be arrested. In 1996, there were 1,919,657 arrests of juveniles ages 13–17 (FBI, 1997:224). If that figure is divided by the total number of such persons—18,786,000 (Day, 1993:18)—the resulting rate per 100,000 population is 10,218.6. Figure 4.1 shows that juveniles and young adults are more likely to be arrested (proportionately speaking) than any other segment of the population. Arrest rates increase rapidly during adolescence, peak at age 18, and then decrease.

"FACTS" THAT MUST BE EXPLAINED

At this point, there are several important questions, such as these: For what offenses are juveniles most likely to be arrested? Are boys or girls arrested most often? Are poor or more affluent children more likely to be arrested?

FIGURE 4.1

Age distribution of arrest rates for all crimes per 100,000 population, 1996

SOURCES: Day, 1993:18; FBI, 1997:224–225.

NOTE: Arrest figures based on 9,666 agencies; 1996 estimated population 189,885,000.

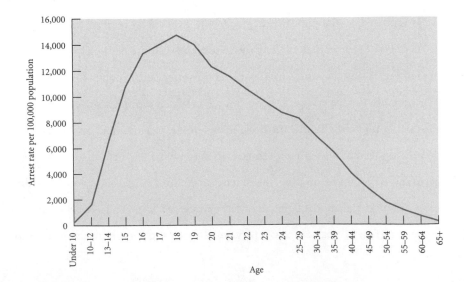

When we reviewed the discovery of childhood and the invention of delinquency, we learned several important things:

1. The discovery of childhood contributed to the notion that children need special care and supervision. Otherwise, it was assumed that they would grow up to be adults with undesirable features.

2. The modern concept of childhood is a product largely of middle-class values and experiences. It was the middle class, in particular, that stressed family and formal schooling as devices for socializing youths.

3. Although great changes occurred in the methods of raising children, role expectations for girls and boys remained markedly different. Boys were granted more freedom than girls, encouraged to pursue more education, and expected to assume positions in commerce, industry, and the professions. Girls, meanwhile, were expected to be less venturesome, limit their educations, marry, and assume domestic roles in support of their husbands and children. Above all, girls were to be more modest, retiring, and virtuous than boys.

4. Opportunities to develop and adhere to these expectations were limited for blacks, Native Americans, and other minority groups. Given those limitations, Americans increasingly believed that the poverty of minorities and their disrupted family lives were inevitable precursors of crime.

5. The creation of the juvenile court was a direct reflection of such developments and assumptions. In the interest of saving wayward boys and girls, particularly the poor, juvenile justice officials were expected not only to detect and suppress their law-violating behavior but to compensate for their poverty, disrupted family life, and failure to heed ideal role expectations.

If these historical developments have any relevance for the present, they should be reflected in arrest statistics. Such factors as age, gender, race, and social class should have some relationship to juvenile arrests. Indeed, if such relationships exist, they become "facts" that criminologists must explain. *Why*, they might ask, is age, or gender, or race related to

JUVENILE MURDERS

The juvenile arrest rate for murder has doubled since 1985. Blumstein (1995:6) argues that the reason is the "rapid growth of the crack markets [beginning] in the mid-1980s" and the diffusion of guns. According to Blumstein, juveniles recently have been recruited into the drug industry and armed with guns for self-protection. Because juveniles tend to be reckless and unskilled at dispute resolution, the diffusion of guns has increased the chances that disputes among juveniles will result in murders.

In contrast, Klein (1995:112–126) argues that recent increases in gang murders are not due to gang members' involvement in crack sales and distribution. Klein (1995:116) agrees with Blumstein that a reason for the increase in gang murders is the "greater lethality of weapons now in the hands of . . . offending gangs." However, Klein (1995:36) claims that although drug use is common among gang members, drug sales and distribution are not. There is a crack, and other drug, connection to some gang murders, according to Klein (1995:125–126), but most of them pertain to non-drug rivalries.

arrest? In pursuit of such "facts," let us first reexamine the relationship between age and arrest.

Age and Arrest

We have already seen that juveniles have very high arrest rates. But for what kinds of offenses are they arrested? Are they largely **status offenses** involving running away, drinking, and violating curfew? Or are they **criminal offenses** involving violence and theft? With those questions in mind, table 4.1 compares juvenile arrest rates per 100,000 population under age 18 with rates for adults ages 18 and over for two kinds of offenses: (1) the eight serious crimes that constitute the FBI's **index offenses** and (2) selected **nonindex offenses.**

Index offenses are serious crimes, reported annually to the FBI by police agencies. These crimes are murder and nonnegligent manslaughter, forcible rape, robbery, aggravated assault, burglary, larceny-theft, motor vehicle theft, and arson. Those offenses, in turn, are divided into two subtypes: (1) **violent crimes** and (2) **property crimes.**

Nonindex offenses include a long list of less serious offenses. For juveniles, they include curfew violations, loitering, nonaggravated assaults, dealing in stolen property, vandalism, possessing weapons, drug abuse, and drinking.

VIOLENT CRIMES The figures for the first four index offenses in table 4.1 indicate that juveniles are less likely than adults to be arrested for violent crimes—murder, rape, robbery, and aggravated assault. The exception is that the adult arrest rate for robbery is lower than that for juveniles (40.3 versus 54.0). However, the adult arrest rate is about twice as high as the juvenile arrest rate for murder, rape, and aggravated assault. Although arrest rates for robbery tend to peak at about age 17, the rates for the other three violent crimes do not peak until the late teens or early twenties (Greenberg, 1977:190; Hirschi and Gottfredson, 1983:557; Steffensmeier et al., 1989: 815).

PROPERTY CRIMES The figures for burglary, larceny-theft, motor vehicle theft, and arson show that arrests of juveniles are more likely to involve property crimes than violent crimes (an arrest rate of 130.5 for burglary, for example, compared with 5.4 for rape). Moreover, arrest rates for property crimes are consistently higher for juveniles than adults, peaking between ages 15 and 17 (Greenberg, 1977:190; Hirschi and Gottfredson, 1983:557; Steffensmeier et al., 1989:815).

The annual publication of official figures like these not only fuels public fear but illustrates the anxieties related to our traditional beliefs about chil-

dren. The modern concept of childhood says that by attending to the moral, economic, and psychological needs of young people, delinquency can be prevented. But these figures suggest that either this assumption is false or our efforts have not been very successful.

NONINDEX OFFENSES The nonindex offenses for which juveniles are arrested most often also are shown in table 4.1. As expected, they account for all of the arrests for curfew violation and running away because those are status offenses applicable only to children. Except for dealing in stolen property and vandalism, arrest rates for the nonindex offenses are higher for adults, although juvenile arrest rates are still very high (more than 100 arrests per 100,000 population) for nonaggravated assaults, drug abuse, liquor law violations, disorderly conduct, and the residual category of *all other offenses.*

Arrest rates for drug abuse and liquor law violations are interesting because they differ somewhat from popular beliefs. Although Americans have been very concerned about juveniles' use of alcohol and other drugs, such as marijuana, cocaine, and heroin, table 4.1 suggests that alcohol and other drug abuse may be more an adult than a juvenile problem. Adults have a higher arrest rate for both offenses (for drug abuse, the adult rate of 469.3 is over twice the juvenile rate of 214.1).

CHRONIC OFFENDERS Another issue has to do with the possibility that high arrest rates are not characteristic of all juveniles, but instead are due to a small group of chronic offenders. Indeed, a longitudinal study by Wolfgang, Figlio, and Sellin (1972) suggested that this is the case. They assembled official records of police contacts with a cohort of 9,945 boys, born in 1945, who lived in Philadelphia between ages 10 and 18. Thirty-five percent (3,475) of the total cohort became officially delinquent (p. 54). However, only 19 percent (1,862 boys) had more than one recorded police contact. This small group of boys accounted for 84 percent of all the police contacts for the cohort, and they were more likely than one-time offenders to be involved in index offenses. In fact, they had 2,935 police contacts for index crimes, while one-time offenders had only 330 (pp. 70–71).

TABLE 4.1

Arrest rates per 100,000 population for index and selected nonindex crimes, juveniles and adults, 1996

type of crime	juveniles	adults
Index crimes		
Murder and nonnegligent manslaughter	3.0	6.0
Forcible rape	5.4	9.7
Robbery	54.0	40.3
Aggravated assault	77.2	160.4
Burglary	130.5	79.6
Larceny-theft	488.5	341.7
Motor vehicle theft	75.0	37.4
Arson	9.8	3.1
Nonindex crimes		
Curfew and loitering	194.7	—
Runaway	189.8	—
Other assaults	228.9	380.9
Stolen property: buying, receiving, possessing	40.3	38.3
Vandalism	137.6	62.5
Weapons: carrying, possessing	53.7	59.2
Drug abuse	214.1	469.3
Liquor laws	145.7	180.5
Disorderly conduct	212.2	220.5
All other offenses except traffic	436.3	1,167.5

SOURCES: Day, 1993:18; FBI, 1997:222.

NOTE: Arrest figures based on 8,275 agencies; 1996 estimated population 175,898,000.

The most chronic offenders of all—those who had five or more recorded police contacts—were selected for further study. Although there were only 627 such boys, they were responsible for *more than half* of all police contacts for the entire cohort. In other words, a group composing only 6 percent of the cohort, and only 18 percent of those who became officially delinquent, was responsible for more than 50 percent of all police contacts. Such findings suggest that only a small percentage of young people become truly serious offenders (p. 88).

SUMMARY Our analysis of the relationship between age and arrest has revealed that (1) juveniles are one of the most frequently arrested segments of the population, (2) they are more likely to be arrested for serious property crimes than violent crimes, and (3) a small group of chronic offenders accounts for a large share of all juvenile arrests. High juvenile arrest rates run counter to the assumption that enlightened methods of child raising protect children from involvement in the debaucheries, misdeeds, and crimes of adults. However, that dismal conclusion tends to

be softened by the finding that there is a small, chronic group of offenders that is contributing disproportionately to the arrests of juveniles. Although the relation between age and arrest is strong, it does not mean that most juveniles should be feared because of their delinquent behavior.

Gender and Arrest

Next, let us examine the relationship between gender and arrest. According to traditional role expectations, girls should be more law-abiding than boys. To address that issue, table 4.2 shows male and female juvenile arrest rates per 100,000 population ages 10–17 for index and nonindex crimes.[1]

INDEX OFFENSES Only 25 percent of all juvenile arrests for index offenses involve girls (FBI, 1997:221). The number of arrests of boys is, therefore, three times that of girls. Table 4.2 reveals that for each

[1]For comparisons among different segments of the youth population (in this case, males versus females), the arrest rates are standardized by the number of juveniles ages 10–17 because arrests are very infrequent before age 10.

TABLE 4.2

Arrest rates per 100,000 population ages 10–17 for index and selected nonindex crimes, males and females, 1996

type of crime	males	females
Index crimes		
Murder and nonnegligent manslaughter	12.7	0.9
Forcible rape	24.1	0.4
Robbery	219.3	24.9
Aggravated assault	276.0	74.8
Burglary	526.8	63.3
Larceny-theft	1,461.7	774.9
Motor vehicle theft	286.5	53.4
Arson	39.2	5.1
Nonindex crimes		
Curfew and loitering	617.5	271.8
Runaway	363.8	516.1
Other assaults	742.8	302.1
Stolen property: buying, receiving, possessing	158.2	24.3
Vandalism	550.3	72.1
Weapons: carrying, possessing	221.0	21.5
Drug abuse	839.7	129.7
Liquor laws	461.3	204.5
Disorderly conduct	724.3	242.5
All other offenses except traffic	1,509.6	476.7

SOURCES: Day, 1993:18; FBI, 1997:223.
NOTE: Arrest figures based on 8,275 agencies; 1996 estimated population 175,898,000.

index offense, the arrest rate is considerably higher for boys. For murder, for example, the arrest rate for boys is 14 times higher than that for girls (12.7 versus 0.9); and, for robbery, the ratio of male-to-female juvenile arrest rates is about 9 to 1 (219.3 versus 24.9). Although girls are more likely to be arrested for larceny-theft than any other offense, the ratio of male to female juvenile arrest rates for that offense is still almost 2 to 1 (1,461.7 versus 774.9). In short, juvenile arrests for index offenses are much more likely to involve boys.

NONINDEX OFFENSES Table 4.2 also shows that arrests of juveniles for nonindex offenses are more likely to involve boys. Girls have a higher arrest rate for only one offense—running away—and this may be due to a double standard that calls for greater concern for unsupervised girls. Overall, arrests of girls constitute only 25 percent of juvenile arrests for nonindex offenses (FBI, 1997:219).

SUMMARY Clearly, girls are arrested far less frequently than boys, suggesting that traditional role expectations may still be strong. But recall that juveniles have higher arrest rates than adults for many offenses, particularly serious property crimes (see table 4.1). This holds for boys and girls alike. That is, for many offenses, both boys and girls have higher arrest rates than their adult counterparts, again suggesting that efforts to nurture and protect children, especially girls, have not always prevented their delinquency.

Race and Arrest

A third important relationship involves race and arrest. During the 1800s, children with white minority parents were far more likely to be considered law violators or in need of institutionalization than children with established, wealthier parents. But now that many minority groups are nonwhite, does the same pattern exist?

TABLE 4.3

Number and percentage of juvenile arrests, by type of crime and race, 1996

type of crime	WHITES		BLACKS		NATIVE AMERICANS OR ALASKAN NATIVES		ASIAN AMERICANS OR PACIFIC ISLANDERS	
	number	percentage	number	percentage	number	percentage	number	percentage
Index crimes	421,675	66.8	187,741	29.7	8,393	1.3	13,737	2.2
Violent crimes	51,335	50.3	48,192	47.2	821	0.8	1,749	1.7
Property crimes	370,340	69.9	139,549	26.4	7,572	1.4	11,988	2.3
Nonindex crimes	1,041,188	70.9	385,757	26.3	17,122	1.2	24,384	1.7
All crimes	1,462,863	69.7	573,498	27.3	25,515	1.2	38,121	1.8

SOURCE: FBI, 1997:233.
NOTE: Figures based on 9,661 agencies; 1996 estimated population 189,885,000.

Most racial groups are so small that their number of arrests is dwarfed by the number of arrests of whites and blacks. As can be seen in table 4.3, neither Native Americans/Alaskan Natives nor Asian Americans/Pacific Islanders account for more than a small percentage of all juvenile arrests. We thus will focus on whites and blacks.

At present, 79 percent of the youth population ages 10–17 is white while 15 percent is black (Day, 1993:18). As table 4.3 shows, however, black juveniles are overrepresented in arrest statistics, accounting for 27 percent of all juvenile arrests; whites account for 70 percent. The difference is particularly striking for index offenses, with 30 percent of all juvenile arrests involving blacks—or twice their percentage in the youth population. On a general level, then, arrest data suggest that black juveniles commit more delinquency. That conclusion, however, does not reflect all of the salient "facts." Those are best revealed by table 4.4, that reports juvenile arrest rates for whites and blacks for specific offenses.

INDEX OFFENSES For index offenses, the number of arrests per 100,000 black juveniles ages 10–17 is considerably higher than the number of arrests per 100,000 white juveniles ages 10–17. Furthermore, there is a greater disparity for violent than property crimes. For example, the ratio of the juvenile arrest rate for blacks to that of whites is approximately 8 to 1 for murder (26.8 versus 3.5) and robbery (484.5

versus 64.5) and approximately 4 to 1 for rape and aggravated assault. In contrast to violent crimes, the arrest rate ratio for blacks and whites is only approximately 2 to 1 for the property crimes of burglary and larceny-theft. For motor vehicle theft, the arrest rate for blacks is three times higher than that for whites; but for arson, the arrest rates are about the same.

Similar findings were reported in the Philadelphia cohort study (Wolfgang, Figlio, and Sellin, 1972:53–129, 245–250). While 29 percent of the whites in the cohort became officially delinquent, 50 percent of the blacks did so. Blacks also were more likely to be **recidivists** (more than one recorded police contact); and among recidivists, they were more likely to be chronic offenders. They were, in fact, five times more likely than whites to be included among the 6 percent who were responsible for over half of all the police contacts for the cohort. Of the fourteen murders recorded for the cohort, all were committed by blacks. According to the index used by the investigators to measure the seriousness of delinquent offenses, the fourteen homicides alone represented more social harm than all the other violent crimes committed by whites.

NONINDEX OFFENSES As with index offenses, the likelihood of arrest for nonindex offenses tends to be greater for black juveniles. For most of the nonindex offenses in table 4.4, the ratio of the juvenile arrest rate for blacks to that of whites is between 2 and 3 to 1. For running away, vandalism, and liquor law

TABLE 4.4

Arrest rates per 100,000 population ages 10–17 for index and selected nonindex crimes, whites and blacks, 1996

type of crime	whites	blacks
Index crimes		
Murder and nonnegligent manslaughter	3.5	26.8
Forcible rape	9.5	38.0
Robbery	64.5	484.5
Aggravated assault	137.0	484.8
Burglary	300.4	490.6
Larceny-theft	1,090.7	2,028.4
Motor vehicle theft	132.3	448.0
Arson	24.4	27.7
Nonindex crimes		
Curfew and loitering	433.2	745.8
Runaway	463.0	506.9
Other assaults	445.6	1,285.5
Stolen property: buying, receiving, possessing	76.0	238.4
Vandalism	344.2	387.5
Weapons: carrying, possessing	104.0	289.3
Drug abuse	411.2	1,227.9
Liquor laws	426.0	134.8
Disorderly conduct	421.7	1,204.1
All other offenses except traffic	978.8	1,814.7

SOURCES: Day, 1993:18; FBI, 1997:233.
NOTE: Arrest figures based on 9,661 agencies; 1996 estimated population 189,885,000.

violations, however, the arrest rate for whites is about as high or higher than the rate for blacks. Indeed, for liquor law violations, the arrest rate is over three times higher for whites (426.0 versus 134.8).

A comparison of the arrest rates for the index and nonindex offenses in table 4.4 raises some provocative questions: Are the behaviors of white and black youngsters glaringly different when it comes to such violent crimes as murder, rape, and robbery but virtually alike when running away and vandalism are involved? Could it be that the police are more protective of whites than blacks when it comes to violent crimes? Is it possible that for liquor law violations, law enforcement officials are more tolerant of black youths? Those are the kinds of questions that arrest data raise but do not answer.

SUMMARY Analysis of the relationship between race and arrest has shown that (1) the number of ar-rests of Native Americans/Alaskan Natives and Asian Americans/Pacific Islanders is dwarfed by that of whites and blacks, (2) black youths are more likely than white youths to be arrested for index offenses, particularly violent crimes, and (3) arrest rates for most nonindex offenses are higher among black juveniles, but for some nonindex offenses, arrest rates are as high or higher among whites. In light of the legacy of slavery and racial discrimination in America and the exclusion of blacks from full economic, political, and social participation, such findings should probably not surprise us. However, they leave questions that beg an explanation: To what extent does the relationship between race and arrest reflect police policy and procedures rather than juvenile behavior? To what extent are the behavioral differences implied by arrest data due to differences in the family lives of white and black youths? In short, the relationship between race and arrest is a "fact" much in need of further research and theoretical attention.

Social Class and Arrest

As we learned previously, Americans have believed that poverty and lower class membership are likely to increase the chances that children will violate the law. If true, this could help to explain the relationship between race and arrest. Black children have long been disadvantaged, both socially and economically. Perhaps, then, their disproportionate representation in arrest statistics is more strongly related to the prejudice, poor education, and poverty they experience than to factors linked strictly to race.

Such a possibility cannot be explored using FBI data because the relationship between social class and arrest is not analyzed in the *Uniform Crime Reports*. However, data that bear on this issue were gathered in the Philadelphia cohort study (Wolfgang, Figlio, and Sellin, 1972:54–129, 244–255). The researchers discovered three things:

1. Social class was strongly related to the chances of arrest. Forty-six percent of the cohort lived in lower-class census tracts, of whom almost half (45 percent) had at least one recorded police contact. By contrast, only 27 percent of those who lived in higher-class tracts had police records, although they composed 54 percent of the cohort.
2. Social class and race overlap; that is, blacks were more likely than whites to reside in lower-class areas. Such double jeopardy was reflected in a host of social afflictions. Compared with other boys, lower-class blacks were more likely not only to have become officially delinquent but also to have experienced the disruption of a greater number of school and residential moves; they also had the lowest IQ scores and completed fewer grades in school.
3. Boys from lower-class census tracts were more likely than those from higher-status tracts to be among the small group of 627 chronic offenders.

In short, the Philadelphia cohort study suggested three points about the relationship between social class and arrest: (1) membership in the lower class is likely to increase the chances of arrest, (2) being black is related to lower-class membership, and (3) lower-class boys are more likely to be serious chronic offenders than are boys from higher social classes. Class membership, therefore, appears to be another "fact" requiring attention in explanations of delinquency.

ARREST TRENDS

Our understanding of delinquency is enhanced if, in addition to the various factors associated with arrest, we examine arrest *trends* and the extent to which they imply that delinquent behavior is increasing or decreasing. If one looks only at the total number of juvenile arrests, the message seems clear: Delinquency has increased considerably over the past several decades. In 1965, the number of juvenile arrests for all nontraffic offenses was 1,074,485; by 1996, it was 2,103,658—an increase of 96 percent (compare FBI, 1966:112 and 1997:224). Such a comparison, however, overlooks two crucial points: (1) The youth population fluctuates in size and (2) today's arrest estimates tend to be based on a larger segment of the total population than they were in 1965. The first point reemphasizes the need for comparing *rates*, as described before. However, the second point requires elaboration. In 1965, FBI data on arrests by age came from agencies covering only about 69 percent of the total population. Since that time, the percentage has increased considerably (to 83 percent in 1993, for example). As a consequence, estimates of increases in arrests may be inflated because the further back one goes in time, the greater the underestimation of the actual number of arrests. To compensate for such underestimations by the FBI, the following adjustment is made in the arrest rates discussed in this section:

$$X = \frac{A \times AP}{OP}$$

where

X = estimated number of actual arrests
A = arrests reported by the FBI

AP = actual population of the United States
OP = population on which FBI arrests are based[2]

Violent Crimes

Arrest trends for violent crimes—murder, rape, robbery, and aggravated assault—are shown in figure 4.2. Juvenile arrest rates per 100,000 population under age 18 are compared with rates for adults ages 18 and older for the period 1965 to 1996. Three observations can be made:

1. The rate at which young people have been arrested for violent crimes has remained lower than the adult rate.
2. Arrest rates for violent crimes have increased markedly for both juveniles and adults since 1965. However, there has been a larger increase for juveniles. While the adult rate has increased 129 percent (from 139 in 1965 to 318 in 1996), the juvenile rate has increased 236 percent (from 61 to 205).
3. All of the increase in the juvenile arrest rate occurred between 1965 and 1975 and between 1985 and 1996; there was little change in the juvenile rate from 1975 to 1985. The adult arrest rate increased 66 percent from 1965 to 1975 (from 139 to 231) but then only another 38 percent from 1975 to 1996 (from 231 to 318).

Property Crimes

The same kinds of information are displayed in figure 4.3 for property crimes—combining burglary, larceny-theft, motor vehicle theft, and arson. However, the findings differ in some respects from those for violent crimes:

1. Since 1965, the rate at which juveniles have been arrested for property crimes has remained higher than the adult rate.
2. The juvenile arrest rate has increased 36 percent during the past thirty or so years (from 781 in

1965 to 1,065 in 1996), compared with a 93 percent increase for adults (from 362 to 697). When these findings are joined with those for violent crimes (see figure 4.2), they suggest that although juveniles appear to have become more delinquent overall, the greatest change has been their increased commission of violent crimes.
3. The gap between juvenile and adult arrest rates for property crimes has decreased since 1975. Since that time, the rate for juveniles has decreased 20 percent (from 1,328 to 1,065), while for adults there has been a slight increase (from 650 to 697).

All Crimes

Figure 4.4 plots the trend in the juvenile arrest rate for all nontraffic offenses—index as well as nonindex—from 1965 to 1996. The rates are calculated per 100,000 youths ages 10–17; and in this figure, changes in the size of this population also are presented for comparison. The following can be observed:

1. The youth population increased between 1965 and 1975 and then decreased until the 1990s.
2. The juvenile arrest rate increased from 1965 to 1975 (42 percent), leveled off from 1975 to 1985, and increased again from 1985 to 1996 (36 percent).
3. Although the size of the youth population was about the same in 1996 as it was in 1965 (30.3 million versus 29.5 million), the juvenile arrest rate has increased 85 percent (from 5,268 to 9,742).

JUVENILE COURT REFERRALS

Following arrest, the juvenile court represents the next step in the processing of offenders. Hence, we now will examine juvenile court referrals.

Number of Referrals

An estimated 982,100 cases were formally processed by juvenile courts in 1994 (Butts et al., 1996:9, 33). To keep that estimate in perspective, note that it

[2]The use of this adjustment requires two assumptions: (1) Arrest rates are the same in areas not covered by the FBI as they are in areas that are covered and (2) the proportions of different segments of the population (juvenile and adult, for example, or male and female) are distributed the same way in uncovered and covered areas. To the extent that these assumptions are not met, error will be introduced. Nonetheless, it is likely that this error will be less than the error that is inherent in unadjusted comparisons.

FIGURE 4.2

Arrest rates for violent crimes per 100,000 population, juveniles and adults, 1965–1996

SOURCES: Bureau of the Census, 1965:15; 1982:29–36, 42–43; 1985:17–24; 1990:12–15; 1992:12; Day, 1993: 12, 14, 16, 18; FBI, 1966:112; 1971:126; 1976:188; 1977: 181; 1978:180; 1979:194; 1980:196; 1981:200; 1982:171; 1983:176; 1984:179; 1985:172; 1986:174; 1987:174; 1988:174; 1989:178; 1990:182; 1991:184; 1992:223; 1993:227; 1994:227; 1995:227; 1996:218; 1997:224; Spencer, 1989:42, 44.

NOTE: Adjusted rates—see text and footnote 2 for detail.

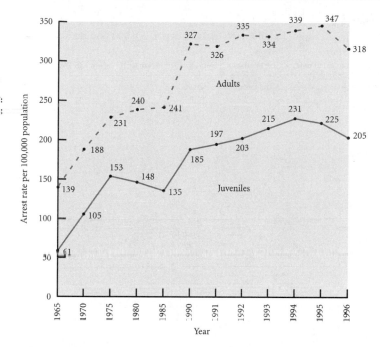

FIGURE 4.3

Arrest rates for property crimes per 100,000 population, juveniles and adults, 1965–1996

SOURCES: Bureau of the Census, 1965:15; 1982:29–36, 42–43; 1985:17–24; 1990:12–15; 1992:12; Day, 1993:12, 14, 16, 18; FBI, 1966:112; 1971:126; 1976:188; 1977:181; 1978:180; 1979:194; 1980:196; 1981:200; 1982:171; 1983:176; 1984:179; 1985:172; 1986:174; 1987:174; 1988:174; 1989:178; 1990:182; 1991:184; 1992:223; 1993:227; 1994:227; 1995:227; 1996:218; 1997:224; Spencer, 1989:42, 44.

NOTE: Rates include arrests for arson. Adjusted rates—see text and footnote 2 for detail.

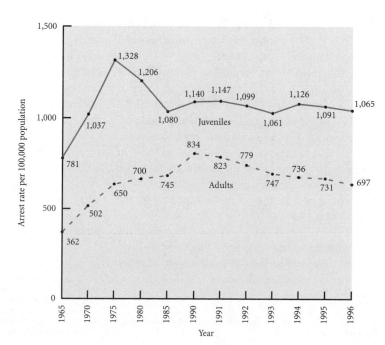

FIGURE 4.4

Trend in arrest rate for all nontraffic crimes per 100,000 population ages 10–17 and in youth population ages 10–17, 1965–1996

SOURCES: Bureau of the Census, 1965:15, 26; 1982:35, 42; 1985:17, 23; 1990:12; Day, 1993:18; FBI, 1966:112; 1971:126; 1976:188; 1981:200; 1986:174; 1991:184; 1997: 224; Spencer, 1989:42.

NOTE: Adjusted rates—see text and footnote 2 for detail.

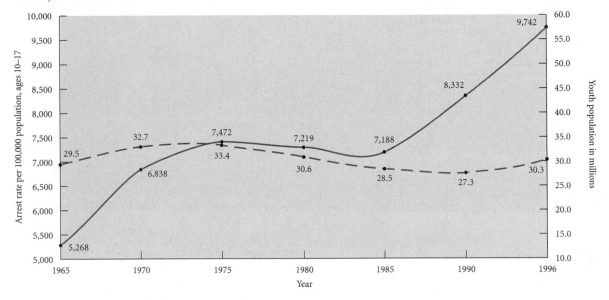

constituted only 3.4 percent of young people ages 10–17 (who numbered about 29 million in 1994) (Day, 1993:14). The nation, in other words, was not inundated by juvenile court cases.

Also, the number of formally processed court cases was only 45 percent of the 2.2 million juvenile arrests reported by the police in the same year (FBI, 1995:227). According to police estimates, then, 7.6 percent of young people ages 10–17 may have committed illegal acts.[3] But because 20 to 40 percent of all juveniles picked up by the police are released, and thus are not subjected to any further legal action, they do not appear in the estimates reported by the juvenile courts (FBI, 1976:177; 1981:258; 1986:240; 1990:233; 1997:271). This fact illustrates a point made at the beginning of the chapter: Compared to juvenile court data, police data provide more accurate estimates of the extent or amount of delinquency.

Reasons for Referral

The kinds of criminal offenses for which juveniles are referred to court are shown in figure 4.5. The data tend to support the notion that the most common criminal offenses among juveniles are property crimes (52–60 percent of all referrals for criminal offenses), followed by violent crimes (16–22 percent) and drug law violations (5–8 percent).

There were 126,900 status offense cases formally processed by juvenile courts in 1994 (up considerably from 76,300 in 1985 and 92,700 in 1990) (Butts et al., 1996:33), most of them involving running away, truancy, ungovernability, and liquor law violations. Furthermore, many more status offense cases were informally processed by the courts.[4]

[3]Because a person may be arrested more than once in any given year, such estimates are crude at best.

[4]Formally processed (petitioned) cases are "those that appear on the official court calendar in response to the filing of a petition, complaint, or other legal instrument requesting the court to adjudicate a youth as a delinquent, status offender, or dependent child" (Butts et al., 1996:58). Informally processed (nonpetitioned) cases have been screened by court personnel (e.g., probation officers) and handled by some means other than the filing of a formal petition (e.g., a warning).

IS THERE A COMING STORM OF JUVENILE MURDERS?

"As if the situation with youth violence was not bad enough already, future demographics are expected to make matters even worse" (Fox, 1996:3). The *demographics* to which that statement refers is an increase in the number of young people as a result of a "baby boomerang" (the large post–World War II cohort of baby boomers having their own children). The number of 14- to 17-year-olds will increase considerably by 2005, leading many criminologists to believe that there also will be an increase in juvenile murders. "Even if the recent surge in teenage homicide rates slows, our nation faces a future juvenile violence problem that may make today's epidemic pale in comparison" (Fox, 1996:3).

Characteristics of Referrals

Several of the assumed "facts" from arrest data are found also in juvenile court data.

AGE Juvenile court data (see figure 4.6) suggest that age is strongly related to the likelihood of being referred to juvenile court for criminal offenses: In 1994, the likelihood of referral increased through age 16, before decreasing among 17-year-olds. But although that pattern is consistent with arrest data, it also raises some important questions. For example, the rate of referral for 16-year-olds (112 per 1,000) is more than twice the rate for 13-year-olds (46 per 1,000). Does this mean that 16-year-olds commit twice as much delinquency? Is it because 16-year-olds have more prior referrals and thus are more likely to be defined as chronic offenders? Or is it because legal officials are more inclined to hold 16-

year-olds responsible for their acts? Because the answers to such questions are known only to the officials who process juveniles and keep official records, it is clear that their responses to the age and other characteristics of young people may be as important in generating juvenile court action and juvenile court records as the acts that young people commit.

GENDER Juvenile court data suggest that boys commit more delinquency than girls. Indeed, since 1985, about 80 percent of all referrals for criminal offenses have involved boys (Butts et al., 1996:21). When one examines the reasons for the referrals, the picture remains largely the same. For every kind of criminal offense—violent crimes, property crimes, and drug law violations—boys account for a higher percentage of court referrals (Butts et al., 1996:21). Only in the case of status offenses does the percentage involving girls (42 percent of all formally processed status offense cases in 1994) approach that of boys (58 percent); and even then, for specific status offenses, there is usually a higher percentage involving boys (Butts et al., 1996:42). For example, boys accounted for about 70 percent of all formally processed cases for liquor law violations in 1994. For only one status offense does the majority of cases involve girls; in 1994, girls were involved in 60 percent of all formally processed cases of running away. Like arrest statistics, then, juvenile court records indicate that delinquency is more likely to be committed by males than females.

RACE About 65 percent of the referrals to juvenile court for criminal offenses involved whites in 1994, and 30 percent involved blacks (Butts et al., 1996: 26). However, when one considers the smaller size of the black youth population (only about 15 percent of youths ages 10–17, as we mentioned previously), it is clear that the chances of referral to juvenile court are greater for blacks than for whites. Like arrest statistics, then, juvenile court records suggest either that black youngsters commit more delinquency or that a racial bias is operating, or both.

Trends in Referrals

Trends in the rate of juvenile court referral per 1,000 population ages 10–17, for 1985, 1990, and 1994, are

FIGURE 4.5

Referrals to juvenile court for
criminal offenses, by type of
offense, 1985, 1990, and 1994

SOURCE: Butts et al., 1996:6.

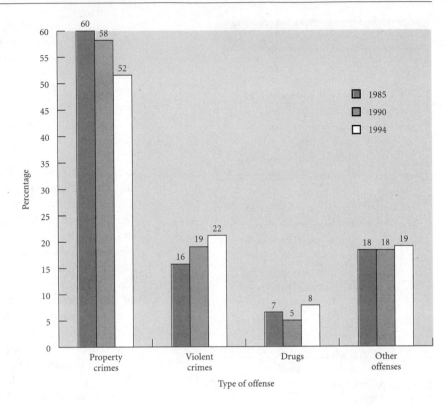

FIGURE 4.6

Referrals to juvenile court for criminal offenses,
by age, 1994

SOURCE: Butts et al., 1996:17.

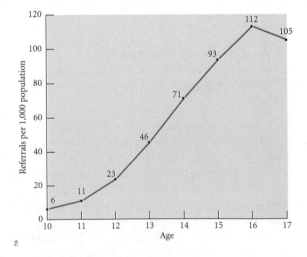

displayed in figure 4.7. Separate trends are shown for
males, females, and both genders combined. Two
points can be made:

1. For both boys and girls, referral rates for criminal offenses increased between 1985 and 1994.
   However, the increase for girls (from 16 to 24,

FIGURE 4.7

Referrals to juvenile court for criminal offenses, by gender, 1985, 1990, and 1994

SOURCE: Butts et al., 1996:6, 22.

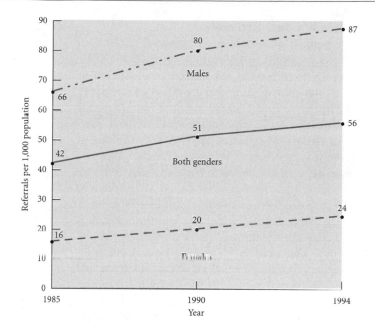

or a 50 percent increase) was greater than the increase for boys (32 percent, from 66 to 87). It seems, then, that the delinquent behavior of girls has increased more rapidly than that of boys.

2. From 1985 to 1994, the juvenile court referral rate for criminal offenses increased 33 percent when both genders are considered together (from 42 to 56).

SUMMARY AND CONCLUSIONS

Arrest records may be cause to question the extent to which the ideology of child saving has served to quarantine children from involvement in delinquent behavior. Indeed, arrest records suggest that juveniles are one of the most criminal segments of the population.

Basic "Facts"

Certain assumed "facts" require explanation.

1. *Age.* Why are arrest rates so strongly related to age? Although a small group of chronic offenders may account for a disproportionate share of all juvenile arrests, apprehensions of young peo-ple by the police increase during adolescence, peak at age 18, and then decrease.

2. *Gender.* Why are arrest rates higher for males than females? It may be that traditional differences between gender roles account for the higher arrest rate of boys.

3. *Race.* Why are arrest rates higher for black than white juveniles? Arrest data imply that centuries of exclusion from the benefits of American life have profoundly affected the lives of young black people. They are much more likely than white youths to be arrested for index offenses, particularly violent crimes.

4. *Social class.* Why are arrest rates higher for lower-class than middle-class juveniles? Like race, membership in the lower class increases the likelihood of arrest. Indeed, those factors tend to be related, putting those young people who possess both characteristics in double jeopardy.

Arrest Trends

Examination of arrest trends also raises important questions: Why have juveniles become more delin-quent during the past thirty years? Why do they appear to be more violent?

Juvenile Court Referrals

The number of cases referred to juvenile court each year is smaller than the number of arrests. Consequently, juvenile court records are not as accurate as arrest statistics in estimating the extent or amount of delinquency. That "fact" notwithstanding, juvenile court records raise many of the same kinds of questions that arrest statistics do: Why does the rate of juvenile court referral increase with age? Why are males referred at a higher rate than females? Why are the chances greater that a black child will be referred to juvenile court than a white child?

In response to such difficult questions, the next two chapters are devoted to a discussion of two additional sources of data: (1) self-reported law violations of juveniles rather than official accounts and (2) data derived from victims. By adding information from those two sources, we can check the accuracy of official accounts and further address the questions they raise.

Discussion Questions

1. What do we mean when we say that police and juvenile court data are *official* accounts of delinquent behavior? What is *official* about police and juvenile court data?
2. How are police data more accurate than juvenile court data in estimating the extent and distribution of delinquency?
3. What is the relationship between age and arrest? Between gender and arrest? Between race and arrest? Between social class and arrest?
4. To what extent do official accounts indicate that there has been a recent epidemic of delinquency in the United States?
5. To what extent do high arrest and juvenile court referral rates suggest that we have failed in our efforts to prevent delinquency?

References

Blumstein, Alfred. 1995. "Violence by Young People: Why the Deadly Nexus?" *National Institute of Justice Journal* 229 (August):2–9.

Bureau of the Census. 1965. *Current Population Reports.* Series P-25, no. 321. Washington, D.C.: U.S. Government Printing Office.

———. 1982. *Current Population Reports.* Series P-25, no. 917. Washington, D.C.: U.S. Government Printing Office.

———. 1985. *Current Population Reports.* Series P-25, no. 965. Washington, D.C.: U.S. Government Printing Office.

———. 1990. *Current Population Reports.* Series P-25, no. 1057. Washington, D.C.: U.S. Government Printing Office.

———. 1992. *Current Population Reports.* Series P-25, no. 1092. Washington, D.C.: U.S. Government Printing Office.

Butts, Jeffrey A., Howard N. Snyder, Terrence A. Finnegan, Anne L. Aughenbaugh, and Rowen S. Poole. 1996. *Juvenile Court Statistics, 1994.* Washington, D.C.: Office of Juvenile Justice and Delinquency Prevention, U.S. Department of Justice.

Day, Jennifer Cheeseman. 1993. *Current Population Reports.* Series P-25, no. 1104. Washington, D.C.: U.S. Government Printing Office.

Federal Bureau of Investigation. 1966. *Crime in the United States: Uniform Crime Reports, 1965.* Washington, D.C.: U.S. Government Printing Office.

———. 1971. *Crime in the United States: Uniform Crime Reports, 1970.* Washington, D.C.: U.S. Government Printing Office.

———. 1976. *Crime in the United States: Uniform Crime Reports, 1975.* Washington, D.C.: U.S. Government Printing Office.

———. 1977. *Crime in the United States: Uniform Crime Reports, 1976.* Washington, D.C.: U.S. Government Printing Office.

———. 1978. *Crime in the United States: Uniform Crime Reports, 1977.* Washington, D.C.: U.S. Government Printing Office.

———. 1979. *Crime in the United States: Uniform Crime Reports, 1978.* Washington, D.C.: U.S. Government Printing Office.

———. 1980. *Crime in the United States: Uniform Crime Reports, 1979.* Washington, D.C.: U.S. Government Printing Office.

———. 1981. *Crime in the United States: Uniform Crime*

Reports, 1980. Washington, D.C.: U.S. Government Printing Office.

1982. *Crime in the United States: Uniform Crime Reports, 1981.* Washington, D.C.: U.S. Government Printing Office.

1983. *Crime in the United States: Uniform Crime Reports, 1982.* Washington, D.C.: U.S. Government Printing Office.

1984. *Crime in the United States: Uniform Crime Reports, 1983.* Washington, D.C.: U.S. Government Printing Office.

1985. *Crime in the United States: Uniform Crime Reports, 1984.* Washington, D.C.: U.S. Government Printing Office.

1986. *Crime in the United States: Uniform Crime Reports, 1985.* Washington, D.C.: U.S. Government Printing Office.

1987. *Crime in the United States: Uniform Crime Reports, 1986.* Washington, D.C.: U.S. Government Printing Office.

1988. *Crime in the United States: Uniform Crime Reports, 1987.* Washington, D.C.: U.S. Government Printing Office.

1989. *Crime in the United States: Uniform Crime Reports, 1988.* Washington, D.C.: U.S. Government Printing Office.

1990. *Crime in the United States: Uniform Crime Reports, 1989.* Washington, D.C.: U.S. Government Printing Office.

1991. *Crime in the United States: Uniform Crime Reports, 1990.* Washington, D.C.: U.S. Government Printing Office.

1992. *Crime in the United States: Uniform Crime Reports, 1991.* Washington, D.C.: U.S. Government Printing Office.

1993. *Crime in the United States: Uniform Crime Reports, 1992.* Washington, D.C.: U.S. Government Printing Office.

1994. *Crime in the United States: Uniform Crime Reports, 1993.* Washington, D.C.: U.S. Government Printing Office.

1995. *Crime in the United States: Uniform Crime Reports, 1994.* Washington, D.C.: U.S. Government Printing Office.

1996. *Crime in the United States: Uniform Crime Reports, 1995.* Washington, D.C.: U.S. Government Printing Office.

1997. *Crime in the United States: Uniform Crime Reports, 1996.* Washington, D.C.: U.S. Government Printing Office.

Fox, James Alan. 1996. "Trends in Juvenile Violence: A Report to the United States Attorney General on Current and Future Rates of Juvenile Offending." Washington, D.C.: Bureau of Justice Statistics, U.S. Department of Justice.

Greenberg, David F. 1977. "Delinquency and the Age Structure of Society." *Contemporary Crisis* 1 (April):189–223.

Hirschi, Travis, and Michael Gottfredson. 1983. "Age and the Explanation of Crime." *American Journal of Sociology* 89 (November):552–584.

Klein, Malcolm W. 1995. *The American Gang: Its Nature, Prevalence, and Control.* New York: Oxford University Press.

Spencer, Gregory. 1989. *Current Population Reports.* Series P-25, no. 1018. Washington, D.C.: U.S. Government Printing Office.

Steffensmeier, Darrell J., Emilie Andersen Allan, Miles D. Harer, and Cathy Streifel. 1989. "Age and the Distribution of Crime." *American Journal of Sociology* 94 (January):803–831.

Wolfgang, Marvin E., Robert M. Figlio, and Thorsten Sellin. 1972. *Delinquency in a Birth Cohort.* Chicago: University of Chicago Press.

SOCIAL SCIENTISTS OFTEN STUDY DELINQUENCY BY ASKING YOUNG PEOPLE TO COMPLETE SELF-REPORT SURVEYS ABOUT THEIR DELINQUENT BEHAVIOR.

CHAPTER FIVE

SELF-REPORTED DELINQUENT BEHAVIOR

Many people are uncomfortable with, and even disbelieving about, official accounts of delinquency. This discomfort is due to the finding not only that law-violating behavior is more common among younger than older people but also that it is more common among males, among racial and ethnic minorities, and among the poor. The likelihood that the police accept such findings adds to the discomfort. It is feared that because the police are more likely to associate crime with youths, males, racial and ethnic minorities, and the poor than with other groups, they are more likely to apprehend these people, producing a disproportionate number of youthful, male, minority, and poor offenders in arrest statistics (Garrett and Short, 1975).

FLAWS IN OFFICIAL STATISTICS

In addition to the possibility that official accounts of delinquency result in a self-fulfilling prophecy, widespread discomfort is fueled by several flaws in official statistics.

The "Dark Figure" of Crime

Official accounts of delinquency are like the tip of an iceberg. Many delinquent acts go unobserved by legal officials or unreported to them. The National Commission on the Causes and Prevention of Violence (1969:18) called this missing body of information the **dark figure of crime**—the gap between the amount of crime recorded by the police and the amount actually committed.

There are two important reasons for this gap. First, most juveniles are able to conceal their illegal acts—shoplifting, truancy, fornication, drinking, gambling, vandalism, joyriding, or even burglary (Blumstein et al., 1986, 1:99). Second, people often fail to report crimes. Some victims, for example, believe that it is a private matter; others believe the police would not want to be bothered or cannot do anything about it; still others do not believe the victimization is important enough to report to the police (Jackson, 1990:32; Maguire and Pastore, 1997: 225; O'Brien, 1985:25–27).

The "Village Watchman"

A second flaw with official statistics is that they are collected on a local level by people who may have a vested interest in seeing their reports turn out in a way that favors them (O'Brien, 1985:27–28, 1995: 62). Nettler (1984:39) quotes Sir Josiah Stamp, an English economist, who put his finger directly on the problem:

> The government are very keen on amassing statistics. They collect them, raise them to the *n*th power, take the cube root, and prepare wonderful diagrams. But you must never forget that every one of these figures comes in the first instance from the village watchman, who just puts down what he damn pleases.

The reason for Stamp's concern about the village watchman is illustrated by this police official's comments:

> The unwritten law was that you were supposed to make things look good. You weren't supposed to report all the crime that actually took place in your precinct—and, if you did, it could be your neck. I know captains who actually lost their commands because they turned in honest crime reports. (National Commission, 1969:18)

The point is that "village watchmen" in police departments, courts, and correctional institutions sometimes distort their reports, either out of ignorance or for self-serving reasons. Their commitment to themselves and their organizations is greater than their commitment to providing accurate information. As with students cheating on a test or taxpayers misreporting their income to the Internal Revenue Service, other concerns can take precedence over accuracy or honesty (Seidman and Couzens, 1974).

Changing Norms and Expectations

Changing norms for behavior and the social expectations that attend them also cause difficulties in interpreting official statistics—often in unexpected ways. For example, one of the results of political inequality traditionally was a tendency for the police to ignore all but the most serious crimes in slum areas (President's Commission, 1967:25). Without political power, poor people were left to take care of their own problems. As a result, many delinquent acts went unchecked and unreported. But as poor people acquired some political clout, they demanded that police take a more active role in suppressing delinquency in their neighborhoods. The likely consequence was an increase in **official delinquency.** Law-violating behavior that customarily had gone unrecorded—for example, **status offenses,** gang behavior, and petty crimes—became a matter of official record. Thus, without a large increase in actual delinquent behavior, arrest and court records may have been inflated considerably.

Changing norms and expectations can alter official crime statistics in other ways. In virtually every state, some types of sexual behavior—fornication, adultery, prostitution, homosexuality, sodomy, oral sex—are against the law. In recent years, however, there have been increasing demands to repeal such laws, and the trend has been not to enforce them. Nettler (1984:40–41) notes that in England, once it was anticipated that the Wolfenden Committee would make similar recommendations, the number of recorded homosexual offenses dropped by half over just a few years. Yet, the laws during that period actually were not changed. The reduction in official offenses was due to changes in police activity, not to changes in the law or sexual behavior.

Police Professionalization

Those who run the Uniform Crime Reporting Program are aware of the flaws with official statistics and have tried to professionalize police reporting practices. One thing that has been done, for example, is to include in the calculation of crime trends only those police departments with comparable reporting practices across the years (FBI, 1997:390).

Paradoxically, one of the reasons for exercising care in interpreting police statistics is that recording practices have improved. With an increase in the number of clerks and improved organization of reporting systems, known crimes now are recorded more faithfully by the police than ever before (Gove, Hughes, and Geerken, 1985:474). Improved recording practices should result in increases in official estimates of crime and delinquency, a notion that reflects a sociological truism: As people become more aware of a problem and attempt to do something about it, the size of the problem seems to increase.

In summary, "it can be argued that official statistics on crime, whether compiled by the police, the courts, or any other administrative agency, can never provide a definitive measure of crime" (Penick and Owens, 1976:153). They are flawed partly because of offenses that are never reported to the police and partly because of variation in police reporting practices. Because of such flaws, researchers have sought alternative ways for estimating delinquent behavior. One of the more important has been the self-report survey.

SELF-REPORTED LAW VIOLATIONS

Instead of using official data on delinquency, social scientists increasingly have turned to juveniles themselves to obtain estimates of law violations. This has been done either by questionnaires or through interviews with youngsters about their behavior. The findings from these **self-report studies** help to answer crucial questions about delinquency.

The Prevalence of Law Violation

The prevalence of law violation refers to the percentage of juveniles who report having violated the law. When delinquent behavior is estimated in that way, self-report studies reveal that virtually all juveniles have committed delinquent acts (e.g., Elliott and Ageton, 1980; Elliott et al., 1983; Erickson and Empey, 1963; Gold, 1966, 1970; Gould, 1969; Hindelang, Hirschi, and Weis, 1981; Murphy, Shirley, and Witmer, 1946; Short and Nye, 1958; Williams and Gold, 1972).

Types of Offenses

Table 5.1 shows the prevalence of law violation by juveniles who were asked if *during the past year* they had committed each of several different types of offenses. The table is derived from self-reported data collected by researchers at the Institute for Social Research at the University of Michigan. Each year since 1975, the institute has collected data from a sample of high school seniors throughout the United States (Maguire and Pastore, 1997:615–619). Each of the values in columns 1–5 in the table represents the percentage of seniors who reported committing a given type of offense at least once during the past year (e.g., during 1995 for the 1996 high school seniors, during 1989 for the 1990 seniors, and so on).

STATUS OFFENSES As shown in the first column of table 5.1, the most commonly reported offense is arguing with parents, which is a status offense. Although girls tend to commit fewer delinquent acts than boys, a higher percentage of 1996 senior girls reported arguing with their parents at least once during the past year (92 percent of girls versus 86 percent of boys).

PROPERTY CRIMES When it comes to **property crimes,** table 5.1 shows that the most commonly reported offenses are theft under $50, shoplifting, and breaking and entering—each involving large percentages of both girls and boys. Vandalism of school is also common. Less commonly reported property crimes are theft over $50, vandalism at work, theft of

SAMPLE QUESTIONS FROM THE NATIONAL YOUTH SURVEY

How many times in the last year have you:

1. purposely damaged or destroyed property belonging to a school
2. stolen (or tried to steal) a motor vehicle, such as a car or motorcycle
3. stolen (or tried to steal) something worth more than $50
4. run away from home
5. attacked someone with the idea of seriously hurting or killing them
6. been involved in gang fights
7. sold marijuana or hashish ("pot," "grass," "hash")
8. hit or threatened to hit a teacher or adult at school
9. sold hard drugs, such as heroin, cocaine, and LSD
10. had (or tried to have) sexual relations with someone against their will
11. used force (strong-arm methods) to get money or things from other students
12. been drunk in a public place
13. broken into a building or vehicle (or tried to break in) to steal something or just to look around
14. skipped classes without an excuse
15. made obscene telephone calls, such as calling someone and saying dirty things

SOURCE: Elliott et al., 1983:12–13.

car parts, and auto theft. Arson is the least commonly reported property crime. Only about 5 percent of 1996 senior boys and 1 percent of 1996 senior girls reported committing arson even once during the past year.

VIOLENT CRIMES   Table 5.1 tends to support official statistics in suggesting that among young people, **violent crimes** are less common than status offenses and property crimes. There are some exceptions, however; for example, fighting (including gang fighting) and, to a lesser extent, serious assaults are commonly reported. Fighting has long been a part of adolescents' lives, and apparently it continues to be so.

According to table 5.1, hitting a teacher is less prevalent than other violent crimes, as is armed robbery. Nonetheless, the fact that *any* girls committed these types of offenses, to say nothing of about 1 in 20 boys, runs contrary to the traditional belief that modern child-raising practices inoculate against serious delinquent behavior.

DRUG USE   Table 5.2 reveals the self-reported lifetime (ever used), annual (past year), and monthly (past month) prevalence of nonprescription drug use by 1996 high school seniors. Several findings are noteworthy:

1. Alcohol, cigarettes, and marijuana are the most commonly used illegal drugs among young people. Almost as many seniors report having used alcohol in the past month (monthly prevalence of 50.8 percent) as having ever used it (lifetime prevalence of 79.2 percent).
2. Large percentages report having ever used other drugs: inhalants (16.6 percent), stimulants (15.3 percent), hallucinogens (14.0 percent), LSD (12.6 percent), tranquilizers (7.2 percent), and cocaine (7.1 percent). However, the percentage reporting having used those drugs during the past month drops off considerably, suggesting that the number of regular users is relatively small (2–4 percent).
3. The prevalence of reported crack cocaine and heroin use among high school seniors is small. However, the estimates do not take into account crack cocaine and heroin use among high school dropouts, for whom the actual prevalence figure is probably higher.

TABLE 5.1

Annual prevalence of self-reported delinquency among high school seniors, males and females, 1996, 1990, 1985, 1980, and 1975

TYPE OF OFFENSE	1996	1990	1985	1980	1975	PERCENTAGE CHANGE 1975–1996
Argue with parents						
Male	86.0	88.8	86.0	85.7	85.6	0
Female	92.3	93.5	91.8	87.6	89.9	3
Theft under $50						
Male	38.7	39.7	38.6	42.5	43.1	−10
Female	26.7	25.0	21.5	24.4	23.3	15
Shoplifting						
Male	36.9	36.9	31.8	38.2	44.7	−17
Female	27.7	26.1	20.8	23.4	27.1	2
Breaking-entering						
Male	29.0	31.7	34.5	33.3	39.5	−27
Female	18.4	18.2	18.0	16.9	18.3	1
Gang fight						
Male	27.0	26.8	26.1	24.2	23.2	16
Female	13.1	15.0	14.9	10.6	12.4	6
Fighting						
Male	22.6	24.1	23.7	21.1	20.0	13
Female	10.0	13.1	12.7	10.5	9.5	5
Serious assault						
Male	22.5	20.2	19.0	20.6	17.5	29
Female	5.4	4.1	3.7	2.8	2.2	145
Vandalism of school						
Male	20.6	18.3	18.9	18.9	21.0	−2
Female	7.5	7.7	8.5	7.6	5.8	29
Theft over $50						
Male	17.8	15.1	11.9	11.7	10.7	66
Female	6.5	4.2	2.1	1.7	1.0	550
Vandalism at work						
Male	10.4	10.8	9.9	12.2	9.6	8
Female	1.8	1.9	1.0	1.6	1.1	64
Theft of car parts						
Male	9.4	11.3	11.1	12.7	10.6	−11
Female	0.9	1.7	2.3	1.4	1.2	−25
Auto theft						
Male	7.4	8.5	7.8	7.3	5.9	25
Female	2.6	4.4	3.4	2.1	2.1	24
Armed robbery						
Male	5.9	5.4	5.3	5.2	4.8	23
Female	1.1	0.8	1.3	0.9	0.8	38
Hit teacher						
Male	5.8	3.4	5.1	5.5	5.5	5
Female	1.1	1.4	1.0	1.0	0.9	22
Arson						
Male	4.9	3.5	2.9	2.7	3.3	48
Female	0.9	0.7	0.6	0.3	0.3	200

SOURCES: Flanagan and McGarrell, 1986:316–319; Flanagan and Maguire, 1990:292–295; Maguire and Pastore, 1997:240–243.
NOTES: 1975 figures are based on 2,879 respondents, 1980 figures on 3,205 respondents, 1985 figures on 3,224 respondents, 1990 figures on 2,516 respondents, and 1996 figures on 2,339 respondents.

TABLE 5.2

Prevalence of self-reported drug use among high school seniors, 1996

TYPE OF DRUG	EVER USED	PAST YEAR	PAST MONTH
Alcohol	79.2	72.5	50.8
Cigarettes	63.5	—	34.0
Marijuana or hashish	44.9	35.8	21.9
Inhalants (e.g., glue, aerosol)	16.6	7.6	2.5
Stimulants (amphetamines, uppers, speed, bennies)	15.3	9.5	4.1
Hallucinogens (e.g., mescaline, peyote)	14.0	10.1	3.5
LSD	12.6	8.8	2.5
Tranquilizers (Librium, Valium, Miltown)	7.2	4.6	2.0
Cocaine	7.1	4.9	2.0
Crack cocaine	3.3	2.1	1.0
Heroin	1.8	1.0	0.5

SOURCE: Maguire and Pastore, 1997:262.
NOTE: Figures based on 14,300 respondents; a dash indicates information not available.

In short, these findings on drug use among high school seniors provide a virtual mirror image of drug use in the larger society. That is, alcohol, cigarettes, and marijuana are the most commonly used illegal drugs, and drug use for recreation and escape is widespread.

THE "DARK FIGURE" OF CRIME

Given that many more juveniles report having violated the law than official statistics indicate, there are two related questions: (1) How large is the dark figure of crime? and (2) What percentage of all offenses reported by juveniles become a part of official records?

Studies indicate that at least 9 out of 10 delinquent acts either go undetected or are unacted upon by anyone in authority (Erickson and Empey, 1963; Gold, 1966; Murphy, Shirley, and Witmer, 1946; Williams and Gold, 1972). These studies use two kinds of information: (1) statements by young people concerning how often they have been caught and (2) official records regarding how often the names of self-reported offenders appear in them. For example, after having checked official records against self-

reports of offending, Williams and Gold (1972:221) found that "less than 1 percent of the chargable offenses committed in the three years prior to the interviews were recorded as official delinquency. . . . And when offenses do come to the attention of police, they often result in warnings, 'station adjustments,' and a host of other possible police actions that fall short of delinquency records for teenagers."

Those outcomes are particularly likely for minor offenses, such as traffic violations, petty theft, buying and drinking alcohol, destroying property, and skipping school. The picture changes, however, for more serious offenses, such as felonious theft, auto theft, breaking and entering, and armed robbery. Fewer of those offenses go undetected and unacted upon. Yet, even in those cases, 8 out of 10 violations remain undetected, and 9 out of 10 do not result in court action (Erickson and Empey, 1963:462; Williams and Gold, 1972:219).

Such findings illustrate the importance of a statement made over fifty years ago by Murphy, Shirley, and Witmer (1946:696) when they first encountered the large gap between actual law-violating behavior and official delinquency: "Even a moderate increase in the amount of attention paid to it [actual law-violating behavior] by law enforcement authorities could create the semblance of a 'delinquency wave' without there being the slightest change in adolescent behavior." If all, or even a large percentage, of law violations became a part of official records, the result would be unprecedented: A large majority of juveniles would be official delinquents.

In light of improvements in police recording practices, such findings raise some important and provocative questions. For example, to what extent are the increases in juvenile arrest rates over the past several decades (discussed in the previous chapter) a result of better police records? If better police records account for the increases, how do we account for the leveling-off of juvenile arrest rates in the late 1970s and early 1980s?

It is difficult to answer those questions. However, the self-report survey of high school seniors by the University of Michigan reveals considerable correspondence with arrest data in terms of trends in delinquent behavior. As shown in columns 3–5 of table 5.1, there was little change in the annual prevalence of many offenses from 1975 to 1985; indeed, among both boys and girls, there were decreases for some offenses (e.g., shoplifting and theft under $50). There were increases, however, in the annual prevalence of many offenses after 1985.

The last column of table 5.1 shows that the annual prevalence for many offenses increased from 1975 to 1996. The increases, however, were mainly among girls. Indeed, among boys, there were decreases for five of the fifteen offenses listed in table 5.1. Among girls, only the prevalence of theft of car parts decreased. For serious offenses—serious assault, theft over $50, and arson—there were substantial increases among girls in annual prevalence.[1]

The University of Michigan also has studied trends in illegal drug use among high school seniors (Maguire and Pastore, 1997:260–261). Key findings based on self-report data include the following:

1. The use of marijuana decreased sharply from 1985 to 1992. The percentage who reported using marijuana during the past year (i.e., annual prevalence) decreased from 41 to 22, while reported use during the past month decreased from 26 percent to 12 percent. In 1993, however, marijuana use began to increase. By 1996, annual prevalence had increased to 36 percent, and monthly prevalence to 22 percent.

2. Like marijuana, reported use of other drugs decreased from 1985 to 1992, only to increase after that. These drugs included stimulants, hallucinogens, tranquilizers, cocaine, and crack cocaine. For example, annual prevalence of stimulant use decreased from 16 percent in 1985 to 7 percent in 1992, but increased to 10 percent in 1996. Moreover, monthly prevalence of stimulant use decreased from 7 to 3 percent from 1985 to 1992, but increased to 4 percent in 1996.

3. The reported use of alcohol decreased throughout the 1985–96 period—from 86 percent to 73 percent for use during the past year and 66 percent to 51 percent for use during the past month. In contrast, the prevalence of cigarette smoking increased, although only late in the period. Reported cigarette smoking changed very little from 1985 to 1993 (monthly prevalence of about 28–30 percent), but it increased regularly from that point (monthly prevalence of 34 percent in 1996).

4. Reported use of two other drugs has increased since 1985: LSD, from 4 percent annually and 2 percent monthly in 1987 to 9 percent annually and 3 percent monthly in 1996; and heroin, from 0.6 percent annually and 0.3 percent monthly in 1985 to 1.0 percent annually and 0.5 percent monthly in 1996.

CHRONIC DELINQUENT BEHAVIOR

In the previous chapter, we reviewed the Philadelphia cohort study of official delinquents by Marvin Wolfgang and his associates (1972), which found that a small group of chronic offenders account for the majority of offenses against persons and property. A basic question, therefore, is whether this finding is confirmed in self-report studies. That is, do all young

---

[1] It is important to note, though, that those increases pertain to offenses with low percentages of girls who reportedly committed them. For example, only 5 percent of the 1996 senior girls reported serious assaults during the twelve months preceding the survey. In 1975 (see column 5 of table 5.1), only 2 percent of the senior girls reported serious assaults; so a 145-percent increase from 1975 to 1996 corresponds to an absolute increase of only about 3 percent. The small base rate (i.e., the small percentage who reportedly committed the offense in 1975) means that any increase from 1975 to 1996 will result in a large percentage increase.

people report being equally delinquent, or are some more delinquent than others?

To answer that question, we must examine not only the prevalence of delinquent behavior—how many juveniles have violated the law—but also its **incidence**—how many delinquent acts juveniles report having committed.[2] Delinquency is not an either-or phenomenon like having the mumps or measles, but rather a more-or-less kind of thing. In other words, delinquency is distributed along a continuum ranging from low to high (Blumstein et al., 1986, 1; Dunford and Elliott, 1984; Elliott and Ageton, 1980; Elliott et al., 1983; Elmhorn, 1965; Erickson and Empey, 1963; Gold, 1970; Huizinga and Elliott, 1987; Nettler, 1984; Short and Nye, 1958; Williams and Gold, 1972). On the low end of the continuum is the majority of young people, most of whom have committed a few minor delinquent acts and an occasional serious offense. Moving along the continuum, we find fewer and fewer young people but more and more delinquency, in terms of both frequency and seriousness. Hence, at the high end of the continuum is a small number of juveniles who are both frequent and serious offenders. All young people, therefore, are not equally delinquent.

But this is not all we need to know about chronic offenders. Because relatively few law violators are caught and punished, two additional questions must be addressed: (1) Is being caught and punished entirely a chance thing? and (2) Are official records at all accurate in identifying those who, by their own admission, are the most delinquent?

Much evidence suggests that being caught and punished is not due entirely to chance—that those youngsters who reportedly have committed the most delinquent acts are the most likely to have been arrested, to have appeared in court, and to have been institutionalized. Consider arrest first. Williams and Gold (1972:219) found that the frequency of offending is related to the likelihood of arrest: the greater the number of delinquent offenses, the greater the chances of apprehension (for a similar finding from

a sample of Seattle youths, see Sampson, 1985:359, 362). To a lesser degree, the seriousness of offenses also was associated with getting caught. In particular, commission of crimes against persons increased the likelihood of arrest.

Dunford and Elliott (1984) reported similar findings in a national survey of youths involving repeated interviews with juveniles who were ages 11–17 in 1976 (they were interviewed initially in 1977 and interviewed again in subsequent years). Four types of juveniles were identified by the frequency of their self-reported offenses and the seriousness of their offenses: (1) *nondelinquents,* (2) *exploratory delinquents* (those committing less than one offense per month and no more than one **index offense** in a given year), (3) *nonserious patterned delinquents* (those committing at least one delinquent act per month and no more than two index offenses in a year), and (4) *serious patterned delinquents* (those committing at least three index offenses in a year). Inspection of arrest records revealed that "serious patterned delinquents were arrested more often than were other types; that nonserious patterned delinquents had more arrests than did exploratory delinquents and nondelinquents; and that exploratory delinquents had more arrests than nondelinquents" (Dunford and Elliott, 1984:72). Yet, despite those findings, the evidence pointed to odds greatly on the side of the lawbreaker. Only 7 percent of juveniles committing as many as 101–200 offenses over a two-year period (1976–1978) were arrested. During that time, just 19 percent of those reporting more than 200 offenses were arrested (Dunford and Elliott, 1984:80).

After arrest, the picture begins to change a bit. For a first offense, especially if it is a petty or status offense, the risks are small that a youngster will be referred to court because the police counsel and release many offenders (FBI, 1997:271). But when some of these offenders get caught more than once in the police net, the likelihood increases that they will be referred to court. Indeed, Erickson (1972: 394–395) found a strong relationship between frequency of self-reported delinquency and likelihood of appearance in juvenile court (also see Erickson and Empey, 1963:465).

Once in court, the same process begins all over again. Like the police, juvenile court officials are

---

[2]While this use of the term *incidence* is conventional in delinquency research, it is defined differently by medical researchers, who in studying the epidemiology of infectious diseases define it as the number of new conditions at some point in time.

lenient with many young people. First offenders who have not committed a serious offense often are warned and supervised informally. But if other court appearances follow, juvenile court officials are inclined to respond more harshly. Juveniles with multiple court appearances are the most likely to end up being institutionalized.

But are institutionalized offenders the most delinquent, or are they just the most unlucky? The evidence is telling. Self-report studies indicate that institutionalized offenders, as well as those who have a record of several court appearances, are by their own admission the most delinquent (Erickson and Empey, 1963; Short and Nye, 1958). Not only have they committed many offenses, most of which are unknown to authorities, but those offenses tend to be quite serious. The evidence is much like that from the Philadelphia cohort study (Wolfgang, Figlio, and Sellin, 1972). Just as that study found that a small, chronic group of offenders is unusually delinquent, self-report studies have found that institutionalized offenders or those with multiple court appearances are not only more delinquent than juveniles who have no official record but also more delinquent than juveniles who have appeared in court only once. Erickson and Empey (1963:462), for example, discovered that if (official) nonoffenders and one-time offenders are combined and compared with a chronic-offender group, the total law violations of the latter group vastly exceeded those of the former for theft (2,851 versus 20,836), violations of property (1,450 versus 10,828), violations of person (457 versus 8,569), and violations involving the purchase and drinking of alcohol (564 versus 21,134). In addition, far smaller percentages of (official) nonoffenders and one-time offenders committed serious offenses than did official repeaters or institutionalized offenders—for example, theft of articles worth more than $50 (2 percent versus 50 percent), auto theft (2 percent versus 52 percent), forgery (0 percent versus 25 percent), and armed robbery (0 percent versus 9 percent).

Such findings suggest that the **juvenile justice system** is like a coarse fishing net that is dragged in a large ocean (Nettler, 1984:90). The odds are small that most fish will be caught. Even when some are caught, most manage to escape or are released be-

cause they are too small. But because a few fish are much bigger and more active than others, they are caught more than once. Each time this occurs, the odds decrease that they will escape or be thrown back. Ultimately, they constitute a very select group whose behavior clearly separates them from most of the fish still in the ocean.

"FACTS" ABOUT DELINQUENCY THAT MUST BE EXPLAINED

A key question at this point is whether the more delinquent juveniles possess any characteristics that differentiate them from the less delinquent juveniles. Official records suggest that they are more likely to be adolescent (approximately ages 13 and older) than preadolescent, male than female, black than white, and lower class than middle class. Indeed, to the extent that self-report surveys confirm those differences, they become "facts" that criminologists must seek to explain.

Age

According to official accounts, age is strongly related to delinquent behavior. Recall from Chapter 4 that both arrest rates and rates of juvenile court referral are low for juveniles at age 10; but after that, they increase sharply, peaking at about age 18. The results of a national survey of youths by Elliott and his associates (1983:95–98) only partially corroborate that pattern. They found that for a general delinquency scale (combining self-report data for twenty-four offenses), annual prevalence increases regularly from ages 12 to 18; but rather than decreasing at that point, it remains high to age 20. Looking at particular offenses, annual prevalence among young people tends to increase with age for hard drug use (e.g., amphetamines, cocaine) and status offenses (running away, truancy, lying about one's age, and sexual intercourse); and, for most types of theft, it peaks at ages 16–17. However, the peak occurs at younger ages for other offenses. For example, aggravated assault involves increasing prevalence to ages 14–16, with a decrease thereafter. In the case of robbery (including strong-arming students and teachers), the peak is at still a younger age—13 or 14—with annual prevalence for 20-year-olds being lower than that for 12-year-olds.

Much the same picture emerges when we consider the annual incidence of delinquent behavior (frequency of self-reported offending during the past year) among various ages (Elliott et al., 1983:101–103). For the general delinquency scale (twenty-four offenses), annual incidence increases with age, with 12-year-olds reporting an average of 10 offenses and 18-year-olds reporting over 30. The same pattern holds for hard drug use and status offenses. For many other offenses, including assault and robbery, however, incidence tends to peak much earlier—as young as 14 or 15.

Although these findings do not refute the idea that juveniles often break the law, they suggest that many offenders are younger than official statistics indicate (Loeber, 1987). Either legal officials are inclined to be more lenient with younger children, or they are concentrating more on the behavior of older juveniles (Farrington, 1986:237).

Gender

As we learned in the previous chapter, police and juvenile court records suggest that gender is a second "fact" that should be taken into account in explaining delinquent behavior. On the one hand, official rates of delinquency tend to be much higher for boys than girls. On the other hand, they suggest that girls are more likely than boys to commit some offenses, such as running away. But are official records accurate? Are girls actually less delinquent than boys? Do girls tend to commit different types of offenses than boys?

Looking again at table 5.1, we can see that the annual prevalence of delinquency is consistently higher for boys. For each offense in every year, a higher percentage of boys than girls report having violated the law.

Based on another national survey of youths (the Elliott survey), Canter (1982:377–379) reports that not only annual prevalence but also annual incidence is higher for boys. The incidence figures for a variety of offenses are shown in table 5.3. The ratio of male to female offending tends to be very high. For example, boys reported an average of 0.28 aggravated assaults during the year preceding the survey com-

pared to 0.05 for girls, or a ratio of about 6 to 1.[3] The ratios for selected other offenses are as follows: sexual assault, 7:1; strong-arming persons other than students or teachers, 5:1; and damaging property, 7:1. Even prostitution (7:1) and truancy (2:1) follow this pattern. The only major exceptions are theft of property worth $5 to $50 (1:1), alcohol and other drug use (1:1 to 1.8:1), and running away (1:1). Otherwise, the strong relationship between being male and frequently committing delinquent acts suggests, once again, that traditional expectations for females may continue to control their delinquent behavior.

Although boys commit more delinquent acts than girls, as table 5.3 shows, they also engage in much the same types of behavior; and that finding is consistent with many other studies (Hindelang, 1971:533; Jensen and Eve, 1976:435; Richards, 1981: 463–466; Wise, 1967:187). So-called *female* offenses such as prostitution and running away comprise only a small fraction of the total law violations committed by girls. Considerably more frequent, by contrast, are drinking, marijuana use, and truancy, the same types of offenses most frequently committed by boys.

In summary, although girls are not as delinquent as boys, they report having committed a long list of law-violating behaviors that historically have been viewed as *male* offenses. Thus, we need explanations to account not only for the greater delinquency of males but also for a picture of female behavior that is far different from that suggested by tradition.

Minority Status

As we learned when considering official accounts of delinquency, both arrest and juvenile court data tend to confirm the long-held assumption that minority groups commit more delinquent acts than other groups. But is that assumption true? Unfortunately, that question cannot be answered for all minority groups because there have been very few self-report

---

[3]There are at least two methods of computing average incidence from self-report data: (1) average frequency of reported crimes among all juveniles and (2) average frequency among offenders only. The second method is preferable because a large number of zero responses from nonoffenders depresses the averages and lessens the chance of observing true group differences (in this case, differences by gender). Most published figures for average incidence from the Elliott et al. (1983) study are based on the first method. Although this undoubtedly causes some distortion, the degree of distortion does not appear to be very great (Canter, 1982:382).

TABLE 5.3

Average annual incidence of self-reported delinquency, males and females, 1976

TYPE OF OFFENSE	MALE	FEMALE	RATIO
Aggravated assault	0.28	0.05	6:1
Sexual assault	0.07	0.01	7:1
Strong-arm other than students or teachers	0.18	0.04	5:1
Burglary	0.22	0.03	7:1
Larceny			
$5–$50	0.29	0.24	1:1
Over $50	0.11	0.01	11:1
Motor vehicle theft			
Stole vehicle	0.03	0.01	3:1
Joyriding	0.15	0.07	2:1
Damaged property	1.48	0.20	7:1
Prostitution	0.14	0.02	7:1
Sexual intercourse	3.42	2.04	2:1
Use of drugs			
Alcohol	9.22	5.51	1.7:1
Marijuana	7.73	6.66	1:1
Hallucinogens	0.15	0.12	1:1
Amphetamines	0.62	0.35	1.8:1
Barbiturates	0.43	0.39	1:1
Truancy	5.42	2.62	2:1
Runaway	0.10	0.08	1:1

SOURCE: Canter, 1982:378–379.
NOTE: Figures based on 1,719 respondents—915 males and 804 females.

studies of such important groups as Mexican Americans, Cuban Americans, and other Hispanic groups; Native Americans; and Asian Americans (Chambliss and Nagasawa, 1969; Jensen, Stauss, and Harris, 1977; and Voss, 1963, are exceptions). Any conclusions, therefore, will have to be drawn from comparisons of whites and blacks.

PREVALENCE Official records have suggested consistently that the prevalence of delinquent behavior is much greater among blacks than whites. Hirschi (1969:43), for example, found that 53 percent of the black and 27 percent of the white boys in a Richmond, California, sample had official police records. These figures are strikingly similar to those reported in the Philadelphia cohort study (Wolfgang, Figlio, and Sellin, 1972:54)—50 percent for blacks and 29

percent for whites—as well as in a more recent Seattle study by Hindelang, Hirschi, and Weis (1981: 35)—47 percent for blacks and 28 percent for whites. Thus, in different places and times, official records have suggested that young black males are far more likely to violate the law than young white males.

But when Hirschi (1969:75–76) compared official accounts with self-reports of delinquent behavior, he found a much smaller difference—49 percent of blacks and 44 percent of whites reported having committed at least one delinquent act during the past year. Compare this difference of only 5 percent with the 26 percent difference in official arrest records (53 percent versus 27 percent).

Such findings are not unique. Along with Hirschi, most self-report surveys have found that the prevalence of delinquent behavior does not differ

TABLE 5.4

Average annual incidence of self-reported delinquency, whites and blacks, 1976

RACE	TOTAL SELF-REPORTED DELINQUENCY	CRIMES AGAINST PERSONS	CRIMES AGAINST PROPERTY	ILLEGAL SERVICE CRIMES	PUBLIC DISORDER CRIMES	HARD DRUG USE	STATUS OFFENSES
White	46.79	7.84	8.93	1.85	14.98	1.26	14.84
Black	79.20	12.96	20.57	1.71	16.50	0.18	16.19

SOURCE: Elliott and Ageton, 1980:102.
NOTE: Figures based on 1,616 respondents—1,357 whites and 259 blacks.

substantially between whites and blacks. The percentage of whites who report having violated the law at least once is about the same as the percentage of blacks (Elliott and Ageton, 1980:103; Elliott et al., 1983:70; Hindelang, Hirschi, and Weis, 1981:169; Huizinga and Elliott, 1987:210–214; Williams and Gold, 1972:215), although there is some evidence that blacks are more likely to commit violent crimes such as aggravated assault (Elliott et al., 1983:70; Hindelang, Hirschi, and Weis, 1981:170; Huizinga and Elliott, 1987:210–214).

INCIDENCE As table 5.4 shows, the incidence of delinquency appears to be a different matter. When Elliott and Ageton (1980:102–103) examined how many delinquent acts youths reported committing in their national survey, they found that for all offenses combined (a total of 47 in this part of their analysis), the ratio of black-to-white offenses was nearly 2 to 1 (although this ratio is smaller in a subsequent analysis of the same data—see Huizinga and Elliott, 1987:216). In other words, black youngsters reported having committed almost twice as many delinquent acts as whites (an average of 79.20 offenses for blacks versus 46.79 for whites). Furthermore, the difference was due primarily to blacks reporting higher frequencies of violent and serious property crimes than illegal service crimes (e.g., prostitution), public disorder crimes (e.g., drunkenness), hard drug use (e.g., amphetamines), or status offenses (e.g., running away).

Other researchers have reported similar findings. Although they have not always found that the over-

all incidence of delinquency is higher among black youths, they have found that blacks are more likely to report having committed serious crimes. Williams and Gold (1972:217), for example, found that "assaults, burglary, theft, and property damage—in that order—account for the greater seriousness of the delinquent behavior of black compared to white boys." Indeed, about the only major exception has to do with cars: Whites, not blacks, are more likely to steal autos, go joyriding, and to drive recklessly (Higgins and Albrecht, 1981:33–34).

CHRONIC OFFENDERS Elliott and Ageton (1980:103–104) also found that differences between whites and blacks are due to a relatively small number of chronic offenders. As shown in table 5.5, ratios of blacks to whites on the low (less delinquent) end of the frequency continuum of total self-reported delinquency (47 offenses) are close to 1 to 1. At the high (most delinquent) end, however, the ratio is greater than 2 to 1.[4] The ratios are very similar for serious property crimes—about 1 to 1 at the low end of the continuum but more than 2 to 1 at the high end.

Elliott and Ageton's (1980:104–105) findings on assault were also illuminating. They found that the average number of simple assaults reported by white juveniles during the year preceding the survey was two times greater than that reported by blacks. But

[4]This finding, however, appears to be limited to juveniles, because, as respondents aged in later years of the survey, "there were no statistically significant differences among the proportion of each racial group . . . included in [the category of high-frequency offenders]" (Huizinga and Elliott, 1987:215).

TABLE 5.5

Percentage of juveniles reporting different levels of delinquency, whites and blacks, 1976

NUMBER OF OFFENSES REPORTED	TOTAL SELF-REPORTED DELINQUENCY			NUMBER OF OFFENSES REPORTED	CRIMES AGAINST PROPERTY		
	black (%)	white (%)	ratios		black (%)	white (%)	ratios
0–24	67.6	71.8	1:1.1	0–4	70.7	70.6	1:1
25–49	8.1	11.0	1:1.4	5–29	22.7	24.1	1:1.1
50–199	15.4	13.1	1.2:1	30–54	2.4	3.4	1:1.4
200 +	9.8	4.1	2.4:1	55 +	4.2	1.9	2.2:1

SOURCE: Elliott and Ageton, 1980:104.

NOTE: Figures based on 1,616 respondents—1,357 whites and 259 blacks.

for aggravated assault and sexual assault, the ratios of white to black offenders (1:4 and 1:5, respectively) were in the opposite direction—like those for arrest statistics.

It seems, then, that minority status is a third "fact" that should be taken into account in any attempt to explain delinquency. However, we need to be cautious in interpreting the findings. On the one hand, they tend to support official accounts by suggesting that black youths are more likely than white youths to commit delinquent acts, especially serious offenses. On the other hand, the self-reported discrepancy between the two groups rarely approaches the discrepancy found in official statistics (Elliott, 1994; Hindelang, Hirschi, and Weis, 1979, 1981:157–165). Although there is a large difference between whites and blacks in official statistics, self-report surveys suggest not only that the difference is much smaller but also that much of it may be due to a small number of chronic offenders.

How, then, does one account for the large racial differences reported in official statistics? To be sure, commission of a serious offense is likely to increase the probability of arrest and referral to juvenile court. But for black youths, law-violating behavior is not the only factor that increases the likelihood they will be processed through the juvenile justice system. Because they are more likely than white juveniles to be poor, to come from single-parent families, and to be school dropouts, they are more likely to be proc-

essed officially. Almost inevitably, their official delinquency rates will be higher. Moreover, because those conditions may apply to other minority groups such as Hispanics, there is an urgent need to gather more self-report data.

Social Class

As recently as 1967, the President's Commission on Law Enforcement and Administration of Justice (1967:57) concluded that "there is still no reason to doubt that delinquency, and especially the most serious delinquency, is committed disproportionately by slum and lower-class youth." But do lower-class juveniles report being more delinquent than middle- or upper-class youths?

When the findings of the first self-report studies on that question were revealed, they hit like a bombshell. Study after study indicated that the presumed relation between social class and delinquent behavior was either small or nonexistent (Akers, 1964; Dentler and Monroe, 1961; Empey and Erickson, 1966; Hirschi, 1969; Short and Nye, 1958; Voss, 1966; Williams and Gold, 1972). Although a few studies found that lower-class juveniles are slightly more delinquent (Clark and Wenninger, 1962; Gold, 1966; Reiss and Rhodes, 1961), others discovered just the opposite (Voss, 1966; Williams and Gold, 1972). However, because the relationship, in either direction, was usually very weak, the best conclusion seemed to be that social class membership was not a good way to distinguish serious delinquents from other youngsters (Krohn et al., 1980:304). Indeed, some researchers concluded that it was a myth that lower-class youths are the most delinquent (Tittle, Villemez, and Smith, 1978:65; also see Tittle and Meier, 1990).

Because many criminologists were inclined to accept that conclusion, efforts were made to explain why the myth had persisted for so long. One explanation was that police officers and juvenile court officials—and indeed, society in general—had been guilty of blatant prejudice. The juvenile justice system had been designed deliberately by those in power to discriminate against the children of the poor. Even though they were not more delinquent, they were future members of society's *dangerous classes* and so had to be controlled (Platt, 1974; Quinney, 1970:18–20, 217–220; Turk, 1969:9–10). A second possible explanation was that although social class may have been an important factor in the past, it was no longer important. Lawbreakers today, if not in the 1800s, are scattered throughout the class structure (Tittle, Villemez, and Smith, 1978:654). Finally, a more technical explanation suggested that official records may have been misinterpreted, not only by laypersons but by social scientists. The assumption that lower-class juveniles are the most delinquent has persisted because people have failed to distinguish between law-violating behavior—that which self-report surveys measure—and official delinquency—that which police and juvenile court records measure.

This last explanation requires some elaboration. Whereas self-report studies are designed to measure only the delinquent acts of juveniles, official records reflect three phenomena: (1) the behaviors that bring young people to the attention of legal officials, (2) the social backgrounds of these young people, and (3) the reactions of legal officials to both the behaviors and the backgrounds of young people. Official delinquency, in other words, is a reflection not only of juveniles' actions but also the way officials interpret these actions and respond to the backgrounds of juveniles (Morash, 1984:98; Sampson, 1986:884). Hence, law-violating behavior should not be equated with official delinquency.

Over the years, self-report surveys have become more sophisticated. Indeed, by comparing the results of three national surveys (Elliott and Ageton, 1980;

Gold and Reimer, 1975; Williams and Gold, 1972), it is possible to be more precise about the relationship between social class and delinquency.

PREVALENCE Although these surveys were conducted at different times—1967, 1972, and 1977—they lead to the same conclusion: The prevalence of delinquent behavior is no greater among lower-class than higher-class juveniles. "A comparison of the proportions of youth reporting one or more offenses [during the past year] . . . reveals no statistically significant class . . . differences" (Elliott and Ageton, 1980:103).[5]

INCIDENCE The same is not true, however, when the incidence of delinquent acts—that is, how many delinquent acts juveniles have committed—is considered. The national studies by Gold and his associates revealed few, if any, class differences (Gold and Reimer, 1975; Williams and Gold, 1972). But these studies were structured so that the frequencies of self-reported acts were collapsed into a few categories. In a more recent analysis, by contrast, Elliott and Ageton (1980) did not collapse frequencies, but rather analyzed the full range of self-reported acts, and in doing so found some significant differences. Their findings are shown in table 5.6, with respondents divided into three class levels: (1) a *lower-class group* whose parents were in semiskilled or unskilled occupations with at most a high school education, (2) a *working-class group* made up of the children of skilled manual workers, clerical workers, salespersons, or owners of small businesses who were high school graduates or possibly had completed some college, and (3) a *middle-class group* whose parents filled professional or managerial occupations and had college educations.

Looking first at *total delinquent acts* (combining data on annual incidence for 47 offenses), we can see that the average number of offenses reported by

---

[5]Elliott and Huizinga (1983:161) showed that as the ages of respondents increased from one survey to the next, there were increasing class differences in the prevalence of serious offenses for males. This suggests that while there may be no class differences among *juveniles* (recall that the Elliott and Ageton data come from respondents who were ages 11–17 in 1976), such differences may appear as young people become *adults,* at least among males.

TABLE 5.6

Average annual incidence of self-reported delinquency by social class, 1976

SOCIAL CLASS	TOTAL SELF-REPORTED DELINQUENCY	CRIMES AGAINST PERSONS	CRIMES AGAINST PROPERTY	ILLEGAL SERVICE CRIMES	PUBLIC DISORDER CRIMES	HARD DRUG USE	STATUS OFFENSES
Lower	60.42	12.02	13.50	2.19	14.32	1.20	14.27
Working	50.63	8.04	9.40	1.36	16.21	0.73	14.47
Middle	50.96	3.32	7.25	1.56	13.81	1.37	15.66

SOURCE: Elliott and Ageton, 1980:102.

NOTE: Figures based on 1,720 respondents—717 lower class, 509 working class, and 494 middle class.

lower-class juveniles (60.42) was greater than that reported by working-class (50.63) or middle-class (50.96) youths. While the incidences of self-reported delinquency in the latter two groups were approximately equal, that for the lower-class group was considerably higher. Second, the average number of *crimes against persons* (sexual assault, aggravated assault, simple assault, and robbery) reported by lower-class juveniles (12.02) was nearly one and a half times greater than that reported by the working-class group (8.04) and nearly four times greater than that reported by the middle-class group (3.32). Third, the average number of reported *crimes against property* (vandalism, burglary, auto theft, larceny, stolen goods, fraud, and joyriding) was also higher for lower-class (13.50) than working-class (9.40) or middle-class youths (7.25). These differences, however, were not statistically significant. Furthermore, there were no significant differences in the average number of self-reported acts for any of the other types of offenses.

Thus, while the overall incidence of delinquent behavior is apparently greatest among lower-class youths, this is not true for all types of crime. It is confined mainly to violent crimes against persons and, possibly, serious property crimes (Elliott and Ageton, 1980:102–103; also see Brownfield, 1986:433; Heimer, 1997; Thornberry and Farnworth, 1982:512).

CHRONIC OFFENDERS One additional issue explored by Elliott and Ageton (1980:103–104) is whether differences among social classes might be due, at least

in part, to a large number of crimes being committed by a small group of juveniles. Indeed, the findings displayed in table 5.7 tend to confirm that notion.

The total self-report measure in table 5.7 (based on 47 offenses) shows that less than 6 in 100 juveniles reported committing 200 or more delinquent acts during the year preceding the survey. By contrast, about 70 in 100 juveniles reported committing from 0 to 24 offenses. Moreover, lower-class youths were most likely to be represented on the high end of this continuum. "The lower-class to middle-class ratios at the low end are ... close to 1:1; but at the high end the ratio is 2:1 for total SRD [self-reported delinquency] and over 3:1 for ... crimes against persons" (Elliott and Ageton, 1980:104). In short, while the data indicate that there are small numbers of chronic offenders in all social classes, they are most heavily concentrated among lower-class juveniles.

This set of findings, then, suggests that there is a strong relationship between social class and delinquent behavior. However, the relationship is qualitatively different from the global one implied by official records. Rather than indicating that all lower-class juveniles are more delinquent than other youths, it suggests that criminologists should seek to answer these questions: (1) Why are there chronic offenders in all social classes? and (2) Why are there higher percentages of chronic offenders among lower-class youths?

Relative to these questions, Clark and Wenninger (1962:833) have suggested that variations in the social climates or social networks of different neighborhoods might help to explain the existence of

TABLE 5.7

Percentage of juveniles reporting different levels of delinquency by social class, 1976

NUMBER OF OFFENSES REPORTED	TOTAL SELF-REPORTED DELINQUENCY			NUMBER OF OFFENSES REPORTED	CRIMES AGAINST PERSONS		
	lower class (%)	working class (%)	middle class (%)		lower class (%)	working class (%)	middle class (%)
0–24	71.7	72.3	70.9	0–4	77.3	80.0	84.6
25–49	10.6	9.4	11.5	5–29	18.2	16.1	13.8
50–199	11.4	14.4	14.4	30–54	1.7	2.1	0.8
200 +	6.3	3.9	3.2	55 +	2.8	1.8	0.8

SOURCE: Elliott and Ageton, 1980:104.
NOTE: Figures based on 1,720 respondents—717 lower class, 509 working class, and 494 middle class.

TABLE 5.8

Self-reported group violation rate (GVR) by community and gender

TYPE OF OFFENSE	URBAN		SMALL TOWN	
	male	female	male	female
Drunk	91	94	93	94
Drinking	86	95	86	92
Marijuana	85	93	87	89
Drugs	82	78	78	84
Vandalism	81	84	72	90
Burglary	74	87	81	86
Grand theft	69	33	68	50
Smoking	67	71	61	66
Auto theft	67	69	52	66
Truancy	63	73	65	80
Petty theft	60	54	45	54
Armed robbery	52	100	58	—
Robbery	48	67	53	50
Shoplifting	45	59	42	61
Runaway	38	33	44	11
Assault	25	36	23	6
Fights	23	21	14	21
Defy parents	23	30	16	42

SOURCE: Erickson and Jensen, 1977:267.
NOTE: GVR = (GD/TD) × 100, where GD = number of delinquent acts committed in the company of other persons and TD = total number of self-reported delinquent acts; figures based on 1,700 respondents—1,273 urban and 427 small town.

chronic offenders in all social classes. In those neighborhoods made up predominantly of lower-class persons, juveniles from all social classes will tend to commit a large number of delinquent acts. Johnstone (1978:69) offers a different possibility: It is being a "have-not" in a neighborhood of "haves" that causes lower-class juveniles to be the most delinquent. Rather than coming from neighborhoods where most persons are lower-class, the most serious offenders are lower-class juveniles who live in higher-class neighborhoods where they are confronted with their own poverty. It is a sense of relative deprivation, then, that leads them to commit a greater number of delinquent acts.

In any case, although social class remains important, it is clearly not in itself sufficient as an explanatory variable. For example, we have seen repeatedly that its effects are so intertwined with race in American society that both factors need careful attention before the influence of one or the other can be sorted out.

Group Delinquency

The final issue for which criminologists must account is the group nature of delinquency. Because offenders are processed through the juvenile justice system one by one, official records often fail to reveal the extent to which delinquent acts usually occur in the company of others, a "fact" that has long been noted (e.g., Cohen, 1955; Glueck and Glueck, 1952; Healy and Bronner, 1936; Scott, 1956; Shaw and McKay, 1931; Zimring, 1981; for a review, see Stafford, 1984).

In the 1970s, Erickson (1971, 1973a, 1973b) and Jensen (Erickson and Jensen, 1977) studied this phenomenon using a self-report survey of Arizona youths. Table 5.8 shows that, whether male or female, or in urban areas or small towns, young people tend to be in groups when they violate the law. Alcohol and drug offenses tend to have the highest group violation rates; that is, the percentage of offenses reportedly committed in the company of others is highest for those offenses (from 78 to 95 percent). Violent and property offenses rank next (from 6 to 100 percent), and status offenses such as defying parents or running away rank last (from 11 to 44 percent).

Using self-report data from a national sample of youths in the 1960s, Warr (1996:221) found a pattern of group offending that is very similar to that reported by Erickson and Jensen (1977). Although looking at different types of offenses than Erickson and Jensen did, virtually all of the twelve offenses considered by Warr had group violation rates of 50 percent or higher. Moreover, group violation rates were highest for alcohol and drug offenses and lowest for violent and property offenses.

The companionate character of delinquency is a strikingly pervasive "fact" that official records fail to reveal and to which many theories have paid scant attention. For example, here are just two important questions that have been largely ignored: (1) Does the onset of delinquency involve primarily lone or group offending? and (2) Why, as many studies have shown, is group offending more characteristic of delinquency than adult crime? (Reiss, 1986:128, 150–152).

LIMITATIONS OF SELF-REPORT SURVEYS

Before summarizing what we have covered in this chapter, it is important to be aware of some of the limitations of self-report surveys (Blumstein et al., 1986, 1:96–98; Elliott and Ageton, 1980:96–98; Hindelang, Hirschi, and Weis, 1979:996–998; Jackson, 1990:39–41; Kleck, 1982:429–432; O'Brien, 1985:71–77, 1995:68–72; Reiss, 1975:214–218):

1. Nationwide self-report surveys of delinquency are limited in number. Hence, caution should be exercised in generalizing about all youths from the data now available.

2. Although a few investigators are now collecting self-report data over time, no permanent mechanisms have been devised by which to regularly collect such data—data that would be analogous to those published in the *Uniform Crime Reports*. Thus, it is difficult to estimate whether delinquency rates are increasing or decreasing, and whether patterns of delinquency are changing.

3. Perhaps most important are issues related to the *reliability*—whether repeated administrations of a questionnaire or interview will elicit the same

MORE ON THE METHODOLOGY OF SELF-REPORT SURVEYS

A question often asked about self-report surveys is this: Why would anyone in his or her right mind inform researchers about the illegal acts he or she has committed? Can't self-reports of delinquency get young people in trouble with legal officials (and perhaps parents and teachers, too)? The answer to the latter question is no, and the reason is that the answers in self-report surveys are either anonymous or confidential. In anonymous questionnaires, respondents are asked to leave off their names so that no one will ever know how they personally answered. If names are requested in the questionnaires or if a survey involves face-to-face interviews, respondents are assured that their answers will be confidential and will not be released to any other persons, including legal officials.

Although social scientists tend to have considerable confidence in the accuracy of self-report data, there are skeptics, such as Lewontin (1995: 28–29), who (perhaps because he is a zoologist/biologist and not a social scientist) sees it as naive to have confidence in self-reports of such sensitive behaviors as delinquency. Such skepticism ought not be discouraged. Indeed, it is important for social scientists themselves to maintain some degree of skepticism and constantly seek ways to collect more accurate data.

In that connection, findings on a new survey methodology from a study by Turner et al. (1998) are important. In the 1995 National Survey of Adolescent Males, respondents were asked questions about a wide range of sensitive behaviors using either standard self-administered questionnaires or audio computer-assisted self-interviewing (audio-CASI) technology. Audio-CASI

> allows respondents to listen over headphones to spoken questions that have been digitally recorded and stored on a laptop computer. To answer, respondents press numbered keys on the computer keyboard. Questions are also displayed on the computer's screen, and respondents may respond to the visual presentation of the question rather than waiting until the audio reading has been completed. (Turner et al., 1998: 867)

The audio-CASI technology seems to allow for greater privacy than standard self-administered questionnaires by immediately storing answers in the computer, making the answers less vulnerable to disclosure to others. Moreover, audio-CASI

> provides . . . (i) a completely standardized measurement system—every respondent (in a given language) hears the same question asked in exactly the same way; (ii) computer-controlled branching through complex questionnaires and automated consistency and range checking; and (iii) efficient multilingual administration of surveys. (Turner et al., 1998:867)

Turner et al. (1988) found that many of the answers differed substantially in the two types of surveys—standard self-administered questionnaires and audio-CASI. Estimated prevalence of male-male sex, injection drug use, and sexual contact with intravenous drug users was three or more times higher when the audio-CASI technology was used. Estimated prevalence also was between one and a half and two times higher for carrying a gun, knife, or razor; pulling a knife or gun on someone; and threatening to hurt someone (Turner et al., 1998:868–870). To the extent it can be concluded that the greater reporting of these behaviors with the audio-CASI technology reflects more accurate reporting (a conclusion cautiously drawn by Turner et al., 1998:871), then this new survey methodology may reveal more of the "dark figure" of crime than we have seen before and provide an even better picture of the extent and distribution of delinquent behavior.

answers from the same juveniles when they are queried two or more times—and *validity*—whether the studies measure what they purport to measure, namely, actual law-violating behavior—of self-report surveys. Fortunately, their exhaustive study of these issues led Hindelang, Hirschi, and Weis (1981:114) to conclude that "reliability measures are impressive and the majority of studies produce validity coefficients in the moderate to strong range." The only major difficulty has to do with validity, primarily because black males often fail to report serious crimes for which they have been arrested. As a result, Hindelang, Hirschi, and Weis (1981:213) urged caution in comparing self-report findings from black males with other groups.

4. There have been few self-report surveys of adults, thus impeding comparisons of lawbreaking among widely varying age groups.

In short, self-report surveys, like other ways of estimating delinquent behavior, have their limitations. Nonetheless, they are probably the single most accurate source of information on the actual illegal acts of young people.

SUMMARY AND CONCLUSIONS

In response to dissatisfaction with official accounts of delinquent behavior, self-report surveys have been conducted. They suggest the following conclusions:

1. Both the *prevalence* and *incidence* of juvenile lawbreaking are far greater than official records indicate. Because these records pertain to only a small fragment of the youth population, they grossly underestimate the extent of lawbreaking by young people.

2. The "dark figure" of crime may be as much as nine times greater than the official figure because approximately 9 out of 10 law violations either go undetected or are unacted upon.

3. Although most juveniles violate the law, only a small minority are chronic offenders who violate the law with great frequency and seriousness.

4. The juvenile justice system is far from totally effective in apprehending all law violators, operating more like a coarse fishing net. Those youngsters who are arrested, who appear in juvenile court, or who are institutionalized are the most delinquent, by their own admission.

5. Official records have suggested that certain issues should be taken into account in trying to explain delinquent behavior. With regard to these "facts," self-report surveys suggest the following:

   • *Age.* Self-report studies do not show that crime increases uniformly from ages 10 to 18. Rather, there are many offenses, some of them serious, for which 13- to 15-year-olds are the most delinquent.

   • *Gender.* Both the prevalence and incidence of delinquent behavior are greater among boys than girls. However, the pattern of offenses reported by girls resembles that of boys.

   • *Minority status.* While conclusions cannot be reached about all minority groups, there is a need to qualify the findings from official records with respect to blacks. On the one hand, self-report studies do not support the idea that the prevalence of delinquency is greater among black juveniles than whites. On the other hand, they suggest that its incidence may be greater among blacks, particularly for serious offenses. However, they also suggest that this variation is due more to an unusually large number of delinquent acts committed by a small group of chronic offenders than to all black youths taken as a whole.

- *Social class.* The same sorts of conclusions apply to the relation between social class and law-violating behavior. While self-report studies do not indicate that the prevalence of law violation is greater among lower- than middle-class youths, they suggest that the incidence is greater among lower-class juveniles. Moreover, lower-class youths are the most likely to be represented on the high end of the delinquency continuum.
- *Group delinquency.* Although official records report nothing about the phenomenon, self-report surveys reveal that most delinquent acts are committed in groups.

In terms of their social and scientific implications, then, these findings suggest that while important qualifications need to be added to the picture of delinquent behavior painted by official records, that picture is not entirely inconsistent with the findings of self-report surveys. It will be interesting to determine whether those conclusions are confirmed by the victimization surveys discussed in the next chapter.

DISCUSSION QUESTIONS

1. What are the flaws with official statistics on delinquency?
2. What are the limitations of self-report surveys of delinquency?
3. Why do self-report surveys reveal more of the "dark figure" of crime than do official statistics?
4. To what extent can it be said that self-report studies reveal substantial age and gender differences in delinquency but insubstantial differences by minority status and social class?
5. Why is it important to know that young people tend to be in groups when they violate the law? Why does it matter whether young lawbreakers tend to be group rather than lone offenders?

REFERENCES

Akers, Ronald L. 1964. "Socio-Economic Status and Delinquent Behavior: A Retest." *Journal of Research in Crime and Delinquency* 1 (January): 38–46.

Blumstein, Alfred, Jacqueline Cohen, Jeffrey Roth, and Christy Visher, eds. 1986. *Criminal Careers and "Career Criminals."* 2 vols. Washington, D.C.: National Academy Press.

Brownfield, David. 1986. "Social Class and Violent Behavior." *Criminology* 24 (August):421–438.

Canter, Rachelle J. 1982. "Sex Differences in Self-Report Delinquency." *Criminology* 20 (November):373–393.

Chambliss, William J., and Richard H. Nagasawa. 1969. "On the Validity of Official Statistics: A Comparative Study of White, Black, and Japanese High-School Boys." *Journal of Research in Crime and Delinquency* 6 (January):71–77.

Clark, John P., and Eugene P. Wenninger. 1962 "Socio-Economic Class and Area as Correlates of Illegal Behavior Among Juveniles." *American Sociological Review* 27 (December):826–834.

Cohen, Albert K. 1955. *Delinquent Boys: The Culture of the Gang.* New York: Free Press.

Dentler, Robert A., and Lawrence J. Monroe. 1961. "Social Correlates of Early Adolescent Theft." *American Sociological Review* 26 (October):733–743.

Dunford, Franklyn W., and Delbert S. Elliott. 1984. "Identifying Career Offenders Using Self-Reported Data." *Journal of Research in Crime and Criminology* 21 (February):57–86.

Elliott, Delbert S. 1994. "Serious Violent Offenders: Onset, Developmental Course, and Termination." *Criminology* 32 (February):1–21.

Elliott, Delbert S., and Suzanne S. Ageton. 1980. "Reconciling Race and Class Differences in Self-Reported and Official Estimates of Delinquency." *American Sociological Review* 45 (February):95–110.

Elliott, Delbert, Suzanne Ageton, David Huizinga, Brian Knowles, and Rachelle Canter. 1983. *The Prevalence and Incidence of Delinquent Behavior: 1976–1980.* Boulder, Colo.: Behavioral Research Institute.

Elmhorn, Kerstin. 1965. "Study in Self-Reported Delinquency Among School Children in Stockholm." Pp. 117–146 in Karl O. Christiansen, ed., *Scandinavian Studies in Criminology.* Vol. 1. London: Tavistock.

Empey, LaMar T., and Maynard L. Erickson. 1966. "Hidden Delinquency and Social Status." *Social Forces* 44 (June):546–554.

Erickson, Maynard L. 1971. "The Group Context of Delinquent Behavior." *Social Problems* 19 (Summer):114–129.
1972. "The Changing Relationship Between Official and Self-Reported Measures of Delinquency: An Exploratory-Predictive Study." *Journal of Criminal Law, Criminology and Police Science* 63 (September):388–395.
1973a. "Group Violations and Official Delinquency: The Group Hazard Hypothesis." *Criminology* 11 (August):127–160.
1973b. "Group Violations, Socioeconomic Status and Official Delinquency." *Social Forces* 52 (September):41–52.

Erickson, Maynard L., and LaMar T. Empey. 1963. "Court Records, Undetected Delinquency, and Decision-Making." *Journal of Criminal Law, Criminology and Police Science* 54 (December):456–469.

Erickson, Maynard L., and Gary F. Jensen. 1977. "'Delinquency Is Still Group Behavior!': Toward Revitalizing the Group Premise in the Sociology of Deviance." *Journal of Criminal Law and Criminology* 68 (June):262–273.

Farrington, David P. 1986. "Age and Crime." Pp. 189–250 in Michael Tonry and Norval Morris, eds., *Crime and Justice: An Annual Review of Research,* Vol. 7. Chicago: University of Chicago Press.

Federal Bureau of Investigation. 1997. *Crime in the United States: Uniform Crime Reports, 1996.* Washington, D.C.: U.S. Government Printing Office.

Flanagan, Timothy J., and Kathleen Maguire, eds. 1990. *Sourcebook of Criminal Justice Statistics—1989.* Washington, D.C.: U.S. Government Printing Office.

Flanagan, Timothy J., and Edmund F. McGarrell, eds. 1986. *Sourcebook of Criminal Justice Statistics—1985.* Washington, D.C.: U.S. Government Printing Office.

Garrett, Marcia, and James F. Short, Jr. 1975. "Social Class and Delinquency: Predictions and Outcomes of Police-Juvenile Encounters." *Social Problems* 22 (February):368–383.

Glueck, Sheldon, and Eleanor Glueck. 1952. *Delinquents in the Making: Paths to Prevention.* New York: Harper.

Gold, Martin. 1966. "Undetected Delinquent Behavior." *Journal of Research in Crime and Delinquency* 3 (January):27–46.
1970. *Delinquent Behavior in an American City.* Belmont, Calif.: Brooks/Cole.

Gold, Martin, and Donald J. Reimer. 1975. "Changing Patterns of Delinquent Behavior Among Americans 13 Through 16 Years Old: 1967–72." *Crime and Delinquency Literature* 7 (December):483–517.

Gould, Leroy C. 1969. "Who Defines Delinquency: A Comparison of Self-Reported and Officially-Reported Indices of Delinquency for Three Racial Groups," *Social Problems* 16 (Winter):325–336.

Gove, Walter R., Michael Hughes, and Michael Geerken. 1985. "Are Uniform Crime Reports a Valid Indicator of the Index Crimes? An Affirmative Answer with Minor Qualifications." *Criminology* 23 (August):451–501.

Healy, William, and Augusta F. Bronner. 1936. *New Light on Delinquency and Its Treatment.* New Haven, Conn.: Yale University Press.

Heimer, Karen. 1997. "Socioeconomic Status, Subcultural Definitions, and Violent Delinquency." *Social Forces* 75 (March):799–833.

Higgins, Paul C., and Gary L. Albrecht. 1981. "Cars and Kids: A Self-Report Study of Juvenile Auto Theft and Traffic Violations." *Sociology and Social Research* 66 (October):29–41.

Hindelang, Michael J. 1971. "Age, Sex, and the Versatility of Delinquent Involvements." *Social Problems* 18 (Spring):522–535.

Hindelang, Michael J., Travis Hirschi, and Joseph G. Weis. 1979. "Correlates of Delinquency: The Illusion of Discrepancy Between Self-Report and Official Measures." *American Sociological Review* 44 (December):995–1014.
1981. *Measuring Delinquency.* Beverly Hills, Calif.: Sage.

Hirschi, Travis. 1969. *Causes of Delinquency.* Berkeley: University of California Press.

Huizinga, David, and Delbert S. Elliott. 1987. "Juvenile Offenders: Prevalence, Offender Incidence, and Arrest Rates by Race." *Crime and Delinquency* 33 (April):206–223.

Jackson, Patrick G. 1990. "Sources of Data." Pp. 21–50 in Kimberly L. Kempf, ed., *Measurement Issues in Criminology.* New York: Springer-Verlag.

Jensen, Gary F., and Raymond Eve. 1976. "Sex Differences in Delinquency: An Examination of Popular Sociological Explanations." *Criminology* 13 (February):427–448.

Jensen, Gary F., Joseph H. Stauss, and V. William Harris. 1977. "Crime, Delinquency, and the American Indian." *Human Organization* 36 (Fall): 252–257.

Johnstone, John W. C. 1978. "Social Class, Social Areas and Delinquency." *Sociology and Social Research* 63 (October):49–72.

Kleck, Gary. 1982. "On the Use of Self-Report Data to Determine the Class Distribution of Criminal and Delinquent Behavior." *American Sociological Review* 47 (June):427–433.

Krohn, Marvin, Ronald Akers, Marcia Radosevich, and Lonn Lanza-Kaduce. 1980. "Social Status and Deviance: Class Context of School, Social Status, and Delinquent Behavior." *Criminology* 18 (November):303–318.

Lewontin, Richard. 1995. "Sex, Lies, and Social Science." *New York Review of Books,* April 20, pp. 24–29.

Loeber, Rolf. 1987. "The Prevalence, Correlates, and Continuity of Serious Conduct Problems in Elementary School Children." *Criminology* 25 (August):615–642.

Maguire, Kathleen, and Ann L. Pastore, eds. 1997. *Sourcebook of Criminal Justice Statistics—1996.* Washington, D.C.: U.S. Government Printing Office.

Morash, Merry. 1984. "Establishment of a Juvenile Police Record: The Influence of Individual and Peer Group Characteristics." *Criminology* 22 (February):97–111.

Murphy, Fred J., Mary M. Shirley, and Helen L. Witmer. 1946. "The Incidence of Hidden Delinquency." *American Journal of Orthopsychiatry* 16 (October):686–696.

National Commission on the Causes and Prevention of Violence. 1969. *Crimes of Violence,* Vol. 11. Washington, D.C.: U.S. Government Printing Office.

Nettler, Gwynn. 1984. *Explaining Crime,* 3rd ed. New York: McGraw-Hill.

O'Brien, Robert M. 1985. *Crime and Victimization Data.* Beverly Hills, Calif.: Sage.

O'Brien, Robert M. 1995. "Crime and Victimization Data." Pp. 57–81 in Joseph F. Sheley, ed., *Criminology: A Contemporary Handbook.* Belmont, Calif.: Wadsworth.

Penick, Bettye K. E., and Maurice E. B. Owens, III, eds. 1976. *Surveying Crime.* Washington, D.C.: National Academy of Sciences.

Platt, Anthony M. 1974. "The Triumph of Benevolence: The Origins of the Juvenile Justice System in the United States." Pp. 356–389 in Richard Quinney, ed., *Criminal Justice in America.* Boston: Little, Brown.

President's Commission on Law Enforcement and Administration of Justice. 1967. *The Challenge of Crime in a Free Society.* Washington, D.C.: U.S. Government Printing Office.

Quinney, Richard. 1970. *The Social Reality of Crime.* Boston: Little, Brown.

Reiss, Albert J., Jr. 1975. "Inappropriate Theories and Inadequate Methods as Policy Plagues: Self-Reported Delinquency and the Law." Pp. 211–222 in N. J. Demerath, III, Otto Larsen, and Karl F. Schuessler, eds., *Social Policy and Sociology.* New York: Academic Press.
    1986. "Co-Offender Influences on Criminal Careers." Pp. 121–160 in Alfred Blumstein et al., eds., *Criminal Careers and "Career Criminals,"* Vol. 2, Washington, D.C.: National Academy Press.

Reiss, Albert J., Jr., and Albert L. Rhodes. 1961. "The Distribution of Juvenile Delinquency in the Social Class Structure." *American Sociological Review* 26 (October):720–732.

Richards, Pamela. 1981. "Quantitative and Qualitative Sex Differences in Middle-Class Delinquency." *Criminology* 18 (February):453–470.

Sampson, Robert J. 1985. "Sex Differences in Self-Reported Delinquency and Official Records: A Multiple-Group Structural Modeling Approach." *Journal of Quantitative Criminology* 1:345–367.
    1986. "Effects of Socioeconomic Context on Official Reaction to Juvenile Delinquency." *American Sociological Review* 51 (December):876–885.

Scott, Peter. 1956. "Gangs and Delinquent Groups in London." *British Journal of Delinquency* 7 (July):4–26.

Seidman, David, and Michael Couzens. 1974. "Getting the Crime Rate Down: Political Pressure and Crime Reporting." *Law and Society Review* 8 (Spring):457–493.

Shaw, Clifford R., and Henry D. McKay. 1931. *Social Factors in Juvenile Delinquency: A Study of the Community, the Family, and the Gang in Relation to Delinquent Behavior.* Report of the National Commission on Law Observance and Enforcement (Wickersham Commission). No. 13, Vol. 2. Washington, D.C.: U.S. Government Printing Office.

Short, James F., Jr., and F. Ivan Nye. 1958. "Extent of Unrecorded Juvenile Delinquency: Tentative Conclusions." *Journal of Criminal Law, Criminology and Police Science* 49 (November–December):296–302.

Stafford, Mark. 1984. "Gang Delinquency." Pp. 167–190 in Robert F. Meier, ed., *Major Forms of Crime.* Beverly Hills, Calif.: Sage.

Thornberry, Terence P., and Margaret Farnworth. 1982. "Social Correlates of Criminal Involvement: Further Evidence on the Relationship Between Social Status and Criminal Behavior." *American Sociological Review* 47 (August):505–518.

Tittle, Charles R., and Robert F. Meier. 1990. "Specifying the SES/Delinquency Relationship." *Criminology* 28 (May):271–299.

Tittle, Charles R., Wayne J. Villemez, and Douglas A. Smith. 1978. "The Myth of Social Class and Criminality: An Empirical Assessment of the Empirical Evidence." *American Sociological Review* 43 (October):643–656.

Turk, Austin T. 1969. *Criminality and Legal Order.* Chicago: Rand McNally.

Turner, C. F., L. Ku, S. M. Rogers, L. D. Lindberg, J. H. Pleck, and F. L. Sonenstein. 1998. "Adolescent Sexual Behavior, Drug Use and Violence: Increased Reporting with Computer Survey Technology." *Science* 280 (May):867–873.

Voss, Harwin L. 1963. "Ethnic Differentials in Delinquency in Honolulu." *Journal of Criminal Law, Criminology and Police Science* 54 (September):322–327.
    1966. "Socio-Economic Status and Reported Delinquent Behavior." *Social Problems* 13 (Winter):314–324.

Warr, Mark. 1996. "Organization and Instigation in Delinquent Groups." *Criminology* 34 (February):11–37.

Williams, Jay R., and Martin Gold. 1972. "From Delinquent Behavior to Official Delinquency." *Social Problems* 20 (Fall):209–229.

Wise, Nancy B. 1967. "Juvenile Delinquency Among Middle-Class Girls." Pp. 179–188 in Edmund W. Vaz, ed., *Middle-Class Juvenile Delinquency*. New York: Harper & Row.

Wolfgang, Marvin E., Robert M. Figlio, and Thorsten Sellin. 1972. *Delinquency in a Birth Cohort*. Chicago: University of Chicago Press.

Zimring, Franklin E. 1981. "Kids, Groups and Crime: Some Implications of a Well-Known Secret." *Journal of Criminal Law and Criminology* 72 (Fall):867–885.

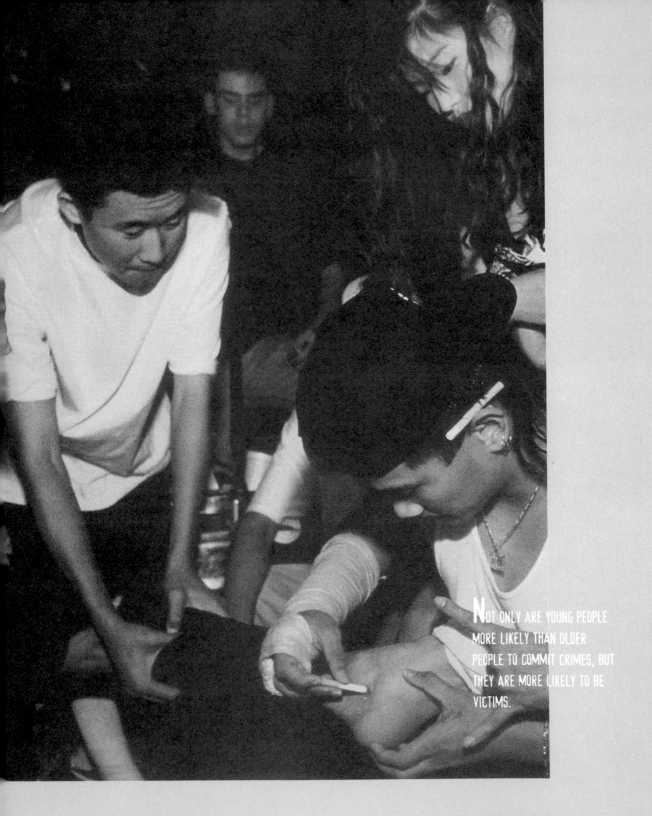

Not only are young people more likely than older people to commit crimes, but they are more likely to be victims.

CHAPTER SIX

VICTIM ACCOUNTS OF DELINQUENT BEHAVIOR

A third source of information on the extent and distribution of delinquent behavior is **crime victimization surveys.** These surveys have an interesting history (Fattah, 1991:31–33; O'Brien, 1985: 12–14, 39–45). In 1965, Lyndon Johnson established a President's Commission on Law Enforcement and Administration of Justice (1967b:v) and charged it with providing a coherent picture of crime and suggesting possible solutions. Almost immediately, knowledgeable staff members and consultants pointed to the well-known difficulties with police data and the need for better data. Consequently, a national survey was conducted with 10,000 representative households to assess what Americans' experiences as victims of crime were, whether they had reported those victimization experiences to the police, and how those experiences had affected their lives.

The findings of the survey were striking. Like the findings from self-report surveys, they indicated that there was far more crime than officially reported. Rape, for example, appeared to be four times as frequent as police data indicated (Ennis, 1967:9). Likewise, many other crimes were underreported, as the commission noted:

> Burglaries occur about three times more often than they are reported to police. Aggravated assaults and larcenies over $50 occur twice as often as they are reported. There are 50 percent more robberies than are reported. In some areas, only one-tenth of the total number of certain kinds of crimes are reported to the police. Seventy-four percent of the neighborhood commercial establishments surveyed do not report to police the thefts committed by their employees. (President's Commission, 1967b:v)

As a result of such findings, the commission expressed concern that crime was eroding the quality of American life. That concern was fueled by another commission study (President's Commission, 1967b:v) conducted in high-crime areas of two cities. Among other things, this second study found the following:

1. Forty-three percent of the respondents stayed off the streets at night because of their fear of crime.
2. Thirty-five percent did not speak to strangers because of their fear of crime.
3. Twenty-one percent used cars and cabs at night because of their fear of crime.
4. Twenty percent would have liked to move to another neighborhood because of their fear of crime.

For these and other reasons, the President's Commission (1967a:2) recommended that additional victimization surveys be conducted and made a part of the nation's regular data-gathering procedures. Likewise, a later commission—the National Advisory Commission on Criminal Justice Standards and Goals (1973:38–39)—noted that it was unrealistic to expect any single measure of crime to be completely accurate. Therefore, victimization surveys might be useful in evaluating police data, and vice versa.

THE NATURE OF VICTIMIZATION SURVEYS

After several years of preparation and pilot study, the first **National Crime Victimization Survey** (NCVS) was conducted in the early 1970s by the U.S. Bureau of the Census in conjunction with the Law Enforcement Assistance Administration (NCJISS, 1975: iii–vii). Information was gathered from a sample of people ages 12 and older in 60,000 households and from 15,000 businesses throughout the nation. The National Crime Victimization Survey of households is still being conducted. The survey of businesses was discontinued in the mid-1970s (NCJISS, 1979:iii), but that is not a serious limitation for us because we are concerned primarily with **crimes against persons** and **households.**

Crimes against persons involve direct contact between offenders and victims. These include the **violent crimes** of rape/sexual assault, robbery, and nonsexual assault and the nonviolent crimes of purse snatching and pocket picking. Crimes against households are **property crimes** that do not involve direct contact between offenders and victims. These include burglary, motor vehicle theft, and theft of other property.

Limitations of Victimization Surveys

Victimization surveys have certain limitations. One of the most important is that they deal only with **criminal offenses,** omitting juvenile **status offenses.** Victimization surveys also omit a long list of other crimes, including murder (because victims cannot be interviewed) and kidnapping. Other types of crimes, such as drunkenness, drug use, gambling, and prostitution, usually do not have immediate victims and thus are omitted. Finally, crimes that are difficult to document from a victim's standpoint, such as employee theft, shoplifting, income tax violations, and even blackmail, also are omitted.

Some of the omissions are serious in that they tend to focus attention on youthful and lower-class crimes while ignoring crimes involving older, affluent, and powerful people, such as embezzlement, bribery, fraud, violation of antitrust laws, stock swindles, and income tax evasion. Admittedly, those crimes are difficult to document—because victims are

SAMPLE QUESTIONS FROM THE NATIONAL CRIME VICTIMIZATION SURVEY

Each person age 12 and over is asked questions like these:

1. During the last 6 months, has anyone raped you or attempted to rape or otherwise sexually attack you?

2. During the last 6 months, has anyone attacked or threatened you in any of these ways: (a) with any weapon, for instance, a gun or knife; (b) with anything like a baseball bat, frying pan, scissors, or stick; (c) by something thrown, such as a rock or bottle; or (d) by grabbing, punching, or choking?

Each head of household is asked questions like these:

1. During the last 6 months, has anyone broken in or attempted to break into your home by forcing a door or window, pushing past someone, jimmying a lock, cutting a screen, or entering through an open door or window?

2. If you owned a car or other motor vehicle during the last 6 months, was it stolen or used without permission?

SOURCE: Bureau of Justice Statistics, 1997:107–108, 115.

Another limitation might seem to be the survey method for collecting victimization data. A question frequently asked about the NCVS is whether accurate estimates of crime can be obtained by interviewing only a sample of Americans rather than all of them. Why not interview all Americans ages 12 and over—over 220 million people (Day, 1993:18)? The answer is that it is unnecessary. By carefully selecting a representative sample of the entire population, it is possible to estimate what that population would have said if everyone had been interviewed. For 1994, the most recent survey available, interviews were conducted with about 90,000 persons in some 48,000 households (Bureau of Justice Statistics, 1997:140). "Each housing unit selected for the National Crime Victimization Survey . . . remains in the sample for 3 years, with each of seven interviews taking place at 6-month intervals" (Bureau of Justice Statistics, 1997:139).

The most serious limitation of victimization surveys probably relates to actually interviewing people—gaining the cooperation of suspicious respondents, overcoming language and communication barriers, and determining whether people are telling the truth and whether they are accurately recalling the events surrounding the crimes in which they were victimized. Sometimes, memories or perceptions are unintentionally, if not intentionally, faulty (Block and Block, 1984:144–145; Bureau of Justice Statistics, 1997:142; Fattah, 1991:38–41). Those who conduct victimization surveys have attempted to deal with problems of recall by asking people to describe only those events taking place within the last six months, because those events can be recalled most accurately (O'Brien, 1985:51–52; Penick and Owens, 1976:21–25). But there is no way of knowing for certain the extent to which other kinds of distortions creep into the survey findings.

Benefits of Victimization Surveys

Despite their limitations, victimization surveys have done much to improve our knowledge of crime and delinquency, not only because they avoid the filtering process through which police and court data are gathered, but because they have provided better information than was available before. Specifically, these surveys give us insight into these areas:

unaware of them, because victims may join in covering them up if they can recover losses, or because the "victim" is all of us. Nevertheless, our knowledge of crime will be improved to the extent that something eventually is done to measure these crimes more effectively (Penick and Owens, 1976:134).

1. *Number of crimes:* How much greater is the number of victimizations than the number of crimes reported to the police? After all, many crimes—64 percent of the crimes in the 1994 National Crime Victimization Survey (Bureau of Justice Statistics, 1997:vii)—are not reported to the police.

2. *Risks of victimization:* What are the chances, say, of being robbed or assaulted or having one's home broken into?

3. *Variations in vulnerability to crime:* Who are the most likely victims of crimes—young or old people, males or females, blacks or whites, poor or well-to-do? Do the victims of one type of crime differ from the victims of another?

The benefits of victim surveys are by no means exhausted by the few examples just cited. The information they provide, although limited in some respects, not only sheds further light on the extent and distribution of crime and delinquency, but also helps to pinpoint both strengths and weaknesses in the ways we explain and respond to them.

NUMBERS OF VICTIMIZATIONS

According to the NCVS data, 42.4 million crimes, completed and attempted, were committed against persons and households in the United States in 1994 (Bureau of Justice Statistics, 1997:6). As table 6.1 shows, the most common victimizations did not involve violence. Instead, 73.2 percent were household burglaries, motor vehicle thefts, and theft of other property. Thus, such violent crimes as nonsexual assault (21.6 percent), robbery (3.1 percent), and rape/sexual assault (1.0 percent) occurred relatively infrequently.

If there were 42.4 million victimizations in 1994, that figure is about three times larger than the number of similar crimes (14.0 million) reported by the police for the same year (FBI, 1995:58). That large discrepancy must be discounted to some degree because of differences in the way police and victim data are collected. Yet, even when those differences are taken into account, data from victimization surveys and self-report surveys together suggest that police data seriously underestimate the amount of crime and delinquency.

TABLE 6.1

Number and percentage of victimizations, by type of crime, 1994

TYPE OF CRIME	NUMBER	PERCENTAGE WITHIN TYPE	PERCENTAGE OF ALL CRIMES
All crimes	42,361,840	—	100.0%
Crimes against persons	11,349,640	100.0%	26.8
Rape/sexual assault	432,750	3.8	1.0
Robbery	1,298,750	11.4	3.1
Assault	9,129,120	80.4	21.6
Purse snatching/pocket picking	489,010	4.3	1.2
Crimes against households	31,012,200	100.0	73.2
Burglary	5,482,720	17.7	12.9
Household theft	23,765,790	76.6	56.1
Motor vehicle theft	1,763,690	5.7	4.2

SOURCE: Bureau of Justice Statistics, 1997:6.

RISKS OF VICTIMIZATION

Because the risks of being a victim of crime are greater than police data indicate, it is useful to examine (1) the risks that the average person will be a victim of crime and (2) variation in the risks of being victimized depending on one's age, gender, race, social class, and place of residence.

In this section, we are concerned with the *average* person's risks. That is important because of prevailing beliefs that crime rates are forever increasing and that the average citizen is at ever-greater risk of being victimized in a crime. Sensationalized media accounts of crime probably do more than any statistical account to shape our views of the risks we face. However, statistical accounts can help to put crime into a larger perspective. Table 6.2 is constructed for that purpose. It compares the rates of various crimes reported by respondents in the NCVS with those reported by the police in the *Uniform Crime Reports.*

The table clearly shows the disparity between victim and police reports of crimes. According to the police, there were 8.4 violent crimes per 1,000 persons in 1994. By contrast, the NCVS puts the rate at 20.4 per 1,000, or more than twice as high.[1] For crimes against property, the disparities tend to be even greater, with victimizations often exceeding police estimates of crime by large amounts: burglary, more than 4 times; motor vehicle theft, 2.5 times; and other theft, almost 7 times. Indeed, because the NCVS calculates property crime rates per 1,000 *households* and police rates are calculated per 1,000 *persons,* the disparities likely would be even greater if a common base were used.[2] Taken at face value, then, such findings seem to suggest that the risks of being victimized are overwhelming. But there is another side to the picture.

Victimization surveys indicate that the odds are against the average person being a victim of a violent crime during any given year. In 1994, the chances that a woman would be raped were less than 3 in 1,000; a person robbed, 6 in 1,000; and a person assaulted, 12 in 1,000. The chances were greater that a household would experience a burglary (54 in 1,000), a motor vehicle theft (18 in 1,000), or some other theft (236 in 1,000). But even then, the odds were against victimization.

TABLE 6.2

Violent and property crimes: Contrasts between victim and police estimates, 1994

TYPE OF CRIME	NATIONAL CRIME VICTIMIZATION SURVEY[a]	UNIFORM CRIME REPORTS[a]
Crimes of violence	20.4	8.4
Murder	—	0.1
Rape	2.7	0.5
Robbery	6.1	2.8
Aggravated assault	11.6	5.0
Crimes against property[b]	307.7	54.7
Burglary	54.4	12.2
Theft	235.8	3.5
Motor vehicle theft	17.5	6.9

SOURCES: Bureau of Justice Statistics, 1997:6–7; Day, 1993:14; FBI, 1995:58.
NOTE: A dash indicates data not collected.
[a]NCVS rate per 1,000 population ages 12 and over; *UCR* rate per 1,000 population ages 10 and over.
[b]Rate per 1,000 households.

SPECIAL VULNERABILITY: "FACTS" THAT MUST BE EXPLAINED

Although we are inclined to breathe a sigh of relief on discovering that the odds are against the average person being victimized in any given year, not all people are equally likely to be a victim of crime. Some people are more likely than others to be victimized because of their age, gender, race, social

[1]Because purse snatching and pocket picking constitute only a small percentage of crimes against persons (4 percent in 1994—Bureau of Justice Statistics, 1997:vi), consideration of crimes against persons in table 6.2 and subsequent tables is limited to violent crimes. The *Uniform Crime Reports* measure only rapes against women and exclude sexual assaults other than forcible rape (FBI, 1997:400). Consequently, the rape rate in table 6.2 is limited to women and excludes other sexual assaults in order to maximize comparability. Similarly, the victimization rate for assault in table 6.2 is limited to aggravated assault because the *Uniform Crime Reports* exclude simple or nonaggravated assaults from their estimates.
[2]In table 6.2, the rates from the *Uniform Crime Reports* are calculated per 1,000 population ages 10 and over. The rates differ only slightly when they are computed for persons ages 12 and over (to make them consistent with the rates from the NCVS).

class, and place of residence. Indeed, the same issues that required explanation when we reviewed official data and self-report surveys tend to reappear when we examine victimization data.

Age

Age is strongly related to the chances of being a victim of crime. As figure 6.1 shows, those most likely to suffer from violent crimes—rape/sexual assault, robbery, and nonsexual assault—are juveniles and young adults. Indeed, what is striking about figure 6.1 is that the victimization rates so closely parallel the arrest rates for persons of various ages (see Chapter 4). The victimization rates for 12- to 15-year-olds are very similar to those for individuals ages 16–19 and 20–24, while the rates for middle-aged and elderly people are much lower. Sixteen- to 19-year-olds, for example, were about 8 times as likely as 50- to 64-year-olds and 24 times as likely as people ages 65 and older to be victims of violent crime.

Victimization data suggest that if any segment of our population lives in a predatory jungle, it is young people. Not only are they more likely to commit crimes, but they also are more likely to be victims. There are at least two possible explanations for the similarity in the ages of violent offenders and victims of violence. First, people are more likely to be victimized when they associate frequently in groups disproportionately made up of offenders. Thus, "younger persons are more likely to be victims of violent crime than older persons because the former are more likely to associate with other youth who are, themselves, disproportionately involved in violence" (Sampson and Lauritsen, 1990:111). Second, violent offenders and victims of violence may be the same people. In that connection, one of the best predictors of victimization is self-reported offending (Sampson and Lauritsen, 1990:113).

Gender

Special vulnerability to crime does not end with age. Gender is also important, and its effects can be demonstrated in two ways. First, the general effects of gender can be considered. Who runs the greater risks of being victimized—males or females? Second, we can determine how gender and age act together to affect the chances of victimization. Are young fe-

males, for example, more likely than older males or older females to be victimized?

Figure 6.2 shows that the ratio of male-to-female victimizations in violent crimes is about 1.5 to 1. The only exception involves rape and other sexual assault; for every age group, the rape victimization rate is much higher for females than males (Bureau of Justice Statistics, 1997:9).

Even then, that conclusion remains true only when males and females of the same age are compared. For example, the violent victimization rate for 16- to 19-year-old girls is 101.2 per 1,000 as compared to 141.3 per 1,000 for 16- to 19-year-old boys. Yet, observe what happens when 16- to 19-year-old girls are compared with men ages 65 and older. The victimization rate for girls is thirteen times greater— 101.2 versus 7.9. Indeed, girls in this age group have a higher rate than all men ages 25 and older.

Equally important is the rate at which young people are victimized in property crimes. Table 6.3 shows that the chances of being burglarized, having household goods stolen, or losing an automobile to thieves decrease steadily as people grow older. Thus, the ratios of property victimization for 12- to 19-year-olds versus people ages 65 and older are also high: burglary, about 5 to 1; household theft, 6 to 1; and motor vehicle theft, 5 to 1.

Given these findings, two conclusions are warranted. First, when age is held constant, males tend to have higher victimization rates than females. But second, young people, whether male or female, have higher victimization rates than middle-aged or older people. In fact, the NCVS indicates that if we were to rank different groups according to their victimization risks, they would rank as follows: (1) young males, (2) young females, (3) older males, and (4) older females.

Such findings are contrary to popular belief. Although most people are aware of the disproportionate contribution of young persons to the commission of crimes, they do not realize that the young are also the most likely to be victimized. A more common belief is that older people run the greatest risks—for example, the defenseless old lady whose purse is snatched or the reputable businessperson who is terrorized by a street gang. Actually, a more likely scenario is one in which a student is backed up against

FIGURE 6.1

Victimization rates for violent crimes, by age, 1994

SOURCE: Bureau of Justice Statistics, 1997:8.

NOTE: Rates per 1,000 in each age group.

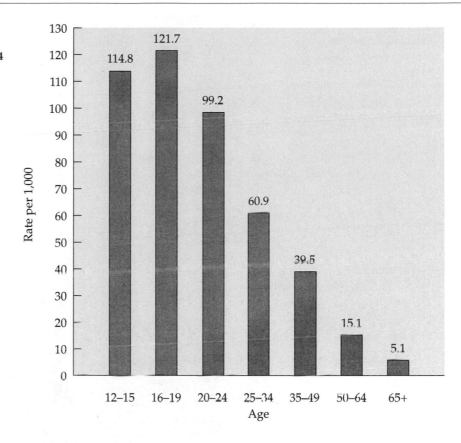

the wall in the school lavatory and robbed of lunch money by peers (Gottfredson and Gottfredson, 1985; Snyder and Sickmund, 1995:22; Whitaker and Bastian, 1991:8). The national survey of high school seniors conducted by the Institute for Social Research at the University of Michigan (Maguire and Pastore, 1997:233), which was described in the last chapter, is also relevant. During the year preceding the survey, about 33 percent of the class of 1996 had something worth less than $50 stolen from them while at school, while about 18 percent had something stolen that was worth more than $50. Almost 22 percent reported being threatened at school by an unarmed person, while about 13 percent were threatened by someone with a weapon (like a gun or a knife).

Race

The NCVS shows that blacks are more likely than whites to report having been victimized in violent crimes (61.8 versus 47.6 per 1,000—Bureau of Justice Statistics, 1997:viii). There is much more to consider, however, about the relationship between race and victimization.

GENDER, RACE, AND VIOLENT CRIMES Table 6.4 shows the relations between gender, race, and victimization in violent crimes. First, observe that males, whether black or white, tend to have higher victimization rates than females. Black males tend to suffer most from violent crimes, followed by white males, black females, and then white females. Second, the rates at which black men and black women are victims of rape/sexual assault, robbery, and aggravated assault are as much as three times the rates for their white counterparts.

RACE, AGE, AND VIOLENT CRIMES Figure 6.3 shows that among both whites and blacks, young people

FIGURE 6.2

Victimization rates for violent crimes, by gender and age, 1994

SOURCE: Bureau of Justice Statistics, 1997:9.

NOTE: Rates per 1,000 in each age group.

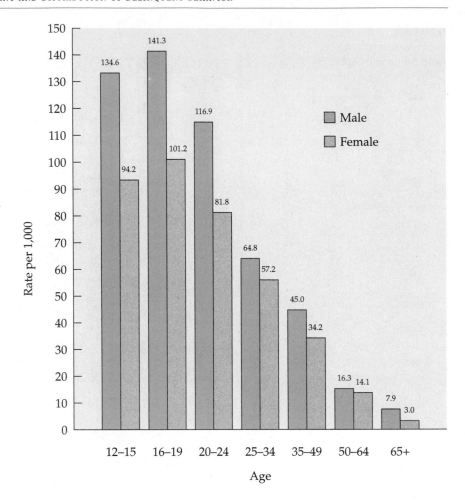

ages 12–19 are more likely than other age groups to suffer from violent crimes. Except for 16- to 24-year-olds, blacks have greater rates of violent victimization than whites. Moreover, while white 16- to 24-year-olds tend to have higher victimization rates for nonsexual assault (simple or nonaggravated assault, in particular), blacks in this age group have higher victimization rates for rape/sexual assault and robbery (Bureau of Justice Statistics, 1997:14).

RACE AND MURDER The foregoing rates of victimization are important, but they pale into insignificance when murder—the most serious of all crimes—is considered:

TABLE 6.3

Household victimization rates, by type of crime and age of head of household, 1994

AGE	BURGLARY	HOUSEHOLD THEFT	MOTOR VEHICLE THEFT
12–19	146.2	532.6	32.3
20–34	66.8	289.8	23.9
35–49	62.4	305.4	21.2
50–64	44.2	193.9	14.0
65 +	32.1	86.4	6.5

SOURCE: Bureau of Justice Statistics, 1997:22.

NOTE: Rates per 1,000 households.

TABLE 6.4

Victimization rates for violent crimes, by gender and race, 1994

TYPE OF CRIME	MALE		FEMALE		RATIO OF BLACK-TO-WHITE RATES	
	black	white	black	white	male	female
Crimes of violence	68.5	58.6	56.2	40.7	1.2:1	1.4:1
Rape/sexual assault	0.5	0.2	4.5	3.5	2.5:1	1.3:1
Robbery	18.5	6.5	10.3	3.2	2.8:1	3.2:1
Assault	49.6	51.8	41.3	34.0	1:1	1.2:1
Aggravated assault	20.6	14.6	13.3	7.4	1.4:1	1.8:1
Simple assault	29.0	37.2	28.0	26.6	1:1.3	1.1:1

SOURCE: Bureau of Justice Statistics, 1997:11.
NOTE: Rates per 1,000 persons ages 12 and over.

FIGURE 6.3

Victimization rates for violent crimes, by race and age, 1994

SOURCE: Bureau of Justice Statistics, 1997:14.
NOTE: Rates per 1,000 in each age group.

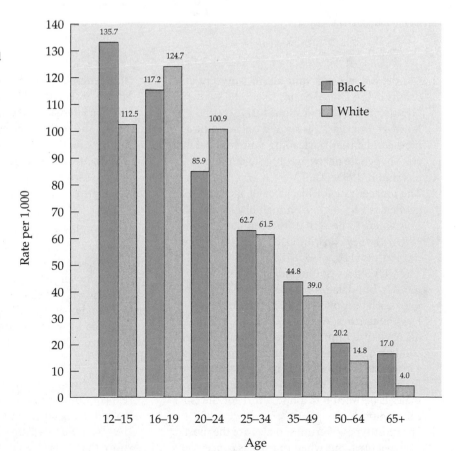

TABLE 6.5

Rates of murder victimization, by race, gender, and age, 1992

| | BLACK | | | | | WHITE | | | | | RATIO OF BLACK TO WHITE | |
| | murder victimization rate | | ratio of male to female | percentage of all causes of death | | murder victimization rate | | ratio of male to female | percentage of all causes of death | | | |
AGE	male	female		male	female	male	female		male	female	male	female
9 and under	6.7	5.9	1.1:1	2.5%	2.7%	1.8	1.5	1.2:1	1.6%	1.7%	3.7:1	3.9:1
10–14	9.6	5.1	1.9:1	21.3	20.1	2.0	1.0	2.0:1	6.9	5.9	4.8:1	5.1:1
15–19	128.5	14.2	9.0:1	58.8	28.2	15.2	3.6	4.2:1	14.4	8.4	8.5:1	3.9:1
20–24	180.5	24.3	7.4:1	56.2	28.8	19.4	4.5	4.3:1	14.4	10.0	9.3:1	5.4:1
25–29	131.7	28.0	4.7:1	36.4	21.4	16.3	4.4	3.7:1	10.6	8.5	8.1:1	6.4:1
30–34	100.6	23.4	4.3:1	21.7	12.7	14.0	3.9	3.6:1	7.2	5.8	7.2:1	6.0:1
35–44	71.4	14.9	4.8:1	10.2	4.7	10.9	3.4	3.2:1	3.9	2.9	6.6:1	4.4:1
45 +	34.6	7.0	4.9:1	1.0	0.3	5.9	2.2	2.7:1	0.2	0.1	5.9:1	3.2:1

SOURCE: National Center for Health Statistics, 1996:Tables 1-27 and 7-2.
NOTE: Rates per 100,000 in each age group.

1. Murder accounts for only about 1 percent of all deaths in the United States (National Center for Health Statistics, 1996:Table 1-27). In 1991, however, murder "was second only to motor vehicle accidents as the leading cause of fatal injuries" to people below age 20 (Snyder and Sickmund, 1995:24).

2. The murder rate for blacks of all ages and both genders is very high. Although blacks make up only about 13 percent of the population (Day, 1993:18), they constitute 48 percent of all murder victims (FBI, 1997:16).

3. The NCVS does not include questions about murder, but data on murder victims are compiled each year by the National Center for Health Statistics. As table 6.5 shows, the most likely victims of murder are black males. Even as children ages 9 and under, their murder victimization rate is almost four times greater than that for white males. The black-to-white ratio for males is between 6 to 1 and 9 to 1 for the older age groups.

4. For most types of crimes, males are the most likely victims. But when murder is concerned, this generalization breaks down. In every age group except ages 15–19, the victimization rate for black females exceeds that of both white males and white females. As a consequence, murder "is the most common cause of death for young African American *females* as well as for young African American males" (American Psychological Association, 1993:12).

Such findings suggest that black slums have become places of terror, particularly for young black males (Wilson, 1987:21–26). In his classic autobiographical novel *Manchild in the Promised Land*, Claude Brown (1965:121–123), supposedly a hardened offender at age 13, described what it meant to be a "bad nigger" in Harlem and how heartsick he was over the expectations associated with that status:

I was growing up now, and people were going to expect things from me. I would soon be expected to kill a nigger if he mistreated me, like Rock, Bubba Williams, and Dewdrop had. . . . I knew now that I had to keep up with these cats; if I didn't, I would lose my respect in the neighborhood. . . . It made life seem so hard. Sometimes I just wanted to give it up.

Then, to a correctional counselor who had befriended him, Brown made a fatalistic remark that is not uncommon among gang members today: "I don't think I'm gonna stay on the street, Papanek, not for much longer. I don't think I'll see Christmas on the streets." Why plan for the future? Violent death is more likely.

RACE AND HOUSEHOLD CRIMES To make matters worse, it is not just from violent crimes that blacks suffer the most. They also suffer from relatively high victimization rates in property crimes against households (Bureau of Justice Statistics, 1997:ix). In 1994, the burglary victimization rate for black households was 70.8 per 1,000 versus 51.7 per 1,000 for white households, 26.6 versus 15.6 for motor vehicle theft, and 243.8 versus 234.6 for theft of other property.

Income

As might be anticipated, income is a fourth factor in considering victimization. The data show that persons in families with the lowest household incomes are the most vulnerable to violent crimes (Bureau of Justice Statistics, 1997:viii). For example, the rates of victimization for people with household incomes of less than $7,500 are several times greater than the rates for those with incomes of $75,000 or more—for rape/sexual assault, 6.7 per 1,000 persons versus 0.9 per 1,000; for robbery, 11.1 versus 4.5; and for assault, 65.8 versus 34.6.

Turning to property crimes, the burglary rate is 78.6 per 1,000 households with incomes of less than $7,500 and 40.9 for households with incomes of $75,000 or more (Bureau of Justice Statistics, 1997: ix). The greater the income, however, the greater the chances that a household will suffer from motor vehicle thefts and other property thefts—for motor theft, for example, a rate of 13.9 for households with incomes of less than $7,500 versus 17.7 for households with incomes of $75,000 or more. In short, poverty is associated with greater violence, while af-

WHAT ACCOUNTS FOR VARIATION IN RISKS OF VICTIMIZATION?

The lifestyle/routine activity perspective, which is fairly new in sociological criminology, treats the risks of victimization as a function of people's everyday behavior. It is people's lifestyles or routine activities—how they tend to spend their time and with whom—that affects their chances of victimization. We will consider the lifestyle/routine activity perspective more fully in a later chapter. However, it might be useful to consider its potential implications here. What is it about the lifestyles or routine activities of young people that might help us to understand why they have higher victimization rates than older people? What is it about the lifestyles or routine activities of females that might help us account for why they are less likely than males to be victimized? How does your own lifestyle increase (or decrease) your risks of being a victim of crime?

fluence is associated with victimization in property crimes.

Victimization data also show that race combines with household income in important ways. On the one hand, the general pattern just described is characteristic of both blacks and whites when comparisons are made *within* races; that is, poor people, whether black or white, suffer the highest rate of victimization in violent crimes (Bureau of Justice Statistics, 1997:20). Furthermore, the greater the family income, the greater the victimization in property crimes (motor vehicle theft and other property theft, but not burglary—Bureau of Justice Statistics, 1997:

23–24). On the other hand, comparisons *across* races reveal that no matter what their household income, blacks tend to suffer more from crime than whites with comparable incomes. Increased income helps to shelter blacks from crime, but it is not sufficient to overcome racial disparities.

Residence

The final factor associated with the risks of being a victim of crime is place of residence. Since the 1800s, Americans have believed that the greatest amount of crime occurs in cities. Victimization surveys tend to confirm that belief (Bureau of Justice Statistics, 1997:49–50). On a continuum from urban to suburban to rural, the rates for violent crimes are as follows: urban, 63.6 per 1,000 persons; suburban, 49.6; and rural, 39.2. The same pattern holds for property crimes: urban, 376.4; suburban, 296.5; and rural, 246.4. Thus, there is a decrease in the risks of victimization from urban to suburban to rural.

TRENDS IN VICTIMIZATION

Police and juvenile court data have suggested that delinquency increased considerably during the late 1960s and early 1970s and then leveled off until the mid-1980s, when it increased again. By contrast, self-report surveys have revealed few changes in delinquency over the past twenty years or so. What have victim surveys shown?

The NCVS was redesigned in the early 1990s, and the data before and after the redesign cannot be compared easily. It is possible, however, to examine trends in victimization prior to 1993. Although victimization rates for violent crimes decreased or remained relatively stable for most age groups from 1973 to 1992, the victimization rate for young people ages 12–19 increased (Zawitz et al., 1993:21–22). However, the rate of victimization for property crimes (burglary, motor vehicle theft, and other theft) decreased. Hence, the findings of victimization surveys tend to concur more with official data than with self-report surveys.

SUMMARY AND CONCLUSIONS

By sampling the general public, victimization surveys have provided valuable information on the extent and distribution of victimization.

Extent and Distribution of Victimization

The number of victim-reported crimes greatly exceeds the number reported by the police. Nonetheless, the odds are against the average citizen being victimized during any given year, especially in a violent crime. Moreover, victimization surveys do not support the belief that it is older people, or white, middle- and upper-class people, who are the most likely victims of crime. Instead, they suggest the following:

1. Young persons are more vulnerable than older persons.
2. Males are more vulnerable than females.
3. Blacks are more vulnerable than whites.
4. Poor people are more vulnerable than the affluent to violent crimes, but not property crimes.
5. Urban residents are more vulnerable than suburban residents, who are more vulnerable than rural residents.

When all of those factors are considered together, they indicate that the prototypical victim, particularly in violent crimes, is the young, poor, black male who lives in an urban slum. The young, poor, white male is not far behind, followed closely by the young, poor, black female.

There is a paradox in such findings. Despite the notion that special steps are taken to nurture and protect young people, they are far more likely than the middle-aged or elderly to be victims. Furthermore, the individuals who are the most disadvantaged economically are also those who suffer most from crimes.

"Facts" That Must Be Explained

There are far more juvenile law violators and victims than there are official offenders and victims. Self-report studies suggest that only about 10 percent of all delinquency is recorded officially, while victimization surveys indicate that the figure may be slightly higher. Whatever the precise figure, it is clear that official data underestimate (1) the actual amount of law-violating behavior by juveniles and (2) the instances in which they are victims.

The three methods of measuring crime and delinquency, however, are in surprising agreement on many of the "facts" to which criminologists must attend. Consider first the similarities between police and victim accounts of crime:

1. Police data show that arrest rates are higher for young people than older adults, higher for males than females, higher for blacks than whites, and higher for low-income than high-income persons.

2. Victimization surveys paint a similar picture (though more for violent crimes than property crimes): Young people are more likely than older people to be victims of crime; males are more likely than females to be victims; blacks are more likely than whites to be victims; and poor people are more likely than affluent people to be victims. In short, while arrest data represent only a portion of those who violate the law and while victim accounts represent only those who are willing to report having been victimized, they seem to be tapping a common universe of behavior.

The picture painted by self-report surveys, while similar in general terms, suggests the need for qualification. For example, while self-report surveys strongly support the idea that crime is concentrated disproportionately among youths and that males are more heavily involved than females, they also suggest that the pattern of female offending is very similar to that of males. Furthermore, self-report surveys raise questions about whether differences in law-violating behavior between low- and high-income persons, and between blacks and whites, are as great as arrest data indicate.

In part three, we will turn our attention to theories of delinquency and examine just how well the theories can explain such phenomena and suggest ways for dealing with them.

DISCUSSION QUESTIONS

1. How have victimization surveys improved our knowledge of the extent and distribution of crime and delinquency?
2. What is the relationship between age and victimization? Gender and victimization? Race and victimization? Social class and victimization? Place of residence and victimization?
3. Why might the victims of some crimes—rape and burglary, for example—be reluctant to report their victimizations to NCVS interviewers?
4. Why do victim-reported crimes exceed the number of crimes reported by the police?
5. In what ways do police, self-report, and victimization data agree on the extent and distribution of crime and delinquency?

REFERENCES

American Psychological Association. 1993. *Violence and Youth: Psychology's Response.* Vol. I: Summary Report of the American Psychological Association Commission on Violence and Youth. Washington, D.C.: American Psychological Association.

Block, Carolyn R., and Richard L. Block. 1984. "Crime Definition, Crime Measurement, and Victim Surveys." *Journal of Social Issues* 40:137–159.

Brown, Claude. 1965. *Manchild in the Promised Land.* New York: Macmillan.

Bureau of Justice Statistics. 1997. *Criminal Victimization in the United States, 1994.* Washington, D.C.: U.S. Government Printing Office.

Day, Jennifer Cheeseman. 1993. *Current Population Reports.* Series P-25, no. 1104. Washington, D.C.: U.S. Government Printing Office.

Ennis, Phillip H. 1967. *Criminal Victimization in the United States: A Report of a National Survey.* Field Surveys II. President's Commission on Law Enforcement and Administration of Justice. Washington, D.C.: U.S. Government Printing Office.

Fattah, Ezzat A. 1991. *Understanding Criminal Victimization: An Introduction to Theoretical Victimology.* Scarborough, Ontario: Prentice-Hall Canada.

Federal Bureau of Investigation. 1995. *Crime in the United States: Uniform Crime Reports, 1994.* Washington, D.C.: U.S. Government Printing Office.
1997. *Crime in the United States: Uniform Crime Reports, 1996.* Washington, D.C.: U.S. Government Printing Office.

Gottfredson, Gary D., and Denise C. Gottfredson. 1985. *Victimization in Schools.* New York: Plenum Press.

Maguire, Kathleen, and Ann L. Pastore, eds. 1997. *Sourcebook of Criminal Justice Statistics—1996.* Washington, D.C.: U.S. Government Printing Office.

National Advisory Commission on Criminal Justice Standards and Goals. 1973. *Criminal Justice System.* Washington, D.C.: U.S. Government Printing Office.

National Center for Health Statistics. 1996. *Vital Statistics of the United States, 1992,* Vol. 2, Part A. Washington, D.C.: U.S. Government Printing Office.

National Criminal Justice Information and Statistics Service. 1975. *Criminal Victimization in the United States, 1973: Advance Report,* Vol. 1. Washington, D.C.: U.S. Government Printing Office.
1979. *Criminal Victimization in the United States, 1977.* Washington, D.C.: U.S. Government Printing Office.

O'Brien, Robert M. 1985. *Crime and Victimization Data.* Beverly Hills, Calif.: Sage.

Penick, Bettye K. Eidson, and Maurice E. B. Owens, III. 1976. *Surveying Crime.* Washington, D.C.: National Academy of Sciences.

President's Commission on Law Enforcement and Administration of Justice. 1967a. *Task Force Report: Crime and Its Impact—An Assessment.* Washington, D.C.: U.S. Government Printing Office.
1967b. *The Challenge of Crime in a Free Society.* Washington, D.C.: U.S. Government Printing Office.

Sampson, Robert J., and Janet L. Lauritsen. 1990. "Deviant Lifestyles, Proximity to Crime, and the Offender–Victim Link in Personal Violence." *Journal of Research in Crime and Delinquency* 27 (May):110–139.

Snyder, Howard N., and Melissa Sickmund. 1995. *Juvenile Offenders and Victims: A National Report.* Washington, D.C.: Office of Juvenile Justice and Delinquency Prevention.

Whitaker, Catherine, and Lisa D. Bastian. 1991. *Teenage Victims: A National Crime Survey Report.* Washington, D.C.: U.S. Government Printing Office.

Wilson, William J. 1987. *The Truly Disadvantaged: The Inner City, the Underclass, and Public Policy.* Chicago: University of Chicago Press.

Zawitz, Marianne, et al. 1993. *Highlights from 20 Years of Surveying Crime Victims.* Washington, D.C.: U.S. Government Printing Office.

PART THREE

EXPLANATIONS OF DELINQUENT BEHAVIOR

C rime theories are much like concepts of childhood; they have changed considerably over time. In the past 200 years, crime theories have ranged from those that locate its causes entirely within the individual to those that locate its causes entirely within the organization of society. The theories' assumptions about human nature are equally diverse. Some assume that people are born inherently evil, while others assume that they are born inherently good. To make sense of such diverse theories, it is necessary to establish a framework for assessing them.

By way of setting the stage, it is useful to reconsider the 18th-century beliefs about the causes of crime that we reviewed in Chapter 3. Recall that American colonists tended to equate crime with sin. Crimes demanded severe punishments, such as whipping, hanging, branding, the stocks, and the pillory. Recall also that this way of explaining and responding to crime changed as Enlightenment philosophers began to stress human reason and pro gress through the application of democratic principles. Indeed, Enlightenment philosophy was largely responsible for what we now call the *classical school of criminology* (Monachesi, 1972; Radzinowicz, 1966:20–28).

CLASSICAL SCHOOL OF CRIMINOLOGY

Led by Cesare Beccaria (1738–1794) in the late 1700s, classical theorists criticized Western criminal justice systems for their arbitrary, cruel, and oppressive practices. The goals of classical theorists were to reduce the severity of existing punishments and to achieve equal justice for all (Beccaria, 1963).

According to Beccaria and Jeremy Bentham (1748–1832), an English philosopher, human nature is characterized by three central features: (1) People are not bound by original sin but have freedom of choice; (2) people are rational and are capable of using reason to govern their lives; and (3) people are motivated to pursue their own self-interests at the expense of others. Consequently, Beccaria and Bentham believed that human behavior, whether law-abiding or criminal, reflects the free exercise of human reason in the pursuit of pleasure (Geis, 1972:56–57).

Believing that people are reasonable and free, classical theorists envisioned a democratic society in which criminal law would be a product of value consensus. In a democratic society, citizens willingly would enter into a social contract to refrain from crime and preserve the *social order* (Monachesi, 1972:40).

Classical theorists did not seek complex explanations of *law-violating behavior*. The explanation lay in their assumptions about human nature: People make free and rational decisions to violate the law in pursuit of personal satisfaction (Bentham, 1948:2).

An enlightened criminal justice system would incorporate all of the due-process protections with which we are familiar—protection against unreasonable search and seizure, and against torture and self-incrimination, to mention just a few. Laws and procedures, not the power of the accused or the discretion of judges, would govern criminal proceedings (Monachesi, 1972:41–43).

People would be deterred from committing crimes if they were threatened with punishment that was certain (unavoidable) and swift (Monachesi, 1972:43–46). Punishments were to be graded by the seriousness of criminal acts—minor punishments for petty crimes and severe punishments for serious crimes. Neither brutality nor the death penalty would be necessary. People did not need to be scourged, disemboweled, or beheaded to convey the idea that crime does not pay.

It is difficult to overstate the impact of classical criminology on Western thought and legal practices. The criminal codes of many Western countries were rewritten in the late 1700s and early 1800s as part of the general growth of democratic institutions. An independent judiciary became a separate arm of government; steps were taken to make due process a regular part of the administration of justice; punishments were reduced in severity and graded according to the seriousness of criminal acts; and newly designed prisons were constructed as more humane places for punishing offenders. Many of those features remain a part of our legal system today.

POSITIVE SCHOOL OF CRIMINOLOGY

Changes took place during the 1800s that eroded the influence of the classical school. One was the growth of science, ironically no less a product of Enlightenment philosophy than was the classical school. But whereas classical theorists joined with Enlightenment philosophers to change the Western legal systems of the 1700s, the growth of science reflected Enlightenment philosophers' emphasis on seeking knowledge and using it to accelerate human progress. As a consequence of that emphasis, a new school of criminology began to take shape—the *positive (or positivist) school.*

Between the emergence of the classical school of criminology in the late 1700s and the emergence of the positive school in the late 1800s, there was a marked "shift in thinking that is of such magnitude that it can well be described as an intellectual revolution" (Vold and Bernard, 1986:35). Beccaria had assumed that human nature involved the rational exercise of free will and that the social contract was responsible for social order. But an increasing number of positivists began to question those assumptions. "What sort of creature is the human animal?" and "How is society organized and maintained?" they asked. But rather than turning to philosophical speculation (e.g., assumptions about human nature) for the answers, they turned to the methods of science—observation, experimentation, and comparison. The application of those methods led to a different approach to explaining and controlling crime. By the time the juvenile court was firmly established in the 1900s, a new set of beliefs tended to dominate criminology:

- *Empirical documentation.* Positivists contended that, as in the natural and physical sciences, the application of reason to a problem is not enough. Despite the plausibility of classical theories, they could be false. If they could not be supported by empirical evidence, other theories must be sought. The job of criminologists was to formulate and test theories of crime and crime control.
- *The doctrine of determinism.* Positivists also argued that crime, like any other phenomenon, is determined by prior causes; it doesn't just happen. The emphasis of the classical school on reason and free will, they said, is too simplistic. People are not always free to do as they wish. Much, if not all, of their behavior is determined by

biological, psychological, and social forces over which they have little personal control. Because certain laws govern the operation of those forces, another job of criminologists was to discover the laws about crime.

- *Value neutrality.* Positivists argued, in addition, that there is a need to be neutral about societal values. Although politicians, citizens, and criminal justice officials had to be concerned with implementing policies that are consistent with prevailing values, criminologists were to be concerned primarily with trying to understand why people violate the law and the effects of alternative crime control policies. This is not to say that criminologists couldn't espouse certain values in their roles as ordinary citizens. But as scientists, they were to confine themselves to "facts" based on objective evidence.

As we will soon see, the most popular theories of the late 19th and early 20th centuries suggested that the causes of crime and delinquency are biological—physical degeneracy, inherited genetic weaknesses, or defective intelligence. Soon *psychodynamic theories* were added, suggesting that law violators suffer from emotional conflicts that originate in the family and result from inadequate socialization in the first few years of life. Finally, 20th-century sociologists and other social scientists theorized that delinquent behavior is caused by such factors as poverty, ignorance, discrimination, social disorganization, and delinquent subcultures.

These ways of explaining crime and delinquency implied the need to alter the classical concept of justice. If lawbreaking was due to factors that offenders could not control, then it would be unjust to punish them for the acts they committed. A more just system, by contrast, would be one that reacted to *criminals,* not to crimes.

As English scientist Charles Goring (1913:12) put it:

> All thinking people today, legislators and judges, as well as the general public, the morality of the age, as well as the voice of science, attest the truth . . . that it is the criminal and not the crime we should study and consider; that it is the criminal and not the crime we ought to penalize.

The positivist strategy was supposed to individualize justice and eliminate delinquent behavior by identifying and eliminating its causes through prevention and rehabilitation.

BEYOND THE CLASSICAL AND POSITIVE SCHOOLS

Twentieth-century positivists have been concerned primarily with one central issue about delinquency: whether there are factors that distinguish law violators from law-abiding youths. The causes of delinquency have been sought in the characteristics of individuals, the ways communities are organized and structured, and the groups in which youths associate; and we will consider a wide range of positivist theories in the next several chapters.

In the 1960s, 1970s, and 1980s, however, there was a shift away from the positive school, initially among a new group of theorists—labeling theorists—who became preoccupied with societal reactions to delinquency (Becker, 1963, 1973; Lemert, 1972; Schur, 1971, 1973). According to *labeling theory,* serious delinquent behavior is not caused by inadequate families, poverty, lack of opportunity, or peer group associations. Instead, society's reactions to youthful lawbreakers produce serious delinquency—what labeling theorists call secondary deviance. The process of identifying, labeling, and stigmatizing children in the juvenile justice system makes their delinquent behavior worse.

Labeling theorists assume that human nature is relatively flexible and subject to change. Most delinquents are viewed as relatively normal youths who eventually will desist from law violations on their own. If they persist, however, in committing delinquent acts, especially serious delinquent acts, it is due not to any evil tendencies on their part, but to the negative effects of the police, judges, and correctional officials on them.

Labeling theorists also assume that the social order is characterized by value conflict, which usually is resolved in favor of people in positions of power and influence. Social rules and the imposition of those rules will reflect their interests, not those of less powerful groups.

The distrust of legal and other social institutions, as implied in labeling theory, was pronounced in the 1970s. The Vietnam War, as well as the burglaries, wiretaps, perjuries, and cover-ups of the Nixon administration, created serious crises. Not only were American streets filled with crime and delinquency, but crime now had penetrated the highest levels of government. Faith in the capacity of American institutions to ensure tranquility and implement reforms had reached a low point.

Given such a situation, it is not surprising that another new group of theorists—radical theorists—picked up on the theme that virtually all social institutions were corrupt. Radical theorists claimed, based on Marxian theory, that the problem lay not with criminals, but with the failures and inequities of capitalism (Platt, 1974; Quinney, 1972, 1974; Taylor, Walton, and Young, 1973). The crises of the 1970s reflected attempts by an awakening citizenry to throw off the political, economic, and legal bonds of an oppressive social order.

Radical theory is sharply at odds with both classical and positive theories. But because the positive school of criminology has been preeminent in the 1900s, radical theorists' main concern has been to discredit it and identify an alternative approach for explaining and controlling crime and delinquency.

To begin with, radical theorists have been quick to point out that positivists inevitably are affected by the values they hold. Crime theories do not grow like plants in a hothouse. Instead, they are social constructions that likely reflect traditional beliefs and prejudices; that is, crime theories not only affect the course of social thought but also are affected by it. No theory is neutral with respect to prevailing values.

Radical theorists have tended to see positivists as unreflective handmaidens of existing power groups because of their stress upon value neutrality. This is especially true of positivists' tendency to use existing laws to determine who is a criminal or delinquent. Such a practice is said to be unjust because laws reflect the values of a powerful elite that seeks to use laws for its own ends, above all as a means of maintaining political and economic power over such powerless groups as the poor, racial/ethnic minorities, and women. Positivists not only fail to support ways to eliminate conditions like poverty, racism, and sexism but, because of their misguided emphasis on value neutrality, tacitly support those who have perpetuated them.

IMPLICATIONS FOR EVALUATING THEORIES

The diverse theories that we will consider in this part of the book make one conclusion very clear: The search for a full understanding of delinquent behavior has been characterized by a mixed bag of values and assumptions. All delinquency theorists, including positivists, are affected by cultural values. Indeed, long before radical criminology came along, William Graham Sumner (1906:98), one of the pioneers of American sociology, commented that "it is vain to imagine that a 'scientific man' can divest himself of prejudice or previous opinion, and put himself in an attitude of neutral independence towards the mores. He might as well try to get out of gravity or the pressure of the atmosphere."

Sumner was correct. Caution, therefore, should be exercised as we consider the theories that follow. Rather than viewing them as pristine statements of reality that somehow transcend all cultural or temporal boundaries, we should recognize that they, too, are artifacts of culture and history. Indeed, if we were to draw a simple diagram of the place of delinquency theories in our cultural life, it might look something like this:

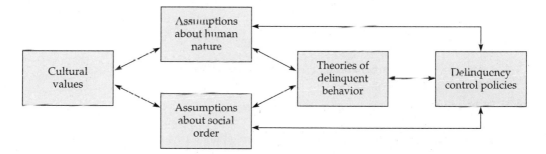

The diagram indicates that cultural values lead to certain assumptions about human nature and social order. Those assumptions, in turn, contribute to both the formulation of theories of delinquent behavior and policies to control it. But the relationship flows in both directions: Although theories of delinquent behavior are affected by prevailing values and assumptions, they also tend to alter those values and assumptions.

Because both are often true, theories play an important role not only in accumulating knowledge but also in constructing new cultural values and ways of controlling delinquency. Moreover, it is not always the scientific adequacy of a theory that will determine its uses, but rather its capacity to capture and give expression to emerging cultural values.

FRAMEWORK FOR ASSESSING THE THEORIES

Given this state of affairs, two steps will be taken to sort out the many theories that exist and draw some overall conclusions about them. First, they will be classified into major types, ranging from the deterministic theories of the late 1800s, which explained delinquent behavior by reference to the inherent characteristics of defective children, to the most recent theories, which are sometimes no less deterministic but offer different explanations. The historical progression of these explanations and the changes they have wrought in our construction of delinquency will be described.

Second, examination of each of the types of theory will be organized to address a series of fundamental questions:

- What are the assumptions about human nature and social order on which the theory is based? What values does it reflect, and what images of children and society does it portray?
- What is its underlying logic and basic content? What are the "facts" on which it concentrates in trying to explain delinquency? Are any of those "facts" among those that we considered while examining the various measures of delinquent behavior: age, gender, race, social class, or the group nature of delinquency?
- What are its implications for social policy, and how has it actually affected policy?
- How well does it stand up to logical and empirical scrutiny?

Once those questions have been addressed, we will be in a position to draw some conclusions about the overall contribution of the theories.

REFERENCES

Beccaria, Cesare. 1963. *On Crimes and Punishments.* Translated by Henry Paolucci. Indianapolis, Ind.: Bobbs-Merrill.

Becker, Howard S. 1963. *Outsiders: Studies in the Sociology of Deviance.* New York: Free Press.
1973. *Outsiders: Studies in the Sociology of Deviance (With a New Chapter—"Labeling Theory Reconsidered").* New York: Free Press.

Bentham, Jeremy. 1948. *An Introduction to the Principles of Morals and Legislation.* Edited by Laurence J. Lafleur. New York: Hafner.

Geis, Gilbert. 1972. "Jeremy Bentham." Pp. 51–68 in Hermann Mannheim, ed., *Pioneers in Criminology.* 2nd ed. Montclair, N.J.: Patterson Smith.

Goring, Charles. 1913. *The English Convict: A Statistical Study.* London: His Majesty's Stationery Office.

Lemert, Edwin M. 1972. *Human Deviance, Social Problems, and Social Control,* 2nd ed. Englewood Cliffs, N.J.: Prentice-Hall.

Monachesi, Elio. 1972. "Cesare Beccaria." Pp. 36–50 in Hermann Mannheim, ed., *Pioneers in Criminology,* 2nd ed. Montclair, N.J.: Patterson Smith.

Platt, Anthony M. 1974. "The Triumph of Benevolence: The Origins of the Juvenile Justice System in the United States." Pp. 356–389 in Richard Quinney, ed., *Criminal Justice in America: A Critical Understanding.* Boston: Little, Brown.

Quinney, Richard. 1972. "The Ideology of Law: Notes for a Radical Alternative to Legal Repression." *Issues in Criminology* 7 (Winter):1–35.
1974. *Criminal Justice in America: A Critical Understanding.* Boston: Little, Brown.

Radzinowicz, Leon. 1966. *Ideology and Crime.* New York: Columbia University Press.

Schur, Edwin M. 1971. *Labeling Deviant Behavior: Its Sociological Implications.* New York: Harper & Row.
1973. *Radical Nonintervention: Rethinking the Delinquency Problem.* Englewood Cliffs, N.J.: Prentice-Hall.

Sumner, William G. 1906. *Folkways: A Study of the Sociological Importance of Usages, Manners, Customs, Mores, and Morals.* Boston: Ginn.

Taylor, Ian, Paul Walton, and Jock Young. 1973. *The New Criminology.* New York: Harper & Row.

Vold, George B., and Thomas J. Bernard. 1986. *Theoretical Criminology,* 3rd ed. New York: Oxford University Press.

EDWARD DINKLEMAN,
ALIAS EDDIE MILLER — HUNTER — BOWMAN,
PICKPOCKET,
SHOP LIFTER AND HOTEL THIEF.

WALTER SHERIDAN,
ALIAS RALSTON — KEENE,
BANK SNEAK, FORGER AND
COUNTERFEITER.

WILLIAM COLEMAN,
ALIAS BILLY COLEMAN,
BURGLAR AND BANK SNEAK.

IKE VAIL,
ALIAS OLD IKE,
CONFIDENCE.

JOHN LARNEY,
ALIAS MOLLIE MATCHES,
BANK SNEAK AND BURGLAR

EDWARD RICE,
ALIAS BIG RICE,
CONFIDENCE AND HOTEL SNEAK.

MANY BIOLOGICAL CONTROL THEORISTS, SUCH AS CESARE LOMBROSO, HAVE POSTULATED THAT LAWBREAKERS ARE DISTINCT PHYSICAL TYPES.

CHAPTER SEVEN

CONTROL THEORY: BIOLOGICAL AND PSYCHODYNAMIC

The earliest scientific theories were **biological and psychodynamic control theories.** They are called **control theories** because they posit that law-violating behavior results from the inability of people to *control* their antisocial impulses. Children commit delinquent acts when they are inherently incapable of controlling those impulses or when they have not been trained properly to do so.

EARLY BIOLOGICAL CONTROL THEORIES

Early biological theories were "kinds-of-people" theories, suggesting that law violators are innately inferior while those who obey the law have inherited the ability to control their antisocial impulses and behave responsibly. Although several such theories were advanced in the 1800s, Cesare Lombroso (1835–1909), an Italian physician, generally is considered the first person to apply the *positive* methods of science to test them (Vold, 1958:28–29; Wolfgang, 1972:280). While a student, Lombroso increasingly disagreed with the free-will philosophy of the **classical school of criminology,** became intrigued by the doctrines of positivistic philosophy, and was excited by the implications of human evolution (Wolfgang, 1972:234).

With medical training in comparative anatomy, Lombroso (1911:xi–xv) quickly accepted the importance of empirical measurement in his studies of brain pathology, mental illness, and criminal behavior; and he postulated a relationship among all such disorders. In contrast to classical criminology's emphasis on *criminal acts* and *legal procedure,* Lombroso stressed the importance of examining the physical characteristics of *law violators* and the conditions under which they violate the law.

Physical Degeneracy

Lombroso came into prominence in 1876 when he published *The Criminal Man.* From observations of Italian prisoners and soldiers, he concluded that criminals were *atavistic*—born lawbreakers who were subhuman throwbacks to an earlier, more primitive stage of evolutionary development. The following three postulates are the essence of his theory (Sutherland and Cressey, 1974:53; Wolfgang, 1972: 250):

1. Law violators are a distinct physical type at birth.
2. Law violators possess physical stigmata that are characteristic of an earlier form of evolutionary development: imbalanced regions of the brain, an asymmetrical face, large ears, an abnormal nose, abundant wrinkles, supernumerary nipples, abnormal sex organs, and other physical anomalies.
3. People with at least five such physical characteristics cannot control their predisposition to crime.

RACE AND CRIME Lombroso (Ferrero, 1911:10–24, 139–140) contended that European criminals possessed many of the characteristics of "African and Oriental" races: flat nose, long arms, curly hair, flat feet, oblique eyes, and thick lips. Gould (1981:126) quotes Lombroso's description of criminals' insensitivity to pain:

Their [criminals'] physical insensibility well recalls that of savage peoples who can bear in rights of puberty tortures that a white man could never endure. All travellers know the indifference of Negroes and American savages to pain: the former cut their hands and laugh in order to avoid work; the latter, tied to the torture post, gaily sing the praises of their tribe while they are slowly burnt.

Lombroso's theory reflected the view of many 19th-century Europeans that people of other races were innately inferior (Gould, 1981:113–135).

GENDER AND CRIME In *The Female Offender,* Lombroso (Lombroso and Ferrero, 1958) also attributed differences between males and females to evolutionary development. Females, he contended, were more primitive than males; in particular, they were more vengeful, jealous, and insensitive to pain, and they lacked any sense of morality (150–151). Nonetheless, the natural deficiencies of females were "neutralized by [their] piety, maternity, want of passion, sexual coldness, by weakness, and an undeveloped intelligence" (p. 151). Indeed, females were so "monotonous and uniform" compared to males that they not only failed to become artists, scientists, and political leaders but also were less inclined to commit crimes (p. 122).

Why, then, did *any* females commit crimes? It was because some inherited male characteristics—a "virile" cranium, excessive body hair, moles, and other masculine features (pp. 28, 82–87). Masculinity among females was itself an anomaly (p. 112). If females were born with feminine features, their innate physiological limitations usually prevented them from committing crimes and predisposed them to unimaginative, dull, and conformist lives (Klein, 1973:9).

ASSESSMENT AND IMPACT OF LOMBROSO'S IDEAS Lombroso's ideas attracted international attention. Nonetheless, it was not long before he and his students began to modify them. By the time of his death in 1909, he had decided that *born* criminals constituted only about one-third of the total criminal population. The remaining two-thirds comprised two additional types: (1) *insane offenders,* whose crimes were caused by any one of several complex mental disorders, and (2) *criminaloids,* whose personalities somehow had been warped by a host of environmental factors (Beirne, 1988:335; Ferrero, 1911:Part 1; Gould, 1981:132–135; Rafter, 1992:537; Vold, 1958: 30; Wolfgang, 1972:251–254).

A study published in 1913 by Charles Goring (1913:173), an English physician, further discredited Lombroso's ideas. After comparing several thousand criminals and noncriminals, Goring concluded that there was no such thing as an atavistic, physical criminal type. Nonetheless, the biological seed had been planted and was growing rapidly.

Arthur MacDonald, an employee of the U.S. Bureau of Education, appealed to Congress in 1908 for funds to establish a laboratory for studying delinquents. He was particularly interested in their height and weight, hair and skin color, nationality, size of hands and ears, thickness of lips, and sensitivity to heat and pain, as well as whether they had been subjected to "hereditary taint" or to the "stigmata of degeneration." MacDonald told Congress that "there is little hope of making the world better if we do not seek the causes of social evils at their beginnings" (Bremner, 1970, 2:562–563).

Defective Intelligence

MacDonald's interest in "hereditary taint" and the "stigmata of degeneration" reflected his awareness of other biological thinking, in particular, the possibility that poor heredity leads to delinquency. Indeed, that was Goring's (1913:287–288, 368) conclusion. Even though his study of English convicts had convinced him that there was no such thing as a physical criminal type, he concluded that the tendency to be criminal was inherited and that the environment contributed little to criminality (Beirne, 1988). Specifically, he concluded that feeblemindedness, or defective intelligence from poor heredity, caused crime.

The theory of feeblemindedness was given greater respectability by attempts in the early 1900s to scientifically measure intelligence. After several years of investigation, French psychologists Alfred Binet and Théodore Simon in 1905 published a scale for measuring intelligence. Then, in 1908, they published a revised scale based on the idea that child-

hood was characterized by developmental stages and that "mental age" could be measured by taking those developmental stages into account (Gould, 1981: 148–154; Vold, 1958:79–81). The concept of mental age suggested that intelligence increased with age and peaked at about age 16. Thus, it should be possible not only to measure the average or normal intelligence of children of different ages but also to determine which ones were feebleminded. Children whose **intelligence quotients** (IQs) fell below the norm for their age were deemed mentally defective.

It wasn't long before intelligence testing was applied to delinquents. Henry Goddard (1911:563, 1914:9), an American psychologist, concluded that at least 25 percent of delinquents, and perhaps up to 90 percent, were mentally defective. However, serious questions were raised about the idea that feeblemindedness caused delinquency when intelligence tests were used to determine the fitness of armed forces draftees during World War I. Goddard (1914: 4, 573) had argued that a mental age of 12 marked the upper limit of feeblemindedness. This standard, therefore, was applied to thousands of young men entering military service. Examiners were astounded, however, to find that about one-third would have to be considered feebleminded if Goddard's standard were retained (Zeleny, 1933:569).

To his credit, Goddard recognized that such a conclusion would be absurd. A high percentage of young men entering military service were not feebleminded (Gould, 1981:172; Vold, 1958:83). Furthermore, when the test scores of criminals and draftees were compared, the two groups were more alike than different. In fact, only about 5 percent of criminals could be considered feebleminded if a mental age of 8 was used as the standard (Zeleny, 1933:576).

More Theories of Physical Inferiority and Defective Intelligence

For a while, the tendency was to discard physical and hereditary explanations of delinquency. Then, in the 1930s, Earnest A. Hooton (1939a, 1939b), a Harvard anthropologist, again made physical inferiority and defective intelligence into topics of scientific discussion.

After studying thousands of criminals in prisons, reformatories, and jails and comparing them with noncriminals—college students, firemen, policemen, and patients in regular and mental hospitals—Hooton (1939a:298–309) came to three major conclusions:

1. Criminals are physically inferior to noncriminals.
2. Physical inferiority is related to mental inferiority.
3. The cause of both types of inferiority is poor heredity.

Unlike in the 1800s, Hooton's conclusions created considerable controversy in the 1930s. By then, the social sciences had grown in stature, and their emphasis on environmental factors had assumed increased importance. There were many criticisms of Hooton's scientific procedures (Sutherland and Cressey, 1974:119; Vold, 1958:63–65). For example, Hooton studied criminals and concluded that their physical characteristics were indicative of inferiority. From a scientific standpoint, such a procedure was unacceptable because Hooton "had no criterion of biological inferiority" (Sutherland and Cressey, 1974:119). Indeed, the superiority of one set of physical characteristics over another tends to be a product of cultural definition rather than some universal biological standard.

So convincing were this and other criticisms that only a few investigators further pursued biological theories of delinquency. An exception was William Sheldon (1949:4), who, like Hooton, maintained that body type and mental type went together and that both were inherited. Sheldon (1949:14–30), identified three major body types: (1) *endomorphs,* who were fat and round, (2) *mesomorphs,* who were large-boned and muscular, and (3) *ectomorphs,* who were lean and delicate. While body types were rarely pure in form, he argued, each produced a different personality and temperament. For example, endomorphs were easygoing, sociable, and comfort-loving; mesomorphs were aggressive, insensitive, impulsive, and inherently deficient in internal controls; and ectomorphs were introverted, sensitive, and nervous. After comparing 200 delinquent boys in a private institution with 4,000 male college students, Sheldon (1949:729) concluded that delinquents were more likely to be mesomorphs.

The Gluecks (1956:215–216, 225–227) reported findings that supported Sheldon, as did Cortes and Gatti (1972:26) many years later. Still other supporting evidence was reported by Hartl, Monnelly, and Elderkin (1982:533–537) from a thirty-year follow-up study of Sheldon's original sample.

The Impact on Social Policy

Early biological theories had considerable impact on social policy. As the first representatives of the **positive school of criminology,** they seriously questioned the classical emphasis on free will and the use of punishment. How could punishment prevent law-breaking if degenerates or mental defectives were products of biological forces over which they had no control?

There were only two ways to prevent crime and delinquency. The first was for the state to remove defective children from their degenerate parents and care for them. Consider the suggestions for public policy by a University of Kansas sociologist in 1897:

> It is seen at once that families of this class . . . are the most difficult to deal with, because they have no place in social life, and it is very difficult to make a place for them. . . . The principle of social evolution is to make the strong stronger that the purposes of social life may be conserved, but to do this the weak must be cared for or they will eventually destroy or counteract the efforts of the strong. We need social sanitation, which is the ultimate aim of the study of social pathology. (Blackmar, 1897:500)

Although the call for "social sanitation" was harsh, it retained a humane flavor by suggesting that defectives should be cared for rather than eliminated. Those sentiments were echoed by Goddard, who said that although defective delinquents should not be turned loose on the streets, neither should they be locked up in a jail or prison. Rather, they "must be cared for . . . in a place we care for irresponsibles" (Goddard, 1911:564). Goddard also believed that delinquency could be prevented by using intelligence tests in the public schools to pick out defectives at an early age. "When we have learned to discriminate and recognize the ability of each child and place upon him such burdens and responsibilities only as he is able to bear, then we shall have largely solved the problem of delinquency" (Goddard, 1911:564).

A second, and even more questionable, way to prevent lawbreaking involved the application of **eugenics,** defined as a "science" concerned with improving the quality of the human race by controlled breeding (Kevles, 1985:ix). Because offenders were biologically inferior, "it follows that the elimination of crime can be effected only by the extirpation of the physically, mentally, and morally unfit, or by their complete segregation in a socially aseptic environment" (Hooton, 1939a:309). Similarly, Sheldon (1949:872) suggested that because delinquency was "mainly in the germ plasm," the only hope for control was selective breeding to weed out harmful constitutional types.

Actually, a eugenics movement had begun many years before Hooton and Sheldon expressed their views. Although the movement was by no means supported universally, it gained some followers in the early 1900s. Its goal was to weed out not only "physical degenerates" and "mental defectives" but also people who were believed to masturbate excessively or overindulge in sex (Kevles, 1985:107–108). In pursuit of such a goal, twenty-four states passed laws between 1907 and the end of the 1920s permitting sterilization of the feebleminded, the mentally ill, and epileptics (Kevles, 1985:111). This method of preventing lawbreaking is a sobering illustration of the extent to which scientific theories can be applied without much evidence that they are accurate.

Scientific Adequacy

We have already seen that early 20th-century criminologists tended to discredit biological theories, for several reasons. First, delinquent behavior was not rare. Second, biological theorists, by and large, relied on biased views and inadequate research techniques. Finally, biological scientists tended to devalue the relative importance of the environment in favor of heredity.

PREVALENCE OF DELINQUENT BEHAVIOR Only if lawbreaking were rare could biological defects be the only, or even a major, cause of delinquency. Yet, as discussed in chapter 5 on self-reported delinquency, its prevalence is great; virtually every young person reportedly has violated the law at one time or another. Unless physical inferiority and defective intelligence are also prevalent, other factors must be more important causes of delinquency.

RESEARCH SHORTCOMINGS Early biological theorists ignored social, economic, and cultural factors. Lombroso's theory, for example, reflected biased views of both race and gender. Not only did his ideas on race reflect the attitudes of 19th-century Europeans toward less developed societies, but his emphasis on the passivity and piety of women failed to recognize that gender relations at the time often were initiated and dominated by males, making females appear passive, conformist, or inferior (Klein, 1973:7–11).

Moreover, in hindsight, poor research designs obviously were used to test early biological theories (Cohen, 1966:53; Sutherland, 1931). The failure of early biological theorists to control for, or even to acknowledge, the effects of environment made their findings suspect.

ENVIRONMENT VERSUS HEREDITY The limits of the research notwithstanding, there have been continued divisions along disciplinary lines regarding the adequacy of biological and social science theories. Like Lombroso, an eminent mid-20th-century biologist contended that genes, not culture, determine human behavior: "The materials of heredity contained in the chromosomes are the solid stuff which ultimately determines the course of history" (Darlington, 1953:404). Meanwhile, an equally eminent anthropologist maintained that biology is insignificant in explaining variation in behavior; instead, "culture is the determinant" (White, 1959:561).

Arguments over the effects of **nature versus nurture** have been fruitless and nonscientific (Raine, 1993:204; Shah and Roth, 1974:102–103, 106–107; Wilson and Herrnstein, 1985:79–80). Such arguments have overlooked the possibility that complex combinations of nature and nurture may shape human behavior (Caspi et al., 1993; Fishbein, 1990:29–30; Mednick, Gabrielli, and Hutchings, 1987:90; Pollock, Mednick, and Gabrielli, 1983:311; Rowe and Osgood, 1984:526). Few modern geneticists, for example, believe that genes by themselves determine behavior; rather, genes help to determine a person's potential, and the development of that potential depends on the social environment.

Furthermore, the way in which biological and environmental factors combine may be related to two "facts" concerning delinquent behavior: the overrepresentation of poor and minority children in both arrest and victimization statistics. Many studies have shown that these children run much greater risks of biological and intellectual impairment than other children (Shah and Roth, 1974:126–129). Rather than indicating that those impairments are always biological in origin, however, the evidence suggests that often they are due to an unfortunate series of environmental events: Poverty and ignorance reduce the likelihood that poor mothers will receive adequate nourishment and prenatal care while they are carrying their babies; the lack of prenatal care, in turn, leads to an excessive number of premature births; and premature births increase the likelihood of even greater impairment. Furthermore, the first few months of life are crucial to growth and maturation. The cells of the brain are not developed fully but continue to grow and divide after birth. Other key developments take place in the early months. Thus, it is not just genetic inheritance but the combination of that inheritance with the environment that spells the difference in a child's physical makeup.

To illustrate the point, investigators in recent decades have found a persistent, though relatively small, difference in IQ between delinquents and nondelinquents (Gordon, 1976; Hirschi and Hindelang, 1977; Raine, 1993:232–235; Wilson and Herrnstein, 1985:Chap. 6). Delinquents—both official and self-reported—tend to have lower IQs than nondelinquents. How, then, should those findings be interpreted?

A strictly biological interpretation suggests that delinquents, particularly chronic offenders, are organically inferior. A strictly social interpretation, by contrast, suggests that IQ scores reflect a person's environment; those who score poorly on intelligence tests have been subjected to environmental deprivations that limit their verbal and problem-solving skills (Simons, 1978). A second strictly social interpretation is that youngsters with low IQs are pushed into delinquent acts because of negative labeling in schools (Menard and Morse, 1984). Yet another interpretation suggests that *both* biological and environmental factors are important and that differences over the meaning of low IQ scores among delinquents cannot be resolved until an integrated, *biosocial* approach is taken.

NEW BIOSOCIAL APPROACHES

A surge in biosocial research over the past few decades has produced several promising leads toward an integrated biosocial approach. Because of "sluggish" nervous systems, some people may not readily learn to inhibit deviant behavior or benefit from punishment; injury to parts of the brain may contribute to uncontrollable fits of rage; and chemical imbalances in the brain may cause some people to be more aggressive than others (Fishbein, 1990:37–38; Konner, 1982:188–197; Mednick and Christiansen, 1977:10, 55; Pollock, Mednick, and Gabrielli, 1983: 311–315).

Perhaps the most promising biosocial advance is a theory recently set forth by Moffitt (1993) and her associates (Moffitt, Lynam, and Silva, 1994), which posits a relationship between neuropsychological impairments and delinquency. By *neuropsychological,* Moffitt (1993:681) means the "anatomical structures and physiological processes within the nervous system [that] influence psychological characteristics such as temperament, behavioral development, cognitive abilities, or all three." Neuropsychological impairments can be inherited, but they also can be caused by maternal alcohol and other drug abuse, poor prenatal nutrition, brain injury, and exposure to toxic agents such as lead (Moffitt, 1993:680; Moffitt, Lynam, and Silva, 1994:296). According to Moffitt, Lynam, and Silva (1994:280), neuropsychological impairments produce poor "verbal skills (e.g., abstract reasoning and language comprehension) and . . . [weak] self-control . . . (e.g., planning, inhibiting, inappropriate responses, attention, and concentration)," which in turn cause delinquency.

How does Moffitt handle a problem with early biological control theories mentioned before—that biological defects could be an important cause of delinquency only if lawbreaking were rare? She does so by positing that there are two kinds of delinquency,

POLICY AND RECENT BIOSOCIAL THEORY

A central theme in this chapter and all of the chapters in Part Three is that there is a close connection between social policy and theory. To illustrate this policy-theory connection, consider recent efforts to rehabilitate offenders in outdoor, physical-challenge programs, such as Outward Bound (Palmer, 1996:137, 142–143, 156). A theoretical rationale for such efforts is provided by Gove and Wilmoth (1990) who posit that the motivation for much delinquency is biosocial. Many types of delinquent behavior, they contend, have few external rewards and involve high risk. "Even when successful, most robberies, burglaries and larcenies [for example] involve modest sums of money and do not appear to be rational" (Gove and Wilmoth, 1990:262). The major reward for such behaviors is mainly the thrill that they produce for offenders, which triggers a "neurophysiologic high" that is positively reinforcing and causes offenders to repeat the behaviors. Because risky behaviors generally result in a neurophysiologic high, the difficult and risky physical challenges (e.g., mountain climbing) in Outward Bound and similar programs can be substituted for much delinquent behavior (Gove and Wilmoth, 1990: 286–287).

only one of which is caused by neuropsychological impairments (Moffitt, 1993:676; Moffitt, Lynam, and Silva, 1994:281–283). The first kind is **adolescence-limited delinquency,** which is restricted to the teen

years. Adolescence-limited offenders form a very large group that first commits delinquency during adolescence but desists from offending by young adulthood, thus accounting for the peak of participation in delinquency during adolescence (as discussed in chapters 4 and 5). The main cause of adolescence-limited delinquency is not neuropsychological impairments, but association with delinquent peers (Moffitt, 1993:686–689). The second kind of delinquency is committed by a small group of **life-course-persistent** offenders who begin to behave antisocially during early childhood, before the adolescent surge, and continue their antisocial behavior through adolescence to adulthood, long after adolescence-limited offenders have desisted. Only the less prevalent, life-course-persistent delinquency is said to be caused by neuropsychological impairments (Moffitt, Lynam, and Silva, 1994:282).

PSYCHODYNAMIC CONTROL THEORY

Following the early biological theories, the next control theories to gain widespread popularity were psychodynamic. These theories attributed delinquent behavior to a youngster's psychological, not biological, makeup. Much of the credit for the formulation of psychodynamic theories goes to the Austrian psychoanalyst Sigmund Freud (1856–1939). Although his ideas have been modified in many ways, they remain a cornerstone on which many later theories have been built.

Freud's Preoccupation with Childhood

Freud was less concerned with explaining delinquency than with explaining how children can be made good. The reasons for his concern become obvious when we consider the main elements of his theory: (1) Human nature is inherently antisocial; (2) good behavior requires effective socialization; and (3) the lifelong features of the personality are determined by the age of 5.

OUR ANTISOCIAL PREDISPOSITION   Unlike early biological theorists, who believed that only some people are born bad or defective, Freud assumed that *every* child possesses a set of primitive and antisocial instincts, which he called the **id.** "The primitive, savage, and evil impulses of mankind," Freud wrote, "have not vanished in any individual, but continue their existence, although in a repressed state" (quoted in Hughes, 1958:143). Humans are not gentle, friendly creatures who simply defend themselves if attacked, Freud continued. Rather, they possess a measure of aggression that will cause them to exploit their neighbor, "to use him sexually without his consent, to seize his possessions, to humiliate him, to cause him pain, and to torture and to kill him" (quoted in Hughes, 1958:151). In short, all of us are born with ample capacity to be bad (Freud, 1966:566–572).

THE IMPORTANCE OF SOCIALIZATION Given his pessimistic view of human nature, Freud (1966:613–615) believed that the antisocial instincts of the id can be overcome only when children are socialized by their parents to have internal controls. To describe how that socialization occurs, Freud posited the existence of two other elements of the mind and personality besides the id.

The first he called the **superego** (Freud, 1949:121–123). In simple terms, this is the individual's conscience that prevents the expression of primitive impulses. To the degree that the superego develops, it becomes an internalized mechanism for keeping antisocial drives in the person's unconscious, preventing them from coming into action, and threatening punishments if they do.

Freud's (1949:15) remaining psychic element is the **ego.** This is the conscious organizer of the personality that permits a person to reflect on available alternatives and make discriminating choices among them. Its main purpose is to act as a rational intermediary between a person's drives and the demands of the external world. In one instance, it may suggest that people should suppress their drives out of self-interest; in another, it may encourage them to release their drives.

Along with the superego, then, the ego is a second means by which basic instincts are controlled. But while the superego is unreflective and repressive, the ego entails greater reason and choice (Freud, 1949:15–17).

EARLY DETERMINATION OF PERSONALITY Freud (1966:611) theorized that by the age of 5, all of the essential features of a person's adult personality will have been determined. Whether the antisocial and aggressive instincts of the id are to become dominant or whether the ego and superego are to be effective in controlling them is a function of parental socialization during the first few years of life (Aichhorn, 1935:119–120).

This socialization occurs in a series of developmental stages (Abrahamsen, 1960:70–74; A. Freud, 1965:passim; S. Freud, 1949:25–32). The first is called the **oral stage** because the mouth is the principal source of gratification to an infant in its sucking, swallowing, gurgling, and kissing. If fondled, fed on time, and weaned at the right time, an infant will feel loved and will develop properly. If not, the infant will experience a sense of deprivation and frustration that can last a lifetime.

The second is the **anal stage,** which lasts from about ages 1 to 3. During that stage, two things happen. First, the child begins to gain erotic satisfaction from the evacuation of bladder and bowels. Second, the superego begins to receive attention because of the importance of toilet training. If children are trained improperly, difficulties will result. Rigid training—too much emphasis on superego controls—can produce a child who is either stubborn and sadistic or totally subdued and passive. Indifferent training, on the other hand, will result in a child who is sloppy, careless, and dirty. Only if training is just right will a child be freed from an anal fixation later in life.

The third is the **phallic stage,** which lasts from about ages 3 to 6. Whereas the child previously sought pleasure from the mouth and anus, he or she now switches to the genitals. Masturbation, voyeurism, and sexual play are common. More importantly, the male child unconsciously develops intense incestuous cravings for his mother (the Oedipus complex) and begins to hate his father, whom he sees as standing in his way (Freud, 1949:90–97). The reverse is true for the female child, except that her problem is compounded. According to Freud (1949:97–99), the girl envies those with a penis, desires to possess one, and so turns to her father. She now experiences sexual attraction for him (the Electra complex) and perceives her mother as a rival. But because both she and her brother still require love from both parents, their incestuous cravings soon arouse intense guilt feelings as a result of a developing superego. If children are socialized properly, they can overcome their negative feelings and learn to identify with the parent of the same sex. If not, emotional illness or delinquent behavior may result. For example, the boy who never gets over his hatred for his rival father will grow up to hate all authority figures. Later in life, he will commit delinquent acts that reflect spite for his father and an immature fixation at the phallic stage.[1]

The implications are clear: The behavior of a person is not the result of personal choice, cultural differences, or changing social conditions. Rather, it is a product of socialization by parents during early childhood.

Sources of Delinquent Behavior

Because Freud believed that delinquent tendencies are inherent in everyone, he devoted little attention to the many ways they might be manifested. His followers, however, have outlined at least four ways that ineffective socialization might allow them to slip through (Feldman, 1969; McCord, McCord, and Zola, 1959:198–200):

1. *Delinquent behavior is neurotic behavior.* Delinquents suffer from a compulsive need for punishment because they feel guilty over some unconscious, socially unacceptable drive, such as a boy's incestuous craving for sex with his mother. Although his superego tells him the craving is wrong, his ego is too weak to rationalize and control it. Hence, he may commit any one of several delinquent acts—theft, robbery, even rape—so that he will be caught and punished. Punishment will help to expiate his overwhelming sense of guilt.
2. *Delinquency results from a defective superego.* Failing to develop internal controls, delinquents readily succumb to primitive impulses. Constantly preying on others, they are both antiso-

cial and amoral—aggressive, affectionless, callous, guiltless persons who have failed to internalize any standard of moral conduct.
3. *Delinquency results from a gap in superego training.* Delinquency can be committed by children who have been socialized properly in the sense that they identify with the appropriate parent. The reason they violate the law is because their parents failed to teach them conventional values and expectations. They did not have the opportunity to learn what is expected of them.
4. *Delinquency represents a search for compensatory gratifications.* Children who were deprived at some early stage of development still seek the gratifications they missed. For example, some may become alcoholics to satisfy an oral craving. Others may be sadistic and cruel because of poor toilet training at the anal stage. Delinquency reflects deeply hidden needs that were unsatisfied in early childhood.

Psychodynamic Theory and Females

These sources of delinquency apply to girls as well as boys. However, females are special cases, requiring additional explanation. Freud (1966:579, 596), like Lombroso, believed that females are inferior to males and are destined to be wives and mothers rather than captains of industry or even Mafia heads. Nature dictated that they be passive and compliant rather than aggressive and domineering. What was his evidence for such a belief? The evidence, Freud (1966:576–599) said, is revealed by the differences between the male and female sex organs. Females are obviously inferior, a fact that boys as well as girls recognize instinctively. Indeed, that is why

> women are exhibitionistic, narcissistic, and attempt to compensate for their lack of a penis by being well dressed and physically beautiful. Women become mothers trying to replace the lost penis with a baby. Women are also masochistic . . . because their *sexual* role is one of receptor, and their sexual pleasure consists of pain. (Klein, 1973:16)

Given the inferiority of girls, the major problem for parents in socializing them is to help them

---

[1]Freud (1949:27, 30) postulated the existence of two additional stages of development—the *latency* and *genital* stages—but they are seen as less crucial than the first three.

overcome their sense of castration. During the phallic stage of development, it will be recalled, the girl recognizes her lack of a penis, may be traumatized by it, and is envious of those who have one. That is why it is so important that she learn to identify with her mother and accept her inferiority. Otherwise, her anger and frustration will cause her to behave in masculine ways; and, according to Freud, masculinity among girls is synonymous with delinquency (Simon, 1975:5). Indeed, "the deviant woman is one who is attempting to be a *man*" (Klein, 1973:17).

In Freudian theory, delinquency is symbolic behavior caused by unconscious motives that lie deep within a person and defy easy detection. The only hope is some kind of psychotherapy. For example, in the case of a delinquent girl, psychotherapy could be used to uncover the sources of her repressed desires and then to bring them to her conscious awareness so that she could examine them and subject them to the controls of her ego and superego. She could then withdraw from the competitiveness of the masculine world (for which she is inherently unfit anyway), marry, and take her place in the calm serenity of a loving home.

The Social Impact of Freudian Theory

Freudian theory profoundly affected our **modern concept of childhood,** probably because it gave expression to many ideas about childhood and human development that had not been articulated before Freud. On the one hand, many of his ideas were by no means radical. For example, his pessimistic view of human nature departed little from age-old religious beliefs that children are inherently inclined to evil. Freud merely stated in secular and psychological terms what the Puritans had said long before in religious terms: Children become good, not by birth, but by education. On the other hand, Freud's preoccupation with childhood and his emphasis on the importance of parental child-raising practices reflected middle-class concerns that had been emerging for centuries. Not only did the formulation of his theory coincide with the disappearance of apprenticeship as a method of raising children, it also reflected the feelings of a growing urban population that increasingly was cut off from extended family ties. Never before had parents and children been left so completely to their own resources (Laslett, 1973).

Freud's complex ideas filtered gradually into public awareness and the organization of social life via intellectual, academic, and professional circles. Subsequent theoretical variations on the Freudian theme are too numerous to list in detail, but certain ones have been expressed repeatedly:

1. The first few years of life are critical. If an infant does not secure satisfying relationships with affectionate, nurturant parents, the damage will be irreversible (Abrahamsen, 1960:42–55; Cohen, 1966:54–55; Friedlander, 1947:45–49). The child will fail to develop as a self-sufficient, responsible person.

2. The ego and superego, if not the id, remain key concepts in most psychodynamic theories. When both are weak, the child is unable to subordinate antisocial impulses, defer gratifications, and adhere to rational and moral courses of action (Redl and Toch, 1979; Redl and Wineman, 1951).

3. Moral maturity is attained when the child moves successfully through a series of developmental stages and is no longer fixated at infantile levels (Jennings, Kilkenny, and Kohlberg, 1983; Kohlberg, 1964; Piaget, 1948). According to one theory (Warren, 1969:52, 54), there are seven stages of interpersonal maturity, but most delinquents remain fixed between the second and fourth stages. Almost half of them are neurotics whose emotional disturbance is characterized by feelings of guilt and inadequacy.

4. Early childhood experiences produce in every person a deeply ingrained and enduring personality. It is this personality that distinguishes between troublemakers and well-adjusted children. Troublemakers possess personality traits that predispose them to antisocial conduct (Abrahamsen, 1960:56–89; Glueck and Glueck, 1952: 173–174, 180–183; Healy and Bronner, 1936: 41–47, 52, 58–59; Warren and Hindelang, 1979: 172–173).

In short, many theories remain in the Freudian tradition, sharing with it "the idea that the wellsprings of behavior, and especially of deviant behavior, are largely irrational, obscure energies relatively inaccessible to observation and conscious control of the actor" (Cohen, 1966:54).

The Impact on Social Policy

Even more than early biological theories, psychodynamic theories found fertile soil in the 20th-century United States. They did much to maintain traditional, middle-class gender roles, suggesting that males are naturally rational, aggressive, and outgoing while females are inherently passive, compliant, and caring. Hence, when it came to considering delinquent acts, not surprisingly, such offenses as robbery, assault, and burglary were viewed as male offenses while sexual promiscuity, running away, and defying parents were seen as female offenses.

The Freudian notion that delinquency is not an intentional defiance of social norms, but rather an unintended response to a combination of antisocial instincts and poor parental practices, helped greatly to legitimize the ideology of the early juvenile court. Delinquents are sick, not wicked. Their acts are not a disease that must be cured, but merely the symptoms of the disease.

Translated into policy, the idea was that judges should sentence delinquents not according to the offenses they committed, but according to experts' diagnosis of their psychological ills. Treatment should be carried out through the entire correctional process, with girls to be trained as *girls* and boys to be trained as *boys*. Moreover, such treatment should include professional counseling, psychotherapy, and medical care, as well as the more traditional academic and vocational training.

Many jurisdictions have not been able to afford treatment programs based on psychodynamic theories. Such programs are very expensive because of the assumption that treatment may require years of effort by a highly skilled staff. Nonetheless, the treatment model suggested by psychodynamic theories remained the standard for many courts and correctional agencies until very recently. As a professional ideology, if not a vehicle, for treating children, few theories have enjoyed as much widespread popularity as psychodynamic theories.

Scientific Adequacy

Despite their widespread impact, most psychodynamic theories have not received a great deal of empirical support, mainly because they are not readily amenable to scientific testing. Some investigators, for example, have used retrospective case studies as a means of testing the theories. After obtaining the life histories of delinquents, analyzing their dreams, or hypnotizing them, they attempt to explain their behavior (Alexander and Healy, 1935; Lindner, 1944). Most such studies, however, have a fatal flaw that is produced by the kind of reasoning often associated with clinical methods of investigation. It goes something like this:

1. Delinquency is the product of psychological abnormality.
2. Joe has committed a delinquent act.
3. Therefore, Joe is psychologically abnormal.

That is circular reasoning. Until Joe commits a delinquent act, he is considered to be normal. But once he has gotten into trouble, he is considered to be abnormal, and his abnormality is used to explain his delinquency (Wootton, 1959:250). The only evidence that he is abnormal, however, is the delinquency that his abnormality is supposed to explain.

Far more defensible tests of psychodynamic theories have used personality tests to measure the various traits that people are assumed to possess (McCord, 1968). In contrast to retrospective case studies, personality tests have permitted researchers to seek independent evidence that some people are psychologically abnormal and then see whether that abnormality is related to delinquent behavior.

Unfortunately, the results have not been very encouraging. Schuessler and Cressey (1950) reviewed 113 studies conducted before 1950 and concluded that they did not demonstrate a consistently strong relationship between specific personality traits and criminal behavior. Later reviews, covering scores of other studies, reached the same conclusion (Arbuthnot, Gordon, and Jurkovic, 1987; Tennenbaum, 1977; Waldo and Dinitz, 1967). While an abnormal personality may be a factor in relatively rare and bizarre cases of criminality, there is little evidence that it is related, strongly and consistently, to **law-violating behavior** in general. Indeed, one review concluded that much personality testing not only fails to reflect the multidimensional differences between criminals and noncriminals but also "allows for more differences to be found *within* groups of criminals and noncriminals than between the two groups" (Tennenbaum, 1977:228).

One of the better studies of personality testing illustrates that conclusion. Hathaway, Monachesi, and Young (1960) selected nearly 15,000 ninth-graders who were first tested with the Minnesota Multiphasic Personality Inventory (MMPI) to determine their personality configurations. The investigators then checked several years later to determine which of the students had become official delinquents. Although some personality differences were related to **official delinquency,** Hathaway and his associates expressed disappointment over the results. Personality measures, they said, "are much less powerful and apply to fewer cases ... than would be expected if one reads the literature on the subject. . . . Surely we cannot say that these data put us far ahead either in prediction or understanding" (Hathaway, Monachesi, and Young, 1960:439; for a review of this and similar studies, see Hanley, 1979:244–248).

Two problems may have contributed to these inconclusive findings. First, it is a gross oversimplification to equate psychological abnormality with delinquency, to state that only emotionally disturbed children commit delinquent acts. By their own accounts, most young people have been delinquent, but it is unlikely that most are abnormal (Klein, 1987:37).

Second, any relation between abnormality and delinquent behavior is probably limited. Hathaway, Monachesi, and Young (1960:433) found, for example, that although psychopathy, schizophrenia, and hypomania were associated with *higher* rates of delinquency, such traits as introversion, depression, and masculinity/femininity were associated with *lower* rates. In short, abnormality is not a unidimensional phenomenon universally associated with delinquent behavior. Sometimes, abnormality may even be associated with excessive or compulsive conformity to the law.

Despite such problems, it would be unwise to dismiss all psychological factors as irrelevant. If nothing else, Freudian psychology has convinced most people that in the process of growing up and developing independent personalities, they must subordinate some of their most powerful and aggressive drives. Furthermore, the idea persists that in the process of learning to control these drives, many of them are pushed below a conscious level, where

they are repressed at considerable personal cost. Yet, despite the cost of repression, inner conflict is inseparable from everyday living and is part of every personality.

In addition, there have been promising new advances in personality theory and testing. Most notably, Caspi and his associates (1994:163) have identified personality correlates of delinquency that hold "in different nations, in different age cohorts, across gender, and across race: greater delinquent participation [is] associated with a personality configuration characterized by high Negative Emotionality and weak Constraint." People high on "Negative Emotionality" are "prone to respond to frustrating events with strong negative emotions, to feel stressed or harassed, and to approach interpersonal relationships with an adversarial attitude" (Caspi et al., 1994: 185). People with weak "Constraint" tend to reject conventional values, seek danger, and are impulsive.

As long as we are concerned with the questions, Why is she delinquent? or Why did he do it?, we must deal with matters of motivation (Toby, 1974). And, as Cohen (1966:65) has pointed out, "sociologists . . . are no less interested in motivation than are psychologists, but they are interested in it from a special point of view." What sociologists want to understand, among other things, is how such variables as social class, minority status, age, gender, and family and peer relations affect a person's psychological state. Thus, as psychiatrist Seymour Halleck (1967: 199) pointed out over thirty years ago, research on the relation between personality and delinquency must take into account this larger set of variables.

Summary and Conclusions

Biological and psychodynamic control theories have contributed to our social construction of delinquency in unique ways. That contribution can be summarized by reference to the basic questions that we will ask about all such theories:

1. What are the assumptions of control theorists about human nature and social order?
2. What is the underlying logic and content of control theories?

3. What are the implications of control theories for social policy, and what has been their impact?
4. How well do control theories stand up to logical and empirical scrutiny?

Underlying Assumptions of Control Theories

The early biological theorists assumed that delinquents and nondelinquents are different kinds of people at birth. Delinquents possess biological traits or depraved tendencies that predispose them to antisocial behavior. Nondelinquents, however, are inherently good people who are predisposed to good conduct.

Psychodynamic theorists, by contrast, assume that *all* children are antisocial at birth—impulsive, self-centered, and lacking the ability to control themselves in socially approved ways. Their tendency to be antisocial "is as original as sin" (Rieff, 1959:274).

Given those views of human nature, both kinds of theory tend to take the **social order** for granted. In other words, they assume that its various elements reflect a high degree of consensus, that morality is self-evident, and that attention must be focused on offenders because the social order does not create problems that might contribute to the commission of delinquent acts.

Underlying Logic and Content of Control Theories

The general logic and content of the early biological theories can be diagrammed as shown in figure 7.1. According to Lombroso, many criminals are born to be criminals and, in fact, are atavistic throwbacks to primitive humans. Hence, their inability to learn and adhere to social rules causes them to be criminal. Other biologists, however, traced delinquent acts to genetic deficiencies that, like atavism, were thought to inhibit learning and to encourage criminal behavior.

Psychodynamic theorists, by contrast, are concerned with explaining why children *conform* to social rules as well as why they are inclined to break them. This body of theory, therefore, can be diagrammed as shown in figure 7.2. Early in life, the child's primitive drives (id) encounter the child-raising practices of the home. If, out of the interaction that occurs, socialization is effective, a well-developed ego and superego will result. That is, the child will have conscious control over his or her primitive drives, and mature, conformist behavior will follow. But if the process of socialization is ineffective, poorly developed controls will result in an unconscious search for compensatory gratifications and in immature, delinquent behavior.

Policy Implications of Control Theories

Early biological theories implied the need to forbid "defective" people from reproducing and to incapacitate those already born. Such theories fostered a eugenics movement and led to the passage of laws that permitted the sterilization of "degenerate" or "defective" people.

Psychodynamic theories imply the importance of early child-raising practices. If those fail, delinquent or predelinquent children should be diagnosed and placed in correctional settings for long-term treatment. As a professional ideology for the juvenile court, psychodynamic theories have been probably more influential than all other theories.

FIGURE 7.1

The underlying logic of biological theory

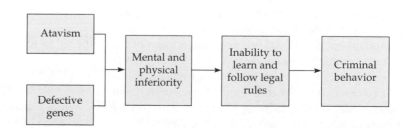

FIGURE 7.2

The underlying logic of psychodynamic theory

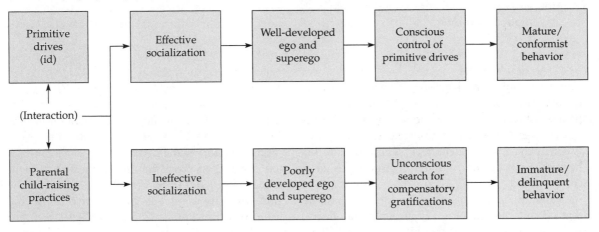

Scientific Adequacy of Control Theories

The fact that biological control theories have been used extensively to guide social policy is striking given their lack of acceptance among positivistic criminologists. The early biological control theories have not been well received, because (1) as originally stated, they were logically inadequate and lacked empirical support, and (2) ideological bickering took place between biological and social scientists over the role of nature versus nurture. Nonetheless, more recent biosocial theories of delinquency reflect a growing body of knowledge about the complex relations among many biological and environmental factors.

Many of the same conclusions apply to psychodynamic theories: (1) Most of them are impossible to falsify, and (2) the tendency to equate an abnormal personality with delinquent behavior has not been confirmed by empirical evidence.

Yet psychological motivation can scarcely be ignored. What has been lacking in the psychodynamic approach, therefore, are postulates that link motivation to social and cultural factors, as well as to those that are familial. Indeed, like biological theory, psychodynamic theory has failed to address many of the "facts" that measures of delinquent behavior suggest are in need of explanation. In the chapters that follow, we will discover that criminologists soon began to attend to some of these "facts" even as control theories reached the apex of their popularity.

DISCUSSION QUESTIONS

1. Many Americans seem to accept the claim of biological theorists that law violators and law abiders are different kinds of people. How do you account for the widespread popularity of such a claim?
2. What is the *nature-versus-nurture* argument? What do we have to gain from an integrated *biosocial* approach to explaining delinquency?
3. What were Sigmund Freud's assumptions about human nature? Why was Freud less concerned with explaining delinquency than with explaining how children can be made good?
4. How is circular reasoning associated with clinical case studies? How does circular reasoning create problems in testing psychodynamic theories (or, for that matter, any theory)?
5. How does Freud's explanation of female delinquency differ from his explanation of male delinquency?

REFERENCES

Abrahamsen, David. 1960. *The Psychology of Crime.* New York: Columbia University Press.

Aichhorn, August. 1935. *Wayward Youth.* New York: Viking Press.

Alexander, Franz, and William Healy. 1935. *Roots of Crime.* New York: Knopf.

Arbuthnot, Jack, Donald A. Gordon, and Gregory J. Jurkovic. 1987. "Personality." Pp. 139–183 in Herbert C. Quay, ed., *Handbook of Juvenile Delinquency.* New York: Wiley.

Beirne, Piers. 1988. "Heredity Versus Environment: A Reconsideration of Charles Goring's *The English Convict.*" *British Journal of Criminology* 28 (Summer):315–339.

Blackmar, Frank W. 1897. "The Smoky Pilgrims." *American Journal of Sociology* 2 (January): 485–500.

Bremner, Robert H., ed. 1970. *Children and Youth in America: A Documentary History.* 3 vols. Cambridge, Mass.: Harvard University Press.

Caspi, Avshalom, Donald Lynam, Terrie E. Moffitt, and Phil A. Silva. 1993. "Unraveling Girls' Delinquency: Biological, Dispositional, and Contextual Contributions to Adolescent Misbehavior." *Developmental Psychology* 29 (January):19–30.

Caspi, Avshalom, et al., 1994. "Are Some People Crime-Prone? Replications of the Personality-Crime Relationship Across Countries, Genders, Races, and Methods." *Criminology* 32 (May): 163–195.

Cohen, Albert K. 1966. *Deviance and Control.* Englewood Cliffs, N.J.: Prentice-Hall.

Cortes, Juan B., and Florence M. Gatti. 1972. *Delinquency and Crime: A Biopsychosocial Approach.* New York: Seminar Press.

Darlington, C. D. 1953. *The Facts of Life.* London: Allen & Unwin.

Feldman, David. 1969. "Psychoanalysis and Crime." Pp. 433–442 in Donald R. Cressey and David A. Ward, eds., *Delinquency, Crime, and Social Process.* New York: Harper & Row.

Ferrero, Gina Lombroso. 1911. *Criminal Man According to the Classification of Cesare Lombroso.* New York: Putnam.

Fishbein, Diana H. 1990. "Biological Perspectives in Criminology." *Criminology* 28 (February):27–72.

Freud, Anna. 1965. *Normality and Pathology in Childhood: Assessments of Development.* New York: International Universities Press.

Freud, Sigmund. 1949. *An Outline of Psychoanalysis.* Translated by James Strachey. New York: Norton. 1966. *The Complete Introductory Lectures on Psychoanalysis.* Translated and edited by James Strachey. New York: Norton.

Friedlander, Kate. 1947. *The Psycho-Analytical Approach to Juvenile Delinquency: Theory, Case Studies, Treatment.* London: Routledge & Kegan Paul.

Glueck, Sheldon, and Eleanor Glueck. 1952. *Delinquents in the Making: Paths to Prevention.* New York: Harper. 1956. *Physique and Delinquency.* New York: Harper.

Goddard, Henry H. 1911. "The Treatment of the Mental Defective Who Is Also Delinquent." Pp. 563–564 in Robert H. Bremner, ed., *Children and Youth in America: A Documentary History,* Vol. 2. Cambridge, Mass.: Harvard University Press. 1914. *Feeble-Mindedness: Its Causes and Consequences.* New York: Macmillan.

Gordon, Robert A. 1976. "Prevalence: The Rare Datum in Delinquency Measurement and Its Implications for the Theory of Delinquency." Pp. 201–284 in Malcolm W. Klein, ed., *The Juvenile Justice System.* Beverly Hills, Calif.: Sage.

Goring, Charles. 1913. *The English Convict: A Statistical Study.* London: His Majesty's Stationery Office.

Gould, Stephen Jay. 1981. *The Mismeasure of Man.* New York: Norton.

Gove, Walter R., and Charles Wilmoth. 1990. "Risk, Crime, and Neurophysiologic Highs: A Consideration of Brain Processes That May Reinforce Delinquent and Criminal Behavior." Pp. 261–293 in Lee Ellis and Harry Hoffman, eds., *Crime in Biological, Social, and Moral Contexts.* New York: Praeger.

Halleck, Seymour. 1967. *Psychiatry and the Dilemmas of Crime.* New York: Harper & Row.

Hanley, Charles. 1979. "The Gauging of Delinquency Potential." Pp. 237–265 in Hans Toch, ed., *Psychology of Crime and Criminal Justice.* New York: Holt, Rinehart & Winston.

Hartl, Emil M., Edward P. Monnelly, and Roland D. Elderkin. 1982. *Physique and Delinquent Behavior: A Thirty-Year Follow-Up of William H. Sheldon's Varieties of Delinquent Youth.* New York: Academic Press.

Hathaway, Starke R., Elio D. Monachesi, and Laurence A. Young. 1960. "Delinquency Rates and Personality." *Journal of Criminal Law, Criminology and Policy Science* 50 (January–February): 433–440.

Healy, William, and Augusta F. Bronner. 1936. *New Light on Delinquency and Its Treatment.* New Haven, Conn.: Yale University Press.

Hirschi, Travis, and Michael J. Hindelang. 1977. "Intelligence and Delinquency: A Revisionist Review." *American Sociological Review* 42 (August): 571–587.

Hooton, Earnest A. 1939a. *The American Criminal: An Anthropological Study,* Vol. 1. Cambridge, Mass.: Harvard University Press.
1939b. *Crime and the Man.* Cambridge, Mass.: Harvard University Press.

Hughes, H. Stuart. 1958. *Consciousness and Society: The Reorientation of European Social Thought, 1890–1930.* New York: Knopf.

Jennings, William S., Robert Kilkenny, and Lawrence Kohlberg. 1983. "Moral-Development Theory and Practice for Youthful and Adult Offenders." Pp. 281–355 in William S. Laufer and James M. Day, eds., *Personality Theory, Moral Development, and Criminal Behavior.* Lexington, Mass.: Lexington Books.

Kevles, Daniel J. 1985. *In the Name of Eugenics: Genetics and the Uses of Human Heredity.* New York: Knopf.

Klein, Dorie. 1973. "The Etiology of Female Crime: A Review of the Literature." *Issues in Criminology* 8 (Fall):3–30.

Klein, Malcolm. 1987. "Watch Out for That Last Variable." Pp. 25–41 in Sarnoff A. Mednick, Terrie E. Moffitt, and Susan A. Stack, eds., *The Causes of Crime: New Biological Approaches.* Cambridge: Cambridge University Press.

Kohlberg, Lawrence. 1964. "Development of Moral Character and Moral Ideology." Pp. 383–431 in Martin L. Hoffman and Lois W. Hoffman, eds., *Review of Child Development Research,* Vol. 1. New York: Russell Sage.

Konner, Melvin. 1982. *The Tangled Wing: Biological Constraints on the Human Spirit.* New York: Holt, Rinehart & Winston.

Laslett, Barbara. 1973. "The Family as a Public and Private Institution: An Historical Perspective." *Journal of Marriage and the Family* 35 (August): 480–492.

Lindner, Robert M. 1944. *Rebel Without a Cause.* New York: Grune & Stratton.

Lombroso, Cesare. 1911. "Introduction." Pp. xi–xx in Gina Lombroso Ferrero, *Criminal Man According to the Classification of Cesare Lombroso.* New York: Putnam.

Lombroso, Cesare, and William Ferrero. 1958. *The Female Offender.* New York: Philosophical Library. (First published in 1895.)

McCord, William. 1968. "Delinquency: Psychological Aspects." Pp. 86–93 in David L. Sills, ed., *International Encyclopedia of the Social Sciences,* Vol. 4. New York: Macmillan/Free Press.

McCord, William, Joan McCord, and Irving K. Zola. 1959. *Origins of Crime: A New Evaluation of the Cambridge-Somerville Youth Study.* New York: Columbia University Press.

Mednick, Sarnoff A., and Karl O. Christiansen, eds. 1977. *Biosocial Bases of Criminal Behavior.* New York: Gardner Press.

Mednick, Sarnoff A., William F. Gabrielli, Jr., and Barry Hutchings. 1987. "Genetic Factors in the Etiology of Criminal Behavior." Pp. 74–91 in Sarnoff A. Mednick, Terrie E. Moffitt, and Susan A. Stack, eds., *The Causes of Crime: New Biological Approaches.* Cambridge: Cambridge University Press.

Menard, Scott, and Barbara Morse. 1984. "A Structuralist Critique of the IQ–Delinquency Hypothesis: Theory and Evidence." *American Journal of Sociology* 89 (May):1347–1378.

Moffitt, Terrie E. 1993. "Adolescence-Limited and Life-Course-Persistent Antisocial Behavior: A Developmental Taxonomy." *Psychological Review* 100 (October):674–701.

Moffitt, Terrie E., Donald R. Lynam, and Phil A. Silva. 1994. "Neuropsychological Tests Predicting Persistent Male Delinquency." *Criminology* 32 (May):277–300.

Palmer, Ted. 1996. "Programmatic and Nonprogrammatic Aspects of Successful Intervention." Pp. 131–182 in Alan T. Harland, ed., *Choosing Correctional Options That Work: Defining the Demand and Evaluating the Supply.* Thousand Oaks, Calif.: Sage.

Piaget, Jean. 1948. *The Moral Judgment of the Child.* Translated by Marjorie Gabain. Glencoe, Ill.: Free Press.

Pollock, Vicki, Sarnoff A. Mednick, and William F. Gabrielli. 1983. "Crime Causation: Biological Theories." Pp. 308–316 in Sanford H. Kadish, ed., *Encyclopedia of Crime and Justice,* Vol. 1. New York: Free Press.

Rafter, Nicole Hahn. 1992. "Criminal Anthropology in the United States." *Criminology* 30 (November):525–545.

Raine, Adrian. 1993. *The Psychopathology of Crime: Criminal Behavior as a Clinical Disorder.* San Diego: Academic Press.

Redl, Fritz, and Hans Toch. 1979. "The Psychoanalytic Perspective." Pp. 183–197 in Hans Toch, ed., *Psychology of Crime and Criminal Justice.* New York: Holt, Rinehart & Winston.

Redl, Fritz, and David Wineman. 1951. *Children Who Hate: The Disorganization and Breakdown of Behavior Controls.* Glencoe, Ill.: Free Press.

Rieff, Philip. 1959. *Freud: The Mind of the Moralist.* New York: Viking Press.

Rowe, David C., and D. Wayne Osgood. 1984. "Heredity and Sociological Theories of Delinquency: A Reconsideration." *American Sociological Review* 49 (August):526–540.

Schuessler, Karl F., and Donald R. Cressey. 1950. "Personality Characteristics of Criminals." *American Journal of Sociology* 55 (March):476–484.

Shah, Saleem A., and Loren H. Roth. 1974. "Biological and Psychophysiological Factors in Criminality." Pp. 101–173 in Daniel Glaser, ed., *Handbook of Criminology.* Chicago: Rand McNally.

Sheldon, William H. 1949. *Varieties of Delinquent Youth: An Introduction to Constitutional Psychiatry.* New York: Harper.

Simon, Rita J. 1975. *The Contemporary Woman and Crime.* Washington, D.C.: U.S. Government Printing Office.

Simons, Ronald L. 1978. "The Meaning of the IQ–Delinquency Relationship." *American Sociological Review* 43 (April):268–270.

Sutherland, Edwin H. 1931. "Mental Deficiency and Crime." Pp. 357–375 in Kimball Young, ed., *Social Attitudes.* New York: Holt, Rinehart & Winston.

Sutherland, Edwin H., and Donald R. Cressey. 1974. *Criminology,* 9th ed. Philadelphia: Lippincott.

Tennenbaum, David J. 1977. "Personality and Criminality: A Summary and Implications of the Literature." *Journal of Criminal Justice* 5 (Fall): 225–235.

Toby, Jackson. 1974. "The Socialization and Control of Deviant Motivation." Pp. 85–100 in Daniel Glaser, ed., *Handbook of Criminology.* Chicago: Rand McNally.

Vold, George B. 1958. *Theoretical Criminology.* New York: Oxford University Press.

Waldo, Gordon P., and Simon Dinitz. 1967. "Personality Attributes of the Criminal: An Analysis of Research Studies, 1950–65." *Journal of Research in Crime and Delinquency* 4 (July): 185–202.

Warren, Marguerite Q. 1969. "The Case for Different Treatment of Delinquents." *The Annals of the*

American Academy of Political and Social Science 381 (January):47–59.

Warren, Marguerite Q., and Michael J. Hindelang. 1979. "Current Explanations of Offender Behavior." Pp. 166–182 in Hans Toch, ed., *Psychology of Crime and Criminal Justice.* New York: Holt, Rinehart & Winston.

White, Leslie A. 1959. "Man's Control over Civilization: An Anthropocentric Illusion." Pp. 548–566 in Morton H. Fried, ed., *Readings in Anthropology,* Vol. 2. New York: Crowell.

Wilson, James Q., and Richard J. Herrnstein. 1985. *Crime and Human Nature.* New York: Simon & Schuster.

Wolfgang, Marvin E. 1972. "Cesare Lombroso." Pp. 232–291 in Hermann Mannheim, ed., *Pioneers in Criminology,* 2nd ed. Montclair, N.J.: Patterson Smith.

Wootton, Barbara. 1959. *Social Science and Social Pathology.* London: Allen & Unwin.

Zeleny, L. D. 1933. "Feeble-Mindedness and Criminal Conduct." *American Journal of Sociology* 38 (January):564–576.

ACCORDING TO SOME CULTURAL
DEVIANCE THEORISTS,
DELINQUENCY IS PRODUCED IN
DISORGANIZED, SLUM
COMMUNITIES.

CHAPTER EIGHT

CULTURAL DEVIANCE THEORY

In this chapter, we will be dealing with a body of theory called **cultural deviance theory,** which is markedly different from control theory. According to control theorists, everyone has antisocial impulses; delinquent acts, therefore, are caused by the *absence* of effective controls. By contrast, cultural deviance theorists reject the notion that antisocial impulses are universal and suggest that delinquent acts are caused by learned values and beliefs that *require* them. Delinquency thus represents conformity to cultural values and beliefs that run counter to those of the larger society. The delinquent is a social individual who is behaving in accordance with the values and beliefs of his or her particular group.

ORIGINS OF CULTURAL DEVIANCE THEORY

The origins of cultural deviance theory can be traced to the pioneering work of two Chicago sociologists, Clifford Shaw and Henry McKay. When Shaw and McKay began their work in the 1920s, they were confronted with a confusing, often contradictory, jumble of explanations of delinquency. On the one hand, religiously oriented social reformers were preoccupied with foreign-born immigrants and rural, native-born Americans who ended up as industrial workers in our growing cities. High rates of urban delinquency, poverty, and vice led the reformers to bemoan the corruption of cities as major sources of trouble. Their commonsense explanations suggested that the moral standards of rural civilization were being destroyed and that urban children were being led into debauchery and sin. On the other hand, prevailing scientific theories reflected biological and psychological determinism. The delinquent was innately inferior, psychologically abnormal, or both. Street-smart and sexually precocious working-class youths were not just deviant but inherently so.

By contrast, the theory eventually advanced by Shaw and McKay rejected both the commonsense and prevailing scientific theories, particularly the idea that delinquents are biological or psychological misfits. Furthermore, Shaw and McKay formulated their theory in an empirical way. They used extensive research, including detailed life histories of delinquents (Shaw, 1931, 1938, 1966), to learn more about delinquency; and only after this was accomplished did they set about trying to explain the "facts" they had uncovered.

Shaw and McKay were trained in the fields of **sociology** and demography, which are concerned with social organization and the size and distribution of populations. Therefore, they sought answers to two central questions: (1) How are official delinquents geographically distributed in the city? and (2) What are the social conditions associated with high-delinquency areas?

Geographical Distribution

Shaw and McKay gathered information in Chicago on all official delinquents who had police records, court hearings, and correctional commitments during various periods between 1900 and 1940—over 60,000 cases in all (Shaw, 1929:22; Shaw and McKay, 1942:45–47). To determine how these thousands of cases were distributed geographically, Shaw and McKay plotted the address of each of them on city maps. They found repeatedly that official delinquents were highly concentrated in particular areas of the city: adjacent to the central business district, around the railroads and stockyards, and in the industrial and steel districts. In short, these youths lived in the most dilapidated, least desirable portions of the city.

The extent of that concentration is illustrated in figure 8.1, a radial map that breaks Chicago into a series of concentric zones. Near the city's center, the number of male official delinquents per 100 boys was 24.5. The number, however, declined to 3.5 in the outermost area. Not only were male delinquents concentrated near the center of the city, but the number of delinquents decreased regularly as one moved farther from this center.

Such findings were not confined only to boys. Shaw (1929:158) found that although rates of delinquency were lower among girls than boys, female delinquents also were concentrated in deteriorated areas adjacent to the center of the city and industrial districts. And, as with the boys, the number of delinquent girls decreased as one moved from the city center to the periphery.

Between the mid-1920s and 1940, Shaw and McKay studied the distribution of delinquents from almost every conceivable angle. They plotted the addresses of truants, juveniles with police records, juveniles committed to correctional schools, and recidivists (repeat offenders). They plotted the locations of delinquents in Philadelphia, Boston, Cincinnati, Cleveland, and Richmond. Finally, after Shaw's death, McKay continued to update delinquency data in Chicago up to 1966 (Shaw, 1929; Shaw and McKay, 1931, 1942, 1969). Yet, for three-quarters of a century and in different locations, the findings remained the same: Official delinquents were concentrated in the overcrowded and deteriorated areas of the city. The second question they sought to answer, therefore, became all the more important.

FIGURE 8.1

Rate of male delinquents, by mile zones surrounding the Loop

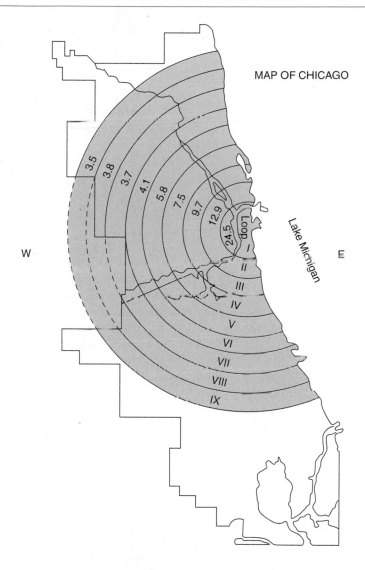

Social Conditions

Shaw and McKay found that certain social conditions were associated with high-delinquency areas.

PHYSICAL DETERIORATION AND POPULATION LOSS As a city expanded outward, commercial and industrial enterprises invaded previously residential areas. As a result, living conditions became progressively worse, and residents fled as soon as they could.

ECONOMIC SEGREGATION The low rents in old, dilapidated buildings and deteriorated neighborhoods attracted low-income people (Shaw and McKay, 1969:147–152). For children, sometimes, there could be enormous distress. In his extraordinary autobiographical novel, Claude Brown (1965:33) described an event that happened in Harlem when he was a child of 6 or 7. He had gone to the home of his friend Bucky and found him choking his younger sister Debbie. Meanwhile, Bucky's older sister Dixie, trying to free Debbie, was hitting Bucky over the head with a broom. All three were crying. When the fight finally stopped, Brown saw what had caused it: "The three of them had been fighting over one egg, and the egg was broken in the scuffle." There was nothing else in the house to eat.

RACIAL/ETHNIC SEGREGATION High-delinquency areas had a high percentage of foreign-born and minority populations who came to American cities seeking economic success (Shaw and McKay, 1931: 79). As Brown (1965:7) related:

> I want to talk about the first Northern urban generation of Negroes. I want to talk about the experiences of a misplaced generation, of a misplaced people in an extremely complex, confused society. . . .
>
> The characters are sons and daughters of former Southern sharecroppers. These were the poorest people of the South, who poured into New York City during the decade following the Great Depression. These migrants were told that unlimited opportunities for prosperity existed in New York and that there was no "color problem" there. They were told that Negroes lived in houses with bathrooms, electricity, running water, and indoor toilets. To them, this was "the promised land." . . . One no longer had to wait to get to heaven to lay his burden down; burdens could be laid down in New York.

African Americans were not the first to migrate into American cities. In the 1880s, residents of inner-city Chicago were mainly German, Irish, and English immigrants. Those groups gradually gave way to Scandinavian, Polish, Italian, and Jewish immigrants around the turn of the century. The large migration of Southern blacks did not begin until after the 1920s. And not until the 1950s did blacks make up a sizable percentage of Chicago's population (Bursik and Webb, 1982:37–38). In each case, the newest immigrants were the poorest and so helped to push the earlier immigrants into more stable working-class areas (Shaw, 1929:17–18). In the process, the inner city became an incredible mixture of people and cultures. "In the naborhood," reported one delinquent, "there were jews, polocks and irish, mostly foreigners and a poor class of people that could hardly read or write but had a flock of 'kids'" (Shaw, 1931:19).

OTHER SOCIAL PROBLEMS In areas with the highest concentrations of official delinquents, there were also high rates of other problems—for example, infant mortality, mental disorder, tuberculosis, and adult crime. All of these problems went hand-in-hand; that is, they were worst near the center of the city and became progressively better as one moved toward the periphery (Shaw and McKay, 1969: 104–106).

The importance of Shaw and McKay's findings about the social conditions in high-delinquency areas could hardly be overstated. Rather than assuming that delinquents are biological or psychological misfits, they reasoned that the spatial, economic, and social distribution of people in deteriorated urban areas must somehow cause delinquency. Furthermore, the "facts" they uncovered were virtually the same as those we encountered when we considered arrest, self-report, and victimization data: Age, gender, race/ethnicity, social class, group association, and community type are related to delinquency. How, then, did Shaw and McKay try to explain those "facts"?

THE SHAW–MCKAY THEORY

Before trying to answer that question, Shaw and McKay had to deal with a provocative and important finding. On the one hand, their research tended to support the 19th-century belief that delinquency is associated with the corruption of American cities. On the other hand, it did not support the belief that delinquency is due to the moral or biological depravity of particular racial and ethnic groups (Shaw and McKay, 1969:152–164). It did not support such a belief because they found that the racial and ethnic composition of high-delinquency areas had changed repeatedly as different racial and ethnic groups had moved in and out of them. Moreover, the delinquency rate for a particular racial or ethnic group decreased when the group moved into more desirable areas. Shaw and McKay thus concluded that delinquency rates are associated more with the kinds of neighborhoods in which juveniles live than with the racial or ethnic composition of the neighborhoods. They believed that the explanation for delinquency lies in the kind of community life found in deteriorated neighborhoods, not in the kinds of people who live in them.

Basic Postulates

The following five postulates capture the essence of that explanation:

1. *The deteriorated areas of the city produce social disorganization.* Shaw and McKay argued that there is **social disorganization** in slum areas, or an almost total absence of a sense of community. They agreed with Frederic Thrasher (1927: 491), another pioneer investigator, that not only do the cultural standards of different racial and ethnic groups conflict with one another, but these groups suffer from many additional problems: "inadequate family life; poverty; deteriorating neighborhoods, and ineffective religion, education, and recreation." These problems, moreover, are compounded by the constant threat of invasion by business and industry and by high levels of population mobility that only make conditions worse. In short, slum conditions produce socially disorganized neighborhoods (Shaw, 1929:204–205; Shaw and McKay, 1969:171–172).

2. *Socially disorganized neighborhoods lead to ineffective control of children.* "The absence of common community ideals and standards prevents cooperative social action . . . to . . . suppress delinquency" (Shaw and McKay, 1931:102). Under such conditions, parents are helpless to control or help their children, even if they try. As Brown (1965:20) noted:

> Mama soon realized that hiding my clothes would not keep me in the house. The next thing she tried was threatening to send me away until I was twenty-one. This was only frightening to me at the moment of hearing it. Ever so often, either Dad or Mama would sit down and have a heart-to-heart talk with me. These talks were very moving. I always promised to mend my bad ways. I was always sincere and usually kept the promise for about a week. During these weeks, I went to school every day and kept my stealing at a minimum. By the beginning of the second week, I had reverted back to my wicked ways,

and Mama would have to start praying all over again.

3. *Ineffective control allows street gangs to develop.* Shaw and McKay (1969:173) found that approximately 8 in 10 delinquent boys had committed their offenses in groups. Hence, they concluded that

> membership in such groups is an important contributing factor in many cases [of delinquency], since it is found that very often the boy's contact with the delinquent group marks the beginning of his career in delinquency and that his initial delinquencies are often identical with the traditions and practices of his group. (Shaw and McKay, 1931: 256)

> So I grew old enough to go out on the street. The life in the streets and alleys became fascinating and enticing. I had two close companions that I looked up to with childish admiration and awe. One was William, my stepbrother. The other one was Tony, a dear friend of my stepbrother, William. They were close friends, four years older than me and well versed in the art of stealing. (Shaw, 1966: 50)

But where did William and Tony learn to steal? Does each small group of boys develop its own delinquent traditions? The answer is no, according to Shaw and McKay. Delinquent traditions have a broader base of support in slum communities.

4. *Delinquent traditions are transmitted from one generation of gang boys to the next.*

> The heavy concentration of delinquency in certain areas means . . . that boys living in these areas are in contact . . . with groups which sanction such behavior and exert pressure upon their members to conform to group standards. . . . This means that delinquent boys in these areas have contact not only with other delinquents who are their contemporaries but also with older offenders, who in turn had contact with delinquents preceding them, and so on back to the earliest history

of the neighborhood. This contact means that the traditions of delinquency can be and are transmitted down through successive generations of boys, in much the same way that language and other social forms are transmitted. (Shaw and McKay, 1942:168)

What this suggests, then, is that a child's immediate peer group becomes a vehicle for perpetuating delinquent traditions and forcing adherence to them, but that such traditions are actually learned from older children:

> Whenever the boys got together they talked about robbing and made more plans for stealing. I hardly knew any boys who did not go robbing. The little fellows went in for petty stealing, breaking into freight cars, and stealing junk. The older guys did big jobs like stick-ups, burglary, and stealing autos. The little fellows admired the "big shots" and longed for the day when they could get into the big racket. Fellows who had "done time" were big shots and looked up to and gave the little fellows tips on how to get by and pull off big jobs. (Shaw, 1966:54)

Although Shaw and McKay wrote mostly about boys, their life history documents imply that girls also were caught up in delinquent gangs and traditions:

> Tony had two sisters who always played with us and went on our stealing adventures. They could steal as good as any boy. Also they had sex relations openly with all the boys in the neighborhood. I remember how the boys boasted that they had had sex relations with each of them. All the boys talked about it and the girls didn't care; they seemed to be proud of it and expect it. The funny thing about it was that Tony knew all about his sisters and their behavior and only made merry about it. (Shaw, 1966:51)

According to this postulate, then, conventional values have little hold on slum children. Unsupervised peer groups and delinquent traditions tend to fill the void.

5. *Delinquent traditions produce high delinquency rates.* In the central city, high delinquency rates are the culmination of a long series of contributing community conditions: Deteriorated areas produce social disorganization; social disorganization leads to ineffective control of children; ineffective control allows street gangs to develop; street gangs perpetuate delinquent traditions; and delinquent traditions produce high delinquency rates. Delinquents are portrayed as inherently sociable people whose response to parental indifference and neighborhood disorganization is the creation of alternative forms of organization. Those alternatives happen to be delinquent according to the standards of the larger society (Kobrin, 1971:124).

Implications for and Impact on Social Policy

The implications of this kind of theory were profound. Delinquency was attributable to the way communities are organized. Indeed, Shaw and McKay stressed that poverty, deteriorating neighborhoods, and racial/ethnic conflict were important in producing delinquency only if they result in social disorganization.

In interpreting their theory, however, two national commissions—the National Commission on Law Observance and Enforcement (1931) and the President's Commission on Law Enforcement and Administration of Justice (1967)—placed greater stress on poverty, recommending that it become the primary focus of social policy. "It is inescapable," said the President's Commission (1967:57), "that juvenile delinquency is directly related to conditions bred by poverty." Therefore, it recommended, the most promising way to address the problem of delinquency would be to ameliorate the conditions that drive juveniles toward it: Strengthen the ability of low-income families to control their children, reduce unemployment, improve housing, enrich slum schools, combat economic and racial segregation, and establish youth service bureaus in slum areas (1967: 58–77).

> The Commission doubts that even a vastly improved criminal justice system can substantially reduce crime if society fails to make it pos-

sible for each of its citizens to feel a personal stake in it—in the good life that it can provide. (1967:58)

In some ways, those recommendations reflected the efforts Shaw himself made to prevent delinquency. Rather than advocating a radical reconstruction of society, Shaw stressed the importance of helping slum residents—most of whom had recently migrated from rural areas—to more effectively conduct their own lives, that is, to develop a better sense of community in their neighborhoods, foster greater opportunities for their children, and find more effective ways for adjusting to a complex urban culture (Bursik and Grasmick, 1993:160–166; Finestone, 1976:124–136). Hence, in the 1930s, Shaw fathered the **Chicago Area Project,** which sought to realize three goals: (1) Induce residents of slum areas to try to prevent delinquency, (2) assist them in gaining greater control of their children by organizing local programs and resources for them, and (3) foster cooperative action among local residents, the schools, the police, and the courts.

Shaw was a charismatic leader who threw himself into the Chicago Area Project for more than a quarter century (Lundman, 1993:66–72) and won the respect of several generations of various racial and ethnic groups. Solomon Kobrin (1959:27–29), a later colleague of Shaw and McKay, noted that the results of the project vindicated Shaw's untiring efforts. His Chicago Area Project has been in operation in Chicago for many years. In no other locale have both theoretical and applied work been combined for such a long period of time.

Despite this outcome, some of today's theorists, who will be discussed in subsequent chapters, argue that Shaw's efforts represented little more than a Band-Aid solution, when radical surgery was needed. Because it is the poverty, overcrowding, and misery of modern capitalist society that are the real causes of delinquency, not social disorganization, critics argue, the Chicago Area Project did nothing more than address symptoms (Snodgrass, 1976:10, 15–17). Radical economic and political changes were required, not efforts to help victims of society adjust more effectively to unacceptable conditions (Schwendinger and Schwendinger, 1985:27–29).

WHAT CAN BE DONE ABOUT GANGS?

Reminiscent of assertions by Clifford Shaw and Henry McKay many decades ago, Malcolm Klein (1995:153) states that

gangs are by-products of partially incapacitated communities. Until we dedicate the . . . resources necessary to alter these community structures, gangs will continue to emerge. . . . I'm talking about the most obvious resources—jobs, better schools, social services, health programs, family support, training in community organization skills, and support for resident empowerment.

Police suppression programs (e.g., "sweeps" through neighborhoods to detain gang members) are not likely to be effective in reducing gang activity because they do little or nothing to address the causes of gangs (p. 233). More effective efforts are likely to involve parent training, job opportunities, and youth–adult contact.

Clearly, serious urban problems have persisted. In recent years, the cores of our largest cities have continued to deteriorate. Unemployment rates among ghetto dwellers have remained staggeringly high. Economic/racial segregation has persisted, as have delinquent gangs. Indeed, the problems of many of today's youths seemingly could have been taken from the pages of Shaw's life histories, written long ago:

At an early age, often even before they start school, [many inner-city] children . . . gravitate to the streets, where they "hang"—socialize with their peers. Children from . . . generally permissive homes have a great deal of latitude and are allowed to "rip and run" up and down the street. They often come home from school, put their books down, and go right back out the door. On school nights eight- and nine-year-olds remain out until nine or ten o'clock (and teenagers come in whenever they want to). On the streets they play in groups that often become the source of their primary social bonds. . . .

By the time they are teenagers, most youths have either internalized the code of the streets or at least learned the need to comport themselves in accordance with its rules. (Anderson, 1994: 86, 88)

Scientific Adequacy

In a sense, the Shaw–McKay theory could be described as a sociological control theory, stressing the social disorganization in city slums and the need to foster more effective ways of controlling the children in them (Bursik, 1988:520–521, 528–529). But rather than seeking to alter the internal states of children, one by one (as would be implied by the psychodynamic control theories reviewed in Chapter 7), the task would be that of understanding and developing more effective social institutions by which to socialize them—modern counterparts of the families, churches, and communities that were so effective in the small rural towns of 18th-century America. Indeed, the hard work by Shaw and McKay to foster the Chicago Area Project suggests that this interpretation is consistent with their theory. To them, delinquent traditions among lower-class youths seemed to have been analogous to Freud's unrestrained, but potentially evil, tendencies in individuals, only in collective form. In this case, however, effective socialization would require the concerted efforts of all social institutions, not just the family.

There is a good reason, however, for describing the Shaw–McKay theory as a cultural deviance theory rather than a sociological control theory. Although Shaw and McKay never used the word *culture* to describe the ties that bind lower-class youths, their emphasis on gang traditions has been a major source of many subsequent theories stressing that delinquency is the product of unique cultures or subcultures. A major question, therefore, is whether that construction of delinquency is accurate.

SOCIAL DISORGANIZATION IN DETERIORATED AREAS
Shaw and McKay attributed the development of delinquent traditions to the disintegration of community controls in slum areas. Yet they offered no direct evidence that the residents of higher-income urban areas engage in collective problem solving any more effectively than do residents in low-income areas (Kobrin, 1971:128–129). Furthermore, they provided no direct evidence that the population in outlying areas is any less heterogeneous than that in the central city. Hence, their assumption that slum areas are more disorganized than other urban areas was not supported by compelling evidence.

Therefore, it became fashionable among sociologists to suggest that we should look not for social disorganization, but for differential social organization in high-delinquency areas (Cohen, Lindesmith, and Schuessler, 1956:21; Kobrin, Puntil, and Peluso, 1967:115–116; Whyte, 1943:272–273). They suggested that while our society often is divided by competing values and beliefs, slum communities are not necessarily jungles, their high rates of delinquency and victimization notwithstanding. Instead, there is an awareness of community among slum residents.

The organization which exists may indeed not be adequate for the effective control of delinquency and for the solution of other social problems, but the qualities and defects of organization are not to be confused with the absence of organization. (Cohen, 1955:33)

Researchers only recently have begun to produce evidence that slum areas are more socially disorganized than are more affluent areas of cities (Elliott et al., 1996; Sampson and Groves, 1989:787–788; Sampson, Raudenbush, and Earls, 1997). Although such evidence is consistent with the Shaw–McKay theory, other recent evidence is not. Elliott and his colleagues (1996:415) have found that neighborhood characteristics (e.g., availability of social activities) are much less important in accounting for delinquency than are characteristics of the youths who live in the neighborhoods.

DELINQUENCY AS A LOWER-CLASS PHENOMENON
Shaw and McKay documented the existence of heavy

concentrations of *official* delinquents in slum areas. Official data, however, may not be accurate measures of **law-violating behavior.** Shaw and McKay treated those data as if they were accurate, because their theory is concerned primarily with explaining why slum children violate the law, not how official rates are created. Yet as we have learned, official data represent not only the way children behave but also the way other people, and legal officials especially, respond to children of different social classes and race/ethnicities.

Furthermore, studies of self-reported delinquency suggest that the relationship between social class and law-violating behavior may not be nearly so strong as the relationship between social class and **official delinquency** (compare Chapters 4 and 5). For these reasons, the Shaw–McKay theory has two additional limitations: (1) It is not a complete explanation of official delinquency because the role of legal officials is not included in it, and (2) it is not a complete explanation of law-violating behavior because it is built on official data.

THE GROUP NATURE OF DELINQUENCY Many studies have confirmed that juveniles tend to violate the law in groups (Erickson, 1971, 1973a, 1973b; Erickson and Jensen, 1977; Eynon and Reckless, 1961; Giordano, 1978; Glueck and Glueck, 1952; Hindelang, 1971; Reiss, 1986; Warr, 1996; Zimring, 1981). However, an important issue is how one interprets that tendency.

Shaw and McKay argued that slum areas give rise to delinquent traditions because of extensive unsupervised peer groups. Consistent with that argument, Sampson and Groves (1989) found more unsupervised teenage peer groups in poor neighborhoods than in affluent neighborhoods. However, Kobrin (1971:130) found that "approximately half the boys of a high delinquency rate area did not participate at all in its juvenile street life." Because some children are unsupervised, all need not be. Many lower-class parents supervise their children carefully.

There are also some problems in assuming that lower-class children have the capacity to develop the group purpose necessary for maintaining delinquent traditions (Klein, 1995:84–85; Kobrin, 1971:130). Shaw and McKay suggested that deteriorated areas are so demoralizing to lower-class adults that they cannot maintain a sense of community, but they then concluded that lower-class children are able to do so. Apparently, children can establish a community where adults cannot!

Whether intentionally or not, this led to a portrayal of lower-class gangs as possessing strong esprit de corps and filled with members whose commitments to the gang exceed their commitments to anything else (Thrasher, 1927:277–281). Several researchers, however, have questioned that portrayal. Klein (1995:passim; Klein and Crawford, 1967:65–67) has argued that gangs are not close-knit and internally strong (also see Morash, 1983:317, 1986:59). Were it not for the external pressures of police and other legal officials or the threats of rival groups, delinquent gangs would have little to unify them. As one South Central Los Angeles gang member indicated: "'Cause if they ain't nobody to fight, it ain't no gangs. It ain't no life. I don't know. . . . It ain't no fun'" (Bing, 1992:49). By themselves, gangs do not develop the kind of group goals and instrumental activities indicative of a high degree of organization.

Similarly, Short and Strodtbeck (1965:280) reported that "the capacity of lower-class gangs to elaborate and enforce norms of reciprocity is very much below what might be required to sustain the group if alternative forms of gratification were available." They found that gang members were characterized by a long list of social disabilities: unsuccessful school adjustment, limited social and technical skills, a low capacity for self-assertion, low intelligence scores, and a tendency to hold other gang members in low esteem (Short and Strodtbeck, 1965:Chap. 10). Interaction within the gang seemed to reflect an aggressive tone rather than close personal ties (but for contrary evidence, based on delinquents in general rather than lower-class gangs, see Giordano, Cernkovich, and Pugh, 1986; and Warr, 1996:30). In short, there is considerable doubt about the extent to which adolescent gangs have developed widely shared and mutually supported norms, to say nothing of a way of life that could qualify as a unique and independent culture.

What is missing in most discussions of this issue, however, is any demonstration of the extent to which lower-class culture in general has been different from

THE CONNECTION BETWEEN GANGS AND DRUGS

Malcolm Klein (1995:40–43), who is one of the most respected authorities on gangs, questions claims by many police officials, politicians, and reporters that there is a close connection between gangs and drug sales and distribution, especially of crack cocaine. "The national hype about crack-selling, crack-controlling street gangs derives in part from the unconsidered assumptions . . . that drug and street gangs are one and the same thing. It just ain't so" (p. 41). Indeed, the characteristics of street gangs argue against a gang–crack connection. A successful conspiracy to sell and distribute drugs requires (1) permanent leadership, (2) strong group cohesiveness, (3) a code of loyalty and secrecy, and (4) avoidance of non-drug-related lawbreaking. "None of these four features is characteristic of the typical street gang," says Klein (p. 43). Although drug use is common among gang members, drug sales and distribution are not (p. 36).

middle-class culture. Some of the descriptions of lower-class youths by Shaw (1931, 1938, 1966) and by his contemporary Frederic Thrasher (1927) were consistent with descriptions of lower-class groups in earlier centuries (Gillis, 1974). In the crowded, teeming streets of the slum, children were attracted by opportunities for fun and adventure. They swiped fruit, tipped over garbage cans, stayed out all night, and mugged drunks. To be sure, they were unsupervised by middle-class standards, but did this mean that their behavior was inconsistent with lower-class traditions? It did, according to Shaw and McKay and

to Thrasher. They implied that the standards of lower-class adults became more middle-class during the 1900s, even though those same adults were ineffective in enforcing their values and beliefs. That was why, as youth groups developed and solidified, they were increasingly at odds with parental expectations.

But this interpretation may be incorrect. It could be that lower-class youths are not at odds with their parents. Rather, their behavior may be consistent with the values and beliefs shared by all lower-class people.

DELINQUENCY AS A PRODUCT OF INTEGRATED LOWER-CLASS CULTURE

In 1958, anthropologist Walter Miller suggested that delinquency is the product of a united, not a divided, lower-class culture.

Basic Postulates

Miller's **lower-class culture theory** has four postulates:

1. *Slums are organized by a distinctive lower-class culture.* According to Miller (1958), delinquent groups are neither produced by disorganized communities nor isolated from adult influence. Adults and children in lower-class communities share a common set of values. In response to economic and racial segregation in American society, "there is . . . a relatively homogeneous and stabilized . . . lower-class culture" (Miller, 1959:225). That culture represents a common adaptation of economically unsuccessful whites and blacks.

2. *Lower-class culture emphasizes membership in single-sex peer groups.* A key to understanding the lower-class culture lies in the way it organizes family life and gender relations. In particular, family life is dominated by females (Miller, 1958:14). Men usually do not play a consistent and predictable role in it, nor do they provide reliable economic support. After generations of failure, conventional work and family roles no longer attract them. Instead, new values emerge that tend to separate males and females into

different groups. As a result, the lower-class family does not possess the close, intimate ties supposedly found in the middle-class family. The mother is responsible for raising the children, who may be the offspring of different men.

This means that children spend the first few years of life under the domination of women, from whom they receive mixed messages about the male role. Children learn from their mothers that men are rogues: simultaneously despicable and desirable, hateful yet alluring, irresponsible but very attractive on a Saturday night. Though this message poses some problems for girls, it is especially difficult for boys because they are faced with issues of sexual identity; A mother does not want her boy to grow up like his father but anticipates that he will.

This problem is resolved during adolescence. While girls continue to identify with their mothers, boys join male street gangs to escape female domination and learn how to be men. Indeed, Miller (1958:17) suggests that gang members are probably the most "able" young members of slum communities. Why, then, do they join gangs?

3. *Single-sex peer groups are organized by a unique set of focal concerns.* Lower-class culture has unique focal concerns related to trouble, toughness, smartness, excitement, fate, and autonomy. *Trouble* involves a desire to avoid entanglement with such officials as the police, as in "staying out of trouble" (Miller, 1958:8). *Toughness* denotes a concern for demonstrating "physical prowess," "masculinity," and "bravery" (p. 9). *Smartness* involves the "capacity to outsmart, outfox, outwit, dupe, 'fake,' 'con' another or others, and the concomitant capacity to avoid being outwitted, 'taken,' or duped oneself" (p. 9). *Excitement* refers to a concern for taking a break from the relatively "routine" and "repetitive" activities of daily life, with "its most vivid expression in the highly patterned practice of the recurrent 'night on the town' . . . [often involving] alcohol, music, and sexual adventuring" (pp. 10–11). *Fate* has to do with the feeling among lower-class persons that their lives are

ruled by "luck" or "destiny," that is, "a set of forces over which they have relatively little control" (p. 11). Finally, *autonomy* reflects a desire to avoid control or domination by others (pp. 12–13).

The lower-class gang is merely an adolescent expression of these focal concerns. Whereas a major criterion for evaluating a man's status in middle-class culture is achievement in education and work, criteria in the lower-class culture suggest that hard work and deferred gratification are for suckers. Consequently, young gang members gain a sense of belonging and acquire status by demonstrating physical prowess, committing delinquent acts that demonstrate an ability to live by their wits, resisting authority, and avoiding the drudgery of a daily job. Thus, while lower-class people, young and old, are aware of middle-class norms, they do not value them. They may express verbal support for them, but they do so to escape getting into trouble with the police (p. 8).

4. *Adherence to lower-class focal concerns produces delinquency.* What this suggests, then, is that the closer the members of lower-class gangs conform to the values and beliefs of their culture, the more likely they are to commit delinquent acts. They commit delinquent acts out of conformity to lower-class values, which are deviant by middle-class standards.

Distinctive Features of Miller's Theory

Compared with the Shaw–McKay theory, Miller's cultural deviance theory has two distinctive features. On the one hand, like Shaw–McKay, it suggests that delinquency is predominantly a lower-class, group phenomenon and that delinquent behavior is due to cultural values and beliefs that require it. On the other hand, it departs from the Shaw–McKay theory in its location of delinquent traditions. Whereas Shaw–McKay suggests that such traditions are the sole possession of unsupervised gangs and peer groups, the Miller theory indicates that they belong to the entire lower-class community. Delinquency is an expression of a distinctive culture in which effective socialization by adults results in deviant values that everyone shares.

Perhaps even more important, Miller "[alerted] us to a possible historical development that has received relatively little attention—the emergence of something like a stable American lower class" (Bordua, 1961:131). Though few people, until recently, have made such an argument, in 1976, Bayard Rustin, a long-time black civil rights activist, argued that "the future advancement of blacks and other poor in this country has very little to do with the color of their skin" (*Los Angeles Times,* August 11, 1976). Instead, poverty and the other social problems associated with it have become a class, not a race, problem. Because technology and a globalized labor force has reduced the need for unskilled labor in the United States, a class of "economic untouchables" has been created, composed of racial and ethnic minorities.

Similarly, some sociologists have observed that Americans increasingly are polarized into middle- and lower-class groups (Moynihan, 1965:5–6; Wilson, 1978:Chap. 7, 1987:7–8, 10–11, 20–21, 125–126). They have contended that, although racism continues, it is no longer the deciding economic factor it once was.[1] The substantial gains made by middle-class blacks, for example, increasingly have separated them from the underclass trapped in the slums, just as affluence has separated middle-class whites from that same underclass. Like Miller, therefore, some sociologists have concluded that American society has become increasingly stratified and may someday witness the development of a lower class with a distinctive culture of its own.

As we will see in later chapters, some theorists take strong exception to this conclusion, arguing that the goal of success is still shared by all Americans. Middle-class values stressing the importance of education, hard work, and deferred gratification, they argue, have filtered down to members of the lower class and are highly motivating to them. Furthermore, Miller's argument may be faulty because he "also forgets that none of the low status groups in the society, with the possible exception of low status Negroes, has any history of his female-based house-

hold, at least not in the extreme form that he describes" (Bordua, 1961:130–131).[2]

According to Miller, lower-class youngsters get into trouble because they remain faithful to values learned from their parents. However, researchers have found that regardless of class background, the closer juveniles are to their parents, the *less* likely they are to commit delinquent acts (e.g., Hindelang, 1973:475–476; Hirschi, 1969:97; Liska and Reed, 1985:555–556; Wiatrowski, Griswold, and Roberts, 1981:535–538). Furthermore, Hirschi (1969:212–223) found little disagreement among adolescents from different social classes on what people ought to do: whether they should obey the law, whether it is right to con others, or whether it is fate rather than personal competence that determines a person's destiny. Hence, Hirschi (1969:97) concluded that "those lower-class boys committing delinquent acts are not finding support for their actions from their parents or from their 'class culture'" (a conclusion shared by Kornhauser, 1978:208; Sampson, 1987:377; and Schwendinger and Schwendinger, 1985:170).

Such findings notwithstanding, some of the delinquency literature continues to depict Americans as divided into competing social class cultures that are linked to the commission of delinquent acts. This is true of theories of both lower-class and middle-class delinquency.

MIDDLE-CLASS SUBCULTURE THEORY

Cultural deviance theories of middle-class delinquency have stemmed from two traditions. The first concerns adolescence in general. It is seen as an ill-defined period in the life cycle, one in which peer relationships become very important. Because adolescents tend to be segregated from adults, a hedo-

---

[1]The Association of Black Sociologists (1978:4) expressed "outrage" at this statement, describing it as a gross misrepresentation of the black experience.

[2]Black families, in fact, *are* an exception. By the early 1980s, almost 50 percent of black families with children under 18 were headed by women (Wilson, 1987:66). For a long time, social scientists believed that the current problems of lower-class black families could be traced back to the disruptive effects of slavery. However, Gutman (1976) has shown that the female-centered black family is a product of more recent social factors. The two-parent family predominated among blacks in the late 19th and early 20th centuries (Gutman, 1976:xvii–xxii), with the situation changing only after World War II (Wilson, 1987:65–66).

nistic and irresponsible **youth subculture** is created (Coleman, 1961:passim; Davis, 1944:13; Glaser, 1971: 35–39; Parsons, 1942:606; Steinberg, 1996:140–143). The second tradition directly concerns delinquency. In the 1950s, the findings of the first self-report studies and some studies based on official data revealed that middle-class delinquency was more extensive than many had believed. These findings led to scattered efforts to explain the delinquent acts of more affluent youths (Bloch and Niederhoffer, 1958; Bohlke, 1961; England, 1960; Scott and Vaz, 1967).[3]

Despite the different concerns of those two traditions, they are remarkably similar. One reason is that they have been constructed from the world-view of the middle class, the view that most social scientists hold. Furthermore, neither tradition has depicted middle-class delinquency as serious. Rather, both tend to describe the values and beliefs of middle-class delinquents as a parody of the worst features of adult values and beliefs. Thus, as Kvaraceus and Miller (1967:234) put it, middle-class delinquency "appears less as a 'social problem' and more as a 'home problem.'"

Basic Postulates

The main theme of this construction of delinquency is captured in the following postulates:

1. *The social status of middle-class adolescents is ill-defined.* Reflecting historical changes in the status of children, most theorists have indicated that adolescents do not possess a clear-cut and responsible position in society. The groundwork

> was laid a century and more ago when youngsters were gradually removed from functional roles in the economy through restrictive apprenticeship codes, protective labor legislation, the compulsory education movement, and the withdrawal of children

from agricultural activities attendant upon urbanization. However diverse the forces were which led to this removal from productive roles, the result was that for probably the first time a major society deactivated a large and energetic segment of its population without clearly redefining the status and function of that segment. (England, 1960:536)

As a result, adolescents find "an absence of definitely recognized, consistent patterns of authority" and are "subjected to a confusing array of competing authorities" (Davis, 1944: 13). They are barred from productive labor but are expected to be hardworking; they attend school to develop their intellects but are not expected to challenge the opinions of parents and teachers; they are sexually mature and encouraged to be socially skilled but are supposed to refrain from adult vices; they are expected to be civic-minded but cannot hold public office, vote, or serve on juries; they often are separated from the direct supervision of parents and are granted considerable freedom but lack the kinds of ties to other adults that might prevent them from getting into trouble (England, 1960:536). As they attempt to deal with such contradictory directives, "boys and girls . . . often find it difficult to tell when and how 'adult' behavior is expected" (Williams, 1952:71).

The problem may have worsened in recent years because middle-class parents have been encouraged to pay greater attention to child development theories that question the wisdom of premature responsibility for children and recommend that they be allowed to develop at a slower, less pressured pace (Scott and Vaz, 1967: 210–213). As a result, parents have become more permissive and have stressed personality development and peer adjustment more than strict adherence to carefully defined rules. Schwartz (1987:238–239) describes one upper-middle-class community:

> In Glenbar, adults are so used to thinking of adolescent behavior in terms of its psychological, social, educational, and legal

---

[3]A noteworthy feature of these theories is their failure to distinguish between young people of the middle and upper classes. There are two reasons for this. First, the term *middle class* is used uncritically; it usually includes all youths whose parents have white-collar jobs, but incomes for white-collar workers range from middle to high. Hence, the children of schoolteachers and small businesspersons are lumped together with those whose parents are highly paid professionals and executives. Second, almost no attention has been paid to the children of very wealthy people. As a result, such children are either ignored in existing theories or are included in middle-class subculture theories.

consequences for a youth's personal development that they are almost incapable of defining modes of conduct that are intrinsically right and wrong. While youth in Glenbar cannot quite put their finger on it, they sense that adults do not operate with a consistent moral vocabulary.

2. *An ill-defined social status separates adolescents from the adult world.* To further complicate matters, the ill-defined adolescent period has been extended (Flacks, 1971; Starr, 1986), and this extension has further limited the contact between young people and adults (Berger, 1971; Coleman, 1961). As recently as about 1950, most students did not finish high school (Glaser, 1971: 34). At about age 16 or 17, they moved into adult roles because jobs were available to them. Since that time, however, increasing numbers have been confined to society's youth ghetto—the school. In the late 1960s, for the first time in history, a majority of American high school graduates entered college (Starr, 1986:324). Many more students have extended their studies into graduate school. As a result, the upper limit of adolescence has increased from around age 16 or 17, not too long ago, to the mid-20s today.

By the time they graduate, 80 percent of American high school students will have held a paying job during the school year, and working while in high school is more common among middle-class than lower-class youths (Greenberger and Steinberg, 1986:11, 20; Steinberg, 1996:166–167). However, most have jobs that isolate them from, rather than connect them to, adults. The reason is that they work mainly in retail stores and restaurants (Greenberger and Steinberg, 1986:63; Steinberg, 1996:168), where

> young people are more likely than not to work side by side with other adolescents. . . . One of the most important functions that early work experience may have served in the past, namely, the integration of young people into adult society, has been considerably eroded. Rather than mingling the generations and providing a context for the informal interaction of young people with their

elders, today's adolescent workplace has become a bastion for the adolescent peer group. (Greenberger and Steinberg, 1986:79)

3. *Social separation produces a middle-class youth subculture.* Virtually all theorists have agreed that the separation of adolescents and adults produces new values and beliefs. However, they have tended to disagree over the extent to which those new values and beliefs differ from those of middle-class adults.

One group of theorists has suggested that there is a substantial difference:

> A fundamental law of sociology and anthropology is that social separation results in cultural differentiation. The more adolescents interact exclusively with each other, the more their customs and values become different from those of other age groups. (Glaser, 1971:35)

A youth **subculture** develops that (1) is isolated, (2) fosters a psychic attachment between young persons and others their own age, (3) rejects adult standards and presses for autonomy, (4) develops an unusual regard for the underdog, and (5) seeks to foster change (Coleman, 1974: 112–125).

"The so-called youth subculture . . . sharply cuts off adolescent experience from that of the child and from that of the adult" (Green, 1952: 95). Eventually, it becomes intolerable for young people to be different from their peers (Parsons, 1950:378). "So extreme is this gap between generations . . . that parents and their adolescent children literally represent [different] subcultures" (Williams, 1952:73). Yet the development of a unique culture by youths "is their natural response to the somewhat unnatural position in which they find themselves in society" (Coleman, 1974:125).

A second group of theorists has suggested that any youth subculture is likely to reflect a great many adult expectations and teachings. For example, middle-class parents want their children to be skilled socially because their success, both as adolescents and adults, depends on it (Berger, 1963:396–400). Hence, for parents as well as adolescents, successful involvement with the youth crowd becomes a moral imperative (Scott and Vaz, 1967:211; Whyte, 1956:392). Not only do parents exhibit great concern over the popularity of their children, but they look to the school as the central agency for facilitating it. Indeed, said Cohen (1967:205), "status in the school is increasingly defined in terms of the standards and values of the adolescent peer groups, and the role of the adult becomes to create a benign atmosphere in which every child can integrate happily with some group." In other words, parents help to facilitate youth relations rather than feeling totally alienated from them.

4   *Middle class youth subculture produces delinquent behavior.* Despite disagreements over the uniqueness of the youth subculture, most theorists have suggested that (1) it helps to produce an adolescent world of hedonism and irresponsibility and (2) the more adolescents are involved in it, the more likely they are to commit delinquent acts. At the same time, most theorists have argued that the subculture encourages petty delinquent acts that tend to evolve from legitimate activities: dating, parties, athletics, extracurricular activities, automobiles, and involvement in the latest fads (England, 1960: 538–539; Scott and Vaz, 1967:214–217). Those activities lead to delinquency because the youth subculture is composed of immature and inexperienced people:

> Delinquent motivations among middle class teenagers arise from . . . [an] adaptive process, in which the teenage world, peopled by immature and inexperienced persons, extracts from the adult world those values having strong hedonistic possibilities, with the result that the values of the teenage culture consist mainly of distorted and caricatured fragments from the adult culture. (England, 1960:538)

Thus, it is argued that middle-class delinquency tends to involve such offenses as joyriding, drinking alcohol, smoking marijuana, staying out late, gambling, and engaging in sex—acts that are scarcely unknown to middle-class adults in their hedonistic moments. Such serious delinquent acts as assault, armed robbery, and burglary are considered outside the boundaries of the middle-class youth subculture. Indeed, according to Kvaraceus and Miller (1967:241), when serious delinquency is committed by a middle-class adolescent, it probably represents pathological rather than group-supported behavior.

Implications for Social Policy

The implications of this kind of theory for social policy are readily apparent and apply as much to lower-class as to middle-class adolescents. Delinquency can be reduced by either (1) ceasing to define such acts as drinking, marijuana use, extramarital sex, joyriding, staying out late, and truancy as delinquent offenses or (2) seeking to reduce the social separation of adolescents and adults by giving adolescents a greater stake in conformity. To some extent, both steps are being tried.

DECRIMINALIZING PETTY OFFENSES For three decades, influential organizations and social scientists have recommended that petty offenses, especially status offenses, be decriminalized (Empey, 1973). As Morris and Hawkins (1970:2) expressed it:

> We must strip off the moralistic excrescences on our criminal justice system so that it may concentrate on the essential. The prime function of the criminal law is to protect our persons and our property; these purposes are now engulfed in a mass of other distracting, inefficiently performed, legislative duties. When the criminal law invades the spheres of private morality and social welfare, it exceeds its proper limits at the cost of neglecting its primary tasks. . . . Man has an inalienable right to go to hell in his own fashion, provided he does not directly injure the person or property of another on the way.

Such expressions imply a greater tolerance for many acts that long have been common among juveniles. The decriminalization of petty offenses, however, would do little to reduce the social separation of adolescents and adults. For example, allowing teenagers to quit school at age 15 will not guarantee them employment. It is likely, therefore, that the social status of out-of-school youths will remain ill-defined.

GIVING ADOLESCENTS A STAKE IN CONFORMITY If the middle-class youth subculture results from the separation of adolescents and adults, then the following remedies are implied: (1) Eliminate the ambiguity and lack of purpose in the adolescent status, (2) close the generation gap, and (3) provide adolescents with socially desirable adult roles—a productive place in the economy, civic responsibilities, and the power of decision making (Toby, 1957). Presumably, if these steps were taken, the youth subculture would no longer exist. Because adolescents are inherently social, they would develop competence and a sense of belonging, generational conflict would be eliminated, and youths would exhibit a firm attachment to the aims, values, and beliefs of a unified, adult–youth culture (Polk and Kobrin, 1972).

In recent years, we have taken some steps in that direction: The voting age, for example, has been lowered to 18; work–study programs, combining work and school, have been initiated; and more young people are becoming active in the political process. Yet when all is said and done, those steps have not been enough to integrate adolescent and adult roles. For that matter, it is hard to imagine that adolescent misconduct will be eliminated by neutralizing the presumed effects of a middle-class youth subculture. Delinquency will continue, if history is any guide. We already have seen that in the 1700s and 1800s, the generations were far less separated than they are today. Work roles for young people were plentiful, and their labor was in great demand. Yet, youthful deviance and adult complaints about it were widespread.

Scientific Adequacy

There are several problems with middle-class subculture theories. First, although there is some disagreement between the generations, adolescents and adults hold to largely the same values and beliefs (Caplow et al., 1982:21, 144–145; Simmons and Blyth, 1987:4). At the very least, there is considerable "selective continuity" between the young and old

(Bengston, Furlong, and Laufer, 1974:9–11; Feather, 1980:278–280; Glass, Bengtson, and Dunham, 1986: 690–695; Kandel and Lesser, 1972:168–169, 181–185). Although young people and adults differ on some issues—for example, child-raising practices and authority relationships—they agree on many others: educational goals, occupational aspirations, even religious affiliations (Elkin and Westley, 1955; Hill, 1970:34–47). It would be difficult, for example, to convince adolescents who are planning middle-class careers in medicine, law, classical music, or science that the older values of delayed gratification, hard work, and self-discipline should always defer to adolescent group values and beliefs. The point is that although there are differences between the generations, the aims, values, and beliefs of adolescents are neither uniformly hedonistic and irresponsible nor uniformly conforming and responsible.

For that matter, Hagan (1991:576) has shown that lower- and middle-class adolescents do not differ with regard to the kinds of values and beliefs that are most likely to be associated with a youth subculture. Specifically, there is no consistent relationship between social class and adolescents' beliefs about how fun it would be to commit both serious delinquent acts, such as theft and fighting, and petty hedonistic acts, such as partying and drinking alcohol.

A second problem is closely related. Middle-class subculture theorists have asserted that the more adolescents are attached to their peers, the more likely they are to commit delinquent acts. As indicated earlier in this chapter, indirect support for this hypothesis has come from findings that delinquency is a group phenomenon. But why do middle-class youths commit delinquent acts in groups? Is it because they are so concerned with acceptance that they will do whatever the group demands, or is there some other reason?

Evidence on those questions is mixed. Hirschi (1969:145–146, 149–150) found that admiration and respect for peers act as a barrier to delinquent behavior: the greater the attachment, the less the delinquency. Hindelang (1973:479–480), by contrast, found the opposite: the greater the attachment to peers, the greater the delinquency (also see Agnew, 1985:56; Massey and Krohn, 1986:124; Smith and Paternoster, 1987:150–153). And by further contrast,

Wiatrowski, Griswold, and Roberts (1981:535–538) reported that there is no relation between attachment to peers and delinquency (also see Smith and Paternoster, 1987:153–155).

In an attempt to resolve the issue, Jensen and Erickson (1976) could find strong support for neither position. It was not clear whether group offenses were due to strong feelings of attachment to friends or whether they were situational acts committed by people who simply went along with the group.

Finally, the assertion that middle-class adolescents do not commit serious delinquent acts is not supported by available data. It is true that recent victimization studies have tended to support official accounts of delinquency, which suggest that lower-class youths are more likely than others to commit serious delinquent acts (see Chapters 4 and 6). But our review of self-report studies (see Chapter 5) also indicated that many middle-class adolescents commit serious property and violent crimes (also see Richards, Berk, and Forster, 1979:148–150). Hence, middle-class theorists seem to have overemphasized social class differences. Furthermore, in assuming that middle-class offending is limited largely to petty offenses, they have failed to account for middle-class offenders like the following:

> In November 1994, six teenagers from Abington Township, a quiet, middle-class suburb of Philadelphia, . . . savagely beat Eddie Polec, age 16, to death with clubs and baseball bats. Law enforcement officials said this might have been part of a "fun outing," although there were reports that the murder was retaliation for the alleged rape of an Abington girl.
>
> One Abington mother, expressing the shock of the community, said, "These are suburban kids—you don't figure them to go bad. It's not their character to be a rough group of kids." . . . But suburbs have become cauldrons of . . . street . . . violence. (Derber, 1996:104–105)

SUMMARY AND CONCLUSIONS

In opposition to the individualistic theories of biologists and psychologists, some sociologists and an-thropologists have constructed an entirely different view of delinquent behavior rooted in subculture and culture.

Assumptions About Human Nature and Social Order

Cultural deviance theorists assume that people are inherently social. No less than law-abiding behavior, delinquency is an expression of a universal tendency to behave in accordance with the values and beliefs of one's own culture. But while human nature is essentially good, the social order is disrupted because there are competing cultures. There is no single standard of good and bad; moral values range from those that are strictly conventional to those that are unconventional.

Underlying Logic and Content of Cultural Deviance Theories

Cultural deviance theories represent a reaction to biological and psychodynamic theories. According to cultural deviance theorists, delinquents are socialized in cultural settings that justify, make attractive, and even require delinquent behavior. Such behavior is as normal to the members of **delinquent cultures** as law-abiding behavior is to members of conventional cultures. However, the various versions of cultural deviance theory differ in indicating the source of delinquent traditions.

LOWER-CLASS THEORY There are two versions of lower-class cultural deviance theory. The Shaw–McKay version suggests that delinquent traditions are produced in disorganized slum communities by unsupervised peer groups and gangs. The only coherent traditions perpetuated from one generation to the next in these communities are delinquent traditions, as shown in the following diagram:

Slum areas → Social disorganization → Loss of adult control → Street gangs → Delinquent youth culture → Delinquent behavior

By contrast, the Miller version suggests that American society has become progressively stratified and has witnessed the development of a lower class with an increasingly distinctive culture of its own. Delinquent behavior is a reflection of widely shared lower-class values, as shown in this diagram:

$$
\text{Slum area} \rightarrow \text{Lower-class culture} \rightarrow \text{Single-sex peer groups} \rightarrow
$$

$$
\text{Unique focal concerns} \rightarrow \text{Delinquent behavior}
$$

MIDDLE-CLASS THEORY Middle-class theory suggests that delinquency is a subcultural variation of the middle class. This kind of delinquency is not very serious and is a distorted caricature of adult values and beliefs, as shown in this diagram:

$$
\text{Ill-defined adolescent status} \rightarrow \text{Separation of generations} \rightarrow \text{Middle-class youth subculture} \rightarrow \text{Delinquent behavior}
$$

Policy Implications of Cultural Deviance Theories

The Shaw–McKay theory implies the need for radical economic and social changes: full employment, improved housing, enriched schools, elimination of economic and racial/ethnic segregation, and more effective control by families and neighborhoods over children—in short, a full assimilation of lower-class people into the middle-class way of life.

Miller's theory implies even more. Either Americans must tolerate a unique, but seemingly deviant, lower-class culture, or they must seek ways for reasserting the importance of the American Dream for everyone. If lower-class people no longer value the things middle-class people value, then they not only need more opportunities but also need to define middle-class goals as worth pursuing. A restructured society, along with a mass conversion, is implied.

Middle-class subculture theory suggests two possible remedies for the delinquency of privileged youths: (1) a new morality in which status offenses are no longer defined as delinquent offenses and (2) a means by which adolescents can be given a greater stake in conformity—closer ties with adults and greater involvement in socially desirable and productive roles.

Logical and Empirical Adequacy of Cultural Deviance Theories

Several of the "facts" on which some or all cultural deviance theories are constructed have continued to receive empirical support: (1) Law-violating behavior occurs frequently among adolescents, (2) rates of official delinquency are high among lower-class youths, (3) delinquent behavior tends to be committed in groups, and (4) there is some discontinuity between the generations. Unless one takes the position that all are due to inherently antisocial or pathological tendencies among large numbers of young people, then one must pay attention to the possible existence of cultural values and beliefs that are deviant.

At the same time, important questions can be raised about cultural deviance theories. Some part of delinquent behavior is due to the ambiguous status of adolescents in American society. Moreover, delinquency often reflects an attempt to establish oneself in a social context in which peers play an important role. But it is a gross oversimplification to suggest that the single most important source of direction and acceptance for adolescents—lower- or middle-class—is that afforded by peers. Young people are not programmed like computers to conform only to delinquent peer standards. Adults also perform a socializing role.

American culture is complex and pluralistic, and people are confronted with alternative guides for behavior—some conventional, some deviant. And, although certain individuals or groups may be influenced by one more than the other, both determine behavior to a considerable degree. What is needed from cultural deviance theorists, therefore, is specification of the conditions under which some individuals or groups resist temptation and remain wedded to conventional alternatives while others succumb to temptation and join in the commission of delinquent acts. Control processes exerted by interested adults, as well as pressures from peers to be delinquent, operate in any setting; and reasonable theories should acknowledge the presence of both factors (Rivera and Short, 1967).

To deal with these issues while reflecting the social character of delinquency, other theorists, some of whom were contemporaries of Shaw and McKay, proceeded in one of two directions. Those in the first group continued to suggest that delinquency is largely a group phenomenon but discarded the notion that it is the function of any particular class culture. Instead, they suggested that it can occur on any class level in response to learning and reinforcement in small groups. This kind of theory will be discussed in the next chapter. Those in the second group followed the lead of Shaw and McKay by suggesting that delinquency is predominantly a lower-class phenomenon. But rather than theorizing that it arises in cultural isolation from middle-class values and beliefs, members of this group have suggested that delinquent acts result from the attractiveness and pursuit of those values. This is called **strain theory** and will be reviewed in Chapter 10.

DISCUSSION QUESTIONS

1. You are a young Chicago sociologist in 1926, and you hear the following statements by a politician:

   "The [name any immigrant group] are ruining America. They are dirty and sexually promiscuous. They have too many children, and they can't control them. They don't know how to live in the American way. They don't save money; they don't teach their kids any manners or send them to school. It's no wonder there's so much juvenile delinquency today. The only solution is to put them all away somewhere. They are simply a menace to society."

   Given your familiarity with the work of Clifford Shaw and Henry McKay, what would you say in response to the politician's statements?
2. What impact has the work of Shaw and McKay had on social policy in the United States?
3. Do you agree or disagree with Bayard Rustin's claim that "the future advancement of blacks and other poor in this country has very little to do with the color of their skin"?
4. How does Walter Miller's cultural deviance theory differ from that of Shaw and McKay?

5. Based on your own experiences, how does the youth subculture separate adolescents and adults?

REFERENCES

Agnew, Robert. 1985. "Social Control Theory and Delinquency: A Longitudinal Test." *Criminology* 23 (February):47–61.

Anderson, Elijah. 1994. "The Code of the Streets." *The Atlantic Monthly* (May), pp. 81–94.

Association of Black Sociologists. 1978. "ABS Statement Assails Book by Wilson." *Footnotes.* Washington, D.C.: American Sociological Association.

Bengston, Vern L., Michael J. Furlong, and Robert S. Laufer. 1974. "Time, Aging, and the Continuity of Social Structure: Themes and Issues in Generational Analysis." *Journal of Social Issues* 30:1–30.

Berger, Bennett M. 1963. "Adolescence and Beyond: An Essay Review of Three Books on the Problems of Growing Up." *Social Problems* 10 (Spring):394–408.
1971. *Looking for America: Essays on Youth, Suburbia, and Other American Obsessions.* Englewood Cliffs, N.J.: Prentice-Hall.

Bloch, Herbert A., and Arthur Niederhoffer. 1958. *The Gang: A Study in Adolescent Behavior.* New York: Philosophical Library.

Bohlke, Robert H. 1961. "Social Mobility, Stratification Inconsistency and Middle Class Delinquency." *Social Problems* 8 (Spring):351–363.

Bordua, David J. 1961. "Delinquent Subcultures: Sociological Interpretations of Gang Delinquency." *Annals of the American Academy of Political and Social Science* 338 (November): 119–136.

Brown, Claude. 1965. *Manchild in the Promised Land.* New York: Macmillan.

Bursik, Robert J., Jr. 1988. "Social Disorganization and Theories of Crime and Delinquency: Problems and Prospects." *Criminology* 26 (November): 519–551.

Bursik, Robert J., Jr., and Harold G. Grasmick. 1993. *Neighborhoods and Crime: The Dimensions of Effective Community Control.* New York: Lexington Books.

Bursik, Robert J., Jr., and Jim Webb. 1982. "Community Change and Patterns of Delinquency." *American Journal of Sociology* 88 (July):24–42.

Caplow, Theodore, Howard M. Bahr, Bruce A. Chadwick, Reuben Hill, and Margaret H. Williamson. 1982. *Middletown Families: Fifty Years of Change and Continuity.* Minneapolis: University of Minnesota Press.

Cohen, Albert K. 1955. *Delinquent Boys: The Culture of the Gang.* New York: Free Press.
1967. "Middle-Class Delinquency and the Social Structure." Pp. 203–207 in Edmund W. Vaz, ed., *Middle-Class Juvenile Delinquency.* New York: Harper & Row.

Cohen, Albert, Alfred Lindesmith, and Karl Schuessler, eds. 1956. *The Sutherland Papers.* Bloomington: Indiana University Press.

Coleman, James S. 1961. *The Adolescent Society: The Social Life of the Teenager and Its Impact on Education.* New York: Free Press.
1974. *Youth: Transition to Adulthood.* Chicago: University of Chicago Press.

Davis, Kingsley. 1944. "Adolescence and the Social Structure." *Annals of the American Academy of Political and Social Science* 236 (November): 8–16.

Derber, Charles. 1996. *The Wilding of America: How Greed and Violence Are Eroding Our Nation's Character.* New York: St. Martin's Press.

Elkin, Frederick, and William A. Westley. 1955. "The Myth of Adolescent Culture." *American Sociological Review* 20 (December):680–684.

Elliott, Delbert S., William Julius Wilson, David Huizinga, Robert J. Sampson, Amanda Elliott, and Bruce Rankin. 1996. "The Effects of Neighborhood Disadvantage on Adolescent Development." *Journal of Research in Crime and Delinquency* 33 (November):389–426.

Empey, LaMar T. 1973. "Juvenile Justice Reform: Diversion, Due Process, and Deinstitutional-ization." Pp. 13–48 in Lloyd E. Ohlin, ed., *Prisoners in America.* Englewood Cliffs, N.J.: Prentice-Hall.

England, Ralph W. 1960. "A Theory of Middle Class Juvenile Delinquency." *Journal of Criminal Law, Criminology and Police Science* 50 (March–April): 535–540.

Erickson, Maynard L. 1971. "The Group Context of Delinquent Behavior." *Social Problems* 19 (Summer):114–129.
1973a. "Group Violations and Official Delinquency: The Group Hazard Hypothesis." *Criminology* 11 (August):127–160.
1973b. "Group Violations, Socioeconomic Status and Official Delinquency." *Social Forces* 52 (September):41–52.

Erickson, Maynard L., and Gary F. Jensen. 1977. "'Delinquency Is Still Group Behavior!': Toward Revitalizing the Group Premise in the Sociology of Deviance." *Journal of Criminal Law and Criminology* 68 (June):262–273.

Eynon, Thomas G., and Walter C. Reckless. 1961. "Companionship at Delinquency Onset." *British Journal of Criminology* 2 (October): 162–170.

Feather, Norman T. 1980. "Values in Adolescence." Pp. 247–294 in Joseph Adelson, ed., *Handbook of Adolescent Psychology.* New York: Wiley.

Finestone, Harold. 1976. *Victims of Change: Juvenile Delinquents in American Society.* Westport, Conn.: Greenwood Press.

Flacks, Richard. 1971. *Youth and Social Change.* New York: Markham.

Gillis, John R. 1974. *Youth and History.* New York: Academic Press.

Giordano, Peggy C. 1978. "Girls, Guys, and Gangs: The Changing Social Context of Female Delinquency." *Journal of Criminal Law and Criminology* 69 (Spring):126–132.

Giordano, Peggy C., Stephen A. Cernkovich, and M. D. Pugh. 1986. "Friendships and Delinquency." *American Journal of Sociology* 91 (March):1170–1202.

Glaser, Daniel. 1971. *Social Deviance.* Chicago: Markham.

Glass, Jennifer, Vern L. Bengtson, and Charlotte C. Dunham. 1986. "Attitude Similarity in Three-Generation Families: Socialization, Status Inheritance, or Reciprocal Influence?" *American Sociological Review* 51 (October):685–698.

Glueck, Sheldon, and Eleanor Glueck. 1952. *Delinquents in the Making: Paths to Prevention.* New York: Harper.

Green, Arnold W. 1952. *Sociology: An Analysis of Life in Modern Society.* New York: McGraw-Hill.

Greenberger, Ellen, and Laurence Steinberg. 1986. *When Teenagers Work: The Psychological and Social Costs of Adolescent Employment.* New York: Basic Books.

Gutman, Herbert G. 1976. *The Black Family in Slavery and Freedom, 1750–1925.* New York: Pantheon Books.

Hagan, John. 1991. "Destiny and Drift: Subcultural Preferences, Status Attainments, and the Risks and Rewards of Youth." *American Sociological Review* 56 (October):567–582.

Hill, Reuben. 1970. *Family Development in Three Generations: A Longitudinal Study of Changing Family Patterns of Planning and Achievement.* Cambridge, Mass.: Schenkman.

Hindelang, Michael J. 1971. "The Social Versus Solitary Nature of Delinquent Involvements." *British Journal of Criminology* 11 (April):167–175.
1973. "Causes of Delinquency: A Partial Replication and Extension." *Social Problems* 20 (Spring): 471–487.

Hirschi, Travis. 1969. *Causes of Delinquency.* Berkeley: University of California Press.

Jensen, Gary F., and Maynard L. Erickson. 1976. "Peer Commitment and Delinquent Conduct: New Tests of Old Hypotheses." Unpublished paper. Tucson: University of Arizona.

Kandel, Denise B., and Gerald S. Lesser. 1972. *Youth in Two Worlds: United States and Denmark.* San Francisco: Jossey-Bass.

Klein, Malcolm W. 1995. *The American Street Gang: Its Nature, Prevalence, and Control.* New York: Oxford University Press.

Klein, Malcolm W., and Lois Y. Crawford. 1967. "Groups, Gangs, and Cohesiveness." *Journal of Research in Crime and Delinquency* 4 (January): 63–75.

Kobrin, Solomon. 1959. "The Chicago Area Project—A 25-Year Assessment." *Annals of the American Academy of Political and Social Science* 322 (March):20–29.
1971. "The Formal Logical Properties of the Shaw–McKay Delinquency Theory." Pp. 101–132 in Harwin L. Voss and David M. Peterson, eds., *Ecology, Crime, and Delinquency.* New York: Appleton-Century-Crofts.

Kobrin, Solomon, Joseph Puntil, and Emil Peluso. 1967. "Criteria of Status Among Street Groups." *Journal of Research in Crime and Delinquency* 4 (January):98–118.

Kornhauser, Ruth R. 1978. *Social Sources of Delinquency: An Appraisal of Analytic Models.* Chicago: University of Chicago Press.

Kvaraceus, William, and Walter B. Miller. 1967. "Norm-Violating Behavior in Middle-Class Culture." Pp. 233–241 in Edmund W. Vaz, ed., *Middle-Class Juvenile Delinquency.* New York: Harper & Row.

Liska, Allen E., and Mark D. Reed. 1985. "Ties to Conventional Institutions and Delinquency: Estimating Reciprocal Effects." *American Sociological Review* 50 (August):547–560.

Lundman, Richard J. 1984. *Prevention and Control of Juvenile Delinquency.* New York: Oxford University Press.

Massey, James L., and Marvin D. Krohn. 1986. "A Longitudinal Examination of an Integrated Social Process Model of Deviant Behavior." *Social Forces* 65 (September):106–134.

Miller, Walter B. 1958. "Lower Class Culture as a Generating Milieu of Gang Delinquency." *Journal of Social Issues* 14:5–19.
1959. "Implications of Urban Lower-Class Culture

for Social Work." *Social Service Review* 33 (September):219–236.

Morash, Merry. 1983. "Gangs, Groups, and Delinquency." *British Journal of Criminology* 23 (October):309–335.
1986. "Gender, Peer Group Experiences, and Seriousness of Delinquency." *Journal of Research in Crime and Delinquency* 23 (February):43–67.

Morris, Norval, and Gordon Hawkins. 1970. *The Honest Politician's Guide to Crime Control.* Chicago: University of Chicago Press.

Moynihan, Daniel P. 1965. *The Negro Family: The Case for National Action.* Washington, D.C.: Office of Policy Planning and Research, U.S. Department of Labor.

National Commission on Law Observance and Enforcement. 1931. *Report on the Causes of Crime.* No. 13, Vol. 2. Washington, D.C.: U.S. Government Printing Office.

Parsons, Talcott. 1942. "Age and Sex in the Social Structure of the United States." *American Sociological Review* 7 (October):604–616.
1950. "Psychoanalysis and the Social Structure." *Psychoanalytic Quarterly* 19 (July):371–384.

Polk, Kenneth, and Solomon Kobrin. 1972. *Delinquency Prevention Through Youth Development.* Washington, D.C.: U.S. Government Printing Office.

President's Commission on Law Enforcement and Administration of Justice. 1967. *The Challenge of Crime in a Free Society.* Washington, D.C.: U.S. Government Printing Office.

Reiss, Albert J., Jr. 1986. "Co-Offender Influences on Criminal Careers." Pp. 121–160 in Alfred Blumstein et al., eds., *Criminal Careers and "Career Criminals,"* Vol. 2. Washington, D.C.: National Academy Press.

Richards, Pamela, Richard A. Berk, and Brenda Forster. 1979. *Crime as Play: Delinquency in a Middle Class Suburb.* Cambridge, Mass.: Ballinger.

Rivera, Ramon J., and James F. Short, Jr. 1967. "Significant Adults, Caretakers, and Structures of Opportunity: An Exploratory Study." *Journal of Research in Crime and Delinquency* 4 (January):76–97.

Sampson, Robert J. 1987. "Urban Black Violence: The Effect of Male Joblessness and Family Disruption." *American Journal of Sociology* 93 (September):348–382.

Sampson, Robert J., and W. Byron Groves. 1989. "Community Structure and Crime: Testing Social-Disorganization Theory." *American Journal of Sociology* 94 (January):774–802.

Sampson, Robert J., Stephen W. Raudenbush, and Felton Earls. 1997. "Neighborhoods and Violent Crime: A Multilevel Study of Collective Efficacy." *Science* 277 (August):918–924.

Schwartz, Gary. 1987. *Beyond Conformity or Rebellion: Youth and Authority in America.* Chicago: University of Chicago Press.

Schwendinger, Herman, and Julia S. Schwendinger. 1985. *Adolescent Subcultures and Delinquency.* New York: Praeger.

Scott, Joseph W., and Edmund W. Vaz. 1967. "A Perspective on Middle-Class Delinquency." Pp. 207–222 in Edmund W. Vaz, ed., *Middle-Class Juvenile Delinquency.* New York: Harper & Row.

Shaw, Clifford R. 1929. *Delinquency Areas: A Study of the Geographic Distribution of School Truants, Juvenile Delinquents, and Adult Offenders in Chicago.* Chicago: University of Chicago Press.
1931. *The Natural History of a Delinquent Career.* Chicago: University of Chicago Press.
1938. *Brothers in Crime.* Chicago: University of Chicago Press.
1966. *The Jack-Roller: A Delinquent Boy's Own Story.* Chicago: University of Chicago Press.

Shaw, Clifford R., and Henry D. McKay. 1931. *Social Factors in Juvenile Delinquency: A Study of the Community, the Family, and the Gang in Relation to Delinquent Behavior.* Report of the National Commission on Law Observance and Enforcement (Wickersham Commission). No. 13, Vol. 2. Washington, D.C.: U.S. Government Printing Office.
1942. *Juvenile Delinquency and Urban Areas: A Study of Rates of Delinquents in Relation to Differ-*

ential Characteristics of Local Communities in American Cities. Chicago: University of Chicago Press.

1969. *Juvenile Delinquency and Urban Areas: A Study of Rates of Delinquency in Relation to Differential Characteristics of Local Communities in American Cities,* rev. ed. Chicago: University of Chicago Press.

Short, James F., Jr., and Fred L. Strodtbeck. 1965. *Group Process and Gang Delinquency.* Chicago: University of Chicago Press.

Simmons, Roberta G., and Dale A. Blyth. 1987. *Moving into Adolescence: The Impact of Pubertal Change and Social Context.* New York: Aldine de Gruyter.

Smith, Douglas A., and Raymond Paternoster. 1987. "The Gender Gap in Theories of Deviance: Issues and Evidence." *Journal of Research in Crime and Delinquency* 24 (May):140–172.

Snodgrass, Jon. 1976. "Clifford R. Shaw and Henry D. McKay: Chicago Criminologists." *British Journal of Criminology* 16 (January):1–19.

Starr, Jerold M. 1986. "American Youth in the 1980s." *Youth and Society* 17 (June):323–345.

Steinberg, Laurence. 1996. *Beyond the Classroom: Why School Reform Has Failed and What Parents Need to Do.* New York: Simon & Schuster.

Thrasher, Frederic M. 1927. *The Gang: A Study of 1,313 Gangs in Chicago.* Chicago: University of Chicago Press.

Toby, Jackson. 1957. "Social Disorganization and Stake in Conformity: Complementary Factors in the Predatory Behavior of Hoodlums." *Journal of Criminal Law, Criminology and Police Science* 48 (May–June):12–17.

Warr, Mark. 1996. "Organization and Instigation in Delinquent Groups." *Criminology* 34 (February): 11–37.

Whyte, William F. 1943. *Street Corner Society: The Social Structure of an Italian Slum.* Chicago: University of Chicago Press.

Whyte, William H., Jr. 1956. *The Organization Man.* New York: Simon & Schuster.

Wiatrowski, Michael D., David B. Griswold, and Mary K. Roberts. 1981. "Social Control Theory and Delinquency." *American Sociological Review* 46 (October):525–541.

Williams, Robin M., Jr. 1952. *American Society: A Sociological Interpretation.* New York: Knopf.

Wilson, William J. 1978. *The Declining Significance of Race: Blacks and Changing American Institutions.* Chicago: University of Chicago Press. 1987. *The Truly Disadvantaged: The Inner City, the Underclass, and Public Policy.* Chicago: University of Chicago Press.

Zimring, Franklin E. 1981. "Kids, Groups and Crime: Some Implications of a Well-Known Secret." *Journal of Criminal Law and Criminology* 72 (Fall):867–885.

DIFFERENTIAL ASSOCIATION AND SOCIAL LEARNING THEORISTS POSTULATE THAT DELINQUENCY RESULTS FROM ASSOCIATION IN DELINQUENT GROUPS.

CHAPTER NINE

DIFFERENTIAL ASSOCIATION THEORY AND SOCIAL LEARNING THEORY

This chapter covers several related theories about delinquency. We first will consider the **theory of differential association** and **drift-neutralization theory,** which are rooted in **symbolic interactionist theory.** Next, we will turn our attention to **social learning theory** and its origins in **learning theory** in psychology.

SYMBOLIC INTERACTIONIST THEORY

Symbolic interactionist theory is not limited to explaining delinquent behavior; instead, it is a theory about human behavior in general. According to symbolic interactionists, **human nature** and **social order** are opposite sides of the same coin. Neither is permanent; both are flexible and subject to change. On the one hand, people constantly are being modified, taking on the expectations and viewpoints of those with whom they interact in small, intimate groups. On the other hand, people contribute to the process of change, helping to shape the groups of which they are part.

Because people participate in intimate groups in different settings, the roles they play often will be inconsistent and conflicting. For example, a high school boy who is known to his friends as a party animal probably will not play the same kind of role at home. The self-concept and rationalizations that make such a role acceptable in one group of intimates do not make it acceptable in another.

This is an important point because it not only implies a human nature that is flexible but suggests that the social order is contradictory: All people are exposed to deviant as well as conformist traditions. Whether youngsters commit delinquent acts depends on the kinds of groups in which they participate. If one or more of the groups includes delinquents, it may provide a person with all the justifications he or she needs for violating the law. If none of the groups includes delinquents, he or she will be more likely to conform to the law.

Delinquency originally was explained in this way by Edwin Sutherland in 1939 in his differential association theory. Symbolic interactionist theory, however, owes its origins to Charles Horton Cooley and George Herbert Mead. Whereas Cooley emphasized the interactional element in symbolic interactionism, Mead stressed the symbolic element.

Cooley: The Interactional Element

Cooley (1902:157–169) concluded from observations of his own children that humans begin to develop a self-image very early in life. He believed that this image is not something with which a child is born; rather, it results from involvement and communication with others. It emerges first as the result of interaction in the family; later, it is developed in play groups, the school, and other social settings.

Cooley (1902:151–153) used an interesting metaphor to illustrate the importance of interactions. He likened the responses of others to a mirror. Just as we can look in the mirror and be pleased or displeased with what we see, we also can see the way people respond to us and judge ourselves in those terms. We develop what Cooley called the *looking-glass self.* We imagine how others perceive our appearance, clothes, manners, and behaviors, and we evaluate ourselves accordingly. If the reflection appears to be favorable, we are pleased; if it appears to be unfavorable, we are mortified and attempt to change our image. This image is a social product, the result of others' responses to us.

Mead: The Symbolic Element

Mead stressed the importance of symbols as the basis for human interaction and communication (Strauss, 1964:127–132, 154–162). A *symbol* acts as a shorthand way of representing something else—an idea, a person, an object, a thing. Some symbols are very complex. The single word **culture,** for example, is used to represent the total way of life of a people—their beliefs, knowledge, values, technology, tastes, and prejudices.

Mead was concerned with symbols because they can become language; and language is essential for communication (Strauss, 1964:187–196, 199–209). Other animals communicate on a primitive level, but only through language can humans acquire a self-concept, engage in systematic thought, or handle complex and abstract ideas. Language, therefore, becomes the means by which a child's view of the world is constructed (Strauss, 1964:209–228).

Like Cooley, Mead also believed that the self is not a fixed entity, but rather is flexible and subject to change. At the same time, he was unclear on just how flexible the self is. According to one interpretation, Mead saw the self mainly, not as a structure but as a process—something that is constantly being shaped and reshaped, something that is never cast into a permanent mold (Blumer, 1969:62–64). According to a second interpretation, however, Mead considered the self to be both a process *and* a structure; it has some stability and is not entirely flexible, but rather is the result of the accumulation of one's experiences and recent social interactions. Although the self changes, it also develops a structure of attitudes and perspectives that are relatively permanent and move with a person from group to group (Strauss, 1964:199–246).

This is an important issue in trying to understand human behavior: If the self is entirely flexible, then we can understand what people do only by looking at their immediate situations, who is present, and how the interaction of the moment results in a particular outcome. If, by contrast, the self is both a process and a structure, to understand people's behavior we would have to be concerned with both the outcomes of their interactions with others and their relatively permanent attitudes and perspectives.

DIFFERENTIAL ASSOCIATION THEORY

Edwin Sutherland's theory of delinquency directly reflected the thinking of theorists like Cooley and Mead. He favored their points of view over those of biological and psychodynamic control theorists, toward whom he was an ardent and persuasive antagonist.

The Postulates of Differential Association Theory

Sutherland's differential association theory of delinquency consists of nine postulates that have remained unchanged since the fourth edition of his book *Principles of Criminology* was published in 1947, three years before his death. Later statements by Donald Cressey, Sutherland's student and co-author, helped to clarify the postulates, which are as follows (Sutherland and Cressey, 1974:75–77):

1. *Criminal behavior is learned.* People are not inherently antisocial. If young people violate the law, it is because they have learned to do it.
2. *Criminal behavior is learned in interaction with other persons in a process of communication.* "What . . . we should study if we are going to establish a theory for explaining criminal conduct is, in a word, *words*" (Cressey, 1965:90). Lawbreaking requires motives and justifications, and those are supplied by language. The learning of deviant values, attitudes, norms, and techniques causes a young person to commit delinquent acts.
3. *The principal part of the learning of criminal behavior occurs within intimate personal groups.*

MEDIA EFFECTS ON VIOLENCE

According to Sutherland, delinquent behavior is caused mainly by association in intimate groups, not by exposure to such impersonal sources of learning as movies and newspapers. Even if Sutherland was correct when he formulated his theory in the first half of the 1900s, is he still correct today? After all, he never could have anticipated the technological advances in the last half of the 1900s—television, cable systems, and videocassette recorders, for example—and their importance in our lives.

In a recent review of the evidence on whether the viewing of media violence causes violent behavior, Felson (1996:123) concludes that there is probably a small effect. However, those effects are "weak and affect only a small percentage of viewers." Felson (1996:123) goes on to say that it is "unlikely that media violence is a significant factor in high crime rates in this country."

We soon will review evidence that association in intimate groups plays a much more important part in causing delinquency. Hence, Sutherland appears to have been correct in postulating that impersonal sources of learning are relatively unimportant, and this holds even in our current media-saturated environment.

"The person (personality) is not separable from the social relationships in which [the person] lives. . . . Criminal behavior is, like other behaviors, attitudes, beliefs, and values which a person exhibits, the *property of groups,* not of individuals" (Cressey, 1965:90). Such impersonal sources of learning as movies and newspapers are relatively unimportant. Although they might provide some motivation to violate the law, that motivation is not likely to be acted upon unless it receives the support of an intimate group of associates.

4. *When criminal behavior is learned, the learning includes (1) techniques of committing the crime, which are sometimes very complicated and sometimes very simple, and (2) the specific direction of motives, drives, rationalizations, and attitudes.* People do not become dancers, schoolteachers, sociologists, or quarterbacks until they learn the necessary techniques. The same is true of delinquents. It takes training to hot-wire a car, become a successful shoplifter, or even smoke marijuana properly. Even more important, lawbreaking requires appropriate motives, rationalizations, and attitudes. These are derived from group definitions that make delinquency acceptable: "Everybody cheats—why shouldn't we?" "What your parents don't know won't hurt them." "Stealing from a crooked company like this is no crime." "Those guys had it coming to them." Delinquency is not likely to occur without those kinds of rationalizations. "It is the presence or absence of a specific, learned, verbal label in a specific situation which determines the criminality or noncriminality of a particular person" (Cressey, 1952:52).

5. *The specific direction of motives and drives is learned from definitions of the legal codes as favorable or unfavorable.* Sutherland (1956:20–21) labeled his theory *differential association* because he believed that the social order is characterized by normative conflict. People associate in groups that put them in contact with norms that favor conformity to law and with norms that encourage lawbreaking. This is differential association—individuals are confronted with mixed definitions of behavior, some conformist and some deviant. The extent to which young people commit delinquent acts, and even the types of delinquent acts they commit, depends on what they learn from the particular groups they encounter

and how those groups define **law-violating behavior.** If they define it unfavorably, a person will be motivated to obey the law. If they define it favorably, the person will be more motivated to violate the law.

6. *A person becomes delinquent because of an excess of definitions favorable to violation of law over definitions unfavorable to violation of law.* According to this postulate, young people commit delinquency when their contacts with delinquent patterns exceed their contacts with nondelinquent patterns. Some young people are almost completely isolated from nondelinquent groups and definitions. Hence, they are likely to commit delinquent behavior because there is nothing to counter the delinquent values and beliefs in their groups.

7. *Differential associations may vary in frequency, duration, priority, and intensity.* These four properties condition the effects of association in different groups. Sutherland did not explain them well, but, presumably, *frequency* refers to how often a person associates in delinquent groups, and *duration* refers to the length of the associations. The greater the frequency and duration of a youngster's delinquent associations, the more likely he or she is to commit delinquent acts. *Priority,* meanwhile, concerns the time in life when delinquent associations begin: The earlier they begin, the more likely they are to persist. Finally, *intensity* "has to do with such things as the prestige of the source of a criminal or anticriminal pattern and with emotional reactions related to the associations" (Sutherland and Cressey, 1974:76). If a group favoring law-violating behavior has high prestige and is emotionally satisfying to its members, they are more likely to commit delinquent acts.

8. *The process of learning criminal behavior by association with criminal and anticriminal patterns involves the same mechanisms as any other learning.* Sutherland considered the meaning of this postulate to be self-evident: The same mechanisms involved in learning nondelinquent behavior—rewards, punishments, imitation, coercion, or a search for self-acceptance—are involved in learning delinquent behavior.

9. *Although criminal behavior is an expression of general needs and values, it is not explained by those general needs and values, because non-criminal behavior is an expression of the same needs and values.* The pursuit of money, success, and prestige does not help to explain delinquent behavior. As Sutherland and Cressey (1974:76–77) put it:

> Thieves generally steal in order to secure money, but likewise honest laborers work in order to secure money. The attempts by many scholars to explain criminal behavior by general drives and values, such as the happiness principle, striving for social status, the money motive, or frustration, have been, and must continue to be, futile, since they explain lawful behavior as completely as they explain criminal behavior.

In other words, it is not the desire to be successful, therefore, that causes delinquency; rather, it is the delinquent motives and rationalizations, learned in intimate groups, that justify the pursuit of money and prestige through illegal means.

Implications for and Impact on Social Policy

In contrast to **control theories** (see Chapter 7), Sutherland's differential association theory suggests that people may be easily affected by others. They are not cast into biological or psychological molds that are impervious to outside influence. Instead, they are malleable. If one wants to reduce delinquency, moreover, one does not have to change an entire community or society, as **cultural deviance theory** suggests (see Chapter 8). The main task is to pay attention to the intimate groups in which children associate and ensure that prosocial values constantly are taught and reinforced.

Despite those potentially critical implications, Sutherland said relatively little about them, leaving it to Cressey (1954, 1955, 1965) to elaborate. According to Cressey, separate detention centers and correctional institutions for delinquents can only become *schools of crime*, causing even more serious delinquent behavior, because the delinquents confined in them will associate only with other delinquents.

If we want them to become nondelinquents, there are two alternatives. First, delinquents and nondelinquents could be integrated in noninstitutional settings, not kept apart. Delinquents could learn from nondelinquents that it is wrong to violate the law. Cressey, however, seemed to prefer a second alternative—using delinquents to change delinquents. Cressey thought that efforts to integrate delinquents with nondelinquents would be impractical. Many people would not stand for it, fearing that good children would be corrupted by bad ones rather than the reverse. In addition, Cressey believed that compared to such professionals as social workers, group therapists, and probation officers, delinquents actually would be more effective in changing each other because they share a better rapport with each other and trust each other more. Even more important, if delinquent behavior results from deviant motives, values, and rationalizations acquired in intimate groups of delinquents, then those groups should be used to change that behavior.

Cressey (1955:119) referred to the process by which delinquents attempt to change other delinquents as **retroflexive reformation.** If delinquents are serious in their attempts to reform others, their membership in the reformation group will cause them to become alienated from their former, delinquent groups. A good example of a setting in which this is presumed to occur is Alcoholics Anonymous, which depends on alcoholics, not professionals, to reform other alcoholics.

The principles of differential association theory, according to Cressey, have not been applied widely because correctional programs have been based more on other theories of delinquency, especially (1) **classical deterrence theory,** which suggests that legal punishment will deter law-violating behavior, and (2) **psychodynamic theory,** which stresses individualized treatment. Even when **group therapy** has been used, leaders have been concerned more with changing the psychological makeup of group members than with changing their values and rationalizations. Psychodynamics are stressed, and the individual is treated *in* the group rather than *through* it.

EXPERIMENTAL PROGRAMS Although the principles of differential association theory have not been applied widely, they have been used in small, experimental programs, such as the **Highfields project** (McCorkle, Elias, and Bixby, 1958), **the Provo experiment** (Empey and Erickson, 1972), and the **Silverlake experiment** (Empey and Lubeck, 1971b). All of those programs were organized and run by adults, but they gave considerable power to the delinquent groups to make decisions and enforce norms.

A boy in the Provo experiment expressed support for Cressey's belief that delinquents are more likely to be changed by each other than by professionals:

> BOY: Boys know more about themselves than grownups do. The first couple months [in this program] don't do any good. Then you find out that the meetin' knows you better than you know yourself. They can tell when you're lyin'. They can tell you things about yourself, an' find out what your problems are. . . . I jus' don't like to listen to adults lecturing . . . it is boring as hell. All the help I got, I got from other guys in the meetin'—nine other guys instead of one stupid adult talkin' to you. I felt they done the same things I done, an' know exactly how I feel, an' why I do them things. (Empey and Erickson, 1972:58, 61)

There also was support for Cressey's confidence in the principles of differential association as a way of producing change:

> BOY: I mentioned that being locked up won't help a guy out of trouble. Understanding why you got there might, but the jail itself won't. You have to get the understanding, an' that comes in the group meeting.
> ADULT: Looking back, did the boys in your group do anything that helped you?
> BOY: They helped me most when they put me in jail for not showin' up. When I got out, I said I wanted to get drunk that night an' the meeting talked to me about it.
> ADULT: How did that help?
> BOY: Well, for one thing, I didn't go out an' get drunk. They talked to me quite a bit. They pointed out to me I was playing a tough role, an' that going on a blast now was the same ol' thing with me.

> ADULT: So what happened?
> BOY: I can't say I was a goodie-goodie right off, but one thing that stuck with me was when they showed me that how I was acting was the way I was talking and treating my mother and my girl. I was being an ass. I thought a lot of my girl an' I saw I was only makin' things worse not better. Her ol' man don't like me anyhow, an' what I wanted to do [get drunk] wouldn't help. (Empey and Erickson, 1972:57)

Besides impressionistic comments like these, systematic research also has indicated that group-centered programs produce a strong commitment to correctional goals. Compared to individualistic programs, members of group-centered programs are less likely to split into competing adult and delinquent groups and are more likely to reinforce antidelinquent values and points of view (Shichor and Empey, 1974). Yet, despite such findings, there is also evidence that the principles of differential association theory are a far cry from a panacea.

PROGRAM LIMITATIONS Programs that develop strong antidelinquent groups often are unable to hold onto many potential members. Thirty-seven percent of the delinquents in the Silverlake experiment ran away, most of them during the first month or two of residence (Empey and Lubeck, 1971b:Chap. 10). Many of them, therefore, persisted in their old patterns of behavior and did not readily accept prosocial values from their peers.

Likewise, group-centered programs may not be very successful in inducing delinquents to refrain from new offenses. Approximately 60 percent of the delinquents in the Provo and Silverlake experiments had no arrests after being released for one year, and about 80 percent had no more than one arrest (Empey and Erickson, 1972:Chaps. 9–10; Empey and Lubeck, 1971b:255). Their commission of serious offenses also decreased markedly following their release. Yet, when the delinquents in the two experiments were compared with control groups of delinquents assigned to regular probation or traditional places of incarceration, their postprogram success rates were not markedly greater. The only time they committed significantly less delinquency was when

PEER GROUP PREVENTION PROGRAMS AND DELINQUENCY

Findings that youths who commit delinquent acts tend to associate in delinquent groups have led to the development of positive peer group prevention programs. Consistent with both differential association and social learning theories, these programs have been based on the assumption that "if affiliating with negative role models encourages the development of deviant behaviors, then sufficient exposure to positive role models might diminish the appeal of deviant friends and hence foster more conventional social ties and behaviors" (Gorman and White, 1995:138). In contrast to the Highfields, Provo, and Silverlake programs, then, positive peer group prevention programs include nondelinquents (positive peers) as participants.

In Project ALERT, for example, seventh-grade students in Oregon and California participated in teacher-led and teacher-led/peer-assisted instructional sessions about how to resist peer pressure to use drugs (Gorman and White, 1995:

140–141). After a review of the evidence, Gorman and White (1995: 138–145) conclude that such programs are largely ineffective in reducing the likelihood of delinquency; and they identify three possible reasons. First, because delinquency is a function of more than merely association in delinquent groups—parental supervision, for example, is also likely to be a factor, as we will consider in the next chapter—successful programs may need to focus on more than simply peer pressure to violate the law. Second, those youths most at risk to commit delinquent acts may not see nondelinquents as their peers and as credible sources of information about lawbreaking. Third, positive peer group prevention programs assume that association in delinquent groups precedes delinquency. To the extent that it is the other way around—that association in delinquent groups follows delinquency—these programs will not affect the causes of delinquent behavior.

---

they were still members of the antidelinquent group in the experimental program (Empey and Erickson, 1972:Chap. 5). Once removed from it, their behavior was much like that of delinquents who had never had contact with it (although a more favorable conclusion is warranted for the Provo than for the Silverlake experiment—Empey and Erickson, 1972:Chaps. 9–11; Gottfredson, 1987:675–686).

ADDITIONAL POLICY IMPLICATIONS Earlier in this chapter, it was noted that according to symbolic interactionist theory, the human self can be viewed in

two ways: (1) as nothing more than a process that undergoes constant modification or (2) as both a process and a structure in which the self retains considerable continuity. The research findings just described do not totally resolve the issue.

On the one hand, many of the delinquents in the Provo and Silverlake experiments resisted involvement in prosocial groups. They were not changed easily; their self-concepts seemed to be structured and inflexible. On the other hand, program participants were not much more inclined than nonparticipants to remain faithful to group standards once they left the programs. This finding, therefore, could be said to confirm the malleability of human nature.

It is also useful to reconsider the way Sutherland's differential association theory has been implemented, particularly taking into account Cressey's belief that delinquents are the best agents of change. Recall that the theory could just as well be interpreted as suggesting that delinquents should be separated from other delinquents and integrated into nondelinquent groups instead. What if delinquents were placed in nondelinquent groups in schools, neighborhoods, and recreation centers rather than in correctional programs? There are at least two possible outcomes. First, nondelinquents might become involved in the task of changing delinquents. Second, delinquents not only might encounter an excess of definitions unfavorable to violation of law but also might have a greater chance to participate in activities that reinforce those definitions. The evidence seems clear that words, attitudes, and rationalizations alone will not suffice. This may be particularly true for those delinquents who lack social skills, are behind in their educational development, or have no access to conventional means for success. Those factors require attention as well.

Scientific Adequacy

Differential association theory has several shortcomings, which cast doubts on its scientific adequacy. First, it does not provide a clear statement of the process by which an individual becomes delinquent. Although it stresses the existence of competing community norms and suggests that someone learns to be delinquent through excessive contact with delinquent patterns, it does not indicate how this comes about—that is, what accounts for association in delinquent groups, how delinquent behavior is learned and reinforced, and at what point definitions favorable to law violation override definitions unfavorable to it and lead to delinquent behavior.

As a result, Cressey and Ward (1969:420) suggested that Sutherland's postulates should be "viewed as a set of directives about the kinds of things that ought to be included in a theory of criminality, rather than as an actual statement of theory." His postulates may be a valuable starting point for a more precise theory, but by themselves they are not enough.

A second shortcoming is that the theory is difficult to test (Short, 1960). For example, at what point has a person been subjected to an *excess of definitions* favorable to violation of law? Even if such a determination could be made (Matsueda, 1982: 494–496; 1988:284–287), is the point the same for all people?

In the same vein, Sutherland said that "differential associations may vary in frequency, duration, priority, and intensity." Yet, he neither defined those terms carefully nor indicated how, when combined in some way, their relationship to delinquent behavior can be assessed.

Drawing on the broader theory of symbolic interactionism, differential association theory suggests that beliefs, rationalizations, and attitudes lead to delinquent behavior. However, many studies have found that beliefs and attitudes actually are poor predictors of behavior (Deutscher, 1973). Words do not always, and indeed often do not, lead to action. For example, Tittle, Burke, and Jackson (1986:426) have shown (albeit in a test of differential association theory among adults) that "attitudes/rationalizations about crime have at best a limited role with respect to . . . particular offenses." More recently, Reed and Rose (1998:261) have reported that although "peers . . . affected attitudes [of youths in the National Youth Survey], . . . attitudes did not influence [youths' serious theft behavior]" (also see Warr and Stafford, 1991).

The theory of differential association suggests that the motives for delinquent behavior result from association in delinquent groups. Other theories, by contrast, suggest that the motives, at least in part, result from other factors. Control theory emphasizes biological factors or early training; cultural deviance theory stresses social class and social organization; and still more factors are stressed by theories we have not yet considered. In each instance, something in a person's life is thought to motivate both delinquent behavior *and* association in delinquent groups, which are seen as ways of solving some problem of adjustment.

These theoretical differences are most apparent when contrasting control theory and differential association theory. Control theorists argue that association in delinquent groups occurs only *after* an individual becomes delinquent, not before (Glueck and Glueck, 1950:163–164; Hirschi, 1969:135–138). It is only then that delinquents, like birds of a feather, flock together. Their flocking is a consequence of their delinquent behavior, not the cause of it. Delinquents take up with other delinquents because they already are detached from parents and school and have nowhere else to turn for support and confirmation.

Which theory is correct—control theory or differential association theory? Much existing research suggests that neither is entirely accurate (Burkett and Warren, 1987:124–126, 128; Empey and Lubeck, 1971a:Chap. 9; Hirschi, 1969:152–158; Jensen, 1972: 568–573; LaGrange and White, 1985:27–35; Marcos, Bahr, and Johnson, 1986:148–152; Massey and Krohn, 1986:124; Patterson and Dishion, 1985:66, 74–75; Smith and Paternoster, 1987:156). Weak attachment to parents and school and association in delinquent groups make independent contributions to the commission of delinquent acts.

Research by Matsueda (1982:499–500; Matsueda and Heimer, 1987:831) is more consistent with differential association theory. Although weak attachment to parents and association in delinquent groups affect delinquency, the effects tend to be mediated by definitions favorable or unfavorable to delinquency. That is, weak attachment to parents and association in delinquent groups lead to the learning of favorable definitions of delinquent behavior, which, in turn, leads to delinquency. The *weight of evidence,* however, certainly does not provide strong support for Sutherland's theory.

As for which comes first, association in delinquent groups or delinquent behavior, several recent studies reveal a complex process. Thornberry and his colleagues (1994:69–70) report that association in delinquent groups leads to delinquent behavior but that delinquent behavior also leads to association in delinquent groups; therefore, association in delinquent groups both precedes and follows the commission of delinquent acts. Similar findings have been reported by Reed and Rose (1998:261–264).

An even more complex pattern has been reported by Elliott and Menard (1996:56), who examined the progression from conformity to the law and association in nondelinquent groups to delinquent behavior and association in delinquent groups. The most frequent pattern is (1) movement into a slightly delinquent peer group, (2) onset of minor delinquency, (3) movement into a more delinquent peer group, (4) onset of serious delinquency, and (5) movement into a predominantly delinquent peer group (also see Warr, 1993:36). There is support, then, for the pattern predicted by differential association theory—association in delinquent groups preceding delinquent behavior—*as well as* the predicted control theory pattern—association in delinquent groups following delinquent behavior.

Scientific Legacy

For several generations of sociologically oriented criminologists, Sutherland's differential association theory has been the orienting scheme around which many new theories have been formulated. Cohen (1955) and Cloward and Ohlin (1960) drew on it in constructing strain theories, which will be discussed in the next chapter. Indeed, Cloward and Ohlin (1960) expressed their indebtedness to Sutherland by dedicating their book to him.

Other criminologists have reformulated differential association theory. Daniel Glaser (1956:440–441), for example, argued that its organizing principle should be "differential identification" rather than differential association. The idea is that "a person pursues criminal behavior to the extent that he identifies himself with real or imaginary persons from whose perspective his criminal behavior seems acceptable" (Glaser, 1956:440). Because people often identify with other people or groups with whom they have little intimate contact, actual group associations are not necessary.

Other theorists, however, have done far more to amplify and reformulate the basic ideas in differential association theory. Next, we will consider the contributions of those theorists.

DRIFT–NEUTRALIZATION THEORY

David Matza and Gresham Sykes (1961; Matza, 1964: Chap. 2) argued that there is a **subculture** of delinquency in the United States but that the subculture is not limited to young people. American culture, they believed, is a mixture of conventional norms and **subterranean,** deviant traditions. Those traditions do not represent ignorance of the law or a general negation of it. Rather, they have a complex relationship to law, one that is symbiotic rather than oppositional. They do not represent a separate set of beliefs that distinguish delinquents from other youths, or youths from adults; instead, deviant traditions make up a part of the overall culture that consists of the personal, less conventional, and less publicized standards for behavior. The two sets of traditions—conventional and deviant—are held simultaneously by almost everyone, according to Matza and Sykes; and although certain groups may be influenced more by one than the other, both affect behavior to a considerable degree.

Daniel Bell's (1953) analysis of crime as an American way of life is a good illustration of Matza and Sykes's point. Bell (1953:132) noted that Americans are characterized by an "extremism" in morality; yet, they also have an "extraordinary" talent for compromise in politics and a "brawling" economic and social history. Those contradictory features form the basis for symbiotic relations between crime and politics, crime and economic growth, and crime and social change. The tradition of cheating to get ahead in school or using any means to succeed in business or politics is no less an American ethic than observing the law.

Illegal acts have been a major means by which many Americans have achieved success and respectability (Bell, 1953:152). Matza and Sykes (1961:715–718) suggested, therefore, that deviant traditions contribute more than we realize to the behavior of young as well as older people. A **delinquent subculture,** rather than being found only among youths, has its roots in the broader culture.

Situational Quality of Delinquent Behavior

Though stressing that delinquency is a product of social interaction, Matza (1964:Chap. 1) placed far less emphasis than Sutherland on the constraining influences of group relations. He considered the theory of differential association (as well as all other theories in the positivist tradition) to be too deterministic, and he called attention to the uncertain status of young people in our society. To understand their behavior, he said, it is necessary to recognize that they exist in a condition of **drift**:

The image of the delinquent I wish to convey is one of drift; an actor neither compelled nor committed to deeds nor freely choosing them; neither different in any simple or fundamental sense from the law abiding, nor the same; conforming to certain traditions in American life while partially unreceptive to other more conventional traditions. . . .

Drift stands midway between freedom and control. . . . The delinquent *transiently* exists in a limbo between convention and crime, responding in turn to the demands of each, flirting now with one, now the other, but postponing commitment, evading decision. Thus, he drifts between criminal and conventional action. (Matza, 1964:28)

Consistent with symbolic interactionist theory, Matza saw human behavior as emerging from a continuous process of interaction. But the process suggested by Matza is more fluid and open than that suggested by Sutherland. In the first place, adolescents have a modicum of choice in deciding whether to violate the law. In the second place, that choice will be determined not by some prior set of causes, but by factors present in the situation in which the choice is made—who is present, what the risks are, and so on. According to this view, then, nobody *has* to commit delinquent behavior. Whether a youth breaks the law will depend on a process that is influenced more by immediate circumstances than by conditions that are predetermined by personality, social position, or membership in a deviant subculture.

To illustrate, about twenty years ago, a young Amish family in Indiana was driving home from a party in their horse-drawn buggy. As they did, a pickup truck pulled up alongside, and someone threw a rock at them. To their horror, they discovered that it had hit their seven-month-old daughter, asleep on her mother's lap, in the head. She was dead of a fractured skull and massive brain injury (*Los Angeles Times,* March 23, 1980).

Shortly thereafter, four teenagers were picked up by the local sheriff, all of them sons of respected families, none of whom had an official record of delinquency or had been drinking alcohol or using other illegal drugs. When asked why they had thrown the rock, one replied that they simply had decided to go out and get some "clapes," a derogatory local term for the peaceful, religious Amish. When asked further why they wanted to harass clapes, another told the sheriff, "I don't even know."

As it turned out, that explanation was not entirely true. People acquainted with the four boys testified that they often bragged about "getting" the Amish; in fact, they did so every weekend as a diversion, like going to see a movie. Nonetheless, as the case unfolded, it served as a classic illustration of symbolic interactionist theory. Not only was the group commission of the act consistent with the theory, but so were the efforts by townspeople to rationalize the killing of the baby. They employed what Sykes and Matza (1957) called **techniques of neutralization**—justifications that serve to lessen the impact of, if not justify, delinquency.

According to Sykes and Matza (1957), neutralization *precedes* delinquency. However, the opposite is also possible—that neutralization occurs *after* delinquency (Hirschi, 1969:208; Minor, 1981, 1984). Indeed, Agnew (1994:572) concludes that it works both ways. Using data from the National Youth Survey to examine the effects of neutralization techniques on violent behavior, he reports that neutralization precedes violence among youths who strongly disapprove of violence. He also reports, however, that "individuals with weak conventional beliefs are more likely to try to justify their delinquency after the fact."

One technique of neutralization is to deny the responsibility of the offender. Local townspeople, for example, contended that the death of the baby was "just a matter of 'kids fooling around,' of a prank that had gone awry. Certainly, 'the boys' did not intend to kill anyone" (*Los Angeles Times*, March 23, 1980).

Similarly, moral indignation over a crime may be neutralized by transforming the victim into someone who, if not deserving injury, could be an understandable target. Although contending that the attacks on Amish people were not motivated by religious bigotry, the local sheriff said that they "just happen to be the best and easiest target. . . . In the buggies, they are a slow-moving target, and young people know they won't retaliate by chasing them or

filing charges." Indeed, if the worth of a peaceful Amish family could be lessened or denied, think how effective the neutralization might have been if applied to the town drunk or a newly arrived Iraqi family.

Other techniques of neutralization identified by Sykes and Matza (1957) might have been used—denying that real injury was done, condemning those who wanted to punish the boys, or contending that loyalty to one's friends takes precedence over loyalty to different people like the Amish—but those techniques ultimately were made unnecessary. Being pacifists, the Amish joined with other local people in suggesting that the boys should not go to jail. Instead, they recommended that the best punishment would be to require the boys to attend the baby's funeral. "We wouldn't push for jail," they said. "We just hope they never do it again."

This local drama illustrated how youths sometimes drift between conventionality and deviance. Hence, when the boys in question committed a delinquent act, it was made possible by their association in a small, intimate group and by their use of momentary justifications—"having fun," "getting some clapes," or "doing what everybody does." But rather than representing a commitment to a delinquent subculture, their lawbreaking was the result of their use of subterranean traditions in a transitory situation.

The Amish incident also illustrated the extent to which other people—law-abiding townspeople as well as lawbreakers—will resort to subterranean traditions to explain away delinquent acts. But rather than suggesting that such traditions should replace the law, these people contend that the law should not be rigorously applied *in this case*. Because it is an exception, the delinquents should be viewed not as bad people, but only as decent people who made a momentary slip.

The delinquents in the Amish incident were from a small town. However, Short and Strodtbeck (1965) reported similar findings from a study of urban delinquents. Specifically, they found that members of lower-class, urban gangs tended to hold to conventional values: "fidelity in marriage, small families, hard work and thrift, and keeping one's sons in school" (Short and Strodtbeck, 1965:250). Yet, those same gang members committed delinquent acts, dropped out of school, and lost their jobs.

Short and Strodtbeck (1965:263–264) concluded that gang members' delinquent behavior was not satisfactorily explained by irrational tendencies, neurotic drives, or a commitment to deviant values. Instead, they emphasized situational elements, such as a serious threat to the status of a gang leader, which can be avoided only by a willingness to commit a delinquent act; the advantages to be gained from committing a delinquent act, which can be realized without entailing much risk of detection; or perceived threats from outside groups, which might require an aggressive response. In most instances, delinquent acts were committed when the range of choice was narrowed because of the presence of others. But contrary to the notion that gang members always felt compelled to commit delinquent acts, some chose not to commit them, as Matza theorized, while others did.

SOCIAL LEARNING THEORY

Like symbolic interactionist theory, *learning theory* is not limited to explaining delinquent behavior. However, just as symbolic interactionist theory provided a foundation for differential association theory, learning theory has been the foundation for a social learning theory of delinquency.

There are two major versions of learning theory in psychology. The first is the **operant behavioral theory** of B. F. Skinner (1953, 1959), who argued that behavior occurs or recurs because of its reinforcing effects. A person learns the consequences of a behavior from direct experience—that is, from experiential learning—and the behavior will persist to the extent that rewards outweigh punishments.

The second version of learning theory is Albert Bandura's (1977, 1986) **cognitive learning theory,** which in many ways is more akin to symbolic interactionist theory than it is to operant behavioral theory. Many behaviorists have rejected theories that deal with thoughts and images, which are not directly observable or measurable (Platt and Prout, 1987:477–478). In contrast, thoughts and images are

central to cognitive learning theory, just as they are to symbolic interactionist theory.

Cognitive learning theory differs from operant behavioral theory in another way. Whereas operant behavioral theory focuses only on learning by direct experience, cognitive learning theory allows for the possibility that people also learn from observing others' behavior. "Imitation is seen as a result of vicarious reinforcement acquired when observing a model's behavior being rewarded" (Krohn, Massey, and Skinner, 1987:458), or at least not being punished. Cognitive learning theory, thus, recognizes both experiential and observational learning.

Impressed by the potential of differential association theory, but believing that it did not go far enough in specifying the process by which a person becomes delinquent, Ronald Akers (1985, 1997, 1998; Burgess and Akers, 1966) has reformulated differential association theory by drawing on learning theory in psychology. However, the resulting social learning theory is closer to cognitive learning theory than it is to operant behavioral theory because it includes such concepts as expected reinforcement and imitation (Akers, 1997:63).[1]

Akers does not see *social learning theory* as a competitor with differential association theory. Instead, it is a

> broader theory that retains all the differential association processes in Sutherland's theory (albeit clarified and somewhat modified) and integrates it with differential reinforcement and other principles of behavioral acquisition, continuation, and cessation. . . . But social learning theory explains criminal and delinquent behavior more thoroughly than does the original differential association theory. (Akers, 1997:62)

The Postulates of Social Learning Theory

The following postulates summarize Akers' social learning theory:[2]

---

[1]Both the theory of human behavior in general (especially the cognitive learning version) and the theory of delinquency often are referred to as social learning theory. To avoid confusion, only the theory of delinquency will be referred to here as social learning theory.

[2]The theory has been modified many times over the past three decades. The postulates, therefore, are taken from many sources, but especially Akers' (1997, 1998) most recent statements about the theory.

1. *Delinquency is learned and modified in the same way as conforming behavior.* This is a restatement of the first and eighth postulates in Sutherland's differential association theory. The likelihood of committing a delinquent act depends on a youth's learning history and the rewards and punishments for that and alternative acts.

2. *The primary learning mechanisms are differential reinforcement, in which behavior is a function of experienced and expected rewards and punishments, and imitation, in which the behavior of others and its consequences are observed and modeled.* "Differential reinforcement refers to the balance of anticipated or actual rewards and punishments that follow or are consequences of behavior" (Akers, 1998:66–67). As such, it helps to explain why a youth may commit a delinquent act rather than conform to the law:

   > The probability that an act will be committed or repeated is increased directly by rewarding outcomes . . . , for example, obtaining approval, status, money, awards, food, or pleasant feelings. This is the process of positive reinforcement. The likelihood that an action will be taken is also enhanced when the act allows the person to avoid or escape aversive or unpleasant events; this is negative reinforcement. Behavior is inhibited, reduced, or extinguished by punishment that may be direct (positive), in which painful or unpleasant consequences are attached to or result from a behavior, or indirect (negative), in which the consequence of the behavior is the removal of a reward or privilege. (Akers, 1998:68)

   Rewards and punishments vary in amount, frequency, and probability. The greater the amount, frequency, and probability of rewards for a delinquent act (as balanced against some alternative behavior), the greater the likelihood that a person will commit and repeat the act. Alternatively, the greater the amount, frequency, and probability of punishments for a delinquent act (again, as balanced against some alternative behavior), the less the likelihood that a person will commit and repeat the act.

   Imitation occurs when a person models his or her behavior on the observed behavior of others and the consequences of that observed behavior. "It is more important in the initial acquisition and performance of novel behavior than in the maintenance or cessation of behavioral patterns once established, but it continues to have some effect in maintaining behavior" (Akers, 1997:67).

3. *Rewards and punishments can be nonsocial—for example, the direct physical effects of drugs and alcohol. Most of the learning of delinquent behavior, however, involves social rewards and punishments, which tend to be highly symbolic.* Examples are the "reinforcing effects [that] come from . . . fulfilling ideological, religious, political, or other goals. Even those rewards [and punishments] that we consider to be very tangible, such as money and material possessions, gain their reinforcing worth from the symbolic . . . value they have in society" (Akers, 1998:72).

   The groups and people who "comprise or control the major sources of social reinforcement for the individual will have the greatest influence on his/her behavior" (Akers, 1998:72). Usually, those are the intimate groups in which people associate, such as families and peer groups; but unlike Sutherland, who referred *only* to learning in intimate groups, Akers (1998:72) allows for the possibility that learning also involves "secondary or more distant groups," including real and imagined people, such as those at school and work.

4. *Learning occurs in a process of differential association, which has both interactional and normative dimensions.* The interactional dimension "is the direct association and interaction with others and their conforming or deviant behavior; the [normative dimension] is the different patterns of norms and values to which an individual is exposed through association" (Akers, 1998:61). The norms and values in Akers' social learning theory are equivalent to Sutherland's definitions favorable or unfavorable to law violation. There are two classes of norms and values in the learning process. The first is the positive definitions

that define delinquent behavior as desirable or permissible; the second is the neutralizing definitions that favor delinquent behavior by justifying or excusing it, like Sykes and Matza's techniques of neutralization. Both classes of definitions—positive and neutralizing—are learned through differential reinforcement and imitation (Akers, 1997:65).

5. *Social learning is a complex process with reciprocal effects.* "Differential association with conforming and non-conforming others typically precedes the individual's committing the acts" (Akers, 1997:68). This is said to be true of association in both families and peer groups. In the case of peer groups, however, the commission of deviant acts can lead to "both the continuation of old and the seeking of new associations" (Akers, 1997:68). "One may choose interaction with others based, in part, on whether they too are involved in similar deviant criminal behavior" (Akers, 1997:69). This means that association in delinquent groups may follow the commission of delinquent acts, as well as the reverse. However, Akers (1997:69) argues that the most likely sequence of events is for association in delinquent groups to precede the onset of delinquency.

Implications for and Impact on Social Policy

Social learning theory has been used in designing a broad range of behavior modification programs for delinquents (Akers, 1997:70). Their defining characteristic has been the systematic manipulation of a person's immediate environment so as to change, or modify, his or her behavior. Some programs have attempted behavior modification by rewarding conforming behavior and punishing deviant behavior in a token economy. Points are earned for conforming behavior and lost for deviant behavior, with the points used to obtain goods (e.g., candy) and privileges (e.g., a weekend movie). Behavior modification sometimes works to decrease deviant behavior among participants in a program, but it has little effect on delinquency after a person leaves the program (Ross and McKay, 1978).

Such an outcome actually is anticipated by social learning theory. A behavior is not forever fixed, according to the theory; it can change depending on the rewards and punishments in given situations. The rewards and punishments in a behavior modification program are not likely to be the same as those outside the program. The balance of rewards and punishments that may have led a young person to violate the law in the first place is not likely to lose its potency after he or she leaves a program.

Scientific Adequacy

Much of the research on Sutherland's theory of differential association is relevant for Akers' social learning theory because "research findings supportive of differential association also support the integrated [social learning] theory" (Akers, 1997:62). Consistent with social learning theory (as well as differential association theory), many studies have found that juveniles who associate in delinquent groups learn norms and values that favor delinquency, are reinforced for delinquency and observe others' delinquency being reinforced, and then commit delinquent acts (e.g., Akers et al., 1979; Matsueda and Heimer, 1987; Reed and Rose, 1998; Warr and Stafford, 1991).

Because in social learning theory, delinquency can be learned through differential reinforcement and imitation as well as through learned definitions favorable to delinquency, Akers' delinquents do not necessarily approve of the delinquent acts they commit. According to Akers (1997:68), "acts in violation of the law can occur in the absence of any thought given to right and wrong." Consistent with such a possibility, Warr and Stafford (1991:857) have found that regardless of youths' attitudes about the rightness or wrongness of delinquency, their delinquent behavior is strongly affected by the delinquent behavior of their friends (also see Reed and Rose, 1998:261).

SUMMARY AND CONCLUSIONS

Differential association theory was instrumental in establishing a new tradition in our social construction of delinquency. It suggested that delinquent behavior is the product of learning and communication in intimate groups, not the product of biological endowment, unconscious psychological drives, or small groups of delinquents who have their own unique way of life. As a consequence, it offered new explanations of delinquent behavior, as have drift-neutralization and social learning theories.

Underlying Logic and Content of the Theories

Although Sutherland's theory of differential association does not provide an adequate description of the process by which a person becomes delinquent, it indicates that all young people are confronted with conflicting standards for behavior. Whether they commit delinquent acts will depend on the groups in which they associate. If they associate in delinquent groups, they will encounter an excess of definitions favorable to violation of law, learn techniques for committing delinquent acts, and acquire motives and rationalizations by which delinquent behavior is made possible. This sequence might be diagrammed as in figure 9.1. Matza suggests, however, that this process will provide a greater degree of choice for individ-

uals and will be more fluid and open than Sutherland suggested.

The underlying logic of social learning theory is depicted in figure 9.2. Delinquent behavior is shown to be a function of differential association, differential reinforcement, imitation, and positive and neutralizing definitions. The double arrows in figure 9.2 reflect the possibility of reciprocal effects; that is, the causes of delinquency—differential association, differential reinforcement, and positive and neutralizing definitions—can be causes and effects of one another, as well as causes and effects of delinquent behavior.

Policy Implications of the Theories

Both differential association theory and social learning theory imply that delinquent behavior can be unlearned by the same process it is learned. When the principles of the theory of differential association have been used in private, experimental programs, they have achieved only partial success. Experiments like those at Provo and Silverlake raise questions

FIGURE 9.1
The underlying logic of Sutherland's theory of differential association

FIGURE 9.2
The underlying logic of Akers' social learning theory

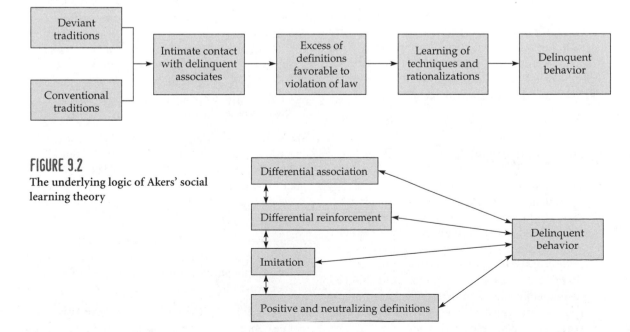

about the flexibility of the human self and suggest that more than words are needed to sustain law-abiding behavior.

When the principles of social learning theory have been applied in behavior modification programs, the results have been no better. Such an outcome, however, is anticipated by social learning theory because the rewards and punishments in a program are not the same as those outside the program.

Logical and Empirical Adequacy of the Theories

Sutherland's theory has several shortcomings: It does not provide a clear statement of the process by which a person becomes delinquent; it is difficult to test; and it probably overestimates the extent to which rationalizations and attitudes, by themselves, provide the necessary motivation for delinquent behavior. The available evidence suggests that some factors stressed by other theories also cause delinquent behavior. Even with all those shortcomings, differential association theory has had an enormous impact on the formulation of other theories, directing our attention to the possibilities that there is cultural conflict, that delinquent acts are highly situational, and that verbal definitions help both to neutralize and to enable delinquent behavior.

The findings of many studies have been consistent with social learning theory. As we will see in a later chapter, moreover, social learning theory also has had an enormous impact on the formulation of other theories, particularly theories that *integrate* social learning with other theoretical principles.

Discussion Questions

1. This chapter suggests that a shortcoming of Sutherland's differential association theory is that it is difficult to determine when a person has been subjected to an *excess of definitions* favorable to violation of law. Why is it necessary in tests of the theory to make such a determination? Why can't we use a youth's commission of delinquent behavior to determine that he or she has been subjected to an excess of definitions favorable to violation of law?

2. In your opinion, what are the reasons that media violence has only a small effect on the likelihood that viewers will commit violent acts? You might find it interesting to compare your answers to those identified by Felson (1996) in his review of the evidence on media effects on violence.

3. Based on your own experiences and on what you have read in this chapter, how does association in delinquent (or nondelinquent) groups affect the likelihood of committing delinquent acts (or conforming to the law)?

4. In what ways are Sutherland's differential association theory and Akers' social learning theory similar? How are they different?

5. Can you think of any instances in which you or someone you know may have used techniques of neutralization to justify law-violating behavior?

References

Agnew, Robert. 1994. "The Techniques of Neutralization and Violence." *Criminology* 32 (November):555–580.

Akers, Ronald L. 1985. *Deviant Behavior: A Social Learning Approach,* 3rd ed. Belmont, Calif.: Wadsworth.
1997. *Criminological Theories: Introduction and Evaluation,* 2nd ed. Los Angeles: Roxbury.
1998. *Social Learning and Social Structure: A General Theory of Crime and Deviance.* Boston: Northeastern University Press.

Akers, Ronald L., Marvin D. Krohn, Lonn Lanza-Kaduce, and Marcia Radosevich. 1979. "Social Learning and Deviant Behavior: A Specific Test of a General Theory." *American Sociological Review* 44 (August):636–655.

Bandura, Albert. 1977. *Social Learning Theory.* Englewood Cliffs, N.J.: Prentice-Hall.
1986. *Social Foundations of Thought and Action: A Social Cognitive Theory.* Englewood Cliffs, N.J.: Prentice-Hall.

Bell, Daniel. 1953. "Crime as an American Way of Life." *Antioch Review* 13 (June):131–154.

Blumer, Herbert. 1969. *Symbolic Interactionism: Perspective and Method.* Englewood Cliffs, N.J.: Prentice-Hall.

Burgess, Robert L., and Ronald L. Akers. 1966. "A Differential Association-Reinforcement Theory of Criminal Behavior." *Social Problems* 14 (Fall): 128–147.

Burkett, Steven R., and Bruce O. Warren. 1987. "Religiosity, Peer Associations, and Adolescent Marijuana Use: A Panel Study of Underlying Causal Structures." *Criminology* 25 (February):109–131.

Cloward, Richard A., and Lloyd E. Ohlin. 1960. *Delinquency and Opportunity: A Theory of Delinquent Gangs.* New York: Free Press.

Cohen, Albert K. 1955. *Delinquent Boys: The Culture of the Gang.* New York: Free Press.

Cooley, Charles H. 1902. *Human Nature and the Social Order.* New York: Scribner.

Cressey, Donald R. 1952. "Application and Verification of the Differential Association Theory." *Journal of Criminal Law, Criminology and Police Science* 43 (May–June):43–52.
1954. "Contradictory Theories in Correctional Group Therapy Programs." *Federal Probation* 18 (June):20–26.
1955. "Changing Criminals: The Application of the Theory of Differential Association." *American Journal of Sociology* 61 (September):116–120.
1965. "Theoretical Foundations for Using Criminals in the Rehabilitation of Criminals." *Key Issues* 2 (January):87–101.

Cressey, Donald R., and David A. Ward, eds. 1969. *Delinquency, Crime, and Social Process.* New York: Harper & Row.

Deutscher, Irwin. 1973. *What We Say/What We Do: Sentiments and Acts.* Chicago: Scott, Foresman.

Elliott, Delbert S., and Scott Menard. 1996. "Delinquent Friends and Delinquent Behavior: Temporal and Developmental Patterns." Pp. 28–67 in J. David Hawkins, ed., *Delinquency and Crime: Current Theories.* Cambridge: Cambridge University Press.

Empey, LaMar T., and Maynard L. Erickson. 1972. *The Provo Experiment: Evaluating Community Control of Delinquency.* Lexington, Mass.: Heath.

Empey, LaMar T., and Steven G. Lubeck. 1971a. *Explaining Delinquency: Construction, Test, and Reformulation of a Sociological Theory.* Lexington, Mass.: Heath.
1971b. *The Silverlake Experiment: Testing Delinquency Theory and Community Intervention.* Chicago: Aldine.

Felson, Richard B. 1996. "Mass Media Effects on Violent Behavior." Pp. 103–128 in John Hagan and Karen S. Cook, eds., *Annual Review of Sociology,* Vol. 22. Palo Alto, Calif.: Annual Reviews.

Glaser, Daniel. 1956. "Criminality Theories and Behavioral Images." *American Journal of Sociology* 61 (March):433–444.

Glueck, Sheldon, and Eleanor Glueck. 1950. *Unraveling Juvenile Delinquency.* New York: The Commonwealth Fund.

Gorman, D. M., and Helene Raskin White. 1995. "You Can Choose Your Friends, but Do They Choose Your Crime? Implications of Differential Association Theories for Crime Prevention Policy." Pp. 131–155 in Hugh D. Barlow, ed., *Crime and Public Policy: Putting Theory to Work.* Boulder, Colo.: Westview Press.

Gottfredson, Gary D. 1987. "Peer Group Interventions to Reduce the Risk of Delinquent Behavior: A Selective Review and a New Evaluation." *Criminology* 25 (August):671–714.

Hirschi, Travis. 1969. *Causes of Delinquency.* Berkeley: University of California Press.

Jensen, Gary F. 1972. "Parents, Peers, and Delinquent Action: A Test of the Differential Association Perspective." *American Journal of Sociology* 72 (November):562–575.

Krohn, Marvin D., James L. Massey, and William F. Skinner. 1987. "A Sociological Theory of Crime and Delinquency: Social Learning Theory." Pp. 455–475 in Edward K. Morris and Curtis J. Braukmann, eds., *Behavioral Approaches to Crime and Delinquency: A Handbook of Application, Research, and Concepts.* New York: Plenum.

LaGrange, Randy L., and Helene Raskin White. 1985. "Age Differences in Delinquency: A Test of Theory." *Criminology* 23 (February):19–45.

Marcos, Anastasios C., Stephen J. Bahr, and Richard E. Johnson. 1986. "Test of a Bonding/Association Theory of Adolescent Drug Use." *Social Forces* 65 (September):135–161.

Massey, James L., and Marvin D. Krohn. 1986. "A Longitudinal Examination of an Integrated Social Process Model of Deviant Behavior." *Social Forces* 65 (September):106–134.

Matsueda, Ross L. 1982. "Testing Control Theory and Differential Association: A Causal Modeling Approach." *American Sociological Review* 47 (August):489–504.
1988. "The Current State of Differential Association Theory." *Crime and Delinquency* 34 (July): 277–306.

Matsueda, Ross L., and Karen Heimer. 1987. "Race, Family Structure, and Delinquency: A Test of Differential Association and Social Control Theories." *American Sociological Review* 52 (December):826–840.

Matza, David. 1964. *Delinquency and Drift*. New York: Wiley.

Matza, David, and Gresham M. Sykes. 1961. "Juvenile Delinquency and Subterranean Values." *American Sociological Review* 26 (October): 712–719.

McCorkle, Lloyd W., Albert Elias, and F. Lovell Bixby. 1958. *The Highfields Story: An Experimental Treatment Project for Youthful Offenders*. New York: Holt.

Minor, W. William. 1981. "Techniques of Neutralization: A Reconceptualization and Empirical Examination." *Journal of Research in Crime and Delinquency* 18 (July):295–318.
1984. "Neutralization as a Hardening Process: Considerations in the Modeling of Change." *Social Forces* 62 (June):995–1019.

Patterson, Gerald R., and Thomas J. Dishion. 1985. "Contributions of Families and Peers to Delinquency." *Criminology* 23 (February):63–79.

Platt, Jerome J., and Maurice F. Prout. 1987. "Cognitive-Behavioral Theory and Interventions for Crime and Delinquency." Pp. 477–497 in Edward K. Morris and Curtis J. Braukmann, eds.,

Behavioral Approaches to Crime and Delinquency: A Handbook of Application, Research, and Concepts. New York: Plenum.

Reed, Mark D., and Dina R. Rose. 1998. "Doing What Simple Simon Says? Estimating the Underlying Causal Structures of Delinquent Associations, Attitudes, and Serious Theft." *Journal of Research in Crime and Delinquency* 25 (June): 240–274.

Ross, Robert R., and H. Bryan McKay. 1971. "Behavioural Approaches to Treatment in Corrections: Requiem for a Panacea." *Canadian Journal of Criminology* 20 (July):279–295.

Shichor, David, and LaMar T. Empey. 1974. "A Typological Analysis of Correctional Organizations." *Sociology and Social Research* 58 (April): 318–334.

Short, James F., Jr. 1960. "Differential Association as a Hypothesis: Problems of Empirical Testing." *Social Problems* 8 (Summer):14–25.

Short, James F., Jr., and Fred L. Strodtbeck. 1965. *Group Process and Gang Delinquency*. Chicago: University of Chicago Press.

Skinner, B. F. 1953. *Science and Human Behavior*. New York: Macmillan.
1959. *Cumulative Record*. New York: Appleton-Century-Crofts.

Smith, Douglas A., and Raymond Paternoster. 1987. "The Gender Gap in Theories of Deviance: Issues and Evidence." *Journal of Research in Crime and Delinquency* 24 (May):140–172.

Strauss, Anselm, ed. 1964. *George Herbert Mead on Social Psychology: Selected Papers*. Chicago: University of Chicago Press.

Sutherland, Edwin H. 1956. "Development of the Theory." Pp. 13–29 in Albert Cohen, Alfred Lindesmith, and Karl Schuessler, eds., *The Sutherland Papers*. Bloomington: Indiana University Press.

Sutherland, Edwin H., and Donald R. Cressey. 1974. *Criminology*, 9th ed. Philadelphia: Lippincott.

Sykes, Gresham M., and David Matza. 1957. "Techniques of Neutralization: A Theory of Delinquency." *American Sociological Review* 22 (December):664–670.

Thornberry, Terence P., Alan J. Lizotte, Marvin D. Krohn, Margaret Farnworth, and Sung Joon Jang. 1994. "Delinquent Peers, Beliefs, and Delinquent Behavior: A Longitudinal Test of Interactional Theory." *Criminology* 32 (February): 47–83.

Tittle, Charles R., Mary Jean Burke, and Elton F. Jackson. 1986. "Modeling Sutherland's Theory of Differential Association: Toward an Empirical Clarification." *Social Forces* 65 (December): 405–432.

Warr, Mark. 1993. "Age Peers and Delinquency." *Criminology* 31 (February):17–40.

Warr, Mark, and Mark Stafford. 1991. "The Influence of Delinquent Peers: What They Think or What They Do?" *Criminology* 29 (November): 851–866.

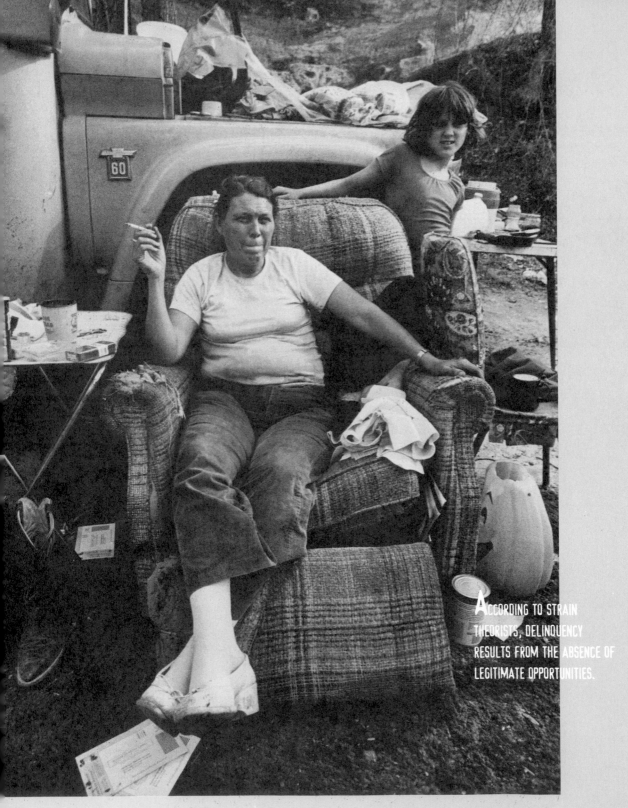

According to strain theorists, delinquency results from the absence of legitimate opportunities.

CHAPTER TEN

STRAIN THEORY

S train theory is the third major body of sociological theory about delinquency. There are several versions of strain theory. Two versions, formulated by Albert Cohen and by Richard Cloward Lloyd Ohlin in the 1950s and 1960s, draw on the earlier theories of Shaw and McKay (social disorganization theory) and Sutherland (differential association theory). A more recent version of strain theory, formulated by Robert Agnew in the 1980s and 1990s, addresses some of the shortcomings with the other two other versions.

Classic strain theory—the Cohen and Cloward–Ohlin versions—assumes that either people are inherently social at birth or human nature is the product of interaction in intimate groups. It also sees delinquency as an expression of conformity to shared values and beliefs. Young people's law violations represent their efforts to adjust collectively to the way society is structured.

At the same time, classic strain theory departs from both of its predecessors—Shaw–McKay and Sutherland—in locating the motive for delinquent behavior. Rather than suggesting that delinquents are motivated by values and beliefs unique to their particular gang or group, it maintains that their law-violating behavior can be explained by values and beliefs that *all* Americans share. The reason is that there is widespread consensus on the importance of achievement and success. According to classic strain theory, delinquency is committed mainly by lower-class boys who are angry and frustrated over their lack of opportunity to fulfill the American Dream. Their aspirations to succeed have been blocked by the prevailing class structure.

This way of explaining delinquency can be traced to Robert Merton, an eminent American sociologist. In a series of statements beginning in 1938, Merton (1938, 1957, 1968) first discounted Freudian explanations of deviant behavior and then proposed an alternative:

> Until recently . . . one could speak of a marked tendency in psychological and sociological theory to attribute the faulty operation of social structures to failures of social control over man's imperious biological drives. . . . In the beginning, there are man's biological impulses which seek full expression. And then, there is the social order, essentially an apparatus for the management of impulses, for the social processing of tensions, for the "renunciation of instinctual gratifications," in the words of Freud. Nonconformity . . . is thus assumed to be anchored in original nature. . . . And by implication, conformity is the result of an utilitarian calculus or of unreasoned conditioning. (Merton, 1968:185)

Such a view, said Merton (1968:185–248), is faulty. Humankind is not, by nature, inherently deviant; rather, deviant impulses are socially induced. In the United States, for example, a great emphasis is placed on monetary success and the achievement of high social status. At the same time, all Americans do not have equal opportunities for that success. Lower-class people, in particular, lack the means to achieve "culturally induced" goals. As a result, they are faced with a dilemma: Either they must give up

the pursuit of the monetary success that everyone values, or they must seek illegal means for achieving it. But, should they choose the latter course, it will be the product not of an inherently evil nature, but of the discrepancy between culturally valued goals and socially available means. "A cardinal American virtue, 'ambition,' promotes a cardinal American vice, 'deviant behavior'" (Merton, 1957:146).

We will first review the the Cohen and Cloward–Ohlin versions of strain theory. Then we will consider the impact of those theories on social policy about delinquency and the empirical evidence on theories. Last, we will consider Agnew's revised strain theory, which is the most recent strain theory.

COHEN: STATUS FRUSTRATION AND DELINQUENCY

Cohen's (1955:Chap. 1) introduction to his theory revealed the extent to which, by the 1950s, cultural explanations of delinquency had gained widespread acceptance, at least among sociologists. His theory, he said, was designed to explain two "facts": (1) the existence and content of the delinquent subculture (pp. 24–32) and (2) the concentration of that subculture among lower-class boys (pp. 36–44).

To Cohen, both facts were inarguable. The existence of delinquent traditions was widely accepted, and the prevailing opinion was that female delinquency was not serious: "Authorities on delinquency are agreed that female delinquency, although it may appear euphemistically in the records as 'ungovernability' or 'running away' is mostly sex delinquency. Stealing, 'other property offenses,' 'orneriness' and 'hell-raising' . . . are primarily practices of the male" (Cohen, 1955:45). On that foundation, Cohen proposed the following postulates to explain the delinquent subculture and its functions for lower-class boys:

1. Lower-class Americans embrace the middle-class success ethic.
2. The socialization of lower-class children hinders their capacity to compete.
3. Decreased ability to compete produces strain.
4. Increased strain produces the delinquent subculture.

5. The delinquent subculture produces delinquent behavior.

Lower-Class Americans and the Middle-Class Success Ethic

According to Cohen (1955:84–93, 102), middle-class values and beliefs, which have been such an important part of American culture and our concept of childhood, are accepted by lower-class Americans. They watch television, go to movies, listen to radios, and attend schools dominated by the middle class (pp. 124–125). Thus, over time, they increasingly have come under the spell of a set of values and beliefs that stress ambition, resourcefulness, achievement, respect for property, and, above all, material success. The American Dream is a valued goal of the lower class.

This acceptance of the American Dream has been encouraged by the democratic belief that every child should be free to compete with every other, regardless of background. "The cards are not dealt and the hands all played . . . before the child appears on the scene" (Cohen, 1955:85). Instead, each boy's achievements, and not the social position into which he was born, should determine his future status.

The Socialization of Lower-Class Children

Unfortunately, the desire to share in the American Dream does not mean that all children have an equal ability to compete (Cohen, 1955:94–102). Lower-class parents do not have the same economic and social resources as middle-class parents—money, clothes, a home in the right neighborhood, or the capacity to intercede effectively with schools or influential employers.

Even more important, according to Cohen (1955:98), lower- and middle-class parents socialize their children in different ways. Middle-class parents are "rational, deliberate, and demanding." They leave little to chance, stressing self-discipline and close adherence to the age-graded demands of childhood. They abhor physical violence and prefer reason and diplomacy. They surround their children with books and educational toys. They budget their children's time and fill their days with such activities as Boy Scouts, Junior Achievement, and music and tennis lessons. Finally, they teach their children that love

and acceptance by parents and teachers are earned by disciplined effort and achievement. Neither comes automatically. Rather, a boy must demonstrate that he deserves them.

In contrast, Cohen (1955:99–100) maintained, lower-class parents are "easy-going" and "permissive." Their children receive less training in self-discipline and are granted greater latitude in the use of their time. They have much less contact with books and highly structured recreational and educational activities. Instead, much earlier in life, they are thrown into the company of their peers, where they are freer to play in the streets or get into trouble. Fighting as a method of settling problems is more acceptable, and parental love is less dependent on self-discipline and achievement. In short, lower-class youths cannot compete effectively because they still are socialized in ways that reflect the lower-class traditions of past centuries—early induction into adult activities and immediate rather than deferred gratification.

Strain Caused by Decreased Ability to Compete

Despite the vast differences in the ways they are socialized, Cohen (1955:109–119) indicated that lower-class children have to compete with middle-class children when they enter school. Indeed, the school is a reflection of the larger society: Its goals are avowedly democratic, and it stresses the development of each child's potential. Yet, the school is a middle-class institution that fosters and rewards middle-class character, skills, and manners. The lower-class boy is found wanting because he lacks those skills and manners.

Like everyone else, this boy wants status and acceptance, but he has not learned middle-class techniques for acquiring them. His boisterous behavior destroys the order and routine of the classroom; he does not read well; and he is not "studious," "docile," and "obedient" (Cohen, 1955:115). In short, he is placed in an arena where he must compete for status against all others, but he has been socialized inappropriately and thus is programmed to fail.

That programming carries over to other middle-class institutions, such as youth centers and church groups. Although the people who run them often have special regard for the "rough" boys in slums, they are drawn more to the "polite, personable, mannerly" child (Cohen, 1955:116). The reason is that, like teachers, they feel compelled to sponsor and reward desirable (middle-class), not disruptive (lower-class), behavior.

Therefore, in youth centers and church groups, as in the schools, lower-class boys find themselves at the bottom of the status ladder, not only among adults but among their peers. Even worse, their low status is accompanied by a sense of personal failure, which would not occur if these boys did not accept the legitimacy of middle-class values and beliefs. But having adopted a *middle-class measuring rod* for judging themselves, lower-class boys view themselves as failures and experience frustration. As Cohen (1955:119) put it, they face a serious problem of adjustment and are in the market for a solution. How is the strain resolved?

Production of the Delinquent Subculture

Cohen (1955:24–32, 121–137) argued that most people adjust to strain by joining with others to seek a solution, not by going it alone or becoming psychologically unstable. Thus, one of three possible role adjustments is likely: the corner boy, the college boy, or the delinquent boy.

THE CORNER BOY Most lower-class boys deal with their frustration by accepting their lower-class status, disengaging themselves from competition, and withdrawing into a "sheltering community of like-minded" peers—the "corner-boy" society of the lower class (Cohen, 1955:129). By so doing, they avoid rupturing ties with parents and neighbors and incurring the hostility of middle-class people (p. 129). They may have a few minor scrapes with the law, but in the main, they will acquire a limited education, a blue-collar job, and a family. To the degree that they still aspire to the American Dream, they will be chronically frustrated, but at least they will not be confronted continually with failure.

THE COLLEGE BOY The second possible adjustment involves the relatively few boys who accept the challenge of the middle-class status system. The "college-boy" adjustment entails considerable sacrifice and acquisition of unfamiliar "linguistic, academic, and 'social' skills" (Cohen, 1955:128). But by working hard and deferring gratification, these college boys can be among the few lower-class boys who attend college and live according to middle-class rules.

THE DELINQUENT BOY The third possible adjustment involves the "delinquent boy," who turns to the delinquent subculture for a solution. According to Cohen (1955:25), the delinquent subculture is "*nonutilitarian, malicious,* and *negativistic.*" Ordinarily, he said, people steal things because they can use them, buy something with them, or wear them. But the delinquency of lower-class boys usually does not have a useful purpose. Instead, they steal things "for the hell of it"—clothes they do not wear, food they do not eat, and other things they do not use (p. 26). They delight in terrorizing "good" kids or older people (p. 28). They vandalize, and even destroy, their own schools; they dump garbage on their neighbors' doorsteps; and they deface buildings and other structures.

Such behavior makes no sense to middle-class people, but that is why it makes sense to those who feel rejected by middle-class society and who view themselves as failures. Hence, said Cohen (1955: 129), "the hallmark of the delinquent subculture is the explicit and wholesale repudiation of middle-class standards and the adoption of their very antithesis." A corner boy may skip school because it is dull and unrewarding, but a member of the delinquent subculture does so because "good" boys are not supposed to be truant (p. 130). A corner boy may steal some hubcaps to dress up his car, but a member of the delinquent subculture merely takes them because he disdains the middle-class love of property.

In short, the delinquent subculture is appealing to lower-class boys because it rejects everything valued by the middle class and compensates for the humiliation that middle-class institutions cause them. It helps delinquents to deal psychologically with the shame and degradation that they have experienced in middle-class settings.

Cohen (1955:132–137) implied that delinquents are boys who, perhaps more than the majority, continue to prize middle-class goals. Thus, the only way they can handle their own sense of failure is to completely deny middle-class values. Their behavior is a collective expression of *reaction formation:* an "'exaggerated,' 'disproportionate,' 'abnormal'" reaction against repressed desires that continue to press for attention (p. 133).

Cohen (1955:135–137, 155–156) maintained that membership in the delinquent subculture is not the only road to delinquency. However, given the problems that lower-class boys face and the group support for delinquency, it is the most likely road. But the delinquent subculture compensates for these problems: It provides the support of like-minded peers; it grants status for nonconformity to middle-class values and beliefs; and it sets the lawbreaker on a higher pedestal than the ordinary corner boy or the upward-bound college boy. In short, it becomes a sort of substitute society for the delinquent, providing an alternative for the middle-class-dominated society in which he has failed (pp. 65–67).

Production of Delinquent Behavior

Because the hallmark of the delinquent subculture is the wholesale repudiation of middle-class standards, the delinquent behavior of its members reflects that spirit (Cohen, 1955:24–32). Delinquent boys are resistant to efforts at home, at school, or in the community to regulate their behavior. They are impulsive and impatient, seeking fun without regard to long-range gains or costs. Their delinquent acts are not well planned or highly specialized. In short, the delinquent subculture is a *contraculture,* that is, a way of life opposed to everything conventional. As an alternative means of avoiding failure and acquiring status, it rewards behavior that attacks the morality of the middle class.

Cohen (1955:147–157) did not explain why some boys choose a delinquent adjustment and others choose a corner-boy or college-boy adjustment. In any case, boys who choose the delinquent adjustment respond in a collective, but irrational and malicious, way. Humiliation is the motive for their delinquent behavior, and the delinquent subculture provides the means for translating the motive into action and for achieving status.

CLOWARD AND OHLIN: DELINQUENCY AND OPPORTUNITY

Cloward and Ohlin's (1960) version of strain theory is similar to Cohen's in several ways. Like Cohen, Cloward and Ohlin (1960:1) assumed that delinquent subcultures and gangs "are typically found among adolescent males in lower-class areas of large urban centers," and they attempted to account for what makes these subcultures arise and persist. They also assumed that virtue promotes vice—that is, the desire to get ahead promotes delinquent behavior.

Beyond those similarities, however, the Cloward–Ohlin theory has many distinctive features. Whereas Cohen's delinquents are irrational and malicious, the opposite of everything middle class, Cloward and Ohlin's lawbreakers are rational and utilitarian. If legitimate channels for success are closed to them, they simply turn to illegitimate ones whenever possible. But conventional goals, if not conventional means, continue to guide them.

Consider the postulates in Cloward and Ohlin's version of strain theory:
1. The success ethic is valued by all Americans.
2. Opportunities for success are not distributed equally throughout the class structure.
3. Blocked opportunities produce strain.
4. Strain produces delinquent subcultures.
5. Delinquent subcultures produce delinquent behavior.

The Success Ethic
Cohen suggested that middle-class values have established only a recent and somewhat tenuous foothold in the lower class. Cloward and Ohlin (1960:86–97) went much further. To them, the success ethic is valued so widely among Americans that it scarcely deserves to be called "middle class." America has been the Promised Land to all its people; everyone wants to get ahead. In fact, lower-class people feel a greater need for upward mobility than do people already higher in the social structure. Because their problems are greater, the pressures to escape them are impelling.

Limited Opportunities for Success

No less than Cohen, Cloward and Ohlin (1960:97–103) indicated that education is indispensable for upward mobility. They also acknowledged that the early socialization of lower-class children may inhibit their capacity to do well in school. But to them, this is not the most serious problem. Educational achievement is not simply a matter of a favorable attitude toward school or the ability of children to behave in school and to defer gratification. The more serious problems are "structural"—the result of the American class system. Many lower-class families simply cannot afford to keep their children in school, particularly beyond high school. That is why so many lower-class children drop out—not because they devalue education, but because they and their parents cannot afford it. If and when lower-class children lower their educational expectations, it is not because they want to; they know that education is important. It is because they must. For them, opportunities for upward mobility are blocked.

Blocked Opportunities and Strain

Serious strain is produced when some people are subjected to confusing and impossible demands. When people value the importance of achieving certain goals but are denied the legitimate means by which to obtain those goals, discontent can be expected.

> The disparity between what lower-class youth are led to want and what is actually available to them is the source of a major problem of adjustment. . . . Faced with limitations on legitimate avenues of access to these [conventional] goals, and unable to revise their aspirations downward, they experience intense frustrations. (Cloward and Ohlin, 1960:86)

However, unlike Cohen's, Cloward and Ohlin's (1960:104–121) boys do not see themselves as failures. It is the system that has failed. Consequently, the strain they feel is due not to low self-esteem, but to a sense of injustice.

Production of Delinquent Subcultures

When people feel that existing norms are unjust, they are likely to withdraw support from them and to search for alternatives. Indeed, Cohen suggested that when delinquents do this, they reject not only the norms governing access to major goals but also the goals themselves. That is why, according to Cohen, the delinquent subculture is malicious and negativistic: It rejects *everything* middle class.

Cloward and Ohlin (1960:104–107, 124–143) argued differently. As they saw it, the American Dream rarely loses its hold on lower-class boys. Thus, when they are frustrated by limited access to legitimate means, they merely turn to illegitimate means. They do not give up easily, but they often fail even in that endeavor. Whether their dreams ever come true depends on the way their slum neighborhoods are organized.

THE CRIMINAL SUBCULTURE Some slum neighborhoods provide opportunities for success through criminal means (Cloward and Ohlin, 1960:22–23, 161–171). There are close ties between adults and children, and the adults transmit traditions that are criminal and career oriented. In other words, a *criminal subculture* exists that provides illegitimate means for success. While middle-class boys are learning to be bankers, lawyers, or businessmen, lower-class boys may be learning to be professional burglars, bookies, or fences. Furthermore, they learn the importance of building strong political ties and hiring the best lawyers so that they can avoid prosecution and conviction. Thus, in neighborhoods where criminal subcultures are found, delinquency is rational and utilitarian, not the opposite, as Cohen suggested. Indeed, where adults and children are linked in criminal activities, the wild, undisciplined delinquent gang is frowned upon because it interferes with business by attracting police.

THE CONFLICT SUBCULTURE The closest thing to Cohen's subculture, according to Cloward and Ohlin (1960:24–25, 171–178), occurs in disorganized neighborhoods like those described by Shaw and McKay. There, young people can find neither legitimate *nor* illegitimate means for success. To be sure, criminals live in these neighborhoods, but they tend to be the unorganized, poorly paid, petty criminals, not the sophisticated, well-organized kinds found in neighborhoods where a criminal subculture exists. The result is a second form of delinquent subculture—a *conflict subculture* characterized by malicious and violent acts that are protests against the meaninglessness of the social experience. This is where one will find the aggressive fighting gangs that people so often associate with lower-class delinquency. Actually, however, their behavior is a way of calling attention to the futility of a life without legitimate or illegitimate opportunities.

THE RETREATIST SUBCULTURE Disorganized neighborhoods also produce a third delinquent subculture—a *retreatist subculture* (Cloward and Ohlin, 1960:25–27, 178–184). The subculture is composed of juveniles who have given up on the struggle for success and have turned to drugs. They are "double failures," individuals who have failed in the use of both legitimate and illegitimate means for success. But rather than blaming society, they blame themselves, retreat from the struggle, and seek solace in escape. It is a mistake, however, to view drug users as total isolates. Even in drug use, where "kicks" become the purpose for existence, one needs other people to learn how to use drugs, gain access to a steady supply, and receive group support for unconventional behavior. In other words, drug use, no less than other types of delinquency, is subcultural behavior.

In summary, all three subcultures—criminal, conflict, and retreatist—are produced by blocked opportunities, not by repudiation of fundamental societal goals. In each instance, illegitimate activity and subcultural standards develop as alternative means for the satisfactions that all people seek.

Production of Delinquent Behavior

Cloward and Ohlin (1960:42–43) suggested that the three kinds of subcultures are specialized. For that reason, they indicated that we should guard against the tendency to see all delinquent behavior as responses to subcultural requirements. For example, drinking, truancy, destroying property, petty theft, and disorderly conduct are all delinquent acts. Yet, said Cloward and Ohlin (1960:7), "we would not necessarily describe as delinquent a group that tolerated or practiced these behaviors *unless they were*

the central activities around which the group was organized" (emphasis added).

This is the key distinguishing factor: Delinquent norms and behavior must have a relatively narrow focus before they can be considered subcultural. Members of a criminal subculture, for example, are rational—they commit delinquent acts for material gain and social status. The fighting of conflict gangs or the drug use of retreatist groups might be intolerable to them. In contrast, the members of a retreatist subculture are preoccupied only with obtaining and taking drugs. Using illegitimate means to get ahead is of little concern to them. Hence, "*a delinquent subculture is one in which certain forms of delinquent activity are essential requirements for the performance of the dominant roles supported by the subculture*" (Cloward and Ohlin, 1960:7).

According to Cloward and Ohlin, the delinquent acts of middle-class groups cannot be considered subcultural unless they are the central concerns of the groups. If their major concerns are with succeeding in school, dating, and going to college, then their delinquency is incidental to other concerns and does not deserve to be called "subcultural delinquency." Likewise, even the Shaw–McKay theory or Cohen's view of the lower-class delinquent subculture would be too broad for Cloward and Ohlin. To them, delinquent subcultures and the acts they endorse are relatively narrow and specialized. That is why the only really serious delinquency arises in the lower class, because it is only in lower-class communities that tightly knit, narrowly focused subcultures exist.

IMPLICATIONS AND IMPACT OF CLASSIC STRAIN THEORY ON SOCIAL POLICY[1]

The idea that delinquency represented a failure of American society was enough to assure the popularity of the Cohen and Cloward–Ohlin versions of strain theory. But in addition, the Cloward–Ohlin version, in particular, became a rationale for some of the most ambitious attempts ever at social engi-

[1]This discussion of implications is drawn from three major sources: Moynihan (1969), Marris and Rein (1973), and Short (1975). For a good journalistic account, see Lemann (1988).

neering. The reason is that it gave expression to long-standing and widely shared beliefs. It was quintessentially American; it was a better reflection of American culture than apple pie:

> A half century of international sociology had produced a set of propositions not far from Father Flanagan's assertion that "There is no such thing as a bad boy." Cloward and Ohlin argued that delinquents were resorting to desperately deviant and dangerous measures in order to *conform* to the routine goals of the larger society. If that society wished them to conform not only in their objectives but in their means for achieving them, it had only to provide the *opportunity* to do so. Opportunity was the master concept. *And what else was America all about?* (Moynihan, 1969:51; emphasis added in last sentence)

The processes by which earlier generations of immigrants were assimilated into the mainstream of American life had broken down, and the solution was the expansion of opportunities for success.

Mobilization for Youth

Cloward and Ohlin did not stand aloof from the implications of their theory. Instead, they set out to see its principles translated into programs for lower-class boys. While writing their book on delinquency, they worked with the Henry Street Settlement on the Lower East Side of New York City to develop a program that would utilize its ideas. To be called "Mobilization for Youth," this program was outlined in a 617-page volume entitled *A Proposal for the Prevention and Control of Delinquency by Expanding Opportunities.* Among other things, Mobilization for Youth was designed to accomplish the following objectives:

1. Improve education—by improving teacher training and curriculum, providing preschool programs for young children, and improving other educational services
2. Create work opportunities—by organizing an urban Youth Service Corps, creating a Youth Jobs Center, and providing better vocational training
3. Organize communities—by taking steps to reach and organize unaffiliated persons, setting up neighborhood councils, and establishing the Lower East Side Neighborhoods Association
4. Provide specialized services to adolescent groups—by initiating a detached worker program for gangs, creating an Adventure Corps, and establishing a Coffee Shop Hangout
5. Provide specialized services to young people and their families—by organizing Neighborhood Service Centers that would provide counseling, assistance to families, and similar services.

This ambitious endeavor was not conceived solely as a service program. It was to be a social experiment, carefully planned and systematically evaluated. Indeed, said Moynihan (1969:51), the proposal "is one of the more remarkable documents in the history of efforts to bring about 'scientific' social change: lucid, informed, precise, scholarly, and above all, candid."

The early 1960s was a period of considerable opportunity for scholars. A new president, John F. Kennedy, had been elected, and his campaign slogan had been "The New Frontier." And, because Cloward and Ohlin's ideas were better formulated than most, they soon came to the attention of the new administration.

Soon after the president was inaugurated, efforts were made to develop a new federal initiative to combat delinquency. David Hackett, a friend and close associate of the president's brother and new attorney general, Robert Kennedy, was named executive director of the **President's Committee on Juvenile Delinquency and Youth Crime.** Seeking information on the latest thinking on delinquency, Hackett was introduced to strain theory and the philosophy of Mobilization for Youth by officers of the Ford Foundation, for which both Cloward and Ohlin were consultants. Cloward and Ohlin's ideas, along with Albert Cohen's, seemed attuned to the spirit of the New Frontier, and Hackett was soon persuaded that the President's Committee should be promoting opportunities for lower-class youths. Thus, he invited Ohlin to help him develop the federal initiative.

New legislation authorized the expenditure of $10 million a year for three years. The key concepts in the disbursement of this money were *opportunity, coordination,* and *community action.* Communities throughout the nation were invited to submit proposals, but they had to indicate how they would mount an interdisciplinary, broad-based attack on delinquency in which the goal was institutional, not personality, change. The federal government would provide planning and seed money, but communities would have to commit local resources and indicate how those resources would be effectively reallocated. Furthermore, they would have to include poor people in the planning process and use research to evaluate their efforts. Because Mobilization for Youth had served as the blueprint for the entire effort, it only made sense that it should be among the first programs funded.

The War on Poverty

Mobilization for Youth and the President's Committee scarcely had gotten under way when classic strain theory became the rationale for even grander social engineering. A nationwide War on Poverty, conceived by President Kennedy and implemented by President Johnson, was declared. Billions of dollars were spent between 1965 and 1970 in an attempt to provide greater opportunities for poor Americans and thereby reduce delinquency and its attendant problems. Despite considerable optimism about its prospects for success, those who have chronicled the history of the War on Poverty have concluded that, at best, it had mixed results.

Even before the War on Poverty got under way in 1964, "the *New York Daily News* declared that Mobilization for Youth had become infected with subversives, or as the phrase became, 'Commies and Commie sympathizers'" (Moynihan, 1969:102). Some of its staff members also were accused of misappropriating funds. Actually, those accusations were levied more because Mobilization for Youth had become involved in a political struggle with city officials than because there was much substance to them. Although some important forces rallied to the defense of Mobilization for Youth and calm was restored temporarily, the damage was done. "The logic of scientific problem solving collapsed in piecemeal pragmatism" (Marris and Rein, 1973:214), and Mobilization for Youth slowly sank in a sea of conflict.

The President's Committee also withered away. From the beginning, it encountered resistance from established old-line departments in the federal bureaucracy. Then, influential members of Congress made it clear that the mandate of the President's Committee was to reduce delinquency, not to reform society or to try out sociological theories on American youths.

The War on Poverty, meanwhile, initiated many new programs, such as Head Start, Job Corps, Vista, and Neighborhood Legal Services, but the crux of its effort was the Community Action Program. Modeled after Mobilization for Youth, this program was designed to establish in every local community an organization in which the poor would join with members of the establishment in planning and operating antipoverty programs. It was this feature of the federal effort, however, that encountered the greatest difficulty.

Moynihan (1969:Chap. 7–8) argued that the Community Action Program harmed the true interests of the poor because it was based on unproven theory and was poorly conceived and poorly run, and, most of all, because it stirred up trouble. As did Mobilization for Youth, the Community Action Program enjoined the poor to engage in rent strikes, organize social protests, and attack the political and welfare establishments.

The goal was to let political leaders know that poor people were an increasingly organized constituency to which they would have to respond with more jobs, better housing, improved education, and extended social services. But the organized protests apparently had the opposite effect. Both Congress and local politicians withdrew support from the War on Poverty, as well as from Mobilization for Youth.

Despite those problems, there was some useful fallout from the War on Poverty. Perhaps the most useful was the formation and training of a strong cadre of minority leadership in the Community Action Program. Increasing numbers of African Americans, Mexican Americans, and Puerto Ricans took up places in American political life and have since organized their constituencies into more potent political forces. Furthermore, preschool programs initiated by Mobilization for Youth and Head Start have become more or less permanent fixtures in our educational system, as has Medicaid for the poor. Those types of programs are central to any effort to achieve equality of opportunity and, therefore, may contribute to achieving the goals of the War on Poverty.

To those of a more radical persuasion, such results were inadequate. Indeed, as we will see in a later chapter on radical theory, some believe that the philosophy of Mobilization for Youth and the War on Poverty was too conservative, little more than a sop to the oppressed masses. Such programs were destined to fail because they did not mount a direct attack on American capitalism and the class structure it has perpetuated. These are seen to be at the root of all our troubles, including delinquency. Indeed, the real lawbreakers are not those who protest oppression, but the capitalist exploiters who have perpetuated it.

SCIENTIFIC ADEQUACY OF CLASSIC STRAIN THEORY

An examination of the scientific adequacy of classic strain theory is important because of the deterministic picture it paints of lower-class youths. In contrast to the boys in the Shaw–McKay groups, who had fun committing delinquent acts, those described by Cohen and by Cloward and Ohlin "are driven by grim economic and psychic necessity into rebellion" (Bordua, 1961:136). Delinquency is no fun for them; they are virtually forced to use desperate measures, either to overcome a sense of inadequacy or to open up new avenues to success. But is that an accurate explanation of delinquency? The answer to that question requires attention to three issues:

1. The idea that serious delinquency is limited largely to lower-class youths
2. The complex series of events that is supposed to produce delinquent behavior: internalization of the American Dream, failure in school, a sense of strain, and the discovery of a solution in one or more delinquent subcultures
3. The failure of strain theory to address female delinquency

The Class Foundation

The assumption that serious delinquency is primarily a lower-class phenomenon needs to be modified. On the one hand, virtually all accounts of delinquent behavior indicate that there are many chronic offenders who are poor (recall the discussion of this issue in Chapters 4 and 5); and, indeed, their serious and repeated lawbreaking requires explanation. On the other hand, those same accounts indicate that there are chronic offenders, even if perhaps fewer in number, in all social classes. Tittle (1983:335), therefore, has pointed out that there is "reason to review conventional wisdom about social status [class] and criminal behavior." First, it is a gross oversimplification to divide our complex class structure into only two strata—lower and middle—and then assume that delinquent behavior is largely explainable in those terms. Second, many studies have indicated that delinquency may be related more strongly to children's relationships with their parents or to their progress in school than to class membership (e.g., Agnew, 1985:160–164; Aultman, 1979: 156–162; Empey and Lubeck, 1971:Chap. 4–6; Hirschi, 1969:66–75; Johnson, 1979:115–120; LaGrange and White, 1985:27–31; Wiatrowski, Griswold, and Roberts, 1981:534–538).

In short, although proponents of classic strain theory are correct in suggesting that a focus on lower-class male gangs is important (e.g., Bernard, 1984:364–366, 368; 1987:270, 275), the subcultures and behaviors of those gangs are not the only things that require explanation. Furthermore, factors other than class membership may better account for delinquent behavior.

The Theoretical Chain

The theoretical chain postulated by classic strain theory actually suggests that social class should relate only weakly to delinquency. After all, social class is but the first in a long series of variables leading to delinquent behavior—from lower-class membership and high aspirations, to failure in school, to a sense of strain, to membership in a delinquent gang, and, finally, to the commission of delinquent acts. Causal inference, in other words, suggests that as we move across the causal chain, each subsequent variable should have a stronger direct relationship to delinquency than the variable(s) that precedes it (Blalock, 1964). What, then, does research reveal about those other variables?

THE AMERICAN DREAM The American Dream seems to be widely shared, as classic strain theorists suggested (Kluegel and Smith, 1981:30, 41). For example, lower-class children are more likely to internalize conventional goals like money, recognition, and status than to adopt a set of goals somehow unique to the lower class. Likewise, they are aware that the legitimate steps for achieving those goals involve getting an education and finding a place in the labor force (Empey, 1956:706–708; Gold, 1963:153–172; Gordon et al., 1963:116–122; Gould, 1941:465–466—for a summary of much of this evidence, see Kornhauser, 1978:168–173). It is unclear, however, how much sophistication lower-class boys possess in their awareness of these goals and means.

The Cloward–Ohlin version of strain theory implies that lower-class boys are quite sophisticated they recognize that success requires many years of education; that gratifications must be deferred to complete high school and college; and that hard work is a precondition for being married, buying a house in the suburbs, and acquiring both a sports utility vehicle and a sports car. But Cohen argued that the socialization of lower-class boys is not that complete. They have learned little about the methods of middle-class success, have had little exposure to books about science and the arts, and have received little or no training on how to defer gratifications.

Tittle (1983:341–342) has cautioned that Cohen's argument may reflect a prejudice that poor people have undesirable attributes. In any case, it is important to look more closely at the extent to which lower-class boys commit delinquency because they are aware of the disparity between their lofty aspirations and their chances for success. Should such an awareness be lacking, then other reasons for difficulties in school, for feelings of alienation, and eventually for delinquent behavior must be explored.

SCHOOL FAILURE AND BLOCKED OPPORTUNITIES
Researchers have found consistently that school performance is related to delinquency. Study after study has indicated that those who do the worst in school or who most strongly believe that their chances for graduating are poor are the most likely to commit delinquency (e.g., Elliott and Voss, 1974:133–137, 175–179, 182–187; Empey and Lubeck, 1971:80–84; Frease, 1973:452–454; Hirschi, 1969:Chap. 7, 170–182; Johnson, 1979:101–103; LaGrange and White, 1985:27–31; Patterson and Dishion, 1985:73; Polk

and Halferty, 1966:84, 90–96; Polk and Schafer, 1972:passim; Rankin, 1980:427–428; Stinchcombe, 1964:143; Wiatrowski, Griswold, and Roberts, 1981:534–538; Wiatrowski et al., 1982:153–158—for a summary, see Maguin and Loeber, 1996).

After having supported that side of strain theory, however, researchers also have raised several questions about it. First, school failure is related to delinquency on all social class levels, not just the lower class (Empey and Lubeck, 1971:34–37, 43–48; Frease, 1973:452–454; Hirschi, 1969:111–120; Johnson, 1979:99–100; Polk and Halferty, 1966:95; Stinchcombe, 1964:143; Wiatrowski, Griswold, and Roberts, 1981:534–538; Wiatrowski et al., 1982:156–157). Second, school failure is related to the delinquency of girls as well as boys (Rankin, 1980:427–428). Third, Bordua (1961:134) suggested that failure in school may *result* from delinquent behavior, not *cause* it: Boys who use the school as a battleground, he says, or who treat its "property as arts and crafts material do not meet the criteria for advancement" (for contrary evidence, see Phillips and Kelly, 1979). Fourth, Maguin and Loeber (1996:147) conclude that "intelligence and attention problems both act as a common cause of both academic performance and delinquency." This means that there may be no causal relationship between school failure and delinquency; instead, "it is possible that the relationship is solely spurious" (Maguin and Loeber, 1996:155).

STRAIN Classic strain theorists described strain as a condition of psychological dissonance that is a necessary bridge between failing in school and joining a delinquent group. To determine whether that is true, we must address several issues.

The first relates to whether school failure produces frustration and a sense of inadequacy. There is some evidence that this is true. Among middle- as well as lower-class students, school failure seems to result in low self-esteem and a belief that one's occupational chances are decreased (Empey and Lubeck, 1971:50; Wiatrowski et al., 1982:154, 156).

Relative to such findings, however, Stinchcombe (1964:8, 134–137, 142–156) argued that it is middle-class, not lower-class, children who are most likely to rebel because of frustration over school failure. Because they are more fully socialized regarding the

VIOLENCE IN SCHOOLS

Recent violence in schools has generated public awareness that not all schools are safe places of learning. What types of schools are most likely to have serious violence problems? As far as this chapter is concerned, it is particularly appropriate to ask: Is violence in schools most likely to involve lower-class (economically disadvantaged) students? Two studies of school violence are useful for addressing those questions. The first is a 1997 survey of principals from a nationally representative sample of elementary, middle, and secondary public schools. According to the principals, about 10 percent of the schools experienced one or more serious violent offenses (murder, rape or other type of sexual assault, suicide, physical attack or fight with a weapon, or robbery) that were reported to police or other law enforcement officials during the 1996–97 school year (Heaviside et al., 1998:iv, 7). Violence is more common in middle schools and high schools than in elementary schools, in large schools than in small schools, and in city schools than in suburban, small town, and rural schools (Heaviside et al., 1998: 57). In contrast to what classic strain theory might lead us to expect, however, there is very little difference in reported school violence by the social class of the students in the schools. When social class is estimated by the percentage of students eligible for free or reduced-price school lunches, there is roughly the same amount of school violence in poor schools (75 percent or more of students are eligible for free lunches) as in more affluent schools (less than 20 percent are eligible).

The second study of school violence is a supplement to the 1995 National Crime Victimization Survey. "Eligible respondents . . . had to be between the ages of 12 and 19, and had to have attended school at some point during the six months preceding the interview" (Chandler et al., 1998:1). Four percent of the students reported violent victimization (physical attacks or theft of property from a student directly by force, weapons, or threats) at school. Violent victimization was more common among students who reported the presence of street gangs at their schools and who reported seeing a student with a gun at school (Chandler et al., 1998:3–5). Again, however, there was little difference in violent victimization at school by the social class of the students. Roughly the same percentage of poor students (household income less than $7,500) as more affluent students (household income of $50,000 or more) reported violent victimization at school. Both studies, then, are consistent with what self-report surveys suggest about the relationship between social class and delinquency—that social class is not strongly related to delinquency. Even the risk of violent victimization is not limited mainly to poor schools and poor students.

long-range importance of education, an inability to achieve not only represents a threat to their upward mobility but actually results in a loss of status and respect. Of all children, therefore, they experience the greatest pressures to succeed or, failing that, to seek out alternative, delinquent means.

Findings by Jensen (1995:151–154) are important. First, he found that the harder students try in school, the less likely they are to commit delinquent acts. Second, that relationship is stronger among students with high or medium grades than among students with low grades. It might be expected that among students with low grades, those who try the hardest should commit the most delinquency. However, Jensen (1995:153) found that among students with low grades, trying harder does not increase the likelihood of law violations; indeed, those who try hardest tend to commit slightly *less* delinquency. Perhaps most surprising, the likelihood of delinquency is not highest among students who try hard but fail; instead, the "highest probability of delinquency appears for those youth who get good grades without trying" (Jensen, 1995:153).

Findings by Hirschi (1969:182–184) and Johnson (1979:107–108) are also important. They found that high occupational aspirations among juveniles, lower- or middle-class, are associated with *low* rates of delinquent behavior, not the reverse. Delinquents, in other words, are not highly ambitious. How, then, could it be said that their lawbreaking is caused by a sense of failure, and by frustrated occupational ambitions? Hirschi's (1969:182–183) answer is straightforward: *"Frustrated occupational ambition cannot be an important cause of delinquency"* (emphasis added). Delinquents must be marching to the beat of a different drummer; strain, if it does exist for them, must not be related to lofty aspirations (Johnson, 1979:108).

Along yet another dimension, Cernkovich and Giordano (1979:148–150) indicate that racial differences may exist for which classic strain theory has failed to account. Contrary to the suggestion that African Americans should experience greater frustration about blocked opportunities than whites and thus should commit more delinquency, they found the opposite: Blocked opportunities were associated more strongly with the delinquency of whites than

African Americans. They speculate that such findings may be due to a tendency for African Americans to develop an attitude of resignation regarding occupational goals and opportunities. Given the racial and economic discrimination African Americans have experienced, they may be less inclined than whites to judge themselves by a middle-class measuring rod.

Some investigators have suggested that it is not frustration over long-range goals that causes delinquency; instead, it is the pressure and tension generated by schools themselves (Elliott and Voss, 1974:26; Frease, 1973:448–451, 454–457; Polk and Schafer, 1972:passim):

> The curriculum and status reward systems of high schools are chiefly oriented toward producing students who will attend college. The teachers unwittingly instill their educational values in students by encouraging the development of college-oriented personalities and rewarding the proper "orderly" and "cooperative" behavior. (Rankin, 1980:423 on Frease, 1973)

For students lacking long-range educational aspirations, the school may become boring and even degrading. In turn, students' negative feelings may lead to rebellion and truancy. According to that explanation, however, strain is created not by frustration at the inability to obtain conventional goals, but by the contact between students who *lack* such goals and teachers and principals who think they ought to have them.

Some studies have suggested that student achievement depends more on a child's family than on the school (Coleman, 1966:21–23, 292–302; Steinberg, 1996:passim). Students who fail are those who have been poorly prepared for achievement by their parents. This is not to suggest that school influences are irrelevant. Indeed, Alexander, Entwisle, and Thompson (1987:672–679) showed that teachers from advantaged social backgrounds (judged from the father's occupation when the teacher was growing up) tend to have low performance expectations for African American students, ultimately impairing their achievement. Hirschi (1969:170–186), however, argued that the problems of such students stem not only from their being black, or coming from the lower class, or failing to please teachers. Instead, they are people whose commitments to legitimate means for success—long-range plans, hard work, and deferred gratification—are minimal. And so Hirschi (1969:174) turned strain theory on its head. It is not that failing and delinquent students do not want money, material goods, and personal pleasures—they certainly do want them. But rather than experiencing strain because the avenues to those desirable goals are blocked, they get into trouble because they are not willing to use legitimate means to achieve them. If they experience strain, it is produced not by the frustration of not achieving long-range goals, but by an unwillingness to pay the conventional price for autonomy and privilege (see Farnworth and Leiber, 1989 for a view that is more consistent with classic strain theory).

The issues raised by these alternative views lead us to consider at least three possibilities concerning the concept of strain as depicted by classic strain theory. First, strain might be linked to the frustration of lofty, but blocked, ambitions, as classic strain theory indicated. But should that be the case, we might find it present among middle-class as well as lower-class juveniles. Second, strain and delinquent behavior may be due more to the degradation and loss of status within schools than to the frustration of not achieving long-range goals. After all, juveniles may not be the highly utilitarian and goal-oriented individuals that Cloward and Ohlin envisioned, particularly those whose fathers and mothers are poorly educated, under- or unemployed, and unable to provide much insight into the nature of success in a highly technological society. Third, if lawbreakers have not been socialized concerning the importance of commitment to legitimate means for success and do not judge themselves by a middle-class measuring rod, strain may be of little help in explaining their behavior. Lawbreakers, then, would be viewed simply as young people who feel that ordinary rules do not apply to them and who could scarcely care that they do not fit the conventional mold.

DELINQUENT SUBCULTURE Issues raised about strain also are relevant to the concept of a delinquent subculture, because classic strain theory postulated that it is in that subculture that shared feelings of strain

are resolved. We have seen repeatedly that delinquent behavior tends to be a group phenomenon (e.g., Erickson, 1971, 1973a, 1973b; Erickson and Jensen, 1977; Hindelang, 1971; Reiss, 1986; Warr, 1996; Zimring, 1981). Indeed, the stability and persistence of this group phenomenon may seem to be persuasive evidence that delinquent subcultures actually exist. Nonetheless, some problems remain when classic strain theory is used to explain such subcultures.

First, neither Cohen nor Cloward and Ohlin explained why, in response to strain, some lower-class boys identify with a delinquent subculture while others select a corner-boy or a college-boy adjustment (Merton, 1997). Although they were concerned more with accounting for the content and nature of delinquent subcultures than with answering that crucial question, some clarification is desperately needed. What are the psychological or sociological mechanisms that affect what a boy chooses? Why do some boys choose a delinquent adjustment, presumably in response to strain, while others do not?

Second, there is conflicting evidence as to whether the delinquent subculture can compensate for the serious problems of adjustment that lower-class boys are supposed to possess. According to Cohen and Cloward–Ohlin, delinquent gangs become a substitute society for lower-class boys, easing the pains produced by frustration and low self-esteem. But many studies indicate that gangs are held together not by feelings of loyalty and solidarity, but by forces much less attractive. According to these studies, delinquent gangs possess a structure, but it is not one that provides much understanding and warmth. Gang members tend to hold one another in low esteem (Klein, 1995:passim; Short and Strodtbeck, 1965:Chap. 10, 12; also see Morash, 1983:317, 1986: 59). Their relationships are characterized by aggression and by a constant need to protect their status and assert their masculinity (Matza, 1964:42–44, 53–55; Miller, 1958:9–10). Moreover, the threatening kind of interaction found in gangs is not the type ordinarily associated with internally strong and emotionally satisfying groups (Yablonsky, 1959). What emerges, instead, is a picture suggesting that delinquent gangs may stay together simply because they have no other alternative. They may appear to outsiders to be dogmatic, rigid, and unyielding in their loyalty to one another; but the sources of the loyalty are external, not internal. Remove the threats of rival gangs and of the authorities, and you remove the ties that bind (Klein and Crawford, 1967).

A different picture, however, emerges from a study by Giordano, Cernkovich, and Pugh (1986:1191) of a large sample of youths ages 12–19:

> Overall, we find that youths who are very different in their levels of involvement in delinquency are nevertheless quite similar in the ways in which they view their friendship relations. There were no differences in the average length of time respondents reported being friends (stability) or in the ongoing frequency of their interactions (contact). Delinquents were somewhat more likely than their less delinquent counterparts to share privacies with one another (self-disclosure) and were about as likely to believe that they can "be themselves" while in the company of these friends (self-confirmation). Contrary to the central assertion of the cold and brittle relationships argument, delinquents were no less likely than others to believe that they have the trust of friends and that these friends "really care about them and what happens to them."

The implication is clear: "Delinquents, at least as much as other adolescents, derive a variety of significant benefits from their friendship relations" (Giordano, Cernkovich, and Pugh, 1986:1192).

Not all was rosy among delinquents. Indeed, Giordano and her associates (1986:1187, 1190) found that delinquents reported more disagreements with their friends, which is at least partial corroboration of previous studies of delinquent groups. However, they cautioned against assuming that disagreements are "necessarily antithetical to intimacy" on the grounds that a certain degree of intimacy probably is required to generate disagreements (Giordano, Cernkovich, and Pugh, 1986:1179, 1192).

The precise nature of delinquent groups is not clearly understood. Warr (1996:23) has reported that most delinquent groups are transitory. Although offenders tend to violate the law with accomplices, an offender will tend to commit only one offense with a particular accomplice. "It is uncommon for offenders to commit more than three or four offenses with the same accomplice." This does not mean, however, that associations among group offenders are "cold and brittle." Indeed, group offenders often are very close friends (Warr, 1996:30).

Unless delinquent groups are cohesive and internally gratifying, it is questionable whether they can provide the motivation to promote and maintain a delinquent subculture in opposition to conventional values. Rather than revealing that delinquent gang members eventually are led to reject such values, however, several studies have indicated just the opposite. Cohen, it will be recalled, argued that in response to humiliation and loss of status, delinquent boys completely repudiate conventional values. The only way they can handle their sense of failure and frustration is to react against those values. The same also would be true, perhaps, of Cloward and Ohlin's conflict and retreatist gangs.

Members of delinquent gangs do not seem to reject the goals of the larger culture. "Even the gang ethic is not one of 'reaction formation' *against* widely shared conceptions of the 'good' life" (Short and Strodtbeck, 1965:271). Gang, lower-class, and middle-class boys, black and white, evaluate "images representing salient features of a middle class style of life equally highly" (Short and Strodtbeck, 1965:59).[2]

Finally, it is necessary to know whether delinquent subcultures of the type described by strain theories actually exist. Cohen suggested the presence of a delinquent subculture characterized by nonutilitarian, malicious, and negativistic behavior, a subculture in which delinquents are not specialized. Cloward and Ohlin, in contrast, argued that delinquent subcultures are specialized, falling into three

---

[2]The Schwendingers (1985:132–133), as well as Bernard (1987:273–274, 279), have identified problems with existing studies about the values of delinquents, especially gang delinquents. Virtually all such studies, they have pointed out, have been surveys of individuals, and "in Cohen's theory the gang culture (i.e., beliefs held in the context of the gang itself) differs from the beliefs of individual gang members" (Bernard, 1987:279). In particular, delinquents may express conventional values in individual interviews, but unconventional values in "a setting dominated by peers" (Schwendinger and Schwendinger, 1985:133). This means that the only appropriate measure of values, as far as classic strain theory is concerned, may come from surveys conducted in the presence of other gang members.

types: criminal, conflict, and retreatist. Before a delinquent subculture can be said to exist, they argued, it has to be organized around a specific activity.

Studies have provided some support for the Cohen version but little for the Cloward–Ohlin version (Short and Strodtbeck, 1965:13). In the first place, even the most delinquent groups of boys spend most of their time in nondelinquent activities (Short, 1963:xlvii). Even in what are considered violent gangs, few boys become involved in actual assault (Miller, 1966:100–102, 105–106). Finally, when delinquent behavior occurs, it does not tend to follow any particular pattern. Delinquent boys drink, steal, burglarize, damage property, smoke marijuana, or even experiment with pills and heroin, but they do not usually limit themselves to any single one of these activities (Erickson and Empey, 1963; Farrington, Snyder, and Finnegan, 1988; Gold, 1970:Chap. 3; Morash, 1983:315; Rojek and Erickson, 1982; Wolfgang, Figlio, and Sellin, 1972:254; Wolfgang, Thornberry, and Figlio, 1987:45–50—for a review, see Klein, 1984).[3]

Thus, although there is little support for the idea that delinquent subcultures are highly specialized, there is some evidence for the existence of subcultures that encourage a "garden variety" of delinquent acts (Cohen and Short, 1958:24–25). About the only time that highly organized criminal gangs appear is when they are linked to the criminal rackets of adults, and that is rare (Kobrin, Puntil, and Peluso, 1967:102–103; Spergel, 1961:42).

Strain Theory and Female Delinquency

Finally, there is the question of female delinquency. When classic strain theories were formulated in the late 1950s and early 1960s, the general assumption was that female delinquency was petty and primarily sexual. Since that time, feminist writers have attacked these and other theories, charging that they tend to stereotype, and thus to ignore, the real problems faced by women (Adler and Simon, 1979; Campbell, 1981; Klein, 1973; Leonard, 1982; Smart, 1976). The roles that women have been expected to play, in both conventional and criminal worlds, have been characterized by a gender-determined *lack of opportunity* (Steffensmeier, 1983). Traditionally, girls have been more passive, more law-abiding, and more acquiescent than boys, not because they are inherently predisposed to such behavior, but because they have not been accorded the same degree of autonomy and opportunity.

But the world is changing. Females, said Adler (1975:14–30), are becoming more like males—more competitive, more "macho." Changes in the roles of girls also have "virilized" this formerly docile segment of the population (Adler, 1975:87). As a consequence, girls may now face more strain than boys. Not only must they compete on an equal footing for a scarce number of prestigious positions, but they also are

> denied access, on the basis of gender, to those legitimate opportunities which are essential for successful achievement. The various pressures associated with this sex-role convergence and competition simply make girls *more vulnerable to delinquency.* (Cernkovich and Giordano, 1979: 146, emphasis added)

Figueira-McDonough and Selo (1980:334) did not agree that the strain experienced by females made them *more* vulnerable to delinquency, but they did contend that equality of opportunity would lead to *similar* behavior among males and females. In contrast to the traditional idea that "lower rates of female delinquency can be explained by low aspirations among females" (p. 341), they hypothesized that "the illegal activities engaged in by girls with high success aspirations and low access to material and legitimate opportunities will be similar to the misbehavior of boys, attributed to strain" (p. 338).

At the same time, Figueira-McDonough and Selo (1980:340) have added a concept to strain theory—the concept of "control": "Low levels of control, under conditions of strain, will result in similar delinquent behavior among males and females." This addition qualified classic strain theory by implying

[3]Farrington, Snyder, and Finnegan (1988:483) have estimated that about 20 percent of delinquents are specialists (also see Bursik, 1980). The extent of specialization, however, appears to increase with age (Blumstein et al., 1986, 1:82–83; Osgood et al., 1988:88–90) and the frequency of offending (Lattimore, Visher, and Linster, 1994). Greater specialization among more frequent offenders "could be due either to escalation in the seriousness of offending . . . or to changes in the composition of the [offending] population" (Lattimore, Visher, and Linster, 1994:314).

that high levels of frustration will produce delinquent, "male" behavior only to the extent that girls no longer are constrained by traditional expectations and that they have internalized the same ambitions as boys. Because the norms that govern female behavior are now in a transitional phase, older norms still may continue to exercise considerable influence.

Given those contrasting positions, what does research suggest? Are the delinquent acts of girls and boys alike? Is delinquency among girls attributable to a denial of opportunity and resultant feelings of frustration and alienation?

FEMALE VERSUS MALE DELINQUENCY We need only recall our review of official and self-report data in Chapters 4 and 5 to know that young girls have not yet become completely macho or virilized. On the one hand, the pattern of female offenses does not fit, and may never have fit, the stereotyped version of the passive female (Morash, 1986:53–54). Furthermore, evidence suggests that in recent decades, delinquency rates among girls have increased more rapidly than among boys. However, gender remains among the strongest and most reliable predictors of delinquency: Boys still commit more delinquency than girls.

FEMALE ASPIRATIONS Undoubtedly, the feminist movement has markedly affected the aspirations of many women. Yet, contentions concerning the virilization of females cannot be confirmed or denied, because there are no studies comparing the aspirations of boys and girls across all social classes and races. Consequently, we cannot say for certain whether boys and girls share the same aspirations.

BLOCKED OPPORTUNITIES Earlier in this chapter, we learned that regardless of gender, delinquents are more likely than nondelinquents to fail in school and to believe that their chances of graduating are poor. Hence, the difficulties generated in schools are no less a problem for girls than boys. But does this mean that girls commit delinquency because they already have experienced strain, particularly that which might be due to discrimination?

STRAIN Pertinent to that question, Datesman, Scarpitti, and Stephenson (1975:120) found that "white female delinquents regarded their opportunities less positively than did their non-delinquent counterparts." One might conclude, then, that blocked opportunities produced strain that produced delinquency. But this was not what Datesman and her associates actually found. They discovered that white female delinquents "seemed to fare no better and no worse in terms of self-esteem than non-delinquents" (p. 119). They concluded, therefore, that in lieu of aspirations similar to those of boys, followed by self-degradation, delinquent girls retained a reasonable sense of self-respect because their offenses were primarily sexual. These girls conformed to traditionally feminine, not masculine, expectations. "Sexual behavior . . . may represent an attempt to gain male attention for either immediate dividends or possible marriage" (p. 120).

Not only was that conclusion the opposite of what was anticipated by feminist strain theory, but the Datesman findings also showed that white females who had committed serious, so-called masculine offenses had worse self-esteem than their white counterparts who had committed less serious offenses (Datesman, Scarpitti, and Stephenson, 1975: 114–115). Therefore, it may be masculine, rather than traditional feminine, behavior that results in a poor self-image.

Cernkovich and Giordano (1979:146) examined whether delinquent behavior by girls is a means of striking back at an unfair, sexist system. But their findings suggested something different: Girls who were inclined to say that females experience discrimination in hiring, firing, and promotion were no more likely to commit delinquent behavior than those who did not (Cernkovich and Giordano, 1979: 148–150). Instead, it was those girls (albeit only whites) who believed that they were unlikely to finish school or get a good job who were the most delinquent—the same pattern that applied to boys (also see Leiber et al., 1994).

DELINQUENT SUBCULTURE Because of the group nature of female delinquency, it is surprising that more recent strain theorists make no mention of the possible role of delinquent subcultures in resolving the strain that girls are presumed to experience. Indeed, Datesman and her associates (1975:112) suggest that there is a "relative absence of subcultural support for female delinquency." Perhaps that is why some girls (white girls who commit serious, "masculine" offenses, according to their findings) experience a loss of self-esteem when they violate the law. "Female delinquency is largely individualistic, and not buttressed by the support and approval of others to as great an extent as male delinquency" (Datesman, Scarpitti, and Stephenson, 1975:112).

This is certainly a provocative conclusion, because it implies that unless girls are an auxiliary appendage to male groups, they are without social support when they commit delinquent acts. However, there is contrary evidence. Giordano, Cernkovich, and Pugh (1986:1193–1194) have found that regardless of their degree of involvement in delinquency, girls are *more,* not less, likely than boys to have intimate relationships with peers. In particular, girls are more likely than boys to disclose personal information with friends and believe that they have their friends' trust. Accordingly, they reached an opposite conclusion from that in the Datesman study: "These data . . . question the image of the female delinquent as a lonely and asocial misfit, unable to establish adequate peer relations" (Giordano, Cernkovich, and Pugh, 1986:1193–1194). That conclusion suggests that strain theorists may need to pay closer attention to delinquent subcultures in their explanations of female delinquency.

AGNEW'S REVISED STRAIN THEORY

The foregoing review of the empirical evidence on classic strain theory has revealed only weak to moderate support for what is perhaps the theory's most fundamental claim—that when young people do not expect to achieve success, they become frustrated and turn to illegitimate means of goal achievement. Because of this and related problems with classic strain theory, Robert Agnew (1985, 1992) has proposed a revised version of strain theory, which expands the notion of strain to include not only blocked achievement of goals but also maltreatment and other types of adversity.

According to Agnew (1995:43), the basic idea in his revised strain theory is simple: "If you treat people badly, they may get mad and engage in crime." The focus is on negative relationships with others—relationships in which an individual is not being treated as he or she would like to be treated. "Adolescents are *pressured* into delinquency by the negative affective states—most notably anger and related emotions—that result from these negative relationships" (Agnew and White, 1992:476).

Agnew (1992) identifies three general types of negative social relations or strain: relationships in which others (1) block the achievement of positively valued goals, (2) remove positively valued stimuli, and (3) present aversive (punishing or degrading) stimuli. The first type of strain includes the focus of classic strain theory (Cohen and Cloward–Ohlin). Agnew (1992), however, goes beyond classic strain theory by considering notions of justice and equity. Just as an inability to achieve valued economic goals might produce a strain toward delinquency, as Cloward and Ohlin argued, so, too, might a concern that valued resources (e.g., grades, attention) are distributed fairly. As Agnew (1995:45) puts it:

> The definition of what constitutes "fair" may differ from situation to situation. A common view, however, is that individuals who contribute more to a relationship should receive more (known as the "equity" rule). So if my inputs to a relationship are greater than those of a similar other, my outcomes should be greater as well. Individuals may respond with delinquency when this is not the case. Delinquency may allow them to increase their outcomes (e.g., by theft), lower their inputs (e.g., truancy from school), lower the outcomes of others (e.g., vandalism, theft, assault), or increase the inputs of others (e.g., by being incorrigible).

The second type of strain—removal of positively valued stimuli—might include the death of a parent or the loss of a boyfriend or girlfriend. The third type of strain—presentation of aversive stimuli—might include criminal victimization, maltreatment by parents or teachers, or a wide range of stressful events. Delinquency may be a corrective action to both types of strain. Young people, for example, may use drugs to manage feelings of despair or depression after the death of a parent, or they may run away to escape an abusive home.

Initial tests of Agnew's revised strain theory have been promising. In these tests, negative social relationships, such as those involving parents and teachers, and stressful life events, such as serious illness or injury and divorce of one's parents, have been found to be associated with a wide range of delinquent behaviors (Agnew, 1985, 1989; Agnew and White, 1992; Hoffman and Miller, 1998; Paternoster and Mazerolle, 1994). Moreover, a recent study by Brezina (1996) has shown that delinquency minimizes some of the negative emotional consequences of strain, suggesting that it may be an effective coping strategy for young people.

It is too early to fully judge the scientific adequacy of Agnew's revised strain theory, but at least one feature of the theory is an improvement over classic strain theory. In contrast to the theories of Cohen and Cloward–Ohlin, the focus of Agnew's theory is not limited to lower-class boys. The types of strain identified by Agnew can be experienced by middle- and upper-class as well as lower-class youngsters. Moreover, they can be experienced by females as well as males. Indeed, the strains can be experienced by all youngsters.

Summary and Conclusions

When strain theory was first formulated, it represented an attempt to explain certain phenomena that had become accepted as "fact": that delinquency is predominantly a male phenomenon, concentrated in the lower class, occurring in groups, and representing a delinquent subculture. It has been broadened in recent years to apply to the feminist movement. It also has been broadened in Agnew's revised strain theory to apply not just to the delinquency committed by lower-class boys, but to the delinquency committed by all youngsters.

Assumptions About Human Nature and Social Order

Classic strain theory assumes that **human nature** is inherently social, that the delinquent is a moral person who prefers to follow conventional rules, given reasonable opportunity to do so. As for the **social order,** strain theory implies that there is a consensus on basic values and goals. Everyone hails these as desirable and lends support to legitimate means for achieving them. Ironically, that very consensus promotes delinquency because some people cannot achieve success by obeying cultural rules. Yet, the impression is pervasive throughout classic strain theory that there would be no conflict, and no delinquency, if only society were organized differently. Were there no structural impediments to self-esteem and material success, the inherently social nature of all males and females would allow them to be law-abiding.

Agnew's assumptions about human nature in his revised strain theory appear to be the same as those in classic strain theory. Unlike classic strain theorists, however, he does not see threats to the social order as being limited to blocked economic opportunities; instead, the social order can be threatened by all manner of stressful life events experienced by people.

Underlying Content and Logic of Strain Theory

As originally formulated, strain theory possessed four distinguishing features. It assumed that (1) while females are conditioned to be passive and law-abiding, males are expected to be status strivers—autonomous, hard driving, and preoccupied with success; (2) these expectations are universal across class lines; (3) because of their socialization, it will be males, not females, who experience a sense of strain if opportunities are blocked; and (4) lower-class males, given their disadvantaged position in the social structure, are those most vulnerable to strain. That is why the latter are the most delinquent segment of the population. In an effort to resolve the intense pressures they feel, they turn to illegitimate means and to like-minded peers for a solution. Delinquent subcultures and behavior are the result. The two expressions of classic strain theory are shown in figure 10.1.

In response to the women's movement, more recent versions of strain theory appear to have modified some, if not all, of the earlier assumptions. They suggest that (1) females as well as males are expected

FIGURE 10.1
The underlying logic of classic strain theory

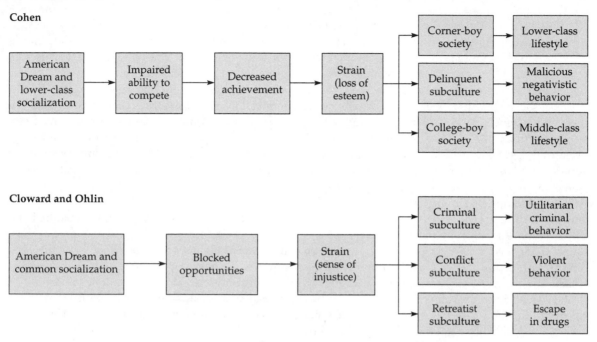

to be autonomous and preoccupied with success; (2) these expectations cut across class and race lines; but (3) it is now females, not males, who are in the greatest bind, because they must confront not only the existence of limited opportunities common to both genders but also the gender-based restrictions of a sexist society. As a consequence, less emphasis is placed on the restrictions of social class and race and more on the disadvantages of being female. Hence, this way of formulating strain theory may be diagramed as follows:

$$\begin{array}{c}\text{American}\\\text{Dream}\end{array} \rightarrow \begin{array}{c}\text{Sexual}\\\text{discrimination}\end{array} \rightarrow \text{Strain} \rightarrow \begin{array}{c}\text{Delinquent}\\\text{behavior}\end{array}$$

An expression of Agnew's revised strain theory is shown in figure 10.2.

Policy Implications of Strain Theory
Classic strain theory implied that there is no such thing as a bad boy or girl: If delinquency occurs, it is because of the failure of the social order; hence, that order must be changed. This construction of delinquency has resulted in some of the most deliberate and comprehensive efforts yet tried to address such root causes of delinquent behavior as poverty, inadequate education, economic segregation, and powerlessness in lower-class communities. It has not, as yet, resulted in similar efforts to reduce gender discrimination. Nonetheless, it is a part of a more general movement that is certainly pointed in that direction.

Scientific Adequacy of Strain Theory
Classic strain theorists have made highly valuable contributions to the delinquency literature by focusing originally on lower-class boys and suggesting that delinquent subcultures may result from the problems they face. It was Cohen, in fact, who first used the term **delinquent subculture** to refer to the delinquent traditions described by Shaw and McKay. And it was Cloward and Ohlin who first alerted us to the possibility that different kinds of subcultures may

FIGURE 10.2

The underlying logic of Agnew's revised strain theory

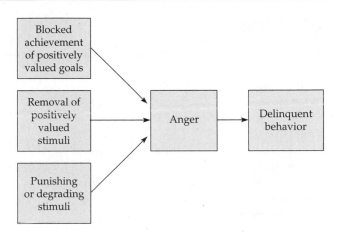

be linked to the opportunity structures of different kinds of communities. Their stress on these matters highlighted the likelihood that lower-class boys have a more difficult transition from childhood to adulthood than middle-class boys.

But do lower-class boys handle the transition in the way that classic strain theory suggests? Are many of them virtually driven to membership in delinquent subcultures? The elements of strain theory that have measured up best to empirical scrutiny are those suggesting that (1) lower-class boys probably want the same goods, pleasures, and statuses that others want; (2) failure in such middle-class institutions as the schools provokes serious problems; and (3) delinquent behavior is a group, and possibly a subcultural, phenomenon. In contrast, the most questioned elements of strain theory are those indicating that (1) serious delinquent behavior is restricted to the lower class; (2) it is a boy's position in the class structure, rather than his relationship with his parents or his unwillingness to pay the legitimate price for success, that is likely to produce problems in school; and (3) the delinquent subculture is capable of solving the serious problems of adjustment that failure in school produces.

Similar difficulties arise with the application of various elements of classic strain theory to girls. Although gender-based discrimination certainly is a serious problem, there is little evidence that it has made girls more, or even equally, vulnerable to delinquency.

In short, classic strain theorists may have attempted to account for too much. In their construction of delinquency, they seemed to forget that delinquents are young and immature people whose understanding of social inequality and pressing contemporary issues is limited. Rather than reflecting an attempt to redress some of society's most serious inequities, therefore, their group behavior may represent little more than an unfettered, irresponsible, and sometimes predatory pursuit of childish desires. To be sure, the deprivations, disillusionments, and frustrations of being lower class may contribute heavily to their problems. But Cohen's humiliated, irrational, angry boys; Cloward's and Ohlin's hard-driving, rational boys; and Adler's macho girls all seem extreme. As Bordua (1961:136) put it, "It seems peculiar that modern analysts have stopped assuming that 'evil' can be fun and see . . . delinquency as arising only when boys [or girls] are driven away from 'good.'"

Although Bordua's comment can apply to Agnew's revised strain theory as much as to classic strain theory, the Agnew theory avoids some of the problems with classic strain theory. Most important, it allows for the possibility that delinquency, even serious delinquency, is not committed just by lower-class boys.

Discussion Questions

1. Which version of classic strain theory—Cohen or Cloward–Ohlin—do you believe is more accurate, and why?
2. What are the main differences between Cohen's version of strain theory and Cloward and Ohlin's version?
3. Why do you think classic strain theory has had such a strong impact on social policy in the United States? Is there anything in early Americans' beliefs about the causes of law-violating behavior that might help us to answer that question?
4. Suppose that a friend unwittingly endorses Cloward and Ohlin's version of strain theory by declaring that lower-class youngsters would commit less delinquency if they had greater access to legitimate opportunities for success. How would you respond?
5. How does Agnew's revised strain theory appear to resolve some of the shortcomings of classic strain theory?

References

Adler, Freda. 1975. *Sisters in Crime: The Rise of the New Female Criminal.* New York: McGraw-Hill.

Adler, Freda, and Rita James Simon, eds. 1979. *The Criminology of Deviant Women.* Boston: Houghton Mifflin.

Agnew, Robert. 1985. "A Revised Strain Theory of Delinquency." *Social Forces* 64 (September): 151–167.
1989. "A Longitudinal Test of the Revised Strain Theory." *Journal of Quantitative Criminology* 5 (December):373–387.
1992. "Foundation for a General Strain Theory of Crime and Delinquency." *Criminology* 30 (February):478–487.
1995. "Controlling Delinquency: Recommendations from General Strain Theory." Pp. 43–70 in Hugh D. Barlow, ed., *Crime and Public Policy: Putting Theory to Work.* Boulder, Colo.: Westview Press.

Agnew, Robert, and Helen Raskin White. 1992. "An Empirical Test of General Strain Theory." *Criminology* 30 (November):475–499.

Alexander, Karl L., Doris R. Entwisle, and Maxine S. Thompson. 1987. "School Performance, Status Relations, and the Structure of Sentiment: Bringing the Teacher Back In." *American Sociological Review* 52 (October):665–682.

Aultman, Madeline G. 1979. "Delinquency Causation: A Typological Comparison of Path Models." *Journal of Criminal Law and Criminology* 70 (Summer):152–163.

Bernard, Thomas J. 1984. "Control Criticisms of Strain Theory: An Assessment of Theoretical and Empirical Adequacy." *Journal of Research in Crime and Delinquency* 21 (November):353–372.
1987. "Testing Structural Strain Theories." *Journal of Research in Crime and Delinquency* 24 (November):262–280.

Blalock, Hubert M., Jr. 1964. *Causal Inferences in Nonexperimental Research.* New York: Norton.

Blumstein, Alfred, Jacqueline Cohen, Jeffrey Roth, and Christy Visher, eds. 1986. *Criminal Careers and "Career Criminals."* 2 vols. Washington, D.C.: National Academy Press.

Bordua, David J. 1961. "Delinquent Subcultures: Sociological Interpretations of Gang Delinquency." *Annals of the American Academy of Political and Social Science* 338 (November): 119–136.

Brezina, Timothy. 1996. "Adapting to Strain: An Examination of Delinquent Coping Responses." *Criminology* 34 (February):39–60.

Bursik, Robert J., Jr. 1980. "The Dynamics of Specialization in Juvenile Offenses." *Social Forces* 58 (March):851–864.

Campbell, Ann. 1981. *Girl Delinquents.* New York: St. Martin's Press.

Cernkovich, Stephen A., and Peggy C. Giordano. 1979. "Delinquency, Opportunity, and Gender." *Journal of Criminal Law and Criminology* 70 (Summer):145–151.

Chandler, Kathryn A., Christopher D. Chapman, Michael R. Rand, and Bruce M. Taylor. 1998. *Students' Reports of School Crime: 1989 and 1995.* Washington, D.C.: U.S. Departments of Education and Justice.

Cloward, Richard A., and Lloyd E. Ohlin. 1960. *Delinquency and Opportunity: A Theory of Delinquent Gangs.* New York: Free Press.

Cohen, Albert K. 1955. *Delinquent Boys: The Culture of the Gang.* New York: Free Press.

Cohen, Albert K., and James F. Short, Jr. 1958. "Research in Delinquent Subcultures." *Journal of Social Issues* 14:20–37.

Coleman, James S. 1966. *Equality of Educational Opportunity.* Washington, D.C.: U.S. Government Printing Office.

Datesman, Susan K., Frank R. Scarpitti, and Richard M. Stephenson. 1975. "Female Delinquency: An Application of Self and Opportunity Theories." *Journal of Research in Crime and Delinquency* 12 (July):107–123.

Elliott, Delbert S., and Harwin L. Voss. 1974. *Delinquency and Dropout.* Lexington, Mass.: Lexington Books.

Empey, LaMar T. 1956. "Social Class and Occupational Aspiration: A Comparison of Absolute and Relative Measurement." *American Sociological Review* 21 (December):703–709.

Empey, LaMar T., and Steven G. Lubeck. 1971. *Explaining Delinquency: Construction, Test, and Reformulation of a Sociological Theory.* Lexington, Mass.: Heath.

Erickson, Maynard L. 1971. "The Group Context of Delinquent Behavior." *Social Problems* 19 (Summer):114–129.
1973a. "Group Violations and Official Delinquency: The Group Hazard Hypothesis." *Criminology* 11 (August):127–160.
1973b. "Group Violations, Socioeconomic Status and Official Delinquency." *Social Forces* 52 (September):41–52.

Erickson, Maynard L., and LaMar T. Empey. 1963. "Court Records, Undetected Delinquency, and Decision-Making." *Journal of Criminal Law, Criminology and Police Science* 54 (December): 456–469.

Erickson, Maynard L., and Gary F. Jensen. 1977. "'Delinquency Is Still Group Behavior!': Toward Revitalizing the Group Premise in the Sociology of Deviance." *Journal of Criminal Law and Criminology* 68 (June):262–273.

Farnworth, Margaret, and Michael J. Leiber. 1989. "Strain Theory Revisited: Economic Goals, Educational Means, and Delinquency." *American Sociological Review* 54 (April):263–274.

Farrington, David P., Howard N. Snyder, and Terrance A. Finnegan. 1988. "Specialization in Juvenile Court Careers." *Criminology* 26 (August): 461–487.

Figueira-McDonough, Josefina, and Elaine Selo. 1980. "A Reformulation of the 'Equal Opportunity' Explanation of Female Delinquency." *Crime and Delinquency* 26 (July):333–343.

Frease, Dean E. 1973. "Delinquency, Social Class, and the Schools." *Sociology and Social Research* 57 (July):443–459.

Giordano, Peggy C., Stephen A. Cernkovich, and M. D. Pugh. 1986. "Friendships and Delinquency." *American Journal of Sociology* 91 (March):1170–1202.

Gold, Martin. 1963. *Status Forces in Delinquent Boys.* Ann Arbor Institute for Social Research at the University of Michigan.
1970. *Delinquent Behavior in an American City.* Pacific Grove, Calif.: Brooks/Cole.

Gordon, Robert A., James F. Short, Jr., Desmond S. Cartwright, and Fred L. Strodtbeck. 1963. "Values and Gang Delinquency: A Study of Street-Corner Groups." *American Journal of Sociology* 69 (September):109–128.

Gould, Rosalind. 1941. "Some Sociological Determinants of Goal Striving." *Journal of Social Psychology* 13 (May):461–473.

Heaviside, Sheila, Cassandra Rowand, Catrina Williams, Elizabeth Farris, Shelley Burns, and Edith McArthur. 1998. *Violence and Discipline Problems in U.S. Public Schools: 1996–97.* Washington, D.C.: U.S. Department of Education, National Center for Education Statistics.

Hindelang, Michael J. 1971. "The Social Versus Solitary Nature of Delinquent Involvements." *British Journal of Criminology* 11 (April):167–175.

Hirschi, Travis. 1969. *Causes of Delinquency.* Berkeley: University of California Press.

Hoffman, John P., and Alan S. Miller. 1998. "A Latent Variable Analysis of General Strain Theory." *Journal of Quantitative Criminology* 14 (March): 83–110.

Jensen, Gary F. 1995. "Salvaging Structure Through Strain: A Theoretical and Empirical Critique." Pp. 139–158 in Freda Adler and William S. Laufer, eds., *Advances in Criminological Theory: The Legacy of Anomie Theory,* Vol. 6. New Brunswick, N.J.: Transaction Books.

Johnson, Richard E. 1979. *Juvenile Delinquency and Its Origins: An Integrated Theoretical Approach.* Cambridge: Cambridge University Press.

Klein, Dorie. 1973. "The Etiology of Female Crime: A Review of the Literature." *Issues in Criminology* 8 (Fall):3–30.

Klein, Malcolm W. 1984. "Offence Specialisation and Versatility among Juveniles." *British Journal of Criminology* 24 (April):185–194.
1995. *The American Street Gang: Its Nature, Prevalence, and Control.* New York: Oxford University Press.

Klein, Malcolm W., and Lois Y. Crawford. 1967. "Groups, Gangs, and Cohesiveness." *Journal of Research in Crime and Delinquency* 4 (January): 63–75.

Kluegel, James R., and Eliot R. Smith. 1981. "Beliefs About Stratification." Pp. 29–56 in Ralph H. Turner and James F. Short, Jr., eds., *Annual Review of Sociology,* Vol. 7. Palo Alto, Calif.: Annual Reviews.

Kobrin, Solomon, Joseph Puntil, and Emil Peluso. 1967. "Criteria of Status Among Street Groups." *Journal of Research in Crime and Delinquency* 4 (January):98–118.

Kornhauser, Ruth R. 1978. *Social Sources of Delinquency: An Appraisal of Analytic Models.* Chicago: University of Chicago Press.

LaGrange, Randy L., and Helen Raskin White. 1985. "Age Differences in Delinquency: A Test of Theory." *Criminology* 23 (February):19–45.

Lattimore, Pamela K., Christy A. Visher, and Richard L. Linster. 1994. "Specialization in Juvenile Careers: Markov Results for a California Cohort." *Journal of Quantitative Criminology* 10 (December):291–316.

Leiber, Michael J., Margaret Farnworth, Katherine M. Jamieson, and Mahesh K. Nalla. 1995. "Bridging the Gender Gap in Criminology: Liberation and Gender-Specific Strain Effects on Delinquency." *Sociological Inquiry* 64 (February): 56–68.

Lemann, Nicholas. 1988. "The Unfinished War." *The Atlantic Monthly* 262 (December), pp. 37–56.

Leonard, Eileen B. 1982. *Women, Crime and Society: A Critique of Criminological Theory.* New York: Longman.

Maguin, Eugene, and Rolf Loeber. 1996. "Academic Performance and Delinquency." Pp. 145–264 in Michael Tonry, ed., *Crime and Justice: A Review of Research,* Vol. 20. Chicago: University of Chicago Press.

Marris, Peter, and Martin Rein. 1973. *Dilemmas of Social Reform: Poverty and Community Action in the United States,* 2nd ed. Chicago: Aldine.

Matza, David. 1964. *Delinquency and Drift.* New York: Wiley.

Merton, Robert K. 1938. "Social Structure and Anomie." *American Sociological Review* 3 (October): 672–682.
1957. *Social Theory and Social Structure,* rev. and enl. ed. New York: Free Press.
1968. *Social Theory and Social Structure,* enl. ed. New York: Free Press.
1997. "On the Evolving Synthesis of Differential and Anomie Theory: A Perspective from the Sociology of Science." *Criminology* 35 (August): 517–525.

Miller, Walter B. 1958. "Lower Class Culture as a Generating Milieu of Gang Delinquency." *Journal of Social Issues* 14:5–19.
1966. "Violent Crimes in City Gangs." *Annals of the American Academy of Political and Social Science* 364 (March):96–112.

Morash, Merry. 1983. "Gangs, Groups, and Delinquency." *British Journal of Criminology* 23 (October):309–335.
1986. "Gender, Peer Group Experiences, and Seriousness of Delinquency." *Journal of Research in Crime and Delinquency* 23 (February):43–67.

Moynihan, Daniel P. 1969. *Maximum Feasible Misunderstanding: Community Action in the War on Poverty.* New York: Free Press.

Osgood, D. Wayne, Lloyd D. Johnston, Patrick M. O'Malley, and Jerald G. Bachman. 1988. "The Generality of Deviance in Late Adolescence and Early Adulthood." *American Sociological Review* 53 (February):81–93.

Paternoster, Raymond, and Paul Mazerolle. 1994. "General Strain Theory and Delinquency: A Replication and Extension." *Journal of Research in Crime and Delinquency* 31 (August):235–263.

Patterson, Gerald R., and Thomas J. Dishion. 1985. "Contributions of Families and Peers to Delinquency." *Criminology* 23 (February):63–79.

Phillips, John C., and Delos H. Kelly. 1979. "School Failure and Delinquency: *Which Causes Which?*" *Criminology* 17 (August):194–207.

Polk, Kenneth, and David S. Halferty. 1966. "Adolescence, Commitment, and Delinquency." *Journal of Research in Crime and Delinquency* 3 (July): 82–96.

Polk, Kenneth, and Walter E. Schafer, eds. 1972. *Schools and Delinquency.* Englewood Cliffs, N.J.: Prentice-Hall.

Rankin, Joseph H. 1980. "School Factors and Delinquency: Interactions by Age and Sex." *Sociology and Social Research* 64 (April):420–434.

Reiss, Albert J., Jr. 1986. "Co-Offender Influences on Criminal Careers." Pp. 121–160 in Alfred Blumstein et al., eds. *Criminal Careers and "Career Criminals,"* Vol. 2. Washington, D.C.: National Academy Press.

Rojek, Dean G., and Maynard L. Erickson. 1982. "Delinquent Careers: A Test of the Career Escalation Model." *Criminology* 20 (May):5–28.

Schwendinger, Herman, and Julia S. Schwendinger. 1985. *Adolescent Subcultures and Delinquency.* New York: Praeger.

Short, James F., Jr. 1963. "Introduction to Abridged Edition." Pp. xv–liii in Frederic M. Thrasher, *The Gang: A Study of 1,313 Gangs in Chicago,* abrg. ed. Chicago: University of Chicago Press.
1975. "The Natural History of an Applied Theory: Differential Opportunity and 'Mobilization for Youth.'" Pp. 193–210 in N. J. Demerath III, Otto Larsen, and Karl Schuessler, eds., *Social Policy and Sociology.* New York: Academic Press.

Short, James F., Jr., and Fred L. Strodtbeck. 1965. *Group Process and Gang Delinquency.* Chicago: University of Chicago Press.

Smart, Carol. 1976. *Women, Crime, and Criminology: A Feminist Critique.* London: Routledge & Kegan Paul.

Spergel, Irving. 1961. "An Exploratory Research in Delinquent Subcultures." *Social Service Review* 35 (March):33–47.

Steffensmeier, Darrell J. 1983. "Organization Properties and Sex-Segregation in the Underworld: Building a Sociological Theory of Sex Differences in Crime." *Social Forces* 61 (June):1010–1032.

Steinberg, Laurence. 1996. *Beyond the Classroom: Why School Reform Has Failed and What Parents Need to Do.* New York: Simon & Schuster.

Stinchcombe, Arthur L. 1964. *Rebellion in a High School.* Chicago: Quadrangle Books.

Tittle, Charles R. 1983. "Social Class and Criminal Behavior: A Critique of the Theoretical Foundation." *Social Forces* 62 (December):334–358.

Warr, Mark. 1996. "Organization and Instigation in Delinquent Groups." *Criminology* 34 (February): 11–37.

Wiatrowski, Michael D., David B. Griswold, and Mary K. Roberts. 1981. "Social Control Theory and Delinquency." *American Sociological Review* 46 (October):525–541.

Wiatrowski, Michael D., Stephen Hansell, Charles R. Massey, and David L. Wilson. 1982. "Curriculum Tracking and Delinquency." *American Sociological Review* 47 (February):151–160.

Wolfgang, Marvin E., Robert M. Figlio, and Thorsten Sellin. 1972. *Delinquency in a Birth Cohort.* Chicago: University of Chicago Press.

Wolfgang, Marvin E., Terence P. Thornberry, and Robert M. Figlio. 1987. *From Boy to Man, From Delinquency to Crime.* Chicago: University of Chicago Press.

Yablonsky, Lewis. 1959. "The Delinquent Gang as a Near-Group." *Social Problems* 7 (Fall):108–117.

Zimring, Franklin E. 1981. "Kids, Groups and Crime: Some Implications of a Well-Known Secret." *Journal of Criminal Law and Criminology* 72 (Fall):867–885.

SOCIAL CONTROL THEORISTS SUGGEST THAT WEAK ATTACHMENT TO SCHOOL IS A CAUSE OF DELINQUENCY.

CHAPTER ELEVEN

SOCIAL CONTROL AND SELF-CONTROL THEORIES

n Chapter 7, we reviewed several control theories that delinquent behavior is due to underlying biological or psychodynamic forces over which children have little control. Those uncontrollable forces are instilled in children by their parents, through either genetic inheritance or improper training. In this chapter, we will examine more recent control theories, which suggest that parents are important in shaping personal controls among children.

HISTORICAL BACKGROUND

To set the stage, let us review a bit of history. During the 1800s, Americans believed that one of the most important causes of youthful lawbreaking was broken or depraved families that were incapable of controlling their children. That is why child-saving institutions were invented—to get the children of disrupted families off the streets and into a moral environment.

In her analysis of the impact of traditional beliefs on 20th-century criminology, Karen Wilkinson (1974:726–732) noted that from 1900 until 1932, the relationship between broken homes and delinquency was widely accepted in the scientific community. Most investigators were rural-born migrants to cities who were convinced that divorce and desertion were serious threats to social stability.

According to Wilkinson (1974:732–734), from about 1933 to 1950, a new generation of criminologists, most of them sociologists, rejected the broken-home explanation of delinquency because (1) early studies lacked scientific rigor and (2) investigators had rural biases (Wilkinson, 1974:732–734). Instead of improving the methods of investigation, however, the new generation rejected the importance of the family altogether. More of the new generation were urban residents, who saw less danger in divorce and social change.

Finally, after mid-century, a few investigators showed a renewed interest in the family (e.g., Chilton and Markle, 1972; Monahan, 1957; Nye, 1958:41–48). Their findings continued to suggest that, indeed, broken or disrupted families are important causes of delinquency. By then, however, the sociological theories that we reviewed in previous chapters had become transcendent. Criminologists were preoccupied not with family relationships, but with the implications of cultural deviance, symbolic interactionist, and strain theories.

In light of that background, more recent control theories are provocative. They suggest that we should not only draw on the past in attempting to understand delinquency, but that we also should rediscover the importance of the family.

SOCIAL CONTROL THEORY

In 1969, Travis Hirschi, a sociologist, reasserted many 19th-century beliefs about the importance of the family. Furthermore, he based his **social control theory** on assumptions about human nature and so-

cial order that were even older than that—beliefs that many 20th-century theorists had long since discarded.

Hirschi (1969:31–34) observed that it had become fashionable to reject the assumptions of philosophers like Hobbes and theorists like Freud that humans are inherently antisocial. Many people today prefer to assume that humans are inherently moral at birth or perhaps that they are a blank slate on which nothing, good or bad, has been inscribed. Hirschi (p. 31) rejected both kinds of assumptions, however, arguing that it is "*not* . . . delinquents and criminals alone [who] are animals, but that we are all animals, and thus all naturally capable of committing criminal acts." If we strip away the "veneer of civilization," we will find that all people are subject to "animal impulses" (p. 31).

If that is true, Hirschi (p. 34) reasoned, then there is nothing to be explained when the question "Why did they do it?" is asked. Because humans are inherently antisocial, all children would commit delinquent acts if they dared. It follows that the central question that a theory of delinquency should ask is why they *don't* do it? That is, why do most children stay out of serious trouble?

The Social Bond

Hirschi (p. 16) answered those questions by suggesting that it is a person's **social bond** that makes the difference (for a similar statement, see Reckless, 1961). To illustrate, he drew from the French sociologist Emile Durkheim (1951:209): "The more weakened the groups to which [a person] belongs, the less he depends on them, the more he consequently depends only on himself and recognizes no other rules of conduct than what are founded on his private interests" (Hirschi, 1969:16). In short, we are moral beings to the extent that we have internalized the norms of society and have become sensitive to the needs of others. Indeed, sensitivity to others *is* the social bond: "To violate a norm is . . . to act contrary to the wishes and expectations of other people. If a person does not care about the wishes and expectations of other people—that is, if he is insensitive to the opinion of others—then he is to that extent not bound by the norms. He is free to deviate" (p. 18).

This way of defining the bond to society requires certain assumptions about the social order. Like rged with remedying their home conditions heir actually having committed more delin- cts (Johnson, 1986; Nye, 1958:51; Sampson aub, 1993:83). Indeed, studies using self- ted law violation to estimate delinquent behav- end to more strongly support Hirschi's social trol prediction.

Self-report studies find a weaker relationship be- ween broken homes and delinquency than do stud- es using official data (for a summary, see Wells and Rankin, 1985:252–254, 1986:85, 1991:85–86). More- over, this tends to hold for both boys and girls (Can- ter, 1982:161–162; Johnson, 1986:68–71; Rankin, 1983:472–476).

Such findings, however, do not mean necessarily that broken homes play no role in causing delin- quency. In the previous chapter, we saw that classic strain theory does not predict a strong relationship between social class and delinquency. This is because social class is only the first in a series of variables in a causal chain leading to the commission of delin- quent acts. Furthermore, as we move across the causal chain, each subsequent variable should have a stronger, more direct relationship to delinquency. The same logic is applicable here. That is, "the over- all correlation between family structure [broken homes] and delinquency . . . may not be large be- cause the two variables are separated by several inter- vening events" (Wells and Rankin, 1986:76). It is possible, for example, that broken homes may result in weak attachment to parents; and weak attachment, in turn, may directly cause delinquency (a possibility acknowledged by Hirschi, 1983:62–63).

Although some studies have found that attach- ment to parents mediates the relationship between broken homes and delinquency (Laub and Sampson, 1988:372–374; Matsueda, 1982:496–500; Matsueda and Heimer, 1987:831; Sampson and Laub, 1993: Chap. 4),[1] others find no such mediating effect (Cern- kovich and Giordano, 1987:305–306, 316; Gove and Crutchfield, 1982:306–309; Johnson, 1986:75–76;

Van Voorhis et al., 1988:248–249, 257). Those latter studies tend to find little or no relationship between broken homes and parental attachment. As Rankin (1983:477) has observed, "the quality of the relation- ship between parent and child is not necessarily good in intact homes nor poor in broken homes."

At the same time, Rankin and Kern (1994:504) have found that "strong attachments to both biolog- ical parents has an additional inhibiting effect on de- linquency over and above strong attachment to only one parent." Although the quality of family relation- ships may be unrelated to whether families are intact or broken, two strong attachments appear to be bet- ter than one (or none) in preventing delinquency.

Many self-report studies tend to show that the children *least* likely to report having violated the law are those who feel loved, identify with their par- ent(s), and respect their wishes. In contrast, *law- breakers* are more likely to come from homes in which (1) cruelty, neglect, erratic discipline, and conflict are present (Baumrind, 1996:412; Cernko- vich and Giordano, 1987:312; Larzelere and Patter- son, 1990:312–314; Norland et al., 1979:230–235; Rankin and Wells, 1990:150–154; Van Voorhis et al., 1988:249–250; Wells and Rankin, 1988:273–280); (2) parental supervision is low (Cernkovich and Giordano, 1987:305–306, 308–316; Gove and Crutch- field, 1982:307–310; Hirschi, 1969:88–90; Jensen, 1972:567–572; Jensen and Eve, 1976:436–438; Lar- zelere and Patterson, 1990:312–314; Patterson and Dishion, 1985:66, 74–75; Smith and Paternoster, 1987:150–153; Van Voorhis et al., 1988:248–250; Warr, 1993:251; Wilson, 1980, 1987); and (3) com- munication and mutual support are lacking (Cern- kovich and Giordano, 1987:305–306, 308–316; Gove and Crutchfield, 1982; Hindelang, 1973:475–476; Hirschi, 1969:89–107; Jensen and Eve, 1976:437– 438; LaGrange and White, 1985:27–31; Liska and Reed, 1985:553–556; Nye, 1958:70–76; Poole and Regoli, 1979:192–193; Rankin and Wells, 1990:151, 154–159; Simons, Miller, and Aigner, 1980:46–49; Wiatrowski, Griswold, and Roberts, 1981:534–536).[2]

other control theorists, Hirschi (p. 23) was dis- inclined to see value conflicts in society as being responsible for a person's insensitivity to others' wishes. Instead, he assumed that people in a given society are tied together by common values, at least where predatory acts are concerned.

That is a crucial assumption. First, it means that Hirschi's theory is not a gender-, social class-, or race/ethnicity-based theory. Rather, because most people believe that they should not kill, rob, or steal, it is only lawbreakers who defy convention and threaten social stability. Second, it implies that devi- ant values are not widely shared. Delinquents are relatively insensitive people who do not adhere to the moral standards of any group, delinquent or con- formist. They violate the law not because they feel obligated to others, but because their natural human impulses remain unrestrained by a lasting bond to any group.

Elements of the Bond

Hirschi (1969:16–30) theorized that the social bond consists of four major elements—attachment, com- mitment, involvement, and belief—that are defined in such a way that their presence can be verified, thus avoiding one of the weaknesses of Freudian theory.

ATTACHMENT The first element, **attachment,** refers to the ties of affection and respect between children and such key people as parents, teachers, and friends. A strong bond with all three will tend to prevent delinquency (p. 83). Attachment to parents, however, is the most important because children are first so- cialized by parents (pp. 29–30). Furthermore, what's most important is not the fact that families may be broken by divorce, separation, desertion, or death, but the quality of the relationship between a child and his or her parent(s) (pp. 86–87). If children are strongly attached to their parents, they are much more likely to internalize conventional norms and to develop feelings of respect for people in authority and for friends (pp. 131, 140–141). But if they are alienated from their parents, they will most likely be alienated from others. They will not learn, or feel obligated by, moral rules, nor will they develop an adequate conscience (p. 86).

In a sense, Hirschi's attachment is analogous to Freud's superego. But it locates "the 'conscience' in

the bond to others rather than making it a part of the personality" (p. 19). In other words, one need not rely on hidden psychodynamic forces to know that the conscience exists. One needs only to dem- onstrate that a person is attached to others and re- spects their wishes.

COMMITMENT The second element of the bond, **commitment,** is a rational component similar to Freud's ego, but it also has roots in long-standing traditions (pp. 20–21). It concerns the extent to which children are committed to such ideal require- ments of childhood as getting an education, post- poning participation in adult activities like drinking and smoking, and aspiring to achieve long-term goals. If children commit themselves to those activi- ties, they will develop a strong **stake in conformity** and will be disinclined to commit delinquent be- havior. To do so would be to endanger their futures (p. 21). And, although commitment refers to an in- ternalized set of expectations, it, too, is amenable to verification, because one can measure how strongly a person is dedicated to the pursuit of conventional goals and means.

INVOLVEMENT The third element, **involvement,** is the modern equivalent of the traditional belief that "idle hands are the devil's workshop" (p. 22). It has particular relevance for teenagers because they are in that phase of the life cycle when they are neither totally under parental domination nor totally free to act as adults. Instead, they are in a limbo, where ex- pectations are not as clear as they might be. Large amounts of unstructured time may weaken the social bond and increase the likelihood of delinquent be- havior. In contrast, children who are busy doing con- ventional things—doing chores around the home, studying, or engaging in sports—may not have time to commit delinquent acts (pp. 21–23). Further- more, the degree to which a person is involved in conventional activities also can be measured.

BELIEF The fourth element, **belief,** refers to accep- tance of the morality of our laws. Some young people simply have not been socialized to respect the law (pp. 23–26). They feel no obligation whatsoever to conform to the expectations of others. This is not to say that they don't know when they are breaking the

---

[1]While Matsueda (1982:496–500) and his associate Karen Heimer (Mat- sueda and Heimer, 1987:835–836) find that attachment to parents medi- ates the relationship between broken homes and delinquency, they also find that the effects of both attachment and broken homes are mediated by the ratio of definitions favorable and unfavorable to delinquency. Hence, they interpret their findings as lending support to Sutherland's differential association theory (see Chapter 9) rather than Hirschi's social control theory.

[2]Not all studies reveal a strong relation between attachment to parents and delinquency. For example, Agnew (1985b:52–54) finds little or no rela- tionship between liking/respect for parents and delinquency. Moreover, Krohn et al. (1983:342–344) find that communication/mutual support has only a small effect on delinquency (at least for cigarette smoking, which is the focus of their study) and that supervision has no effect at all.

law or that they fail to recognize that they may incur the wrath of others when they do; it is just that their consciences are not offended by delinquent behavior. Lacking any moral constraints, they are free to violate the law. Hence, the less that young people believe in the morality of law, the more likely they are to commit delinquent acts (p. 26).

Like Freud's theory, Hirschi's social control theory is more about conformity than delinquency. Because it assumes that we all are animals at birth and will rob, cheat, and steal unless restrained, delinquency needs no explanation. As Durkheim (1953: 45) suggested, many of us "find charm in the accomplishment of a moral act prescribed by a rule that has no other justification than that it is a rule. We feel a . . . pleasure in performing our duty simply because it is our duty." But why? Because the performance of duty inevitably requires effort, why do we find it attractive? Hirschi implied that it is because we have a strong **stake in conformity** (Toby, 1957). If we enjoy the respect of our parents, teachers, and friends, and are committed to long-range goals, we are threatened with a loss of those things if we fail to do our duty, particularly if we violate the law. That is why the social bond is so important. We have learned that we have more to lose than to gain from violating the law. It will threaten whatever chances we have of completing school, launching a career, and earning the esteem of other people.

IMPLICATIONS OF SOCIAL CONTROL THEORY FOR SOCIAL POLICY

Hirschi's (1969) social control theory has not had an impact on social policy that is anywhere near that of strain theory. Nevertheless, it has continued to reinforce a set of widely shared beliefs and practices.

To begin with, it appeals to common sense. For example, Claude Lewis (1993), a nationally syndicated columnist, states that "for too long blacks have believed that any and everything that affects them in negative ways . . . is the fault of someone else: mainly white people. . . . Black-on-black crime is not the fault of whites. . . . [The fault for] such massive misbehavior . . . lies with blacks themselves." Sounding like a social control theorist, he suggests that the so-

lutions to black youth violence are parental responsibility, education, and hard work among blacks themselves.

The same view is held by many legal officials, who, in contrast to criminologists, actually encounter delinquents, one by one. As official delinquents are filtered through the juvenile justice system, they are less likely than other children to have strong ties to anyone, even their parents. For example, consider the comments of a physician about the delinquents who come to hospitals because of their wounds in street battles:

> The kids we get are real tough kids. They make you feel afraid. You know they wouldn't hesitate to take a knife to your throat. But when they come in here for care, they've been hurt so badly that they have no fight left. They have been stabbed or shot, but they never ask for anyone. They expect to die and would just as soon die as live.
>
> The thing that shocks me is that many of their parents never show up to see them. They just watch with a hopeless attitude; they've given up on their children. They ask questions like, "Why did you call me in?" "Why do I have to sign this paper?" "Isn't he a ward of the court?" The parents don't want anything to do with their children, and the children seem to have lost all sense of caring. (unpublished personal interview)

Given their repeated exposure to distressing situations like these, legal officials are inclined not only to sound like social control theorists but also to agree with one study of official delinquents that indicated "(1) that children charged with delinquency live in disrupted families substantially more often than children in the general population, [and] (2) that children referred for more serious delinquency are more likely to come from incomplete families than juveniles charged with minor offenses" (Chilton and Markle, 1972:93). It takes no stretch of the imagination for these officials to associate disrupted families and a weak social bond with delinquent behavior. (For the policy implications of social control theory as applied to the family, see Hirschi, 1983, 1995: 138–139).

Consequently, whereas Freud's psychodynamic control theory may have served as a kind of sophisticated legitimizing rationale for legal officials' roles as professionals, Hirschi's (1969) social control theory has done a far better job of capturing the commonsense side of the problems they face. They readily can understand the need to (1) *attach* youngsters to some kind of family, (2) *commit* them to the long-range conventional goals that childhood demands, (3) *involve* them in school and other constructive activities, and (4) have them acquire *beliefs* in the morality of law.

In short, whether legal officials are aware of Hirschi's social control theory, it is the kind of explanation that makes sense to them and on which they base many of their interventions. An important question, therefore, is whether the theory is adequate from a scientific standpoint.

SCIENTIFIC ADEQUACY OF SOCIAL CONTROL THEORY

Hirschi (1969) did an unusual thing by testing his own theory. Indeed, he even examined one of social control theory's basic assumptions, namely, that the social order is characterized by value consensus and that most people agree about what is right and wrong. We will examine Hirschi's notion of social order first and then the findings about the various elements of the social bond: attachment, commitment, involvement, and belief.

Social Order

Along with other researchers, Hirschi (1969:212–223) found that there is considerable consensus among young people from different racial/ethnic groups and social classes about the importance of obeying the law, getting an education, and refusing to take advantage of others (also see Gold, 1963: 160–162; Short and Strodtbeck, 1965:59, 271). Similarly, researchers have found that—whether white or black, middle or lower class, educated or uneducated—most people agree about the seriousness of various crimes and believe that offenders should be punished severely if they commit offenses that harm others (Blumstein and Cohen, 1980; Chilton

and DeAmicis, 19[...]
Rossi, Simpson, and [...]
Warr, Meier, and Eric[...]
334–336; Wolfgang et al., [...]

There seems to be agreem[...]
values and beliefs about what is [...]
do the elements of the social [...]
commitment, involvement, and bel[...]
between those who conform to the [...]
who violate it?

Attachment

Recall that attachment refers to ties of affectio[...]
respect between children and such key person[...]
parents, teachers, and friends. Strong attachmen[...]
are supposed to act as barriers against delinquency.
Thus, if attachments are weak, children should be free to commit delinquent acts.

ATTACHMENT TO PARENTS Hirschi's social control theory includes two basic predictions: (1) The quality of the relationship between a child and one or both parents is a more important cause of delinquency than whether the home is broken by divorce, separation, desertion, or death, and (2) the weaker a child's attachment, the greater the likelihood that he or she will commit delinquent acts.

Several studies, based on comparisons of official delinquents and official nondelinquents, would seem to cast doubts on those predictions, especially the first one—that broken homes are less important than the quality of the parent–child relationship in causing delinquency (Chilton and Markle, 1972; Cockburn and Maclay, 1965:298–299; Cowie, Cowie, and Slater, 1968:Chap. 5; Datesman and Scarpitti, 1975; Monahan, 1957; Rodman and Grams, 1967: 196–197). Not only are officially delinquent boys and girls more likely to come from broken homes, but among girls "the proportions from incomplete families are so high . . . that there can hardly be any doubt as to the importance of parental deprivation to them" (Monahan, 1957:258).

A problem with these studies, however, is their use of official data. When official delinquents are compared with official nondelinquents, there is a danger that the high proportion of delinquents from broken homes will be due more to legal officials

Furthermore, although occasional studies indicate that those variables may have a slightly greater effect on girls than boys, most studies suggest that gender makes little difference.

Given such findings, the existing evidence suggests two basic conclusions with respect to the family (for a comprehensive review, see Loeber and Stouthamer-Loeber, 1986). First, most investigators are inclined to support Hirschi's hypothesis that "the nature of relationships between children and parents is more relevant to explaining delinquency than is the broken or intact nature of the home" (Jensen and Rojek, 1992:308). Second, most studies suggest that the juveniles who are most likely to commit delinquent behaviors—whether male or female, black or white, lower or middle class—are those whose attachment to their parents is weak. Conversely, the stronger their attachment, the less likely that they will commit delinquency.

ATTACHMENT TO SCHOOL In considering attachment to school, Hirschi (1969) alluded to the importance of education in the lives of children. "Insofar as this institution [the school] is able to command his attachment," he claimed, ". . . the adolescent is presumably able to move from childhood to adulthood with a minimum of delinquent acts" (p. 110). As discussed in prior chapters, the evidence tends to support that claim. Moreover, the results can be devastating for those young people who fail in school. Whether male or female, black or white, lower or middle class, those who do the worst in school are the most likely to commit delinquent acts (Agnew, 1991:143–144; Elliott and Voss, 1974:133–137, 175–179, 182–187; Empey and Lubeck, 1971:80–84; Frease, 1973:452–454; Hindelang, 1973:476–477; Hirschi, 1969:115–116; Johnson, 1979:101–103; LaGrange and White, 1985:27–31; Polk and Halferty, 1966:84, 90–96; Polk and Schafer, 1972:passim; Rankin, 1980:427–428; Stinchcombe, 1964:143; Wiatrowski, Griswold, and Roberts, 1981:534–538; Wiatrowski et al., 1982:153–158).

A basic question, therefore, is not whether attachment to school is important, but to what its absence should be attributed. Why is it that delinquents are more likely than nondelinquents to have weak ties to the educational system? Classic strain theory suggests that it is due either to frustration over blocked opportunities or to a sense of inadequacy because of failure to live up to the standards of the middle-class measuring rod. Hirschi's (1969:113, 115, 120) social control theory, in contrast, suggests that it represents insensitivity to the opinions of teachers, parents, and friends, and a lack of commitment to long-range goals. Students who fail in school simply do not care about others' opinions and are not interested in the hard work that conventional success requires.

Evidence regarding those contrasting views is equivocal. On the one hand, much of it appears to support Hirschi's social control theory by showing that students who fail in school and commit delinquent acts tend to have lower, not higher, aspirations—and thus to challenge the idea that poor attachment to school is due to frustrated ambitions (Hirschi, 1969:178–179; Polk and Halferty, 1966:84, 93–96; Wiatrowski et al., 1982:153 158). On the other hand, research does not clearly indicate whether weak attachment to school precedes or follows low aspirations. If Hirschi (1969:117) is correct, low aspirations should be preceded by weak attachment. But Cohen (1955:112–116, 129–137) maintained that although lower-class boys start out with high aspirations, it is the loss of status they suffer in school that eventually causes them to reject everything that is middle class, including long-range goals. In other words, weak attachment to school does not precede, but rather follows the frustration of aspirations.

It is possible, at least for some youths, that weak attachment to school is a result, not a cause, of low aspirations. Although perhaps interested in school as elementary students, these youths have become alienated from it by the time they reach adolescence. Their weak attachment and their delinquent behavior are certainly real, but their problems may not be due to a lifelong disregard for conventional people and conventional goals. Instead, it may be due to unpleasant experiences that the school itself has fostered.

In the same vein, there is the question of intellectual ability. If children have the ability to do well in school, the chances are greater that they will become strongly attached to it. But if they lack that ability, their poor performance will lead to a dislike of school, followed in turn by the rejection of authority and the commission of delinquent acts.

General support for that kind of causal chain is provided by Wiatrowski, Griswold, and Roberts (1981:535) and by Wiatrowski et al. (1982:154–157) from research on a national sample of high school males. We already have seen that delinquents tend to get poorer grades in school than do nondelinquents. Moreover, a variety of studies find that delinquents do less well on achievement tests (Hirschi, 1969:113–115; Jensen, 1976; Patterson and Dishion, 1985:73; Wolfgang, Figlio, and Sellin, 1972:245–248) and are more likely to reject school authority (Hindelang, 1973:478; Hirschi, 1969:123–124; Stinchcombe, 1964: 27–32).

One of the most serious challenges to Hirschi's social control theory about the relationship between attachment to school and delinquency again involves causal ordering: whether weak attachment precedes or follows delinquency. Hirschi's (1969:Chap. 7) position on that issue is clear: Weak attachment to school should precede delinquent behavior. Studies by Agnew (1985b:57–58) and by Liska and Reed (1985:553–556), however, have suggested just the opposite causal ordering. Looking at youths' attitudes toward school and their satisfaction with school experiences, both studies have indicated that weak attachment to school follows delinquency. To explain such a causal chain, Liska and Reed (1985: 557) observed that much delinquency is committed in schools and that

> street delinquency may be correlated with troublesome school behavior in classrooms, school halls and schoolyards. . . . This leads to reactions by teachers and school administrators, which in turn decrease school attachment. Also, adolescents involved in delinquency simply have less time for school; thus, delinquency, independently of teacher reactions, may decrease school attachment.

In summary, research regarding attachment to school has been inconsistent. On the one hand, it leaves little doubt that attachment to school is crucial in explaining the difference between conformity to the law and delinquency (although it seems that delinquency leads to poor attachment to school, and not the opposite, as Hirschi suggested), and it indicates that high aspirations are more likely to act as

barriers to delinquency than as motivators for it. The evidence, in other words, tends to support social control rather than classic strain theory. On the other hand, research does not permit us to determine whether delinquents have always been insensitive to conventional goals and people or whether they acquire such feelings as a result of their school experiences.

ATTACHMENT TO FRIENDS Affinity with friends is the final dimension of attachment. As we have seen, Hirschi (1969) theorized that young people who do not like and respect their parents and teachers are more likely to commit delinquent acts. But he also theorized that delinquents are not as likely to respect their friends, either (pp. 140–141). The reason is that they have never developed feelings of compassion and responsibility for anyone. Although delinquents may join together in groups or gangs, their relations will be exploitive rather than warm and supportive.

This aspect of Hirschi's theory has been one of the most difficult to confirm or deny. On the one hand, we have seen in previous chapters that delinquency is overwhelmingly a group phenomenon. Furthermore, as Johnson (1979:109) has demonstrated, the school is a place where children are sifted and sorted into different groups—some delinquent, some conformist. In an attempt to explain those phenomena, cultural deviance and classic strain theorists (see Chapters 8 and 10) have suggested that in delinquent groups, friends become a sort of substitute society, providing satisfactions that nondelinquents find through conventional friends.

Several studies have suggested that this may be the case. Juveniles with weak attachments to parents and school seem to compensate by seeking out delinquent friends (Johnson, 1979:99–111; Johnson, Marcos, and Bahr, 1987:333–335; Marcos, Bahr, and Johnson, 1986:147–154; Matsueda and Heimer, 1987: 831–833; Patterson and Dishion, 1985:74–75). Moreover, in general, delinquents (although evidence is limited to delinquent boys) are more likely than nondelinquents to be influenced by the expectations of their friends (Empey and Lubeck, 1968:769–770; Erickson and Empey, 1965:275–279).

At the same time, those studies do not necessarily show that delinquents are as inclined as nondelinquents to hold their friends in high esteem. With regard to that issue, Hirschi (1969:145–152) found that boys who were least respectful of their friends were most likely to have committed delinquent acts. Although that finding has not been replicated in subsequent studies (Hindelang, 1973:478–479; Krohn and Massey, 1980:534–536; Krohn et al., 1983:344; Wiatrowski, Griswold, and Roberts, 1981:535), it tends to support the contentions of others that members of delinquent groups are not characterized by relaxed or laid-back feelings. Indeed, delinquent gangs have been described more in terms of aggression, threat, and insult than warmth, respect, and solidarity (Matza, 1964:42–44, 53–55; Miller, 1958: 9–10; Short and Strodtbeck, 1965:221–234; Yablonsky, 1970:191–192). Klein and Crawford (1967) argued that, were it not for the external pressures of rival gangs, neighbors, and police, delinquent gangs would have little to hold them together. Members' loyalty to one another is an expression of the need to resist outside pressure more than to repay internal debts of kindness and mutual esteem.

We have seen, however, in previous chapters (especially Chapter 10) that such characterizations have not gone unchallenged. Giordano, Cernkovich, and Pugh (1986), for example, have reported that delinquents have the same kinds of friendship relationships as nondelinquents and that those relationships are often stable and mutually supportive.

In light of such conflicting findings, two conclusions are warranted. First, Hirschi's social control theory appears to overlook the important role played by peers in the commission of delinquent acts. Second, given the doubts that have been raised about Hirschi's contention that compared to law-abiding children, delinquents are less attached to friends, more research on the character of delinquent, as well as conventional, groups is needed.

Commitment

As the second element of the social bond, commitment assumes that the motivation to adhere to the ideal concept of childhood and strive for conventional goals is a built-in constraint on delinquent behavior. An individual has a stake in conformity that he or she feels will be jeopardized by delinquency. For example, Hirschi (1969:165–166) con-

tended that those children who engage in such adult activities as smoking, drinking, dating, and driving at an early age are also more likely to commit delinquent acts (recognizing, of course, that smoking and drinking may themselves be status offenses). By doing such things, they deny their status as children, express contempt for the expectations of parents and teachers, and free themselves from the norms governing childhood.

The evidence in support of those contentions has been rather consistent. Juveniles who willingly violate the expectations of childhood at an early age are most likely to commit delinquent acts (Agnew, 1985a:160–163; Hindelang, 1973:480–482; Hirschi, 1969:166–169; Polk and Halferty, 1966:84; Wiatrowski, Griswold, and Roberts, 1981:534–537).

So much for the deviant side of the coin (i.e., smoking, drinking, and the like). What effect does commitment to an education or a career have on delinquency? We have already seen in both this and the previous chapter that ambition, with its implied commitment to long-term educational and occupational goals, is more likely to operate as a barrier to than a cause of delinquency. Therefore, it is not difficult to anticipate the results of research. They indicate that those girls and boys most committed to staying in school and otherwise conforming to the requirements of childhood are the least likely to commit delinquent acts (Briar and Piliavin, 1965:42–45; Hindelang, 1973:481–482; Hirschi, 1969:170–184; Johnson, 1979:108–109; Krohn et al., 1983:345; LaGrange and White, 1985:32–35; Massey and Krohn, 1986:124; Polk and Halferty, 1966:91–93).[3]

Involvement

The third element of the bond, involvement, predicts that participation in conventional activities should prevent delinquency. The evidence, however, is mixed. On the one hand, the greater the involvement in studying or doing homework, the less the chances of committing delinquent acts (Hindelang, 1973:481, 483; Hirschi, 1969:191–192; Polk and Halferty, 1966:

---

[3]Krohn and Massey (1980:534–536) and Wiatrowski, Griswold, and Roberts (1981:535), however, report contrary evidence. Moreover, Krohn et al. (1983:344) suggest that such variables as commitment may explain minor delinquent acts better than they do serious offenses.

84; Wiatrowski, Griswold, and Roberts, 1981:534–536). On the other hand, participation in sports, clubs, hobbies, or even a job does not seem to have the predicted preventive effect. Young people who engage in those activities are almost as likely to commit delinquent acts as are those who do not (Agnew, 1984:439, 445; Hindelang, 1973:483; Hirschi, 1969:189–190; Rankin, 1976:475–476, 479, 1980: 428; Smith and Paternoster, 1987:150–155). Consequently, of those types of activities, it is involvement in academic activities rather than other conventional activities that is the strongest barrier to delinquency.

Belief

As the final element of the bond, Hirschi's (1969) social control theory suggests that beliefs are relatively stable attributes of a person and are generally impervious to transitory relationships. If children have been trained to believe in the morality of law, they will be less inclined to commit delinquent acts, no matter what groups they encounter.

In contrast, symbolic interactionist theory (see Chapter 9) tends to suggest that beliefs are relatively transitory attitudes that can be shaped and reshaped, depending on the groups with whom one associates. Even though a young person might have been a member of law-abiding groups in the past, association with a delinquent group can lead that individual to alter his or her beliefs and commit delinquent acts.

Research to examine those opposing points of view has supported neither one totally. On the one hand, a number of studies lend some support to Hirschi's social control theory. Boys and girls who are not strongly attached to parents and school have the least respect for the law and the police. Those same juveniles, in turn, are most likely to commit delinquent acts (Hindelang, 1973:483–486; Hirschi, 1969: 200–205; Krohn and Massey, 1980:535; Marcos, Bahr, and Johnson, 1986:147–152).

On the other hand, some investigators have sought to separate the effects of peer group associations from the effects of beliefs about the law. In doing so, they have found that beliefs affect delinquency, but probably in a different way than Hirschi suggested. Indeed, Hirschi (1969:138, 156) argued that beliefs should affect association with delinquent friends; in particular, attenuation of beliefs in the

moral validity of law should increase the likelihood of having delinquent friends. And he suggested that both a lack of respect for the law and association with delinquent friends should lead to delinquent behavior.[4]

In contrast to that argument, Sutherland's theory of differential association suggests that association with delinquent friends increases the likelihood of delinquency because it is more likely than association with nondelinquent friends to transmit definitions favorable to delinquency. Hence, Sutherland's theory posits that (1) association with delinquent friends should attenuate beliefs in the moral validity of law, not the other way around, and (2) only beliefs should have a direct effect on delinquency, because the effects of delinquent friends on delinquent behavior should be mediated by beliefs.

Reanalyzing the same data that Hirschi (1969) used to test his theory, Matsueda and Heimer (1987: 831, 835) found more support for the causal chain suggested by Sutherland than for Hirschi's (and, using different data, Matsueda [1989:442–446] again finds, in contrast to Hirschi's basic argument, that delinquency affects beliefs, not the other way around).

Still other studies, however, have reported evidence contrary to that of Matsueda and Heimer (1987), although not totally consistent with Hirschi's theory either (Marcos, Bahr, and Johnson, 1986:155; Massey and Krohn, 1986:124). Those studies have shown that when association with delinquent friends and beliefs about law are considered simultaneously, only association with delinquent friends has a direct effect on delinquency. The effects of beliefs on delinquency are indirect, in that they influence juveniles' peer associations. That is, juveniles become friends with delinquents after questioning the moral validity of law, and then association with delinquent friends leads to delinquency.

---

[4]In Chapter 9, it was said that most control theorists argue that membership in delinquent groups occurs only *after* an individual becomes delinquent (delinquents, like birds of a feather, flock together). Here, it is being said that, according to Hirschi (1969), association with delinquent friends *precedes* delinquency. Hirschi himself tends to waffle on this issue, demonstrating the point that peer relations are generally of secondary importance to control theorists. After analyzing his data, however, Hirschi (1969: 156) concluded that association with delinquent friends probably leads to delinquent behavior, not the opposite.

other control theorists, Hirschi (p. 23) was disinclined to see value conflicts in society as being responsible for a person's insensitivity to others' wishes. Instead, he assumed that people in a given society are tied together by common values, at least where predatory acts are concerned.

That is a crucial assumption. First, it means that Hirschi's theory is not a gender-, social class-, or race/ethnicity-based theory. Rather, because most people believe that they should not kill, rob, or steal, it is only lawbreakers who defy convention and threaten social stability. Second, it implies that deviant values are not widely shared. Delinquents are relatively insensitive people who do not adhere to the moral standards of any group, delinquent or conformist. They violate the law not because they feel obligated to others, but because their natural human impulses remain unrestrained by a lasting bond to any group.

Elements of the Bond

Hirschi (1969:16–30) theorized that the social bond consists of four major elements—attachment, commitment, involvement, and belief—that are defined in such a way that their presence can be verified, thus avoiding one of the weaknesses of Freudian theory.

ATTACHMENT The first element, **attachment,** refers to the ties of affection and respect between children and such key people as parents, teachers, and friends. A strong bond with all three will tend to prevent delinquency (p. 83). Attachment to parents, however, is the most important because children are first socialized by parents (pp. 29–30). Furthermore, what's most important is not the fact that families may be broken by divorce, separation, desertion, or death, but the quality of the relationship between a child and his or her parent(s) (pp. 86–87). If children are strongly attached to their parents, they are much more likely to internalize conventional norms and to develop feelings of respect for people in authority and for friends (pp. 131, 140–141). But if they are alienated from their parents, they will most likely be alienated from others. They will not learn, or feel obligated by, moral rules, nor will they develop an adequate conscience (p. 86).

In a sense, Hirschi's attachment is analogous to Freud's superego. But it locates "the 'conscience' in the bond to others rather than making it a part of the personality" (p. 19). In other words, one need not rely on hidden psychodynamic forces to know that the conscience exists. One needs only to demonstrate that a person is attached to others and respects their wishes.

COMMITMENT The second element of the bond, **commitment,** is a rational component similar to Freud's ego, but it also has roots in long-standing traditions (pp. 20–21). It concerns the extent to which children are committed to such ideal requirements of childhood as getting an education, postponing participation in adult activities like drinking and smoking, and aspiring to achieve long-term goals. If children commit themselves to those activities, they will develop a strong **stake in conformity** and will be disinclined to commit delinquent behavior. To do so would be to endanger their futures (p. 21). And, although commitment refers to an internalized set of expectations, it, too, is amenable to verification, because one can measure how strongly a person is dedicated to the pursuit of conventional goals and means.

INVOLVEMENT The third element, **involvement,** is the modern equivalent of the traditional belief that "idle hands are the devil's workshop" (p. 22). It has particular relevance for teenagers because they are in that phase of the life cycle when they are neither totally under parental domination nor totally free to act as adults. Instead, they are in a limbo, where expectations are not as clear as they might be. Large amounts of unstructured time may weaken the social bond and increase the likelihood of delinquent behavior. In contrast, children who are busy doing conventional things—doing chores around the home, studying, or engaging in sports—may not have time to commit delinquent acts (pp. 21–23). Furthermore, the degree to which a person is involved in conventional activities also can be measured.

BELIEF The fourth element, **belief,** refers to acceptance of the morality of our laws. Some young people simply have not been socialized to respect the law (pp. 23–26). They feel no obligation whatsoever to conform to the expectations of others. This is not to say that they don't know when they are breaking the law or that they fail to recognize that they may incur the wrath of others when they do; it is just that their consciences are not offended by delinquent behavior. Lacking any moral constraints, they are free to violate the law. Hence, the less that young people believe in the morality of law, the more likely they are to commit delinquent acts (p. 26).

Like Freud's theory, Hirschi's social control theory is more about conformity than delinquency. Because it assumes that we all are animals at birth and will rob, cheat, and steal unless restrained, delinquency needs no explanation. As Durkheim (1953: 45) suggested, many of us "find charm in the accomplishment of a moral act prescribed by a rule that has no other justification than that it is a rule. We feel a . . . pleasure in performing our duty simply because it is our duty." But why? Because the performance of duty inevitably requires effort, why do we find it attractive? Hirschi implied that it is because we have a strong **stake in conformity** (Toby, 1957). If we enjoy the respect of our parents, teachers, and friends, and are committed to long-range goals, we are threatened with a loss of those things if we fail to do our duty, particularly if we violate the law. That is why the social bond is so important. We have learned that we have more to lose than to gain from violating the law. It will threaten whatever chances we have of completing school, launching a career, and earning the esteem of other people.

IMPLICATIONS OF SOCIAL CONTROL THEORY FOR SOCIAL POLICY

Hirschi's (1969) social control theory has not had an impact on social policy that is anywhere near that of strain theory. Nevertheless, it has continued to reinforce a set of widely shared beliefs and practices.

To begin with, it appeals to common sense. For example, Claude Lewis (1993), a nationally syndicated columnist, states that "for too long blacks have believed that any and everything that affects them in negative ways . . . is the fault of someone else: mainly white people. . . . Black-on-black crime is not the fault of whites. . . . [The fault for] such massive misbehavior . . . lies with blacks themselves." Sounding like a social control theorist, he suggests that the so-

lutions to black youth violence are parental responsibility, education, and hard work among blacks themselves.

The same view is held by many legal officials, who, in contrast to criminologists, actually encounter delinquents, one by one. As official delinquents are filtered through the juvenile justice system, they are less likely than other children to have strong ties to anyone, even their parents. For example, consider the comments of a physician about the delinquents who come to hospitals because of their wounds in street battles:

> The kids we get are real tough kids. They make you feel afraid. You know they wouldn't hesitate to take a knife to your throat. But when they come in here for care, they've been hurt so badly that they have no fight left. They have been stabbed or shot, but they never ask for anyone. They expect to die and would just as soon die as live.
>
> The thing that shocks me is that many of their parents never show up to see them. They just watch with a hopeless attitude; they've given up on their children. They ask questions like, "Why did you call me in?" "Why do I have to sign this paper?" "Isn't he a ward of the court?" The parents don't want anything to do with their children, and the children seem to have lost all sense of caring. (unpublished personal interview)

Given their repeated exposure to distressing situations like these, legal officials are inclined not only to sound like social control theorists but also to agree with one study of official delinquents that indicated "(1) that children charged with delinquency live in disrupted families substantially more often than children in the general population, [and] (2) that children referred for more serious delinquency are more likely to come from incomplete families than juveniles charged with minor offenses" (Chilton and Markle, 1972:93). It takes no stretch of the imagination for these officials to associate disrupted families and a weak social bond with delinquent behavior. (For the policy implications of social control theory as applied to the family, see Hirschi, 1983, 1995: 138–139).

Consequently, whereas Freud's psychodynamic control theory may have served as a kind of sophisticated legitimizing rationale for legal officials' roles as professionals, Hirschi's (1969) social control theory has done a far better job of capturing the commonsense side of the problems they face. They readily can understand the need to (1) *attach* youngsters to some kind of family, (2) *commit* them to the long-range conventional goals that childhood demands, (3) *involve* them in school and other constructive activities, and (4) have them acquire *beliefs* in the morality of law.

In short, whether legal officials are aware of Hirschi's social control theory, it is the kind of explanation that makes sense to them and on which they base many of their interventions. An important question, therefore, is whether the theory is adequate from a scientific standpoint.

SCIENTIFIC ADEQUACY OF SOCIAL CONTROL THEORY

Hirschi (1969) did an unusual thing by testing his own theory. Indeed, he even examined one of social control theory's basic assumptions, namely, that the social order is characterized by value consensus and that most people agree about what is right and wrong. We will examine Hirschi's notion of social order first and then the findings about the various elements of the social bond: attachment, commitment, involvement, and belief.

Social Order

Along with other researchers, Hirschi (1969:212–223) found that there is considerable consensus among young people from different racial/ethnic groups and social classes about the importance of obeying the law, getting an education, and refusing to take advantage of others (also see Gold, 1963: 160–162; Short and Strodtbeck, 1965:59, 271). Similarly, researchers have found that—whether white or black, middle or lower class, educated or uneducated—most people agree about the seriousness of various crimes and believe that offenders should be punished severely if they commit offenses that harm others (Blumstein and Cohen, 1980; Chilton

and DeAmicis, 1975; Hamilton and Rytina, 1980; Rossi, Simpson, and Miller, 1985; Rossi et al., 1974; Warr, Meier, and Erickson, 1983; Wellford, 1975: 334–336; Wolfgang et al., 1985:77).

There seems to be agreement, therefore, on basic values and beliefs about what is right and wrong. But do the elements of the social bond—attachment, commitment, involvement, and belief—differentiate between those who conform to the law and those who violate it?

Attachment

Recall that attachment refers to ties of affection and respect between children and such key persons as parents, teachers, and friends. Strong attachments are supposed to act as barriers against delinquency. Thus, if attachments are weak, children should be free to commit delinquent acts.

ATTACHMENT TO PARENTS Hirschi's social control theory includes two basic predictions: (1) The quality of the relationship between a child and one or both parents is a more important cause of delinquency than whether the home is broken by divorce, separation, desertion, or death, and (2) the weaker a child's attachment, the greater the likelihood that he or she will commit delinquent acts.

Several studies, based on comparisons of official delinquents and official nondelinquents, would seem to cast doubts on those predictions, especially the first one—that broken homes are less important than the quality of the parent–child relationship in causing delinquency (Chilton and Markle, 1972; Cockburn and Maclay, 1965:298–299; Cowie, Cowie, and Slater, 1968:Chap. 5; Datesman and Scarpitti, 1975; Monahan, 1957; Rodman and Grams, 1967: 196–197). Not only are officially delinquent boys and girls more likely to come from broken homes, but among girls "the proportions from incomplete families are so high . . . that there can hardly be any doubt as to the importance of parental deprivation to them" (Monahan, 1957:258).

A problem with these studies, however, is their use of official data. When official delinquents are compared with official nondelinquents, there is a danger that the high proportion of delinquents from broken homes will be due more to legal officials being charged with remedying their home conditions than to their actually having committed more delinquent acts (Johnson, 1986; Nye, 1958:51; Sampson and Laub, 1993:83). Indeed, studies using self-reported law violation to estimate delinquent behavior tend to more strongly support Hirschi's social control prediction.

Self-report studies find a weaker relationship between broken homes and delinquency than do studies using official data (for a summary, see Wells and Rankin, 1985:252–254, 1986:85, 1991:85–86). Moreover, this tends to hold for both boys and girls (Canter, 1982:161–162; Johnson, 1986:68–71; Rankin, 1983:472–476).

Such findings, however, do not mean necessarily that broken homes play no role in causing delinquency. In the previous chapter, we saw that classic strain theory does not predict a strong relationship between social class and delinquency. This is because social class is only the first in a series of variables in a causal chain leading to the commission of delinquent acts. Furthermore, as we move across the causal chain, each subsequent variable should have a stronger, more direct relationship to delinquency. The same logic is applicable here. That is, "the overall correlation between family structure [broken homes] and delinquency . . . may not be large because the two variables are separated by several intervening events" (Wells and Rankin, 1986:76). It is possible, for example, that broken homes may result in weak attachment to parents; and weak attachment, in turn, may directly cause delinquency (a possibility acknowledged by Hirschi, 1983:62–63).

Although some studies have found that attachment to parents mediates the relationship between broken homes and delinquency (Laub and Sampson, 1988:372–374; Matsueda, 1982:496–500; Matsueda and Heimer, 1987:831; Sampson and Laub, 1993: Chap. 4),[1] others find no such mediating effect (Cernkovich and Giordano, 1987:305–306, 316; Gove and Crutchfield, 1982:306–309; Johnson, 1986:75–76;

Van Voorhis et al., 1988:248–249, 257). Those latter studies tend to find little or no relationship between broken homes and parental attachment. As Rankin (1983:477) has observed, "the quality of the relationship between parent and child is not necessarily good in intact homes nor poor in broken homes."

At the same time, Rankin and Kern (1994:504) have found that "strong attachments to both biological parents has an additional inhibiting effect on delinquency over and above strong attachment to only one parent." Although the quality of family relationships may be unrelated to whether families are intact or broken, two strong attachments appear to be better than one (or none) in preventing delinquency.

Many self-report studies tend to show that the children *least* likely to report having violated the law are those who feel loved, identify with their parent(s), and respect their wishes. In contrast, *lawbreakers* are more likely to come from homes in which (1) cruelty, neglect, erratic discipline, and conflict are present (Baumrind, 1996:412; Cernkovich and Giordano, 1987:312; Larzelere and Patterson, 1990:312–314; Norland et al., 1979:230–235; Rankin and Wells, 1990:150–154; Van Voorhis et al., 1988:249–250; Wells and Rankin, 1988:273–280); (2) parental supervision is low (Cernkovich and Giordano, 1987:305–306, 308–316; Gove and Crutchfield, 1982:307–310; Hirschi, 1969:88–90; Jensen, 1972:567–572; Jensen and Eve, 1976:436–438; Larzelere and Patterson, 1990:312–314; Patterson and Dishion, 1985:66, 74–75; Smith and Paternoster, 1987:150–153; Van Voorhis et al., 1988:248–250; Warr, 1993:251; Wilson, 1980, 1987); and (3) communication and mutual support are lacking (Cernkovich and Giordano, 1987:305–306, 308–316; Gove and Crutchfield, 1982; Hindelang, 1973:475–476; Hirschi, 1969:89–107; Jensen and Eve, 1976:437–438; LaGrange and White, 1985:27–31; Liska and Reed, 1985:553–556; Nye, 1958:70–76; Poole and Regoli, 1979:192–193; Rankin and Wells, 1990:151, 154–159; Simons, Miller, and Aigner, 1980:46–49; Wiatrowski, Griswold, and Roberts, 1981:534–536).[2]

---

[1]While Matsueda (1982:496–500) and his associate Karen Heimer (Matsueda and Heimer, 1987:835–836) find that attachment to parents mediates the relationship between broken homes and delinquency, they also find that the effects of both attachment and broken homes are mediated by the ratio of definitions favorable and unfavorable to delinquency. Hence, they interpret their findings as lending support to Sutherland's differential association theory (see Chapter 9) rather than Hirschi's social control theory.

[2]Not all studies reveal a strong relation between attachment to parents and delinquency. For example, Agnew (1985b:52–54) finds little or no relationship between liking/respect for parents and delinquency. Moreover, Krohn et al. (1983:342–344) find that communication/mutual support has only a small effect on delinquency (at least for cigarette smoking, which is the focus of their study) and that supervision has no effect at all.

Furthermore, although occasional studies indicate that those variables may have a slightly greater effect on girls than boys, most studies suggest that gender makes little difference.

Given such findings, the existing evidence suggests two basic conclusions with respect to the family (for a comprehensive review, see Loeber and Stouthamer-Loeber, 1986). First, most investigators are inclined to support Hirschi's hypothesis that "the nature of relationships between children and parents is more relevant to explaining delinquency than is the broken or intact nature of the home" (Jensen and Rojek, 1992:308). Second, most studies suggest that the juveniles who are most likely to commit delinquent behaviors—whether male or female, black or white, lower or middle class—are those whose attachment to their parents is weak. Conversely, the stronger their attachment, the less likely that they will commit delinquency.

ATTACHMENT TO SCHOOL In considering attachment to school, Hirschi (1969) alluded to the importance of education in the lives of children. "Insofar as this institution [the school] is able to command his attachment," he claimed, ". . . the adolescent is presumably able to move from childhood to adulthood with a minimum of delinquent acts" (p. 110). As discussed in prior chapters, the evidence tends to support that claim. Moreover, the results can be devastating for those young people who fail in school. Whether male or female, black or white, lower or middle class, those who do the worst in school are the most likely to commit delinquent acts (Agnew, 1991:143–144; Elliott and Voss, 1974:133–137, 175–179, 182–187; Empey and Lubeck, 1971:80–84; Frease, 1973:452–454; Hindelang, 1973:476–477; Hirschi, 1969:115–116; Johnson, 1979:101–103; LaGrange and White, 1985:27–31; Polk and Halferty, 1966:84, 90–96; Polk and Schafer, 1972:passim; Rankin, 1980:427–428; Stinchcombe, 1964:143; Wiatrowski, Griswold, and Roberts, 1981:534–538; Wiatrowski et al., 1982:153–158).

A basic question, therefore, is not whether attachment to school is important, but to what its absence should be attributed. Why is it that delinquents are more likely than nondelinquents to have weak ties to the educational system? Classic strain theory suggests that it is due either to frustration over blocked opportunities or to a sense of inadequacy because of failure to live up to the standards of the middle-class measuring rod. Hirschi's (1969:113, 115, 120) social control theory, in contrast, suggests that it represents insensitivity to the opinions of teachers, parents, and friends, and a lack of commitment to long-range goals. Students who fail in school simply do not care about others' opinions and are not interested in the hard work that conventional success requires.

Evidence regarding those contrasting views is equivocal. On the one hand, much of it appears to support Hirschi's social control theory by showing that students who fail in school and commit delinquent acts tend to have lower, not higher, aspirations—and thus to challenge the idea that poor attachment to school is due to frustrated ambitions (Hirschi, 1969:178–179; Polk and Halferty, 1966:84, 93–96; Wiatrowski et al., 1982:153–158). On the other hand, research does not clearly indicate whether weak attachment to school precedes or follows low aspirations. If Hirschi (1969:117) is correct, low aspirations should be preceded by weak attachment. But Cohen (1955:112–116, 129–137) maintained that although lower-class boys start out with high aspirations, it is the loss of status they suffer in school that eventually causes them to reject everything that is middle class, including long-range goals. In other words, weak attachment to school does not precede, but rather follows the frustration of aspirations.

It is possible, at least for some youths, that weak attachment to school is a result, not a cause, of low aspirations. Although perhaps interested in school as elementary students, these youths have become alienated from it by the time they reach adolescence. Their weak attachment and their delinquent behavior are certainly real, but their problems may not be due to a lifelong disregard for conventional people and conventional goals. Instead, it may be due to unpleasant experiences that the school itself has fostered.

In the same vein, there is the question of intellectual ability. If children have the ability to do well in school, the chances are greater that they will become strongly attached to it. But if they lack that ability, their poor performance will lead to a dislike of school, followed in turn by the rejection of authority and the commission of delinquent acts.

General support for that kind of causal chain is provided by Wiatrowski, Griswold, and Roberts (1981:535) and by Wiatrowski et al. (1982:154–157) from research on a national sample of high school males. We already have seen that delinquents tend to get poorer grades in school than do nondelinquents. Moreover, a variety of studies find that delinquents do less well on achievement tests (Hirschi, 1969:113–115; Jensen, 1976; Patterson and Dishion, 1985:73; Wolfgang, Figlio, and Sellin, 1972:245–248) and are more likely to reject school authority (Hindelang, 1973:478; Hirschi, 1969:123–124; Stinchcombe, 1964: 27–32).

One of the most serious challenges to Hirschi's social control theory about the relationship between attachment to school and delinquency again involves causal ordering: whether weak attachment precedes or follows delinquency. Hirschi's (1969:Chap. 7) position on that issue is clear: Weak attachment to school should precede delinquent behavior. Studies by Agnew (1985b:57–58) and by Liska and Reed (1985:553–556), however, have suggested just the opposite causal ordering. Looking at youths' attitudes toward school and their satisfaction with school experiences, both studies have indicated that weak attachment to school follows delinquency. To explain such a causal chain, Liska and Reed (1985: 557) observed that much delinquency is committed in schools and that

> street delinquency may be correlated with troublesome school behavior in classrooms, school halls and schoolyards. . . . This leads to reactions by teachers and school administrators, which in turn decrease school attachment. Also, adolescents involved in delinquency simply have less time for school; thus, delinquency, independently of teacher reactions, may decrease school attachment.

In summary, research regarding attachment to school has been inconsistent. On the one hand, it leaves little doubt that attachment to school is crucial in explaining the difference between conformity to the law and delinquency (although it seems that delinquency leads to poor attachment to school, and not the opposite, as Hirschi suggested), and it indicates that high aspirations are more likely to act as

barriers to delinquency than as motivators for it. The evidence, in other words, tends to support social control rather than classic strain theory. On the other hand, research does not permit us to determine whether delinquents have always been insensitive to conventional goals and people or whether they acquire such feelings as a result of their school experiences.

ATTACHMENT TO FRIENDS Affinity with friends is the final dimension of attachment. As we have seen, Hirschi (1969) theorized that young people who do not like and respect their parents and teachers are more likely to commit delinquent acts. But he also theorized that delinquents are not as likely to respect their friends, either (pp. 140–141). The reason is that they have never developed feelings of compassion and responsibility for anyone. Although delinquents may join together in groups or gangs, their relations will be exploitive rather than warm and supportive.

This aspect of Hirschi's theory has been one of the most difficult to confirm or deny. On the one hand, we have seen in previous chapters that delinquency is overwhelmingly a group phenomenon. Furthermore, as Johnson (1979:109) has demonstrated, the school is a place where children are sifted and sorted into different groups—some delinquent, some conformist. In an attempt to explain those phenomena, cultural deviance and classic strain theorists (see Chapters 8 and 10) have suggested that in delinquent groups, friends become a sort of substitute society, providing satisfactions that nondelinquents find through conventional friends.

Several studies have suggested that this may be the case. Juveniles with weak attachments to parents and school seem to compensate by seeking out delinquent friends (Johnson, 1979:99–111; Johnson, Marcos, and Bahr, 1987:333–335; Marcos, Bahr, and Johnson, 1986:147–154; Matsueda and Heimer, 1987: 831–833; Patterson and Dishion, 1985:74–75). Moreover, in general, delinquents (although evidence is limited to delinquent boys) are more likely than nondelinquents to be influenced by the expectations of their friends (Empey and Lubeck, 1968:769–770; Erickson and Empey, 1965:275–279).

At the same time, those studies do not necessarily show that delinquents are as inclined as nondelinquents to hold their friends in high esteem. With regard to that issue, Hirschi (1969:145–152) found that boys who were least respectful of their friends were most likely to have committed delinquent acts. Although that finding has not been replicated in subsequent studies (Hindelang, 1973:478–479; Krohn and Massey, 1980:534–536; Krohn et al., 1983:344; Wiatrowski, Griswold, and Roberts, 1981:535), it tends to support the contentions of others that members of delinquent groups are not characterized by relaxed or laid-back feelings. Indeed, delinquent gangs have been described more in terms of aggression, threat, and insult than warmth, respect, and solidarity (Matza, 1964:42–44, 53–55; Miller, 1958: 9–10; Short and Strodtbeck, 1965:221–234; Yablonsky, 1970:191–192). Klein and Crawford (1967) argued that, were it not for the external pressures of rival gangs, neighbors, and police, delinquent gangs would have little to hold them together. Members' loyalty to one another is an expression of the need to resist outside pressure more than to repay internal debts of kindness and mutual esteem.

We have seen, however, in previous chapters (especially Chapter 10) that such characterizations have not gone unchallenged. Giordano, Cernkovich, and Pugh (1986), for example, have reported that delinquents have the same kinds of friendship relationships as nondelinquents and that those relationships are often stable and mutually supportive.

In light of such conflicting findings, two conclusions are warranted. First, Hirschi's social control theory appears to overlook the important role played by peers in the commission of delinquent acts. Second, given the doubts that have been raised about Hirschi's contention that compared to law-abiding children, delinquents are less attached to friends, more research on the character of delinquent, as well as conventional, groups is needed.

Commitment

As the second element of the social bond, commitment assumes that the motivation to adhere to the ideal concept of childhood and strive for conventional goals is a built-in constraint on delinquent behavior. An individual has a stake in conformity that he or she feels will be jeopardized by delinquency. For example, Hirschi (1969:165–166) con-

tended that those children who engage in such adult activities as smoking, drinking, dating, and driving at an early age are also more likely to commit delinquent acts (recognizing, of course, that smoking and drinking may themselves be status offenses). By doing such things, they deny their status as children, express contempt for the expectations of parents and teachers, and free themselves from the norms governing childhood.

The evidence in support of those contentions has been rather consistent. Juveniles who willingly violate the expectations of childhood at an early age are most likely to commit delinquent acts (Agnew, 1985a:160–163; Hindelang, 1973:480–482; Hirschi, 1969:166–169; Polk and Halferty, 1966:84; Wiatrowski, Griswold, and Roberts, 1981:534–537).

So much for the deviant side of the coin (i.e., smoking, drinking, and the like). What effect does commitment to an education or a career have on delinquency? We have already seen in both this and the previous chapter that ambition, with its implied commitment to long-term educational and occupational goals, is more likely to operate as a barrier to than a cause of delinquency. Therefore, it is not difficult to anticipate the results of research. They indicate that those girls and boys most committed to staying in school and otherwise conforming to the requirements of childhood are the least likely to commit delinquent acts (Briar and Piliavin, 1965:42–45; Hindelang, 1973:481–482; Hirschi, 1969:170–184; Johnson, 1979:108–109; Krohn et al., 1983:345; LaGrange and White, 1985:32–35; Massey and Krohn, 1986:124; Polk and Halferty, 1966:91–93).[3]

Involvement

The third element of the bond, involvement, predicts that participation in conventional activities should prevent delinquency. The evidence, however, is mixed. On the one hand, the greater the involvement in studying or doing homework, the less the chances of committing delinquent acts (Hindelang, 1973:481, 483; Hirschi, 1969:191–192; Polk and Halferty, 1966:

[3]Krohn and Massey (1980:534–536) and Wiatrowski, Griswold, and Roberts (1981:535), however, report contrary evidence. Moreover, Krohn et al. (1983:344) suggest that such variables as commitment may explain minor delinquent acts better than they do serious offenses.

84; Wiatrowski, Griswold, and Roberts, 1981:534–536). On the other hand, participation in sports, clubs, hobbies, or even a job does not seem to have the predicted preventive effect. Young people who engage in those activities are almost as likely to commit delinquent acts as are those who do not (Agnew, 1984:439, 445; Hindelang, 1973:483; Hirschi, 1969:189–190; Rankin, 1976:475–476, 479, 1980:428; Smith and Paternoster, 1987:150–155). Consequently, of those types of activities, it is involvement in academic activities rather than other conventional activities that is the strongest barrier to delinquency.

Belief

As the final element of the bond, Hirschi's (1969) social control theory suggests that beliefs are relatively stable attributes of a person and are generally impervious to transitory relationships. If children have been trained to believe in the morality of law, they will be less inclined to commit delinquent acts, no matter what groups they encounter.

In contrast, symbolic interactionist theory (see Chapter 9) tends to suggest that beliefs are relatively transitory attitudes that can be shaped and reshaped, depending on the groups with whom one associates. Even though a young person might have been a member of law-abiding groups in the past, association with a delinquent group can lead that individual to alter his or her beliefs and commit delinquent acts.

Research to examine those opposing points of view has supported neither one totally. On the one hand, a number of studies lend some support to Hirschi's social control theory. Boys and girls who are not strongly attached to parents and school have the least respect for the law and the police. Those same juveniles, in turn, are most likely to commit delinquent acts (Hindelang, 1973:483–486; Hirschi, 1969:200–205; Krohn and Massey, 1980:535; Marcos, Bahr, and Johnson, 1986:147–152).

On the other hand, some investigators have sought to separate the effects of peer group associations from the effects of beliefs about the law. In doing so, they have found that beliefs affect delinquency, but probably in a different way than Hirschi suggested. Indeed, Hirschi (1969:138, 156) argued that beliefs should affect association with delinquent friends; in particular, attenuation of beliefs in the

moral validity of law should increase the likelihood of having delinquent friends. And he suggested that both a lack of respect for the law and association with delinquent friends should lead to delinquent behavior.[4]

In contrast to that argument, Sutherland's theory of differential association suggests that association with delinquent friends increases the likelihood of delinquency because it is more likely than association with nondelinquent friends to transmit definitions favorable to delinquency. Hence, Sutherland's theory posits that (1) association with delinquent friends should attenuate beliefs in the moral validity of law, not the other way around, and (2) only beliefs should have a direct effect on delinquency, because the effects of delinquent friends on delinquent behavior should be mediated by beliefs.

Reanalyzing the same data that Hirschi (1969) used to test his theory, Matsueda and Heimer (1987:831, 835) found more support for the causal chain suggested by Sutherland than for Hirschi's (and, using different data, Matsueda [1989:442–446] again finds, in contrast to Hirschi's basic argument, that delinquency affects beliefs, not the other way around).

Still other studies, however, have reported evidence contrary to that of Matsueda and Heimer (1987), although not totally consistent with Hirschi's theory either (Marcos, Bahr, and Johnson, 1986:155; Massey and Krohn, 1986:124). Those studies have shown that when association with delinquent friends and beliefs about law are considered simultaneously, only association with delinquent friends has a direct effect on delinquency. The effects of beliefs on delinquency are indirect, in that they influence juveniles' peer associations. That is, juveniles become friends with delinquents after questioning the moral validity of law, and then association with delinquent friends leads to delinquency.

---

[4]In Chapter 9, it was said that most control theorists argue that membership in delinquent groups occurs only *after* an individual becomes delinquent (delinquents, like birds of a feather, flock together). Here, it is being said that, according to Hirschi (1969), association with delinquent friends *precedes* delinquency. Hirschi himself tends to waffle on this issue, demonstrating the point that peer relations are generally of secondary importance to control theorists. After analyzing his data, however, Hirschi (1969:156) concluded that association with delinquent friends probably leads to delinquent behavior, not the opposite.

SELF-CONTROL THEORY

Gottfredson and Hirschi's (1990) **self-control theory** is a variation of social control theory. Identified by them as a general theory of crime, self-control theory is grounded in the classical view of human behavior: "All human conduct can be understood as the self-interested pursuit of pleasure or the avoidance of pain" (p. 5). Lawbreaking is perceived to be a universally desirable strategy for pursuing self-interest because it provides "immediate, easy, and certain short-term pleasure" (p. 41). Thus, consistent with social control theory, the central question in self-control theory is not what causes lawbreaking, but rather what constrains it.

For Gottfredson and Hirschi, the answer is self-control, which is the "differential tendency of people to avoid criminal acts whatever the circumstances in which they find themselves" (p. 87). People with high self-control resist the immediate pleasures associated with criminal behavior. Conversely, people with low self-control are impulsive, prone to risk-taking, self-centered, and hot-tempered, and they prefer easy gratification and physical rather than mental activities (pp. 87–89; also see Grasmick et al., 1993:13–18). Low self-control, coupled with criminal opportunity, frees people to act out their natural antisocial impulses. The principal cause of low self-control is ineffective child rearing: parents failing to (1) monitor a child's behavior, (2) recognize deviant behavior when it occurs, and (3) punish such behavior (p. 97).

Gottfredson and Hirschi offer a few additional arguments. First, in addition to breaking the law, people with low self-control will "tend to pursue immediate pleasures that are *not* [necessarily] criminal: they will tend to smoke, drink, use drugs, gamble, have children out of wedlock, and engage in illicit sex" (p. 90). Thus, this is a theory not merely of crime and delinquency, but also of deviance, broadly defined to include such things as job and marital instability, accidents, addiction, and poor health maintenance. All such things supposedly are manifestations of low self-control.

Second, Gottfredson and Hirschi point to the stability of deviant behavior—childhood deviance often is followed by deviance at later points in life—in order to argue that low self-control is established early, remains stable over the life course, and is *the* cause of law-violating behavior at all points of life, regardless of circumstances. Associating with delinquent friends or dropping out of school, for example, are not causes of deviance, but rather are consequences of low self-control.

Despite its newness, self-control theory has received a surprising amount of attention in the way of tests. By and large, most tests have supported the theory. Researchers consistently have found a relationship between self-control and crime/delinquency (Arneklev et al., 1993; Burton et al., 1998; Evans et al., 1997; Grasmick et al., 1993; Kean, Maxim, and Teevan, 1993; Polakowski, 1994). Evans and his colleagues (1997) found that low self-control increases the likelihood of violating the law. People with low self-control also were less likely to be married or to have high occupational status, and they reported lower-quality family relationships and friendships. Burton and his colleagues (1998) studied a sample of adults and found that low self-control was an important cause of crime for both males and females.

In one of the few studies that considered opportunity, Grasmick and his colleagues (1993) found that the combination of low self-control and perceived criminal opportunities increased the likelihood of committing crimes. In contrast to self-control theory, however, perceived opportunities affected crime independently of low self-control. (According to the theory, perceived criminal opportunities should increase the likelihood of violating the law only when combined with low self-control.)

Although many studies have examined the relationship between self-control and crime/delinquency, very little attention has been paid to Gottfredson and Hirschi's claim that self-control is a function of child-rearing practices. Several studies, however, have considered whether criminal/delinquent behavior is due to a single, stable trait, and therefore not responsive to changing life circumstances (e.g., Bartusch et al., 1997; Paternoster and Brame, 1997; Sampson and Laub, 1993; Warr, 1998). Those studies have tended to suggest, in contrast to the theory, that such life course transitions as marriage and employment affect the likelihood of committing crime and deviance.

An obvious question about self-control theory is its connection to Hirschi's (1969) social control theory. Gottfredson and Hirschi have been silent on the issue. Reflecting confusion about the issue, Akers (1991:205) mused: "Can self-control be subsumed under social bonding [control] theory or does self-control now supersede social bonding? Can all previous control perspectives be subsumed under self-control?" Polakowski (1994:42–43) has interpreted Gottfredson and Hirschi as implying that neither self-control nor social control subsumes the other. Instead, they can be seen as independent constraints on the natural impulse to offend:

> Classical theory is . . . based on the idea that the costs of crime depend on the individual's current location in or bond to society. What classical theory lacks is an explicit idea of self-control, the idea that people also differ in the extent to which they are vulnerable to the temptations of the moment. Combining the two ideas thus merely recognizes the simultaneous existence of social and individual restraints on behavior. (Gottfredson and Hirschi, 1990:87–88)

Polakowski (1994:60) found that low self-control was more strongly associated with criminal convictions than were social bonds. But the two were strongly associated with each other because they both were affected by early childhood socialization: "Inadequate socialization simultaneously creates an individual who acts upon impulse and who is less likely to have developed a moral bond consistent with the customary rules of society."

SUMMARY AND CONCLUSIONS

The publication of Hirschi's social control theory in 1969 was valuable because it helped to rectify a serious shortcoming in criminology: the tendency to eschew the importance of family relationships. Although a host of social scientists in other disciplines had long felt that those relationships were vital in determining the course of child development, criminologists had argued for almost half a century that they were relatively unimportant when compared with socioeconomic, racial, and subcultural factors.

Following the publication of Hirschi's theory, research on the family began to increase. Nonetheless, it sparked reactions that were negative as well as positive, ideological as well as scientific.

Assumptions About Human Nature and Social Order

Hirschi's theory resurrected some old, very conservative points of view about human nature—namely, that all people would violate the law if given the chance. Without adequate socialization or strong social controls, law-violating behavior would be common. Rather than working to pay for a car, for example, people would simply steal one. What children must be taught, therefore, is not how to break the law, but how to restrain their natural impulses and how to be law-abiding.

Meanwhile, Hirschi, like other control theorists, also assumed that the social order is characterized by value consensus. People are not divided into subcultures according to differing values; rather, most people agree that crime is wrong. It is only delinquents and adult criminals who defy convention and threaten social stability.

Underlying Logic and Content of Social Control Theory

Social control theory has as much to do with conformity as with delinquency. Because all of us are animals at birth and will prey on others unless restrained, we must seek to explain what spells the difference between delinquency and conformity.

As shown in figure 11.1, the answer is the social bond. If socialization is effective—if children are attached to others, committed to long-range goals, and involved in conventional activities, and if they believe in the morality of law—the social bond will develop. In turn, a strong stake in conformity will be created, and conformity to the law will result. But if socialization is ineffective, natural human impulses will remain unrestrained. Children will be free to violate the law, and delinquency will be a consequence.

Policy Implications of Social Control Theory

Hirschi's assumption about human nature aside, his version of control theory is the kind of explanation that makes sense to legal officials and on which they base many of their interventions. They can readily understand the need to reattach delinquents to some kind of family, to recommit them to long-range goals, to involve them in constructive activities, and to cultivate their belief in the morality of law.

Empirical Adequacy of Social Control Theory

Hirschi contended that social control theory will explain delinquency among genders, social classes, and races. Relative to the concepts of attachment, commitment, and involvement, that contention has held up rather well. Those elements of the theory that have best stood the test of empirical scrutiny are those that (1) stress the idea that attachment to family and school is important in distinguishing between conformity and delinquency, (2) indicate that commitment to long-term educational and occupational goals is a barrier to, rather than a cause of, delinquent behavior, and (3) suggest that involvement in

academic activities, if not other conventional activities, is useful in promoting conformity.

In contrast, the areas most in question are Hirschi's view of the delinquent as someone who lacks strong feelings and compassion for other people. Just as cultural deviance, symbolic interactionist, and strain theories are extreme in painting delinquents as moral and gregarious people who violate the law only because they feel compelled to adhere to the expectations of others, social control theory probably goes too far in the opposite direction. When it indicates that delinquents are unsocialized predators, it underestimates the role of peers in generating support for delinquency and overstates the importance of acquired beliefs as barriers to it.

Self-Control Theory

The newest variation of social control theory is Gottfredson and Hirschi's self-control theory, first advanced in 1990. As shown in figure 11.2, delinquency

FIGURE 11.1

The underlying logic of social control theory

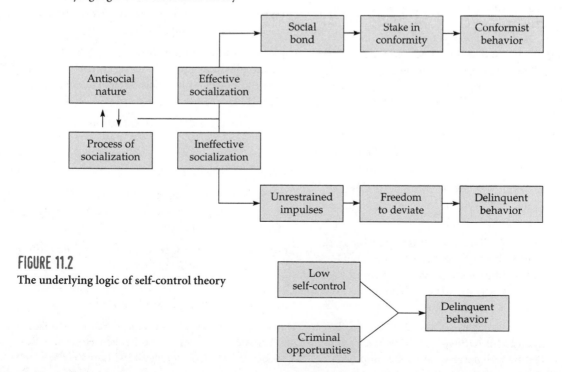

FIGURE 11.2

The underlying logic of self-control theory

is caused by a combination of low self-control and criminal opportunities to violate the law. Although there have been few tests of self-control theory to date, most tests have generally supported it.

Discussion Questions

1. What historical and traditional beliefs did Hirschi incorporate into his social control theory?
2. What are the elements of the social bond, and what is its significance in social control theory?
3. What implications does social control theory have for social policy?
4. Has research confirmed Hirschi's theory that the social order is characterized by value consensus and that most people agree about what is right and wrong?
5. In what ways is self-control theory a variation on social control theory?

References

Agnew, Robert. 1984. "Goal Achievement and Delinquency." *Sociology and Social Research* 68 (July):435–451.
1985a. "A Revised Strain Theory of Delinquency." *Social Forces* 64 (September):151–167.
1985b. "Social Control Theory and Delinquency: A Longitudinal Test." *Criminology* 23 (February): 47–61.
1991. "A Longitudinal Test of Social Control Theory and Delinquency." *Journal of Research in Crime and Delinquency* 28 (May):126–156.

Akers, Ronald L. 1991. "Self-Control as a General Theory of Crime." *Journal of Quantitative Criminology* 7 (June):201–211.

Arneklev, Bruce J., Harold G. Grasmick, Charles R. Tittle, and Robert J. Bursik. 1993. "Low Self-Control and Imprudent Behavior." *Journal of Quantitative Criminology* 9 (September): 225–247.

Bartusch, Dawn R. Jeglum, Donald R. Lynam, Terrie Moffitt, and Phil A. Silva. 1997. "Is Age Important? Testing a General Versus a Developmental Theory of Antisocial Behavior." *Criminology* 35 (February):13–38.

Baumrind, Diana. 1996. "The Discipline Controversy Revisited." *Family Relations* 45 (October): 405–414.

Blumstein, Alfred, and Jacqueline Cohen. 1980. "Sentencing of Convicted Offenders: An Analysis of the Public's View." *Law and Society Review* 14 (Winter):223–261.

Briar, Scott, and Irving Piliavin. 1965. "Delinquency, Situational Inducements, and Commitment to Conformity." *Social Problems* 8 (Summer):35–45.

Burton, Velmer S. Jr., Francis T. Cullen, T. David Evans, Leanne Fiftal Alarid, and R. Gregory Dunaway. 1998. "Gender, Self-Control, and Crime." *Journal of Research in Crime and Delinquency* 35 (May):123–147.

Canter, Rachelle J. 1982. "Family Correlates of Male and Female Delinquency." *Criminology* 20 (August):149–167.

Cernkovich, Stephen A., and Peggy C. Giordano. 1987. "Family Relationships and Delinquency." *Criminology* 25 (May):295–321.

Chilton, Roland, and Jan DeAmicis. 1975. "Overcriminalization and the Measurement of Consensus." *Sociology and Social Research* 59 (July): 318–329.

Chilton, Roland, and Gerald E. Markle. 1972. "Family Disruption, Delinquent Conduct and the Effect of Subclassification." *American Sociological Review* 37 (February):93–99.

Cockburn, James J., and Inga Maclay. 1965. "Sex Differentials in Juvenile Delinquency." *British Journal of Criminology* 5 (July):289–308.

Cohen, Albert K. 1955. *Delinquent Boys: The Culture of the Gang.* New York: Free Press.

Cowie, John, Valerie Cowie, and Eliot Slater. 1968. *Delinquency in Girls.* London: Heineman.

Datesman, Susan K., and Frank R. Scarpitti. 1975. "Female Delinquency and Broken Homes: A Reassessment." *Criminology* 13 (May):33–55.

Durkheim, Emile. 1951. *Suicide: A Study in Sociology.* Translated by John A. Spaulding and George Simpson. New York: Free Press.
1953. *Sociology and Philosophy.* Translated by D. F. Pocock. Glencoe, Ill.: Free Press.

Elliott, Delbert S., and Harwin L. Voss. 1974. *Delinquency and Dropout.* Lexington, Mass.: Lexington Books.

Empey, LaMar T., and Steven G. Lubeck. 1968. "Conformity and Deviance in the 'Situation of Company.'" *American Sociological Review* 33 (October):760–774.
1971. *Explaining Delinquency: Construction, Test, and Reformulation of a Sociological Theory.* Lexington, Mass.: Heath.

Erickson, Maynard L., and LaMar T. Empey. 1965. "Class Position, Peers and Delinquency." *Sociology and Social Research* 49 (April):268–282.

Evans, T. David, Francis T. Cullen, Velmer S. Burton, Jr., R. Gregory Dunaway, and Michael L. Benson. 1997. "The Social Consequences of Self-Control: Testing the General Theory of Crime." *Criminology* 35 (August):475–504.

Frease, Dean E. 1973. "Delinquency, Social Class, and the Schools." *Sociology and Social Research* 57 (July):443–459.

Giordano, Peggy C., Stephen A. Cernkovich, and M. D. Pugh. 1986. "Friendships and Delinquency." *American Journal of Sociology* 91 (March):1170–1202.

Gold, Martin. 1963. *Status Forces in Delinquent Boys.* Ann Arbor, Mich.: Institute for Social Research at the University of Michigan.

Gottfredson, Michael R., and Travis Hirschi. 1990. *A General Theory of Crime.* Stanford, Calif.: Stanford University Press.

Gove, Walter R., and Robert D. Crutchfield. 1982. "The Family and Juvenile Delinquency." *Sociological Quarterly* 23 (Summer):301–319.

Grasmick, Harold G., Charles R. Tittle, Robert J. Bursik, Jr., and Bruce J. Arneklev. 1993. "Testing the Core Empirical Implications of Gottfredson and Hirschi's General Theory of Crime." *Journal of Research in Crime and Delinquency* 30 (February):5–29.

Hamilton, V. Lee, and Steve Rytina. 1980. "Social Consensus on Norms of Justice: Should the Punishment Fit the Crime?" *American Journal of Sociology* 85 (March):1117–1144.

Hindelang, Michael J. 1973. "Causes of Delinquency: A Partial Replication and Extension." *Social Problems* 20 (Spring):471–487.

Hirschi, Travis. 1969. *Causes of Delinquency.* Berkeley: University of California Press.
1983. "Crime and the Family." Pp. 53–68 in James Q. Wilson, ed., *Crime and Public Policy.* San Francisco: Institute of Contemporary Studies.
1995. "The Family." Pp. 121–140 in James Q. Wilson and Joan Petersilia, eds., *Crime.* San Francisco: Institute for Contemporary Studies.

Jensen, Gary F. 1972. "Parents, Peers, and Delinquent Action: A Test of the Differential Association Perspective." *American Journal of Sociology* 78 (November):562–575.

Jensen, Gary F., and Raymond Eve. 1976. "Sex Differences in Delinquency: An Examination of Popular Sociological Explanations." *Criminology* 13 (February):427–448.

Jensen, Gary F., and Dean G. Rojek. 1992. *Delinquency: A Sociological View,* 2nd ed. Lexington, Mass.: Heath.

Johnson, Richard E. 1979. *Juvenile Delinquency and Its Origins: An Integrated Theoretical Approach.* Cambridge: Cambridge University Press.
1986. "Family Structure and Delinquency: General Patterns and Gender Differences." *Criminology* 24 (February):65–84.

Johnson, Richard E., Anastasios C. Marcos, and Stephen J. Bahr. 1987. "The Role of Peers in the Complex Etiology of Adolescent Drug Use." *Criminology* 25 (May):323–339.

Keane, Carl, Paul S. Maxim, and James J. Teevan. 1993. "Drinking and Driving, Self-Control, and Gender: Testing a General Theory of Crime." *Journal of Research in Crime and Delinquency* 30 (February):30–46.

Klein, Malcolm W., and Lois Y. Crawford. 1967. "Groups, Gangs, and Cohesiveness." *Journal of Research in Crime and Delinquency* 4 (January): 63–75.

Krohn, Marvin D., and James L. Massey. 1980. "Social Control and Delinquent Behavior: An Examination of the Elements of the Social Bond." *Sociological Quarterly* 21 (Autumn):529–543.

Krohn, Marvin D., James L. Massey, William F. Skinner, and Ronald M. Lauer. 1983. "Social Bonding Theory and Adolescent Cigarette Smoking: A Longitudinal Analysis." *Journal of Health and Social Behavior* 24 (December):337–349.

LaGrange, Randy L., and Helen Raskin White. 1985. "Age Differences in Delinquency: A Test of Theory." *Criminology* 23 (February):19–45.

Larzelere, Robert E., and Gerald R. Patterson. 1990. "Parental Management: Mediator of the Effect of Socioeconomic Status on Early Delinquency." *Criminology* 28 (May):301–324.

Laub, John H., and Robert J. Sampson. 1988. "Unraveling Families and Delinquency: A Reanalysis of the Gluecks' Data." *Criminology* 26 (August): 355–380.

Lewis, Claude. December 22, 1993. "Jackson's Challenge: Keeping Black Youth Marching Ahead." *The Pueblo Chieftain*, p. 4A.

Liska, Allen E., and Mark D. Reed. 1985. "Ties to Conventional Institutions and Delinquency: Estimating Reciprocal Effects." *American Sociological Review* 50 (August):547–560.

Loeber, Rolf, and Magda Stouthamer-Loeber. 1986. "Family Factors as Correlates and Predictors of Juvenile Conduct Problems and Delinquency." Pp. 29–149 in Michael Tonry and Norval Morris, eds., *Crime and Justice: An Annual Review of Research,* Vol. 7. Chicago: University of Chicago Press.

Marcos, Anastasios C., Stephen J. Bahr, and Richard E. Johnson. 1986. "Test of a Bonding/Association Theory of Adolescent Drug Use." *Social Forces* 65 (September):135–161.

Massey, James L., and Marvin D. Krohn. 1986. "A Longitudinal Examination of an Integrated Social Process Model of Deviant Behavior." *Social Forces* 65 (September):106–134.

Matsueda, Ross L. 1982. "Testing Control Theory and Differential Association: A Causal Modeling Approach." *American Sociological Review* 47 (August):489–504.
1989. "The Dynamics of Moral Beliefs and Minor Deviance." *Social Forces* 68 (December): 428–457.

Matsueda, Ross L., and Karen Heimer. 1987. "Race, Family Structure, and Delinquency: A Test of Differential Association and Social Control Theories." *American Sociological Review* 52 (December):826–840.

Matza, David. 1964. *Delinquency and Drift.* New York: Wiley.

Miller, Walter B. 1958. "Lower Class Culture as a Generating Milieu of Gang Delinquency." *Journal of Social Issues* 14:5–19.

Monahan, Thomas P. 1957. "Family Status and the Delinquent Child: A Reappraisal and Some New Findings." *Social Forces* 35 (March):250–258.

Norland, Stephen, Neal Shover, William E. Thornton, and Jennifer James. 1979. "Intrafamily Conflict and Delinquency." *Pacific Sociological Review* 22 (April):223–240.

Nye, F. Ivan. 1958. *Family Relationships and Delinquent Behavior.* New York: Wiley.

Paternoster, Raymond, and Robert Brame. 1997. "Multiple Routes to Delinquency? A Test of Developmental and General Theories of Crime." *Criminology* 35 (February):49–84.

Patterson, Gerald R., and Thomas J. Dishion. 1985. "Contributions of Families and Peers to Delinquency." *Criminology* 23 (February):63–79.

Polakowski, Michael. 1994. "Linking Self- and Social Control with Deviance: Illuminating the Structure Underlying a General Theory of Crime and Its Relation to Deviant Activity." *Journal of Quantitative Criminology* 10 (March):41–78.

Polk, Kenneth, and David S. Halferty. 1966. "Adolescence, Commitment, and Delinquency." *Jour-*

nal of Research in Crime and Delinquency 3 (July): 82–96.

Polk, Kenneth, and Walter E. Schafer, eds. 1972. *Schools and Delinquency.* Englewood Cliffs, N.J.: Prentice-Hall.

Poole, Eric D., and Robert M. Regoli. 1979. "Parental Support, Delinquent Friends and Delinquency: A Test of Interaction Effects." *Journal of Criminal Law and Criminology* 70 (Summer): 188–193.

Rankin, Joseph H. 1976. "Investigating the Interrelations Among Social Control Variables and Conformity." *Journal of Criminal Law and Criminology* 67 (December):470–480.
1980. "School Factors and Delinquency: Interactions by Age and Sex." *Sociology and Social Research* 64 (April):420–434.
1983. "The Family Context of Delinquency." *Social Problems* 30 (April):466–479.

Rankin, Joseph H., and Roger Kern. 1994. "Parental Attachments and Delinquency." *Criminology* 32 (November):495–515.

Rankin, Joseph H., and L. Edward Wells. 1990. "The Effect of Parental Attachments and Direct Controls on Delinquency." *Journal of Research in Crime and Delinquency* 27 (May):140–165.

Reckless, Walter C. 1961. "A New Theory of Delinquency and Crime." *Federal Probation* 25 (December):42–46.

Rodman, Hyman, and Paul Grams. 1967. "Juvenile Delinquency and the Family: A Review and Discussion." Pp. 188–221 in President's Commission on Law Enforcement and Administration of Justice, *Task Force Report: Juvenile Delinquency and Youth Crime.* Washington, D.C.: U.S. Government Printing Office.

Rossi, Peter H., Jon E. Simpson, and Joann L. Miller. 1985. "Beyond Crime Seriousness: Fitting the Punishment to the Crime." *Journal of Quantitative Criminology* 1 (March):59–90.

Rossi, Peter H., Emily Waite, Christine E. Bose, and Richard E. Berk. 1974. "The Seriousness of Crimes: Normative Structure and Individual Dif-

ferences." *American Sociological Review* 39 (April): 224–237.

Sampson, Robert J., and John H. Laub. 1993. *Crime in the Making: Pathways and Turning Points Through Life.* Cambridge, Mass.: Harvard University Press.

Short, James F., Jr., and Fred L. Strodtbeck. 1965. *Group Process and Gang Delinquency.* Chicago: University of Chicago Press.

Simons, Ronald L., Martin G. Miller, and Stephen M. Aigner. 1980. "Contemporary Theories of Deviance and Female Delinquency: An Empirical Test." *Journal of Research in Crime and Delinquency* 17 (January):42–57.

Smith, Douglas A., and Raymond Paternoster. 1987. "The Gender Gap in Theories of Deviance: Issues and Evidence." *Journal of Research in Crime and Delinquency* 24 (May):140–172.

Stinchcombe, Arthur L. 1964. *Rebellion in a High School.* Chicago: Quadrangle Books.

Toby, Jackson. 1957. "Social Disorganization and Stake in Conformity: Complementary Factors in the Predatory Behavior of Hoodlums." *Journal of Criminal Law, Criminology and Police Science* 48 (May–June):12–17.

Van Voorhis, Patricia, Francis T. Cullen, Richard A. Mathers, and Connie C. Garner. 1988. "The Impact of Family Structure and Quality on Delinquency: A Comparative Assessment of Structural and Functional Factors." *Criminology* 26 (May): 235–261.

Warr, Mark. 1993. "Age, Peers, and Delinquency." *Criminology* 31 (February):17–40.
1998. "Life-Course Transitions and Desistance from Crime." *Criminology* 36 (May):183–216.

Warr, Mark, Robert F. Meier, and Maynard L. Erickson. 1983. "Norms, Theories of Punishment, and Publicly Preferred Penalties for Crimes." *Sociological Quarterly* 24 (Winter):75–91.

Wellford, Charles. 1975. "Labelling Theory and Criminology: An Assessment." *Social Problems* 22 (February):332–345.

Wells, L. Edward, and Joseph H. Rankin. 1985. "Broken Homes and Juvenile Delinquency: An Empirical Review." *Criminal Justice Abstracts* 17 (June):249–272.

1986. "The Broken Homes Model of Delinquency: Analytic Issues." *Journal of Research in Crime and Delinquency* 23 (February):68–93.

1988. "Direct Parental Controls and Delinquency." *Criminology* 26 (May):263–285.

1991. "Families and Delinquency: A Meta-Analysis of the Impact of Broken Homes." *Social Problems* 38 (February):71–93.

Wiatrowski, Michael D., David B. Griswold, and Mary K. Roberts. 1981. "Social Control Theory and Delinquency." *American Sociological Review* 46 (October):525–541.

Wiatrowski, Michael D., Stephen Hansell, Charles R. Massey, and David L. Wilson. 1982. "Curriculum Tracking and Delinquency." *American Sociological Review* 47 (February):151–160.

Wilkinson, Karen. 1974. "The Broken Family and Juvenile Delinquency: Scientific Explanation or Ideology?" *Social Problems* 21 (June):726–739.

Wilson, Harriett. 1980. "Parental Supervision: A Neglected Aspect of Delinquency." *British Journal of Criminology* 20 (July):203–235.

1987. "Parental Supervision Re-Examined." *British Journal of Criminology* 27 (Summer): 275–301.

Wolfgang, Marvin E., Robert M. Figlio, and Thorsten Sellin. 1972. *Delinquency in a Birth Cohort.* Chicago: University of Chicago Press.

Wolfgang, Marvin E., Robert M. Figlio, Paul E. Tracy, and Simon I. Singer. 1985. *The National Survey of Crime Severity.* Washington, D.C.: U.S. Government Printing Office.

Yablonsky, Lewis. 1970. *The Violent Gang,* rev. ed. Baltimore: Penguin Books.

NEOCLASSICAL THEORISTS
EMPHASIZE PUNISHMENT RATHER
THAN REHABILITATION FOR YOUNG
LAWBREAKERS.

CHAPTER TWELVE

NEOCLASSICAL THEORY

L ike labeling and radical theory, **neoclassical theory** initially sought to make sense of the crime and turbulence of the 1960s. However, in contrast to those theories, which question whether any system of justice can be fair, neoclassical theory has stressed that the legal system should focus exclusively on *doing justice*. Neoclassical theorists have supported a revival of the principles of the **classical school of criminology** and a return to the practice of responding to crime, not criminals (see the introduction to Part Three). According to those principles, humans are rational, have freedom of choice, and are motivated to pursue their own self-interests. Thus, a person's lawbreaking cannot be blamed on his or her family, peers, or community. Rather, that person made a rational decision to violate the law in pursuit of personal satisfaction.

Neoclassical theorists can be divided into three groups. **Utilitarian philosophers** believe that legal punishments serve two vital functions: (1) deterring persons from committing crimes and (2) protecting society from those whose acts threaten the social order. **Just deserts philosophers,** in contrast to utilitarians, question the utility of legal punishment as a means of deterring crime and advocate its use only because those who commit crimes deserve to be punished. They claim that the rehabilitative ideal is a vehicle for abuse and that the only alternative is to restrict its power and replace it with a system based on classical principles. Lastly, **rational choice theorists** argue that the principles of classical criminology can do more than merely shed light on the appropriate legal reactions to crime. They can be used to construct scientific theories that explain such behavior. To determine the grounds on which these divergent constructions of reality are based and to assess their implications for juvenile justice, each will be analyzed separately.

UTILITARIANISM

Two persons—Ernest van den Haag (1975) and James Q. Wilson (1975, 1983)—have been primarily responsible for articulating utilitarian principles. Whereas positivist theories and the rehabilitative ideal appeal to our compassionate sentiments, utilitarian theory and legal punishment appeal to our punitive feelings.

Assumptions About Human Nature
According to van den Haag (1975:263–264), many theorists over the past two centuries have argued that crime should be blamed on society's institutions, which corrupt naturally good people. Like Freud, however, van den Haag asserted that the reverse is actually true: "For the most part, offenders are not sick. They are like us. Worse, we are like them. Potentially, we could all be or become criminals" (p. 118). People, not society's institutions, are corrupt. Van den Haag continued: "If man were good by nature, no morality would be needed; he would always want to do what he should" (p. 22). But because people

are naturally evil, the threat of legal punishment is imperative:

> If it became known that there are no conductors on trains anymore, the habit of paying would soon disappear. Driven only by their internalized moral sense, unsupported by conductors or policemen, fewer and fewer passengers would buy tickets. Cheating might even be accepted enough to lose its disrepute. Ultimately, those who pay might be as few as those are who now cheat. (p. 23)

Wilson (1975) has been somewhat more cautious on this matter. On the one hand, like most social scientists, he assumed that people are neither naturally good nor evil (pp. 57, 62–63). On the other hand, he asserted that "wicked people [do] exist" (p. 235). And like van den Haag, he suggested that if not for the threat of legal punishment, many people would quickly take advantage of others.

Assumptions About Social Order
Like classical criminologists, van den Haag (1975:16) assumed that society is held together by an implied social contract: "Human beings cannot exist but in society, and society is inconceivable without some order—we all owe society some allegiance in exchange." Because that allegiance constantly is threatened, however, people must be taught that lawbreaking is wrong. "Acts are forbidden either because [they are] regarded as inherently wicked (murder) or because, although not intrinsically wicked (e.g., driving on the wrong side of the street), they interfere with securing some good. Once forbidden, acts become offenses because [they are] unlawful, *whatever their moral quality*" (p. 9, emphasis added). Thus, utilitarians assume that because most people will commit crimes if given the chance, society is held together by a social contract based on the threat of legal punishment for law violations.

Bankruptcy of Positive Criminology
Given their assumptions about human nature and social order, both van den Haag and Wilson argued that positive criminology is bankrupt because its theories are irrelevant and because the rehabilitative ideal is futile.

IRRELEVANCE OF THEORY Positive criminology is irrelevant for three reasons. First, positivist criminologists have tried to discover crime's ultimate causes. But while that effort might help to make crime more understandable, it is irrelevant for social policy (van den Haag, 1975:77–78; Wilson, 1975:53):

> Ultimate causes cannot be the object of policy efforts precisely because, being ultimate, they cannot be changed. For example, criminologists have shown beyond doubt that men commit more crimes than women and younger men more (of certain kinds) than older ones. It is a theoretically important and scientifically correct observation. Yet it means little for policy makers concerned with crime prevention, since men cannot be changed into women or made to skip over the adolescent years. (Wilson, 1975:55)

Second, because most people will commit crimes if given the chance, "the line between the offender and the nonoffender is as blurred as is the line between ordinary and extraordinary temptation" (van den Haag, 1975:82). Finally, it has been argued that the policy recommendations of positivists have been based on personal beliefs rather than scientific evidence (Wilson, 1975:67–70). For example, in recommending the War on Poverty, improvements in the quality of family life, or the enrichment of slum schools, positivists have gone beyond their data. Because they have never been able to prove that such efforts would reduce crime, they have used liberal ideology to justify their recommendations.

FUTILITY OF REHABILITATION By the same token, if positivist theories are irrelevant, then the rehabilitative ideal, which is based on them, is futile:

> If a child is delinquent because his family made him so or his friends encourage him to be so, it is hard to conceive what society might do about his attitudes. No one knows how a government might restore affection, stability, and fair discipline to a family that rejects these characteristics; still less can one imagine how even a family once restored could affect a child who has passed the formative years and in any event has developed an aversion to one or both of his parents. (Wilson, 1975:54)

But even if offenders could be rehabilitated, it is far more important to do justice—to establish a direct link between crime and legal punishment (van den Haag, 1975:187). Consequently, there is need for another view:

> I believe that our society has not done as well as it could have in controlling crime because of erroneous but persistent views about the nature of man and the capacities of his institutions. . . . I argue for a sober view of man and his institutions that would permit reasonable things to be accomplished, foolish things abandoned, and utopian things forgotten. (Wilson, 1975:222–223)

Utilitarian Principles

The view suggested by utilitarians is based on two fundamental principles: (1) Punishment deters people from committing crimes, and (2) punishment vindicates the social order.

BELIEF THAT PUNISHMENT DETERS CRIME A cornerstone of utilitarianism is **deterrence theory.** The earliest versions of deterrence theory were put forth independently by 18th-century social philosophers Cesare Beccaria (1963) and Jeremy Bentham (1948). Beccaria and Bentham presented an array of ideas, but many can be reduced to this generalization: Certain, severe, and swift punishments will *deter* people from committing crimes (Gibbs, 1975:5).

Positivists often have rejected the classical idea that legal punishment deters crime; specifically, they have rejected the idea that people are rational—that in pursuit of their own self-interest, people decide to commit crimes after having weighed the rewards and the punishments. Both Wilson and van den Haag agreed with positivists that people are not entirely rational. Yet, this does not mean that they are undeterrable:

> Prospective offenders need be no more rational than rats are when taught by means of rewards or punishments to run a maze. . . . Legal threats are effective if those subjected to them are capable of responding to threats (whether or not capable of grasping them intellectually), of learning from each other, and of forming habits. Deterrence depends on the likelihood and on the

regularity of human responses to danger, and not on rationality. (van den Haag, 1975:113)

It should be remembered, moreover, that legal punishment is directed not only at criminals but also at *potential* criminals. This points to the distinction between specific and general deterrence (Stafford and Warr, 1993). *Specific deterrence* involves the effects of legal punishment on those who have suffered it. If a burglar is imprisoned, for example, in the hope that upon release, he or she will refrain from committing more burglaries (and perhaps all crimes) in order to avoid further legal punishment, then the hope is that the imprisonment will have a specific deterrent effect. By contrast, *general deterrence* involves the effects of legal punishment on those persons who have not suffered it. Van den Haag (1975: 60–61) described this function of legal punishment in this way:

> It [punishment] is a message addressed to the public at large. The punishment of the offender deters others by telling them: "This will happen to you if you violate the law." Deterrence protects the social order by restraining not the actual offender, who, *eo ipso,* has not been deterred, but other members of society, potential offenders, who still can be deterred. As an English judge succinctly remarked: "Men are not hanged for stealing horses, but that horses may not be stolen."

BELIEF THAT PUNISHMENT VINDICATES THE SOCIAL ORDER In addition to its deterrence function, utilitarians see legal punishment as indispensable for the maintenance of social order. In particular, it can be seen as **retribution**—fair payment exacted for the committing of crimes. That fair payment, in turn, serves two key functions. First, it vindicates the legal order: "Prescribed by the law broken, and proportioned to the gravity of the offense committed, retribution is not inflicted to gratify or compensate anyone who suffered a loss or was harmed by crime—even if it does so—but to enforce the law and to vindicate the legal order" (van den Haag, 1975:11). Second, retribution reinforces the social sentiments that oppose crime: "A great part of the general detes-

tation of crime . . . arises from the fact that the commission of offenses is associated . . . with the solemn and deliberate infliction of punishment wherever crime is proved" (Stephens, 1973:80–81, as quoted by Wilson, 1975:229). If criminals were not punished, people who resisted temptation would feel cheated. And if the threat of legal punishment proved altogether empty, "those who did not break the law would have been deceived" (van den Haag, 1975:21). Consequently, "the purpose of the criminal justice system is not to expose would-be criminals to a lottery in which they either win or lose, but to expose them . . . to the solemn condemnation of the community should they yield to temptation" (Wilson, 1975:230).

Implications for Social Policy

Both van den Haag and Wilson spelled out the policy implications of their ideas in considerable detail.

DECRIMINALIZATION OF STATUS OFFENSES Like other theorists, utilitarians stress the importance of decriminalizing status offenses. The purpose of any legal system should be to catch and punish offenders, not to serve as a social service conduit for for wayward children (van den Haag, 1975:173–175).

LOWER AGE OF ACCOUNTABILITY "Children surely should not be held responsible for their conduct to the extent that adults are" (van den Haag, 1975:174). But juveniles over the age of 13 are another matter: "The victim of a fifteen-year-old mugger is as much mugged as the victim of a twenty-year-old mugger, the victim of a fourteen-year-old murderer or rapist is as dead or as raped as the victim of an older one" (p. 174).

ABOLISHMENT OF JUVENILE COURT Given their common emphasis on treating adults and juveniles alike, both van den Haag and Wilson suggested that the juvenile court should be abolished. Neglected children, and perhaps young offenders under the age of 13, should be handled by family courts, while those ages 13 and over should be tried in criminal courts. Not only would their rights be better protected, but they would gain a greater sense of the meaning of justice and the gravity of their acts.

USE OF DETERMINATE SENTENCES   The sentencing of offenders should be governed by strict procedures. Too often, sentencing decisions have been guided by the utopian view that judges and correctional officials can reform offenders. Utilitarians reject that view and argue that all sentences should be predetermined by law and governed by procedures that ensure uniformity in sentencing (Wilson, 1975: Chap. 8).

GRADING OF PUNISHMENTS   Because most people would commit crimes if given the chance, the costs of crime must be increased so that they exceed the benefits (van den Haag, 1975:250–251). A calculus is needed by which legal punishments can be graded according to both an offender's current offense and his or her prior record.

For first offenders, "every conviction for a nontrivial offense would entail a penalty that involved a deprivation of liberty, even if brief. . . . Only the most serious offenses would result in long penalties" (Wilson, 1975:202). "Unless they are dangerous, these convicts should be kept in prison only as long as is needed to stigmatize their offenses" (van den Haag, 1975:241). This does not mean, however, that there should be efforts to rehabilitate them:

> [Although] the gravity of the offense must be appropriately impressed on the first offender, . . . [any] effort to devise ways of reeducating or uplifting him in order to insure that he does not steal again is likely to be wasted—both because we do not know how to reeducate or uplift and because most young delinquents seem to reeducate themselves no matter what society does. (Wilson, 1975:223)

As a result, such rehabilitative measures as probation should be abolished (Wilson, 1975:202).

Meanwhile, sentences for recidivists should be far more severe, because the offenders pose greater problems: "What we do with first offenders is probably far less important than what we do with habitual offenders" (Wilson, 1975:223). Consequently, "conviction for a subsequent offense would invariably result in an increased deprivation of liberty. If the second offense were minor, the increase would be small; if grave, the increase would be substantial" (Wilson, 1975:202). The length of a sentence could be doubled for a second offense or tripled for a third.

USE OF PREVENTIVE INCAPACITATION   Increased sentences for recidivists would pose some difficulties for the concept of equal justice, because such sentences would be much longer than those given to first offenders. Because recidivists pose a greater danger to other people, however, **preventive incapacitation** should be used until they are no longer a threat (van den Haag, 1975:241–250).

To ensure that the incapacitation is both regularized and humane, three steps should be taken. First, recidivists should complete their prison sentences, based on the last crimes they committed. Then, once these sentences are completed, special supervisory courts should be employed to determine the length of their postprison incapacitation. And because "few [offenders] are dangerous after age forty, hardly any after age sixty," these might be the best ages to which to hold them (van den Haag, 1975:241). Finally, to make the incapacitation humane, new alternatives should be sought. Rather than confinement in prison, recidivists should be *banished* from "certain areas" (their homes and communities?), *exiled* to some "small and distant place" (a deserted island?), or *confined* in some "secure" but "non-punitive" setting where their families could join them and where they might receive visitors (perhaps detention centers?). But because those extraordinary measures are more in the interest of protecting society than in serving justice, offenders should be treated decently, as long as they do not attempt to escape. And if they do try to escape, they should be returned to prison (van den Haag, 1975:256–257).

USE OF CAPITAL PUNISHMENT   Wilson (1975:Chap. 9; 1983:181–188) acknowledged that research on the deterrent effects of the death penalty is equivocal. However, the tendency for people to fall back on scientific studies of the death penalty is really an attempt to avoid the most crucial issue—that of doing justice. "The point is not whether capital punishment prevents future crimes, but whether it is a proper and fitting penalty for crimes that have occurred. . . . [Because] such a question forces us to weigh the value we attach to human life against the horror in which we hold a heinous crime," that is the issue toward which we should be directing our attention (Wilson, 1975:221).

Van den Haag (1975:205–228) was more prescriptive. Although acknowledging the many arguments, pro and con, he suggested that they boil down mainly to the symbolic importance of the death sentence:

> No matter what can be said for abolition of the death penalty, it will be perceived symbolically as a loss of nerve: social authority no longer is willing to pass an irrevocable judgment on anyone. Murder is no longer thought grave enough to take the murderer's life. . . . Life becomes cheaper as we become kinder to those who wantonly take it. . . . Yet if life is to be valued and secured, it must be known that anyone who takes the life of another forfeits his own. (p. 213)

Assessment of Utilitarian Philosophy

KNOWLEDGE OF PUNISHMENT Because utilitarians assume that all people would violate the law given the chance, they have suggested that the only way crime can be controlled is if persons are sufficiently threatened by punishments. If the threat of legal punishment is to deter individuals from committing crimes, they must have some knowledge of that threat. But are people well enough informed of the statutory penalties associated with crime?

To answer that question, the California Assembly Committee on Criminal Procedure (1968) obtained responses from a sample of several populations—students from both low- and high-delinquency high schools, college students, members of the general adult population, and convicted delinquents and criminals confined in California institutions. The high school students—at least potentially one of the more criminal populations—and the members of the general public were extremely ignorant of the statutory penalties associated with eleven crimes. By contrast, the most informed groups were the insti-

tutionalized delinquents and criminals (California Assembly Committee on Criminal Procedure, 1968: 13). Hence, the committee concluded, "It appears that knowledge of penalties comes *after* the crime—that is, penalties cannot act as deterrents since these are unknown until after a person has committed a crime or become a prisoner" (p. 13).

Likewise, both students and the general public were almost totally unaware that the California legislature recently had increased penalties for several offenses, including a minimum of fifteen years for rape, robbery, and burglary, when great bodily injury was involved. The institutionalized adult criminals were the best informed. In this instance, however, the institutionalized delinquents were no better informed about the increased penalties than were the high school students (California Assembly Committee on Criminal Procedure, 1968:13–14, 17).

Other studies have reached similar conclusions regarding knowledge about criminal penalties (Williams and Gibbs, 1981; Williams, Gibbs, and Erickson, 1980). In short, there is little evidence that the public is very knowledgeable about statutory penalties.

THE THREAT OF PUNISHMENT Beginning in the 1960s, several studies were undertaken to determine whether deterrence works. Many of these early studies examined general deterrence among U.S. states; in particular, they focused on how crime rates were related to the certainty and severity of legal punishments and to use of the death penalty (e.g., Bedau, 1967; Gibbs, 1968; Schuessler, 1952; Tittle, 1969).

Because these studies sometimes reached different conclusions, a panel was convened by the most prestigious scientific body in the United States—the National Academy of Sciences—to examine the evidence and report its findings (Blumstein, Cohen, and Nagin, 1978). With respect to the death penalty, the panel concluded that "the available studies provide no useful evidence on the deterrent effect of capital punishment" (p. 9). Research conducted after the panel's report was issued has generated a similar conclusion (Peterson and Bailey, 1988, 1991). If the death penalty is to be used, therefore, it will have to be justified on grounds other than deterrence, because the studies conducted thus far are simply insufficient to draw any definitive conclusions.[1]

Other kinds of legal punishment, however, still could have deterrent effects. "Certainly, most people will agree that increasing sanctions will deter crime somewhat, but the critical question is, By how much? There is still considerable uncertainty over whether that effect is trivial (even if statistically detectable) or profound" (Nagin, 1978:136). The National Academy of Sciences panel went on to state that its "reluctance to draw stronger conclusions does not imply support for a position that deterrence does not exist, since the evidence certainly favors a proposition supporting deterrence more than it favors one asserting that deterrence is absent" (Blumstein, Cohen, and Nagin, 1978:7).

Evidence for general deterrence should be viewed cautiously for several reasons. First, legal punishment may help to reduce crime for reasons other than deterrence—reasons that often get confused with deterrence (Gibbs, 1975:Chap. 3). For example, suppose that chronic offenders were imprisoned for long periods of time, as utilitarians have recommended. Suppose further that during the same period, crime rates decreased. What would explain that decrease? Would it be because potential offenders were deterred when they saw what happened to chronic offenders? Or would it be because chronic offenders could not commit crimes while imprisoned—that is, because they were *incapacitated* from committing crimes? Also, the long prison sentences might have strengthened people's beliefs about the wickedness of engaging in crime. Thus, a decrease in the crime rate in the wake of increased imprisonment is not conclusive evidence of deterrence.

Another basis for caution has already been mentioned: If people lack knowledge of legal punishments, how can they be deterred by them? That question plagued many early studies, and the response has been to adopt new research designs that focus on *perceptions* of legal punishments. Surveys have been conducted to inquire into individuals' perceptions of the certainty and severity of legal punishment and then to determine how they are related to self-reported offending. Much of the research supports deterrence theory (for a thorough review, see Paternoster, 1987:175–179, 187–194). A consistent finding is that the perceived certainty of punishment is negatively related to offending—the greater the perceived certainty of punishment, the less the self-reported offending (Bachman, Paternoster, and Ward, 1992; Erickson, Gibbs, and Jensen, 1977). The same is true of the perceived severity of punishment, provided that perceived certainty is high (Anderson, Chiricos, and Waldo, 1977; Grasmick and Bryjak, 1980; Grasmick, Bursik, and Arneklev, 1993).

A STAKE IN CONFORMITY What about the idea that the best way to control delinquency is to give young people a stake in conformity? Is nothing to be gained by strengthening their attachments to home and school, designing educational programs that give them access to legitimate opportunities, and providing them with a sense that they can affect their own destinies through conventional means of success? Even though legal punishments may have some deterrent effect, additional policies may be necessary if delinquency is to be controlled.

At issue, of course, is our concept of justice. Should it be defined in narrow utilitarian terms? Or should it take into account the relationship between delinquency and the malfunction of such social institutions as the family, the school, and political and economic systems? Relative to these questions, let us consider several points:

1. Juvenile unemployment rates in some slum areas run as high as 50 percent.
2. Rates of illegitimacy and single parenthood among ghetto teenage girls have reached alarmingly high levels.
3. Juvenile gang wars in poor urban communities have become as deadly as the wars between the Palestinians and the Israelis or between Northern Ireland's Catholics and Protestants.

[1] In spite of this research, states increasingly are sentencing offenders to death, even juvenile offenders (Streib, 1987). Indeed, in three recent cases (*Stanford v. Kentucky,* 1989; *Thompson v. Oklahoma,* 1988; *Wilkins v. Missouri,* 1989), the U.S. Supreme Court has ruled that it is constitutional to execute a person who was at least age 16 at the time of committing a capital crime, but not younger. (For an evaluation of *Thompson v. Oklahoma,* see Ricotta, 1988; for a journalistic account of the Wilkins case, see Rosenbaum, 1989.)

Hirschi (1979:208–210) contended that when utilitarian philosophers argue that nothing can or should be done about these kinds of problems, their confusion over the logic of positive theories is "absolute." For example, is it reasonable to assume that as long as these problems continue, increases in the threat of legal punishment alone will successfully reduce delinquency? Indeed, without stakes in conformity, legal punishments may not pose the threat that they otherwise would. And are we to assume that social and legal justice will be served by greater legal punishment?

Furthermore, let us recall the findings of self-report studies (Chapter 5), which indicate that only 1 in 10 delinquent acts receives any official attention. How realistic is it, then, to assume that the threat of legal punishment can serve as the primary mechanism for preventing or controlling delinquency? By all counts, therefore, it seems that unless policies are directed toward helping families, schools, employers, and communities, we cannot expect legal punishment alone to control delinquency.

PREVENTIVE INCAPACITATION This possibility notwithstanding, utilitarian philosophers argue that the incapacitation of violent and chronic offenders may prove to be the answer. Society will be protected by longer prison terms, exile, banishment, and preventive detention.

To assess the accuracy of that argument, three major questions must be addressed: (1) By how much would crime rates be reduced if violent or chronic offenders were locked up for longer periods of time? (2) How many of those locked up would not have committed additional serious offenses had they remained free in the community? and (3) Would we be willing to bear the costs of confining larger numbers of offenders?

Estimates vary considerably concerning the extent to which crime rates would be reduced if offenders were institutionalized for longer periods of time. Greenberg (1975:572) concluded that a one-year increase in prison sentences would reduce the commission of all index offenses by about 10 percent. By contrast, Shinnar and Shinnar (1975:605–607) suggested that the effect might be considerably larger, particularly if specific offenses, such as robbery,

were analyzed separately. After examining these and other studies, however, the panel at the National Academy of Sciences, mentioned earlier, as well as a more recent National Academy of Sciences panel, recommended caution in interpreting the findings. Estimating the effects of incapacitation is so difficult, using arrest and confinement rates, that the validity of existing estimates must be questioned; more research, therefore, is badly needed (Blumstein, Cohen, and Nagin, 1978:64–80; Blumstein et al., 1986: 122–154; Cohen, 1978).

As an example of the kind of research that is needed, Van Dine, Conrad, and Dinitz (1979:36) identified a population of 342 persons in Franklin County, Ohio, who were charged with violent offenses in 1973. They then sought to determine how much violent crime would have been prevented if those offenders had been kept in prison, based on their crimes committed some time during the previous five years. The findings were striking. If all 342 offenders had been kept in prison, only 111, or 3.8 percent, of the 2,892 violent crimes committed in the county in 1973 would have been prevented (p. 62). In short, this research suggested that the preventive effects of incapacitation would have been very slight. Examining other studies, the more recent panel at the National Academy of Sciences reached the same conclusion: "While incarceration leads to some reduction in crime through incapacitation," there is little basis for expecting dramatic reductions (Blumstein et al., 1986:142–143).

Such findings may be surprising, given that almost by definition, imprisonment prevents an offender from committing crime. The factor that most minimizes the effect of incapacitation is the inability to select out chronic offenders in advance. Also, for offenses committed by gangs or organized crime rackets, if only one or a few offenders is imprisoned, the collective criminal activities will persist (Blumstein, Cohen, and Nagin, 1978; Ekland-Olson and Kelly, 1993). Imprisoned offenders simply will be replaced through an illegitimate labor market. Ekland-Olson and Kelly (1993:107) have noted that in cases like this, "all incapacitation does in the long term is expand the pool of experienced [criminal] labor."

The research by Van Dine, Conrad, and Dinitz (1979:Chap. 5) showed that most of the 342 offenders would have been kept in prison unnecessarily had preventive incapacitation been strictly enforced. They would have been *false positives*—people who were imprisoned even though they would have committed no crimes if left free in the community.

To determine how many false positives there would be due to a policy of incapacitation, the earlier panel at the National Academy of Sciences carefully reviewed the relevant studies (Blumstein, Cohen, and Nagin, 1978:75–78; Monahan, 1978). Again, the findings were startling: *Predictions of future criminality were wrong between 50 and 99 percent of the time.* Whether based on prior records, personal characteristics, or clinical diagnoses, these estimates were wrong more often than they were right.

This was a disappointing finding, in one sense, considering the undeniable existence of chronic offenders. However, in advocating the use of preventive incapacitation, utilitarians did not reckon with the extreme difficulty of identifying these offenders *before*, rather than after, they engage in a series of offenses. Noted the earlier National Academy of Sciences panel: "Even good prediction procedures would suffer very high false-positive rates" (Blumstein, Cohen, and Nagin, 1978:77).

False-positive rates are high for several reasons. Some offenders continue to violate the law but evade detection; law-violating behavior by juveniles begins to decline after the middle to late teens; and many criminals, both juvenile and adult, commit violent offenses only once in their lives (Hamparian et al., 1978; Petersilia, Greenwood, and Lavin, 1977). Thus, if incapacitation is used as a method for controlling crime, many offenders may be denied freedom even though they may not have committed crimes had they remained free.

Let us consider the economic and social costs of incapacitation. The economic burdens associated with housing, feeding, and guarding ever-increasing numbers of offenders might be more than we would be willing to bear. Consider but one example. Van Dine, Conrad, and Dinitz (1979:123) estimated that if Ohio had adopted a strict incapacitative policy, the number of inmates in its prisons would have risen from 9,000 to 42,000 within five years. Thus, if the annual costs for confining each inmate for one year were $20,000, annual expenditures would have in-

creased from $180 to $840 million. This figure does not include the capital costs of constructing new prisons, the increases in welfare to care for inmates' families, or the possible diversion of funds from educational and social programs to give potential offenders a stake in conformity. In short, such a policy would entail incredible expenditures (also see Cullen and Gilbert, 1982:183).

Still another estimate of the costs of incapacitation comes from the more recent National Academy of Sciences panel. To reduce all index crimes by 10 percent, "prison population increases of at least 100 to 200 percent would . . . be required" (Blumstein et al., 1986:127). A policy to reduce the rate of some specific index crimes by the same amount would require a smaller increase in prison populations, but it still would be very costly. For example, "5 to 10 percent reductions in robbery [could be achieved] with 10 to 20 percent increases in the population of robbers in prison" (Blumstein et al., 1986:143).

JUST DESERTS PHILOSOPHY

Just deserts philosophy is similar to utilitarian philosophy in that it would have us concentrate on doing justice rather than rehabilitating offenders. But the two greatly differ in other respects.

Basic Assumptions

Whereas utilitarians stress the need to protect the state from the wickedness of its citizens, just deserts philosophers seek to protect citizens from the wickedness of the state. They would revive the use of classical principles, not because they believe the state requires more power to arrest and punish, but because they believe its use of this power has been oppressive. People who violate the law have a right to be free of such things as (1) unwanted intervention into their lives (as is the case with rehabilitation), (2) scapegoating designed to scare others into conformity (as is the case with general deterrence), and (3) extended imprisonment that punishes them for crimes they have not yet committed (as is the case with selective incapacitation). In short, individuals have the right simply *to be punished for the acts they have committed.* Any other consideration is unjustified and gives the state more power than what is needed to do justice.

Just Deserts Principles

Just deserts principles were derived from several sources: (1) a committee of scholars set up to analyze the weaknesses of prisons and recommend improvements (Gaylin and Rothman, 1976; von Hirsch, 1976), (2) a practicing correctional administrator and former executive director of the Illinois Law Enforcement Commission (Fogel, 1975), and (3) a legal scholar who sought to reform the juvenile justice system (Fox, 1974). Persons from a variety of perspectives, therefore, joined in condemning not only the rehabilitative ideal but also utilitarianism. Five guiding principles of this perspective are presented here:

1. *Treat legal punishment as a "desert."* Legal punishment for a crime is not justified by the need for retribution—a fair payment for a criminal act. Furthermore, legal punishment is not justified because it serves the utilitarian function of deterring persons from committing crimes. Rather, it is justified only because the offender deserves it (von Hirsch, 1976:Chap. 6).

2. *Avoid doing harm.* The idea of legal punishment as a just desert entails pessimism about the prospects for rehabilitation. The rehabilitative ideal "was a scheme born to optimism, and faith, and humanism. It viewed the evils in man as essentially correctable" (Gaylin and Rothman, 1976:xxxvii). However, "there is virtually no sound proof that, short of killing him, anyone knows how to stop another person from committing crimes" (Fox, 1974:3), so the time has come to discard our maudlin beliefs.

   Although supporters of the rehabilitative ideal sought to do good by giving legal officials the discretion to adapt individual treatment to individual needs, such discretion has proved to be an unmitigated evil:

   Both in tone and in content, the recommendations of the Committee represent a departure from tradition. Permeating this report is a determination to do less rather than more—an insistence on not doing harm. The quality of heady optimism and confidence of reformers in the past, and their belief that they could solve the problem of crime . . . will not be found in this document. Instead, we have here a crucial shift in perspective from a commitment to do good to a commitment to do as little mischief as possible. . . . The Committee insists that the potential benefit done to any one offender under a system of massive discretion is more than offset by the harms done to the vast majority of persons through such a normless scheme. (Gaylin and Rothman, 1976:xxxiv–xxxv)

3. *Sentence delinquency, not the delinquent.* To avoid doing harm, we should adopt a mechanized system of justice that sentences delinquent acts, not delinquents (Fox, 1974:6). Decisions concerning offenders' sentences should be based not on their needs or circumstances, but on the penalties they deserve for their acts (von Hirsch, 1976:98).

4. *Interfere parsimoniously.* Because the rights of individuals are paramount and the only justification for legal punishment is a just desert, the state is obligated to observe "strict parsimony" in interfering in the lives of convicted offenders. Not only should it have to justify the use of severe punishments for them, but it should have to justify *any* intrusion into their lives (von Hirsch, 1976:5).

5. *Restrain efforts to prevent crime.* The pursuit of justice must override every other consideration. It therefore requires that we restrain efforts to prevent crime. A major concern is that the utilitarian notions of deterrence and incapacitation "could lead to punishing the offender more severely than he deserves" (von Hirsch, 1976:70), but rehabilitation is discarded as well:

   The concept of [just] deserts is intellectual and moralistic; in its devotion to principle, it turns back on such compromising considerations as generosity and charity, compassion and love. It emphasizes justice, not mercy, and while it need not rule out tempering justice with mercy, by shifting the emphasis from concern for the individual to devotion to the moral right, it could lead to an abandonment of the former altogether. (Gaylin and Rothman, 1976:xxxix)

In other words, social policy should be concerned "less with the administration of justice and more . . . with the *justice of administration*" (Fogel, 1975:xv).

Implications for Social Policy

Although based on different principles, many of the policy implications of just deserts philosophy are similar to those of utilitarianism. Just deserts philosophers imply that we should do several things:

1. Decriminalize status offenses, not only because justice requires it but because attention to non-criminal offenses encourages legal oppression in the name of benevolence.
2. Lower the age of accountability for crime, because justice demands attention to crimes, not criminals.
3. Abolish the juvenile court in the interest of both eliminating its powers and protecting the rights of juveniles.
4. Use **determinate sentences** as a means of eliminating official discretion.
5. Punish rather than treat offenders.
6. Grade punishments along two dimensions: "(a) the seriousness of the crime for which the offender currently stands convicted, and (b) the seriousness of his prior record" (von Hirsch, 1976:133—although primary emphasis should be placed on the first dimension according to von Hirsch, 1985:Chap. 7). The greater the seriousness and the longer the history of crime, the greater the legal punishment.

Despite these similarities, there is an important difference between utilitarian and just deserts philosophers. Whereas the former would make legal punishments more severe and would exile, banish, or incapacitate chronic offenders, just deserts philosophers would not only discard the death penalty but also reduce sentence lengths to the point where it satisfies our sense of equity, but no more than that: "'warnings' for crimes low on a scale of seriousness [fines based on ability to pay], intermittent confine-

ment (weekends or evenings) for more serious offenses, and . . . full-time incarceration only for the most serious crimes" (Gaylin and Rothman, 1976: xxxv; also see von Hirsch, 1976:119–123). Rather than severity of sanctions, therefore, the principle that should govern the imposition of legal punishments, according to just deserts philosophers, is the *least restrictive alternative* commensurate with the seriousness of the criminal act.

In fact, the only reason just deserts philosophers would continue to institutionalize offenders at all is that they cannot think of a better alternative (von Hirsch, 1976:111). Because imprisonment is a necessary evil, however, "the preference should be for open facilities, without bars or restraining walls. There should also be strict limits on the size of institutions, to reduce the need for regimentation" (von Hirsch, 1976:115). And even then, "it bears repeating: incarceration, even with shorter sentences, should only be invoked against offenders whose crimes are serious" (von Hirsch, 1976:114).

Assessment of Just Deserts Philosophy

Two points must be made about the implications of just deserts philosophy. On the one hand, it emphasizes doing justice—protecting the rights of the accused, seeing that legal prcedures are fair, respecting the worth of the offender, and, where possible, mitigating the destructive impact of legal punishments. Such emphases are basic to the precepts of Enlightenment philosophy and must form the cornerstone of any continuing effort to promote justice. Their importance cannot be denied.

On the other hand, just deserts philosophers express a depressing pessimism. Because legal bureaucracies have not always been successful in doing so in the past, the humane sentiments that gave rise to them must be discarded. Rather than seeking new social inventions by which to combine justice with mercy, we must become even more legalistic and resort to a system that is based on "despair, not hope," on "a determination to do less rather than more" (Gaylin and Rothman, 1976:xxxix, xxxiv). It is as though we no longer have the will or the inventiveness by which to incorporate compassion, love, and charity in our dealings with law violators. Consider

UTILITARIAN VERSUS JUST DESERTS: THE CASE OF KARLA FAYE TUCKER

Although the policy implications for the utilitarian and just deserts philosophies tend to be similar, every few years a controversy reveals the contrast between the two. This recently happened in Texas as the execution date neared for death row inmate Karla Faye Tucker. Tucker was convicted in 1983 for an abhorrent murder in which she and an accomplice robbed two victims and then repeatedly struck them with a pickaxe. She later claimed that each swing of the pickaxe gave her a sexual thrill. Despite the brutality of her crime, her pending execution attracted widespread attention as many people—including Pope John Paul II—called for her death sentence to be commuted to life in prison. They argued that Tucker had experienced a true rehabilitation during her fifteen years in prison. She had embraced Christianity, and for the first time in her adult life she was not abusing drugs. She also was actively involved in counseling other inmates. Although supporters of Tucker tended to be opponents of the death penalty, they invoked utilitarian arguments in her defense. They argued that her transformation could have positive future consequences. She would symbolize to all offenders that embracing religion, acknowledging guilt, and accepting punishment could lead to their own transformation. She could even correspond with troubled offenders who were seeking to change their ways. In short, Karla Faye Tucker *could help prevent future crime.* This argument obviously did not sit well with just-deserts-minded policymakers and citizens, who believed that regardless of the future good Tucker could do, her crime justified the use of the death penalty. In refusing to call off the execution, Governor George W. Bush commented that "judgments about the heart and soul of an inmate on death row are best left to a higher authority" and that the state's decision must be based on the crime she committed. In February 1998, Tucker became the first woman executed in Texas since 1863. Source: *The Economist,* February 7, 1998, pp. 28–29.

---

a few of the problems that are left unattended by the just deserts philosophers.

JUST DESERTS IN AN UNJUST SOCIETY Von Hirsch identified some serious moral problems associated with sentencing and punishing offenders in an unjust society: "Consider the impoverished and alienated ghetto-dweller who turns to crime in the absence of lawful opportunities for making a decent living: what, if any are his deserts?" (von Hirsch, 1976:145). But while the inventors of the juvenile court considered it their responsibility to do something about these matters (to say nothing of the implications of positive or radical theories), von Hirsch (1976:147) concluded that with a mechanized system of justice, "it may not be feasible to treat social deprivation as a mitigating factor."

Just deserts philosophy is no more capable of promoting social justice than is utilitarianism. Because its proposals for reform are based on despair and on mistrust of the state, no attempt would be made to remedy the discrimination, inequality, or powerlessness that so often are associated with delinquency.

THE ELIMINATION OF DISCRETION The individualized concept of justice requires that considerable discretion—the capacity to exercise judgment and make decisions—be granted to judges and correctional officials. Because discretion has been misused in the past, however, just deserts philosophers would like to see it eliminated. On the surface, the rationale is a sound one: In a discretionary system, a rich man's son or daughter may be given probation for smoking marijuana while a poor youth may be institutionalized. "In a nondiscretionary system, everyone—or no one—must go to prison" (Greenberg and Humphries, 1980:209).

However, discretion may be used to avoid as well as promote injustice. For example, similar offenses are not necessarily committed by similar persons: A 16-year-old joyrider is not the same as, nor is he or she motivated by the same interests as, a professional auto thief. Rather than always discriminating against the powerless, judges may do the reverse: They may seek ways to soften the severity of statutory penalties in an effort to avoid imposing pain unnecessarily or unfairly (Cressey, 1977:24).

THE RIGHT TO PUNISHMENT In their desire to overcome the evils of individualized justice, just deserts philosophers also have stressed juveniles' rights to punishment. Rather than focusing on causes of their delinquency or factors that may lead them to future law-violating behavior, justice requires that the focus be on their past offenses and the legal punishment they deserve for them.

The implications of this position are horrendous. Suppose, for example, that a 15-year-old girl is arrested for shoplifting. Suppose further that upon investigation, the court discovers that she has a rather common problem: She is a runaway who left home because her mother refused to protect her from the sexual abuses of her stepfather and who stole in order to survive. If the just deserts philosophy was followed to the letter, the court would be required to punish the girl for shoplifting and would be precluded from taking action based on her home condition or her sexual abuse. To be sure, authorities could seek to have her stepfather prosecuted. But unless her mother was willing to testify against her stepfather—and in many cases she is not—it is unlikely that any charges could be sustained. Thus, short of convicting the stepfather, the court would have no recourse for protecting the young girl.

The same sorts of problems might be encountered in places of confinement for more serious delinquents. Said von Hirsch (1976:115): "We favor minimum interference with confined offenders. The sanction should consist only of the deprivation of the freedom to leave." If delinquents wished, they might participate in vocational training, traditional schooling, or counseling, but any such participation would have to be strictly voluntary.

A New Version of Just Deserts

Just deserts philosophers and utilitarians have a shared vision of the legal system. Indeed, it has been argued that the policy implications of just deserts philosophy (determinate sentencing, graded punishment, lower age of accountability, etc.) so closely resemble those of utilitarian philosophy (Forst and Blomquist, 1992) that the distinctions between the two are merely academic.

In recent years, however, a variation of just deserts philosophy, **restorative justice,** has presented a new set of policy implications (Galaway, 1988; Wright, 1991; Zehr, 1982). Proponents of restorative justice share just deserts philosophers' concern with doing justice. However, they argue that a focus on punishment prevents true justice from being served. Restorative justice is concerned with achieving justice for both victims and offenders. The problem with a punishment-based system is that officials become preoccupied with securing convictions and imposing sanctions, and in so doing, ignore the financial, physical, and emotional losses that victims have suffered. Also, when crimes are perceived as offenses against the state and when the debt to be paid is a *debt to society,* then offenders seldom are required to face their victims and "understand the real human costs of their actions" (Zehr, 1982:4).

Proponents of restorative justice would change this by stressing that in the wake of a crime, true justice is served only when offenders make restitution so as to return victims, to the greatest extent possible, to their original circumstances (Barnett, 1981). That strategy clearly runs into difficulty with respect to victimless crimes or crimes so serious that restitution would be impossible. For other offenses, however, victim–offender mediation can be used to negotiate a restitution agreement, including such things as an apology and replacement or repair of damaged property.

The number of victim–offender mediation programs in the juvenile justice system has expanded greatly in the past decade (Umbreit and Coates, 1993), and evaluations of those programs suggest that participants believe that justice is being served. In a study of mediation programs in St. Paul, Galaway (1988) found that over 95 percent of mediation sessions resulted in restitution agreements and about 80 percent of agreements were fulfilled. The rate of satisfaction among victims with the mediation process exceeded 60 percent and often was as high as 80 percent (Marshall and Merry, 1990; Umbreit and Coates, 1993). Rates of satisfaction appear to be high among offenders as well (Coates and Gehm, 1989). Some studies also suggest that **recidivism** may be lower among offenders whose cases are referred to victim–offender mediation rather than to some other program (Schneider, 1986; Umbreit and Coates, 1993). However, Umbreit and Coates (1993) are quick to point out that such a consideration is secondary. True to its philosophy, restorative justice is devoted principally to doing justice.

RATIONAL CHOICE THEORY

Rational choice theory has flourished in recent decades. Whereas utilitarians and just deserts philosophers have revived principles of the classical school to determine the appropriate legal reactions to crime, rational choice theorists have done so to explain such behavior.

Basic Assumptions
Like utilitarians and just deserts philosophers, rational choice theorists assume that people violate the law as a result of a rational exercise of free will: "Offenders seek to benefit themselves by their criminal behavior; ... this involves the making of decisions and of choices, however rudimentary on occasion these processes might be; and ... these processes ex-

hibit a measure of rationality" (Cornish and Clarke, 1985:1). In some senses, we have already considered rational choice theory. Both social control theory and self-control theory, covered in Chapter 11, contain aspects of rational choice. For example, social control theory assumes that humans pursue their self-interests and that bonds to conventional society prevent most people from doing so in antisocial ways. Self-control theory takes a similar view of human nature but assumes that the primary restraint on antisocial impulses derives more from internal than from external controls.

Two recent theories—routine activities theory and expanded deterrence theory—extend rational choice theory. As we will see, they conceive of criminal offenders in different ways. **Routine activities theory** assumes a ready supply of motivated offenders and tends to focus on opportunities for violating the law. By contrast, offenders are the main focus of **expanded deterrence theory,** which assumes a knowledgable and thoughtful law violator, one who considers not just the certainty and severity of legal punishments, but many other factors as well.

Routine Activities Theory
As we have seen, classical theorists rejected the positivist notion that crime is caused by personal defects of offenders. Rather, all people are inherently inclined to pursue their own interests and will commit crimes if given the chance. There is little reason, therefore, to focus on offenders because the real issue involves the presence or absence of opportunities for law-violating behavior.

Routine activities theorists take that view even further. They ignore the characteristics of offenders and instead focus on crime *situations*. The basic premise of routine activities theory is that for a predatory crime to occur, there must be a convergence in time and space of three elements: (1) a motivated offender, (2) a suitable target, and (3) the absence of capable guardians—that is, people who could prevent or interfere with the commission of a crime. *Routine activities* affect where, when, and how often these elements converge, with routine activities defined as "recurrent and prevalent activities which provide for basic population and individual needs, whatever their biological or cultural origins" (Cohen and Felson, 1979:593). Routine activities include such things as "formalized work, . . . provision of standard food, shelter, sexual outlet, leisure, social interaction, learning, and childrearing" (p. 593). In short, any activity that is part of everyday life influences the convergence of the three necessary elements of predatory crimes.

Cohen and Felson (1979) illustrated the importance of routine activities by showing that an increase in U.S. crime rates between 1947 and 1974 was closely related to a decrease during the same period in household activity, as measured by the portion of U.S. households with a married female not participating in the labor force. There were several reasons for this. First, because most crimes involving direct contact between victim and offender occur away from the home (p. 595), increased activity away from the home places people at greater risk. Second, activity away from the home removes people who could act as capable guardians of a household's material possessions. Third, an increase in dual-income households is associated with increased ownership of such suitable targets for theft as vehicles and electronic appliances.

The Cohen–Felson findings generated considerable interest in routine activities theory. Several years later, Cohen, Kluegel, and Land (1981) formulated an alternative version of the theory, which they termed *opportunity theory*. Although continuing to emphasize the convergence of motivated offenders, suitable targets, and the absence of capable guardians, they argued that *four* principle opportunity variables affect individuals' and communities' risks of crime victimization: (1) exposure to high-risk environments, (2) physical proximity to motivated offenders, (3) availability of attractive targets for crime, and (4) the absence of guardians. Cohen, Kluegel, and Land's (1981) analysis revealed general support for opportunity theory: For a sample of U.S. households and individuals, measures of the four opportunity variables tended to be positively related to the risks of crime victimization.

Subsequent studies, however, have provided only partial support for the theory. No consistent evidence has emerged regarding the effects of target attractiveness and capable guardianship on rates of crime (Miethe and Meier, 1994:50–51). But many studies have found that exposure to high-risk environments and proximity to motivated offenders are associated with high victimization rates. Kennedy and Forde (1990), for example, found that non-household, nighttime activity—such as going to bars or going for a walk or drive—increased people's risk of assault and robbery, presumably by exposing them to more dangerous environments. Similarly, Kennedy and Baron (1993) and Jensen and Brownfield (1986) found that people heavily involved in the commission of crimes had lifestyle patterns that increased their exposure to dangerous situations, thus increasing their own risk of crime victimization. As for proximity to motivated offenders, the most commonly used measures have been residence in an urban or low-income area and perceptions of danger in the immediate neighborhood, which several studies have found to be positively associated with victimization (Ennis, 1967; Miethe and Meier, 1990, 1994:Chap. 6; Smith and Jarjoura, 1989).

The argument actually can be made that routine activities theory has never been tested fully or adequately. As Miethe and Meier (1994:54–55) have noted, data limitations have led researchers to rely on "inadequate measures of proximity, exposure, attractiveness, and guardianship [that] do not tap each of the underlying concepts and have ambiguous meanings." For example, guardianship refers to the extent to which household members or neighbors are able to protect their households from victimization. Lacking the resources to directly measure this concept, researchers have relied on indirect measures, such as the number of members in a household—which may or may not be indicative of guardianship as conceived by routine activities theorists.

Furthermore, data limitations at times have led researchers to measure different opportunity variables in the same way. For example, the socioeconomic status of a neighborhood has been used as a measure for both proximity to motivated offenders (in which case it should be negatively related to crime) and target attractiveness (in which case it should be positively related to crime). Similarly, is mothers' employment outside the home indicative of high exposure to risky situations or the absence of capable guardianship? Until those measurement

SOLUTION TO THE CRIME PROBLEM? WATCH MORE TELEVISION

People often have speculated that violence on television causes high rates of violent crime. Combining data on violent crime and television viewing patterns, Steven Messner (1986) examined whether the Standard Metropolitan Statistical Areas (SMSAs) with the highest viewership of the five most violent television shows in 1980 also would have the highest violent crime rates. To his surprise, he found the opposite—SMSAs with the highest viewership of violent programming had the *lowest* rates of violent crime. Messner used routine activities theory to explain this finding. People who watched violent programming also tended to watch more television in general, and this in-the-household activity decreased their risk of victimization for street crimes while also decreasing their risk of household victimization (e.g., burglary) by increasing guardianship of their household.

problems are resolved, the empirical adequacy of routine activities theory cannot be fully known.

Expanded Deterrence Theory

Expanded deterrence theory is not so much a distinct theory as it is a line of empirical research that examines the different costs of law-violating behavior. That research is rooted in the premise that people refrain from committing crimes as a result of perceived costs but that those costs include more than the perceived certainty and severity of legal punishment. Of central importance are *informal sanctions,* which include embarrassment, loss of respect from one's friends or family, and diminished educational

and occupational chances. The *moral* costs of crime also have been considered—people who are morally opposed to violating the law may anticipate the guilt they will suffer and consequently refrain from violating the law. Closely related are the costs associated with shame and loss of self-respect: "Shame, a self-imposed sanction, occurs when actors violate norms they have internalized. It is experienced most immediately as the pain of feeling guilt or remorse . . . and it can occur even if no one but the actor is aware of the transgression" (Grasmick, Bursik, and Arneklev, 1993:43).

Tests of expanded deterrence theory have received strong support. Virtually every test to date has found evidence of crime-reducing effects of informal sanctions (e.g., Anderson, Chiricos, and Waldo, 1977; Jensen and Erickson, 1978; Nagin and Paternoster, 1994; Petee, Milner, and Welch, 1994; Tittle, 1980). This also has been the case for moral costs and shame (Bachman, Paternoster, and Ward, 1992; Grasmick, Bursik, and Arneklev, 1993; Nagin and Paternoster, 1994).

Some of the more interesting speculation has involved the ways that formal (legal) and informal sanctions combine to affect crime. For example, Gibbs (1975:84–86) argued that informal sanctions that result from legal punishments may deter crime as much or more than the legal punishments themselves. Similarly, Salem and Bowers (1970:22) wrote that "formal sanctions' primary effect is through their capacity to . . . reinforce and mobilize . . . informal social disapproval." Consistent with this, Tittle (1980:Chap. 7) found that the deterrent effects of the perceived certainty of arrest were due entirely to fear of the perceived interpersonal loss of respect that would follow from arrest. Similarly, Williams and Hawkins (1989) found a deterrent effect of the perceived certainty of arrest for wife assault in part because of the negative reactions that would follow from friends, family, neighbors, and employers.

In a study of thirty-four drug dealers, Ekland-Olson, Lieb, and Zurcher (1984) found that dealers' concerns about legal punishments often derived not from the punishments themselves, but from the way the punishments would affect their interpersonal networks. One dealer commented on what being caught by police would mean for his relationships with "straight" people:

My paranoia resulted from my being straight. It was a straight kind of paranoia. It was also like I had a lot to lose if I got busted. . . . The problem wasn't the thought of going to prison or jail . . . you [just] certainly didn't want to get caught doing anything like I was. (Ekland-Olson, Lieb, and Zurcher, 1984:162)

In addition to the fear of how an arrest would affect ties with law-abiding people, a principal concern of drug dealers was how it would affect their dealing connections. Ekland-Olson and his colleagues (1984: 169) observed that "an arrest and the accompanying investigation were often perceived to be just as threatening as a prison sentence. Not only was the person arrested affected, but a network of relations built over a period of years could instantly collapse." One dealer commented on how a large-scale marijuana deal had gone awry for one of his suppliers: "His whole source [of marijuana] . . . dried up because of the police investigation. So he was out of business, and that not only put me out of business, but it put the guy in Kansas City [who I supplied] out of business [also]" (p. 169). The researchers concluded that a focus on how formal sanctions disrupt people's interpersonal relationships "better explains the deterrent impact of criminal sanctions than does a more strictly psychological approach to fear" (p. 160).

In sum, there is strong support for expanded deterrence theory. Moreover, there is opportunity for further development of the theory as criminologists conceive of additional costs of crime. And, as some have suggested (e.g., Nagin and Paternoster, 1994; Paternoster and Simpson, 1993), expanded deterrence theory could be incorporated into a broader rational choice theory. In such a theory, the benefits of crime would not be taken as a given, but would be clearly identified and examined in terms of how they are distributed across the population and how, in conjunction with perceived costs, they affect the commission of crime.

Policy Implications of Rational Choice Theories

The principal policy implication of routine activities theory is that efforts must be made to reduce opportunities for crime. This might involve broad-based

measures, such as Neighborhood Watch programs, increased police patrols, or architectural designs that enable greater supervision of an area. It also could include narrowly tailored strategies that make a specific target less vulnerable to victimization. Routine activities theorists refer to this as *target hardening*, which includes such actions as installing private security alarms and extra locks, increasing lighting in dark areas, and having neighbors watch one's property.

One cautionary note is that target-hardening and other opportunity reduction strategies may *displace* crime rather than prevent it. That is, target hardening in one area may decrease crime there but increase crime in nearby areas that are less protected. There is some reason to believe that this does, in fact, occur (Gabor, 1990). As Miethe and Meier (1994:176) indicate, "under criminal displacement, the efficacy of current crime prevention efforts is called into question since there would be no overall reduction in crime rates following the implementation of crime control actions." From a policy standpoint, displacement must be seriously considered, because the neighborhoods that are most plagued by crime problems may be poor and socially disorganized, and therefore the least capable of enacting thorough target-hardening strategies.

When one considers expanded deterrence theory's policy implications, its relation to social control theory becomes obvious. The principle implication of expanded deterrence theory is that policymakers should pursue any policy that encourages children to internalize prosocial norms, become attached to conventional others, and develop committment to conventional goals. These things prevent crime by sensitizing people to the various costs of law-violating behavior, such as moral regret and shame, loss of respect among family and friends, and diminished occupational and educational chances.

SUMMARY AND CONCLUSIONS

Convinced that the rehabilitative ideal has failed and that positivist criminology is bankrupt, three groups of philosophers have revived the principles of classical criminology. One group—the utilitarians—stress the use of legal punishment for deterrence and the protection of society. The second group—the just deserts philosophers—object to the use of legal punishment as a deterrent and advocate its application only as a means of doing justice. The third group—rational choice theorists—uses the classical view of human nature to construct theories to explain law-violating behavior.

Assumptions About Human Nature and the Social Order

Utilitarian philosophers and rational choice theorists assume that people will violate the law if given the chance. The threat of punishment and a reduction in criminal opportunities, therefore, are the only means for protecting the state and maintaining social order. Just deserts philosophers, by contrast, assume that the state is the wicked party and that its citizens require protection.

Based on those contrasting assumptions, each group has different reasons for rejecting individualized justice. Utilitarians would reject it because it is utopian and optimistic, and assumes that the wicked inclinations of young people can be changed. Meanwhile, just deserts philosophers would reject it not because it is utopian and benevolent, but because the state cannot be trusted to be utopian and benevolent.

Underlying Principles of Neoclassical Theories

Utilitarian philosophy is based on two fundamental principles: (1) The threat of legal punishment deters persons from committing crimes, and (2) legal punishment is indispensable for the maintenance of social order.

Just deserts philosophy, by contrast, is built on principles of despair. It supports (1) mechanizing justice to avoid doing harm; (2) sentencing delinquency, not the delinquent; (3) viewing legal punishment as a just desert; and (4) restraining efforts to prevent delinquency or rehabilitate offenders. In short, just deserts proponents would shift the emphasis from a concern with the individual to a higher morality of uniform legal punishments. A recent variation of this philosophy is restorative justice, which emphasizes that justice is served when offenders provide victims with restitution that returns them,

to the greatest extent possible, to their original circumstances.

Rational choice theory is based on the idea that differences in the risks of victimization can be explained by differences in opportunities and the informal sanctions for criminal behavior.

Implications for Policy of Neoclassical Theories

Utilitarian and just deserts philosophies share many policy implications. Both support (1) decriminalizing status offenses, (2) lowering the age of accountability for crime, (3) abolishing juvenile court, (4) using determinate sentences, and (5) grading legal punishments to fit current and past offenses. Within these general policies, however, are some important differences. Utilitarians would use the death penalty, punish offenders more severely, and incapacitate recidivists for long periods of time. By contrast, just deserts philosophers would eliminate the death penalty, lessen the severity of legal punishments, and use incarceration only as a last resort. A recent variation of just deserts philosophy—restorative justice—advocates the use of restitution and mediation to assure that justice is served for both victims and offenders.

The principal policy implication of rational choice theory is that efforts must be made simultaneously to decrease opportunities for crime and to increase the perceived costs of crime. Routine activities theory advocates increased guardianship and target hardening in the form of Neighborhood Watch programs, increased police patrols, security alarms, increased lighting, and so on. Expanded deterrence theory advocates any policy that increases youths' moral commitments, attachment to conventional others, or commitment to conventional goals—each of which will increase their awareness of the informal costs of crime.

Assessment of Neoclassical Theories

With regard to utilitarianism, studies have revealed that (1) the deterrent effects of legal punishment are limited by the public's lack of knowledge about criminal penalties; (2) the threat of legal punishment does have some deterrent effect, but it is difficult to estimate the magnitude of that effect; (3) the possibility that the legal system can control delinquency is slight, unless efforts are made by other social institutions to provide young people with a stake in conformity; and (4) despite incredible costs in human and monetary terms, preventive incapacitation is not likely to result in large decreases in crime rates.

Given their commitment to minimizing harm, just deserts philosophers (1) would not attempt to provide juveniles with a stake in conformity, (2) would prevent judges and correctional officials from exercising discretion, and (3) like utilitarian philosophers, would discard any concern with individual differences and needs. Restorative justice, a new version of just deserts theory, places a similar emphasis on doing justice but would achieve this by having offenders provide restitution to victims. That practice may reform offenders by encouraging them to be accountable for their behavior, but such concerns are secondary to the goal of doing justice. A limitation of restorative justice is that it cannot achieve justice for serious or traumatic offenses (such as homicide, rape, or assault) for which restitution would be impossible.

Perhaps we should not be too surprised by some of the limitations of neoclassical philosophies. The reason that efforts were made to refine classical principles and practices in the 1800s was because the legal system alone could not be expected to ensure justice and control crime. After all, its role in socializing young persons is more negative than positive—that is, better designed to indicate what young people should not do than what they should do.

Thus, society must depend on other institutions to accomplish those tasks. Indeed, if it is serious about wanting to reduce delinquency, society must pursue policies that, in addition to improving the legal system, are designed to (1) identify those institutions—the family, school, church, or community—that are most likely to provide desirable models for conduct and legitimate avenues for success; (2) strengthen those institutions or invent new ones so that these desirable goals are enhanced; and (3) discard those institutions that now tend to foster delinquent behaviors and identities.

To be sure, neoclassical philosophers are correct in suggesting that such a task is profoundly complex. Yet, if nothing else, we should have learned by now that delinquency is a historical phenomenon that does not lend itself to easy solutions.

DISCUSSION QUESTIONS

1. According to utilitarian philosophers, how is criminological theory irrelevant?
2. How effective is preventive incapacitation?
3. What do just deserts philosophers find unacceptable about deterrence and preventive incapacitation?
4. What have studies revealed about the empirical adequacy of routine activities theory?
5. What is the difference between deterrence theory and expanded deterrence theory?

REFERENCES

Anderson, Linda S., Theodore G. Chiricos, and Gordon P. Waldo. 1977. "Formal and Informal Sanctions: A Comparison of Deterrent Effects." *Social Problems* 25 (October):103–114.

Bachman, Ronet, Raymond Paternoster, and Sally Ward. 1992. "The Rationality of Sexual Offending: Testing a Deterrence/Rational Choice Conception of Sexual Assault." *Law and Society Review* 26 (May):343–372.

Barnett, R. 1981. "Restitution: A New Paradigm of Criminal Justice." Pp. 245–261 in Burt Galaway and Joe Hudson, eds., *Perspectives on Crime Victims*. St. Louis: Mosby.

Beccaria, Cesare. 1963. *On Crimes and Punishments.* Translated by Henry Paolucci. Indianapolis, Ind.: Bobbs-Merrill.

Bedau, Hugo A. 1967. *The Death Penalty in America,* rev. ed. Garden City, NY.

Bentham, Jeremy. 1948. *An Introduction to the Principles of Morals and Legislation.* Edited by Laurence J. Lafleur. New York: Hafner.

Blumstein, Alfred, Jacqueline Cohen, and Daniel Nagin, eds. 1978. *Deterrence and Incapacitation: Estimating the Effects of Criminal Sanctions on*

Crime Rates. Washington, D.C.: National Academy of Sciences.

Blumstein, Alfred, Jacqueline Cohen, Jeffrey A. Roth, and Christy A. Visher, eds. 1986. *Criminal Careers and "Career Criminals,"* Vol. 1. Washington, D.C.: National Academy Press.

California Assembly Committee on Criminal Procedure. 1968. *Deterrent Effects of Criminal Sanctions.* Sacramento: Assembly of the State of California.

Coates, Robert, and John Gehm. 1989. "Victim–Offender Mediation: An Empirical Assessment." Pp. 251–263 in Martin Wright and Burt Galaway, eds., *Mediation and Criminal Justice: Victims, Offenders, and Community.* London: Sage.

Cohen, Jacqueline. 1978. "The Incapacitative Effect of Imprisonment: A Critical Review of the Literature." Pp. 187–243 in Alfred Blumstein, Jacqueline Cohen, and Daniel Nagin, eds., *Deterrence and Incapacitation: Estimating the Effects of Criminal Sanctions on Crime Rates.* Washington, D.C.: National Academy of Sciences.

Cohen, Lawrence, and Marcus Felson. 1979. "Social Change and Crime Rate Trends: A Routine Activity Approach." *American Sociological Review* 44 (August):588–608.

Cohen, Lawrence, James R. Kluegel, and Kenneth C. Land. 1981. "Social Inequality and Predatory Criminal Victimization: An Exposition and Test of a Formal Theory." *American Sociological Review* 46 (October):505–524.

Cornish, Derek, and Ronald Clarke, eds. 1985. *The Reasoning Criminal: Rational Choice Perspectives on Offending.* New York: Springer-Verlag.

Cressey, Donald R. 1977. "Doing Justice: The Rule of Law Includes More Than the Statutes." *The Center Magazine* 10 (January/February):21–28.

Cullen, Francis T., and Karen E. Gilbert. 1982. *Reaffirming Rehabilitation.* Cincinnati: Anderson.

Ekland-Olson, Sheldon, and William R. Kelly. 1993. *Justice Under Pressure: A Comparison of Recidivism Patterns Among Four Successive Parolee Cohorts.* New York: Springer-Verlag.

Ekland-Olson, Sheldon, John Lieb, and Louis Zurcher. 1984. "The Paradoxical Impact of Criminal Sanctions: Some Microstructural Findings." *Law and Society Review* 18 (Spring):159–178.

Ennis, Philip H. 1967. *Criminal Victimization in the United States: A Report of a National Survey.* Washington, D.C.: U.S. Department of Justice.

Fogel, David. 1975. *We Are the Living Proof: The Justice Model for Corrections.* Cincinnati: Anderson.

Forst, Martin L., and Martha-Elin Blomquist. 1992. "Punishment, Accountability, and the New Juvenile Justice." *Juvenile and Family Court Journal* 43(1):1–9.

Fox, Sanford J. 1974. "The Reform of Juvenile Justice: The Child's Right to Punishment." *Juvenile Justice* 25 (August):2–9.

Gabor, Thomas. 1990. "Crime Displacement and Situational Prevention: Toward the Development of Some Principles." *Canadian Journal of Criminology* 32 (January):41–73.

Galaway, Burt. 1988. "Crime Victim and Offender Mediation as a Social Work Strategy." *Social Service Review* 62 (December):668–683.

Gaylin, Willard, and David J. Rothman. 1976. "Introduction." Pp. xxi–xli in Andrew von Hirsch, *Doing Justice: The Choice of Punishments.* New York: Hill & Wang.

Gibbs, Jack P. 1968. "Crime, Punishment, and Deterrence." *Social Science Quarterly* 48 (March): 515–530.
1975. *Crime, Punishment, and Deterrence.* New York: Elsevier.

Grasmick, Harold G., and George J. Bryjak. 1980. "The Deterrent Effect of Perceived Severity of Punishment." *Social Forces* 59 (December): 471–491.

Grasmick, Harold G., Robert J. Bursik, Jr., and Bruce J. Arneklev. 1993. "Reduction in Drunk Driving as a Response to Increased Threats of Shame, Embarrassment, and Legal Sanctions." *Criminology* 31 (February):41–67.

Greenberg, David F. 1975. "The Incapacitive Effect of Imprisonment: Some Estimates." *Law and Society Review* 9 (Summer):541–580.

Greenberg, David F., and Drew Humphries. 1980. "The Cooptation of Fixed Sentencing Reform." *Crime and Delinquency* 26 (April):206–225.

Hamparian, Donna M., Richard Schuster, Simon Dinitz, and John P. Conrad. 1978. *The Violent Few: A Study of Dangerous Juvenile Offenders.* Lexington, Mass.: Heath.

Hirschi, Travis. 1979. "Reconstructing Delinquency: Evolution and Implications of Twentieth-Century Theory." Pp. 183–212 in LaMar T. Empey, ed., *Juvenile Justice: The Progressive Legacy and Current Reforms.* Charlottesville: University Press of Virginia.

Jensen, Gary F., and David Brownfield. 1986. "Gender, Lifestyles, and Victimization: Beyond Routine Activity." *Violence and Victims* 1 (Summer): 85–99.

Jensen, Gary F., and Maynard L. Erickson. 1978. "The Social Meaning of Sanctions." Pp. 119–136 in Marvin Krohn and Ronald Akers, eds., *Crime, Law, and Sanctions: Theoretical Perspectives.* Beverly Hills, Calif.: Sage.

Kennedy, Leslie W., and Stephen W. Baron. 1993. "Routine Activities and a Subculture of Violence: A Study of Violence on the Street." *Journal of Research in Crime and Delinquency* 30 (February): 88–112.

Kennedy, Leslie W., and David R. Forde. 1990. "Routine Activities and Crime: An Analysis of Victimization in Canada." *Criminology* 28 (February):137–152.

Marshall, Tony, and Susan Merry. 1990. *Crime and Accountability: Victim–Offender Mediation in Practice.* London: HMSO.

Messner, Steven F. 1986. "Television Violence and Violent Crime: An Aggregate Analysis." *Social Problems* 33 (February):218–235.

Miethe, Terance D., and Robert F. Meier. 1990. "Opportunity, Choice, and Criminal Victimization Rates: A Test of a Theoretical Model." *Journal of Research in Crime and Delinquency* 27 (August): 243–266.
———. 1994. *Crime and Its Social Context: Toward an Integrated Theory of Offenders, Victims, and Situations.* Albany: State University of New York Press.

Monahan, John. 1978. "The Prediction of Violent Criminal Behavior: A Methodological Critique and Prospectus." Pp. 244–269 in Alfred Blumstein, Jacqueline Cohen, and Daniel Nagin, eds., *Deterrence and Incapacitation: Estimating the Effects of Criminal Sanctions on Crime Rates.* Washington, D.C.: National Academy of Sciences.

Nagin, Daniel. 1978. "General Deterrence: A Review of the Empirical Evidence." Pp. 95–139 in Alfred Blumstein, Jacqueline Cohen, and Daniel Nagin, eds., *Deterrence and Incapacitation: Estimating the Effects of Criminal Sanctions on Crime Rates.* Washington, D.C.: National Academy of Sciences.

Nagin, Daniel S., and Raymond Paternoster. 1994. "Personal Capital and Social Control: The Deterrence Implications of a Theory of Individual Differences in Criminal Offending." *Criminology* 32 (November):581–606.

Paternoster, Raymond. 1987. "The Deterrent Effect of the Perceived Certainty and Severity of Punishment: A Review of the Evidence and Issues." *Justice Quarterly* 4 (June):173–217.

Paternoster, Raymond, and Sally Simpson. 1993. "A Rational Choice Theory of Corporate Crime." Pp. 37–58 in Ronald V. Clarke and Marcus Felson, eds., *Routine Activity and Rational Choice.* Advances in Criminological Theory, Vol. 5. New Brunswick, N.J.: Transaction Publishers.

Petee, Thomas A., Trudie F. Milner, and Michael R. Welch. 1994. "Levels of Social Integration in Group Contexts and the Effects of Informal Sanction Threat on Deviance." *Criminology* 32 (February):85–106.

Petersilia, Joan, Peter W. Greenwood, and Marvin Lavin. 1977. *Criminal Careers of Habitual Felons.* Santa Monica, Calif.: Rand.

Peterson, Ruth D., and William C. Bailey. 1988. "Murder and Capital Punishment in the Evolving Context of the Post-*Furman* Era." *Social Forces* 66 (March):774–807.
———. 1991. "Felony Murder and Capital Punishment:

An Examination of the Deterrence Question." *Criminology* 29 (August):367–395.

Ricotta, Dominic J. 1988. "Eighth Amendment— The Death Penalty for Juveniles: A State's Right or a Child's Injustice?" *Journal of Criminal Law and Criminology* 79 (Fall):921–952.

Rosenbaum, Ron. 1989. "Too Young to Die?" *The New York Times Magazine,* March 12, pp. 33–35, 58–61.

Salem, Richard G., and William J. Bowers. 1970. "Severity of Formal Sanctions as a Deterrent to Deviant Behavior." *Law and Society Review* 5 (1): 21–40.

Schneider, Anne L. 1986. "Restitution and Recidivism Rates of Juvenile Offenders: Results from Four Experimental Studies." *Criminology* 24 (August):533–552.

Schuessler, Karl. 1952. "The Deterrent Effect of the Death Penalty." *The Annals* 284:54–62.

Shinnar, Shlomo, and Reuel Shinnar. 1975. "The Effects of the Criminal Justice System on the Control of Crime: A Quantitative Approach." *Law and Society Review* 9 (Summer):581–611.

Smith, Douglas A., and G. Roger Jarjoura. 1989. "Household Characteristics, Neighborhood Composition and Victimization Risk." *Social Forces* 68 (December):621–640.

Stanford v. *Kentucky.* 1989. 109 S. Ct. 2969.

Stephens, James F. 1973. *A History of the Criminal Law in England,* Vol. 2. New York: Burt Franklin. (First published in 1883.)

Streib, Victor L. 1987. *Death Penalty for Juveniles.* Bloomington: Indiana University Press.

Thompson v. *Oklahoma.* 1988. 108 S. Ct. 2687.

Tittle, Charles R. 1969. "Crime Rates and Legal Sanctions." *Social Problems* 16 (Spring):405–423. 1980. *Sanctions and Social Deviance: The Question of Deterrence.* New York: Praeger.

Umbreit, Mark, and Robert Coates. 1993. "Cross-Site Analysis of Victim–Offender Mediation in Four States." *Crime and Delinquency* 39(October): 565–585.

van den Haag, Ernest. 1975. *Punishing Criminals: Concerning a Very Old and Painful Question.* New York: Basic Books.

Van Dine, Stephan, John P. Conrad, and Simon Dinitz. 1979. *Restraining the Wicked: The Incapacitation of the Dangerous Criminal.* Lexington, Mass.: Heath.

von Hirsch, Andrew. 1976. *Doing Justice: The Choice of Punishments.* New York: Hill & Wang. 1985. *Past of Future Crimes: Deservedness and Dangerousness in the Sentencing of Criminals.* New Brunswick, N.J.: Rutgers University Press.

Wilkins v. *Missouri.* 1989. 109 S. Ct. 2969.

Williams, Kirk R., and Jack P. Gibbs. 1981. "Deterrence and Knowledge of Statutory Penalties." *Sociological Quarterly* 22 (Autumn):591–606.

Williams, Kirk R., Jack P. Gibbs, and Maynard L. Erickson. 1980. "Public Knowledge of Statutory Penalties: The Extent and Basis of Accurate Perception." *Pacific Sociological Review* 23 (January): 105–128.

Williams, Kirk R., and Richard Hawkins. 1986. "Perceptual Research on General Deterrence: A Critical Review." *Law and Society Review* 20 (Winter):545–572. 1989. "The Meaning of Arrest for Wife Assault." *Criminology* 27 (February):163–181.

Wilson, James Q. 1975. *Thinking About Crime.* New York: Vintage Books. 1983. *Thinking About Crime,* rev. ed. New York: Vintage Books.

Zehr, Howard. 1982. *Mediating the Victim/Offender Conflict.* Akron, Pa.: Mennonite Central Committee.

ACCORDING TO LABELING
THEORISTS, LEGAL REACTIONS
ARE STIGMATIZING AND WILL
LEAD OFFENDERS TO COMMIT
MORE SERIOUS DELINQUENT ACTS.

CHAPTER THIRTEEN

LABELING THEORY

As noted in the introduction to Part Three, positivist theories of delinquency have been concerned primarily with whether certain factors distinguish law violators from law-abiding juveniles. These theories located the causes of delinquency in such things as the characteristics of individuals, the ways communities are organized and structured, and the groups in which delinquents associate.

In the 1960s and 1970s, however, an alternative to the positivist school emerged in the form of **labeling theory.** Rather than devoting primary attention to the presumed *causes* of delinquent behavior, labeling theorists were concerned with *societal reactions to delinquency.*

Labeling theorists tend to be symbolic interactionists. Their assumptions about human nature and social order, therefore, are generally the same as those of symbolic interactionists, but with a special twist. Like symbolic interactionists, labeling theorists assume that human nature is relatively flexible and subject to change. Yet, they are far more concerned with the stigmatizing effects of arrest and adjudication on lawbreakers than with the processes of interaction that produce their illegal behavior in the first place. The reason is that labeling theorists are inclined to believe that lawbreakers are relatively normal people. Hence, if they persist in delinquent behavior and become serious offenders, it is due less to their own evil nature than to the negative ways in which police, judges, and correctional authorities react to their behavior.

The assumptions of labeling theorists about social order reflect this same bias. Although they acknowledge that society is characterized by cultural conflict, they suggest that this conflict usually is resolved in favor of people in positions of power and influence. Thus, the definition and imposition of social rules will reflect their interests, not those of less powerful groups.

These assumptions about human nature and social order together suggest that delinquent characteristics are not an inherent property of individuals, but rather a property that is conferred on them by others—by legal officials and those who have the power to legislate their own brand of morality. Hence, children become delinquent not because of their behavior or some sort of predisposition to crime, but because they are labeled as delinquents by persons in positions of power.

THE DRAMATIZATION OF EVIL

The historian Frank Tannenbaum (1938) was probably the first person to set forth some of the principles of labeling theory. Tannenbaum argued that the last steps in the making of a serious delinquent occur not when a child violates the law, but when he or she becomes enmeshed in the juvenile justice system (pp. 17–21). With this official step, an insignificant problem turns into a serious one.

Many children break windows, push over garbage cans, skip school, shoplift, and otherwise annoy people. From a child's perspective, those acts are "play, adventure, excitement, interest, mischief, [and] fun" (p. 17). But adults perceive them as nuisances, evils, and delinquency. Hence, such acts often result in chastisement, juvenile court action, and punishment.

To the extent that these acts continue, and to the extent that the different perceptions of them persist, two things will happen. First, adults' views will harden. That is, their tendency to view specific acts as evil will be transformed into a tendency to view mischievous children as evil: "The individual who used to do bad and mischievous things now [will] become a bad and unredeemable human being" (p. 17). Second, a view of mischievous children as evil will have a lasting and destructive effect. That is, these children will come to believe that they are different from other children: "The young delinquent becomes bad because he is defined as bad and because he is not believed if he is good" (pp. 17–18). In short, these children will have acquired new, delinquent self-images from the negative reactions to them.

Tannenbaum called this process the dramatization of evil and said that it becomes a self-fulfilling prophecy that tends to evoke and emphasize the very behavior that was complained about in the first place (pp. 19–21). "The process of making the criminal," he maintained, ". . . is a process of tagging, defining, identifying, segregating, describing, emphasizing, making conscious and self-conscious; it becomes a way of stimulating, suggesting, emphasizing, and evoking the very traits that are complained of. . . . The person becomes the thing he is described as being" (pp. 19–20).

The relatives of mischievous children, the police, and juvenile court and correctional officials often are enthusiastic and well intentioned in their efforts to reform them, but their very enthusiasm can undermine their objective. "The harder they work to reform the evil, the greater the evil grows under their hands" (p. 20). Left alone, mischievous children will not become serious delinquents or adult criminals. As long as they are defined as bad and isolated from conventional groups and activities, however, their only resource is to join other children like themselves—those who also have been defined as bad.

It is when this occurs that truly serious problems begin to emerge. Delinquent gangs develop that provide the only source of security for labeled children (pp. 8–21). Even worse, gangs begin to generate their own delinquent norms. In other words, a new game is set up in which "innocent maladjustment" escalates into law-violating behavior and in which the delinquent gang becomes a child's major reference group (p. 20).

According to Tannenbaum, the only solution is to refuse to dramatize evil in the first place: "The less said about it the better" (p. 20). The act of labeling children as evil and then making them aware of that label is the major source of gangs and serious delinquency, not some evil inherent in the children themselves.

PRIMARY AND SECONDARY DEVIANCE

In 1951, about thirteen years after Tannenbaum's contribution, Edwin Lemert, a professor at the University of California at Los Angeles, added two new concepts to labeling theory. First of all, said Lemert (1951:75–76), it is necessary to distinguish between two kinds of deviant behavior: primary deviance and secondary deviance.[1]

Primary Deviance

Tannenbaum failed to mention that many delinquent acts go undetected. This is **primary deviance**—deviance that is neither detected nor punished by anyone in authority. Such deviance is common, as self-report studies have indicated, and can be due to a variety of causes. In fact, said Lemert (1951:75), there are an "embarrassingly large number of [causal] theories"—control theories, cultural deviance theories, strain theories, and others that we have already examined. Although most of those theories contain elements of truth and thus are important from a scientific standpoint, they are unimportant in terms of actually explaining how official delinquents are created. The reason is that until pri-

mary deviance is detected, there are no delinquents. Hence, the impact of primary deviance on children will be minimal because they will not develop a deviant identity. Rather, they will be inclined, like most people, to use **techniques of neutralization** to disavow the implications of their deviant acts and to continue defining themselves as good (see Chapter 9). Because their reputations have not been destroyed by labeling, they will tend to retain a conformist self-concept and avoid the negative consequences of being viewed as evil persons.

If their primary deviance is detected, however, the results may resemble those described by Tannenbaum (1938)—the evil will be dramatized, and the status of the offenders will be transformed. For example, labeled offenders not only must deal with the stigma of their delinquent status but also must respond to new clues regarding what is expected of them. The reactions of parents, teachers, and friends, as well as legal officials, will tend to affirm their delinquent status. To the extent that labeled delinquents are sensitive to the expectations of others, their behavior may mirror not their normal, conventional roles, but deviant ones. Even their clothes, speech, and mannerisms may be altered, reflecting the delinquent status now expected of them (Lemert, 1951:76).

Lemert (1971:13) also suggested that once people are labeled, they are expected to adhere to an additional set of official rules that apply only to them. Rather than helping to reduce people's problems, however, those new rules only increase them. When children are placed on probation, for example, they can be forbidden from living with "unfit" parents or associating with their old friends, or they can be expected to suddenly reverse their patterns of failure in school. Any slip in adhering to those special rules can, in itself, constitute a new act of defiance. Hence, in attempting to treat delinquents, juvenile justice officials actually may increase the number of rules whereby their future behavior can be considered delinquent—rules that do not apply to nondelinquents.

Secondary Deviance

This increase in rules, coupled with the tendency for delinquents to behave in accordance with the

---

[1]Lemert did not restrict his discussion to law-violating behavior. Although we will focus on the relevance of labeling theory for delinquency, Lemert's version of the theory has implications for violations of any agreed-upon rule (i.e., deviance), not just violations of the law.

FIGURE 13.1

Early version of labeling theory, showing serious delinquent behavior (secondary deviance) as the product of labeling

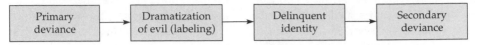

expectations of their deviant status, may result in what Lemert (1951:76) termed **secondary deviance.** This kind of deviance evolves from the adaptations that labeled persons make to the problems created by reactions to their primary deviance. "When a person begins to employ his deviant behavior or a role based upon it as a means of defense, attack, or adjustment to the overt and covert problems created by the consequent societal reaction to him, his deviation is secondary" (Lemert, 1951:76). Thus, even though personal or situational factors may cause a child's *primary* deviance, the reactions to it are likely to increase the chances that more serious *secondary* deviance will result. According to Lemert (1951:76–77), these are the most important causes of serious delinquent behavior. As Tannenbaum (1938:20) suggested, "the person becomes the thing he is described as being."

Lemert (1951:76–77) did not suggest that secondary deviance will follow closely on the heels of any particular, even punitive, reaction to an individual. Rather, as Tannenbaum (1938:8–22) indicated, it is the product of a rather long process—primary deviance, punitive reactions, further deviance, more punitive reactions, until eventually children accept their deviant status and become full-fledged delinquents. Inherent in the arguments of both theorists, then, are three basic ideas:

1. Some kind of deviant behavior—namely, primary deviance—must occur to initiate the labeling process.
2. Community norms act against primary as well as secondary deviance. Although overreaction by parents, teachers, and legal officials inevitably makes the problem worse, these people subscribe to a shared set of rules that define certain acts as deviant.
3. Primary deviance is not learned in intimate groups; rather, *serious delinquent behavior (secondary deviance) is the product of labeling and*

stigma. In other words, both Tannenbaum and Lemert were symbolic interactionists.

When people react to juveniles as if they are deviant, they dramatize evil unnecessarily and are *themselves* the major cause of delinquent identities and lifestyles (Gove, 1980:27–28). The sequence can be diagrammed as shown in figure 13.1.

THE SOCIAL CREATION OF DELINQUENCY

There was a wave of excitement in the 1960s and 1970s over this new way of constructing delinquency. Were it not for punitive reactions to mischievous children, entangling them in a self-fulfilling prophecy, there would be few career criminals.

To be sure, Tannenbaum and Lemert described the child as someone whose own behavior might contribute to the process by which he or she is labeled as delinquent—a fact that subsequent theorists acknowledged. Howard Becker (1963:14), for example, noted that "whether a given act is deviant or not depends in part on the nature of the act (that is, whether or not it violates some rule) and in part on what other people do about it." But as increased attention was paid to this exciting conception of the problem, newer versions tended to concentrate less on acts of mischievous children and more on how reactions made them delinquents.

As Schur (1971:19) described it, labeling theorists began to exhibit considerable ambivalence. Early versions of labeling theory described delinquents as persons who had a hand in shaping their own fate by committing deviant acts. Later versions, however, described delinquents as being at the mercy of those who react to them. More and more, they were treated as passive objects. The emphasis of symbolic interactionists on social process was eschewed in favor of a structural approach in which the organization of society became the center of attention (Finestone, 1976:208–211; Gove, 1980:27–30). What emerged was a new kind of determinism that paid almost exclusive attention to (1) the nature and construction of social rules, (2) the selective enforcement of rules, and (3) the social functions of deviance.

Social Rules and Moral Crusaders

In an influential series of statements, Becker (1963) argued that it is not just the way control agents react to people that determines whether they will be defined as deviant. The process of defining deviants begins earlier. It is rooted in the inclinations of all group members, particularly the "moral crusaders," to create rules:

> Social groups create deviance by making the rules whose infraction constitutes deviance, and by applying those rules to particular people and labeling them as outsiders. From this point of view, deviance is *not* a quality of the act the person commits, but rather a consequence of the application by others of rules and sanctions to an "offender." The deviant is one to whom that label has successfully been applied; deviant behavior is behavior that people so label. (p. 9)

Becker's argument was not entirely new. Criminologists had long known that rules are important because definitions of crime and delinquency vary considerably from place to place and over time. As Becker suggested, deviance is behavior that people so label. However, deviance also implies the existence of rules that define the behavior as either good or evil. For example, a prehistoric man who took food from a weaker person did not really commit *theft* until the group of which he was a part decided that such an action was bad. Likewise, there was little chance that a child in the 1200s could commit truancy, given that schools were not created until centuries later. In short, it is not merely reactions to behavior that must be considered in understanding why some people are labeled as deviant, but also the rules that serve to direct attention to certain behaviors and not others.

But Becker (1963:147–163) was not interested merely in calling attention to something that was already well known. Instead, he wanted to direct attention to people he called *moral entrepreneurs*—people who become crusading reformers. They are the ones most likely to seek the new rules by which new forms of deviance are created. They are disturbed by some evil and will not be content until it is corrected.

Moral crusaders, however, are not simply busybodies. Often, they are like the environmentalists of today or the child savers of past centuries who, in seeking to correct a set of problems, exhibit humanitarian concerns. They want new rules by which to address problems they consider serious. Nonetheless, said Becker (1963:149), moral crusades typically are dominated by influential and powerful people on the "upper levels of the social structure." As a result, it is their vision of good and bad that usually is imposed on society.

In their zeal, moral crusaders frequently fail to anticipate the consequences of doing good. For example, to correct some evil, it is not enough merely to pass a new set of rules. Rules also must be enforced, and this often requires new agencies and officials. A humanitarian drive that initially seeks to convince the world of the moral necessity of a new set of rules eventually becomes a bureaucracy devoted to their enforcement.

It is in the self-interests of the rule enforcers to see to it that the rules are perpetuated. After all, rules provide them with a job, a profession, a reason for being (Becker, 1963:156–157). Rule enforcers must justify their existence by convincing others of the importance of the rules and by seeing to it that they are enforced. But sometimes the cure is worse than the disease. For example, in seeking to reduce sex crimes, "sexual psychopaths" have been institutionalized indefinitely, though psychiatrists and psychologists do not know for sure what a sexual psychopath is.

In seeking to prevent the reproduction of lawbreakers, a eugenics movement was started and laws passed that permitted authorities to sterilize "hereditary criminals" and "moral degenerates" (see Chapter 7). This was done despite the absence of scientific proof that crime is inherited or is the result of moral depravity.

In seeking to keep "giddy," "headstrong," and "restless" teenage girls away from temptation, some of them have been charged with status offenses and kept "safe" for a year or two in state-run institutions. It has been deemed more important that these girls

CURFEW COUNTRY?

Since the 1980s, many U.S. cities have passed curfew laws that make it illegal for children under age 16 or 18 to be away from home unsupervised after a certain hour, usually 11 P.M. or midnight. Indeed, 76 percent of U.S. cities with a population of 200,000 or more now have such laws (Ruefle and Reynolds, 1995). This is a clear exception to the pattern of *decriminalization* that is discussed in this chapter. From the perspective of labeling theorists, however, it is an important exception because it raises this question: How many kids might go from committing normal mischief to committing serious delinquency largely as a result of being labeled as official delinquents *simply for being away from home past midnight?*

be institutionalized than that they run the risk of violating the moral rules associated with childhood.

Selective Enforcement of Rules

According to Becker (1963:159–162), rules tend to be enforced selectively. Not every rule violator, and not every rule violator who is caught, is labeled. The actual labeling of people depends on many things other than their behavior: their race and social class, whether they show proper respect to legal officials, and whether the violated rule is high or low on an agency's list of rules to be enforced.

Other labeling theorists, writing during the same period, agreed with Becker. Universal definitions of good and bad, John Kitsuse (1962:248) argued, exist only in principle, not in fact. In any complex society like ours, it is difficult to establish a set of moral rules that will be universally supported and enforced. Consequently, "the socially significant differentiation of deviants from the non-deviant population is increasingly contingent upon circumstances of situation, place, social and personal biography, and the bureaucratically organized activities of agencies of control" (p. 256).

Kai Erikson (1962:308) argued that the most crucial factor is the "social audience":

> Deviance is not a property *inherent* in certain forms of behavior; it is a property *conferred upon* these forms by the audiences which directly or indirectly witness them. Sociologically, then, the critical variable in the study of deviance is the social *audience* rather than the individual *person*, since it is the audience which eventually decides whether or not any given action or actions will become a visible case of deviation.

Even the most deviant person, Erikson (1962: 308) noted, commits deviant behavior only a fraction of the time. When a community sanctions him or her, "it is responding to a few deviant details set within a vast context of proper conduct. Thus a person may be jailed . . . for a few scattered moments of misbehavior" (p. 308). One of the most pressing questions is how society decides which behaviors will be singled out for attention.

Social Functions of Deviance

In seeking to answer that question, Erikson (1962) concerned himself not with the characteristics of deviants, as most criminologists had done before, but with the characteristics of societies. Drawing on the ideas of Emile Durkheim (1966), he said that "specialists in crime . . . have long suggested that deviance can play an important role in keeping the social order intact" (p. 309). Deviance serves important social functions.

Any social system requires boundaries—some geographical, and some normative. For people to do business with one another, there must be rules, and people must have some assurance that the rules will be obeyed. Yet, the only material found in the system for marking its boundaries is the deviant behavior of its group members. In contrast to acts of conformity, deviant acts help to establish the outer limits of the kinds of behavior that can be tolerated. Should the boundaries become too extreme, the system will de-

FIGURE 13.2

Later version of labeling theory, showing permanent delinquent status as the product of selective labeling

| Creation of rules | → | Selective labeling | → | Stigmatization of the offender | → | Permanent delinquent status |

teriorate. Therefore, said Erikson (1962:310), "each time the community censures some act of deviance, . . . it sharpens the authority of the violated norm and reestablishes the boundaries of the group." Moreover,

> as a trespasser against the norm, he [the deviant] represents those forces excluded by the group's boundaries: he informs us, as it were, what evil looks like, what shapes the devil can assume. In doing so, he shows us the difference between kinds of experience which belong within the group and kinds of experience which belong outside it.
>
> Thus deviance cannot be dismissed as behavior which *disrupts* stability in society, but is itself, in controlled quantities, an important condition for *preserving* stability. (p. 310)

According to Erikson, then, the selective labeling of persons by control agents can be viewed as a boundary-maintaining activity. But, if that is the case, some delicate, and possibly frightening, questions are raised: Is it possible that control agents use labeled persons as resources? Because not all rule violators can be caught, is it possible that control agents selectively label some persons because they feel it is necessary to mark society's boundaries and deter others?

Although such questions are difficult to answer, Erikson (1962:311) suggested that "the institutions devised by human society for guarding against deviance sometimes seem so poorly equipped for this task that we might well ask why this is considered their 'real' function at all." Self-report studies have indicated that only a small fraction of lawbreakers are apprehended. Yet, those caught sometimes are ushered into a deviant status by a dramatic ceremony—a trial or an adjudicatory hearing—a ritual that is clearly visible to everyone. Once that is

completed, many deviants are then warehoused in institutions where, instead of being separated from deviant influences, they are tightly segregated into groups in which the opportunity to learn more deviant behavior is ever present. Furthermore, once having completed their sentences, they are retired from their deviant status with little or no public notice. Nothing equivalent to a trial is used as a rite of passage out of that status.

Hence, it could be that one of the major functions of control agencies is to dramatize the deviance of a select few. Deviants can be used as signposts, indicating to others the outer limits of society. If that is the case, the labeled person is a resource and may be of greater worth to society as a deviant than as a nondeviant.

In summary, then, in the course of its development, labeling theory moved farther away from a consideration of the deviant acts that might bring an individual to the attention of legal officials. Likewise, the reasons for those acts assumed less importance. Consequently, the delinquency-generating sequence suggested by this line of thought can be diagrammed as shown in figure 13.2. The figure implies that if children are lucky enough to avoid the labeling process, they will be the masters of their own fates and will grow up to be **insiders**—law-abiding persons. But if they acquire a deviant status, they will be known forever as **outsiders**—permanent pariahs whose only worth to society lies in helping to define its outer limits.

IMPLICATIONS AND IMPACT ON POLICY

These ideas have had a profound impact on social policy. Indeed, labeling theory became a legitimizing rationale for many criticisms of the juvenile justice system that were first made in the 1960s and 1970s. Writing for the President's Commission on Law Enforcement and Administration of Justice, Lemert (1967:96) stated its implications in classic form:

> The aims of preventing delinquency and the expectation of definitively treating a profusion of child and parental problems have laid an impossible burden upon the juvenile court, and they may be seriously considered to have no proper part in its philosophy. *If there is a defensible philosophy for the juvenile court it is one of judicious nonintervention.* It is properly an agency of last resort for children, holding to a doctrine analogous to that of appeal courts which require that all other remedies be exhausted before a case will be considered. (emphasis added)

Based on such statements, several reforms were proposed. All, coincidentally, started with the letter *D* and stressed the importance of keeping the hands of child savers off young people whenever possible. They were decriminalization, diversion, due process, and deinstitutionalization.

Decriminalization

The first reform suggested that status offenses such as running away, defying parents, sexual promiscuity, and truancy should be **decriminalized.** Indeed, a statement by the President's Commission (1967a:25) clearly reflected the contention of labeling theorists that moral crusades, like that which led to the invention of the juvenile court, are likely to produce rules and practices with cures worse than the diseases they are supposed to correct:

> The provisions on which [legal] intervention . . . is based are typically vague and all-encompassing: Growing up in idleness and crime, engaging in immoral conduct, in danger of leading an immoral life. . . . They establish the judge as arbiter not only of the behavior but also of the morals of every child (and to a certain extent the parents of every child) appearing before him. The situation is ripe for overreaching, for imposition of the judge's own code of youthful conduct.

The solution was to protect children from overly zealous officials. "It has become equally or more im-

portant to protect children from unanticipated and unwanted consequences of organized movements, programs and services in their behalf than from the unorganized, adventitious 'evils' which gave birth to the juvenile court" (Lemert, 1967:97). Hence, according to the President's Commission (1967a:27), "serious consideration should be given [to] complete elimination from the court's jurisdiction of conduct illegal only for a child." In other words, status offenses should be decriminalized.

Diversion

A second reform—**diversion**—was closely related to decriminalization. It, too, was based on the premise that the evils of children have been overdramatized. To avoid labeling and stigmatization, potential arrestees or court referrals should be diverted from the juvenile justice system into other, less harmful agencies, such as youth services bureaus, welfare agencies, or special schools.

Although this reform represented a marked change, it still tended to compromise the intent of labeling theory. Both Tannenbaum and Lemert had implied that *nothing* should be done about the offenses of any but the most serious offenders. The less said about their acts, the better. Likewise, Schur (1973:155) suggested that children should be left alone wherever possible. Our policy should be one of "radical nonintervention," a policy that would "accommodate society to the widest possible diversity of behavior and attitudes, rather than forcing as many individuals as possible to 'adjust' to supposedly common societal standards" (Schur, 1973:154).

Policymakers, however, were not prepared to act so radically. Instead, the President's Commission (1967b:81–88) recommended a more modest course in which delinquent offenders would be protected from the negative effects of the juvenile court but would be guided and helped nonetheless.

It was suggested that this could be accomplished in several ways. Every police department should provide juvenile specialists who would decide promptly which juveniles might be referred elsewhere rather than to court. Community agencies should be available to juveniles to provide counseling and tutorial, occupational, and recreational services. Even better, every community or large neighborhood should have a Youth Services Bureau to provide all of those services in one setting for all children, delinquent and nondelinquent. Not only the police, but families, schools, and other agencies could refer children to such bureaus. In short, the President's Commission was not prepared to go all the way with labeling theory, but it was willing to go part of the way. If unwilling to adopt radical nonintervention, society should at least be prepared to divert juveniles from the juvenile justice system.

Due Process

The third reform stressed the importance of **due process** in juvenile court proceedings. The Supreme Court of the United States concluded in 1966, in *Kent* v. *United States,* that when a child is referred to court, he (or she) "receives the worst of both worlds: that he gets neither the [constitutional] protections accorded to adults nor the solicitous care and regenerative treatment postulated for children." In this and subsequent decisions, the Supreme Court concluded that except for jury trials, children should receive most of the protections that adults receive.

By no means was labeling theory totally responsible for those decisions. Instead, they reflected in part the growing distrust of governmental and other institutions in the 1960s. Nonetheless, one of the main themes of labeling theory was evident in the actions of the Supreme Court: the need to limit the discretion of child savers and control their power over young people. Because all delinquent acts could not be decriminalized and some offenders could not be diverted, those who were referred to juvenile court should be protected by constitutional procedures. In this sense, labeling theory contributed to sentiments favoring greater due process for juveniles.

Deinstitutionalization

The fourth reform to which labeling theory contributed was **deinstitutionalization**—the removal of children from detention centers, jails, and reformatories. Like diversion, the goal of deinstitutionalization was to limit the destructive effects of legal processing. Clearly, however, strain and other positivist theories also contributed to the reintegrative beliefs favoring this reform. These theorists had long stressed that if delinquents are to be reformed, steps should be taken to improve their attachments to home and school, increase their academic skills, open up legitimate opportunities for them, and reduce their association with delinquent peers. But, as the following comments indicate, the President's Commission (1967b:165) also was concerned with using deinstitutionalization to eliminate the harmful consequences of labeling:

> Institutions tend to isolate offenders from society, both physically and psychologically, cutting them off from schools, jobs, families, and other supportive influences and increasing the probability that the label of criminal will be indelibly impressed upon them. The goal of reintegration is likely to be furthered much more readily by working with offenders in the community than by incarceration.

In summary, labeling theory helped to legitimize four alternative and alliterative reforms: decriminalization, diversion, due process, and deinstitutionalization. Although these reforms were due, in part, to other constructions of the delinquency problem, they clearly reflected the major doctrine of labeling theory: Hands off children whenever possible!

SCIENTIFIC IMPACT AND ADEQUACY

The initial impact of labeling theory on scientific criminology was as great as its impact on social policy. No longer, as labeling theorists suggested, could reactions to delinquent behavior be taken for granted. All of the frustrations associated with a hundred years of trying to explain delinquency now took on a new light. In concentrating on the characteristics of offenders—family backgrounds, failures in school, blocked opportunities, or affiliations with subcultures and groups—researchers had been looking in the wrong places. According to labeling theorists, it is the reactions to delinquents, not delinquents themselves, that create the problem. Therefore, researchers should examine the process by which societal reactions to law-violating behavior create serious delinquents.

Although this new conception of delinquency generated an initial flurry of excitement, its prominence eventually would wane. In the past few decades, there has been a general retreat from labeling theory, due in part to empirical research that has provided only mixed support for labeling theorists' central claim—that official reactions to delinquency mark offenders with a "delinquent identity," which in turn leads to further delinquency. To be sure, some studies have supported such a claim (Kaplan and Johnson, 1991; Klein, 1974; Ward and Tittle, 1993). But these studies have tended to find that although punitive reactions sometimes lead to deviant identities and increase the likelihood of subsequent delinquency, these things are affected more by prior delinquency. In the terminology of labeling theorists, *one of the most important causes of secondary deviance is primary deviance.* Frequent, serious offending at one point in time tends to be related to frequent, serious offending at a later time, regardless of punitive reactions. Although that finding does not conflict directly with the more moderate versions of labeling theory (Becker, 1973; Lemert, 1951), it nevertheless reveals the need to understand the causes of primary deviance, a task that generally is eschewed by labeling theorists.

Some studies have failed to find any delinquency-generating effects of punitive reactions (Foster, Dinitz, and Reckless, 1972; Hepburn, 1977; Mahoney, 1974; Thomas and Bishop, 1984). In one of the more sophisticated analyses of the issue, Smith and Paternoster (1990) examined the relationship between juvenile court processing and subsequent referrals to the juvenile court. Consistent with labeling theory, they initially found that after controlling for differences in prior offending, offenders who were referred to the juvenile court (compared to offenders who were diverted) were more likely to be referred again to the court for subsequent offenses. However, they went on to demonstrate that this presumed labeling effect was only illusory. What seemed to be occurring was that offenders referred to the juvenile court were different from diverted offenders, not just in terms of prior offending but in other unmeasured ways that affected the likelihood of further offending (p. 1127). Hence, there was a *selection effect*: Juvenile court referral did not cause further delinquency; in-

stead, the children who were referred to the juvenile court were more likely to commit delinquency for other reasons.

Given such evidence, it is difficult to know if official reactions to crime lead to the sort of labeling and secondary deviance described by labeling theorists. That some studies support labeling theory while others do not probably suggests that the theory holds only for some types of people and/or only under some conditions. The challenge is to identify those people and conditions. Toward that end, some evidence suggests that official processing has a greater effect on the self-identities of infrequent as compared to frequent offenders (Ageton and Elliott, 1974; Jensen, 1980; Shoemaker, 1990). On the whole, however, labeling theory has not received the degree of support that its proponents envisioned.

RETHINKING LABELING THEORY

Once the empirical evidence began to accumulate and the initial excitement over the theory subsided, it was easier to identify both the positive and negative aspects of labeling theory. On the positive side, labeling theorists successfully challenged the deterministic views of many positivist theorists. Even more important, labeling theorists clearly demonstrated that in attempting to understand delinquency, positivist theories tended to ignore secondary deviance and the possible parts played by labeling and stigmatization in producing it. More than ever before, there was a need to study the effects of child saving on delinquents. No longer could the concepts of childhood and juvenile justice be taken for granted. At the same time, however, there was clearly a need to avoid some of the extremism in some versions of labeling theory. Indeed, some serious questions have been raised about those versions.

The Existence of Crime
In their concern with moral crusaders, labeling theorists tended to imply that virtually all rules are reflections of some elite group's special brand of morality and that the rules disadvantage less powerful groups and are not shared by them. Among children,

for example, such acts as truancy, premarital sex, drinking, or talking back to parents were defined as evil by child savers in the 1800s and thus were criminalized. But whereas those rules originally reflected a middle-class conception of childhood, they have become so common in all social classes today that it is difficult to separate deviants from conformists.

And what about the rules that prohibit serious, predatory crimes such as murder, assault, robbery, and rape? Should they be viewed in the same way as those covering status offenses? Wellford (1975:335) has maintained that "all societies have found it functional to control certain kinds of [predatory] behavior," which casts doubt on the notion that no behavior is intrinsically deviant today. Although labeling theorists have been correct in suggesting that acts do not constitute crimes until they are defined as such by some group, the predatory character of some acts has led virtually every civilization in history to establish laws prohibiting them.

Many researchers have found that, whether white or black, middle- or lower-class, educated or uneducated, Americans tend to agree on the types of offenses they consider to be serious law violations (Chilton and DeAmicis, 1975; Hamilton and Rytina, 1980:1131–1132, 1140; Rossi et al., 1974; Wolfgang et al., 1985:77). Hence, in assessing the nature and function of social rules, we must recognize that not all definitions of crimes can be attributed to the unique standards of some elite group of moral crusaders.

The Existence of Criminals

There also are problems with the contention of labeling theorists that criminals are only individuals who have been labeled as such. On the one hand, it is true that *official* delinquents do not exist until they are caught and labeled. Until legal action is taken, they cannot be distinguished from *official* nondelinquents. It is also true that because most young people report having violated the law at one time or another, young people cannot be divided easily into law-violating and law-abiding segments. On the other hand, *chronic* law violators—those who are both frequent and serious offenders—can be distinguished from occasional, and usually petty, offenders (D'Unger et al., 1998; Laub, Nagin, and Sampson,

1998; Moffitt, 1993). Self-report studies have indicated that at the high end of the delinquency continuum is a small group of young people whose law-violating behavior clearly distinguishes them from the majority. Whether their acts have been detected or not, one could scarcely say that their criminal behavior is normal, any more than one could say that people whose IQs are above 160 are normal.

What is more, the results of longitudinal studies of official delinquents tend to corroborate self-report studies. In Chapter 4, we learned that a group of chronic offenders, composing only 6 percent of a birth cohort of boys in Philadelphia, was responsible for over 50 percent of all the police contacts for the cohort. These chronic offenders were a small part of the total cohort, but it would be foolish to suggest that their delinquency could not be distinguished from the cohort's less delinquent members.

The Determinism of Labeling Theory

The more extreme versions of labeling theory imply that labelers are the only creators of deviance (Mankoff, 1971:211–213):

> One sometimes gets the impression from reading this literature that people go about minding their own business, and then—"wham"—bad society comes along and slaps them with a stigmatized label. Forced into the role of deviant the individual has little choice but to be deviant. This is an exaggeration, of course, but such an image can be gained easily from an overemphasis on the impact of labelling. (Akers, 1968:463)

Significantly, Lemert (1974:459) himself has objected to the "wham" conception of deviance, with its tendency to view the delinquent as a helpless "underdog":

> Labeling unfortunately conveys an impression of interaction that is both sociologistic and unilateral; in the process deviants who are "successfully labeled" lose their individuality; they appear, as Bordua (1967) says, like "empty organisms" or, as Gouldner (1968) puts it, "like men on their backs" (Walton, 1973). The extreme subjectivism made explicit by the underdog perspective, reflecting sympathy for the victim and antipathy

towards the establishment, also distorts by magnifying the exploitative and arbitrary features of the societal reaction. But more important, it leaves little or no place for human choice at either level of interaction.

Lemert's comments raise some profound questions: What if labeling theory became the sole concern in criminology? What if no attention was paid to human choice, or to the idea that people are motivated by different factors? What if it was assumed that children do not begin to commit serious acts of delinquency until they are labeled? If all those things actually occurred, criminologists would become blind to the differences among individuals. It is not that studies of reactions to delinquency are unimportant. Rather, an exclusive focus on them would deny the possibility that the label of delinquent is ever earned or that children differ from one another (Nettler, 1984:283). Such a denial would prove both misleading and inaccurate. Children do differ from one another, as we have seen, and the factors that contribute to these differences also contribute to the commission of delinquent acts.

Radical Nonintervention

A final problem with labeling theory is its emphasis on "radical nonintervention"—the idea that legal officials should react to delinquent acts only as a last resort. Given the basic logic of the theory, it is not surprising that labeling theorists would emphasize that idea, but it also is ironic. After all, more than any other delinquency theory, labeling theory has drawn attention to the "social functions of deviance." In one of the most famous statements on the issue— one drawn upon heavily by labeling theorists— Durkheim (1933:85–103) argued that punishment of deviance reinforces a society's shared beliefs about how persons ought to behave, thereby increasing commitment to the law and its underlying moral principles. If that is the case, then at the same time that radical nonintervention avoids labeling a child as a delinquent, it also avoids sending a message to the child and to the rest of the community that the delinquent act is outside the boundaries of acceptable behavior. At least one study supports that line of reasoning. In a study of Arizona high school students, Erickson, Stafford, and Galliher (1984) found that among students who had committed delinquent acts, those who had been referred to a juvenile court with a noninterventionist approach later perceived a wide range of offenses as less serious than those who had not been referred to such a court. This was true even when comparing court-referred youths to nonreferred youths who had frequently committed delinquent acts.

In short, labeling theorists' calls for radical nonintervention have ignored the possible ways this strategy may *increase* delinquency. And the extreme position—that we should avoid any reaction to delinquent acts—has distracted criminologists from identifying ways we can react to delinquency without placing a stigmatizing label on the child.

RECONCILING LABELING AND OTHER THEORIES

Such problems have not been lost on labeling theorists and the rest of the sociological community. Numerous people have pointed out that labeling theory does not contain some of the elements of a sound substantive theory—for example, a careful delineation and definition of concepts, and a logically developed and integrated set of postulates (Gibbs, 1966; Goode, 1975; Schrag, 1971:94; Schur, 1971:35). Indeed, the most eminent labeling theorists have maintained that they were misinterpreted and that their statements never were intended as a full explanation of deviance. Hence, such statements do not warrant being called theories in any rigorous sense (Becker, 1973:178–179; Lemert, 1972:16–18).

Becker (1973:178–179) maintained that labeling theorists never intended to suggest that a person begins to do deviant things only after being labeled. Such a notion, he indicates, is ridiculous:

The act of labelling, as carried out by moral entrepreneurs, while important, cannot possibly be conceived as the sole explanation of what alleged deviants actually do. It would be foolish to propose that stick-up men stick people up simply because someone labelled them stick-up men, or

Labeling theorists seem to assume that a labeled delinquent *accepts* the label—that he or she will adopt a delinquent identity. However, that often is not the case. Quite the opposite of what labeling theorists have assumed, official delinquents frequently go to great lengths to reject or deny a delinquent label. Rogers and Buffalo (1974:107) found that

> the court plea of "not guilty!", the "I've been framed!" of the inmate, and the "I'm the same as you are!" statements are familiar rebuttals to judges, wardens, and psychiatrists. Although the label itself may, in fact, have been inflicted on an innocent person, this mode may be employed by the guilty as well.

that everything a homosexual does results from someone having called him homosexual. (p. 179)

People do these things for reasons quite apart from the way others react to them. Hence, the causes of delinquent behavior, no less than reactions to it, need to be studied.

Given that need, both Lemert and Becker propose doing away with one-sided approaches and substituting an interactional model for studying delinquency. While we "can't go home again" to the old positivistic criminology, Lemert said, neither can we rely totally on the study of reactions to deviance (1974:466–467). Becker (1973:181) agreed and recommended that the term *labeling theory* be discarded and a new term adopted: *interactionist theory*. In its simplest form, interactionist theory would be concerned with all the actors involved in any episode of deviance: rule creators, rule breakers, and rule enforcers. All three, not just one or the other, would be treated as raw materials for scientific analysis (Gibbs and Erickson, 1975; Rains, 1975; Scheff, 1974). Toward that end, two recent theories to be discussed in Chapter 15—Braithwaite's (1989) theory of reintegrative shaming and Matsueda's (1992) theory of differential social control—integrate certain claims by labeling theorists into their broader theories of delinquency.

SUMMARY AND CONCLUSIONS

Labeling theorists challenged the preoccupation of positivistic criminology with the presumed causes of delinquent behavior and directed our attention to another part of the mosaic of which delinquency is comprised: the roles of rule makers and rule enforcers. They made an exceedingly valuable contribution, markedly extending the range of behavioral phenomena with which both social scientists and policymakers must be concerned.

Assumptions About Human Nature and Social Order
Like symbolic interactionists, labeling theorists have tended to assume that human nature is flexible and subject to change. By humanizing the delinquent and normalizing his or her acts, they have been inclined to believe that most children will be good if they are not pushed into adopting a delinquent self-image by the punitive reactions of others to them. The assumptions of labeling theorists about social order reflect the same bias. Although there are conflicting definitions of behavior, it is the tendency of rule makers and rule enforcers to dramatize the conflict that exacerbates the delinquency problem.

Underlying Content and Logic of Labeling Theory
Early proponents of labeling theory stressed the notion that delinquents become bad because of the unnecessary dramatization of their primary deviance. If that drama is repeated several times, offenders are likely to adopt a delinquent self-image and engage in acts of secondary deviance.

By contrast, more recent proponents of labeling theory have tended to treat the delinquent as a passive social object, helplessly transported from a normal to a delinquent status. Moral crusaders create unnecessary and arbitrary rules; rule enforcers selectively impose those rules; and the unlucky labelee is stigmatized and used as a symbol for maintaining social stability and marking society's boundaries.

Policy Implications of Labeling Theory

The more modest implication of labeling theory is to use the juvenile court as an agency of last resort for only the most serious offenders. The more radical implication is to do absolutely nothing—to refuse to dramatize evil. Policymakers have tended to adopt the first implication. Consequently, four reforms have been pursued: (1) decriminalization, narrowing the jurisdiction of the juvenile court, particularly over status offenders; (2) diversion, turning juveniles away from the juvenile justice system and toward other social agencies; (3) due process, requiring the juvenile court to provide alleged delinquents with the constitutional protections accorded adults; and (4) deinstitutionalization, removing delinquents from detention centers, jails, and reformatories.

Logical and Empirical Adequacy of Labeling Theory

In their more extreme interpretations of labeling theory, some have contended that there are no crimes and no criminals, and that the only justifiable paradigm for criminology is one that focuses attention on reactions to delinquency. Along with others, however, most labeling theorists have discounted such intemperate interpretations. Rather, there are crimes, though societies create the definitions that define them as injurious; there are criminals, though societies distinguish their extreme behaviors from those of the majority; and punitive reactions to crime are not the only factors that produce law-violating behavior and deviant identities. Thus, interpretations of labeling theory suggesting that punitive reactions are sufficient to explain delinquency are unacceptably deterministic.

Recent statements by labeling theorists suggest that we should return to an interactionist frame of reference. Although we cannot rely solely on the older models of positivistic criminology, neither can we adopt a one-sided approach stressing only reactions. Instead, all of the actors in the drama of creating delinquency—rule makers, rule breakers, and rule enforcers—must be taken into account.

DISCUSSION QUESTIONS

1. What is the difference between primary and secondary deviance?
2. What do Erikson and Durkheim mean by "the social functions of deviance"?
3. What major policy reforms have stemmed from labeling theory?
4. To what extent has labeling theory been supported in empirical tests?
5. How does *interactionist theory* differ from *labeling theory*? Why have some suggested that the first term be adopted?

REFERENCES

Ageton, Suzanne, and Delbert Elliott. 1974. "The Effects of Legal Processing on Self-Concept." *Social Problems* 22 (October):87–100.

Akers, Ronald L. 1968. "Problems in the Sociology of Deviance: Social Definitions and Behavior." *Social Forces* 46 (June):455–465.

Becker, Howard S. 1963. *Outsiders: Studies in the Sociology of Deviance.* New York: Free Press. 1973. *Outsiders: Studies in the Sociology of Deviance (With a New Chapter—"Labeling Theory Reconsidered").* New York: Free Press.

Bordua, David J. 1967. "Recent Trends: Deviant Behavior and Social Control." *Annals of the American Academy of Political and Social Science* 369 (January):149–163.

Braithwaite, John. 1989. *Crime, Shame and Reintegration.* Cambridge: Cambridge University Press.

Chilton, Roland, and Jan DeAmicis. 1975. "Overcriminalization and the Measurement of Consensus." *Sociology and Social Research* 59 (July): 318–329.

D'Unger, Amy V., Kenneth C. Land, Patricia L. McCall, and Daniel S. Nagin. 1998. "How Many Latent Classes of Delinquent/Criminal Careers? Results from Mixed Poisson Regression Analyses." *American Journal of Sociology* 103 (May): 1593–1630.

Durkheim, Emile. 1933. *The Division of Labor in Society.* Glencoe, Ill.: The Free Press. (Originally published in 1893.)
1966. *The Rules of Sociological Method.* Translated by Sarah A. Solovay and John H. Mueller, and edited by George E. G. Catlin. New York: Free Press.

Erickson, Maynard L., Mark C. Stafford, and James M. Galliher. 1984. "The Normative Erosion Hypothesis: The Latent Consequences of Juvenile Justice Practices." *Sociological Quarterly* 25 (Summer):373–384.

Erikson, Kai T. 1962. "Notes on the Sociology of Deviance." *Social Problems* 9 (Spring):307–314.

Finestone, Harold. 1976. *Victims of Change: Juvenile Delinquents in American Society.* Westport, Conn.: Greenwood Press.

Foster, Jack, Simon Dinitz, and Walter C. Reckless. 1972. "Perceptions of Stigma Following Public Intervention for Delinquent Behavior." *Social Problems* 20 (Fall):202–209.

Gibbs, Jack P. 1966. "Conceptions of Deviant Behavior: The Old and the New." *Pacific Sociological Review* 9 (Spring):9–14.

Gibbs, Jack P., and Maynard L. Erickson. 1975. "Major Developments in the Sociological Study of Deviance." Pp. 21–42 in Alex Inkeles, ed., *Annual Review of Sociology,* Vol. 1. Palo Alto: Annual Reviews.

Goode, Erich. 1975. "On Behalf of Labeling Theory." *Social Problems* 22 (June):570–583.

Gouldner, Alvin W. 1968. "The Sociologist as Partisan: Sociology and the Welfare State." *American Sociologist* 3 (May):103–116.

Gove, Walter R. 1980. "The Labelling Perspective: An Overview." Pp. 9–33 in Walter R. Gove, ed., *The Labelling of Deviance,* 2nd ed. Beverly Hills, Calif.: Sage.

Hamilton, V. Lee, and Steve Rytina. 1980. "Social Consensus on Norms of Justice: Should the Punishment Fit the Crime?" *American Journal of Sociology* 85 (March):1117–1144.

Hepburn, John R. 1977. "The Impact of Police Intervention upon Juvenile Delinquents." *Criminology* 15 (August):235–262.

Jensen, Gary F. 1980. "Labeling and Identity: Toward a Reconciliation of Divergent Findings." *Criminology* 18 (May):121–129.

Kaplan, Howard B., and Robert J. Johnson. 1991. "Negative Social Sanctions and Juvenile Delinquency: Effects of Labeling in a Model of Deviant Behavior." *Social Science Quarterly* 72 (March): 98–122.

Kent v. *United States.* 1966. 383 U.S. 541, 16L. Ed. 2d 84, 86 S. Ct. 1045.

Kitsuse, John I. 1962. "Societal Reaction to Deviant Behavior: Problems of Theory and Method." *Social Problems* 9 (Winter):247–256.

Klein, Malcolm W. 1974. "Labeling, Deterrence, and Recidivism: A Study of Police Dispositions of Juvenile Offenders." *Social Problems* 22 (December): 292–303.

Laub, John H., Daniel S. Nagin, and Robert J. Sampson. 1998. "Trajectories of Change in Criminal Offending: Good Marriages and the Desistance Process." *American Sociological Review* 63 (April):225–238.

Lemert, Edwin M. 1951. *Social Pathology: A Systematic Approach to the Theory of Sociopathic Behavior.* New York: McGraw-Hill.
1967. "The Juvenile Court—Quest and Realities." Pp. 91–106 in the President's Commission on Law Enforcement and Administration of Justice, *Task Force Report: Juvenile Delinquency and Youth Crime.* Washington, D.C.: U.S. Government Printing Office.

1971. *Instead of Court: Diversion in Juvenile Justice.* Public Health Service Publication No. 2127. Washington, D.C.: U.S. Government Printing Office.

1972. *Human Deviance, Social Problems, and Social Control,* 2nd ed. Englewood Cliffs, N.J.: Prentice-Hall.

1974. "Beyond Mead: The Social Reaction to Deviance." *Social Problems* 21 (April):457–468.

Mahoney, Anne R. 1974. "The Effect of Labeling upon Youths in the Juvenile Justice System: A Review of the Evidence." *Law and Society Review* 8 (Summer):583–614.

Mankoff, Milton. 1971. "Societal Reaction and Career Deviance: A Critical Analysis." *Sociological Quarterly* 12 (Spring):204–218.

Matsueda, Ross L. 1992. "Reflected Appraisals, Parental Labeling, and Delinquency: Specifying a Symbolic Interactionist Theory." *American Journal of Sociology* 97 (May):1577–1611.

Moffitt, Terrie E. 1993. "Adolescence-Limited and Life-Course-Persistent Antisocial Behavior: A Developmental Taxonomy." *Psychological Review* 100 (October):674–701.

Nettler, Gwynn. 1984. *Explaining Crime,* 3rd ed. New York: McGraw-Hill.

President's Commission on Law Enforcement and Administration of Justice. 1967a. *Task Force Report: Juvenile Delinquency and Youth Crime.* Washington, D.C.: U.S. Government Printing Office.

1967b. *The Challenge of Crime in a Free Society.* Washington, D.C.: U.S. Government Printing Office.

Rains, Prudence. 1975. "Imputations of Deviance: A Retrospective Essay on the Labeling Perspective." *Social Problems* 23 (October):1–11.

Rogers, Joseph W., and M. D. Buffalo. 1974. "Fighting Back: Nine Modes of Adaptation to a Deviant Label." *Social Problems* 22 (October):101–118.

Rossi, Peter H., Emily Waite, Christine E. Bose, and Richard E. Berk. 1974. "The Seriousness of Crimes: Normative Structure and Individual Dif-

ferences." *American Sociological Review* 39 (April): 224–237.

Ruefle, William, and Kenneth M. Reynolds. 1995. "Curfews and Delinquency in Major American Cities." *Crime and Delinquency* 41 (July): 347–363.

Scheff, Thomas J. 1974. "The Labelling Theory of Mental Illness." *American Sociological Review* 39 (June):444–452.

Schrag, Clarence. 1971. *Crime and Justice: American Style.* National Institute of Mental Health Publication No. HSM-72-9052. Washington, D.C.: U.S. Government Printing Office.

Schur, Edwin M. 1971. *Labeling Deviant Behavior: Its Sociological Implications.* New York: Harper & Row.

1973. *Radical Nonintervention: Rethinking the Delinquency Problem.* Englewood Cliffs, N.J.: Prentice-Hall.

Shoemaker, Donald J. 1990. *Theories of Delinquency: An Examination of Explanations of Delinquent Behavior,* 2nd ed. New York: Oxford University Press.

Smith, Douglas A., and Raymond Paternoster. 1990. "Formal Processing and Future Delinquency: Deviance Amplification as Selection Artifact." *Law and Society Review* 24 (December):1109–1131.

Sutherland, Edwin H., and Donald R. Cressey. 1974. *Criminology,* 9th ed. Philadelphia: Lippincott.

Tannenbaum, Frank. 1938. *Crime and the Community.* Boston: Ginn.

Thomas, Charles W., and Donna M. Bishop. 1984. "The Effect of Formal and Informal Sanctions on Delinquency: A Longitudinal Comparison of Labeling and Deterrence Theories." *The Journal of Criminal Law and Criminology* 75 (4): 1222–1245.

Walton, Paul. 1973. "The Case of the Weathermen: Social Reaction and Radical Commitment." Pp. 157–181 in Ian Taylor and Laurie Taylor, eds., *Politics and Deviance.* London: Penguin Books.

Ward, David A., and Charles R. Tittle. 1993. "Deterrence or Labeling: The Effects of Informal Sanctions." *Deviant Behavior* 14 (January):43–64.

Wellford, Charles. 1975. "Labelling Theory and Criminology: An Assessment." *Social Problems* 22 (February):332–345.

Wolfgang, Marvin E., Robert M. Figlio, Paul E. Tracy, and Simon I. Singer. 1985. *The National Survey of Crime Severity.* Washington, D.C.: U.S. Government Printing Office.

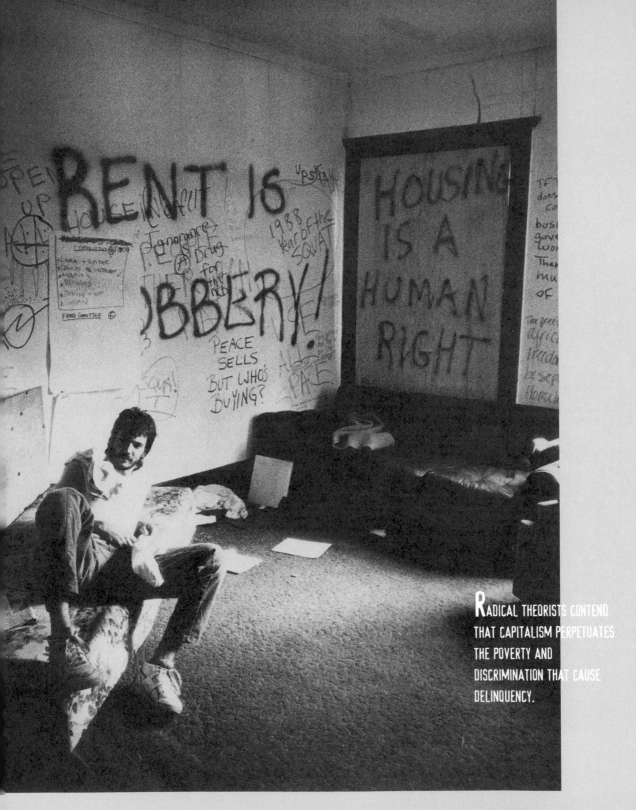

RADICAL THEORISTS CONTEND THAT CAPITALISM PERPETUATES THE POVERTY AND DISCRIMINATION THAT CAUSE DELINQUENCY.

CHAPTER FOURTEEN

RADICAL THEORY

Radical theory gained prominence in the 1960s and 1970s. Like labeling theory, it stemmed from a line of social thought that moved progressively away from the notion that delinquent tendencies are inherent in individuals and toward the notion that such tendencies are inherent in the way rules are made and enforced to selectively punish some people and not others.

According to **radical theory,** delinquency results from a perpetual class struggle in which the ruling segments of capitalist society (1) define what delinquent behavior is, based on their particular self-interests, (2) create the social conditions that make delinquents out of the children of working-class people, and then (3) devise legal machinery to maintain control over these children. Therefore, the rules and practices that govern delinquency and the criminogenic conditions that produce it are products of the inequities and injustices of a capitalist social order.

Radical theorists strongly imply that human nature is inherently good. Although children may possess some selfish tendencies, they become truly bad only if people define or make them that way. If they were liberated from the evils of the class struggle, the cooperative instincts of young people would become dominant, and a humane, crime-free society would emerge.

ORIGINS OF RADICAL THEORY

Radical beliefs of this type are not really new. Why, then, did they experience a revival in the last third of the 20th century? In part, they can be traced to events in America during the 1960s and 1970s: the civil rights protests and urban riots, the Vietnam War, the Watergate cover-up, and evidence of corruption among America's political leaders (Krisberg and Austin, 1978:4). When those events were coupled with growing dismay over the decay of American cities, the Third World struggles against colonialism, the persistence of sexual inequality, and the worldwide destruction of the environment, faith in traditional values and the American system was weakened.

This crisis of legitimacy (Schaar, 1974) not only undermined the principles on which order and obedience are based but also contributed to widespread social despair. Pessimistic critics renounced their faith in the American system of justice and the capitalist division of labor. In such a climate, it is not surprising that a new view of the American system of justice should emerge. Thus, a new generation of criminologists began to search for political and legal alternatives, with radical theory being one result. Radical theorists expressed dismay over the past, blamed capitalists for creating crime and injustice, and provided a different course of action for the future. In constructing this new view of delinquency and justice, however, radical theorists did not create an entirely new theory. Rather, they borrowed heavily from conflict theory and Marxian theory.

CONFLICT THEORY

In support of their belief in widespread social injustice and class conflict, radical theorists have argued that greater attention should be paid to existing laws and the persons served by those laws. They pointed out that until the early 20th century, little attention was paid to those matters. At that time, however, a number of legal scholars developed a legal philosophy known as *sociological jurisprudence*. In order to understand the law, these scholars argued, one must examine its relation to the social order.

The Social Nature of Law

Sociological jurisprudents emphasized that the law is not merely a set of unchangeable formal rules, but rather is a dynamic body of norms heavily influenced by the society of which it is a part (Pound, 1942: Chap. 2). The law not only reflects the society but also influences the society. As Quinney (1974:6) put it, the law is "both social product and social force." Like other cultural elements, it originally reflects the course of a civilization and its people, and then, in a sense, takes on a life of its own—it shapes the course of a civilization and is shaped by it.

A second point emphasized by sociological jurisprudents is that the law represents social engineering that will improve the social order. Roscoe Pound (1922:99), for example, argued that the law regulates social behavior and establishes a social organization that eventually will improve society:

> I am content to see in legal history the record of a continually wider recognizing and satisfying of human wants or claims or desires through social control; a more embracing and more effective securing of social interests; a continually more complete and effective elimination of waste and precluding of friction in human enjoyment of the goods of existence—in short, a continually more efficacious social engineering.

Finally, sociological jurisprudents have suggested that the law serves as a means for reconciling competing interests in society. It provides a way of protecting the *little* people from the powerful, of ensuring justice for lawbreakers, and of mediating between the demands of conflicting interest groups (Fuller, 1971; Selznick, 1968). The law, in short, represents an attempt to accomplish the greatest good for the greatest number of people.

Few scholars today would deny that the law is deeply rooted in our cultural history and that it strongly shapes our society. But radical criminologists have sharply disagreed with the notion that the law necessarily improves society or that it equitably serves the interests of all. Such a view, they have suggested, represents a consensual view of social order, which assumes that there is general agreement among the members of society on basic goals and on the laws that should govern the pursuit of those goals.

This view, radicals have argued, is a mythical construction of reality designed to preserve order in an unjust society. Society is organized not by a widespread consensus, but by the exercise of power by a small, ruling class (Quinney, 1974:18). "Those who control the means of production also control the production of values in the society" (Chambliss, 1976:3). As a consequence, legal scholars have based their views of law on a misguided conception of the way social order is maintained. Perhaps even worse, the same is true of most social scientists. From Lombroso to Sutherland, from Freud to Cloward and Ohlin, they have developed theories of delinquency that not only provide misleading descriptions of its causes but also furnish the ruling class with an ideology for maintaining its own self-serving brand of social control (Quinney, 1974:3–4). To understand how this came about, said radical criminologists, it is necessary to contrast the consensus framework of social order, within which positivists have conducted their analyses of delinquency, with the conflict framework, within which radical theorists have conducted their research.

The Consensus Framework

The **consensus framework** evolved from a long tradition in science that stressed the importance of trying to understand any phenomenon in its entirety, whether it be the human body, the solar system, or society (Merton, 1968:Chap. 2). How do all parts of society contribute to its ongoing operation? Which of its parts are necessary for its survival? If some key part is destroyed, how does society adapt?

Advocates of the consensus framework have assumed that even though the various parts of society are never integrated fully, they tend toward stability and equilibrium (van den Berghe, 1963:695–697). Change is more likely to proceed gradually rather than in a revolutionary or violent way. But, above all, societal integration and stability are made possible by the general agreement among members of society on basic values and beliefs. In its ideal form, therefore, the consensus framework suggests that "(1) society is a relatively persistent, stable structure, (2) it is well integrated, (3) every element [in it] has a function—it helps maintain the system, and (4) [it possesses] a functioning social structure . . . based on a consensus of values" (Quinney, 1970:9, from Dahrendorf, 1959:161).

According to the consensus framework, then, there would be little disagreement in identifying lawbreakers because these people reject a community's basic values, commit prohibited acts, and threaten the stability of the whole. As the French sociologist Emile Durkheim (1964:73) put it, "the only common characteristic of all crimes is that they consist . . . in acts *universally disapproved* of by members of each society" (emphasis added).

Because the consensus framework assumes that values and beliefs are widely shared in society, it implies that lawbreakers are somehow different from law-abiding people—lawbreakers suffer some psychological abnormalities, are undersocialized, or have values and beliefs that run counter to those of the larger community.

The Conflict Framework

In sharp contrast to proponents of the consensus framework, radical criminologists have argued that the analysis of social order should be cast within the framework of conflict. Like the consensus framework, the conflict framework has a long history (Dahrendorf, 1959:Part 1). But unlike the consensus framework, it assigns much less importance to shared values and beliefs. Instead, the **conflict framework** stresses the importance of social change and the exercise of power by a limited few. It assumes that "(1) at every point society is subject to change, (2) it displays at every point dissensus and conflict, (3) every element contributes to change, and (4) it is based on the coercion of some of its members by others" (Quinney, 1970:9, from Dahrendorf, 1959:162).

According to the conflict framework, then, society is held together not by consensus, but by force and constraint. Although certain values and beliefs predominate, they are enforced more by dominant power groups than by members of society as a whole (Chambliss, 1973:6; Dahrendorf, 1958; Turk, 1969: 30–34). Hence, conflict theorists have believed that although different social classes may cling to their own unique values and customs, social order throughout society is maintained by the power exercised by a ruling class. Some acts are defined as delinquent because it is in the interests of the ruling class to so define them.

If that is true, it is fruitless to try to explain the behavior of children who commit delinquent acts. If we wish to understand delinquency, we must concentrate on the distribution of power in society and the processes by which laws are written and labels are attached to some children and not others.

MARXIAN THEORY

Radical criminologists' interest in class conflict and social order also sprang from a second theoretical source: **Marxian theory.** Karl Marx (1818–1883) was a German philosopher whose writings reflected the economic and social ferment that accompanied the growth of Western, industrial capitalism in the early and middle 1800s. Like radicals today, Marx favored a dialectical theory of human progress: He viewed history as a reflection of a perpetual struggle between the economic classes.

The seeds for Marx's dialectical theory came from Georg Wilhelm Friedrich Hegel (1770–1831), another German philosopher. Hegel was concerned that philosophers had not developed an explanatory system for the world because it was constantly changing (Taylor, 1967:8). To fill that void, he constructed a dialectical theory of change.

Webster's Dictionary defines **dialectic** as "any systematic reasoning, exposition, or argument that juxtaposes opposed or contradictory ideas and . . . seeks to resolve their conflict." Hegel suggested that whenever some basic idea prevails in society—he called it the *thesis*—that idea eventually is challenged by an opposing idea—the *antithesis*. A conflict between the two ideas usually ensues, but rarely is there a clear victory for either side. Rather, a new *synthesis* of the two ideas emerges, which, in time, is accepted and becomes the prevailing thesis. But, true to the march of history, the new thesis eventually is challenged by a new antithesis, and then a new synthesis emerges. That was Hegel's way of accounting for human progress and social change.

Although Marx made use of Hegel's dialectical theory, he believed that change is due not to the conflict of contrasting ideas, but to the conflict of competing economic systems. According to Marx, history is a succession of economic arrangements in which the weak forever struggle against exploitation by the powerful. The inevitable consequence of that struggle is a succession of ever-improving economic orders. That is, time after time, the powerful eventually will be overthrown by angry workers who rise up against their oppressors and install a more just order. Marx's theory, therefore, became a theory of **dialectical materialism.**

Marx argued that there have been three major economic and social epochs: ancient slave society, feudal society of the Middle Ages, and **capitalism** (Meyer, 1968:41). Each has represented a step forward in the progress of humanity, but each also has included the seeds of its own destruction. Capitalism, for example, represents the peak of social development thus far. It has overthrown the stagnating influence of feudalism, provided abundant material goods, and instituted constitutional government. But capitalism also possesses weaknesses that will lead to its destruction.

The ruling class under capitalism—the *bourgeoisie*—has pursued the accumulation of wealth and property rather than human rights or the elimination of human misery and chaos. The result has been the movement of most people—the *proletariat*—into dehumanizing positions in society. Although people are inherently social and inclined to pursue freedom, those virtues have been distorted by capitalist economic arrangements. Workers have been converted into commodities whose labor, talents, and personalities are sold. Human dignity and the worth of the individual have been sacrificed to the prevailing interests of the bourgeoisie in accumulating wealth (Taylor, Walton, and Young, 1973: 219–220).

Even though this has dehumanized the proletariat, it has served at least one valuable purpose: It has helped to create the conditions that will lead to a liberated civilization. "Society as a whole is more and more splitting up into two great hostile camps, . . . bourgeoisie and proletariat" (Marx and Engels, 1948: 9). That split eventually will lead to a new and final synthesis—an epoch of socialism, a dictatorship by the proletariat—in which all vestiges of capitalism will be liquidated, class struggle will cease, and the historical dialectic will come to an end. "In place of the old bourgeois society, with its classes and class antagonisms, we shall have an association, in which the free development of each is the condition for the free development of all" (Marx and Engels, 1948:31). The proletariat will rise above narrow interests and ideologies to liberate humankind from the curses of property and class.

POSTULATES OF RADICAL THEORY

Radical theorists have made several stinging indictments of positivist criminology and its concern with identifying characteristics that distinguish lawbreakers from law-abiding people. According to radical theorists, the key issue is how capitalism leads to crime by enabling a small ruling class to make and enforce laws that perpetuate its control over other members of society. By ignoring this and concentrating on the characteristics of lawbreakers, positivists have reinforced an unjust system. They have constructed a stereotype of law-violating children "designed to convince us that the delinquent is different

from the 'normal child,'" and in so doing have diverted attention away from the problems of capitalism (Krisberg and Austin, 1978:118–119). In short, positivists' technical skills and research have become *tools* that are used to operate the capitalist system of social control (Platt, 1974:357). As Quinney (1974: 15) noted, "criminologists today are furnishing the information and knowledge necessary for the manipulation and control of those who threaten the social system."

Radical theorists have called for criminologists to stop "systematically ignor[ing] moral questions about the legal order" (Quinney, 1974:13). The following six postulates put forth by Quinney (1974:24) are a standard expression of radical theory:

1. *American society is based on an advanced capitalist economy.* The term *capitalism* generally refers to an "economic system in which the greater proportion of economic life, particularly ownership of and investment in production goods, is carried on under private (i.e., non-governmental) auspices through the process of economic competition . . . and the avowed incentive of profit" (Cole, 1964:70). Those who favor such a system argue that if left free from governmental interference, capitalism maximizes production and results in the most equitable distribution of scarce resources.

   Radical theorists have maintained, however, that with capitalism the private owners of the means of production extract a profit by paying laborers less than the full value of their labor, thus exploiting them. That is particularly true in an advanced capitalist economy like ours, in which control has passed into the hands of fewer and fewer financiers, bankers, and corporate investors who, although divorced from the day-to-day management of industrial enterprises, extract huge profits from them.

2. *The state is organized to serve the interests of the dominant economic class, the capitalist ruling class.* The few people who dominate the huge corporations and financial institutions constitute the ruling class in American society. It is "that class which owns and controls the means of production and which is able, by virtue of the

economic power thus conferred upon it, to use the state as its instrument for the domination of society" (Miliband, 1969:23).

The domination is not limited to the oppression of working-class people; it overlaps with, and includes, other groups as well:

- Youths: "Young people form a subservient class, alienated, powerless, and prone to economic manipulation" (Krisberg and Austin, 1978:1).
- Women: "Capitalism and sexism are intimately related . . . Sexism is not merely the prejudice of individuals; it is embedded in the very economic, legal, and social framework of life in the United States" (Rafter and Natalizia, 1981:81).
- Racial and ethnic minorities: The United States is a racist country in which capitalism has resulted not only in the systematic oppression of African Americans but the oppression of other racial and ethnic minorities as well (Burns, 1974; Takagi, 1981).

3. *Criminal law is an instrument of the state and ruling class to maintain and perpetuate the existing social and economic order.* Law is "the ultimate means by which the state secures the interests of the ruling class. Laws institutionalize and legitimize the existing property relations" (Quinney, 1974:23). Even delinquency laws are designed to accomplish this purpose. They were written by elitist child savers who

> were concerned not with championing the rights of the poor against exploitation by the ruling classes but rather with integrating the poor into the established social order and protecting "respectable" citizens from the "dangerous classes." Given this perspective, it is not surprising that the child savers sought curbs on immigration, staunchly defended the unequal distribution of wealth, and discussed ways of imposing birth control on the lower classes. The child savers regarded the children of the urban poor with a mixture of paternalism and contempt. (Platt, 1971:ix)

The only concern of the child savers was with keeping such children under control, thereby se-

curing their selfish economic interests (Sinclair, 1983:21).

4. *Crime control in capitalist society is accomplished through a variety of institutions and agencies established and administered by a governmental elite, representing ruling class interests, for the purpose of establishing domestic order.* In the simple, undeveloped societies of previous centuries, the modern state with its governing elite of armed police officers, judges, prison wardens, and other legal officials was unknown. Order was maintained, instead, by democratic means in a communal social system. But with the rise of capitalism, new methods of control were required. The emergence of a new ruling class required that the state be invented as a means for coercing the rest of the population into economic and political submission (Engels, 1942: 154–163):

> It is through the legal system, then, that the state explicitly and forcefully protects the interests of the capitalist ruling class. Crime control becomes the coercive means of checking threats to the existing social and economic arrangements. The state defines its welfare in terms of the general well-being of the capitalist economy. (Quinney, 1974:24)

5. *The contradictions of advanced capitalism—the disjunction between existence and essence—require that the subordinate classes remain oppressed by whatever means necessary, especially through the coercion and violence of the legal system.* Capitalism dehumanizes and alienates people because of the contradictions inherent in it (Edwards, Reich, and Weisskopf, 1974:430–431):

- Although it has created a wealth of consumer goods, it has failed to provide for "creative and socially useful work, meaningful community, and liberating education for individual development."
- It has been based on the pursuit of profit by creating obsolescent consumer goods and military waste, a pursuit that undermines the legitimacy of the system that produced it.

- It has made promises it cannot deliver. It cannot, for example, provide the means by which women, the poor, racial and ethnic minorities, and persons in Third World countries can be liberated.
- It has drawn an increasingly larger share of the world's population into "alienating wage and salary work," expanding the number of exploited people.
- By fostering education and worldwide communication, it has created a sophisticated proletariat that grows increasingly dissatisfied with the present division of labor and unequal distribution of power.

Given that state of affairs, the legal system clearly must resort to whatever means necessary to maintain control over the exploited and dehumanized classes (Chambliss, 1976:6):

- The criminal law is not the product of a consensus, but "is a set of rules laid down by the state in the interests of the ruling class."
- "Some criminal behavior is no more than the 'rightful' behavior of persons exploited by extant economic relations—what makes their behavior criminal is the coercive power of the state to enforce the will of the ruling class."
- "Criminal behavior results either from the struggle between classes wherein individuals of the subservient classes express their alienation from established social relations or from competition for control of the means of production."

Even the juvenile justice system was designed to advance the interests of the capitalist system and to ensure an excess labor supply:

The juvenile court system was part of a general movement directed towards developing a specialized labor market and industrial discipline under corporate capitalism by creating new programs of adjudication and control for "delinquent," "dependent," and "neglected" youth. This in turn was related to augmenting the family and enforcing compulsory education in order to guarantee the proper reproduction of the labor force. (Platt, 1974:377)

In other words, children involved in delinquency are idle, obscene, dirty youngsters, and there is a need to change them. Otherwise, the ruling class will be unprepared to staff the alienating system of capitalist work.

6. *Only with the collapse of capitalist society and the creation of a new society, based on socialist principles, will there be a solution to the crime problem.* Because capitalist rulers have defined as criminal any behavior that threatens the capitalist system, crime and delinquency can never be eliminated until that system is destroyed. The only alternative is a socialist system of government that places the ownership and control of the means of production into the hands of the community as a whole. "When there is no longer the need for one class to dominate another, where there is no longer the need for a legal system to secure the interests of a capitalist ruling class, then there will no longer be the need for crime" (Quinney, 1974:25). Once humankind is liberated from the curses of property and class, as Marx suggested, a crime-free, truly egalitarian society will emerge.

POLICY IMPLICATIONS

The policy implications of radical theory are unconventional (Sinclair, 1983:23–26). Unlike other theories, it denies that the delinquency problem can be solved by working within the framework of capitalist society, tampering with its system of juvenile justice, or trying to rehabilitate offenders. Because crime is inherent in the alienating and oppressive character of the capitalist system, it is the ageist, sexist, and classist rulers of that system who are the real criminals, not the ordinary street offenders who are their victims. The only solution is socialist revolution.

Prescriptions for Revolution

In the 19th century, Marx and Friedrich Engels (1948:44) argued that change was possible only by the "forcible overthrow" of capitalist society. Radical criminologists, however, have not gone that far, at least not explicitly. Instead, they have tended to take the position that as criminologists, they should join others in promoting a political movement to promote radical change by peaceful means:

> Our task as students of crime is to consider the alternatives to the capitalist legal order. . . . At this advanced stage of capitalist development, law is little more than a repressive instrument of manipulation and control. We must make others aware of the current meaning of crime and justice in America. The objective is to move beyond the existing order. And this means ultimately that we are engaged in socialist revolution. (Quinney, 1974:25)

The success of such a revolution requires two steps:

1. *Understand the contradictions of capitalist society.* We must become better aware of the dialectical nature of history and the contradictions inherent in capitalism, as mentioned earlier. The mere acknowledgment of the contradictions, however, is not enough, nor are individual rebellions, strikes, or campus protests. "The capitalist class is a privileged and exploiting class, and it is not about to give up its special place without resistance. . . . [It will] mystify discontent, offer sham concessions, co-opt leaders and causes . . . and suppress movement organizations" (Edwards, Reich, and Weisskopf, 1974: 432). Thus, a second step is required.

2. *Create class consciousness.* "Fundamental social change will occur only if a self-conscious class emerges and engages in organized political struggle" (Edwards, Reich, and Weisskopf, 1974: 432). This class "must articulate and struggle for a vision of a liberated society, in which all social relations are transformed and all hierarchical divisions of labor are abolished" (Edwards, Reich, and Weisskopf, 1974:432). But what is the vision for which people should struggle? What are the goals of a liberated society? How would it be organized?

The Liberated Society

The goals of a **liberated society** are (1) an end to all status differences (such as those based on gender and race) and a reliance on nonalienating work and co-operation to meet human needs, (2) respect for group differences and guarantees for individual rights, (3) an end to human greed, and (4) the elimination of all sexism, racism, poverty and crime (Edwards, Reich, and Weisskopf, 1974:433–434). Although the history of civilization has been characterized by value conflict and clashing interests, order in the liberated society apparently would be maintained by an enlightened consensus.

Despite those impressive goals, radical theorists have not clearly described the organization of a liberated society. They have suggested that (1) private ownership of capital would be abolished and the wealth redistributed, (2) all government bureaucracies and other social hierarchies would be destroyed, (3) monolithic criminal law would be eliminated and replaced with local community laws, and (4) people would become self-governing and self-managing (Edwards, Reich, and Weisskopf, 1974:433–434; Quinney, 1972:25–26). But if all people are to be equal and self-managing, without any differences in wealth or status and without the need for any governmental or industrial bureaucracies, an institutional redesign of the greatest magnitude is implied. Presumably, the U.S. Constitution, its Bill of Rights, our system of government, and our legal, economic, and educational institutions all would have to be changed drastically, if not eliminated. The need for a socialist blueprint of some kind is strongly implied, particularly because we are talking about the alteration of a complex, heterogeneous, highly technological society of more than 265 million people.

Regrettably, however, radical theorists have not provided such a blueprint. That is the case even though some have argued that the primary function of radical theory is the creation of "workable recipes" for social change: "The ultimate test of a theory's utility is not its logical structure or its 'fit' with empirical data but its ability to create workable recipes for changing the existing set of social conditions (both material conditions and the superstructure derived therefrom)" (Chambliss, 1976:3). At the same time, some radical theorists have openly disavowed the need to be specific. To do so, Edwards, Reich, and Weisskopf (1974:433) suggest, would be to appear excessively utopian:

We cannot present a blueprint or an exact specification of how a socialist "utopia" would work; nor should we attempt to do so, since constructing imaginary utopias bears little relation to the actual task of building a decent society. Any *real* alternatives to capitalism will be historically linked to the forces and movements generated by the contradictions of capitalist society itself. *New institutions which liberate rather than oppress can only be created by real people confronting concrete problems in their lives and developing new means to overcome oppression.* The political movements arising from capitalism's contradictions therefore constitute the only means for society to move from its present condition to a new and more decent form, and only out of these movements will humane as well as practical new institutions be generated. (emphasis added)

In other words, radical theory should be accepted on faith. Having experienced considerable social despair over the contradictions of capitalism, Americans should pursue a socialist vision of tomorrow, even if it is somewhat fuzzy.

THE IMPACT ON POLICY

Although radical theory's impact on policy has been indirect and complex, it has been significant nonetheless. Most importantly, radical theory and its search for justice have enriched our sense of human possibility. This, in turn, has had profound implications for a number of social movements. Indeed, the period of social unrest from which radical theory grew, as well as the theory itself, resulted in the emergence of two activities that radicals have felt must be present before revolution can occur: (1) the emergence of social movements that further highlight the contradictions of capitalism, and (2) the creation of self-conscious groups, as a result of those movements, that continue the struggle for economic and political power. Four of these movements are discussed here.

Civil Rights
During the 1960s, the franchise was extended to many people. Their consciousness was raised regard-

ing the importance of organized political action and protest; the Civil Rights Act of 1964 prohibited discrimination in schools and the workplace, as well as in the voting booth; and the economic position of the black middle class, along with others, was improved (Geshwender, 1980a, 1980b; Glazer, 1980; Grimshaw, 1980; Williams, 1977; Wilson, 1978:129).

Poverty
Efforts were made to reduce some of the more extreme effects of poverty through federal programs—job training, preschool programs, Medicaid, community action programs, legal services for the poor, and increased welfare benefits. And while there are still questions about the extent to which these programs were successful (Marris and Rein, 1973; Moynihan, 1969; Piven and Cloward, 1971:256–282), the ideas that gave birth to them were radical for many Americans.

Women's Rights
The same was true of the women's rights movement (Friedan, 1963; Millet, 1970). The Civil Rights Act of 1964 prohibited discrimination based on sex, and more women entered the workforce than ever before (Waite, 1981:4). Although women have not yet achieved political and economic equality, affirmative action on their behalf has produced a marked change in their favor in virtually every social institution.

Children's Rights
Finally, efforts to eliminate oppression have been extended to children. "We are on the threshold of a new consciousness of children's rights," said Richard Farson (1975), "a dramatically new concept of childhood itself. The fundamental change will be a recognition of the child's right to live with the same guarantee of freedom that adults enjoy, the basic right being that of self-determination."

Children's rights would be granted by writing into the Constitution a Bill of Rights for children. In addition to bringing about reforms in juvenile justice, these rights would permit children of all ages to (1) decide whether they wished to live with their parents, with someone else, or in state-run, child-care centers, (2) choose and design their own educational programs, including the option of no school attendance at all, (3) use alcohol or drugs and experience sex with no more restrictions placed on them than those placed on adults, (4) obtain employment, (5) manage their own money, (6) own credit cards, (7) enter binding contracts, (8) vote, and (9) share completely in the political process (Farson, 1974; Holt, 1974).

To be sure, these four movements did not begin to give full expression to the implications of radical theory. Few of them, for example, were designed to eliminate capitalist ownership and place it in the hands of workers. Furthermore, a conservative counterrevolution in the 1980s sought to undo some of the changes that had been introduced. Nonetheless, social movements emerged that did produce significant changes.

ASSESSMENT OF RADICAL THEORY

Three major issues merit careful scrutiny in assessing radical theory: (1) its use of history to *demystify* law, (2) its explanation of delinquency, and (3) its contention that crime could be eliminated if the means of production were controlled by the working class.

Demystification of Law

Like labeling theorists, radical theorists have performed a valuable service in directing our attention to the sources and effects of law. Indeed, this book borrows heavily from some of the insights of labeling and radical theorists.

THE MEANING OF DELINQUENCY We have seen that delinquency was invented in the 1800s as a result of changes that had been taking place for centuries. But that invention occurred not because the behavior of children had changed, but because the methods for controlling children had been reorganized and the meaning of their behavior had been redefined. Hence, our analysis has helped to demystify that segment of our history and to suggest that to understand delinquency, we must look at the creation of law and systems of control, as well as at the behavior of children.

THE CREATION OF LAW Radical theorists also may have been correct in suggesting that vagrancy and other laws were written as a means of controlling adults in the labor force and ensuring that members of the working class did not disrupt the prevailing system of production (Chambliss, 1964, 1973:10–11; 1984:11–41; Krisberg and Austin, 1978:7–11; Nelson, 1974—although for a critique of a radical interpretation of the development of vagrancy laws, see Adler, 1989). Yet, research has not always supported the view that the poor and racial/ethnic minorities are subjected to harsher penalties than other people (Cohen and Kluegel, 1978, 1979; Dannefer and Schutt, 1982; McCarthy and Smith, 1986; Peterson and Hagan, 1984; Sampson, 1986; Terry, 1967; Thornberry, 1973, 1979). Furthermore, Hagan and Leon (1977:596–597) found that the creation of the juvenile court did not result in greater incarceration for working-class children, as radicals have contended:

> Although this legislation substantially changed the operations of the juvenile and criminal courts, probably with consequences both good and bad, intended and unintended . . . , the overall effect was not to intensify a formal and explicit system of coercion, but rather to reinforce and increasingly intervene in informal systems of social control, particularly the family.

Thus, whereas historical analyses have helped to demystify the juvenile court, they have not always supported the radical belief that the only reason for the court's existence is political and economic discrimination.

SOCIAL SCIENCE AS OPPRESSOR Radicals also have contended that social science has served to legitimize the existing social order. Although that contention contains some truth, it has been grossly overstated. One of the greatest achievements of social scientists is that they have played leading roles in altering prevailing views. For example, anthropologists have helped to demolish the belief that Western values and institutions are preeminent; the findings of social scientists have been instrumental in legal proceedings, such as the 1954 Supreme Court decision that led to the desegregation of public schools; sociologists and psychologists have helped to discount the notion that delinquency is solely the result of biological defects by pointing to cultural and structural factors; self-report and victimization studies have revealed the error and bias in police and court statistics; and, throughout this century, criminologists and other social scientists have called attention to society's protection of white-collar and other powerful criminals.

In short, the process of demystifying the law is not new (Meier, 1976). Yet, radical theory holds out the promise of a better understanding of law and justice, informed by a greater awareness of history. It directs our attention to persistent discrimination and to collusion between governmental and ruling-class interests—issues to which criminologists have not paid enough attention. And it reminds us, as the 19th-century child savers needed reminding, that delinquency is not merely an expression of pathological individuals or depraved immigrant groups colliding with a just legal system. Rather, that legal system and its underlying values must be considered, and its contribution to delinquency must be assessed. That lesson may be radical theory's greatest contribution to the demystification of law.

Explanations of Delinquency

The contribution of radical theory to the explanation of delinquency is much less certain. According to radicals, delinquency exists only because capitalism is oppressive and because the ruling class creates laws to discriminate against and thereby control the working class. That is a questionable claim for several reasons.

THE EXISTENCE OF CRIME IN EVERY SOCIETY There is no doubt that poverty and discrimination are found in capitalist societies and that they are associated with delinquent behavior. However, in asserting that those problems are peculiar to capitalism and would disappear in a socialist society, radical theorists fell prey to two of the same problems that have plagued labeling theorists.

The first problem is the assumption that if capitalists did not create the laws that defined crime, there would be none of the behaviors—murders, thefts, and burglaries—that those laws condemn. Clearly, such a contention is questionable, if not to-

tally false. These behaviors are committed in all societies—whether capitalist or socialist, developed or undeveloped.

The second problem is that radicals, like labeling theorists, have viewed lawbreakers as underdogs. Although that view has merits, it also can lead to excessive claims, such as the view that lawbreakers are courageous opponents of an oppressive system and should be defined not as offenders, but as victims. In reality, however, few lawbreakers see their behavior as political crimes intended to overthrow oppression. Furthermore, crime victims tend not to be wealthy elites (those supposedly responsible for oppression), but rather are more likely to be poor, to be members of racial/ethnic minorities, and to live in urban areas (Karmen, 1995:152–153). In short, whether in capitalist or noncapitalist societies, there always have been predators who violate laws for personal gain.

THE CAUSES OF CRIME Although crime exists in all societies, radicals have condemned other criminologists for seeking to explain it, asserting that their theories are nothing more than sophisticated rationalizations that justify oppression of poor people, minorities, women, and children. In light of that assertion, several issues should be considered.

First, Marx's view of lawbreakers was unlike that of contemporary radicals. Marx was vitriolic in condemning lawbreakers, whom he viewed as members of the *lumpenproletariat*—a "dangerous class," a "social scum," a "passively rotting mass thrown off by the lowest layers of old society" (Marx and Engels, 1948:20). Such people could not be relied upon for any constructive actions. They were "a parasitic class, living off productive labour by theft, extortion and beggary, or by providing 'services' such as prostitution and gambling" (Hirst, 1975:216). Hence, Marx clearly regarded lawbreakers as different and suggested that valuable insights might be gained by trying to understand why that is so. Why do the lumpenproletariat, but not other working-class people, succumb to the problems and pressures of capitalist society?

Second, radical theory rests on the assumption that because capitalist societies oppress the lower and working classes, class membership should be the best predictor of official delinquency and law-violating

CRIME IN PRIMITIVE SOCIETIES

Radical theorists' argument that capitalism is the cause of crime is immediately called into question when one hears of the story of Guibode, a tribesman of the Kiowa Indians of the western U.S. plains:

> Guibode belonged to the *Kiep* group, which was supposed to camp on the south side of the camp circle. He didn't like the location, so he moved over to where the *Koiga* group was.... They told him to move back where he belonged ... [but] Guibode then raised his bow as if to shoot. The Chief acted quickly and knocked him cold with a blow on the head.... When Guibode came to ... [he] got up without a word and went back to the *Kiep* territory. A year later he caught his wife *in flagrante delicto* with Pokongiai, son of a wealthy man. The adulterer got away, but the enraged Guibode beat his wife unmercifully.... Guibode [then] went out in the camp crying threats of death against the life of Pokongiai ... [and then] went and killed a number of horses from the herd of the adulterer's father. (Hoebel, 1976 [1954]:174–175)

In the absence of capitalism, Guibode somehow managed to commit a range of offenses, including trespassing, attempted homicide, domestic violence, threatened homicide, and cruelty to animals. He also was the victim of adultery and perhaps even police brutality!

behavior. Although the poor and members of racial/ethnic minorities are overrepresented in the juvenile justice system, class membership is not the best predictor of official delinquency.[1] Rather, delinquency is much more strongly related to age and gender than to social class (see Chapters 4, 5, and 6). Whether in capitalist or noncapitalist societies, the highest crime-producing years tend to occur during adolescence and young adulthood and to involve males more than females. To be sure, it has been suggested that children are oppressed and that this may account for much of their lawbreaking (Greenberg, 1977). But even if we accept suggestion, how do we account for the differences between males and females? Because females are the more oppressed of the two, one should expect more delinquency among them. But that clearly is not the case, so oppression alone cannot explain delinquency.

Third, the findings of positivist research often are contrary to radical theory. Radicals have stated that poverty and discrimination are solely responsible for delinquency, and particularly for arrest and adjudication. However, positivist research has shown that weak attachment to home and school, a weak commitment to conventional means for success, poor achievement in school, and association with delinquent peers predict these outcomes among youths from all social classes, not just among those from the working or lower classes.

Indeed, what about the delinquent behavior of advantaged youths? Why do they vandalize property, steal autos, use drugs, rape, and burglarize? Not only does the delinquency of advantaged youths require explanation, but the evidence indicates that juvenile justice officials have not ignored them in favor of punishing only the poor.

In summary, this short review suggests that (1) there are lawbreakers in every society, not just capitalist societies; (2) lawbreakers possess characteristics that distinguish them from law-abiding per-

---

[1]Farnworth et al. (1994) found that the relationship between social class and self-reported delinquency and official delinquency depended in large part on how social class is measured. Social class is most strongly related to delinquency when measured in a way that is sensitive to the differences between the lowest social classes and all others rather than differences between the middle and upper-middle classes. Nevertheless, regardless of the measure used, the relationship between social class and delinquency is not extraordinary.

EXCESS MORTALITY IN HARLEM

Radical theorists believe that although capitalist societies are interested in punishing offenders, they rarely are interested in addressing the root causes of crime and delinquency—poverty, inequality, and racism. This leads to a society divided between those who have power and those who do not. The experiences and life chances of those two groups diverge so much that it is as though they live in two entirely different societies. One recent study reported in *The New England Journal of Medicine* confirms that view. In the Harlem district of New York City, where 96 percent of the inhabitants are black and 41 percent live below the poverty line, mortality rates are more than double those of white Americans. Moreover, for men over the age of 40, Harlem mortality rates are higher than that for a typical rural area in Bangladesh (McCord and Freeman, 1990).

sons; (3) age and gender are better predictors of delinquency than class membership; (4) oppression alone cannot explain differences in the delinquency of various segments of the population; and (5) positivist theories have been useful in identifying factors that account for delinquency in all social classes, not just the lower class.

Why, then, have radical theorists disavowed a concern with such matters? The answer lies in their preoccupation with capitalist rules and practices. Like labeling theorists, radicals are not concerned with primary deviance, individual differences, or reasons for crime. Because they believe it is political and economic oppression that determines the course of human events, the inclinations and motivations of

people are unimportant. Indeed, if capitalism was replaced by a socialist system, we would not need to worry about motives for crime or about ageism, sexism, racism, or classism. All would disappear. But how good a case have radical theorists made that a society could evolve in that way or that this plan should be pursued? We will consider that question next.

Elimination of Crime

Radical theorists have pointed to a way of solving the crime problem that is different from traditional American perspective:

> Characteristically, Americans are individualists. If some good is achieved in the social order, Americans assume that some individuals deserve credit and reward for the accomplishment. On the other hand, existence of a social problem is assumed to imply that some persons must be individually to blame. If unemployment is too high, it must be the President's fault. If use of heroin proliferates, some organized crime boss must be responsible. If crime in general proliferates, it must be the doing of some perverse group of offenders. Curing or eliminating social problems is regarded as synonymous with curing or eliminating individual culprits. Identify the culprits, bring them to justice (or perhaps help them to overcome personal deficiencies), and the problem will be solved. (Pepinsky, 1980:307)

By contrast, radical theory "assumes the dynamics of a social structure to be the source of crime and its control" (Pepinsky, 1980:308). Far more important than individuals are industrialization, technology, the division of labor, bureaucratic growth, and **social stratification.** Those elements of the social structure organize social relationships, govern the passage of law, and cause crime. If crime is to be controlled, "it is unnecessary and even counterproductive to identify criminals or potential criminals as a prelude to implementing crime control measures" (Pepinsky, 1980:309). Rather, attention should be devoted to changing the elements of the social structure that cause crime.

The idea of structural change, however, is not new. It was suggested by classic strain theorists, for example, when they recommended programs to improve educational and economic opportunities among lower-class youths. Nonetheless, the idea is a challenging one. In place of identifying and blaming individuals for delinquency, much might be accomplished by changing the structure and organization of social institutions. However, because radicals have failed to outline a strategy for doing this, radical theory has been seriously criticized; a few of those criticisms are described here.

ESCHEWING REFORMS Downes (1979:11) suggested that "by equating specifiable and documented proposals for change with 'mere' reformism, by—indeed—dismissing the ideal of gradual and therefore reversible change as contemptible," radicals have left us without any clue as to what should be done. Thus, because they have made a virtue out of obfuscation, they should not be too surprised when others view their proposals with caution.

Pepinsky (1980:299–300), himself a radical theorist, was even more caustic. He contended that by suggesting that the only real criminals are rich capitalists, Marxists have done no better than liberal criminologists. Instead of outlining ways for changing the social structure, they simply blame the rich and "would resocialize, or even liquidate," them (p. 300). Even more importantly, they have provided no assurance that if working-class people were to assume power, they would somehow be more humane, more wise, and more just than those whom they were replacing:

> Even Marx ... himself conceded that political revolution alone was insufficient to rid a social system of class oppression and its by-product, crime. Incapacitation of the rich and powerful cannot succeed in ending class oppression unless the revolutionaries themselves are disinclined to achieve wealth and power for themselves. Incapacitation of the rich and powerful itself implies a lust by some to gain power over others. It presages the rise to power of a "new class" (Djilas, 1957) of offenders, not an end to criminality. (Pepinsky, 1980:307; for similar statements, see Bohm, 1982:581–582)

It is little wonder, then, that criminologists have been slow to consider the notion that the only solu-

tion to the crime problem is a proletarian revolution. There is little to suggest that such a solution would be viable.

LOGICAL DEFICIENCIES Radical theory also possesses some logical deficiencies that make it virtually impossible to prove or disprove. The most serious deficiency is its circularity—repression is inferred from capitalist society, and capitalist society is explained by repression. Values that produce sexism, racism, poverty, and crime are, at one and the same time, both the causes and consequences of capitalism.

But circularity is not the only problem with radical theory. In relying on the dialectical-conflict theory of social order, radical theorists have maintained that history is characterized by a succession of economic orders in which the law inevitably reflects the interests of the powerful. "The problem with this position is that it can never specify the conditions under which law would not be simply an instrument of a currently powerful interest" (Taylor, Walton, and Young, 1973:266).

Every society allocates power and status according to some set of criteria. Indeed, social stratification is not unique to capitalism. The Egyptians, for example, enslaved the Jews, as did the Romans and the Babylonians. Moreover, women in most societies have been subservient to men, and children tend to be treated differently from adults. Yet, "critical criminologists too often write as if imperialism was monopolised by capitalist societies, as if the tanks had never rolled into Prague or Budapest, as if people in capitalist societies were utterly dehumanised (except where they are struggling heroically against the bosses)" (Downes, 1979:9).

This does not mean that exploitation and discrimination should be considered inevitable. Nor does it mean that radicals have failed to ask important questions about capitalism. Rather, the problem is that they have allowed their inquiry to *stop* at capitalism, as if oppression and corruption were limited to capitalist societies (Downes, 1979:9). China and Cuba often are cited as socialist countries whose streets are relatively safe. But the same is also true of Norway, Finland, and Sweden, all of which are capitalist, welfare countries. Why is this? Moreover, countries such as China and Cuba are not democratic; their citizens scarcely possess such things as freedom of choice, speech, and movement (consider the 1989 massacre of student protesters in Tiananmen Square in Beijing, China). Yet, because of their preoccupation with the weaknesses of capitalism, radical theorists have paid scant attention to those matters. As a result, radicals supply no alternative body of knowledge by which their assertions can be assessed (Bottomore, 1972:4–5; Schichor, 1980: 10–14).

ALTERNATIVES FOR VIEWING RADICAL THEORY
Given those problems, there are two alternatives for interpreting radical theory. The first is to ignore its deficiencies and accept it as a perspective that is not to be confused with scientific theory. This is an attractive alternative because humankind always has aspired to create a civilized utopia in which intolerance, exploitation, and crime no longer exist. Once the repressive rules of modern society are eliminated, love, brotherhood, and freedom will prevail.

The second alternative is to formulate and test new theories in which the insights of radical theory are combined with those of other theories (Groves and Sampson, 1987). As we will see shortly, a few theorists have used radical theory in exactly this way. Cultural deviance, strain, control, and even symbolic interactionist theories can be integrated with radical theory to shed light on the effects of social structure and the need for altering that structure to reduce delinquency (for a contrasting view, see Barak, 1987; Bohm, 1987).

Likewise, neither a conflict nor a consensus framework alone is adequate for explaining the origins and maintenance of social order, but both have something to offer (Dahrendorf, 1959:Chap. 5; Greenberg, 1976:611–612; Hills, 1971:5–6; Hopkins, 1975:612–614). Many of our laws, for example, seem to reflect a high degree of *consensus*—laws that prohibit murder, assault, fraud, embezzlement, or rape. The interests of most people, not just the powerful, are served by them. Other laws produce *conflict* and seem to be expressions of special interests—for example, laws that prohibit marijuana use, gambling, or vagrancy. More attention could be devoted to the historical and structural origins of both types of laws.

If that second alternative were chosen, however, it would not lend itself to the optimistic outlook inherent in radical theory. Radicals are correct in ob-

serving that most criminologists are skeptical that delinquency and other forms of deviant behavior can ever be eliminated. Most scholars believe that we must be leery of utopian schemes because crime is a normal aspect of human life (Durkheim, 1966: Chap. 3). It is virtually impossible to conceive of a society in which all passion, innovation, and inclination to rebel would be so effectively controlled that deviant behavior would be nonexistent. Hence, the idea that crime can be eliminated "involves a particularly trivial kind of utopian dreaming" (Bittner, 1970:49).

The argument is not merely that people will forever remain bad, but that the standards of morality are changing constantly. Consider Durkheim's (1966: 68–69) classic allegory:

> Imagine a society of saints, a perfect cloister of exemplary individuals. Crimes, properly so called, will there be unknown; but faults which appear venial to the layman will create there the same scandal that the ordinary offense does in ordinary consciousness. If, then, this society has the power to judge and punish, it will define these acts as criminal and will treat them as such.

What Durkheim meant was that

> if all those acts we know as crime were extinguished, small differences in behaviour that have no moral significance [at present] would take on new and larger meaning [in the future]. Small improprieties and breaches of manners and good taste would become serious crimes; lesser improprieties would become crimes of a lesser degree, and so on. In short, there *cannot* be a society of saints because a process of social redefinition operates continuously to insure that all the positions on the scale from wickedness to virtue will always be filled and that some will always be holier than others. (Cohen, 1974:5)

In other words, the solution to a current set of problems inevitably produces its own set of new problems. Humans seem to have a chronic tendency to redefine misery, injustice, delinquency, or poverty in such a way that regardless of what we do about them, they are always with us (Cohen, 1974:5). For example, rates of malnutrition, infant mortality, and disease no doubt were higher during the Middle Ages than they are today. But we are no less concerned about them. Even if life is improved according to today's standards, it will be marked by serious problems according to tomorrow's standards; and some people will be defined as deviant for violating those standards.

RECENT DEVELOPMENTS IN RADICAL THEORY

Like many delinquency theories, radical theory has been revised in response to criticism of initial statements of the theory. In fact, since the mid-1980s, at least four new variations of radical theory have emerged, the most prominent of which is the **power-control theory** developed by John Hagan and his colleagues. It is too early to establish with any precision how accurate these new versions of radical theory are, but there is some cause for optimism. At the very least, all four versions are more sophisticated than the simple radical invective that capitalist exploitation leads to crime among the oppressed. Importantly, several of the new versions combine radical theory's emphasis on class analysis with concepts and arguments from other delinquency theories. The four new variants of radical theory, and when possible their empirical adequacy, are summarized here.

Hagan's Power-Control Theory of Gender and Delinquency

We have seen that because females tend to be more oppressed than males, radical theorists have considerable difficulty in explaining why males are more likely to violate the law. Furthermore, it has been argued that much might be gained from combining radical theory with other theories. With those points in mind, a new theory by Hagan, Gillis, and Simpson (1985; Hagan, 1985:267–274; Hagan, Simpson, and Gillis, 1987) merits attention in that it focuses on gender differences in delinquency by integrating insights from Marxian theory with those from social control theory and the classical school of criminology.

Hagan and his associates (1985) described their theory as a "neo-Marxian, class-based, power-control theory of gender and delinquency" (p. 1151), one that focuses on minor types of delinquency such as petty theft and vandalism (pp. 1161–1162). While observing that delinquency is related more strongly to gender than to social class, they contended that the class membership of parents should condition the relationship between gender and delinquency. The emphasis on social class is not unique to radical theory. As we saw earlier, it is a key variable in many other theories of delinquency (recall, for example, Cohen's version of strain theory). Instead, what makes the Hagan–Gillis–Simpson theory Marxian is the way they conceptualized class. Rather than categorizing people into upper, middle, and lower classes (categorizations based on gradational differences), they focused on occupational control regarding the means of production. That is, they distinguished two class positions related to whether parents' occupations place them in positions of control over other persons (1987:795). If they are employers or supervisors (and, hence, exercise control over others), they are members of the **command class.** If they do not have control over others in their jobs (they take orders or are under someone else's supervision), they belong to the **obey class.**

The class position of parents is important because of its implications for child-rearing styles. Hagan and his associates (1987:791–798) saw contemporary families as varying between two extremes: patriarchal and egalitarian. In *patriarchal* families, typically, the husband is in the command class while the wife is in the obey class, either because of the nature of her occupation (one that does not involve control over other persons) or because she is not employed outside of the home. In *egalitarian* families, both parents are in the same class, either command or obey. Families with both parents in command occupations are higher class, and families with both parents in obey occupations (including families in which the husband is a worker with no control over others and the wife is not employed) are lower in the class structure. Female-headed households are considered to be egalitarian families because of the absence of male domination, and they usually are low in the class structure.

The theory's basic argument was that the power of spouses relative to each other strongly affects the social control of sons and daughters. In patriarchal families, daughters are expected to focus on domestic tasks and thus are subjected to more intense control than sons, who are given more freedom and are more strongly encouraged to take risks. The situation in egalitarian families is different. Even in families in which both the husband and wife are in the command (higher) class, parents "will redistribute their control efforts so that daughters are subjected to controls more like those imposed on sons" (p. 792). Both daughters and sons in egalitarian families have more freedom, are encouraged by their parents to take risks, and perceive a lower risk of punishment. Hence, in egalitarian families, including female-headed households, the delinquency of girls should be more equal to that of boys. The general logic of power-control theory can be diagrammed as shown in figure 14.1.

Because power-control theory is so new, there have been only a few tests of its adequacy. By and large, those studies have provided a mixed picture of its accuracy. One test by Hill and Atkinson (1988) addressed a key argument in the theory: whether the objects of parental control are more likely to be girls than boys. In a sample of Illinois youths, Hill and Atkinson (1988:142–143) found some evidence for such a pattern, but the main difference among boys and girls was the *kind* of parental control to which they were subjected rather than the *degree*. Boys reported that they were subjected to more appearance rules (with appearance rules inferred from responses to such questions as, "In your home, are there any rules about how you wear your hair?"). In contrast, girls indicated that they were more likely to have curfew rules (inferred from answers to such questions

as, "In your home, are there any rules for you about weeknight curfews?").

Hagan, Gillis, and Simpson's (1987) test of the theory provided much stronger support. They found greater male–female differences in delinquency among patriarchal families than among egalitarian and single-parent families. This was due mainly to the higher level of female delinquency in the latter two family types, which led the researchers to conclude that "daughters are freest to be delinquent in families in which mothers either share power equally with fathers or do not share power with fathers at all" (Hagan, Gillis, and Simpson, 1987:812).

However, findings from a test by Singer and Levine (1988) contradicted power-control theory in many ways. Singer and Levine found that male–female differences in parental controls, risk taking, and self-reported delinquency were greater in egalitarian than in patriarchal households. Moreover, mothers in egalitarian households exerted relatively more control over their daughters than did mothers in patriarchal households. However, at least partially consistent with power-control theory, Singer and Levine (1988:639) reported that "girls who become delinquent in balanced [egalitarian] households do so because they are more willing to take risks than girls in unbalanced [patriarchal] households. Not only are they more willing to take risks, but girls in balanced households also perceive less chance of punishment than do girls in unbalanced households."

In another test, Jensen and Thompson (1990: 1013–1015) found little or no relationship between class and minor self-reported delinquency (which is consistent with most findings on that issue—see

FIGURE 14.1

The underlying logic of power-control theory

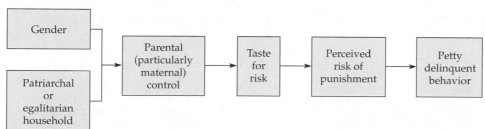

Chapter 5). Moreover, like Singer and Levine, Jensen and Thompson did not find greater male–female differences in delinquency in the higher classes (pp. 1015–1016).[2]

Two studies by Harold Grasmick and his colleagues examined risk taking among adults rather than youths, and each strongly supported power-control theory. Analyzing survey data from adults in Oklahoma City, Grasmick, Blackwell, and Bursik (1993) found that between 1982 and 1992, there was a convergence between males and females in their perceived risk of legal punishments for theft. That finding is important because there was a gradual shift to less patriarchal family structures during that same period. Moreover, using similar Oklahoma City data for 1993, Grasmick and his colleagues (1996:188) found that among adults, "men and women whose families of origin were less patriarchal do not differ significantly in their risk preferences, but among those raised in more patriarchal families men have a greater preference for risk than women."

Colvin and Pauly's Integrated Structural-Marxist Theory

The **integrated structural-Marxist theory** put forth by Colvin and Pauly (1983) was similar to power-control theory in its focus on how parents' social control experiences in the workplace affect control strategies used at home. But Colvin and Pauly's focus was different in two ways. First, they were concerned with the type of control to which workers *are exposed,* not the amount of control that they *exert.* Second, they did not address the role that gender plays either in workplace or family control or in delinquency. Rather than explaining convergence or divergence in male and female rates of minor delinquency, Pauly and Colvin attempted to explain both minor and serious delinquency among all youths.

Their theory's basic premise is this: "The relations of workplace control, which take various class-related forms under capitalism, shape the con-

sciousness and behavior of parents who repeatedly produce and reproduce control relations with children" (Colvin and Pauly, 1983:514). In short, people's occupations affect the type of control they experience at work, which in turn affects their perspectives on authority and the manner in which they control their children.

Colvin and Pauly (1983:532) borrowed heavily from Edwards (1979) and Etzioni (1970) in distinguishing among three different types of workers and the workplace control to which they are exposed. *Fraction I* workers have low-skill, nonunion jobs in which the principal control mechanism is *coercive* power—power that relies on such sanctions as job dismissal, which effectively removes workers' means for satisfying basic needs. *Fraction II* jobs are higher-skill jobs that may be unionized. The required higher skills and the protective benefits of unionization preclude employers' reliance on job dismissal. Instead, control follows from *remunerative* power—the manipulation of behavior through such positive rewards as job promotions and pay raises. *Fraction III* workers also are highly skilled and include technical staff, craft workers, and salaried professionals. The key aspects of these jobs are that they "require independent initiative and self-pacing," involve less external oversight, and tend to hold considerable intrinsic meaning for workers (Edwards, 1979:174). The principal control mechanism is *normative* power, which "rests on the allocation and manipulation of symbolic rewards" and elicits a "moral involvement" among workers toward their jobs and employers (Etzioni, 1970:104).

Colvin and Pauly argued that parents use on their children the same type of control as they are exposed to at work. This, in turn, affects the strength of a child's *bond* to authority (used here in a way very similar to Hirschi's [1969] use of the term), which affects the likelihood that the child will commit delinquency. Colvin and Pauly (1983:536) made the following predictions:

> Parents from Fraction I of the working class, typified by more coercive workplace controls and more sporadic associations with specific workplaces, tend to enforce an uneven and erratic family control structure that swings unpredict-

---

[2]In a response to this study, Hagan, Gillis, and Simpson (1990) argued that the first finding is not contrary to power-control theory, given that the theory posits that social class should condition the effect of gender on delinquency, rather than predict delinquency itself (p. 1025). As for the second finding, they have been sharply critical of Jensen and Thompson's "gradational measures" of social class, which in their opinion, do not adequately assess respondents' control in the workplace (pp. 1025–1026).

ably between being lax and being highly punitive. . . . We expect more alienated bonds to be produced in children who experience such arbitrary, inconsistent, and coercive family control structures. Parents from fraction II of the working class, characterized by more steady and long-term association with a utilitarian compliance structure at work, tend to enforce a more utilitarian compliance structure in the family that produces calculative bonds of intermediate intensity in their children, who can dependably predict external consequences for behavior. Parents in more "self-directing" workplace situations [fraction III workers] . . . tend to enforce a more normative family compliance structure in which positive social bonds of high intensity are produced in children.

Moreover, a weak bond to the family has important implications for a child's school experiences. It results in such things as disruptive behavior and low IQ and academic motivation, which, in turn, lead the child to be placed in lower-level academic tracks that rely on the same coercive power used at home. Delinquent peer associations are likely to be developed in lower-level academic tracks because other students come from similarly coercive households. The main point, therefore, is that with each step down the class structure—from fraction III through fraction I—coercive family control increases and the strength of the bond to family authority decreases. In turn, coercive school control, delinquent peer associations, and involvement in delinquency all increase (Colvin and Pauly, 1983:544).

Because few tests have been conducted, it is difficult to assess the empirical adequacy of Colvin and Pauly's structural-Marxist theory. Indeed, only two tests have been conducted, and each shows that, consistent with the theory, parental work affects family and school control structures and peer associations, which, in turn, affect delinquency (Messner and Krohn, 1990; Simpson and Ellis, 1994).

Messerschmidt's Theory of Masculinities and Crime

Messerschmidt's (1993) variation on radical theory also was similar to power-control theory in its focus

on the intersection of class and gender in the production of delinquency. Messerschmidt's main emphasis was on the ways that youths from different social classes construct and express *masculinity*. Although many criminologists have focused on gender differences in delinquency, the focus typically has been on why females *do not* commit delinquency, not on why males *do* (Messerschmidt, 1993:4–25). Messerschmidt turned this around and argued that we need to understand male gender identity and how it is constructed differently in different social classes.

Messerschmidt's (1993:82) theory began with the premise that in Western, industrialized societies, masculinity involves "authority, control, competitive individualism, independence, aggressiveness, and the capacity for violence." Masculinity creates a tendency for rebellion among all adolescent males, but the nature and extent of rebellion varies by social class. Among middle-class males, masculinity can be achieved through academic success and involvement in sports. However, that is only partially satisfying because the school's emphasis on authority and obedience is emasculating. Outside of the school, the quest for masculinity involves minor "pranks" and "mischief," including vandalism, petty theft, and alcohol use. Importantly, those acts do not directly confront authority and are not likely to interfere with one's standing in school and pursuit of a good career, goals that are important among middle-class youths (pp. 93–96).

The situation is quite different for working-class white males. They also experience school authority as emasculating, but their disregard for education leads them to seek masculinity in terms of both in-school opposition and out-of-school rebellion. They perceive office jobs and bookwork as "sissy stuff" and believe that "'real men' choose manual, not mental labor" (p. 97). Their construction of delinquency, therefore, centers on a rejection of these things and those who represent them, such as teachers and good students, as well as a preference for such physical activities as fighting. Within school, they will be involved in "pranks," "mischief," and "mock fights"; their delinquency outside of school will be more frequent, and more violent, and sometimes will be motivated by a desire for money. Over time, however, they may commit less delinquency because of attachments to paid labor.

The situation for lower-class minority group members is the most extreme. Like working-class whites, they perceive the school as unrelated to future success, emasculating, and better suited for "wimps" (p. 104). But unlike working-class whites, they lack the resources to obtain a stable manual labor position. Under such conditions, they are "likely to employ other means of accomplishing gender. In particular, violent behavior, as a resource for an opposition masculine construction, is more likely to increase relative to youth of other class and race backgrounds" (p. 104). They are more likely to become members of street gangs that commit such violent crimes as robbery and engage in group violence such as "turf wars" (p. 105). Drawing on Katz (1988), Messerschmidt argued that robbery is unique because it provides "the ideal opportunity to construct an 'essential' toughness and 'maleness'; it provides a means with which to construct that certain type of masculinity—hardman" (p. 107).

No tests of Messerschmidt's theory have been conducted, although Messerschmidt (1993:87–153) himself argued that many ethnographic studies can be reinterpreted in ways that support the idea that a search for masculinity, conditioned by class, is a central cause of delinquency. However, Messerschmidt's reliance on ethnographic research may reveal a logical problem with the theory—namely, it predicts *too much* delinquency, especially violent behavior among working-class youths. The theory seems to imply that *all* lower-class youths, especially minority youths, will commit violence—masculinity can be gained in no other way.

Currie's Market Theory of Postindustrial Violence

One of the main problems with radical theory and other class-based theories is that many studies have found little or no relationship between social class and delinquency. However, Elliott Currie's (1997) version of radical theory differs from others in that it does not necessarily rely on the existence of such a relationship. Rather than asking why lower-class youths commit more delinquency than middle-class youths, Currie asks this question: Why do some capitalist societies have much higher rates of violence

than others? Currie's (1997:151) answer is that "varying levels of serious criminal violence across the 'post-industrial' societies are closely tied to the greater or lesser growth of what I call 'market society.'" By **market society,** Currie (1997:151–152) means a society in which

> the pursuit of personal economic gain becomes increasingly the dominant organizing principle of social life; a social formation in which market principles, instead of being confined to some parts of the *economy*, and appropriately buffered and restrained by other social institutions and norms, come to suffuse the whole social fabric. . . . Market societies, in short, are Darwinian societies. . . . They are "sink or swim" societies.

Currie argues that to the extent that society is dominated by market principles, it will have high rates of violence. Currie argues further that seven mechanisms work *in conjunction with one another* to increase rates of violence:

1. *Market society breeds violent crime by destroying livelihood.* The long-term absence of opportunities for stable and rewarding work leads to alienation and reduces people's stakes in legitimate society:

   > The fundamental problem is that in market society labor appears simply as a cost to be reduced rather than a social institution valuable in its own right. . . . [The] central thrust of market society [is] . . . to cheapen labor and/or eliminate it altogether. The result is a . . . proliferation of low-wage, high turnover jobs, endemic structural unemployment, or some combination of both. (p. 155)

2. *Market society has an inherent tendency toward extremes of inequality and material deprivation* (p. 157). Although inequality and material deprivation may not always explain why some individuals, and not others, commit violence, they do explain why violence rates are higher in some societies than others (Gartner, 1990; Messner, 1989).

3. *Market society weakens other kinds of public support that act as strong buffers against crime.* Because a "basic operating principle of market society [is] to keep the public sector small, it

forces individuals and families to rely on individual efforts to secure some of the basics of healthy human development" that other societies, even poor ones, may provide more readily (p. 159). For example, low wages and a lack of public support may lead workers to hold several part-time jobs, which may deprive their children of attention and support.

4. *Market society erodes informal social supports and networks of care that act as buffers against crime.* The rapid movement of financial capital, and thus, jobs, necessitates the geographic mobility of workers, thereby eroding the stability and cohesion of families and communities: Worker flexibility "translates into rootlessness for individuals and families and atomization for communities" (p. 160).

5. *Market society promotes a culture that exalts individual competition and consumption over the values of community, contribution, and productive work.* Although much attention has been devoted to the violent culture of the *underclass,* we cannot hope to understand violent crime "unless we view it within the context of the growth and spread of a dominant culture of exploitation, predation and indifference to human life" (p. 162).

6. *Market society deregulates the technology of violence.* Free-market principles increase the availability of a product, regardless of its potential harms (pp. 164–165).

7. *Market society weakens or erodes alternative political values and institutions.* Many of the problems described here could be reduced by organized social movements, such as labor movements, but the individualist culture of a market society discourages people from defining their problems in collective terms and envisioning a collective response (p. 166).

Before tests of Currie's theory can be conducted, a way for measuring a society's *market orientation* will need to be identified. One possible measure is the *gross national product* per capita—the total value of goods and services produced by a society in a given year, divided by the number of people in the population. However, using a similar measure, Kick and Lafree's (1985) study of forty societies provides evidence that is inconsistent with Currie's theory—namely, that the more economically developed societies have *lower* rates of homicide, not higher rates.[3]

SUMMARY AND CONCLUSIONS

Radical theory cannot be viewed in the same way that positivist theories are viewed. Instead, it is built on an entirely different set of philosophical principles.

The cornerstone of the positivistic philosophy is the Enlightenment notion that the scientific study of human affairs will lead to a better world. Although knowledge can be gained only by patience, skepticism, and tolerance of uncertainty, scientific investigation will contribute ultimately to humankind's long search for a more just and humane society.

Radical theorists have argued that faith in science not only reflects questionable values but also is naive. By clinging to a positivistic philosophy, scientists not only fail to eliminate oppression and injustice but give tacit approval to those who have perpetuated them. Radical theorists, as a consequence, have suggested that criminologists should be guided by values that oppose the status quo. Because delinquency results from capitalist oppression, criminologists should be documenting that oppression, making the public aware of it, and joining in socialist revolution.

Radical theorists have stressed research and action that involve predetermined socialist goals, while positivists have stressed tentativeness and scholarly detachment in the pursuit of goals that are not always predetermined. Because ultimate truth is unknown, scientists must keep an open mind while pursuing it. More than positivist theories, radical theory is doctrinal in character: It expresses beliefs that are laid down as true and beyond serious dispute. What, then, are those beliefs?

Assumptions About Human Nature and Social Order

Radical theorists have assumed that human nature is good. Were people not enslaved by the historical

---

[3]The findings might have been different if only advanced industrial societies—the focus of Currie's theory—had been included in the study. Additionally, Currie's discussion seems to imply a more elaborate conceptualization of market society than GNP per capita.

struggle among the classes, their humane inclinations would produce an enlightened and liberated society. The social order, by contrast, is characterized by conflict and coercion, and maintained through the oppression of the masses by society's rulers.

Underlying Logic and Content of Radical Theory

The history of civilization has been characterized by a succession of economic arrangements in which the powerful have always exploited the weak. The period of advanced capitalism now existing in the United States is the latest development in that series of arrangements. A modern society like ours, its laws, and its legal system are organized to serve the capitalist ruling class. Delinquency, therefore, is any behavior that threatens the interests of that class.

Policy Implications of Radical Theory

Delinquency cannot be eliminated by working within the framework of a capitalist society or by attempting to reform its system of juvenile justice. The only solution lies in the formation of class consciousness, the overthrow of capitalism, and the creation of a socialist society.

Assessment of Radical Theory

Radical theorists have extended the boundaries of knowledge in several important ways. They have cast doubts on the usefulness of positivistic philosophy, analyzed social conflict and its role in maintaining social order, stressed a better understanding of law and legal practice, and pointed out the persistence of sexism, racism, and exploitation in modern society. Moreover, Marxian theory, one of the principal sources for radical theory, has been an impetus for several new theories that could bridge the gap between radical and positive theories.

At the same time, radical theory is marked by serious deficiencies:

1. It presents a circular argument that is virtually impossible to test.
2. By insisting that social order is always characterized by conflict, it cannot specify the conditions under which the law would not be an instrument of some powerful group. Yet, it concludes that socialist societies will be characterized by cooperation, fraternity, and equality.
3. In relying solely on the notion that crime is an artifact of political and economic oppression, it tends to deny that the criminal label is ever earned by offenders or that their personal motivations, however induced, are important in explaining their behaviors.
4. It holds that crime will disappear in liberated societies, but it also maintains that capitalists are criminals. How will these enemies of socialism be treated? Will they not be defined as criminals?
5. It denies the possibility that cultural forces other than those that are political and economic have been instrumental in the creation of childhood and the invention of delinquency.
6. In concentrating on class conflict, it ignores that age and gender are more closely related to the commission of delinquent acts than is social class.

Given those deficiencies, several questions might be raised. The first is concerned with the nature of radical philosophy. Radicals are correct in suggesting that positivist criminologists have tended to confine their research to the context provided by existing values and laws and that this practice sometimes gives tacit approval to injustice. But what about the radical approach to research? What if investigators insisted on conducting research in which only their values provided the context for analysis? Would this not be like the anthropologist who goes to a foreign country, and without trying to understand the values that give rise to behavior there, judges that society as inferior because it does not conform to his or her values?

In some ways, that is what radical theorists have done. Like Marx, they have been more intent on using research to justify conclusions they have already reached than on weighing carefully both the pros and cons of their arguments. That approach to research is an old one, but it is closer to the version used by lawyers and debaters than that used by scientists. The object of science is not to win a legal case or a debate, but to weigh evidence on both sides of a question.

It must be pointed out, however, that positivists also have not been free of this problem. For a century now, the changing construction of delinquency has sometimes been as much the result of new values and beliefs as of scientific evidence. Earlier groups of social scientists did not reject biological explanations or Freudian theory for scientific reasons alone. Instead, their objections often were as value-laden and political as those of the radical movement today.

Hence, the differences between radicals and positivists are not absolute, but rather a matter of degree. Although positivists remain relatively more skeptical about the ultimate truth of their theories and proposed reforms, their personal values are apparent in their work nonetheless.

For those reasons, the ultimate test of radical theory will remain much the same as it has for the positivist school. Its acceptance as a philosophy and as a method for studying and responding to delinquency will depend, in part, on its doctrinal character and, in part, on the evidence that can be found to support it. Thus far, the doctrine is stronger than the evidence.

DISCUSSION QUESTIONS

1. How did Hegel account for human progress and social change? How did Marx modify Hegel's ideas?
2. What has been the main policy impact of radical theory?
3. What critiques have been made of radical theorists' attempts to explain delinquency?
4. What is the basic argument in power-control theory?
5. What is the basic argument in Colvin and Pauly's integrated structural-Marxist theory?

REFERENCES

Adler, Jeffrey S. 1989. A Historical Analysis of the Law of Vagrancy." *Criminology* 27 (May): 209–229.

Barak, Gregg. 1987. "Comment on 'Traditional Contributions to Radical Criminology' by Groves and Sampson." *Journal of Research in Crime and Delinquency* 24 (November):332–335.

Bittner, Egon. 1970. *The Functions of the Police in Modern Society: A Review of Background Factors,* *Current Practices, and Possible Role Models.* Washington, D.C.: U.S. Government Printing Office.

Bohm, Robert M. 1982. "Radical Criminology: An Explication." *Criminology* 19 (February): 565–589.
1987. "Comment on 'Traditional Contributions to Radical Criminology' by Groves and Sampson." *Journal of Research in Crime and Delinquency* 24 (November):324–331.

Bottomore, Tom. 1972. "Introduction." Pp. 1–8 in *Varieties of Political Expression in Sociology.* Special issue of *American Journal of Sociology* 78 (July):1–220.

Burns, Hayward. 1974. "Racism and American Law." Pp. 263–274 in Richard Quinney, ed., *Criminal Justice in America: A Critical Understanding.* Boston: Little, Brown.

Chambliss, William J. 1964. "A Sociological Analysis of the Law of Vagrancy." *Social Problems* 12 (Summer):67–77.
1973. *Functional and Conflict Theories of Crime.* New York: MSS Modular Publications.
1976. "Functional and Conflict Theories of Crime: The Heritage of Emile Durkheim and Karl Marx." Pp. 1–28 in William J. Chambliss and Milton Mankoff, eds., *Whose Law? What Order?: A Conflict Approach to Criminology.* New York: Wiley.
1984. *Criminal Law in Action,* 2nd ed. New York: Wiley.

Cohen, Albert K. 1974. *The Elasticity of Evil: Changes in the Social Definition of Deviance.* Oxford: Oxford University Penal Research Unit by Basil Blackwell.

Cohen, Lawrence E., and James R. Kluegel. 1978. "Determinants of Juvenile Court Dispositions: Ascriptive and Achieved Factors in Two Metropolitan Courts." *American Sociological Review* 43 (April):162–176.
1979. "The Detention Decision: A Study of the Impact of Social Characteristics and Legal Factors in Two Metropolitan Juvenile Courts." *Social Forces* 58 (September):146–161.

Cole, G. D. H. 1964. "Capitalism." Pp. 70–72 in Julius Gould and William L. Kolb, eds., *A*

Dictionary of the Social Sciences. New York: Free Press.

Colvin, Mark, and John Pauly. 1983. "A Critique of Criminology: Toward an Integrated Stuctural-Marxist Theory of Delinquency Production." *American Journal of Sociology* 89 (November): 513–551.

Currie, Elliott. 1997. "Market, Crime and Community: Toward a Mid-Range Theory of Post-Industrial Violence." *Theoretical Criminology* 2 (May):147–172.

Dahrendorf, Ralf. 1958. "Out of Utopia: Toward a Reorientation of Sociological Analysis." *American Journal of Sociology* 64 (September):115–127.
1959. *Class and Class Conflict in Industrial Society.* Stanford, Calif.: Stanford University Press.

Dannefer, Dale, and Russell K. Schutt. 1982. "Race and Juvenile Justice Processing in Court and Police Agencies." *American Journal of Sociology* 87 (March):1113–1132.

Djilas, Milovan. 1957. *The New Class: An Analysis of the Communist System.* New York: Praeger.

Downes, David. 1979. "Praxis Makes Perfect: A Critique of Critical Criminology." Pp. 1–16 in David Downes and Paul Rock, eds., *Deviant Interpretations.* New York: Barnes & Noble.

Durkheim, Emile. 1964. *The Division of Labor in Society.* Translated by George Simpson. New York: Free Press.
1966. *The Rules of Sociological Method.* Translated by Sarah A. Solovay and John H. Mueller; edited by George E. G. Catlin. New York: Free Press.

Edwards, Richard. 1979. *Contested Terrain: The Transformation of the Workplace in the Twentieth Century.* New York: Basic Books.

Edwards, Richard C., Michael Reich, and Thomas E. Weisskopf. 1974. "Toward a Socialist Alternative." Pp. 429–434 in Richard Quinney, ed., *Criminal Justice in America: A Critical Understanding.* Boston: Little, Brown.

Engels, Friedrich. 1942. *The Origin of the Family, Private Property and the State.* New York: International.

Farnworth, Margaret, Terence P. Thornberry, Marvin D. Krohn, and Alan J. Lizotte. 1994. "Measurement in the Study of Class and Delinquency: Integrating Theory and Research." *Journal of Research in Crime and Delinquency* 31 (February): 32–61.

Farson, Richard. 1974. *Birthrights.* New York: Macmillan.
1975. "Busing Violates the Rights of Children." *Los Angeles Times,* January 28, Section 2, p. 5.

Friedan, Betty. 1963. *The Feminine Mystique.* New York: Norton.

Fuller, Lon L. 1971. "Human Interaction and the Law." Pp. 171–217 in Robert P. Wolff, ed., *The Rule of Law.* New York: Simon & Schuster.

Gartner, Rosemary. 1990. "The Victims of Homicide: A Temporal and Cross-National Comparison." *American Sociological Review* 55 (February): 92–106.

Geshwender, James A. 1980a. "On Analyzing Race Relations Without Theory." *Contemporary Sociology* 9 (March):215–218.
1980b. "Response to Grimshaw and Glazer." *Contemporary Sociology* 9 (September):601–603.

Glazer, Nathan. 1980. "Comment on a Review Which Denies Black Progress." *Contemporary Sociology* 9 (September):599–600.

Grasmick, Harold G., Brenda Sims Blackwell, and Robert J. Bursik, Jr. 1993. "Changes in the Sex Patterning of Perceived Threats of Sanctions." *Law and Society Review* 27 (November):679–705.

Grasmick, Harold G., John Hagan, Brenda Sims Blackwell, and Bruce J. Arneklev. 1996. "Risk Preferences and Patriarchy: Extending Power-Control Theory." *Social Forces* 75 (September): 177–179.

Greenberg, David F. 1976. "On One-Dimensional Marxist Criminology." *Theory and Society* 3 (Winter):611–621.
1977. "Delinquency and the Age Structure of Society." *Contemporary Crises* 1 (April):189–223.

Grimshaw, Allen D. 1980. "A Different Perspective on *Mutual Accommodation.*" *Contemporary Sociology* 9 (September):600–601.

Groves, W. Byron, and Robert J. Sampson. 1987. "Traditional Contributions to Radical Criminology." *Journal of Research in Crime and Delinquency* 24 (August):181–214.

Hagan, John. 1985. *Modern Criminology: Crime, Criminal Behavior, and Its Control.* New York: McGraw-Hill.

Hagan, John, A. R. Gillis, and John Simpson. 1985. "The Class Structure of Gender and Delinquency: Toward a Power-Control Theory of Common Delinquent Behavior." *American Journal of Sociology* 90 (May):1151–1178.
1990. "Clarifying and Extending Power-Control Theory." *American Journal of Sociology* 95 (January):1024–1037.

Hagan, John, and Jeffrey Leon. 1977. "Rediscovering Delinquency: Social History, Political Ideology and the Sociology of Law." *American Sociological Review* 42 (August):587–598.

Hagan, John, John Simpson, and A. R. Gillis. 1987. "Class in the Household: A Power-Control Theory of Gender and Delinquency." *American Journal of Sociology* 92 (January):788–816.

Hill, Gary D., and Maxine P. Atkinson. 1988. "Gender, Familial Control, and Delinquency." *Criminology* 26 (February):127–149.

Hills, Stuart L. 1971. *Crime, Power, and Morality.* Scranton, Pa.: Chandler.

Hirschi, Travis. 1969. *Causes of Delinquency.* Berkeley: University of California Press.

Hirst, Paul Q. 1975. "Marx and Engels on Law, Crime and Morality." Pp. 203–232 in Ian Taylor, Paul Walton, and Jock Young, eds., *Critical Criminology.* Boston: Routledge & Kegan Paul.

Hoebel, E. Adamson. 1976. *The Law of Primitive Man.* New York: Atheneum. (Originally published in 1954 by Harvard University Press.)

Holt, John. 1974. *Escape from Childhood.* New York: Dutton.

Hopkins, Andrew. 1975. "On the Sociology of Criminal Law." *Social Problems* 22 (June):608–619.

Jensen, Gary F., and Kevin Thompson. 1990. "What's Class Got to Do with It? A Further Examination of Power-Control Theory." *American Journal of Sociology* 95 (January):1009–1023.

Karmen, Andrew A. 1995. "Crime Victims." Pp. 145–164 in Joseph F. Sheley, ed., *Criminology: A Contemporary Handbook.* Belmont, CA: Wadsworth.

Katz, Jack. 1988. *Seductions of Crime: Moral and Sensual Attractions in Doing Evil.* New York: Basic Books.

Kick, Edward L., and Gary D. Lafree. 1985. "Development and the Social Context of Murder and Theft." *Comparative Social Research* 8:37–57.

Krisberg, Barry, and James Austin. 1978. *The Children of Ishmael: Critical Perspectives on Juvenile Justice.* Palo Alto, Calif.: Mayfield.

Marris, Peter, and Martin Rein. 1973. *Dilemmas of Social Reform: Poverty and Community Action in the United States,* 2nd ed. Chicago: Aldine.

Marx, Karl, and Friedrich Engels. 1948. *The Communist Manifesto.* Edited by S. H. Beer. New York: International.

McCarthy, Brenda R., and Brent L. Smith. 1986. "The Conceptualization of Discrimination in the Juvenile Justice Process: The Impact of Administrative Factors and Screening Decisions on Juvenile Court Dispositions." *Criminology* 24 (February):41–64.

McCord, Colin, and Harold P. Freeman. 1990. "Excess Mortality in Harlem." *The New England Journal of Medicine* 322 (January):173–177.

Meier, Robert F. 1976. "The New Criminology: Continuity in Criminological Theory." *Journal of Criminal Law and Criminology* 67 (December):461–469.

Merton, Robert K. 1968. *Social Theory and Social Structure,* enlarged ed. New York: Free Press.

Messerschmidt, James M. 1993. *Masculinities and Crime: Critique and Reconceptualization of Theory.* Lanham, MD: Rowman & Littlefield.

Messner, Steven F. 1989. "Economic Discrimination and Homicide Rates: Further Evidence on the

Cost of Inequality." *American Sociological Review* 54 (August):597–612.

Messner, Steven F., and Marvin Krohn. 1990. "Class Compliance Structures and Delinquency: Assessing Integrated Structural-Marxist Theory." *American Journal of Sociology* 96 (September): 300–328.

Meyer, Alfred G. 1968. "Marxism." Pp. 40–46 in David L. Sills, ed., *International Encyclopedia of the Social Sciences,* Vol. 10. New York: Macmillan.

Miliband, Ralph. 1969. *The State in Capitalist Society.* London: Weidenfeld & Nicolson.

Millett, Kate. 1970. *Sexual Politics.* New York: Doubleday.

Moynihan, Daniel P. 1969. *Maximum Feasible Misunderstanding: Community Action in the War on Poverty.* New York: Free Press.

Nelson, William E. 1974. "Emerging Notions of Modern Criminal Law in the Revolutionary Era: An Historical Perspective." Pp. 100–126 in Richard Quinney, ed., *Criminal Justice in America: A Critical Understanding.* Boston: Little, Brown.

Pepinsky, Harold E. 1980. "A Radical Alternative to 'Radical' Criminology." Pp. 299–315 in James A. Inciardi, ed., *Radical Criminology: The Coming Crises.* Beverly Hills, Calif.: Sage.

Peterson, Ruth D., and John Hagan. 1984. "Changing Conceptions of Race: Towards an Account of Anomalous Findings of Sentencing Research." *American Sociological Review* 49 (February): 56–70.

Piven, Frances F., and Richard A. Cloward. 1971. *Regulating the Poor: The Functions of Public Welfare.* New York: Pantheon Books.

Platt, Anthony M. 1971. "Introduction to the Reprint Edition." Pp. v–xvi in *National Conference of Charities and Correction, History of Child Saving in the United States.* Montclair, N.J.: Patterson Smith.
1974. "The Triumph of Benevolence: The Origins of the Juvenile Justice System in the United States." Pp. 356–389 in Richard Quinney, ed.,

Criminal Justice in America: A Critical Understanding. Boston: Little, Brown.

Pound, Roscoe. 1922. *An Introduction to the Philosophy of Law.* New Haven, Conn.: Yale University Press.
1942. *Social Control Through Law.* New Haven, Conn.: Yale University Press.

Quinney, Richard. 1970. *The Social Reality of Crime.* Boston: Little, Brown.
1972. "The Ideology of Law: Notes for a Radical Alternative to Legal Repression." *Issues in Criminology* 7 (Winter):1–35.
1974. *Criminal Justice in America: A Critical Understanding.* Boston: Little, Brown.

Rafter, Nicole Hahn, and Elena M. Natalizia. 1981. "Marxist Feminism: Implications for Criminal Justice." *Crime and Delinquency* 27 (January): 81–98.

Sampson, Robert J. 1986. "Effects of Socioeconomic Context on Official Reaction to Juvenile Delinquency." *American Sociological Review* 51 (December):876–885.

Schaar, John H. 1974. "Legitimacy in the Modern State." Pp. 62–92 in Richard Quinney, ed., *Criminal Justice in America: A Critical Understanding.* Boston: Little, Brown.

Schichor, David. 1980. "The New Criminology: Some Critical Issues." *British Journal of Criminology* 20 (January):1–19.

Selznick, Philip. 1968. "The Sociology of Law." Pp. 50–59 in David L. Sills, ed., *International Encyclopedia of the Social Sciences,* Vol. 9. New York: Macmillan.

Simpson, Sally S., and Lori Ellis. 1994. "Is Gender Subordinate to Class? An Empirical Assessment of Colvin and Pauly's Structural Marxist Theory of Delinquency." *Journal of Criminal Law and Criminology* 85 (Fall):453–480.

Sinclair, Catherine M. 1983. "A Radical/Marxist Interpretation of Juvenile Justice in the United States." *Federal Probation* 47 (June):20–28.

Singer, Simon I., and Murray Levine. 1988. "Power-Control Theory, Gender, and Delinquency: A

Partial Replication with Additional Evidence on the Effects of Peers." *Criminology* 26 (November): 627–647.

Takagi, Paul. 1981. "Race, Crime, and Social Policy: A Minority Perspective." *Crime and Delinquency* 27 (January):48–63.

Taylor, A. J. P. 1967. "Introduction." Pp. 7–47 in Karl Marx and Friedrich Engels, *The Communist Manifesto*. Baltimore: Penguin Books.

Taylor, Ian, Paul Walton, and Jock Young. 1973. *The New Criminology*. New York: Harper & Row.

Terry, Robert M. 1967. "Discrimination in the Handling of Juvenile Offenders by Social-Control Agencies." *Journal of Research in Crime and Delinquency* 4 (July):218–230.

Thornberry, Terence P. 1973. "Race, Socioeconomic Status and Sentencing in the Juvenile Justice System." *Journal of Criminal Law and Criminology* 64 (March):90–98.

1979. "Sentencing Disparities in the Juvenile Justice System." *Journal of Criminal Law and Criminology* 70 (Summer):164–171.

Turk, Austin T. 1969. *Criminality and Legal Order*. Chicago: Rand McNally.

van den Berghe, Pierre L. 1963. "Dialectic and Functionalism: Toward a Theoretical Synthesis." *American Sociological Review* 28 (October): 695–705.

Waite, Linda J. 1981. "U.S. Women at Work," *Population Bulletin* 36(2). Washington, D.C.: Population Reference Bureau.

Williams, Robin W., Jr. 1977. *Mutual Accommodation: Ethnic Conflict and Cooperation*. Minneapolis: University of Minnesota Press.

Wilson, William J. 1978. *The Declining Significance of Race: Blacks and Changing American Institutions*. Chicago: University of Chicago Press.

THE COMPLEXITY OF BEHAVIOR
IS ONE REASON WHY EXISTING
THEORIES DO NOT ALWAYS
ADEQUATELY EXPLAIN
DELINQUENCY.

CHAPTER FIFTEEN

INTEGRATED THEORIES AND SOME CON-CLUSIONS ABOUT THEORIES OF DELIN-QUENT BEHAVIOR

We have considered various theories of delinquent behavior and research findings. We now should identify general conclusions that can be drawn from this vast array of information. This involves answering three questions: (1) Have the theories identified any causes that actually predict delinquent behavior? (2) Do the theories predict delinquent behavior with considerable accuracy? and (3) Given the causes identified, what are the appropriate policy implications? As we will see, answers to the first two questions affirm the value of several theories of delinquent behavior but also point to their limited capacities to predict delinquent behavior. **Theoretical integration** has emerged in response to that limitation. This involves combining the arguments of two or more theories to create a new theory.

CAUSES OF DELINQUENT BEHAVIOR

Delinquency theories have included several variables that actually predict delinquent behavior. These are discussed here.

Attachment to Parents

To a greater or lesser degree, several theories indicate that the ties between parents and children are important. If families lose control over their children (Shaw–McKay theory), if they are unable to prepare them to achieve in middle-class institutions (strain theory), or if the quality of their interpersonal relations is poor (social control theory), delinquent behavior is more likely.

Much more information is needed on the techniques used by parents to effectively raise their children. But research does suggest that if children have been disciplined with love and concern and if they like and respect their parents (social control theory), they will be less likely to be delinquent. Consequently, a postulate for which there is considerable empirical support is this: *The weaker the attachment between parents and children, the greater the likelihood of delinquent behavior.*

Attachment to School and Academic Achievement

Difficulty in school may be one of the best predictors of delinquency. If schools are disorganized or unduly segregate children from adult role models (cultural deviance theory), if schools frustrate students (strain theory), or if children do not respect their teachers and the authority of the school (social control theory), delinquent behavior will be more likely. In general, research has tended to confirm this postulate: *The weaker the attachment to school, the greater the likelihood of delinquent behavior.*

But attitudinal and emotional ties are not the only predictors to emerge from research on schools. Another is academic achievement. Those children who do less well on achievement tests, get poorer grades, and are not on track to go to college are most likely to be delinquent. Hence, a second, school-related postulate is this: *The poorer the academic achievement, the greater the likelihood of delinquent behavior.*

Commitment to the Means for Success

Both strain and social control theories suggest that lack of achievement in school, as well as delinquent behavior, is somehow related to young people's long-range plans and goals. In seeking to explain that relationship, however, both theories use concepts that are ambiguous and unclear.

Strain theory stresses *aspirations* and *means*. It hypothesizes that virtually all children have lofty aspirations and are highly motivated to achieve them. If they become delinquent, it is because legitimate means for success have been blocked or frustrated. Social control theory, in contrast, places greater stress on *commitment* to success *goals*. All children do not have high aspirations. Instead, those who fail in school and commit delinquent acts do so because of a lack of commitment to long-range goals.

Before we can resolve the theoretical differences, we must clarify the meaning of those concepts. For example, aspirations can be viewed in two ways. On the one hand, if young people are asked to identify the important goals in American society, virtually all of them will point to a good job, wealth, material possessions, and prestige. In this sense, therefore, it could be said that they recognize and endorse traditional American values.

On the other hand, if the same young people are asked whether they aspire to complete high school, get a college education, and pursue a demanding career, some will not share those aspirations. Indeed, when defined that way, high aspirations appear to be an insulator against delinquency—the higher the aspirations, the less the chance of committing delinquency.

The problem with defining aspirations in terms of completing school and getting a job is that they become virtually synonymous with the means for success. That is, if people become wealthy and prestigious, most will have to use those conventional means. Hence, strain and social control theories are confusing when they use aspirations and means interchangeably.

Finally, the concept of commitment, in conjunction with the other concepts, also is used ambiguously in strain and social control theories. First, it is employed to reflect the degree to which young people aspire to the good life (strain theory); then it is used to determine the degree to which they are committed to the means for success (social control theory).

In short, the same confusion concerning aspirations and means is perpetuated, but with the third concept of commitment added. Fortunately, steps can be taken to eliminate the confusion. Because most young people aspire to such general *goals* as wealth, happiness, and prestige, we can safely eliminate those concepts. Then we can concentrate on using the other two concepts—*means* and *commitment*. Various studies indicate that if the conventional means for achieving success are defined to include such activities as studying hard, getting as much education as possible, and finding a job, and if commitment is defined as including personal obligation and the desire to employ those means in the pursuit of success, there is a fourth postulate for which there is considerable empirical support: *The weaker the commitment to conventional means for success, the greater the likelihood of delinquent behavior.* Despite aspiring to the good life, those individuals who are unwilling or unable to pay the conventional price for it are the most likely to commit delinquent acts.

Association with Delinquent Peers

Cultural deviance, strain, and symbolic interactionist theories suggest that disorganized or age-stratified communities, along with schools, are arenas where children are sifted and sorted into different groups— some delinquent, some conformist. The sorting process eventually results in the creation of a delinquent subculture. The traditions and associations that subculture generates become a sort of substitute

family for marginal youths, providing the satisfactions that nondelinquents find through conventional means.

There is only partial support for those ideas. On the one hand, there is not support for two ideas that are central to several theories: (1) Delinquent peers are effective family substitutes for delinquents, and (2) delinquents possess the skills to develop and maintain a coherent system of deviant values, beliefs, and practices.

On the other hand, peer relationships are important. Research reveals that the juveniles most likely to commit delinquent acts are those who (1) have a preponderance of delinquent friends and (2) are inclined to follow those friends in some situations, even if this places them in serious conflict with parents, teachers, or legal officials. As a result, another postulate is this: *The greater the association with delinquent peers, the greater the likelihood of delinquent behavior.*

Perceptions of Formal and Informal Sanctions

Central to the classical school of criminology is the idea that the threat of punishments for law-violating behavior deters such behavior. Research has revealed that the perceived certainty of legal punishment is negatively related to delinquency—the greater the perceived certainty of punishment, the less the likelihood of delinquency. This is also true of the perceived severity of legal punishment, provided that perceived certainty is high. The perceived certainty and severity of such informal sanctions as embarrassment, loss of respect from one's friends or family, and diminished educational and occupational chances also are negatively related to delinquency. Indeed, the deterrent effect of formal sanctions may be due in large part to their triggering of informal sanctions. In general, therefore, this postulate receives support: *The less the perceived certainty and severity of formal and informal sanctions, the greater the likelihood of delinquent behavior.*

Labeling

Although not all aspects of labeling theory have been supported, there is evidence that for some individuals, under some circumstances, sanctions have detrimental results. Those results include such things as delinquent identities, feelings of self-rejection, and isolation from conventional people, all of which increase the likelihood of delinquent behavior. Thus, the following postulate is proposed: *The greater the exposure to stigmatizing sanctions that label children as deviants, the greater the likelihood of delinquent behavior.*

In summary, youthful lawbreakers have weak bonds or a weak stake in conformity. Their attachment to parents and school is tenuous; their academic achievement is poor; their commitment to the conventional requirements of childhood is weak; their association with delinquent peers often places them in serious conflict with authority; they perceive few costs to committing delinquent behavior; and they have been sanctioned in a way that labels them as deviants. Such a portrayal conforms more closely to the *undersocialized* image of delinquents often painted by social control theory than to the highly motivated, *socialized* image painted by strain and cultural deviance theories. Judged by conventional standards, at least, delinquents conform less readily than other children to the ideal requirements of childhood.

THE PREDICTIVE POWER OF DELINQUENCY THEORY

Next, we need to consider the extent to which the various theories predict delinquent behavior with a high degree of accuracy. The predictive power of a theory is based on the strength of the relationships between its variables and delinquent behavior. If those variables are able to explain delinquent behavior with complete accuracy, it is said that they account for 100 percent of the variation.

Whether in the physical or social sciences, few, if any, theories approach that degree of accuracy. Compared with those in some of the other sciences, however, criminological theories are relatively inaccurate. Even when their effects are combined, such variables as attachment to parents and school, commitment to conventional means for success, and association with delinquent peers tend to account for less than 50 percent of the variation. This means that while we can say that certain juveniles are more likely than others to violate the law, we must also be aware that most of the variation goes unexplained.

Why is the predictive power of the theories so low? There are three possible answers. The first comes from Matza (1964), who criticized the hard determinism of positivist criminologists. Matza argued that lawbreakers are not compelled to violate the law. If they were, they would not become progressively less delinquent as they grew up, nor would they violate the law only intermittently while young. Matza proposed that we discard the assumption of hard determinism in favor of soft determinism—a doctrine that stands somewhere between the emphasis of classical criminology on *free will* and that of positivist criminology on *compulsion*. Almost all people, Matza (1964:5–7) contended, exercise some degree of choice in deciding whether to violate the law. He argued that lawbreakers can be seen as *drifters*:

> The image of the delinquent I wish to convey is one of drift; an actor neither compelled nor committed to deeds nor freely choosing them; neither different in any simple or fundamental sense from the law abiding, nor the same; conforming to certain traditions in American life while partially unreceptive to other more conventional traditions. (Matza, 1964:28)

That image is important because of the profound issues it raises. If, for example, the behavior of delinquents is highly determined, as most theories suggest, then it should be possible for science to isolate its causes and predict its occurrence with considerable accuracy. But if Matza is correct that the youthful lawbreaker is merely unconstrained and uncommitted, drifting in and out of delinquency, then specific causes for his or her behavior will be less pronounced and less easily predicted. To the extent that is true, delinquent behavior may never be explained: "Though we may explore and perhaps specify the conditions that activate the will to crime, we cannot definitively state that a crime will be committed" (Matza, 1964:191). A study by Agnew (1995) finds some support for this idea.

A second possibility is that the complexities of delinquency make it extremely difficult to explain. At present, our theories are inadequate for the task. Hence, criminologists need more time to improve their knowledge. The third possibility is that it is inappropriate to model criminology after the physical sciences. The physical sciences model stresses the importance of measuring observables; however, because human thought and consciousness cannot be readily observed, other models must be sought.

In light of all this, positivist criminology is left with two possibilities: (1) It can improve its theories, or (2) it can find other ways for exploring human thought and consciousness. One of the major developments of recent decades involves the former—specifically, attempts to integrate two or more theories to produce better explanations of delinquent behavior.

A GLUT OF DELINQUENCY THEORIES?

Some criminologists have proposed theoretical integration as a way to rid the field of some of its theories; that is, if theories are combined with one another, we will have less of them. Bernard and Snipes (1996:301–302) argue that this is necessary because the abundance of theories impedes scientific progress by fragmenting the discipline. To support their case that there are too many theories, they point out that between 1985 and 1994, criminologists put forth at least sixteen new theories of crime.

THEORETICAL INTEGRATION

Theory Competition

Positivist criminologists generally agree about the need for better theory. There is little consensus, however, regarding how this should be done. One strategy involves *theory competition,* in which the predictive power of different theories are compared. The acceptability of a theory depends on how well it fares in scientific tests. Critical to this strategy are *crucial tests*—tests of postulates that follow from one theory but are in direct conflict with the postulates of another theory. Theories that survive such tests are retained, those that do not are discarded, and the result should be progressively better theories of delinquent behavior (Liska, Krohn, and Messner, 1989:2–3).

Theory competition has received strong endorsements (Akers, 1989:34–36; Hirschi, 1989), but it also has come under attack in recent decades. Delbert Elliott (1985), one of its more vocal critics, has pointed to some of its limitations. First, as indicated previously, even theories that fare well in theory competition have low predictive power, typically accounting for no more than 10 to 20 percent of the variation in delinquent behavior. This may be due to

the "overly simple" nature of delinquency theories, some of which can be reduced to a single explanatory variable (Elliott, 1985:124–125, 127).

Crucial tests also have proved to be problematic: "Theories of crime and delinquency rarely provided competing postulates that were testable, theories with different assumptions and causal propositions frequently predicted similar outcomes, and in those instances where such tests were possible the results were seldom definitive" (Elliott, 1985:125). Crucial tests rarely have supported one theory while rejecting the other; more commonly, they have indicated that one theory is more plausible than the other but that neither is a powerful explanation of delinquency. Indeed, Bernard and Snipes (1996:301–302) have argued that because most theories receive *some* empirical support, crucial tests and theory competition have not dismissed theories as expected. Instead, theory competition has led to a glut of delinquency theories—with new theories frequently added but old ones rarely removed.

Another limitation is that theory competition encourages us to protect the purity of simple theories with little predictive power. Attention is directed to the differences between theories rather than their commonalities and the ways they can be combined to produce more powerful explanations. Combining different theories is necessary, Elliott (1985:126–127) argued, because the causes of delinquency are multiple. Social control, strain, social learning, and several other theories all receive empirical support, but not enough to deem any one as *the* explanation of delinquency. More competition among these theories is not likely to change the situation. What is needed, instead, is more complex theoretical statements that combine the supported postulates from different theories (Elliott, 1985:127). Although this is a formidable task, Tittle (1985:109) argued that the nature of science mandates that it be pursued: "The object of theory building is to rise above the confines of everyday categorization and causal assumptions to grasp the ways in which phenomena [and different theories] are abstractly connected." Elsewhere, Tittle (1989:162) asserted that

> the objective of [science] is to build general theories; i.e., to encompass observations of specific phenomena into explanatory schemes subsumed within larger, more general theories that satisfactorily answer questions of how and why posed by critical scholars. . . . Hence, theoretical science *requires* integration.

In sum, sharply demarcating the different theories and then pitting them against one another has gotten us only so far. It is now necessary to consider the ways in which they are compatible and in which they may be integrated to produce more powerful explanations of delinquent behavior. The profusion of integrated theories in recent years suggests that many positivist criminologists have found this argument to be convincing. We will consider five such theories, but before doing so, we must address an issue considered only implicitly thus far.

Different Models of Causal Arguments

Theories of delinquent behavior do not merely identify variables that are related to delinquency; ideally, they also specify *how* those variables are related to delinquency. Although this is important for any theory, it is especially important for integrated theories. The uniqueness of these theories often derives not so much from their causal variables, which are bor-

rowed from preexisting theories, but from the way that the variables are argued to affect delinquency. In developing and testing theories, criminologists have used four different kinds of causal arguments: independent, interdependent, reciprocal, and conditional.

INDEPENDENT The first model is designed to treat each postulate as an *independent* explanation for delinquent behavior. If that is done, one assumes that the effects of each variable—for example, social control theory's four elements of the social bond—are independent of the effects of all other variables. A child's attachment to parents, for example, is not affected by his or her attachment to school. Each has a separate and independent effect. The independent model is diagrammed in figure 15.1. The advantage of this model is that it is conceptually simple, but it may oversimplify the processes by which children become delinquent. For example, besides being related to delinquent behavior, weak attachment to parents also may weaken attachment to school, which, in turn, may affect commitment to conventional goals, such as going to college. Consequently, many criminologists opt for a second, more complex, model.

INTERDEPENDENT The interdependent model suggests that many of the influences in a child's life are *interdependent*. Although this interdependence may be portrayed in numerous ways, one way is to develop a set of postulates that reflect it, as is the case with labeling theory:

1. Primary deviance often leads to the dramatization of evil (labeling).

FIGURE 15.1
Independent effects

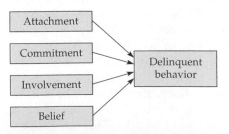

2. The greater the dramatization of evil, the greater the delinquent identity of the one being labeled.
3. The greater the delinquent identity, the greater the secondary deviance.

When stated this way, the postulates of the theory may be diagrammed as follows:

Primary deviance → Dramatization of evil (labeling) → Delinquent identity → Secondary deviance

This model implies that delinquency results from a complex series of events. It further implies that each variable in the causal chain not only is dependent on those preceding it but also is linked to delinquency only through the variable or variables following it. For example, a child who commits primary deviance and has been labeled will commit secondary deviance only after acquiring a delinquent identity. Unless each step occurs, a child will be unlikely to commit secondary deviance.

But what if variables in the causal chain have both an independent and an interdependent effect on delinquency? The dramatization of evil could lead to secondary deviance not merely by causing a delinquent identity but also by having an independent effect. Labeling theory, in particular, does not make that argument, but because both kinds of effects are possible, theory and research often are designed to take both into account. If that were done with labeling theory, the model shown in figure 15.2 would be used.

RECIPROCAL   There is also reason to believe that not only independent and interdependent effects but also *reciprocal* effects—effects that move backward as well as forward—lead to delinquent behavior. Consider deterrence theory's postulate that people who perceive a low certainty of legal punishment are more likely to violate the law. Because most law violations are not detected by the police, offenders are able to avoid punishment, further lowering their perceptions of punishment certainty. The cycle may then repeat itself. A model of these effects is shown in figure 15.3.

CONDITIONAL   The conditional model suggests that the effects of some causes on delinquency are dependent—or *conditional*—on the presence of other causes. Gottfredson and Hirschi's (1990) self-control theory, for example, posited that low self-control leads to delinquency only when it is combined with opportunities to violate the law. Similarly, Cloward and Ohlin (1960) argued that the effects of blocked legitimate opportunities on gang delinquency are dependent on the availability of illegitimate opportunities.

As we will see, conditional effects are common in integrated theories. Like the interdependent and reciprocal models discussed previously, the conditional model reflects a view that delinquency results from a combination of many variables rather than from a single, independent cause. With that in mind, let us turn now to a discussion of key integrated theories.

The Integrated Theories

Our earlier discussion isolated seven postulates for which empirical support tends to be the strongest:
1. The weaker the attachment between parents and children, the greater the likelihood of delinquent behavior.

FIGURE 15.2
Interdependent and independent effects

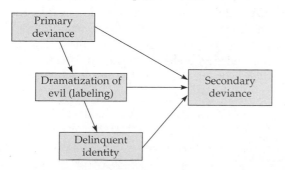

FIGURE 15.3
Reciprocal effects

2. The weaker the attachment to school, the greater the likelihood of delinquent behavior.

3. The poorer the academic achievement, the greater the likelihood of delinquent behavior.

4. The weaker the commitment to conventional means for success, the greater the likelihood of delinquent behavior.

5. The greater the association with delinquent peers, the greater the likelihood of delinquent behavior.

6. The less the perceived certainty and severity of formal and informal sanctions, the greater the likelihood of delinquent behavior.

7. The greater the exposure to stigmatizing sanctions that label children as deviants, the greater the likelihood of delinquent behavior.

In varying ways, integrated theories weave those postulates into their explanations. But beyond that similarity, integrated theories often are very different from one another. This is probably due to the lack of consensus over how theoretical integration should be achieved (Messner, Krohn, and Liska, 1989). Some integrated theories are complex, while others are almost as simple as the theories they build upon. Some integrated theories introduce new causal variables, while others combine only preexisting variables.

BRAITHWAITE'S THEORY OF REINTEGRATIVE SHAMING[1]
Braithwaite (1989:44–50) began by explicitly providing a list of the "facts a theory of crime ought to fit," which includes six of the seven postulates listed here. He argued that no existing theory could encompass all of those facts, and thus, there is need for some integrating framework. For Braithwaite, that framework was provided by the concept of *shaming*, which involves a particular way of reacting to deviant behavior. Shaming refers to "all social processes of expressing disapproval which have the intention or effect of invoking remorse in the person being shamed and/or condemnation by others who become aware of the shaming" (p. 100).

Braithwaite distinguished between two types of shaming. Shaming is *reintegrative* when it is followed by efforts to reintegrate deviants back into the community of law-abiding citizens. This can be done through words or gestures of forgiveness or through ceremonies to decertify the offender as deviant (1989:100–101). Reintegrative shaming reduces deviance in two main ways. First, it reinforces the underlying rule that was violated, such that both shamed individuals and those who participate in or become aware of the shaming will be more likely to deem deviance "unthinkable" (p. 81). Second, it has a deterrent effect. The shamed person will want to avoid the discomfort of guilt and shame that would follow from further deviance. This preventive effect is enhanced by coupling shame with reintegration, which strengthens attachments between offenders and those who might shame future deviance, thereby increasing the perceived costs of future shaming.[2]

Reintegrative shaming is contrasted with *stigmatization*, which is shaming with little or no effort to forgive offenders or affirm the basic goodness of their character, and thus, to reconcile them with the members of their community (1989:101). Stigmatization weakens attachments to those who might shame future deviance, essentially rejecting offenders as outcasts:

> Shaming that is stigmatizing, in contrast, makes criminal subcultures more attractive because these are in some sense subcultures which reject the rejectors. . . . The deviant is both attracted to criminal subcultures and cut off from other interdependencies (with family, neighbors, church, etc.). (Braithwaite, 1989:102)

A key factor in Braithwaite's theory is *interdependency*, which refers to the extent to which people are involved in networks in which they are dependent on others to achieve valued goals and others are dependent on them (1989:99–100). People high in interdependency are more likely than those low in interdependency to be reintegratively shamed (as opposed to stigmatized), and thus are less likely to

---

[1]This description of Braithwaite's theory closely parallels the one provided by Hay (1998:421–423).

[2]Braithwaite's theory is relevant for multiple units of analysis. Just as individuals who are exposed to reintegrative shaming should engage in less law-violating behavior, territorial units (e.g., communities, regions, societies) with high levels of reintegrative shaming should have low rates of crime.

commit crimes. Characteristics associated with high interdependency, such as age (being under 15 and over 25), being married, female, and employed, and having high educational and occupational aspirations, therefore, should be negatively related to delinquent behavior.

As figure 15.4 shows, Braithwaite's theory combines many of the variables that have been found to predict delinquency. Indeed, Braithwaite (1989:15) was explicit about the connection between his theory and previous ones:

> Interdependency is the stuff of control theory; stigmatization comes from labeling theory; subculture formation is accounted for in [classic strain] theory terms; subcultural influences are naturally in the realm of subcultural theory; and the whole theory can be understood in integrative cognitive social learning theory terms such as are provided by differential association.

ELLIOTT, AGETON, AND CANTER'S INTEGRATED THEORY
In some sense, Elliott, Ageton, and Canter's (1979)

integrated theory is the archetypal integration. They introduced no new theoretical concepts; instead, they devoted attention entirely to weaving together certain arguments of social control, classic strain, and social learning theories.

They began with social control theory's emphasis on weak social bonds. They argued that low integration (akin to Hirschi's [1969] involvement and commitment) and low commitment (akin to Hirschi's [1969] attachment and belief) among children weakens their bonds to the conventional order. This occurs as a result of such things as failure in conventional social contexts (e.g., school), negative labeling, and social isolation. Weak bonds increase association in delinquent peer groups and increase the likelihood of delinquent behavior. Figure 15.5 shows the theory's key predictions.

THORNBERRY'S INTERACTIONAL THEORY The integrated theory put forth by Thornberry (1987) and his colleagues (Thornberry et al., 1994) is in many ways similar to Elliott, Ageton, and Canter's theory:

FIGURE 15.4
Braithwaite's theory of reintegrative shaming

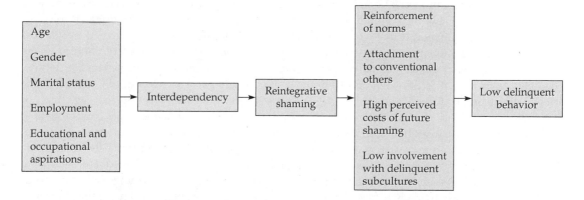

FIGURE 15.5
Elliott, Ageton, and Canter's integrated theory

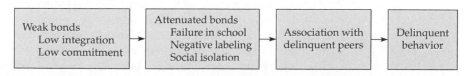

No new theoretical concepts were introduced; social control theory was the starting point; and association with delinquent peers was an important cause of delinquency. Thornberry's interactional theory, however, was inspired in large part by an ongoing debate about the relationship between delinquent peer association and delinquent behavior. Although criminologists agree that those variables are strongly associated with each other, there is much debate about what that association means theoretically. Social control theorists have argued that children with weak bonds to society will commit delinquency and then seek out the company of delinquent peers. Social learning theorists have proposed a different causal order: Children associate with delinquent peers and then commit delinquency. Interactional theory combines these two positions: "Rather than assigning unidirectional causal priority to one of these variables over the others, [interactional theory] argues that they are likely to be interrelated over the life course and to have bi-directional [reciprocal] causal influences on one another" (Thornberry et al., 1994:49).

Of course, something must initiate the process. The weakening of a child's bond to conventional society is seen as the fundamental cause of delinquency (Thornberry et al., 1994:50). But weak bonds merely free children to violate the law; weak bonds are not sufficient to produce delinquency. If that freedom is to lead to delinquency, children must be in environments in which delinquency can be learned and reinforced. "This environment is provided largely by associations with delinquent peers and by the formation of delinquent beliefs" (p. 50). The principal argument, therefore, is that weak bonds lead to delinquent peer associations and the learning of delinquent beliefs, which, in turn, lead to delinquency. Once that has occurred, causation turns the other direction: "Delinquency eventually becomes its own indirect cause precisely because of its ability to weaken further the person's bonds to family, school, and conventional beliefs" (Thornberry, 1987:876).

To be sure, Thornberry (1989:56–57) himself suggested that interactional theory is not theoretical integration, but rather is best described as theoretical *elaboration*. Interactional theory essentially is a social control theory that has incorporated association with delinquent peers while also considering the consequences of delinquency on bonds and the consequences of bonds on delinquency. Those changes reflect a desire to increase the predictive power of social control theory rather than a preference for "melding together . . . differing theories as an end in itself" (Thornberry, 1989:60). Nevertheless, that others (e.g., Akers, 1997; Bernard and Snipes, 1996) see interactional theory as an integrated theory reflects the confusion that persists over the meaning of theoretical integration.

MATSUEDA'S THEORY OF DIFFERENTIAL SOCIAL CONTROL At no point is Matsueda's theory (1992; Heimer, 1996; Heimer and Matsueda, 1994) referred to as an integrated theory, but his weaving together of social control, social learning, and labeling variables justifies such a designation. Matsueda's differential social control theory is rooted in symbolic interactionism and, specifically, the idea that a person's behavior results from the role identities he or she develops in response to social interactions. People develop role commitments and identities based on their past behavior and their perception of how others have appraised that behavior. When placed in a problematic situation (one in which there are alternative behaviors), they will act in a way consistent with their role commitments and identities. In this way, Heimer and Matsueda (1994:367) argued, people "adjust to emergent events and discontinuities in the present by aligning them with the past and the future."

The important variables in differential social control theory are social location (e.g., age, race, or family structure), prior delinquency, commitment to conventional roles, delinquent role-taking, and delinquent behavior. Although the effects of these variables tend to be interdependent, there are several principal arguments. First, youngsters' social location and prior delinquency influence their commitment to conventional rather than delinquent roles. Commitment to conventional roles for the most part encompasses Hirschi's (1969) elements of both commitment and attachment (Heimer and Matsueda, 1994:374). Commitment to conventional roles then influences delinquency by affecting the extent of delinquent role-taking—the extent to which someone identifies with delinquent roles. There are various aspects of delinquent role-taking: perceiving that others see oneself as a rule violator, holding delinquent attitudes, not anticipating negative reactions from significant others in response to delinquent behavior, associating with delinquent peers, and having a history of delinquent habits (Heimer and Matsueda, 1994:367–368). Figure 15.6 provides a model of this theory's arguments.

TITTLE'S CONTROL BALANCE THEORY The most complicated integrated theory is Tittle's (1995) control balance theory. Its complexity follows from many things, including its introduction of a new concept (control balance), its relevance to all forms of deviance and not just law-violating behavior, and its attention to interdependent and conditional causation. Key to the theory is the *control ratio*, which Tittle defined as "the amount of control to which the person is subject relative to the amount that he or she can exercise" (p. 145). The basic premise of the theory is that individuals' control ratios affect the probability that they will commit deviant acts and the probability that they will commit specific types of deviance. Tittle (p. 142) argued that deviant behavior is "a device, or maneuver, that helps people escape deficits and extend surpluses of control." Thus, when people experience a control *imbalance,* they are motivated to deviance. If they are subject to more control than they exercise (a control deficit), they will be motivated to commit defiant or predatory acts (such as armed robbery) designed to gain the control they

lack. If they are subject to less control than they exercise (a control surplus), they will be motivated to commit plunderous or exploitative acts (such as corporate price-fixing) designed to extend their control surplus (p. 189).

The predisposition toward deviant motivation is not, however, a sufficient cause of deviance. Rather, said Tittle, that predisposition must converge with three other variables: (1) provocation (the situational stimulation for the motivation), (2) opportunity to commit deviance, and (3) a lack of restraint (the likelihood that a particular deviant act will not meet with restraining responses by others) (1995:142). When applied to the explanation of delinquent behavior, these variables encompass many of the variables from other theories, including social control, differential association, and expanded deterrence. The convergence of the four variables significantly influences the probability that a deviant act will be committed. But a number of factors, referred to by Tittle as *contingencies* (p. 201), condition the effects of these variables, especially those of the control ratio. As Tittle noted, the effect of the control ratio "does not occur with the same strength or likelihood in all circumstances. Contingencies impinge on, and alter, the 'ordinary' operation of the control balancing process" (p. 201). Included among these conditional variables are moral commitments, habits, impulsivity, and ability to commit deviant acts. For example, although most young people have a control deficit, and therefore should be motivated to engage

FIGURE 15.6
Matsueda's theory of differential social control

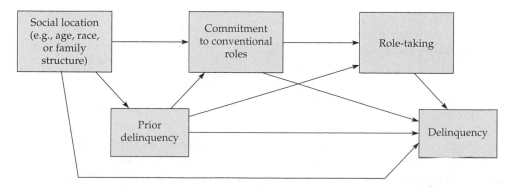

in deviant acts, some will not do so because they consider such acts morally unacceptable.

There are many obstacles to testing integrated theories. A few of the theories, such as Braithwaite's and Tittle's, are complex and present new concepts that are not easily measured (see Hay, 1998:424–426; Tittle, 1995:261). Even those theories that use only pre-existing variables make reciprocal causal arguments that require complex statistical models and repeated measurements over long periods of time. Nevertheless, early tests of the theories put forth by Elliott and colleagues, Thornberry, and Matsueda are promising. But the impact of integrated theories on criminology is unknown at this time. Although many criminologists support theoretical integration in principle, the integrated theories of the past often have not received much attention, leaving the fate of more recent ones unclear. As Akers (1989:35–36) commented,

> While some [integrated theories] have received some empirical support, I must say that by and large they have not widely replaced the different theories they supposedly integrated. It is as if the integration never took place. . . . They have basically been ignored or have simply taken their places alongside the original theories as either something very different or variations on a common theme.

POLICY IMPLICATIONS: PRINCIPLES OF PREVENTION AND REHABILITATION

In considering the policy implications of delinquency theory and research, let us return to the seven postulates for which support has been greatest. Because empirical evidence for many theories has been weak or lacking, these postulates provide the best guide for policymakers concerned reducing delinquent behavior.

Drawn from several theories, these postulates suggest that delinquents are more likely than other young people to lack a *stake in conformity*. Their attachments to the basic child-raising institutions of family and school are weak or disrupted; their academic achievement is poor; they are not committed to conventional means for success; they associate with delinquent peers; they do not perceive many costs to their delinquent behavior; and they have been sanctioned in a way that labels them as delinquents. This description suggests that the best way for authorities to protect society, as well as to serve marginal youths, is to construct programs that are based on three interrelated principles:

1. The primary focus of efforts to prevent nondelinquents (or predelinquents) from committing delinquent acts and to rehabilitate those who are already delinquent should be on establishing a stake in conformity in young people.
2. A stake in conformity is most likely to occur if children are effectively socialized.
3. Effective socialization is a product of institutional design and process—a result of the way families, schools, and communities are organized.

The implication is clear: Rather than emphasizing punishment, removal from society, or isolation in treatment programs, prevention and rehabilitation should be pursued actively by policymakers.

Guidelines for Prevention

With regard to prevention, the following guidelines are suggested for authorities:

1. Strengthen families to create a strong attachment between parents and children.
2. Design educational programs so that children learn to respect their teachers, the authority of the school, and the importance of learning.
3. Promote academic achievement so that children are prepared to assume adult roles.
4. Commit children to the conventional means by which success is achieved—hard work, deferred gratification, and job preparation.
5. Help children associate with law-abiding peers.
6. Educate parents about how to convey to their children the various formal and informal costs of delinquency and how to punish their children in a way that does not label them as delinquents.

Guidelines for Rehabilitation

The guidelines for rehabilitating delinquents differ only in their emphasis. Instead of punishment, they

POLICY INTEGRATION

At the same time that criminologists have focused on theoretical integration, policymakers increasingly are concentrating on policy integration. Multisystemic therapy (MST) is one of the newest approaches to treating serious antisocial behavior (Henggeler, 1997). Premised on the idea that previous treatment strategies have been too specialized or have not been cost-effective, MST provides an array of treatments that do not involve expensive out-of-home placements. Most importantly, treatments are selected on the basis of information about known causes of delinquency. MST interventions focus on all delinquency-generating factors, including the individual youth and his or her family, peer relationships, school/vocational performance, and neighborhood/community.

stress the need to undo the effects of improper or inadequate socialization, to achieve these goals:

1. Strengthen the weak attachment of delinquents to family and school.
2. Provide delinquents with renewed opportunities for education—opportunities that not only appeal to their present levels of learning but also pose the possibility of later sources of reward and satisfaction.
3. Turn delinquents away from illegitimate sources of satisfaction and recommit them to conventional means for success.
4. Assimilate delinquents into law-abiding groups and alienate them from delinquent groups.
5. Reverse delinquent labels that have been adopted and sensitize offenders to the formal and informal costs of their behavior.

In short, the principles of positivist criminology suggest that programs designed to promote a stake in conformity and adoption of legitimate roles will be most successful if the family, school, and community are involved in the process. It is these institutions, and not jails, reformatories, or training schools, that must be responsible for keeping delinquents on the road that leads from childhood to adulthood. To lock them up with other delinquents or further isolate them from conventional pursuits may make their behavior worse rather than better, and it may act to postpone the needed reforms rather than hasten them.

SUMMARY AND CONCLUSIONS

Many theories of delinquency have been proposed, and each has implications for new theoretical developments and policy.

Predicting Delinquent Behavior

Some factors can be identified that predict delinquent behavior: attachment to parents, attachment to school, academic achievement, commitment to conventional means for success, association with delinquent peers, perceptions of formal and informal sanctions, and adoption of delinquent labels. Nevertheless, those factors do not predict delinquency with a high degree of accuracy, possibly supporting Matza's belief that the majority of delinquents are drifters who are neither entirely free nor entirely compelled to commit delinquency.

Given such evidence, some softening of positivist doctrines and goals seems appropriate. But while all law violators cannot be viewed as atypical and without choice, there are some chronic offenders whose behavior may be determined. Hence, there remains the hope that by improving scientific methods, the power of positivist theories to explain their behavior can be improved.

Theoretical Integration

Theoretical integration has been used in an attempt to construct better theories. Theoretical integration involves combining the arguments of two or more theories to create a better explanation of delinquency.

Integrated theories incorporate various models of causation, including independent, interdependent, reciprocal, and conditional. These different models often are used to weave together variables from already-existing theories. This is the case for integrated theories put forth by Elliott, Ageton, and Canter (1979), Thornberry (1987), and Matsueda (1992). However, some integrated theories, such as those from Braithwaite's (1989) and Tittle's (1995) blend social control, differential association, strain, and expanded deterrence variables with new theoretical concepts. All of these integrated theories are relatively new and have not been fully tested, although early tests of the Elliott, Thornberry, and Matsueda theories are promising. There is some question, however, whether these integrated theories will attract the attention of criminologists, who have been partial to the traditional theories.

Implications for Prevention and Rehabilitation

The limitations of positivist theory notwithstanding, the ideology of juvenile justice has stressed the need to apply scientific principles to programs of prevention and rehabilitation. They suggest that because delinquent behavior is determined, efforts must be made to socialize youths more effectively. By strengthening their family bonds, promoting their attachment to school, improving their academic achievement, committing them to legitimate roles, discouraging their associating with delinquent peers, sensitizing them to the formal and informal costs of delinquency, and avoiding the use of delinquent labels, they can be given a stake in conformity. This knowledge places us in the unique position to use these principles and problems as a backdrop against which we can examine and evaluate the organization and operation of the juvenile justice system.

DISCUSSION QUESTIONS

1. What are the seven postulates for which there is great support?
2. What are some reasons delinquency theories have not been able to explain 100 percent of the variation in delinquency?
3. What is theory competition?
4. What is reciprocal causation?
5. What is a control ratio, and how is it related to deviant behavior?

REFERENCES

Agnew, Robert. 1995. "Determinism, Indeterminism, and Crime: An Empirical Exploration." *Criminology* 33(February):83–109.

Akers, Ronald L. 1989. "A Social Behaviorist's Perspective on Integration of Theories of Crime and Deviance." Pp. 23–36 in Steven F. Messner, Marvin D. Krohn, and Allen E. Liska, eds., *Theoretical Integration in the Study of Deviance and Crime: Problems and Prospects.* Albany: State University of New York Press.

Bernard, Thomas J., and Jeffrey B. Snipes. 1996. "Theoretical Integration in Criminology." Pp. 301–348 in Michael Tonry, ed., *Crime and Justice: A Review of Research.* Chicago: University of Chicago Press.

Braithwaite, John. 1989. *Crime, Shame and Reintegration.* New York: Cambridge University Press.

Cloward, Richard A., and Lloyd E. Ohlin. 1960. *Delinquency and Opportunity: A Theory of Delinquent Gangs.* New York: Free Press.

Elliott, Delbert. 1985. "The Assumption That Theories Can Be Combined with Increased Explanatory Power: Theoretical Integrations." Pp. 123–149 in Robert F. Meier, ed., *Theoretical Methods in Criminology.* Beverly Hills, Calif.: Sage.

Elliott, Delbert S., Suzanne S. Ageton, and Rachelle J. Canter. 1979. "An Integrated Theoretical Perspective on Delinquent Behavior." *Journal of Research in Crime and Delinquency* 16 (January): 3–27.

Gottfredson, Michael R., and Travis Hirschi. 1990. *A General Theory of Crime.* Stanford, Calif.: Stanford University Press.

Hay, Carter. 1998. "Parental Sanctions and Delinquent Behavior: Toward Clarification of Braithwaite's Theory of Reintegrative Shaming." *Theoretical Criminology* 2 (November):419–443.

Heimer, Karen. 1996. "Gender, Interaction, and Delinquency: Testing a Theory of Differential Social Control." *Social Psychology Quarterly* 59 (March): 39–61.

Heimer, Karen, and Ross L. Matsueda. 1994. "Role-Taking, Role Commitment, and Delinquency: A Theory of Differential Social Control." *American Sociological Review* 59 (June):365–390.

Henggeler, Scott W. 1997. "Treating Serious Antisocial Behavior in Youth: The MST Approach." *The OJJDP Juvenile Justice Bulletin*. Washington, D.C.: U.S. Government Printing Office.

Hirschi, Travis. 1969. *Causes of Delinquency*. Berkeley: University of California Press.
1989. "Exploring Alternatives to Integrated Theory." Pp. 37–50 in Steven F. Messner, Marvin D. Krohn, and Allen E. Liska, eds., *Theoretical Integration in the Study of Deviance and Crime: Problems and Prospects*. Albany: State University of New York Press.

Liska, Allen E., Marvin D. Krohn, and Steven F. Messner. 1989. "Strategies and Requisites for Theoretical Integration in the Study of Crime and Deviance." Pp. 1–19 in Steven F. Messner, Marvin D. Krohn, and Allen E. Liska, eds., *Theoretical Integration in the Study of Deviance and Crime: Problems and Prospects*. Albany: State University of New York Press.

Matsueda, Ross L. 1992. "Reflected Appraisals, Parental Labeling, and Delinquency: Specifying a Symbolic Interactionist Theory." *American Journal of Sociology* 97 (May):1577–1611.

Matza, David. 1964. *Delinquency and Drift*. New York: Wiley.

Messner, Steven F., Marvin D. Krohn, and Allen E. Liska, eds. 1989. *Theoretical Integration in the Study of Deviance and Crime: Problems and Prospects*. Albany: State University of New York Press.

Thornberry, Terence P. 1987. "Toward an Interactional Theory of Delinquency." *Criminology* 25: 863–887.
1989. "Reflections on the Advantages and Disadvantages of Theoretical Integration." Pp. 51–60 in Steven F. Messner, Marvin D. Krohn, and Allen E. Liska, eds., *Theoretical Integration in the Study of Deviance and Crime: Problems and Prospects*. Albany: State University of New York Press.

Thornberry, Terence P., Alan J. Lizotte, Marvin D. Krohn, Margaret Farnworth, and Sung Joon Jang. 1994. "Delinquent Peers, Beliefs, and Delinquent Behavior: A Longitudinal Test of Interactional Theory." *Criminology* 32 (February): 47–83.

Tittle, Charles. 1985. "The Assumption That General Theories Are Not Possible." Pp. 93–121 in Robert F. Meier, ed., *Theoretical Methods in Criminology*. Beverly Hills, Calif.: Sage.
1989. "Prospects for Synthetic Theory: A Consideration of Macro-Level Criminological Activity." Pp. 161–178 in Steven F. Messner, Marvin D. Krohn, and Allen E. Liska, eds., *Theoretical Integration in the Study of Deviance and Crime: Problems and Prospects*. Albany: State University of New York Press.
1995. *Control Balance: Toward a General Theory of Deviance*. Boulder, Colo.: Westview Press.

PART FOUR

JUVENILE JUSTICE

I n this last section of the book, we consider another part of the delinquency picture—the juvenile justice system. From 1899 until well into the 1960s, that system remained relatively unchallenged. The ideology of child saving was transcendent; and reformers, legislators, and judges believed that the new system was not only revolutionary but desirable.

The invention of the juvenile court in the state of Illinois was hailed universally as a triumph of benevolent progressivism over reactionism and ignorance (Chute, 1949:3; Mead, 1918:594–595; Platt, 1969:10). By 1920, all states except three had enacted juvenile court laws, although it was not until almost mid-century that Wyoming became the last state to do so. Meanwhile, the juvenile court became the model in many other nations as well (Caldwell, 1961:496).

Not only did the rehabilitative philosophy of the juvenile court spread geographically, but its jurisdiction was extended to older youths (Caldwell, 1961:496). Most states raised the upper limit of jurisdiction from 16 to 18 years of age, and a few raised it to 21. The definition of delinquency was broadened to include cases of illegitimacy and mental or physical defectiveness. Adults could be brought into court and charged with contributing to the delinquency of minors. Some cities created family or domestic relations courts to deal with family problems of any kind: dependency and neglect, illegitimacy, and offenses committed by one family member against another.

THE REHABILITATIVE IDEOLOGY

The beliefs that sustained the juvenile court movement are best understood as an ideology about the best way to nurture and protect children. For example, the modern concept of childhood assumed that children are qualitatively different from adults and that their immaturity makes them more malleable. The positivist school also assumed that because delinquent behavior is due to forces over which children have little control, they simply cannot anticipate the consequences of their acts. When those two sets of assumptions were combined, they suggested that rehabilitation and prevention were required for controlling juvenile lawbreaking. Indeed, the juvenile court could accomplish those goals simultaneously.

Rehabilitation would work for those who had gone so far as to commit delinquent acts. These youths could be restored to a condition of social repute by scientifically designed programs of care and treatment. Furthermore, by using the same techniques, delinquency could be prevented among those who were still at the dependent and neglected stage or were status offenders. In pursuit of those twin goals, there was little need to distinguish between the child who was neglected, rude, or intemperate, and the child who had broken a criminal law. The purpose of the court was to deal with the problems of children, not to judge their behaviors.

Until well after mid-century, the theories of delinquency that contributed most to these ideas were biological and psychological—theories that concentrated on the defects of individuals. Hence, in addition to suggesting that delinquent behavior is due to causes over which the child has little control, they suggested that the primary problems were defective intelligence, uncaring parents, and an unacceptable home life. Relatively little thought was given to the possible effects of differential opportunities, delinquent peers, or pluralistic culture.

According to the rehabilitative ideology, differential responses to children were the only way to protect society. Short of killing off all delinquents or permanently institutionalizing them, the only way citizens could be protected was to cure lawbreakers of their criminal tendencies. In pursuit of that goal, juvenile court officials were not acting unconstitutionally if they denied juveniles the due process rights that were guaranteed for adults. Indeed, rather than taking issue with the rehabilitative ideology, important higher court decisions served only to sustain it. For example, in *Commonwealth* v. *Fisher* in 1905, an appellate court ruled that "the manner in which a child was brought into court was irrelevant . . . given the state's benevolent intent" (Schlossman, 1983:963). Furthermore, the constitutional protections of adult criminal trials were unnecessary in juvenile court because "there was no trial for any crime here. . . . The very purpose . . . is to prevent trial" (Schlossman, 1983:963).

This ideology had changed little by 1962. In that year, Orman Ketcham (1962:25), judge of the juvenile court in the District of Columbia, observed that "the juvenile in America may [still] be brought within the protective power of the juvenile court without the operation of legal safeguards customarily offered to a person accused of law violations." Caldwell (1961:497) added that "the balance between rights, on the one hand, and duties and responsibilities, on the other, which every court must seek to maintain, has been upset as the juvenile court has been pushed more and more into the role of a social work agency."

For much of this century, then, the conception of the juvenile court as a rehabilitative instrument has provided juvenile justice officials not only with a broad mandate but with awesome responsibilities. On the one hand, this meant that delinquents should be treated in a much more thoughtful and humane way than adult offenders are treated. Retribution should be avoided; the care, custody, and discipline of delinquents should approximate that of loving parents. On the other hand, officials should not wait until children "become criminal in habits and tastes" before they act (Platt, 1969:138). Rather, they should respond at the first sign of parental neglect or departure on the part of any child from accepted moral and legal standards, even if this required stern and arbitrary methods.

So pervasive was the rehabilitative ideology that little thought was given to the possibilities that its basic assumptions might be faulty or that the interventions by the court might be more harmful than helpful. Consequently, the development of sociological theories of delinquency had relatively little impact on the juvenile court philosophy and practice until after 1960. It was not until the early 1960s, for example, that strain theory became the rationale for the creation of both the President's Committee on Juvenile Delinquency and Youth Crime, and Mobilization for Youth. But because those programs were concerned more with preventing delinquency than with judging or rehabilitating known offenders, they did not have much impact on the practices of judges and correctional officials. Little attention was paid to the implications of positivist theories suggesting that programs designed to promote a stake in conformity would be most successful if families, schools, neighborhoods, and law-abiding peers, as well as probation officers and correctional officials, were involved in the process.

Partly as a result of this neglect, the juvenile justice system recently has been in a state of ferment. Its rehabilitative ideology has been challenged; its effectiveness has been questioned; and some of its basic procedures have been altered.

- *Chapter 16* examines the police: their historical development in this country, their perceptions of the rehabilitative ideology and its impact on them, and their responses to conflicting social expectations as they actually process juveniles.
- *Chapter 17* conducts the same sort of analysis of the juvenile court: the historical expansion of its benevolent ideology, its original procedures for dealing with juveniles, and the events, scientific findings, and ideologies that eventually tarnished its image and led to reforms.
- *Chapter 18* focuses on society's efforts to reform delinquents, from the time when they were whipped or disfigured to the mid-1900s when they were placed in diagnostic and treatment programs. Although the prevailing approach stressed rehabilitation, attitudes toward it began to change in the 1960s. People began to question not only whether rehabilitation was effective but whether it had even been tried.
- *Chapter 19* draws some conclusions about childhood, scientific efforts to understand delinquency, the juvenile justice system, and efforts to prevent and control delinquency.

REFERENCES

Caldwell, Robert G. 1961. "The Juvenile Court: Its Development and Some Major Problems." *Journal of Criminal Law, Criminology and Police Science* 51 (January–February):493–511.

Chute, Charles L. 1949. "The Juvenile Court in Retrospect." *Federal Probation* 13 (September):3–8.

Ketcham, Orman W. 1962. "The Unfulfilled Promise of the American Juvenile Court." Pp. 22–43 in Margaret K. Rosenheim, ed., *Justice for the Child: The Juvenile Court in Transition*. New York: Free Press.

Mead, George H. 1918. "The Psychology of Punitive Justice." *American Journal of Sociology* 23 (March):577–602.

Platt, Anthony M. 1969. *The Child Savers: The Invention of Delinquency*. Chicago: University of Chicago Press.

Schlossman, Steven L. 1983. "Juvenile Justice: History and Philosophy." Pp. 961–969 in Sanford H. Kadish, ed., *Encyclopedia of Crime and Justice*, Vol. 3. New York: Free Press.

The police see themselves as the First line of defense in the war on crime.

CHAPTER SIXTEEN

POLICING JUVENILES

The police are the most visible symbol of the juvenile justice system. When lawbreaking, a family quarrel, or some other disturbance occurs, most citizens turn to the police. Indeed, most youths in the juvenile court have been referred by the police. To understand how the police play such a crucial role, one must be aware of not only the rehabilitative ideal for juveniles but also the history and organization of police work, public perceptions of the police, and police officers' views of themselves. Taken together, those topics create a view of delinquency that is unique to the police and that, for much of this century, has determined how police respond to juveniles.

HISTORY OF POLICE WORK

Perhaps surprisingly, large, organized police departments have not been in existence for much longer than the juvenile court.[1] Like the juvenile court, they seem to have been created in response to the growth of large cities, technology, and industrialization. As the informal controls of rural communities gradually broke down, people turned increasingly to more impersonal, formal controls—juvenile institutions and juvenile courts, as well as the police.

The origin of police departments in this country can be traced to prior developments in Western European countries, particularly England. France and several other European countries had professional police forces of a sort as early as the 1600s. England, however, did not begin to create them until the 1800s. The delay was due, in part, to a fear of police oppression (Lane, 1992:6). "During the period of the absolute monarchy the police came to represent the underground aspects of tyranny and political repression, and they were despised and feared even by those who ostensibly benefitted from their services" (Bittner, 1970:6–7). Instead of large police departments, England used the **mutual pledge system** for apprehending criminals. Local citizens were encouraged to maintain law and order, and were responsible for their own actions and those of their neighbors. When a crime was committed, citizens were expected to raise the **hue and cry,** join their neighbors, and pursue the criminal. If citizens failed in that task, they could be fined. Those efforts were coordinated by a local constable or sheriff who performed three functions: (1) organize citizens into groups of ten families to enforce laws, (2) supervise the **watch and ward** (people expected to protect property against fire, guard the gates, and arrest criminals between sunset and daybreak), and (3) inquire into offenses, serve summonses, take charge of prisoners, and assist local justices responsible for judging cases in each county.

As long as England was rural, such a system was adequate. But with the Industrial Revolution, accompanied by the migration of thousands of people to factory towns, it became inadequate. Anonymity increased; neighborhood networks disappeared; and the people were no longer willing or able to enforce laws. In the second quarter of the 19th century, therefore, England's first professional police departments were organized.

AMERICAN POLICE

The same pattern characterized the development of the police in this country. American colonists in the 1600s and 1700s installed the mutual pledge, the watch and ward, and the constable system in their small towns. Those were adequate to supplement the informal controls of family, church, and community. But, as some towns began to expand in the late 1700s and early 1800s, informal controls no longer were adequate to cope with the increasing disorder:

> New York City was alleged to be the most crime-ridden city in the world, with Philadelphia, Baltimore and Cincinnati not far behind.
>
> Gangs of youthful rowdies in the larger cities . . . threatened to destroy the American reputation for respect for law. . . . Before their boisterous demonstrations the crude police forces of the day were often helpless. (Cole, 1934:154–155)

In response, in the 1830s and 1840s, New York, Boston, and Philadelphia created police departments. By the 1870s, all large cities had full-time police departments. But they proved to be less than a panacea: Police officers were poorly educated and poorly trained (Lane, 1992:13). Worse still, police forces often became instruments of political corruption when elected officials used them for personal gain and political advantage:

> Rotation in office enjoyed so much popular favor that police posts of both high and low degree were constantly changing hands, with political fixers determining the price and conditions of each change. . . . The whole police question simply churned about in the public mind and eventually became identified with the corruption and

---

[1]Except where indicated, this brief history is drawn from the *Task Force Report: The Police* by the President's Commission on Law Enforcement and Administration of Justice (1967:3–7).

degradation of the city politics and local governments of the period. (Smith, 1960:105–106)

The police, in short, became objects of distrust. Earlier fears of political corruption and oppression were confirmed.

In the small towns and mining communities of the West and in the rural South, police departments were much slower to develop than in the larger eastern cities. In both areas, modern police departments did not begin to emerge on any scale until the early 1900s. Until then, local constables or sheriffs, along with the citizenry, were responsible for maintaining law and order.

The real expansion of police departments and citizens' interest in them began after World War I. By that time, most state legislatures had created state police forces because local departments could not or would not enforce laws beyond their own jurisdictions. Then, in 1924, J. Edgar Hoover organized the Federal Bureau of Investigation to deal with federal crimes. Finally, in 1931, the first National Commission on Law Observance and Enforcement (pp. 1–10), aware of a growing number of police problems, issued a call for reform. For example, the average police chief was too subject to political manipulation and control; there were too few competent, honest police officers; there was little effort to educate, train, and discipline officers; and the police lacked the necessary equipment, skill, and personnel to enforce the flood of new laws produced by an increasingly complex society.

In recent decades, considerable progress has been made in correcting such problems. Local, state, and federal governments have spent large sums of money to improve police training and record-keeping systems and to expand crime control techniques. Government expenditures for police services totaled $44 billion for fiscal year 1993 (Maguire and Pastore, 1997:4).

PUBLIC PERCEPTIONS OF THE POLICE

Given the long-standing distrust and spotty history of the police, experts have alluded repeatedly to the public's ambivalence about them (Bittner, 1970:

Chap. 2; Blumberg and Niederhoffer, 1985; Moore, 1992:110; Wilson, 1970:24–29, 41–43). Ben Whitaker, an English lawyer who studied the police system there, described this ambivalence as follows:

> The public use the police as a scapegoat for its neurotic attitude towards crime. Janus-like we have always turned two faces toward a policeman. . . . We employ him to administer the law, and yet ask him to waive it. We resent him when he enforces the law in our own case, yet demand his dismissal when he does not elsewhere. We offer him bribes, yet denounce his corruption. We expect him to be a member of society, yet not to share its values. We admire violence, even against society itself, but condemn force by the police on our behalf. We tell the police that they are entitled to information from the public, yet we ostracize informers. We ask for crime to be eradicated, but only by use of "sporting" [constitutional] methods. (Morris and Hawkins, 1970:89)

Whitaker's description is valuable because it indicates that police behavior, good or bad, often mirrors public attitudes. To be sure, mixed feelings are inevitable as a result of the storm-trooper image that police often project. Dressed in jodhpurs and boots, wearing helmets and dark glasses, with pistols and clubs strapped to their belts, they can trigger a tinge of panic in even the most innocent citizen. But for many citizens who are themselves law-violating hypocrites, the suspicion cannot be allayed that the police are likewise hypocritical and less than law-abiding. The notion lingers that "those who do battle against evil cannot themselves live up fully to the ideals they presumably defend" (Bittner, 1970:7).

Sometimes the suspicions are confirmed. We all have read or heard accounts of police corruption:

> A store's door is tried and found open; officers loot the place. A cop is sent to guard a DOA [dead-on-arrival], and cash and jewelry mysteriously disappear. A motorist is pulled over, and a large bill is attached to the license. Prisoners regularly complain that more money was taken from them at the time of arrest than was returned on release. (Bouza, 1990:53; also see McAlary, 1987; Skolnick and Fyfe, 1993)

Although public indignation over such behavior is justified, the police are not the only people who violate the law. Indeed, consider just a few examples: taxpayers who cheat on their income taxes, workers who steal property from their places of employment, businesspeople who report personal expenditures on their company accounts, and motorists who drive under the influence of alcohol or other drugs. It appears, then, that police officers may be judged by standards that are applied otherwise only to such guardians of public morality as ministers and teachers. As Whitaker said, we always have turned two faces to police officers: on the one hand, distrusting them, but on the other, expecting exemplary behavior from them. That position is made worse by the different roles that the police are expected to play: the crime fighter when dealing with lawbreakers versus the social service provider when responding to citizens' cries for help (e.g., providing emergency medical aid or getting cats out of trees).

Crime Fighter

In a rather remarkable account, a group of police officers once analyzed, from their perspective, the media-created image of the main protagonists in the war on crime: the criminals and the crime fighters. They noted that criminals often are more famous than the police who fight them, and they listed a large number of famous criminals, spanning many decades:

> John Dillinger, "Baby Face" Nelson, "Pretty Boy" Floyd, "Machine Gun" Kelly, [Bonnie and Clyde], . . . "Willie the Actor" Sutton, the Boston Strangler, nurse killer Richard Speck, Charles Whitman of University of Texas notoriety, Charles Manson and his family, Lindbergh kidnapper Bruno Hauptmann, Alcatraz "Birdman" Robert Stroud, Caryl Chessman, Hickok and Smith of "In Cold Blood" infamy, . . . San Francisco's Zodiak [sic] killer, and a host of Mafia-type hoodlums, including "Scarface Al" Capone, "Lucky" Luciano, Frank Costello, Albert Anastasia, and Vito Genovese. (Carter et al., 1971:80)

One could add the names of many other criminals: Ted Bundy, Lyle and Erik Menendez, Jeffrey Dahmer, Michael Milken, Bernard Goetz, Patty Hearst, and Carla Faye Tucker, to name just a few. "The list," as the police officers noted, "is seemingly endless" (Carter et al., 1971:80), and some on the list not only are famous but have been viewed as folk heroes (Kooistra, 1989).

But who remembers real-life crime fighters? Who are they? At best, people can name only a few: J. Edgar Hoover (who, today, is as notorious as he is famous), Elliott Ness of "Untouchables" fame, and perhaps O. W. Wilson, August Vollmer, and William Parker. Even though the latter were police chiefs, they are not well known outside of law enforcement circles. Instead, police officers generally are seen by the public in terms of a series of stereotypes: the dumb Irish cop, the flatfoot, the dick, the gumshoe, the fuzz, or the pig. Sad, but true, "the 'good guys'" have been "very bad at being good" (Carter et al., 1971: 80). This is ironic in that the crime problem usually has been portrayed in American folklore as black and white, as good guys versus bad guys.

If regular police officers are distrusted and unknown, who are the good guys? They are not ordinary police officers, but are fictional characters. Carter and his associates (1971:82, 86) called them "SUPERcrimefighters": Dick Tracy, Batman, Superman, Mighty Mouse, and the Lone Ranger, for example, and to that list we can add the Mighty Morphin Power Rangers, Robocop, and the X-Men. Ordinary police officers are incapable of waging the war on crime, so SUPERcrimefighters have been created to fill the void. Moreover, certain themes running through America's crime-fighting mentality suggest that unusual characteristics and techniques are required of SUPERcrimefighters (pp. 82–88):

1. SUPERcrimefighters are not mere mortals, but rather possess exceptional intuition, intelligence, and toughness, which makes them indestructible and all-powerful.
2. Crime is best stamped out by gimmicks, hardware, and the products of science. Dick Tracy has a two-way wrist radio; Batman's belt is loaded with sophisticated devices; and James Bond's car has a bullet-proof shield, machine guns, an ejection seat, and a device for spilling oil on the road to thwart evil pursuers.
3. SUPERcrimefighters always triumph over evil; the bad guys are always caught, and so crime never pays.

4. Violence is inevitably present in crime and its control. Most comic strips and television shows portray heroes and villains who are involved in an almost endless orgy of violence. Even Mighty Mouse dispatches cat villains by punching them in the nose.
5. SUPERcrimefighters usually must operate outside the law in order to control crime.

Chester Gould, the creator of Dick Tracy noted:

> The trend of the times seemed to be exactly right for a straight shoot-'em-down detective. We had a crime situation . . . that was beyond coping with legally—or what we would call legally today. So I brought out this boy Tracy and had him go out and get his man at the point of a gun, and, if necessary, shoot him down. (Carter et al., 1971:82)

Not surprisingly, therefore, most SUPERcrimefighters burglarize to collect evidence, use illegal wiretaps, obtain confessions through threats or brutality, and engage in a long list of other acts that are contrary to law.

Given such a construction of the way crime is fought, ordinary police officers are losers. The image of the successful crime fighter cannot possibly fit a law-abiding police officer who is constrained by constitutional provisions protecting the rights of individuals. Furthermore, the popular image of what it is that police officers do bears little resemblance to their actual work.

Social Service Provider

Only about half of all police work involves crime-related activities (Greene and Klockars, 1991:280–281). In addition, "patrol officers individually make few important arrests. The 'good collar' is a rare event" (Skolnick and Bayley, 1986:4). Unlike fictional SUPERcrimefighters, most police officers never fire a shot away from the range, nor do they engage in wild confrontations involving karate chops and judo holds or duck bullets zinging through the air (Carter et al., 1971:86). How, then, do police officers spend their time?

They spend much of it providing social services or, as Cumming and her associates (1965:283) described it, playing "philosopher, guide, and friend." To be sure,

> a large portion of them [social services] involve emergencies that could deteriorate rapidly and lead to bad consequences unless someone responds quickly with help. But these are rarely crime emergencies. More often, they are social emergencies such as domestic disputes that have not yet become knife fights or children on the street alone at night or the sudden fears of an elderly woman who hears noises or health emergencies like drug overdoses or miscarriages. (Moore, 1992:114–115)

For the poor, in particular, the police must often play this role of social service provider—calming unruly children, providing information to people in trouble, or acting as counselors in interpersonal conflicts (Bouza, 1990:109). Other resources may be unavailable to them: "All citizens can count on emergency help from the police when there is sudden illness at night, but only a certain kind of citizen takes his marital troubles to them" (Cumming, Cumming, and Edell, 1965:286). Perhaps efforts to deal with problems like those counteract some of the negative public perceptions of the police, but the evidence is by no means conclusive that it does:

1. Many citizens express attitudes that are inconsistent with the actual demands they place on the police. They want them to be SUPERcrimefighters, not social service providers, and they want "more police protection rather than improvement in the quality of service" (Walker, 1992:230–231).
2. Although most Americans hold generally favorable views of the police, many do not—particularly poor people and racial/ethnic minorities (Maguire and Pastore, 1997:119,126). Some in this latter group view the police as intruders in poor neighborhoods who are often unfair, racist, and brutal (Lohman and Misner, 1966; Skolnick, 1973; Walker, 1992:224).
3. Many crime victims do not report their victimization to the police. This is due, in part, to a belief that the police cannot or will not do anything, and also to a reluctance to become involved in time-consuming criminal justice

activities: identifying offenders, going to court, and testifying as witnesses (Maguire and Pastore, 1997:225).

Given such a state of affairs, how do the police respond to the public's ambivalence toward them?

POLICE VIEWS OF POLICE WORK

The police tend to view themselves in two ways: as social outcasts and as crime fighters.

Social Outcasts

Police officers share the public's view that they have a tainted occupation. They see themselves as pariahs, as outcasts:

> [The police officer] regards the public as his enemy, feels his occupation to be in conflict with the community, and regards himself to be a pariah. The experience and the feeling give rise to a collective emphasis on secrecy, an attempt to coerce respect from the public, and a belief that almost any means are legitimate in completing an important arrest. (Westley, 1953:35)

The police, as a result, are sensitive to criticism and are impatient with abstract, academic definitions of their work. Consider a Los Angeles police sergeant's response to one such definition by Bittner (1970:46):

> BITTNER: The role of the police is best understood as a mechanism for the distribution of non-negotiably coercive force employed in accordance with the dictates of an intuitive grasp of situational exigencies.
>
> SERGEANT: What the fuck does that mean? (Carter, 1976:121)

Police officers tend to have feelings of frustration, anger, anxiety, alienation, and hostility about their work:

> People don't like cops. Now, maybe some cops did some stupid things, but most of us are trying to do good. . . . You wonder why we stick together; you almost have to. . . . Nobody under-

stands; non-cops can't understand it. Maybe we don't understand it ourselves. Next time you're in a bar, tell the dude next to you that you're a cop. Watch him come apart. Or try to make it with some broad and tell her you're a cop. Shit. Nothing. People want you around and they don't want you around. They love you, they hate you. They need you, they don't need you. God, if the role is fuzzy, it's probably because no one really knows what they want from police. (Carter, 1976:122–123)[2]

Crime Fighters

Despite feelings of frustration and anger, police officers share the public's view that they should be crime fighters, not social service providers. Police officers are:

> inclined to see . . . calls [for social services] as "garbage calls" that waste their resources and special capabilities and distract them from the main job of being ready to deal with serious crime whenever it occurs. . . . [P]olice who are committed to professional law enforcement believe it is wrong for them to waste much time with these nonmission-related calls. (Moore, 1992:115)

Even those citizens believe that their family quarrels and neighborhood disturbances require police attention, the police tend to resent them. "You ought to talk to Sergeant ———; he's a classic. He'll tell you straight out that prevention isn't our job: parents ought to be doing more, the schools ought to get rid of the fuckups, and people ought to go to church" (Carter, 1976:130).

POLICE ATTITUDES TOWARD JUVENILE WORK

Given such views of themselves, it is not difficult to imagine police views on the rehabilitative ideal for

---

[2]This excerpt and others from "The Police View of the Justice System" by Robert M. Carter are reprinted from The *Juvenile Justice System*, Vol. 5, Sage Criminal Justice System Annuals, Malcolm W. Klein (ed.), 1976, by permission of the author and the publisher, Sage Publications, Inc., Beverly Hills/London.

juveniles—and the criminology professors whom they believe herald it:

> Nothing personal, but most professors don't know what they are talking about. They sit on the campus putting out all this good shit about rehabilitation and causes of crime. Most of them haven't ever been on the street; and if you want to know what's happening, you have to be on the street. They haven't seen these assholes after the sun goes down, laughing and scratching, shucking and jiving. Instead of them telling us about crime, we ought to be telling them. If they would spend a couple of days with us, they might find out what's happening. No, they don't want to do that, it might upset all their theories. I've heard some of those theories in school. Bullshit! What has toilet training got to do with anything? Nothing. They ought to be teaching stuff we can use, not all that sociology and social work. Like they say in the army: they don't know shit from shinola. It's a shuck. (Carter, 1976:123)

To many police officers, the traditional concept of juvenile justice is distorted and unrealistic. It has forced them to play the role of social service provider to neglected children and status offenders while hindering their attempts to control serious crime among young "hoodlums" and "pukes":

> I don't want to sound like a hardass, but we have some really bad young hoodlums on the streets of L.A. These aren't the nickel and dime kid shoplifters; they are hardcore. Some of them have dozens of arrests, but they're still out there ripping off people. Some of them have killed people, but they are still out there. . . . These pukes are into juvenile hall and out twenty minutes later; seriously, some of these hoodlums are back on the street before I finish the paperwork. If you are going to correct kids, they have to get their hands whacked the first time they put them in the cookie jar, not six months later. Juvenile justice is slow. Jesus, the rights these kids have got. They have more rights than I have: lawyers, witnesses, the whole bag. I'm not talking about the Mickey Mouse cases; I mean the hoodlums. (p. 124)

As one officer suggested, the juvenile justice system on the streets does not include kindly judges or probation officers, but only two people in a squad car:

> When you turn a corner, drive into an alley, or respond to a 211 IP or 459 silent, you don't know what's going to happen. It might be a psycho, a street junkie, some kid on speed, or even some dude who wants to waste a cop. Might not be anything. You don't know. But let me tell you what the justice system is then. It is me and my partner. We have a car, a radio, a backup unit, two 38s, one shotgun in the rack. That is the justice system on the street. To make it complete, you add one criminal. (p. 123)

More and more people today side with the police. American society is in a transitional phase in which many laws and procedures with respect to children are being changed radically, and those changes already have affected how the police process juveniles.

POLICE PROCESSING OF JUVENILES

Police processing of juveniles can be understood best by considering the following questions:

1. How do the police respond to widespread law violation by juveniles?
2. How many juveniles are actually arrested each year?
3. For what kinds of offenses are juveniles arrested most often?
4. What do the police do with arrested juveniles?
5. When questioned by police, are juveniles warned of their rights and protected against self-incrimination?
6. What criteria contribute to police decision making?

Police Response to Law Violations

In Chapter 5, we learned that there is an enormous amount of undetected law violation among juveniles. Almost every child breaks the law, sometimes repeatedly and sometimes seriously. Are the police aware of that? The evidence indicates that they are but that they regard much delinquency as not serious and, therefore, do not take formal action against it. Instead, the police exercise discretion in deciding which of the many children who come to their attention will be arrested (Levine, 1973:558).

Bordua (1967:161), for example, found that the police in Detroit had contacts with juveniles eleven times more frequently than they made arrests. Of well over 100,000 encounters with juveniles, only 9 percent resulted in actual arrest. Findings of the same sort were reported by Terry (1967a:223) in Racine, Wisconsin. Of 9,023 offenses known to the police, only 9 percent were referred to the probation department, and only 3 percent actually resulted in court hearings. Such figures vary from department to department, but overall, they suggest that the police are disinclined to arrest many juveniles who otherwise might be sent to court for disposition (Black and Reiss, 1967:67–80; Goldman, 1969:284; Terry, 1967b:177; Williams and Gold, 1972:221).

Arrests

In relation to their part of the total population, the percentage of juveniles actually arrested in a given year is not large. In 1996, for example, there were approximately 30.3 million juveniles, ages 10–17, in the United States (Day, 1993:18); yet there were only about 1.9 million juvenile arrests (FBI, 1997:218). If each arrest represented one juvenile, 6 percent of all juveniles would have been arrested, but because a person can be arrested more than once, the actual figure was less than 6 percent.

Obviously, when arrests are accumulated over a period of several years, the percentage of juveniles who have been arrested increases considerably. In their study of a birth cohort in Philadelphia, for example, Wolfgang, Figlio, and Sellin (1972:54) found that 35 percent (3,475) of the 9,945 boys in the cohort had at least one official police contact by age 18. However, because a contact does not necessarily lead to an arrest, the arrest rate was lower than 35 percent.

Offenses Leading to Arrests

The laws in most states empower the police to take custody of dependent/neglected children and status offenders, as well as those who violate the criminal law (Murray, 1983:51–52; Rubin, 1985:Chap. 3). Given that power, official statistics are revealing.

In 1996, persons under age 18 accounted for 35 percent of all arrests for serious property crimes— burglary, larceny, motor vehicle theft, and arson—and 19 percent of all arrests for violent crimes—murder, rape, robbery, and aggravated assault (FBI, 1997: 218). Although juveniles account for a larger share of arrests for serious crimes than we might like, these still represent a relatively small proportion of all arrests of juveniles (Sampson, 1985:350). Indeed, juveniles tend to be arrested more frequently for such less serious offenses as fighting, disorderly conduct, liquor- and other drug-related offenses, and status offenses. Indeed, in 1996, about 70 percent of all juvenile arrests involved nonindex offenses (see Chapter 4)—those other than murder, rape, robbery, aggravated assault, burglary, larceny, motor vehicle theft, and arson (FBI, 1997:218).

Treatment of Arrested Juveniles

In principle, laws should apply equally to all juveniles; that is, once arrested, all youths should be treated uniformly. But that is not what actually happens. Instead, the police are inclined to make use of several dispositional alternatives, some of which are not prescribed by law. They may (1) take the child to the station and release him or her to the custody of a parent; (2) refer the child to the juvenile bureau of the police department, if it has one, and leave further decisions to the officers working there; (3) refer the child to some community welfare agency; (4) refer the child directly to juvenile court; or (5) refer the child to adult criminal court.

Until recently, the police referred about half of arrests to juvenile court, handling most of the rest entirely within their own departments (FBI, 1976: 177). This latter procedure is known as **counsel and release**—the juvenile's parents are summoned to the station and, if they seem interested and willing, both they and the child are warned about the evils of misbehavior and urged to take steps to see to it that it does not happen again. "Generally, petty offenders and first offenders receive a warning and a return home; for more serious or repetitive offenders, the police decision is a referral to court" (Rubin, 1985: 93). The police also have the option of referring a child to a private or public welfare agency, but the number of children thus referred has not been large. In 1975, for example, only 1.4 percent of all arrested youths were referred to welfare agencies (FBI, 1976:177).

By 1996, more arrestees—69 percent—were referred to juvenile court, with fewer being counseled and released (FBI, 1997:271). There are several possible reasons for the change in police practices from earlier decades, but they all involve the fact that the juvenile justice system is in a transitional phase. The "clear picture emerging from these data is of more formal and restrictive police responses to youth crime" (Krisberg et al., 1986:12).

Questioning of Juveniles

According to the Fifth Amendment of the Constitution, any person charged with a crime is protected from self-incrimination; that is, the individual should not be required to answer questions that might result in prosecution and conviction. Children, however, traditionally did not enjoy the protection of that amendment. Because the presumed purpose of the juvenile justice system was treatment, not punishment, ordinary protections were not guaranteed, and the practices of the police and juvenile courts were not subjected to the scrutiny of higher courts.

In the mid-1960s, however, the Supreme Court closely reviewed the practices of the juvenile justice system for the first time (*In re Gault,* 1967; *Kent* v. *United States,* 1966; *Miranda* v. *Arizona,* 1966). As a consequence, most states ordered the police and juvenile courts to change their practices. Specifically, the courts required police to advise juveniles that (1) they need not answer any questions; (2) anything they might say could be used against them; (3) they had the right to have an attorney present during interrogation; and (4) if they could not afford an attorney, one would be provided (Bird, Conlin, and Frank, 1984:475–479; Levine, 1973:559). The Supreme Court noted further that juveniles might not fully appreciate the consequences of waiving their rights. Because they were immature and likely to be incapable of resisting a threatening or persuasive adult, advice might not be enough. Instead, the child's parents should be notified of any proposed

interrogation and should be present when one occurred (Bird, Conlin, and Frank, 1984:478–479; Levine, 1973:559).

The implications of such procedural changes have been great. However, because there is always a considerable lag between the time legal decisions are handed down and the time police actually put them into practice, their full effects are still being debated (Holtz, 1987). In fact, this is one reason the juvenile justice system is in a state of transition—the old practice of ignoring the rights of juveniles is being replaced.

Police Decision Making

Thus far, we have considered some perplexing issues. We have seen that the police traditionally have been inclined to avoid arresting juveniles. Because they have been granted considerable discretion, however, the police continue to counsel and release many of those whom they have arrested, albeit less frequently than in the past. Even more perplexing, we have seen that about 70 percent of juvenile arrests are for non-index offenses. Are there criteria by which to make sense of police behavior? The answer is that there are criteria, in addition to those that are strictly legal, that influence police decision making.

OFFENSE SERIOUSNESS The seriousness of an offense is a factor in determining the course of police response. Virtually all alleged felony encounters end in arrest, while only a small percentage (5–15 percent) of those apprehended for rowdiness or status offenses are arrested (Black and Reiss, 1970:68–69; Lundman, Sykes, and Clark, 1978:79–80; Piliavin and Briar, 1964:209; Terry, 1967a:224–228).

CITIZENS AS COMPLAINANTS Many potential arrest situations result from citizens' complaints, not police patrols (Black and Reiss, 1970:66–67; Terry, 1967a: 223). Except for traffic offenses, citizens initiate many of the contacts (Lundman, Sykes, and Clark, 1978:76–78, 80–83). And when they do, police decisions may hinge on whether the complainants are present and what their wishes are. "In not one instance," reported Black and Reiss (1970:71), "did the police arrest a juvenile when the complainant lobbied for leniency." But if the citizen demanded action, it was taken (Emerson, 1969:42). Clearly, then, police sensitivity to citizen complainants affects police processing of juveniles. A child who might be counseled and released in one setting might be arrested and processed further in another.

DEPARTMENTAL POLICY Police practices vary widely from community to community, depending not only on differences in law but also on differences in departmental policy. In his study of four Pennsylvania communities, for example, Goldman (1969:280) found that the percentage of juvenile arrests that were referred to court varied enormously from one community to the next—from a low of 9 percent in one community to a high of 71 percent in another. Similarly, in a study of forty-eight police departments in southern California, Klein (1970) found that virtually all arrested juveniles in one department were referred to court, while in another, 4 out of 5 juveniles were counseled and released.

Such widely varying policies often reflect the sentiments of the communities in which the departments are located. Sometimes, however, they are associated with internal departmental policies and structures (Lundman, Sykes, and Clark, 1978:78). In one highly professionalized department, Wilson (1968) found that the police were very impersonal toward juveniles, went strictly by the book, arrested many of them, and released very few. In another city, he found a much less professionalized department in which officers were permitted a wide latitude of choice, often lived in the neighborhoods in which they worked, dealt with juveniles in a highly personal manner and viewed their arrests as "Mickey-Mouse," low-status arrests.

Smith (1984:30) found much the same thing in a comparison of four types of departments: "In legalistic [highly professional and bureaucratic] departments, 17.6% of suspects under the age of eighteen were arrested," compared with between 5 and 9 percent in less legalistic departments. Thus, he noted, "police officers in legalistic departments appear to treat the infractions of youthful offenders more formally, whereas officers in other types of police agencies handle problems with juveniles without resorting to the legal system."

Such findings once again illustrate that justice does not operate uniformly throughout the United States. Instead, it takes on widely different meanings, depending not only on varying policies among departments but also on community sentiments, the wishes of complainants, the type of offense committed, and possibly other criteria such as the gender, race, and social class of the offender.

GENDER Legal rules supposedly apply equally to girls and boys. Realistically, however, their application often has reflected a double standard, one that has had striking and paradoxical consequences. Our analysis of self-reported delinquency in Chapter 5 revealed that compared to boys, girls report fewer delinquent acts, but the kinds of offenses they commit are similar. Like boys, girls commonly drink alcohol, smoke marijuana, shoplift, skip school, destroy property, commit theft, and burglarize. The police, however, have not always reacted to their offenses in similar ways. Criminal offenses, for example, traditionally have been defined as male behaviors; and some investigators, after controlling for the seriousness of the offense and the offender's prior record, have found that girls have been less likely than boys to be arrested and referred to court for them (e.g., Krohn, Curry, and Nelson-Kilger, 1983:425–427; Morash, 1984:104–107). Instead, girls have received chivalrous treatment from the police.

Not all studies, however, have reported evidence of chivalry. For example, Krohn, Curry, and Nelson-Kilger (1983:425) have indicated that police bias favoring girls who commit crimes is limited to misdemeanors and probably is decreasing over time. Moreover, other studies have suggested that the police do not discriminate at all in arresting boys and girls for criminal offenses; that is, they are not chivalrous toward girls (Dannefer and Schutt, 1982: 1123–1124; Sampson, 1985:358, 362; Williams and Gold, 1972:223).

Although the latter studies imply that male and female youths receive the same treatment from police officers, Visher (1983:22) has shown that gender bias may exist even when initial appearances suggest otherwise. In a study of 785 police–suspect encounters in twenty-four police departments in three cities, she found that although arrest rates for males and females (juveniles *and* adults) were essentially the same, "the police use different criteria in their arrest decisions for male and female suspects" (p. 22). For example, "younger females receive harsher treatment among female suspects than do older females," probably because of "different gender expectations for younger and older women. Police officers adopt a more paternalistic and harsher attitude toward younger females to deter any further violation of appropriate sex-role behavior" (p. 15). By contrast, the age of the suspect was irrelevant in arrest decisions for male suspects (pp. 15–17). Thus, although superficially the police seemed to react the same to males and females, closer examination revealed considerable bias.

There is additional evidence of discriminatory treatment of girls by the police. After examining over 10,000 police contacts with juveniles in a Midwestern city over approximately a twenty-five-year period, Krohn, Curry, and Nelson-Kilger (1983:424–425) found that girls were more likely than boys to be referred to juvenile court for status offenses (also see Staples, 1987:14–15, 17, 21). Furthermore, there was "no evidence for a decline in the paternalistic treatment of female status offenders"; indeed, it appeared to increase over time (p. 425). "Females who commit juvenile status offenses (e.g., sexual misbehavior, running away from home, truancy) may be seen as needing protection from themselves or from immoral influences" (p. 419).

Similar findings were reported by Teilmann and Landry (1981:74–75). Using self-reports of both offending and arrests from high school students in an Arizona county, they found that girls accounted for 47 percent of self-reported running away and the same percentage of incorrigibility. However, they constituted 58 percent of the arrests for running away and 78 percent of the arrests for incorrigibility, indicating that girls are "overarrested for status offenses when compared with boys" (Teilmann and Landry, 1981:74).

A tendency to overarrest female status offenders may not be due entirely to police actions, because it is usually parents who bring ungovernable girls to the attention of legal officials (Teilmann and Landry, 1981:75–76). Nonetheless, when the police are asked to intervene, their responses tend to reflect the views of the complaining parents—that girls should be obedient and protected from "unladylike" behavior. Boys, on the other hand, are allowed to "sow [their] wild oats" (Chesney-Lind, 1977:129).

RACE AND SOCIAL CLASS The race and social class of children are additional criteria that affect police decision making. It is uncertain, however, whether the effects are due to bigotry unique to the police or to more pervasive attitudes in our society.

Minority children historically have been overrepresented in arrest statistics. Many social scientists, as a result, have concluded that they are the scapegoats of frustrated police officers (Clinard, 1963:Chap. 18; Cloward and Ohlin, 1960:12; Lemert, 1951:311). Furthermore, racial/ethnic minorities often have agreed with that conclusion. To them, the police have been symbolic of oppression:

> Their very presence is an insult, and it would be, even if they spent their entire day feeding gumdrops to children. They represent the force of the white world, and that world's . . . criminal profit and ease, to keep the black man corralled up here, in his place. The badge, the gun in the holster, and the swinging club, make vivid what will happen should his rebellion become overt. (Baldwin, 1961:65–66)

It should come as no surprise that racial/ethnic minorities and the police often have viewed each other as enemies. Anyone familiar with the war mentality that characterizes their relationship knows that minor incidents quickly can escalate into battles (Skolnick and Fyfe, 1993:Chap. 6). Each group fears and distrusts the other, and it does little good to realize that in earlier times, the same kind of relationship existed between the police and white gang members.

Likewise, it does little good to learn that studies have not always found that the police discriminate against minority and lower-class youths. On the one hand, some researchers have concluded that is the case. After controlling for offense seriousness and prior record, they have found that the police are more inclined to arrest minority and/or lower-class youngsters or to refer them to court (e.g., Dannefer and Schutt, 1982:1123–1124; Ferdinand and Luchterhand, 1970:511–513; Sampson, 1986:880–884; Thornberry, 1973:93–97; 1979:168–169). Piliavin and Briar (1964: 210, 212–213) concluded that boys whose race, group affiliations, grooming, and language suggested to the police that they were "tough" guys were more likely to be arrested. Those characteristics, perhaps more than any offense they might have committed, determined police response.

On the other hand, other researchers have failed to find much evidence of discrimination by the police (Black, 1970:744–746; Hohenstein, 1969:146–149; Kurtz, Giddings, and Sutphen, 1993:50–51; Lundman, Sykes, and Clark, 1978:81–84; Morash, 1984:104–107; Shannon, 1963:27; Terry, 1967a:226–228; 1967b:177–178; Weiner and Willie, 1971:204, 208–209; Williams and Gold, 1972:223–225). However, most of them point out that one can reach this conclusion only by taking into account that (1) arrest rates vary widely from one community to another, (2) the highest arrest rates are in minority and lower-class areas, and (3) black complainants tend to be more insistent than white complainants that law-breakers be arrested.

When one sorts through all such factors, one finds that race and social class are not the major determinants of arrest. Rather, arrest rates in minority and lower-class areas are higher mainly because the young people living there are somewhat more likely to violate the law frequently and to commit serious offenses. Recall from our analysis of self-reported delinquency that the juveniles arrested most often are persons who, by their own admission, are the most frequent and serious law violators (see Chapter 5). Even though minority and lower-class youths are overrepresented in arrest statistics, therefore, it may be that they are more likely to be chronic offenders.

Because the scientific community is divided over this issue, we are faced with a dilemma in interpreting existing evidence. Gibbons and Krohn (1986:91) have concluded that one cannot really generalize about police bias. Rather, in all likelihood, "what these discrepant findings reflect are real differences among communities and police departments." Just as other policies vary from department to department, so practices with respect to minority and lower-class youths also are likely to vary. For example, Dannefer and Schutt (1982:1118–1119, 1122–1123) found that discriminatory practices by the police were most pronounced in the largest of two counties they studied, which also had the largest minority population. Perhaps, as "the proportion of the population that belongs to minority groups . . . increases, majority group members' fears . . . are

likely to increase" the motivation to discriminate (p. 115). That sort of finding may be generalizable to other locations; unfortunately, it does not begin to exhaust the complexities of the issue.

Throughout our history, Americans have tended to believe that the poverty, disrupted families, and ignorance of minority and poor people are the inevitable precursors of child neglect and lawbreaking. As a consequence, laws were written and the juvenile court was created to locate dependent and neglected, as well as law-violating, children, and to bring them into conformity with the ideal concept of childhood. Given such a construction of the nature and causes of delinquency, it should not be surprising that minority and lower-class children have become special targets of the police and other legal officials. Those children are more likely to be members of one-parent families and to be neglected, malnourished, and otherwise deprived, and the police have been conditioned to expect higher rates of delinquency among them (Garrett and Short, 1975). As a result, we may be confronted with a self-fulfilling prophecy: The very problems the police and citizens have been conditioned to expect actually occur.

If generations of minority and poor people have not enjoyed the economic, familial, and educational advantages that lead to success in our society, we should expect the consequences to be evident among their children. Indeed, they are: Minority and lower-class children have higher infant death rates, run much greater risks of biological impairment due to environmental deprivation, and are victimized in serious crimes far more often than other children. They experience difficulties in social adjustment, fail in school, and turn to street gangs for alternative sources of satisfaction and protection. Not having been socialized according to the dictates of the ideal concept of childhood and lacking a stake in conventional society, they often exhibit behaviors that are not only socially debilitating to themselves but also contrary to law.

If there is merit in this interpretation, then the tendency of the police to find and report higher rates of law-violating behavior, child abuse, and neglect among minority and poor children clearly is not simply the product of a bigotry peculiar to them. Rather, it is a function of real conditions for which the police are not solely responsible. Instead, the police are merely the frontline troops of conventional society who are expected to mop up messes of poor communities after a long war of attrition in which racism and social segregation have taken a heavy toll.

The actions of the police and the criteria they use in processing offenders are reflections of our sociocultural history and the kind of society it has produced. The ambivalent attitude of the police toward juveniles, their differential treatment of boys and girls, and their behavior in poor communities are the result not only of their own views but also of the way delinquency is defined and constructed in our society. If we are to understand how and why the police behave as they do, we must look not merely at them but at the roles into which they have been cast. During the 1900s, those roles have become increasingly important while the social control functions of the family, workplace, and community have declined. As long as new social inventions do not reverse that trend, the roles of the police will continue to increase in importance and will likely become more, not less, controversial.

Summary and Conclusions

Throughout their history, the police have been viewed with considerable public ambivalence: on the one hand, distrusted and feared, but on the other, expected to play the roles of social service provider and crime fighter. Police officers' views of themselves have reflected those views. Their chosen profession has been tainted, and they have seen themselves as outcasts, particularly in poor communities where they have been viewed as symbols of oppression. Hence, while much of their time has been spent assisting distressed adults or calming unruly children, they have received relatively little recognition for this type of work.

This conflicting situation affects the way the police handle and process juveniles:

1. *The police exercise discretion in deciding whom to arrest and whom to refer to juvenile court.* This discretion produces a filtering process, as shown in figure 16.1. Based on what we have learned in this and previous chapters, it presents an esti-

mate of the actual number of juveniles who violate the law and the actions the police take concerning them. Briefly, the evidence summarized in figure 16.1 is this:

- Given that most juveniles, ages 10–17, report having violated the law, the actual number of offenders probably numbered many millions nationwide in 1996.
- The police had contacts with many of those law violators. Although the exact number is unknown, they could have arrested many of them. The police, however, took no formal action against most law violators.
- The number of arrests of juveniles in 1996 was less than the number of juvenile contacts with the police.[3]
- About 69 percent of juvenile arrests resulted in a referral to juvenile court in 1996. Most of the remaining arrestees were counseled and released.

2. *The police filtering process is not random, but is affected by several criteria that help to determine who will be arrested and for what reasons.*

- Police practices have reflected society's concern with enforcing traditional moral rules for children. Even though the police are more likely to arrest serious than petty offenders, arrests for petty offenses still outnumber those for serious offenses.
- The police are highly sensitive to public attitudes, arresting or releasing offenders according to the wishes of complainants.
- The police sometimes have applied a double standard in making decisions about girls and boys. The evidence is equivocal about whether the police are less inclined to process girls than boys for criminal offenses, but most studies suggest that the police discriminate against girls when status offenses are involved.
- The actions of the police have helped to produce high arrest rates among minority and

---

[3]The number of arrests of juveniles in figure 16.1 (i.e., 1,315,578) is less than the 1.9 million arrests mentioned earlier. The reason is that the figures in figure 16.1 are based on reports from police agencies representing about 166 million of the U.S. population, while the other figure is based on reports from agencies representing about 168 million people (FBI, 1997:218, 271).

FIGURE 16.1

The police filtering process, 1996

SOURCES: Day, 1993:18; FBI, 1997:271.

NOTE: Figures based on 8,062 agencies; 1996 estimated population 165,572,000.

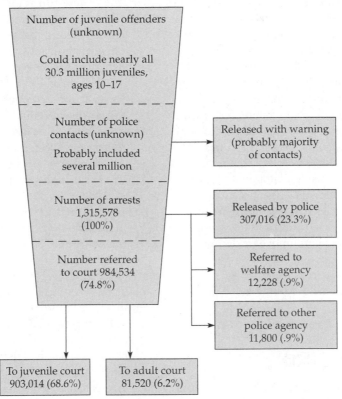

lower-class youths. These high rates may be partially due to the frequency and seriousness of their law-violating behavior, but they also reflect a tendency on the part of the police to respond to the social ills in those populations.

3. *Many, probably most, of the important decisions made by juvenile justice officials are made by the police—on the streets and in the stations—not by probation officers or judges.* Given the discretion exercised by the police, their actions could be said to be contrary to the original child-saving philosophy of the juvenile court—that all children with problems should be referred to court, not merely the ones whom the police chose to refer. It should be a wise, deliberate judge, with his or her supporting cast of experts, who decides whether intervention is required, not the cop on the street.

The actions of the police, however, reflect the ambivalent attitudes of our society and the practical problems of day-to-day police work. Indeed, if the police always followed the letter of the law, the courts would be inundated with offenders, and the resulting increase in official delinquency would be unprecedented—without the slightest change in juvenile behavior. Whether right or wrong, therefore, the police probably play the most crucial role in determining the nature and character of juvenile justice.

DISCUSSION QUESTIONS

1. How has the modern American police force evolved in the last century?

2. What is the public perception of the police, and what roles does the police officer play?
3. How do the police tend to view themselves?
4. How do the police view juvenile work, and how do they view delinquents?
5. What are the various components of police processing of juveniles, and what factors contribute to police decision making?

REFERENCES

Baldwin, James. 1961. *Nobody Knows My Name: More Notes of a Native Son.* New York: Dial Press.

Bird, John R., Marcia L. Conlin, and Geri Frank. 1984. "Children in Trouble: The Juvenile Justice System." Pp. 461–514 in Robert M. Horowitz and Howard A. Davidson, eds., *Legal Rights of Children.* New York: McGraw-Hill.

Bittner, Egon. 1970. *The Functions of the Police in Modern Society.* Washington, D.C.: U.S. Government Printing Office.

Black, Donald J. 1970. "Production of Crime Rates." *American Sociological Review* 35 (August): 733–748.

Black, Donald J., and Albert J. Reiss, Jr. 1967. "Patterns of Behavior in Police and Citizen Transactions." Section 1 of *Studies in Crime and Law Enforcement in Major Metropolitan Areas,* Vol. 2. Washington, D.C.: U.S. Government Printing Office.
1970. "Police Control of Juveniles." *American Sociological Review* 35 (February):63–77.

Blumberg, Abraham S., and Elaine Niederhoffer, eds. 1985. *The Ambivalent Force: Perspectives on the Police,* 3rd ed. New York: Holt, Rinehart & Winston.

Bordua, David J. 1967. "Recent Trends: Deviant Behavior and Social Control." *Annals of the American Academy of Political and Social Science* 369 (January):149–163.

Bouza, Anthony V. 1990. *The Police Mystique: An Insider's Look at Cops, Crime, and the Criminal Justice System.* New York: Plenum.

Carter, Robert M. 1976. "The Police View of the Justice System." Pp. 121–131 in Malcolm W. Klein, ed., *The Juvenile Justice System.* Beverly Hills, Calif.: Sage.

Carter, Robert M., et al. 1971. "SUPERcop and SUPERcriminal: The Media Portrait of Crime." *Daily Variety* 153, 38th Anniversary Issue (October):80–88.

Chesney-Lind, Meda. 1977. "Judicial Paternalism and the Female Status Offender: Training Women to Know Their Place." *Crime and Delinquency* 23 (April):121–130.

Clinard, Marshall B. 1963. *Sociology of Deviant Behavior,* rev. ed. New York: Holt, Rinehart & Winston.

Cloward, Richard A., and Lloyd E. Ohlin. 1960. *Delinquency and Opportunity: A Theory of Delinquent Gangs.* New York: Free Press.

Cole, Arthur C. 1934. *The Irrepressible Conflict, 1850–1865.* Vol. 7 in Arthur M. Schlesinger and Dixon R. Fox, eds., *A History of American Life.* New York: Macmillan.

Cumming, Elaine, Ian Cumming, and Laura Edell. 1965. "Policeman as Philosopher, Guide, and Friend." *Social Problems* 12 (Winter):276–286.

Dannefer, Dale, and Russell K. Schutt. 1982. "Race and Juvenile Justice Processing in Court and Police Agencies." *American Journal of Sociology* 87 (March):1113–1132.

Day, Jennifer Cheeseman. 1993. *Current Population Reports.* Series P-25, no. 1104. Washington, D.C.: U.S. Government Printing Office.

Emerson, Robert M. 1969. *Judging Delinquents: Context and Process in Juvenile Court.* Chicago: Aldine.

Federal Bureau of Investigation. 1976. *Crime in the United States: Uniform Crime Reports, 1975.* Washington, D.C.: U.S. Government Printing Office.
1997. *Crime in the United States: Uniform Crime Reports, 1996.* Washington, D.C.: U.S. Government Printing Office.

Ferdinand, Theodore N., and Elmer G. Luchterhand. 1970. "Inner-City Youth, the Police, the

Juvenile Court, and Justice." *Social Problems* 17 (Spring):510–527.

Garrett, Marcia, and James F. Short, Jr. 1975. "Social Class and Delinquency: Predictions and Outcomes of Police-Juvenile Encounters." *Social Problems* 22 (February):368–383.

Gibbons, Don C., and Marvin D. Krohn. 1986. *Delinquent Behavior,* 4th ed. Englewood Cliffs, N.J.: Prentice-Hall.

Goldman, Nathan. 1969. "The Differential Selection of Juvenile Offenders for Court Appearance." Pp. 264–290 in William J. Chambliss, ed., *Crime and the Legal Process.* New York: McGraw-Hill.

Greene, Jack R., and Carl B. Klockars. 1991. "What Police Do." Pp. 273–284 in Carl B. Klockars and Stephen D. Mastrofski, eds., *Thinking About Police: Contemporary Readings,* 2nd ed. New York: McGraw-Hill.

Hohenstein, William F. 1969. "Factors Influencing the Police Disposition of Juvenile Offenders." Pp. 138–149 in Thorsten Sellin and Marvin E. Wolfgang, eds., *Delinquency: Selected Studies.* New York: Wiley.

Holtz, Larry E. 1987. "*Miranda* in a Juvenile Setting: A Child's Right to Silence." *Journal of Criminal Law and Criminology* 78 (Fall):534–556.

In re Gault. 1967. 387 U.S. 1.

Kent v. *United States.* 1966. 383 U.S. 541.

Klein, Malcolm W. 1970. "Police Processing of Juvenile Offenders: Toward the Development of Juvenile System Rates." Los Angeles County Sub-Regional Board, California Council on Juvenile Justice, Part III.

Klein, Malcolm W., ed. 1976. *The Juvenile Justice System.* Beverly Hills, Calif.: Sage.

Kooistra, Paul. 1989. *Criminals as Heroes: Structure, Power and Identity.* Bowling Green, Ohio: Bowling Green State University Popular Press.

Krisberg, Barry, Ira M. Schwartz, Paul Litsky, and James Austin. 1986. "The Watershed of Juvenile Justice Reform." *Crime and Delinquency* 32 (January):5–38.

Krohn, Marvin D., James P. Curry, and Shirley Nelson-Kilger. 1983. "Is Chivalry Dead?: An Analysis of Changes in Police Dispositions of Males and Females." *Criminology* 21 (August):417–437.

Kurtz, P. David, Martha M. Giddings, and Richard Sutphen. 1993. "A Prospective Investigation of Racial Disparity in the Juvenile Justice System." *Juvenile and Family Court Journal*:43–59.

Lane, Roger. 1992. "Urban Police and Crime in Nineteenth-Century America." Pp. 1–50 in Michael Tonry and Norval Morris, eds., *Modern Policing.* Chicago: University of Chicago Press.

Lemert, Edwin M. 1951. *Social Pathology: A Systematic Approach to the Theory of Sociopathic Behavior.* New York: McGraw-Hill.

Levine, Martin. 1973. "The Current Status of Juvenile Law." Pp. 547–606 in Gary B. Adams et al., eds., *Juvenile Justice Management.* Springfield, Ill.: Thomas.

Lohman, Joseph D., and Gordon E. Misner. 1996. *The Police and the Community: The Dynamics of Their Relationship in a Changing Society.* 2 vols. Washington, D.C.: U.S. Government Printing Office.

Lundman, Richard J., Richard E. Sykes, and John P. Clark. 1978. "Police Control of Juveniles: A Replication." *Journal of Research in Crime and Delinquency* 15 (January):74–91.

McAlary, Mike. 1987. *Buddy Boys: When Good Cops Turn Bad.* New York: Putnam.

Maguire, Kathleen, and Ann L. Pastore, eds. 1997. *Sourcebook of Criminal Justice Statistics—1996.* Washington, D.C.: U.S. Government Printing Office.

Miranda v. *Arizona.* 1966. 384 U.S. 436.

Moore, Mark Harrison. 1992. "Problem-Solving and Community Policing." Pp. 99–158 in Michael Tonry and Norval Morris, eds., *Modern Policing.* Chicago: University of Chicago Press.

Morash, Merry. 1984. "Establishment of a Juvenile Police Record: The Influence of Individual and Peer Group Characteristics." *Criminology* 22 (February):97–111.

Morris, Norval, and Gordon Hawkins. 1970. *The Honest Politician's Guide to Crime Control.* Chicago: University of Chicago Press.

Murray, John P. 1983. *Status Offenders: A Source-book.* Boys Town, Nebr.: Boys Town, Nebraska Center, Communications & Public Service Division.

National Commission on Law Observance and Enforcement. 1931. *Report on Police,* No. 14. Washington, D.C.: U.S. Government Printing Office.

Piliavin, Irving, and Scott Briar. 1964. "Police Encounters with Juveniles." *American Journal of Sociology* 70 (September):206–214.

President's Commission on Law Enforcement and Administration of Justice. 1967. *Task Force Report: The Police.* Washington, D.C.: U.S. Government Printing Office.

Rubin, H. Ted. 1985. *Juvenile Justice: Policy, Practice, and Law,* 2nd ed. New York: Random House.

Sampson, Robert J. 1985. "Sex Differences in Self-Reported Delinquency and Official Records: A Multiple-Group Structural Modeling Approach." *Journal of Quantitative Criminology* 1:345–367.
1986. "Effects of Socioeconomic Context on Official Reaction to Juvenile Delinquency." *American Sociological Review* 51 (December):876–885.

Shannon, Lyle W. 1963. "Types and Patterns of Delinquency Referral in a Middle-Sized City." *British Journal of Criminology* 4:24–36.

Skolnick, Jerome H. 1973. "The Police and the Urban Ghetto." Pp. 223–238 in Arthur Niederhoffer and Abraham S. Blumberg, eds., *The Ambivalent Force: Perspectives on the Police.* San Francisco: Rinehart Press.

Skolnick, Jerome H., and David H. Bayley. 1986. *The New Blue Line: Police Innovation in Six American Cities.* New York: Free Press.

Skolnick, Jerome H., and James F. Fyfe. 1993. *Above the Law: Police and the Use of Excessive Force.* New York: Free Press.

Smith, Bruce. 1960. *Police Systems in the United States,* 2nd ed. New York: Harper.

Smith, Douglas A. 1984. "The Organizational Context of Legal Control." *Criminology* 22 (February): 19–38.

Staples, William G. 1987. "Law and Social Control in Juvenile Justice Dispositions." *Journal of Research in Crime and Delinquency* 24 (February): 7–22.

Teilmann, Katherine S., and Pierre H. Landry, Jr. 1981. "Gender Bias in Juvenile Justice." *Journal of Research in Crime and Delinquency* 18 (January): 47–80.

Terry, Robert M. 1967a. "Discrimination in the Handling of Juvenile Offenders by Social-Control Agencies." *Journal of Research in Crime and Delinquency* 4 (July):218–230.
1967b. "The Screening of Juvenile Offenders." *Journal of Criminal Law, Criminology and Police Science* 58 (June):173–181.

Thornberry, Terence P. 1973. "Race, Socioeconomic Status and Sentencing in the Juvenile Justice System." *Journal of Criminal Law and Criminology* 64 (March):90–98.
1979. "Sentencing Disparities in the Juvenile Justice System." *Journal of Criminal Law and Criminology* 70 (Summer):164–171.

Visher, Christy A. 1983. "Gender, Police Arrest Decisions, and Notions of Chivalry." *Criminology* 21 (February):5–28.

Walker, Samuel. 1992. *The Police in America: An Introduction,* 2nd ed. New York: McGraw-Hill.

Weiner, Norman L., and Charles V. Willie. 1971. "Decisions by Juvenile Officers." *American Journal of Sociology* 77 (September):199–210.

Westley, William A. 1953. "Violence and the Police." *American Journal of Sociology* 59 (July):34–41.

Williams, Jay R., and Martin Gold. 1972. "From Delinquent Behavior to Official Delinquency." *Social Problems* 20 (Fall):209–228.

Wilson, James Q. 1968. "The Police and the Delinquent in Two Cities." Pp. 9–30 in Stanton Wheeler, ed., *Controlling Delinquents.* New York: Wiley.
1970. *Varieties of Police Behavior: The Management of Law and Order in Eight Communities.* New York: Atheneum.

Wolfgang, Marvin E., Robert M. Figlio, and Thorsten Sellin. 1972. *Delinquency in a Birth Cohort.* Chicago: University of Chicago Press.

JUVENILE COURTS TODAY TEND TO BE A BLEND OF TRADITIONAL AND MODERN ELEMENTS.

CHAPTER SEVENTEEN

JUVENILE COURT

R ecall that the modern concepts of both childhood and the juvenile court resulted from centuries of change in both Europe and America. By the 1800s, people no longer tolerated the practice of killing or abandoning unwanted children. Instead, children were entitled to a series of nurturance rights. Not only were they guaranteed the right to life, food, clothing, and shelter, but they were to be raised and loved by their own parents, permitted to attend school to learn moral principles and reading and writing, and protected from evil city streets, immoral associates, and places of vice and corruption.

Such beliefs meant that the social status and influence of children inevitably would be subordinate to that of adults. They could not be both protected from and equal to adults. Persons who are supposedly guileless and immature cannot enjoy equal rights with those who know what is best for them and who are expected to safeguard and discipline them (Stafford, 1995). Thus, throughout much of the 19th century, children were committed to institutions, not merely to preserve order and protect society but also to serve their best interests.

Then, in 1899, when such commitments proved to be less than a panacea and it became clear that children still were being exploited, the juvenile court was invented. It would succeed where other means had failed.

JURISDICTION OF THE JUVENILE COURT

Although new state laws varied in their definitions of the powers of the juvenile court, all agreed that it would have jurisdiction over four kinds of children:

1. *Delinquent children*—those who committed an act that, if committed by an adult, would be a crime
2. *Status offenders*—those who were beyond the control of their parents or engaged in conduct thought to be harmful to themselves
3. *Neglected children*—those whose parents failed to provide proper care and guidance when they were able to do so
4. *Dependent children*—those whose parents, through no fault of their own, were unable to care for them (Paulsen and Whitebread, 1974:32)

In short, the new laws endowed the juvenile court with unprecedented powers. Whereas the Constitution of the United States protected adults from unreasonable invasions of privacy and governed any criminal proceedings against them with carefully prescribed procedures, such would not be the case where children were concerned. Instead, the concept of juvenile justice implied that such procedures would frustrate the child-saving functions of the court.

FUNCTIONS OF THE COURT

As envisioned by its inventors, the juvenile court would fulfill several important functions: (1) enforce the modern concept of childhood, (2) act as a surrogate for the family and school, (3) prevent delinquency, (4) decriminalize the behavior of young lawbreakers, and (5) rehabilitate juvenile offenders.

Enforcing the Modern Concept of Childhood

The first function of the juvenile court was to enforce the modern concept of childhood—the idea that (1) children go through several stages of development; (2) throughout those stages, they are qualitatively different from adults; and (3) until their full emotional, moral, physical, and rational skills are cultivated, children should be quarantined from adult vices and responsibilities.

Mandatory education and child labor laws of the late 1800s, along with the creation of the juvenile court, represented an embodiment of those ideas. That is why children have been referred to court not only for violating the criminal law but also for displaying idle conduct or intractability, associating with lewd or lascivious persons, being truant, being alone with someone of the opposite sex at night, or committing a host of other offenses. Legal definitions of youthful misbehavior reflected the moral principles inherent in the modern concept of childhood—that the ideal child should be obedient, self-controlled, hard-working, modest, and chaste. A paternalistic court was expected to ensure that children were safeguarded, formally educated, and carefully protected from adult behavior until they had outlived the quarantine associated with childhood.

Acting as a Surrogate for Family and School

The second function of the juvenile court was closely related to the first. Its creators hoped that the court would become a benevolent surrogate for uncaring families and ineffective schools. That is why the first juvenile court act in Illinois specified that the law should be "liberally construed, to the end . . . that the care, custody and discipline of a child shall approximate . . . that which should be given by its parents" (*Revised Statutes of Illinois*, 1899, Sec. 21).

By way of illustrating that expectation, the Educational Commission of Chicago complained in 1899 that its Compulsory Attendance Act was not adequate to ensure schooling for marginal children: "They cannot be received or continued in the regularly organized schools; . . . their parents cannot or will not control them; teachers and committees fail to correct their evil tendencies and vicious conduct. What shall be done with them?" (Harpur, 1899:161).

The answer, of course, was that the juvenile court would discipline them. It would rescue them from their dissolute parents and see to it that they were properly educated: "The welfare of the city demands that such children be put under restraint. . . . We should rightfully have the power to arrest all the little beggars, loafers, and vagabonds that infest our city, take them from the streets, and place them in schools where they are compelled to receive education and learn moral principles" (Harpur, 1899:163–164). In short, the juvenile court would act as a helpful and stern parent, stepping in when all else had failed.

Preventing Delinquency

By taking over for inadequate parents, teachers, and communities, the juvenile court could not only keep children in school but also perform a greater function: prevent delinquency. According to the Chicago Bar Association, the court should not have to wait until a child "has become criminal in habits and tastes" or is "in jails, bridewells and reformatories" before it acts. Instead, the court should "seize upon the first indications . . . of neglect or delinquency" and thereby prevent innocent children from wandering down the path to criminality (Platt, 1969:138–139). Furthermore, in fulfilling that role, the court would not be encumbered with all the inhibiting strictures of due process, because its primary goal was to surround chidren with good, not punish them for evil.

Decriminalizing Juvenile Lawbreaking

Besides using the juvenile court to prevent delinquency, reformers believed that it also could be used to decriminalize the behavior of young lawbreakers. In the past, as Judge Julian W. Mack (1910:296) indicated, children generally were "huddled together" with older criminals in the station houses, jails, and

workhouses of America. "Instead of the state training its bad boys so as to make of them decent citizens, it permitted them to become the outlaws and outcasts of society; it *criminalized* them by the methods that it used in dealing with them" (1910:293; emphasis added).

Judge Mack's lament reflected the fact that the treatment of children throughout the 1800s had not caught up with the belief that they were qualitatively different from adults. "Children tried for committing crimes were routinely processed primarily by lower municipal courts, which presumably did not adhere to the most libertarian conceptions of due process and adversary rights" (Schultz, 1974:248). At the discretion of their parents and guardians, as well as the police and courts, children were committed to industrial and training schools for being "destitute of proper parental care, or growing up in mendicancy, ignorance, idleness or vice" (Platt, 1969:103). Many also were confined in adult jails and prisons for the "blanket charge of disorderly conduct," which covered everything from committing assault with a deadly weapon to building bonfires in the street or playing on railroad tracks (Lathrop, 1917:2). To address those problems and avoid making outlaws out of children, the juvenile court would destigmatize them by calling them delinquents rather than criminals, and it would devise a set of remedies—as opposed to punishments—better suited to their needs.

Rehabilitating Juvenile Offenders

The idea that youthful lawbreaking should be decriminalized and its perpetrators reformed was symptomatic of the growing popularity of the concept of **rehabilitation.** Indeed, the growth of the school of positivist criminology only enhanced that popularity. Because crime in the streets and misconduct in schools were presumed to be due to causes over which children had no control, each misbehaving child was thought to require personal attention. Reflecting those ideas, William Healy, an influential psychiatrist who directed the Psychopathic Institute of the first Chicago Juvenile Court, argued that suitable remedies could be found only by a detailed analysis of each offender (Rothman, 1979:42–45). Poverty, alone, does not cause bad behavior, he concluded. Rather, it is due to "bad habits of mind" and "mental imagery of low order," both of which result from some combination of "defective interests," depraved parents, poverty, and "bad companions."

Indeed, when studying an urban juvenile court, Emerson (1969:249) noted the persistence of psychodynamic theory. "Illegal behavior," he observed, "is held to be 'pathological' and to reflect psychological conflicts which the psychiatrist can identify." His quotation from the guidelines of the court's psychiatric clinic illustrates his point:

> The commission of an offense must, by its antisocial nature, indicate some breakdown, overpowering, or remission of that facility which human beings have, or are expected to have, to maintain their status as law-abiding citizens. In a sense, then, an offense may be seen as symptomatic of an inner conflict which the ego is not able to effectively deal with. (p. 250)

The passage suggests that the only solution to delinquency is to attempt to discover the causes of delinquency for each child. Fortunately, it was believed, the juvenile court could act as the screening mechanism for the process.

In summary, then, the needs to be served and the remedies for meeting them were clear. The juvenile court would be endowed with all the discretion and power it needed to save America's children. There would be little need to draw sharp distinctions between 9-year-olds and 16-year-olds or between children who commit crimes and those who are poor, neglected, or failing in school. Judge Mack (1910: 297) proudly proclaimed that it is the duty of the state not merely to ask whether a child has committed a specific offense but also "to find out what he is, physically, mentally, morally, and then, if it learns that he is treading the path that leads to criminality, to take him in charge, not so much to punish as to reform, not to degrade but to uplift, not to crush but to develop, not to make him a criminal but a worthy citizen."

THE IDEAL PROCEDURES

In pursuit of that noble objective, the procedures of the juvenile court generally have been divided into three major steps: intake, adjudication, and disposition. A simplified version of those steps is displayed in figure 17.1. By reviewing each of them, we can determine how, according to proponents, each child is supposed to have been treated by the juvenile court.

Intake

Intake was to be the process during which a juvenile referral was received by the court and a series of important decisions was made. Specifically the court would decide whether to (1) hold the child in detention while his or her case was being investigated, (2) release the child with a warning, (3) file a petition for a formal court hearing, or (4) refer the child to some other agency, or to adult criminal court if he or she had committed a serious offense.

One of the major innovations of the juvenile court was the appointment of probation officers to conduct this screening process, as well as to supervise children following court action. Indeed, early judges were eloquent in their praise of that innovation. "The ideal probation officer," said Judge Harvey Baker (1910:326) of Boston, "should have all the consecration of the devoted clergyman, all the power to interest and direct of the efficient teacher, and all the discernment of the skillful physician." Likewise, Richard Tuthill, who was one of the first juvenile judges in Chicago, along with Julian Mack, called **probation** "the cord upon which all the pearls of the juvenile court are strung. . . . Without it, the juvenile court could not exist" (Rothman, 1979:50).

The intake inquiry conducted by the probation officer was supposed to fulfill two major functions. The first was diagnostic. The officer was charged with obtaining detailed information on the background, character, and needs of a child in order to enable the judge to look beyond the offense to the child's condition. As a result, the officer was given authority to obtain case histories from police, parents, teachers, neighbors, welfare workers, and any other relevant persons. The officer also was expected to seek information from such court-appointed experts as psychologists, physicians, and social workers. Depending on the officer's findings, he or she might dismiss the case, authorize a full court hearing, or dispose of it by informal methods, such as the counsel-and-release procedures used by the police. Judge

FIGURE 17.1

Juvenile court processing

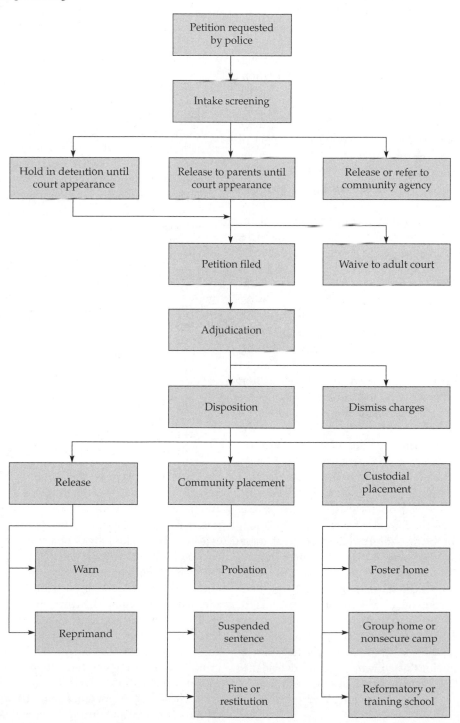

Baker (1910:322) likened the role of the probation officer to that of the medical technician who gathers the information necessary to make a diagnosis and recommend a cure.

The second major function of the probation officer was that of deciding, prior to a court hearing, whether the juvenile should be held in **detention.** This was a key function because one of the major goals of juvenile court legislation was to remove juveniles from adult jails. This goal was all the more important because few states extended the right of bail to children; therefore, it fell to probation officers to decide which children would be held in custody. If, in the officer's judgment, parents or guardians were unfit to supervise their children, or if children were viewed as serious threats to themselves or the community, they were to be detained. Otherwise, they could be released pending court action.

Adjudication

For those juveniles for whom intake resulted in the filing of a petition, adjudication was to be the formal hearing conducted by a judge, with the probation officer assisting. In contrast to a criminal proceeding, in which a defendant is found guilty or not guilty, the judge was to determine whether the allegations in the petition were to be sustained and whether the child should be defined as delinquent or as dependent or neglected.

Because, in principle, the juvenile court was charged with exploring the mental and social condition of a child, every state moved to relax the style of the adjudicatory proceedings. Judges were supposed to be selected on the basis of their special qualifications—their knowledge of child psychology and social problems—more than their legal training. Though they were not legally empowered to banish lawyers from their courts, that, in effect, was what happened. It was done on the grounds that the hearing of a case should be similar to what thoughtful parents might administer. Hence, judges were inclined neither to adhere to accepted rules of evidence used in adult proceedings nor to restrict admissions of guilt by youthful defendants. As Judge Orr of Minnesota put it, "the laws of evidence are sometimes forgotten or overlooked" (Rothman, 1979:49).

A description of the way in which juvenile courts were conceived and operated can be found in an important book, *Preventive Treatment of Neglected Children,* published in 1910. In it, one of the leading reformers of that time, Judge Baker (1910:319), described how he conducted juvenile court:

> The judge excludes all newspaper reporters and all other persons having only a general interest in the proceedings. The sheltered location of the room, the absence of decoration, the dispensing with attendants and the exclusion of outsiders give the simplicity which is necessary to gain the undivided attention of the child, and give the quiet which is indispensable for hearing clearly what the child says and speaking to him in the calmest tone.
>
> When the judge is ready to hear a case the probation officer brings in the child from the waiting room. The child does not stand in front of the desk, because that would prevent the judge from seeing the whole of him, and the way a child stands and even the condition of his shoes are often useful aids to a proper diagnosis of the case. The child stands at the end of the platform, where the judge can see him from top to toe, and the judge sits near the end, so he is close to the child and can reassure him if necessary by a friendly hand on the shoulder. The platform is just high enough to bring the average child's eye about on a level with the eye of the judge.

Boys and girls were treated somewhat differently. Judge Baker wanted to see a boy alone at first to spare him the embarrassment and the fear "which he often feels in speaking the truth in the presence of his parents" (p. 319). The judge's objective was to get the boy to admit his guilt. "The child is told . . . that in this court there is only one thing worse than stealing (or whatever the child is supposed to have done), and that is not telling the truth about it afterwards" (p. 320). If the boy continued to deny his guilt, Judge Baker, like a good father, continued to reason with him, pointing out why such a denial was harmful. Lying to protect oneself, one's friends, or one's parents only made things worse.

Such beliefs and practices have been neither exceptional nor isolated throughout the 1900s. In 1962,

Judge Paul W. Alexander, a former president of the National Council of Juvenile Court judges, agreed with Judge Baker in virtually the same terms, even though their careers were half a century apart:

> To help the child change his attitude, a confession is a primary prerequisite. Without it the court is aiding the child to build his future on a foundation of falsehood and deceit, instead of on the rock of truth and honesty. . . . Anything that may tend to discourage a child from making a clean breast of it, that may tend to encourage him to try to escape the consequences of his actions by denial or other means, must retard, and possibly defeat, the court's efforts to correct the child. (p. 88)

If the child persisted in denying his guilt, parents, police, and sometimes defense counsel could be brought in, and the case would be heard formally. But this was not the most desirable procedure. Judge Alexander (1962:89) indicated that "the question is almost never 'Did he or didn't he?' but rather 'What is the best way to change his wrong attitude and correct his unlawful behavior?'" Or, as Judge Baker (1910:320) related, a confession of guilt would enable the judge to say to a boy's parents, the police, and aggrieved parties: "John says it is true that he took Mrs. Doe's money and I adjudge him delinquent, and he has the right to appeal."

By contrast, Judge Baker was more chivalrous with girls. He warned that every step should be taken to protect their reputations, as well as the judge's. From the time of arrest, a girl should be turned over to an "accredited" woman. "When she [the girl] comes into the judge's chamber she is attended by a woman. . . . The judge never talks with girls alone as he sometimes does with boys" (p. 325). With the chaperone present, however, he could go on to conduct his fatherly hearing.

Cases sometimes were dismissed for lack of evidence. However, the major concern of a judge was not with establishing guilt or innocence, but with using the court hearing to begin reforming the delinquent. The general reasoning seemed to be that if children were in enough trouble to be in court, they probably needed help regardless of whether they were technically guilty of a delinquent act.

Disposition

Disposition refers to the process by which a judge decides what should be done with a juvenile for whom guilt is established—whether the child should be released to his or her parents or separated from them, and whether the child should be placed on probation or institutionalized. When an adult is tried, the disposition (i.e., sentencing) is separated from the adjudicatory process so as not to confuse it with decisions regarding a person's guilt or innocence. Because the inventors of the juvenile court were concerned less with a child's guilt than with his or her condition, however, the two hearings often were intermixed:

> Of course the court does not confine its attention to just the particular offense which brought the child to its notice. For example, a boy who comes to court for some trifle as failing to wear his badge when selling papers may be held on probation for months because of difficulties at school; and a boy who comes in for playing ball in the street may (after the court has caused more serious charges to be preferred against him) be committed to a reform school because he is found to have habits of loafing, stealing or gambling which cannot be corrected outside. (Baker, 1910:322)

The differences between these procedures and those in adult criminal courts are obvious: An adult could not be brought to court on one offense and found guilty of additional offenses; an adult is defended by a lawyer; and an adult could not be institutionalized on an initial charge of playing ball in the street.

The Indeterminate Sentence

Another striking feature of the juvenile court was its use of the **indeterminate sentence.** To secure the best possible long-term care for children, most states empowered the court to maintain supervision over them until age 21. In the event of some trifling matter, such as playing ball in the street, a child could be given a light punishment, such as copying the laws governing the proper use of public thoroughfares. Once that was done, probation officers and judges could check their work, "just as a physician might do in the case of a burn or a bruise" (Baker, 1910:323).

If the "burn" had healed, the patient could be released. But if the offense was serious, the child was "seen by the judge at frequent intervals, monthly, weekly, or sometimes even daily, just as with the patient and the physician in case of tuberculosis or typhoid" (p. 323). A disease such as delinquency might take a long time to cure.

PUBLIC ACCEPTANCE

Early reactions to the juvenile court and its rehabilitative ideology were overwhelmingly favorable; opposition was weak and divided. Some municipal judges objected to their loss of jurisdiction over juveniles, and a few police departments expressed fears that probation would send many serious offenders back to the streets. A leading scholar, Roscoe Pound, also warned in 1913 that "the powers of the court of star chamber were a bagatelle compared with those American juvenile courts. . . . If those courts chose to act arbitrarily and oppressively they could cause a revolution quite as easily as did the former" (Rothman, 1979:61). Yet, when he addressed a meeting of the National Council of Juvenile Court Judges in the 1950s, Pound described the juvenile court as "one of the most significant advances in the administration of justice since the Magna Carta" (National Probation and Parole Association, 1957:127).

As a result of that kind of acceptance, the philosophy and ideal procedures just described went largely unchallenged until well after mid-century. The concern of most authorities was not with protecting children from possible arbitrary procedures, but with finding ways by which those procedures could be made more effective.

THE TARNISHED SUPERPARENT: JUVENILE COURT IN THE 1960S AND 1970S

With any social institution, whether it is the family, church, school, or political system, there is always a gulf between expressed ideals and actual practices. The same is true of the juvenile court. Between 1960 and the mid-1970s, reformers became increasingly critical of it. The gap between its expressed ideals and actual practices, they contended, had become so large that it could no longer be tolerated. Their criticisms centered on the wide net of the juvenile court, lack of due process, assembly line justice, extensive use of detention, jailing of juveniles, rising crime rates, and liberal ideology.

The Wide Net of the Juvenile Court

The first criticism involved jurisdiction of the juvenile court over status offenses. At its meeting in London in 1960, the Second United Nations Congress on the Prevention of Crime and the Treatment of Offenders recommended that "the meaning of the term *juvenile delinquency* should be restricted as far as possible to violations of the criminal law" (United Nations, 1961:61). Such misbehaviors as running away, defying parents, or truancy should not be defined as delinquent.

The President's Commission on Law Enforcement and Administration of Justice (1967b:25) agreed:

> The provisions on which intervention . . . is based are typically vague and all-encompassing: Growing up in idleness and crime, engaging in immoral conduct, in danger of leading an immoral life. Especially when administered with the informality characteristic of the court's procedures, they establish the judge as arbiter not only of the behavior but also of the morals of every child (and to a certain extent the parents of every child) appearing before him. The situation is ripe for overreaching, for imposition of the judge's own code of youthful conduct. . . . One need not expound the traditional American virtues of individuality and free expression to point out the wrongheadedness of so using the juvenile court.

It recommended, therefore, that "serious consideration should be given to complete elimination from the court's jurisdiction of conduct illegal only for a child" (p. 27). The wide net of the juvenile court should be made much smaller.

It is worth noting that in subsequent years, most states have followed the recommendation of the

President's Commission (1967b) through diversion, deinstitutionalization, and decriminalization (Feld, 1998:521). Although those efforts reflected an attempt to narrow the net of the juvenile justice system, in many instances they actually may have expanded it. For example, diversion has involved the provision of services through informal, non-court-ordered programs. Those programs, however, have provided a means by which to expand rather than narrow juvenile justice efforts by applying informal interventions to those who previously might have been released (Feld, 1993b).

Similarly, deinstitutionalization represented an attempt to eliminate the practice of committing of status offenders to secure or long-term institutions. The federal government took the initiative in 1974 by passing the Juvenile Justice and Delinquency Prevention Act, which mandated that states deinstitutionalize status offenders if they were to continue to receive federal juvenile justice funding (Holden and Kepler, 1995; Raley, 1995). Yet many states today retain the authority to commit status offenders to group homes or other types of nonsecure institutions (Feld, 1998:522).

Finally, decriminalization involved attempts to relabel behaviors that previously were illegal only for children—for example, status offenses, such as truancy and running away from home. Those behaviors have become the basis for establishing alternative juvenile court jurisdiction, which is reflected by such labels as "persons in need of supervision" (PINS) or "children in need of supervision" (CHINS). It remains unclear whether such labels work to the benefit of children. As Barry Feld (1998:523), a prominent juvenile justice scholar, observed:

> Label changes simply shift youths from one jurisdictional authority to another without significantly limiting courts' dispositional authority. By manipulating classifications, states and juvenile justice personnel may relabel former status offenders downward as dependent or neglected youths, upward as delinquent offenders, or laterally into private-sector treatment facilities.

The result, historically, has been that "the child welfare, juvenile justice, and mental health systems dealt with relatively interchangeable youth populations and shifted them from one system to another depending on social attitudes, available funds, and imprecise legal definitions" (p. 523).

Lack of Due Process

The second criticism was based on the lack of due process in the juvenile court. In the 1960s and early 1970s, the Supreme Court of the United States rendered several decisions requiring that judges and other juvenile justice officials grant constitutional protections to children. In a now celebrated case, *Kent v. United States,* the Court observed that while there can be no doubt

> of the original laudable purpose of juvenile courts, studies and critiques in recent years raise serious questions as to whether actual performance measures well enough against theoretical purpose to make tolerable the immunity of the process from the reach of constitutional guaranties applicable to adults. . . . *There is evidence, in fact, that there may be grounds for concern that the child receives the worst of both worlds: that he gets neither the protections accorded to adults nor the solicitous care and regenerative treatment postulated for children.* (*Kent,* 383 U.S. 541, 555–556 [1966]; emphasis added)

In a second landmark case, *In re Gault,* the Supreme Court held in 1967 that the code and practices of the state of Arizona deprived children of procedural safeguards guaranteed by the Fourteenth Amendment. Gerald Gault was a 15-year-old boy charged with making an obscene phone call to a neighbor. After a juvenile court hearing, Gault was committed to an industrial school where he could have been held up to the age of 21. The maximum punishment he could have received had he been an 18-year-old adult would have been a fine of from $5 to $50 or confinement in jail for not more than two months.

Although the institutionalization alone was questionable, it was but one of many dubious practices that the Supreme Court noted in reversing the original decision. Gault, for example, was arrested and held in detention without notification of his parents.

A petition outlining the charges was not served on his parents prior to a hearing; indeed, the petition made no reference to any factual basis for taking court action. It stated only that "said minor is under the age of eighteen years, and is in need of the protection of this Honorable Court; [and that] said minor is a delinquent minor" (*In re Gault*, 387 U.S. 1, 5 [1967]).

The police and court actions leading to the institutionalization of Gault were based on a verbal complaint by his neighbor, but she never appeared in court to give sworn testimony. In fact, no one was sworn in at the hearing, no transcript or recording was kept, and Gault was not represented by counsel. He was alleged to have confessed to making the call, but his confession was never set down on paper, and it was obtained without the presence of his parents, without legal counsel, and without any advice of his right to remain silent.

Expressing his opinion of the case, Justice Abe Fortas wrote:

> Under our constitution, the condition of being a boy does not justify a kangaroo court. The traditional ideas of Juvenile Court procedure, indeed, contemplated that time would be available and care would be used to establish precisely what the juvenile did and why he did it—was it a prank of adolescence or a brutal act threatening serious consequences to himself or society unless corrected? Under traditional notions, one would assume that in a case like that of Gerald Gault, where the juvenile appears to have a home, a working mother and father, and an older brother, the Juvenile Judge would have made a careful inquiry and judgment as to the possibility that the boy could be disciplined and dealt with at home, despite his previous transgressions.... The essential difference between Gerald's case and a normal criminal case is that safeguards available to adults were discarded in Gerald's case. The summary procedure as well as the long commitment was possible because Gerald was 15 years of age instead of over 18. (*In re Gault*, 387 U.S. 1, 28–29 [1967])

The Supreme Court also suggested that the failure to exercise adequate safeguards characterized many jurisdictions, not just the Arizona court in question. It added that "Juvenile Court history has again demonstrated that unbridled discretion, however benevolently motivated, is frequently a poor substitute for principle and procedure" (*In re Gault*, 387 U.S. 1, 18 [1967]). Most of the justices concluded that "due process of law is the primary and indispensable foundation of individual freedom" (*In re Gault*, 387 U.S. 1, 20 [1967]).

The Supreme Court reaffirmed many of those ideas in 1970 in *In re Winship*. Again, the Court broke new ground by noting that proof of guilt beyond a reasonable doubt is required in juvenile as well as adult cases. Justice William Brennan wrote: "The same considerations that demand extreme caution in factfinding to protect the innocent adult apply as well to the innocent child" (*In re Winship*, 397 U.S. 358, 365 [1970]). Along with *Kent* and *Gault*, then, *Winship* set forth two important guidelines for the juvenile court: (1) Procedures that ensure fairness could not be discarded merely because the juvenile court purports to be benevolent and rehabilitative, and (2) guarantees of due process need not interfere with the rehabilitative and other traditional goals of the juvenile court (Paulsen and Whitebread, 1974:20).

The march to grant juveniles the same constitutional protections as adults was sidetracked in 1971, when the Supreme Court held, in *McKeiver* v. *Pennsylvania*, that the right to a trial by jury does not extend to delinquency cases in state courts (*McKeiver*, 403 U.S. 528 [1971]). States, however, were not prohibited from authorizing jury trials by statute or interpretation of state constitutions.

The march toward due process for juveniles did not stop altogether after 1971. In *Breed* v. *Jones* in 1975, the Supreme Court ruled that a juvenile court could not adjudicate a youngster for an offense and then transfer the case to adult criminal court for the same offense because that would constitute double jeopardy.

The Supreme Court, however, shifted directions again in the 1984 case of *Schall* v. *Martin*. That case dealt with a section of the New York Family Court Act that authorized "pretrial detention of an accused juvenile delinquent based on a finding that there is a 'serious risk' that the child 'may before the return date commit an act which if committed by an adult would constitute a crime'" (*Schall*, 467 U.S. 253, 255 [1984]). Originally, the plaintiffs had filed a suit in Federal District Court, claiming that the act was unconstitutional because of its vagueness and because it allowed for preadjudicatory detention:

> The District Court struck down the statute as permitting detention without due process and ordered the release of all class members. The Court of Appeals affirmed, holding that since the vast majority of juveniles detained under the statute either have their cases dismissed before an adjudication of delinquency or are released after adjudication, the statute is administered, not for preventive purposes, but to impose punishment for unadjudicated criminal acts, and that therefore the statute is unconstitutional as to all juveniles. (*Schall*, 467 U.S. 253 [1984])

The Supreme Court reversed the appellate court's decision. Justice William Rehnquist wrote that "preventive detention under the FCA [Family Court Act] serves a legitimate state objective, and that the procedural protections afforded pretrial detainees by the New York statute satisfy the requirements of the Due Process Clause of the Fourteenth Amendment to the United States Constitution" (*Schall*, 467 U.S. 253, 256–257 [1984]). Remarkably, the Supreme Court seemed to endorse a kind of second-class citizenship for juveniles: "*The juvenile's . . . interest in freedom from institutional restraints . . . must be qualified by the recognition that juveniles, unlike adults, are always in some form of custody*" (*Schall*, 467 U.S. 253, 265 [1984]; emphasis added).

Assembly Line Justice

A third criticism of the juvenile court was that it administered assembly line justice. As juvenile court was originally conceived, wise judges and probation officers were to have access to a wide array of resources for helping children. But considerable evidence suggests that this often was not the case.

To begin with, the structure of the juvenile court had taken many different forms. In some states, it was a unit of county government; in others, it was a statewide system. In some states, it was exclusively a family court; in others, it was part of a broad-based trial court system, on either the highest superior court level or the municipal court level, where lesser criminals were tried; in still others, it was a part of a probate court that heard both civil and criminal matters. In short, there was no uniform, nationwide system of juvenile justice (Rubin, 1976:133–134).

To make matters worse, juvenile court judges were not uniformly qualified. In 1963, one-fifth of these judges had received no college education; almost half had not earned a college degree; and one-fifth were not members of the bar. Rather than being selected for their expert knowledge of child psychology and social problems, three-fourths of them had been elected to office. Almost two-thirds were probably continuing political careers, having previously been elected to other offices (President's Commission, 1967b:6–7). Clearly, the juvenile court had not attained much stature in the court system or in the legal profession. Few law schools had courses on juvenile justice, and in those jurisdictions where the juvenile court was part of a superior or district court system, the feeling among judges was that assignment to the juvenile division was "a journey to Siberia" (Rubin, 1976:135).

Given those problems, many courts likely were operating a kind of assembly line justice. For example, Cohen (1975b:13) discovered that in one court, it took an average of 76 days for intake personnel to decide what to do about a case. If the case required judicial action, the average waiting period doubled, to 130 days; if it was contested in court, the wait was 211 days. But when a court hearing finally took place, it often lasted no longer than 10 or 15 minutes (President's Commission, 1967b:7).

Although probation was to be the "cord upon which all the pearls of the juvenile court are strung," one-third of all full-time judges in 1965 reported that they had no probation officer to assist them, and 83 percent said that they also had no psychiatric or psychological assistance (President's Commission, 1967b:6). Most states made provision for probation services, and 74 percent of the nation's counties had probation officers. However, their caseloads were large, and their pay was low (p. 6). As a result, the average probation officer had between 71 and 80 delinquents to supervise at any given time, in addition to the investigations he or she was supposed to make of new cases coming before the court.

Extensive Use of Detention

The fourth criticism of the juvenile court had to do with the large number of young people being held in detention while awaiting disposition of their cases. In the mid-1970s, approximately 520,000 youths were admitted to juvenile detention centers each year (Poulin et al., 1980:5–6). Because some jurisdictions did not have any juvenile detention centers, many youths also were detained in adult jails and police lockups—about 120,000 annually (p. 11). Overall, therefore, in the mid-1970s, about 640,000 young people each year were separated from their families and held in custody while the court decided what to do with them.

There were also wide disparities among states in the rate at which they detained juveniles (Poulin et al., 1980:5–15). For example, five states (California, Florida, Ohio, Texas, Washington) accounted for 50 percent of all the young people held in detention facilities nationwide, although less than 20 percent of the juvenile population, ages 5–17, lived in those states. The detention rate per 100,000 in California (4,734) was more than 100 times greater than the rate in North Dakota (45). Worse still, the same pattern prevailed in the use of jails: More than half of all the juveniles detained in jails were from ten states that included less than 20 percent of the juvenile population.

The extensive use of detention was disconcerting because the National Probation and Parole Association had set standards in 1957 that the number of children detained by the court normally should not exceed "20 percent of those referred to the court for delinquency" (Poulin et al., 1980:48). Then, in 1961, this figure was reduced to 10 percent (National Council on Crime and Delinquency, 1961:18). Such figures notwithstanding, only seven states in 1975 remained within the 20 percent guideline, to say nothing of the 10 percent level. Indeed, some states were detaining more than 90 percent of all referrals; the percentage for the nation as a whole was about 50 percent (Poulin et al., 1980:23–24).

Jailing of Juveniles

As if those problems were not enough, the National Council on Crime and Delinquency found in the mid-1960s that 93 percent of the nation's counties had no juvenile detention facilities at all (President's Commission, 1967a:121). As mentioned previously, detained juveniles in those counties were held in adult jails, police lockups, and drunk tanks despite the fact that the laws in most states severely restricted such practices.

Such a discrepancy between ideology and practice dated back to the first juvenile court in Illinois. After enacting laws that created the juvenile court and prohibited the use of jails for young people, Illinois legislators refused to approve the necessary funds to construct detention facilities (Schultz, 1974: 245). Most other states also continued to put children in jail.

In the 1970s, about two-thirds of the juveniles in jails nationwide were awaiting a formal hearing (Law Enforcement Assistance Administration, n.d.). Almost half of them were status offenders, the majority of whom were not segregated from adult criminals (Children's Defense Fund, 1976:20; Sarri, 1974:7–9). Some judges, in fact, reported that they "chose jails for juveniles to 'teach them a lesson'" (Sarri, 1974: 10). Meanwhile, others were being held in protective custody because they were abused or neglected children. "One child was in jail because her father was suspected of raping her. Since the incest could not be proven, the adult was not held. The child, however, was put in jail for protective custody" (Children's Defense Fund, 1976:21).

In numerous cases, children in jails suffered brutal treatment and even death at the hands of adult offenders. For example, three brothers—Billy (age 12), Brian (age 13), and Dan (age 14)—were suspected of stealing some coins from a local store and were placed in an adult jail:

> After the lights were out in the jail, the men ordered the boys to take off their clothes. When they refused ... the men tore off the boys' clothing, and then, one by one, each of the men forcibly raped the three brothers. Pointing to a long electric cord hanging in the cell, one of the men warned the boys that if they uttered a sound ... he would choke them to death. ... The boys obeyed ... and were silent. (Children's Defense Fund, 1976:1)

Wald (1976:124–125) summed up the opinions of most critics regarding such practices—an opinion not much different from those expressed in 1899:

There is no responsible evidence to indicate that we know how to predict dangerous or violent behavior in a juvenile any more than we do in an adult. Yet juvenile courts have operated on the premise that they are authorized to detain for possible future criminal behavior. . . . [Equally bad,] status offenders are also held for the longest periods in detention. It is ironically and bitterly true that most lawbreakers can go back home but those who offend against their parents usually cannot.

Rising Crime Rates

The sixth criticism of the juvenile court stemmed from a large increase in crime rates during the 1960s and 1970s (see Chapter 4). During that turbulent period, civil rights protests, urban riots, campus rebellions, and opposition to the Vietnam War gave the United States the appearance of a nation gone berserk, especially among its young people.

Although the juvenile court obviously could not have been responsible for those events, many Americans began to believe that it was incapable of dealing with them. Its progressive philosophy had contributed to anarchy, not order. As a result, Richard Nixon promised in 1968 that, if elected president, he would wage a war on crime, even if young people had to be numbered among the enemy. The pervasive feeling was that the nation was in danger of losing everything. The only solution was to return to a more retributive concept of justice, favoring legal punishment rather than rehabilitation.

Liberal Ideology

Criticism of the juvenile court came from both ends of the ideological spectrum—conservative as well as liberal. The rehabilitative ideology of the court was built on assumptions derived primarily from psychodynamic control theory—in particular, the idea that delinquency is due to the defective socialization of children and that to be rehabilitated they had to be personally treated and cared for.

But other theories emerged and became much more popular during this chaotic period. From the social disorganization theory of Shaw and McKay to strain theory, each new body of scientific thought supported the idea that delinquent behavior could not be prevented and controlled by tinkering with the minds of delinqunts. To do so would be to treat symptoms, not causes. It was society that segregated people by age, social class, and race. Hence, it was society that produced delinquent subcultures among children, defined rules as favoring the powerful, and then labeled and stigmatized the powerless who broke them.

If that was the case, it was a "brave idea" to suggest that the juvenile court could both prevent and control youthful misbehavior (Lemert, 1967:93). Twentieth-century criminology had constructed an ideological superstructure that not only lent support to critics of the juvenile court but also helped to erode the notion that such a court could be effective. Except for serious offenders, youthful lawbreakers would be best dealt with by other than legal means—reducing unemployment, enriching schools, combating racial and economic segregation, shrinking the generation gap, and giving young people a stake in conformity. In short, such ideas helped to tarnish the image of the juvenile court and cast doubts on the entire concept of juvenile justice.

RECENT PRACTICES: JUVENILE COURT IN THE 1980s AND 1990s

Despite the many criticisms of the juvenile court, it has remained surprisingly resistant to reform. Schlossman (1983:968–969) has observed that although changes have occurred, much about the juvenile court today "would be easily recognizable to its founders":

> The practices of juvenile courts in diverse jurisdictions appear to be as variegated as ever, although, generally speaking, they are more careful and constrained in procedure, deal less frequently with status offenders, and must increasingly accommodate to the presence of lawyers. As previously, few commentators on juvenile courts have much good to say about them. But the juvenile court—founded . . . to dispense love to society's most needy children—has grown inured to survival without being loved itself.

Schlossman's (1983) observations notwithstanding, there was much debate in the late 1980s and early 1990s about the merits of maintaining separate juvenile justice and criminal justice systems (Feld,

1998). That debate was embodied by federal and state "get-tough" juvenile justice reforms aimed at increasing (1) the procedural formality of juvenile court processing (e.g., increased reliance on sanctioning guidelines and decreased confidentiality of juvenile court records and proceedings), (2) the ease with which juveniles could be transferred to juvenile court for criminal processing, and (3) the severity of sanctions (e.g., Bernard, 1992; Feld, 1998; Howell, 1996; Miller, 1995; National Criminal Justice Association, 1997; Sickmund, Snyder, and Poe-Yamagata, 1997; Snyder and Sickmund, 1995; Torbet et al., 1996). Such reforms suggested that the juvenile court increasingly was becoming "criminalized"; that is, both procedurally and substantively, it appeared to be converging with the procedural and substantive focus typically associated with criminal court processing (Feld, 1998; Singer, 1996a, 1996b).

Some have argued that from these recent reforms may emerge eventually a more balanced system of sanctioning that maintains the distinction between the juvenile and the criminal court (Guarino-Ghezzi and Loughran, 1996; see also Moore and Wakeling, 1997). The balance likely would reflect public opinion that consistently has supported rehabilitation of delinquents but more severe punishment for serious or violent offenders, regardless of their age (Roberts and Stalans, 1998:52). It would provide, in short, for more severe punishment of serious or violent juvenile offenders (Zimring, 1991), with commensurate procedural safeguards, while maintaining the traditional *parens patriae* philosophy for less serious offenders.

Let us look at the way young people have been processed in recent years through the three major steps of the juvenile court.

Intake

Intake procedures can be understood best in terms of the following: number of delinquency cases referred to court, number of abuse and neglect cases, distribution of delinquency cases by gender, sources of court referrals, reasons for court referral, detention, and results of intake procedures.

THE NUMBER OF DELINQUENCY CASES REFERRED TO COURT As shown in table 17.1, approximately

TABLE 17.1

Estimated number and rate of delinquency cases disposed by juvenile courts, 1959–94

YEAR	ESTIMATED DELINQUENCY CASES[a]	RATE PER 1,000[b]	PERCENT INCREASE IN RATE
1959	483,000	19.6	—
1967	811,000	26.3	34
1975	1,317,000	38.8	48
1984	1,304,000	45.7	18
1991	1,428,200	54.8	20
1994	1,682,100	60.7	11
Total percent increase in rate, 1959–94		210	

SOURCES: Bureau of the Census, 1985:17; NIJJDP, 1987a:10; 1987b:5; OJJDP, 1994:5–6, 33; 1996:5–6, 33.

[a]Estimates for 1959–67 are from a national sample of juvenile courts.

[b]The number of delinquency cases per 1,000 population ages 10–17.

483,000 cases (criminal and status offenses) were received at intake in 1959, at a rate of 19.6 cases per 1,000 juveniles ages 10–17. By 1975, the overall number of cases had almost tripled, to 1,317,000, and the rate had increased to 38.8 per 1,000.

By 1984, the number of delinquency cases had decreased to 1,304,000, but because of a declining number of children ages 10–17, the referral rate had increased to 45.7 per 1,000. By 1994, the referral rate had reached 60.7 per 1,000, a 56 percent increase over the 1975 figure.[1]

The largest increase in the rate of referral occurred between 1967 and 1975 (48 percent). It bears emphasizing again that those were the years when, among other things, civil rights protests, campus riots, and demonstrations against the Vietnam War were at their peak. Moreover, that was a period when juvenile arrest rates increased substantially (see Chapter 4). That large increase notwithstanding, it is striking that the rate of referral has increased steadily since 1959, with a tripling of the rate between 1959 and 1994.

[1]For 1991 and 1994, the estimated number of delinquency cases included petitioned and nonpetitioned nonstatus offenses and petitioned status offenses (i.e., nonpetitioned status offenders are not included in the estimates).

TABLE 17.2

Estimated number and percentage distribution of delinquency cases disposed by juvenile courts, by gender, 1959–94

YEAR	MALES		FEMALES	
	NUMBER	PERCENT	NUMBER	PERCENT
1959	393,000	81	90,000	19
1967	640,000	79	171,000	21
1975	1,001,700	76	315,300	24
1984	986,000	76	318,000	24
1991	1,140,100	80	288,100	20
1994	1,304,000	78	378,200	22

SOURCES: NJJDP, 1987a:13; 1987b:24 25; OJJDP, 1989:10, 21, 31, 40, 1994.20, 43, 1996:22, 42.

THE NUMBER OF ABUSE AND NEGLECT CASES In contrast to the 1,682,100 delinquency cases processed in juvenile courts in 1994 (see table 17.1), approximately 2 million reports of child abuse and neglect were made to child protective service agencies in that same year (Sickmund, Snyder, and Poe-Yamagata, 1997:9). Of those 2 million reports, 1.6 million (82 percent) were investigated, and of those cases, 592,000 (37 percent) were substantiated (Sickmund, Snyder, and Poe-Yamagata, 1997:9). The jurisdiction of the juvenile justice system, therefore, extends to roughly equal numbers of delinquency and abuse and neglect cases.

THE DISTRIBUTION OF DELINQUENCY CASES BY GENDER Table 17.2 documents changes between 1959 and 1994 in the gender distribution of juvenile court referrals.[2] From the late 1950s to the mid-1960s, there was little or no change: About one-fifth of all delinquency cases involved females. By 1975, however, 24 percent of all cases involved females, a relatively large increase in a short period. Indeed, merely from 1967 to 1975, the number of female cases increased by 84 percent (from 171,000 to 315,300), compared to a 57 percent increase in male

cases (from 640,000 to 1,001,700). By 1991, however, the percentage of delinquency cases involving females had again decreased to 20 percent—approximately the same percentage as in 1959 (19 percent)—a figure that remained relatively stable through 1994 (22 percent).

SOURCES OF COURT REFERRALS In 1994, the police or other law enforcement officers were responsible for the vast majority—86 percent—of juvenile court referrals for criminal offenses (OJJDP, 1996:7). The rest were made by parents and relatives, schools, social service agencies, probation officers, and a variety of other sources.

Unlike what they did with criminal offenses, the police were the primary source of juvenile court referral for only 44 percent of petitioned status offenses (OJJDP, 1996:34). Although 94 percent of cases for liquor violations were referred by the police, that was true of only 40 percent of the cases for running away, 9 percent for truancy, and 10 percent for ungovernability (incorrigibility).

The figures for status offenses suggest that one of the major functions of the juvenile court has remained virtually unchanged: that of acting as a "backup institution" to help communities enforce the moral rules governing childhood (Emerson, 1969:269–271). Parents, schools, and social service agencies continue to make referrals to the court when their authority is seriously challenged or when they are sufficiently concerned about the insubordination and misconduct of troublesome children.

REASONS FOR COURT REFERRAL As shown in table 17.3, however, juvenile court processing of status offenses clearly has decreased over the past several decades.[3] In 1976, a research group at the University of Michigan reported that most court referrals involved property and status offenses, with each accounting for 36.2 percent of all cases referred to juvenile courts (Hasenfeld, 1976:68). About 60 percent of referrals for status offenses involved curfew violations, running away, and incorrigibility. When the figures for status offenses were added to those for drug

[2]See footnote 1 in this chapter.

[3]See footnote 1 in this chapter.

TABLE 17.3

Reasons for court referral, 1970s–94

TYPE OF OFFENSE	EARLY 1970s	1985	1994
Offenses against persons	7.3	15.3	20.0
Offenses against property	36.2	47.4	47.8
Drug offenses	7.3	5.3	7.1
Status offenses	36.2	14.1	7.5
All other offenses	13.0	17.8	17.6

SOURCES: Hasenfeld, 1976:68; OJJDP, 1989:11, 31; 1994:5, 33.

violations, they constituted almost half of all court referrals. Only about 7 percent of referrals at the time were for offenses against persons.

By 1985, however, only about 14 percent of juvenile court referrals involved status offenses, considerably less than the figure reported by the Michigan group. Nearly two-thirds of the referrals in 1985 were for property offenses (47 percent) and offenses against persons (15 percent). That trend continued through 1994, such that only about 8 percent of juvenile court referrals involved status offenses, whereas 20 percent were for property offenses and about 48 percent were for offenses against persons.

One interpretation of the difference over time is that there were relatively fewer status offenses in the 1980s and 1990s than in the 1970s, and relatively more property and violent crimes were committed by juveniles. Hence, changes in the kinds of cases referred to juvenile courts could simply reflect changes in law-violating behavior. However, we learned in the previous chapter that in the 1980s, the police began to counsel and release relatively fewer of those juveniles whom they arrested and to refer more of them to juvenile court. This reflects "more formal and restrictive police responses to youth crime" (Krisberg et al., 1986:12; also see Torbet et al., 1996). At the same time, as discussed previously, efforts have been made in recent years to decriminalize status offenses, or at least to divert rebellious youngsters from the juvenile justice system (Holden and Kepler, 1995; Raley, 1995). Thus, it is more likely that criminal offenses now constitute a larger percentage of juvenile court referrals because of changing laws

and procedures (Torbet et al., 1996), not because of changes in what children have been doing (Sickmund, Snyder, and Poe-Yamagata, 1997:24–25; Snyder and Sickmund, 1995:47–51).

DETENTION   Juveniles can be held in preadjudicatory detention for three basic reasons: (1) to protect the child, (2) to prevent the child from committing new offenses considered dangerous to the community, and (3) to prevent the child from running away (Cohen and Kluegel, 1979:149; Frazier, 1989:149; Mulvey and Saunders, 1982:262–268). With increasing arrest rates of juveniles for violent crime in the late 1980s and early 1990s (Snyder and Sickmund, 1995:116), increased delinquency caseloads (OJJDP, 1996:5), and increasingly tougher juvenile laws (Torbet et al., 1996), one would expect an increase in the use of detention in recent years. However, between 1988 and 1992, the percentage of delinquents detained was relatively constant, with approximately 20 percent of all youths detained in any given year (Snyder and Sickmund, 1995:141). In 1992, 47 percent of detained cases were for property offenses, 24 percent for person offenses, 20 percent for public order offenses, and 9 percent for drug offenses (Snyder and Sickmund, 1995:141).

Although the percentage of all delinquency cases detained has remained relatively constant, the median time to disposition has increased 26 percent, from 43 days in 1985 to 54 days in 1994 (Butts, 1997: 1–2). Given recent "get-tough" laws, which increasingly have formalized juvenile justice processing, the time to disposition is unlikely to decrease anytime soon. The issue is important because of the increasingly crowded conditions in detention centers. In 1995, almost 75 percent of all public detention center residents were held in facilities operating above design capacity. That figure represents a significant increase since 1991, when close to half of all detention residents were in facilities operating above design capacity (Sickmund, Snyder, and Poe-Yamagata, 1997:41).

The issue of detention also is important for subsequent juvenile justice processing. For example, in research on a juvenile court in Pennsylvania, Cohen (1975a:36–39, 42–51) found that those held in preadjudicatory detention are more likely than comparable, nondetained youths to receive severe dispositions. Clarke and Koch (1980:293–295) discovered much the same thing for detainees in North Carolina, as did Frazier and Cochran (1986:297–300) in Florida, Dannefer (1984:260) in a northeastern state, Bortner and Reed (1985:417–420) in a midwestern juvenile court, and Feld (1988:409, 412) in several states. (For contrary or inconsistent findings, however, see Aday, 1986:114; Bishop and Frazier, 1988: 254–257; and Frazier and Bishop, 1985:1151.) Bortner (1982:31) has described some of the biases that may operate against detained juveniles:

> Minimally, the fact that juveniles have been detained is considered evidence that they are not able to deal with their problems and require immediate supervision and court involvement. . . . if a juvenile is detained, it is commonly regarded as a sign that there is a lack of self-control, problems are immediate, and the illegal behavior is likely to reoccur.

Although those biases are consequences of detention, other biases may affect who gets detained.

DETENTION OF STATUS OFFENDERS   Generally, the courts are more likely to detain younger offenders and recidivists—juveniles with previous court referrals—than older and first-time offenders (Bookin-Weiner, 1984:46–47; Bortner, 1982:31; Bortner and Reed, 1985:415–418; Cohen, 1975c:28–29; Cohen and Kluegel, 1979:157; Dungworth, 1977:31–32; Frazier and Cochran, 1986:296; McCarthy and Smith, 1986:52, 54–55; OJJDP, 1996:40; Pawlak, 1977:158–161). That generalization, however, should not be interpreted to mean that recidivists include only juveniles who repeatedly commit criminal offenses. Many recidivists are status offenders, and status offenders are detained as frequently as, if not more than, those charged with criminal offenses (Bortner and Reed, 1985:415–418; Cohen, 1975c:29–32, 41–42; Dungworth, 1977:27–28; Pawlak, 1977:31–32; Sumner, 1971:174; Teilmann and Landry, 1981:64–65). Mulvey and Saunders (1982:275–276) have argued that the "relationship between offense seriousness and detention is probably U-shaped, with the highest likelihood of detention being for both serious crimes against persons and status offenses."

DETENTION OF FEMALES   In 1994, females and males who had committed status offenses were equally likely to be detained. For both groups, 7 percent of all status offenders were detained; similarly, roughly equal percentages of both groups were detained for running away, truancy, ungovernability, liquor violations, and miscellaneous other offenses (OJJDP, 1996:43). By contrast, in the mid-1970s, Pawlak (1977:162) found that "females who commit juvenile code [status] offenses, regardless of race and of prior court contacts, have a larger percentage of detention than males who commit such offenses." Such findings are difficult to reconcile or interpret, particularly because, as Chesney-Lind and Shelden (1998: 160) have suggested, "bias against girls may be less overt" today than in the past and may operate differently across different geographic locations (see also Bishop and Frazier, 1992; Poe-Yamagata and Butts, 1996:14–19).

Such biases or double standards assume particular significance when we consider the horror stories associated with the detention of females. Chesney-Lind (1977:125) noted, for example, that all females brought before the courts in New York and Philadelphia were given vaginal smears to test for venereal disease, even if the charges against them were nonsexual. Similarly, Wakin (1975:45) reported that in one detention center, all females were required to undergo a pelvic examination to determine if they were pregnant. Describing the same sort of situation in Philadelphia, an official noted that females had no choice in the matter:

> "We do put a girl on the table in the stirrups and we do have a smear. . . . We do have a swab. You go in and get a smear." When asked whether a girl who refused to undergo this pelvic exam would be placed in "medical lock-up"—a polite term for solitary confinement—he responded, "Yes, we may have to." (Chesney-Lind, 1977:125)

It is impossible to say how widespread such practices are. But, in general, they have reflected a rather common assumption that if a young female comes to the attention of court officials, particularly for status offenses, she must be sexually promiscuous (Chesney-Lind and Shelden, 1998:passim; Datesman and Scarpitti, 1977). Thus, the courts apparently have sometimes subjected females not only to a legal double standard but also to physical degradation.

RACE AND SOCIAL CLASS Despite the tendency of Americans to equate poverty with crime and delinquency, the evidence is by no means clear that minority and poor youths suffer from bias in detention decisions. Minority and lower-class juveniles have slightly higher rates of detention, but differences between those rates and those for white, middle-class youths are surprisingly small (Bishop and Frazier, 1988; Bookin-Weiner, 1984; Cohen, 1975c; Cohen and Kluegel, 1979; Dungworth, 1977; Fagan, Slaughter, and Hartstone, 1987; Frazier and Bishop, 1985; Frazier and Cochran, 1986; McCarthy, 1985; McCarthy and Smith, 1986; Pawlak, 1977; Schutt and Dannefer, 1988; however, see Bortner and Reed, 1985; Pope and Feyerherm, 1993).

Two factors seem to be operating. On the one hand, the relatively high arrest rates of minority and poor youths for criminal offenses, particularly for violent offenses, may explain why they have slightly higher rates of detention. On the other hand, court officials may be inclined to discriminate against white, middle-class youths, particularly females, in that they sometimes have high detention rates for status offenses (Cohen, 1975c:43; Pawlak, 1977:159–160; Schutt and Dannefer, 1988:513).

Although the results of a few studies cannot be taken to represent court practices nationwide, they are contrary to expectations. The tendency for officials to act paternalistically toward some higher-status young people by confining them in detention centers could mean that officials have been more concerned about the morality of higher-status than lower-status youths (Schutt and Dannefer, 1988:515). Detention may be a way of disciplining those whom juvenile court officials consider worth saving.

JUVENILES IN JAIL As noted previously, in response to rising juvenile arrest rates and perceived injustices in the juvenile justice system, the U.S. Congress in 1974 enacted the Juvenile Justice and Delinquency Prevention Act. For those states participating in the federal juvenile justice program, the legislation required that juveniles in jails and police lockups be kept completely separate from adult inmates. More-

over, it prohibited any confinement of dependent/ neglected children and status offenders. Congress amended the act in 1980, requiring that participating states completely eliminate the jailing of children by December 1985, though this date was later extended to December 1988 (Holden and Kepler, 1995; Raley, 1995; Schwartz, Harris, and Levi, 1988; Soler, 1988; Swanger, 1988).

Even though the federal mandate seemed to be clear, compliance "has been another story. . . . The use of adult jails to confine juveniles continues to be prevalent" (Swanger, 1988:211). For example, in California, 15 of 58 counties (26 percent), mainly in rural areas, still lacked juvenile detention facilities in 1986 (Steinhart, 1988:170–173). The result was that thousands, possibly even tens of thousands, of juveniles were confined in adult jails, even though California law restricted that practice (albeit weakly so, a situation that has been corrected with new legislation "outlawing the use of adult jails and lockups for the confinement of minors" [Steinhart, 1988:169]).

California is not the only state that continued to use jails to confine juveniles after enactment of the Juvenile Justice and Delinquency Prevention Act. It was estimated that as many as twenty-two states had not complied with federal standards by the mid-1980s (Chesney-Lind, 1988b:155; Schwartz, Harris, and Levi, 1988:134; Soler, 1988:205). "Twelve of the 14 years allowed had passed by 1986, but Federal experts stated that 240,000 youths would be held in jails in 1986" (Polier, 1989:32). Some progress has been made in subsequent years. For example, between 1983 and 1991, the number of juveniles admitted to jails declined by 43 percent, from 105,366 to 60,181 (OJJDP, 1995:51).

Nevertheless, elimination of the jailing of children is far from being a reality. In 1994, a one-day count of juveniles revealed that there were 6,725 juveniles in adult jails, which approximated the average daily population of juveniles in adult jails on any given day (Bureau of Justice Statistics, 1996:24). One obstacle to reform is, by now, a familiar one: As in Illinois when the first juvenile court was created, many states have not provided adequate financing for detention facilities or other alternatives to jails, such as twenty-four-hour on-call crisis intervention and home detention (Guarino-Ghezzi and Loughran, 1996; Schwartz, Harris, and Levi, 1988). However, reform also has been impeded by the attitudes and beliefs of key political and juvenile justice officials who "do not feel that the jailing of juveniles is a serious problem" (Schwartz, Harris, and Levi, 1988: 145). Until all such obstacles to reform are overcome, it is unlikely that the practice of confining juveniles in adult jails will be brought to an end. Indeed, a further obstacle is the possibility that recent "get-tough" legislation in many states (Feld, 1998; Torbet et al., 1996) will exert considerable pressure upon juvenile facilities to house ever-greater numbers of juveniles for longer periods of time.

RESULTS OF INTAKE PROCEDURES The intake staff exercises "substantial power," according to Rosenheim (1983:972), because, "with the advice of the prosecutor's office, [it] decides whether to release the offender or to prepare a delinquency petition" for a formal hearing. In its study of several hundred juvenile courts, the research group at the University of Michigan found that approximately 40 percent of all cases during the early 1970s were handled formally, whereas 60 percent were handled informally (i.e., without the filing of a petition):

> The most typical pattern is either to dismiss the case, or to counsel, warn, and release the youth. Only a small fraction ... are put on informal probation (16%) or referred to other social service agencies. In other words, most courts seem to cope with the inflow of juvenile cases through very minimal intervention, which may, at most, produce a court record, but no significant action by court staff. (Hasenfeld, 1976:69)

That situation changed very little until the early 1990s, when formal processing became more common. "The likelihood of formal processing for delinquency referrals increased between 1985 and 1994, rising from 46% to 55%" (OJJDP, 1996:8; see also Krisberg and Schwartz, 1983; McCarthy, 1987; Rosenheim, 1983). Furthermore, the intake decisions for formally petitioned cases in 1994 changed considerably from those in 1985:

> A detailed analysis of referral offenses showed that the likelihood of formal handling was greater for more serious offenses within the same general offense category. In 1994, for example, 64% of aggravated assault cases but only 49% of simple assault cases were handled formally. Similarly, more than 70% of burglary and motor vehicle theft cases were handled informally by juvenile courts, compared with 42% of larceny-theft cases and 45% of cases in which vandalism was the most serious charge. (OJJDP, 1996:8)

Perhaps the most significant changes in intake procedures have involved the handling of status offenses. The study by the Michigan group, conducted in the early 1970s, found that juveniles charged with status offenses were just as likely to be handled formally as those charged with property crimes (Creekmore 1976:127). Only juveniles charged with violent crimes were more likely than status offenders to receive a formal court hearing. In the 1980s, however, a relatively smaller percentage of status offense cases were handled formally. For example, only 29 percent of status offense cases in 1984 were handled formally with the filing of a petition, as opposed to 48 percent of cases involving criminal offenses (NIJJDP, 1987b: 16–17). This trend may have reflected an increasing tendency to bring mainly serious and chronic offenders before the court for a hearing (Rubin, 1989). Unfortunately, with the advent of more diverse court reporting and the involvement of multiple agencies in performing juvenile court functions, national data collection on the informal processing of status offenders has not been possible (OJJDP, 1996:1). It therefore remains unclear whether the trends of the late 1980s have continued into the 1990s.

Adjudication

As we have seen, the juvenile court was subjected to a series of reviews by the Supreme Court in the 1960s and early 1970s—reviews designed to alter the adjudicatory process, if nothing else (*In re Gault,* 1967; *Kent,* 1966; *In re Winship,* 1970). In contrast to earlier court practices, the Supreme Court concluded that juveniles should receive many of the same constitutional protections that adults have in criminal trials. If these constitutional protections have been translated into practice, they should be evident in the actions of juvenile courts.

The national study by the University of Michigan group revealed that some changes occurred. By the early 1970s, virtually all courts had begun to give written notice to juvenile defendants of the specific charges made against them; no new charges could be sprung on them in court as Judge Baker had done in Boston in the early 1900s. Likewise, 7 in 10 judges indicated that they tried to explain charges in simple as well as legal language (Sosin and Sarri, 1976:195).

Also by the early 1970s, virtually all judges agreed that juveniles had a right to legal counsel and that one would be appointed if necessary (Sosin and Sarri, 1976:195). However, the actual number of defense attorneys participating in juvenile court proceedings has remained small. In many courts, half or more of adjudicated offenders do not have lawyers (Aday, 1986:114; Bortner, 1982:139; Clarke and Koch, 1980:297; Feld, 1988:400–402; 1989:1217–1223).

Usually, the facts in a case are not contested in a formal hearing. Reflecting a practice that would have pleased juvenile court judges of the early 1900s, between 70 and 95 percent of young people admit their delinquency rather than deny it (Bortner, 1982:39–44; Clarke and Koch, 1980:297; Feld, 1989:1210; Rubin, 1985:195; 1989:129). Surprisingly, the presence of legal counsel does not greatly affect whether a child confesses to committing an offense. Clarke and Koch (1980:298) reported, in a study of two North Carolina juvenile courts, that "79.7 percent of children without counsel admitted an offense, but 68.3 percent of those with counsel also did so."

One of the best predictors of whether a juvenile is represented by legal counsel at adjudication is the type of offense with which he or she is charged. Those charged with violent or serious property crimes are much more likely to have attorneys than those charged with status or other petty offenses (Feld, 1988:401–402; 1989:1220–1221; Sosin and Sarri, 1976:196).

> Judges may . . . predetermine the likely disposition they will impose on a juvenile, and decline to appoint counsel when they anticipate a probationary sentence. In many instances, juveniles may plead guilty and judges dispose of their case at the same hearing without benefit of counsel. (Feld, 1998:519)

Even if juveniles are represented by lawyers, however, the quality of representation sometimes leaves much to be desired. While not true of all defense attorneys, many are not

> capable of or committed to representing their juvenile clients in an effective adversarial manner. Organizational pressures to cooperate, judicial hostility toward adversarial litigants, role ambiguity created by the dual goals of rehabilitation and punishment, reluctance to help juveniles "beat a case," or an internalization of a court's treatment philosophy may compromise the role of counsel in juvenile court. (Feld, 1988:395; also see Bortner, 1982:136–139)

In the University of Michigan study, only about half of the judges reported that attorneys always confronted prosecution witnesses, only 20 percent of attorneys called their own witnesses, and few made legal motions for dismissal of cases (Sosin and Sarri, 1976:196). Even in serious cases, lawyers did not take an active role in formal proceedings as they would in adult criminal court:

> For the most part, attorneys tended to prefer to plea-bargain with the judge on small points rather than on the adjudication decision itself. For example, some lawyers would have their clients admit guilt on three of six counts if the other three would be dropped. Judges often agreed to this arrangement, and for good reasons: once a child is adjudicated delinquent, three rather than six counts makes no legal difference, as legally the judge need not fit the disposition to the number of charges. (p. 196)

To make matters worse, representation by legal counsel may be detrimental to juveniles in the disposition of their cases. Feld (1989:1236) indicated that "youths *with counsel* are substantially more likely to receive severe dispositions [out-of-home placement or secure confinement] than are those *without counsel*." Moreover, this holds even with controls for prior record and the seriousness of the alleged offense (Feld, 1989:1251, 1305–1311; also see Bortner, 1982:139–140; Clarke and Koch, 1980:300–302; Feld, 1988:413, 415–417; for inconsistent evidence, suggesting variation among courts in the relation between attorney use and the severity of disposition, see Aday, 1986:112–116). One possible reason for this harsh treatment is that judges may feel less constrained in issuing severe dispositions to youths who have lawyers because "adherence to formal due process may insulate sentences from appellate reversal. Such may be the price of formal procedures" (Feld, 1989:1333). Or it is also possible that "before *Gault*, . . . juvenile courts were trying to be as lenient as they possibly could; perhaps the advent of the attorney as a new participant in the process only made it more difficult for them to be lenient" (Clarke and Koch, 1980:305–306).

Among adjudicated offenders who are represented by legal counsel, private attorneys appear to be less detrimental than public defenders or court-appointed counsel:

> Juveniles represented by private attorneys have the lowest rates of out-of-home placement and secure confinement dispositions . . . ; those represented by court appointed attorneys have intermediate rates; and those represented by public defenders appear to have the highest rates of removal. (Feld, 1989:1242)

The worst possible situation, then, at least from the perspective of the offender, may be one in which he or she cannot afford a private attorney and, as a result, is assigned to a public defender for the sake of due process.

In short, this review of adjudication illustrates the extent to which the decisions of the Supreme Court have been tempered by traditions favoring the informal treatment of children. In some juvenile courts, those decisions have, in fact, been incorporated into judicial proceedings; but in many, their effects have been slow in coming.

Disposition

As was the case in the early 1900s, most states continue to use indeterminate sentences. However, juvenile justice reforms in the late 1980s and early 1990s revealed a greater willingness on the part of most state legislatures to include **determinate sentencing** and combinations of juvenile and adult sanctions, in what have been termed "blended sentencing" statutes:

Blended sentencing refers to the imposition of juvenile and/or correctional sanctions to cases involving serious and violent juvenile offenders who have been adjudicated in juvenile court or convicted in criminal court. Blended sentencing options are usually based on age or on a combination of age and offense. (Torbet et al., 1996:11; also see Feld, 1998:531; Forst, Fisher, and Coates, 1985; Guarino-Ghezzi and Loughran, 1996)

Moreover, as in the early juvenile court, adjudication and disposition often are intermixed; that is, the dispositional hearing is not always separated from the adjudicatory hearing as it is in adult criminal court (Aday, 1986:111; Bortner, 1982:43–44; President's Commission, 1967b:5; Rubin, 1985:195, 200, 399; 1989:131).

Before we consider the results of dispositional hearings, it should be recalled that close to half of all delinquency cases are handled informally at intake— 45 percent of all cases in 1994. Only 55 percent of all cases in 1994, therefore, were processed formally through the filing of a petition for an adjudicatory hearing. However, 41 percent of petitioned cases were never actually adjudicated in juvenile court, with most involving either outright release without further court action or some form of informal (voluntary) probation (OJJDP, 1996:9).

Of those cases that were adjudicated (at this point, 32 percent of the original number of cases at intake), 3 percent were dismissed (OJJDP, 1996:9). Furthermore, 53 percent of adjudicated cases resulted in formal probation, 29 percent resulted in out-of-home placement in a correctional facility, and 15 percent resulted in a variety of dispositions, such as fines, restitution, and suspension of a driver's license (p. 9). While those percentages undoubtedly varied from court to court, the same pattern generally prevails—most adjudicated offenders are put on probation rather than institutionalized.

LONG-TERM VERSUS SHORT-TERM CONFINEMENT Such practices raise a provocative question: Why, after a formal hearing by a judge, are so few juveniles sent to long-term facilities when, during the period prior to court action, so many are locked up in detention centers and jails? In 1994, approximately

321,200 juveniles were admitted to short-term detention facilities and shelters awaiting intake, adjudicatory, or dispositional decisions (OJJDP, 1996:7). Yet only about 141,300 were admitted to long-term public facilities following disposition (p. 15)—a ratio of almost 2 to 1.

The answer to the question is clear. It is decision making by the police, prosecutors, and probation officers, not judges, that results in the early detention of most juveniles, even if only for short periods of time. As a consequence, the President's Commission on Law Enforcement and Administration of Justice (1967a:23) concluded that detention is used for punishment, even though proof of guilt or the precise character of a child's problems has not been established.

RACE AND SOCIAL CLASS Minority and lower-class youths are more likely than other juveniles to be institutionalized following court action. For example, Krisberg and his associates (1987:186) reported that in 1982, black males were committed to training schools at a rate almost five times that of white males. Like the police, therefore, the juvenile court has been accused of being discriminatory.

The evidence regarding this accusation, however, is contradictory (Pope and Feyerherm, 1993:passim). Some studies suggest that the accusation is true (Arnold, 1971; Bishop and Frazier, 1988; Bortner and Reed, 1985; Fagan, Slaughter, and Hartstone, 1987; Feld, 1989, 1998; McCarthy and Smith, 1986; Thornberry, 1973, 1979; Wordes, Bynum, and Corley, 1994). However, other studies suggest that dispositional decisions are more likely to reflect an offender's prior record and the seriousness of the offense than outright bigotry (Aday, 1986; Cohen, 1975b; Cohen and Kluegel, 1978; Clarke and Koch, 1980; Eaton and Polk, 1961; Staples, 1987; Terry, 1967). Furthermore, there is evidence that decisions vary widely from court to court, reflecting bias in some courts but not in others (Cohen, 1975a:23–28; Dannefer and Schutt, 1982:1122–1124, 1126). For example, Tittle and Curran (1988:49–50), in a study of thirty-one counties in Florida, show that "minorities are significantly more severely treated only when there are simultaneously large proportions young and large proportions nonwhite in a court jurisdiction," which they interpret as meaning that "minorities are differentially sanctioned when they reflect youthfulness that threatens adults."

The issue is complicated by the fact that while the effect of race and social class on dispositions may be small, discrimination that occurs in earlier processing decisions may mask later discrimination (Pope and Feyerherm, 1993). To illustrate, we have seen that there is evidence that detained juveniles are more likely than nondetained juveniles to receive severe dispositions. To the extent that detention decisions are biased against minority and lower-class youths, dispositions will be discriminatory even if juvenile court judges do not take race or social class into account in deciding the dispositions of detainees. Bortner and Reed (1985:418–421), for example, found that race had no direct effect on dispositions of cases. However, race had a substantial effect on detention decisions, with black juveniles more likely to be detained than whites (pp. 417–418). Because detention affected the severity of dispositions (pp. 418–421), race had an indirect effect on dispositions, which would have remained hidden if Bortner and Reed had not examined both processing steps: "There is an interdependence between processing variables and juvenile characteristics, but the relationship may be obscured at the final decision point" (p. 421). As Pope and Feyerherm (1993:10) observed: "Race effects at any one stage of processing may be canceled out or enhanced at later stages. Only by examining multiple decision points can we gain a more complete picture of how minority status does or does not influence outcome decisions."

DISPOSITIONS OF MALES AND FEMALES In 1994, about seven times as many males as females were admitted to or placed in secure facilities (OJJDP, 1996:25). Moreover, the percentage adjudicated delinquency cases for females that resulted in out-of-home placements decreased from 26 percent to 23 percent between 1985 and 1994, while for males it increased from 29 percent to 30 percent.

Given that sort of distribution for training school admissions, it is not surprising that studies of male and female dispositions tend to conclude that for most offenses, there is little or no bias against females once prior record and seriousness of the offense are taken into account (Aday, 1986; Bishop and Frazier, 1988; Clarke and Koch, 1980; Dannefer and Schutt, 1982; McCarthy and Smith, 1986; Staples, 1987; Teilmann and Landry, 1981; Tittle and Curran, 1988; see, however, Bishop and Frazier, 1992; Terry, 1967). If anything, males are more likely to receive severe dispositions.

Dispositions of status offenses, however, tend to represent an exception to this general pattern. Indeed, several studies have shown that compared to males, female status offenders receive more severe dispositions (see, however, U.S. General Accounting Office, 1995). For example, Datesman and Scarpitti (1977:63) found in an eastern state that "female juveniles brought before the court as status offenders were least likely to be dismissed or warned and most likely to be placed under supervision by a probation officer and institutionalized." For white female status offenders with one or more prior offenses, 33 percent were institutionalized, compared with 4 percent of their white male counterparts (p. 70). Moreover, Feld (1989:1279–1280) found that in the state of Minnesota in 1986, 15 percent of female status offenders received some "out-of-home placement" (group home, foster care, psychiatric or chemical dependency treatment facility, secure institution, and the like); such was the case for only 11 percent of male status offenders. "The disproportionate intervention with female offenders charged with . . . status offenses may reflect the 'double standard' and 'paternalistic' attitudes for which scholars have criticized juvenile courts" (p. 1279; for a general discussion of this issue, see Chesney-Lind, 1988a:153–157; Chesney-Lind and Shelden, 1998:passim).

As we have seen in considering the effects of race and social class on dispositions, it is also important to bear in mind that gender bias in early processing decisions may obscure discrimination in later decisions (Chesney-Lind and Shelden, 1998; Pope and Feyerherm, 1993). To the extent that female status offenders are more likely to be detained, for example, dispositions may be discriminatory even if juvenile court judges do not use gender as a dispositional criterion. Again, research by Bortner and Reed (1985:416–419) is informative. First, female status offenders were more likely than other offenders to be detained and more likely to have formal petitions

filed against them. Gender was not directly related to disposition, but it would be misleading to conclude that dispositional decisions were unbiased, because the earlier processing decisions—detention and the filing of a petition—affected the severity of dispositions (pp. 418–421).

THE DEATH PENALTY   Although rare, the death penalty on occasion has been applied to juveniles (Streib, 1987). The Supreme Court traditionally has avoided addressing the constitutionality of capital punishment in juvenile cases. In the 1980s, however, it addressed the issue in a series of cases that culminated with *Stanford* v. *Kentucky,* which established the constitutionality of the death penalty for crimes committed by 16- or 17-year-olds. In the past twenty-five years, few youths who committed a capital offense while under the age of 18 have been given a death sentence. "Between 1973 and 1993, 121 death sentences were handed down to youth who were under age 18 at the time of their crime, accounting for about 2% of the total number of death sentences imposed since 1973" (Snyder and Sickmund, 1995: 179). Nonetheless, as with discussions about the death penalty generally (Bedau, 1992), considerable debate exists concerning capital punishment for juveniles (Baird and Rosenbaum, 1995) despite the fact that public opinion polls consistently reveal a lack of support for applying the death penalty to juveniles (Roberts and Stalans, 1998).

SUMMARY AND CONCLUSIONS

Reflecting the growth of the modern concept of childhood, the juvenile court was supposed to fulfill a grand mission:

1. *Guarantee nurturance rights for children:* the rights to life, food, shelter, loving parents, education, and protection from immorality and crime
2. *Have jurisdiction over four types of young people:* delinquents, status offenders, neglected children, and those who were dependent and in need of care
3. *Fulfill five major functions:* enforce the modern concept of childhood, act as a surrogate for

failing families and schools, prevent delinquency, decriminalize the conduct of children, and rehabilitate those who required special care

In pursuit of these goals, the juvenile court was granted almost unlimited power and discretion. Its procedures, consisting of three major steps—intake, adjudication, and disposition—would operate without the constitutional constraints imposed on adult criminal courts, because its goal was to save children, not punish them.

Criticisms

Few serious challenges were levied against the juvenile court until well after the mid-20th century. However, because of the large gap between its professed ideals and actual practices, the juvenile court was subjected to increasingly strident criticisms between 1960 and the mid-1970s:

1. Reflecting changes in social values and the concept of childhood, the laws that permitted the juvenile court to have jurisdiction over status offenders were condemned as vague, discriminatory, and unworkable.
2. The Supreme Court disavowed the discretionary powers of the juvenile court and demanded that it provide young people with most of the constitutional protections afforded adults.
3. Juvenile court officials were accused of administering assembly line justice.
4. The practice of confining large numbers of children in detention centers and jails was attacked as cruel and inhumane.
5. Rising crime rates were cited as evidence that the juvenile court had failed.
6. Conservatives and liberals, citing the same presumed defects in the system, came to contrary conclusions—the court was too lenient, or it was too punitive and treated symptoms, not causes, of delinquency.

Recent Practices

While juvenile court practices have, in fact, changed in response to such criticisms, the continued viability of the juvenile court is being challenged by recent and widespread reforms—including the constitutionality of the death penalty for juvenile offenders—that increasingly blur the distinction between juvenile and adult justice. Nonetheless, the historical and ideological trends that led to the invention of the juvenile court have retained considerable vigor:

1. The rate at which juveniles have been referred to court has increased since 1959. Females constitute about 20 percent of these referrals.
2. Juvenile court processing of status offenses has decreased over the past several decades because of changing laws and procedures with regard to children. However, the court has continued to act as a "backup institution" to enforce the moral rules governing childhood. Indeed, most court referrals for status offenses are made by parents, teachers, and welfare workers who are seeking help with troublesome youths.
3. Juvenile court officials continue to exercise a great deal of discretion, particularly at the intake stage, reflecting highly contradictory behaviors. On the one hand, court officials release close to half of all court referrals at the intake stage, using informal procedures much like those used by the police. On the other hand, these same officials confine far more juveniles in detention centers and jails at this stage than are ultimately confined in long-term facilities following adjudication and disposition.
4. Despite Supreme Court decisions in the 1960s and early 1970s asserting that juveniles should have the same constitutional protections as adults, including the right to legal counsel, most adjudicated offenders still do not have lawyers. Moreover, there is a question about the quality of representation even if juveniles have lawyers. As in the juvenile court in the early 1900s, most adjudicated offenders admit their delinquency instead of contesting it.
5. Although only a small fraction of all juveniles referred to court are eventually institutionalized, minority and lower-class youths are overrepresented among them. It is unclear whether this reflects bias among juvenile court judges. Even if judges do not discriminate on the basis of race or social class, however, dispositions may still be biased if earlier processing decisions—arrest, detention, or intake—are discriminatory.

FIGURE 17.2
The juvenile court filtering process, 1994
SOURCE: OJJDP, 1996:9.

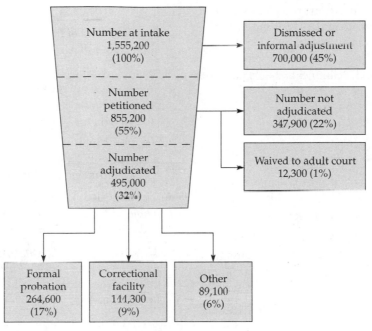

Figure 17.2 provides a graphic portrayal of recent juvenile court practices.[4] Because it is simplified, it serves better as a general, rather than a precise, illustration of how juveniles are handled in the court. It should be noted that the percentage of cases formally handled (i.e., petitioned) increased from 46 percent to 55 percent between 1985 and 1994. For drug offense and weapons cases, this increase was even larger—43 percent formal handling of drug offense cases in 1985, compared with 61 percent in 1994, and 45 percent formal handling of weapons offense cases in 1985, compared with 62 percent in 1994 (Butts, 1997; also see OJJDP, 1996:5). The relatively larger increases for those two offenses perhaps reflect greater attention by law enforcement agencies and states to drug and violent offending (Snyder and Sickmund, 1995:108, 120; Torbet et al., 1996).

Dilemmas

The juvenile court is confronted with numerous dilemmas: Should it be concerned more with the nurturance rights of juveniles or with their constitutional rights? Should it be engaged in doing justice for young offenders or in trying to save truants, runaways, and neglected children as well? Should it risk censure for being too punitive by detaining and institutionalizing delinquents or for being too lenient by releasing them to the community? What principles should govern its operation? Should the concept of juvenile justice be discarded entirely? When we examine the results of efforts to rehabilitate delinquents in the next chapter, we will find that there are even more dilemmas to consider.

DISCUSSION QUESTIONS

1. What is the jurisdiction of the juvenile court, and what specific functions does it serve?

[4]Status offenses are not included in this figure.

2. What is the ideal procedure by which youthful offenders are supposed to be treated by the juvenile justice system?

3. Why was the juvenile court regarded as a "tarnished superparent" in the 1960s and 1970s?

4. How has the juvenile court changed in the 1980s and 1990s?

5. How do you think delinquents should be treated by society?

REFERENCES

Aday, David P., Jr. 1986. "Court Structure, Defense Attorney Use, and Juvenile Court Decisions." *Sociological Quarterly* 27 (Spring):107–119.

Alexander, Paul W. 1962. "Constitutional Rights in the Juvenile Court." Pp. 82–94 in Margaret K. Rosenheim, ed., *Justice for the Child: The Juvenile Court in Transition.* New York: Free Press.

Arnold, William R. 1971. "Race and Ethnicity Relative to Other Factors in Juvenile Court Dispositions." *American Journal of Sociology* 77 (September):211–227.

Baird, Robert M., and Stuart E. Rosenbaum. 1995. *Punishment and the Death Penalty: The Current Debate.* Amherst, N.Y.: Prometheus Books.

Baker, Harvey H. 1910. "Procedure of the Boston Juvenile Court." Pp. 318–327 in Hastings H. Hart, ed., *Preventive Treatment of Neglected Children.* New York: Russell Sage.

Bedau, Hugo A. 1992. *The Case Against the Death Penalty.* Washington, D.C.: American Civil Liberties Union, Capital Punishment Project.

Bernard, Thomas J. 1992. *The Cycle of Juvenile Justice.* New York: Oxford University Press.

Bishop, Donna M., and Charles E. Frazier. 1988. "The Influence of Race in Juvenile Justice Processing." *Journal of Research in Crime and Delinquency* 25 (August):242–263.
1992. "Gender Bias in Juvenile Justice Processing: Implications of the JJDP Act." *The Journal of Criminal Law and Criminology* 82 (Winter): 1162–1182.

Bookin-Weiner, Hedy. 1984. "Assuming Responsibility: Legalizing Preadjudicatory Juvenile Detention." *Crime and Delinquency* 30 (January):39–67.

Bortner, M. A. 1982. *Inside a Juvenile Court: The Tarnished Ideal of Individualized Justice.* New York: New York University Press.

Bortner, M. A., and Wornie L. Reed. 1985. "The Preeminence of Process: An Example of Refocused Justice Research." *Social Science Quarterly* 66 (June):413–425.

Bureau of the Census. 1985. *Current Population Reports.* Series P-25, no. 965. Washington, D.C.: U.S. Government Printing Office.

Bureau of Justice Statistics. 1996. *Correctional Populations in the United States, 1994.* Washington, D.C.: Bureau of Justice Statistics.

Butts, Jeffrey A. 1997. *Juvenile Court Processing of Delinquency Cases, 1985–1994.* Washington, D.C.: Office of Juvenile Justice and Delinquency Prevention.

Chesney-Lind, Meda. 1977. "Judicial Paternalism and the Female Status Offender: Training Women to Know Their Place." *Crime and Delinquency* 23 (April):121–130.
1988a. "Girls and Status Offenses: Is Juvenile Justice Still Sexist?" *Criminal Justice Abstracts* 20 (March):144–165.
1988b. " Girls in Jail." *Crime and Delinquency* 34 (April):150–168.

Chesney-Lind, Meda, and Randall G. Shelden. 1998. *Girls, Delinquency, and Juvenile Justice.* Belmont, Calif.: Wadsworth.

Children's Defense Fund. 1976. *Children in Adult Jails.* New York: Washington Research Project.

Clarke, Stevens H., and Gary G. Koch. 1980. "Juvenile Court: Therapy or Crime Control, and Do Lawyers Make a Difference?" *Law and Society Review* 14 (Winter):263–308.

Cohen, Lawrence E. 1975a. *Delinquency Dispositions: An Empirical Analysis of Processing Decisions in Three Juvenile Courts.* Washington, D.C.: U.S. Government Printing Office.
1975b. *Juvenile Dispositions: Social and Legal Factors Related to the Processing of Denver Delin-*

quency Cases. Washington, D.C.: U.S. Government Printing Office.

1975c. *Pre-Adjudicatory Detention in Three Juvenile Courts: An Empirical Analysis of the Factors Related to Detention Decision Outcomes.* Washington, D.C.: U.S. Government Printing Office.

Cohen, Lawrence E., and James R. Kluegel. 1978. "Determinants of Juvenile Court Dispositions: Ascriptive and Achieved Factors in Two Metropolitan Courts." *American Sociological Review* 43 (April):162–176.

1979. "The Detention Decision: A Study of the Impact of Social Characteristics and Legal Factors in Two Metropolitan Juvenile Courts." *Social Forces* 58 (September):146–161.

Creekmore, Mark. 1976. "Case Processing: Intake, Adjudication, and Disposition." Pp. 119–150 in Rosemary Sarri and Yeheskel Hasenfeld, eds., *Brought to Justice? Juveniles, the Courts, and the Law.* Ann Arbor: University of Michigan, National Assessment of Juvenile Corrections.

Dannefer, Dale. 1984. "'Who Signs the Complaint?': Relational Distance and the Juvenile Justice Process." *Law and Society Review* 18:249–271.

Dannefer, Dale, and Russell K. Schutt. 1982. "Race and Juvenile Justice Processing in Court and Police Agencies." *American Journal of Sociology* 87 (March):1113–1132.

Datesman, Susan K., and Frank R. Scarpitti. 1977. "Unequal Protection for Males and Females in the Juvenile Court." Pp. 59–77 in Theodore N. Ferdinand, ed., *Juvenile Delinquency: Little Brother Grows Up.* Beverly Hills, Calif.: Sage.

Dungworth, Terence. 1977. "Discretion in the Juvenile Justice System: The Impact of Case Characteristics on Prehearing Detention." Pp. 19–43 in Theodore N. Ferdinand, ed., *Juvenile Delinquency: Little Brother Grows Up.* Beverly Hills, Calif.: Sage.

Eaton, Joseph W, and Kenneth Polk. 1961. *Measuring Delinquency: A Study of Probation Department Referrals.* Pittsburgh: University of Pittsburgh Press.

Emerson, Robert M. 1969. *Judging Delinquents: Context and Process in Juvenile Court.* Chicago: Aldine.

Fagan, Jeffrey, Ellen Slaughter, and Eliot Hartstone. 1987. "Blind Justice?: The Impact of Race on the Juvenile Justice Process." *Crime and Delinquency* 33 (April):224–258.

Feld, Barry C. 1988. "*In re Gault* Revisited: A Cross-State Comparison of the Right to Counsel in Juvenile Court." *Crime and Delinquency* 34 (October):393–424.

1989. "The Right to Counsel in Juvenile Court: An Empirical Study of When Lawyers Appear and the Difference They Make." *Journal of Criminal Law and Criminology* 79 (Winter):1185–1346.

1993a. *Justice for Children: The Right to Counsel and Juvenile Courts.* Boston: Northeastern University Press.

1993b. "Juvenile (In)Justice and the Criminal Court Alternative." *Crime and Delinquency* 39 (October):403–424.

1998. "The Juvenile Court." Pp. 509–541 in Michael H. Tonry, ed., *The Handbook of Crime and Punishment.* New York: Oxford University Press.

Forst, Martin L., Bruce A. Fisher, and Robert B. Coates. 1985. "Indeterminate and Determinate Sentencing of Juvenile Delinquents: A National Survey of Approaches to Commitment and Release Decision-Making." *Juvenile and Family Court Journal* 36 (Summer):1–12.

Frazier, Charles E. 1989. "Preadjudicatory Detention." Pp. 143–168 in Albert R. Roberts, *Juvenile Justice: Policies, Programs, and Services.* Chicago: Dorsey.

Frazier, Charles E., and Donna M. Bishop. 1985. "The Pretrial Detention of Juveniles and Its Impact on Case Dispositions." *Journal of Criminal Law and Criminology* 76 (Winter):1132–1152.

Frazier, Charles E., and John C. Cochran. 1986. "Detention of Juveniles: Its Effects on Subsequent Juvenile Court Processing Decisions." *Youth and Society* 17 (March):286–305.

Guarino-Ghezzi, Susan, and Edward J. Loughran. 1996. *Balancing Juvenile Justice.* New Brunswick, N.J.: Transaction.

Harpur, W. R. 1899. *The Report of the Educational Commission of the City of Chicago.* Chicago: Lakeside Press.

Hasenfeld, Yeheskel. 1976. "Youth in the Juvenile Court: Input and Output Patterns." Pp. 60–71 in Rosemary Sarri and Yeheskel Hasenfeld, eds., *Brought to Justice? Juveniles, the Courts, and the Law.* Ann Arbor: University of Michigan, National Assessment of Juvenile Corrections.

Holden, Gwen A., and Robert A. Kepler. 1995. "Deinstitutionalization Status Offenders: A Record of Progress." *Juvenile Justice* 2 (Fall/Winter):3–10.

Howell, James C. 1996. "Juvenile Transfers to the Criminal Justice System: State of the Art." *Law and Policy* 18(1/2):17–60.

In re Gault. 1967. 387 U.S. 1.

In re Winship. 1970. 397 U.S. 358.

Kent v. *United States.* 1966. 383 U.S. 541.

Krisberg, Barry, and Ira Schwartz. 1983. "Rethinking Juvenile Justice." *Crime and Delinquency* 29 (July):333–364.

Krisberg, Barry, et al. 1987. "The Incarceration of Minority Youth." *Crime and Delinquency* 33 (April): 173–205.

Krisberg, Barry, Ira M. Schwartz, Paul Litsky, and James Austin. 1986. "The Watershed of Juvenile Justice Reform." *Crime and Delinquency* 32 (January):5–38.

Lathrop, Julia C. 1917. "Introduction." Pp. 1–10 in Sophonisba P. Breckinridge and Edith Abbott, *The Delinquent Child and the Home: A Study of the Delinquent Wards of the Juvenile Court of Chicago.* New York: Russell Sage.

Law Enforcement Assistance Administration (LEAA). n.d. *Children in Custody.* Washington, D.C.: U.S. Government Printing Office.

Lemert, Edwin M. 1967. "The Juvenile Court—Quest and Realities." Pp. 91–106 in President's Commission on Law Enforcement and Administration of Justice, *Task Force Report: Juvenile Delinquency and Youth Crime.* Washington, D.C.: U.S. Government Printing Office.

McCarthy, Belinda. 1985. "An Analysis of Detention." *Juvenile and Family Court Journal* 36 (Summer): 49–50.
1987. "Case Attrition in the Juvenile Court: An Application of the Crime Control Model." *Justice Quarterly* 4 (June): 238–255.

McCarthy, Belinda R., and Brent L. Smith. 1986. "The Conceptualization of Discrimination in the Juvenile Justice Process: The Impact of Administrative Factors and Screening Decisions on Juvenile Court Dispositions." *Criminology* 24 (February):41–64.

Mack, Julian. 1910. "The Juvenile Court as a Legal Institution." Pp. 293–317 in Hastings H. Hart, ed., *Preventive Treatment of Neglected Children.* New York: Russell Sage.

McKeiver v. *Pennsylvania.* 1971. 403 U.S. 528.

Miller, Neal. 1995. *State Laws on Prosecutors' and Judges' Use of Juvenile Records.* Washington, D.C.: National Institute of Justice.

Moore, Mark H., and Stewart Wakeling. 1997. "Juvenile Justice: Shoring Up the Foundations." Pp. 253–301 in Michael H. Tonry, ed., *Crime and Justice: A Review of Research,* Vol. 22. Chicago: University of Chicago Press.

Mulvey, Edward P., and J. Terry Saunders. 1982. "Juvenile Detention Criteria: State of the Art and Guidelines for Change." *Criminal Justice Abstracts* 14 (June):261–289.

National Council on Crime and Delinquency. 1961. *Standards and Guides for the Detention of Children and Youth,* 2nd ed. New York: National Council on Crime and Delinquency.

National Criminal Justice Association. 1997. *Juvenile Justice Reform Initiatives in the States: 1994–1996.* Washington, D.C.: Office of Juvenile Justice and Delinquency Prevention.

National Institute for Juvenile Justice and Delinquency Prevention (NIJJDP). 1987a. *Juvenile Court Statistics, 1983.* Washington, D.C.: U.S. Government Printing Office.
1987b. *Juvenile Court Statistics, 1984.* Washington, D.C.: U.S. Government Printing Office.

National Probation and Parole Association. 1957. *Guide for Juvenile Court Judges.* New York: National Council on Crime and Delinquency.

Office of Juvenile Justice and Delinquency Prevention (OJJDP). 1989. *Juvenile Court Statistics, 1985.* Washington, D.C.: U.S. Government Printing Office.
1994. *Juvenile Court Statistics, 1991.* Pittsburgh: National Center for Juvenile Justice.
1995. *Juveniles Taken Into Custody: Fiscal Year 1992.* Washington, D.C.: Office of Juvenile Justice and Delinquency Prevention.
1996. *Juvenile Court Statistics, 1994.* Pittsburgh: National Center for Juvenile Justice.

Paulsen, Monrad G., and Charles H. Whitebread. 1974. *Juvenile Law and Procedure.* Reno, Nev.: National Council of Juvenile Court Judges.

Pawlak, Edward J. 1977. "Differential Selection of Juveniles for Detention." *Journal of Research in Crime and Delinquency* 14 (July):152–165.

Platt, Anthony. 1969. *The Child Savers.* Chicago: University of Chicago Press.

Poe-Yamagata, Eileen, and Jeffrey A. Butts. 1996. *Female Offenders in the Juvenile Justice System.* Washington, D.C.: Office of Juvenile Justice and Delinquency Prevention.

Polier, Justine Wise. 1989. *Juvenile Justice in Double Jeopardy: The Distanced Community and Vengeful Retribution.* Hillsdale, N.J.: Lawrence Erlbaum.

Pope, Carl E., and William Feyerherm. 1993. *Minorities and the Juvenile Justice System: Research Summary.* Washington, D.C.: Office of Juvenile Justice and Delinquency Prevention.

Poulin, John E., John L. Levitt, Thomas M. Young, and Donnell M. Pappenfort. 1980. *Juveniles in Detention Centers and Jails: An Analysis of State Variations During the Mid 1970s.* Washington, D.C.: National Institute for Juvenile Justice and Delinquency Prevention.

President's Commission on Law Enforcement and Administration of Justice. 1967a. *Task Force Report: Corrections.* Washington, D.C.: U.S. Government Printing Office.
1967b. *Task Force Report: Juvenile Delinquency and Youth Crime.* Washington, D.C.: U.S. Government Printing Office.

Raley, Gordon A. 1995. "The JJDP Act: A Second Look." *Juvenile Justice* 2 (Fall–Winter):11–18. Washington, D.C.: Office of Juvenile Justice and Delinquency Prevention.

Revised Statutes of Illinois. 1899. Section 21.

Roberts, Julian V., and Loretta J. Stalans. 1998. "Crime, Criminal Justice, and Public Opinion." Pp. 31–57 in Michael H. Tonry, ed., *The Handbook of Crime and Punishment.* New York: Oxford University Press.

Rosenheim, Margaret K. 1983. "Juvenile Justice: Organization and Process." Pp. 969–977 in Sanford H. Kadish, ed., *Encyclopedia of Crime and Justice,* Vol. 3. New York: Free Press.

Rothman, David J. 1979. "The Progressive Legacy: Development of American Attitudes Toward Juvenile Delinquency." Pp. 34–68 in LaMar T. Empey, ed., *Juvenile Justice: The Progressive Legacy and Current Reforms.* Charlottesville: University Press of Virginia.

Rubin, H. Ted. 1976. "The Eye of the Juvenile Court Judge: A One-Step-Up View of the Juvenile Justice System." Pp. 133–159 in Malcolm W. Klein, ed., *The Juvenile Justice System.* Beverly Hills, Calif.: Sage.
1985. *Juvenile Justice: Policy, Practice, and Law,* 2nd ed. New York: Random House.
1989. "The Juvenile Court Landscape." Pp. 110–142 in Albert R. Roberts, *Juvenile Justice: Policies, Programs, and Services.* Chicago: Dorsey Press.

Sarri, Rosemary C. 1974. *Under Lock and Key: Juveniles in Jails and Detention.* Ann Arbor: University of Michigan, National Assessment of Juvenile Corrections.

Sarri, Rosemary, and Yeheskel Hasenfeld, eds. 1976. *Brought to Justice? Juveniles, the Courts, and the Law.* Ann Arbor: University of Michigan, National Assessment of Juvenile Corrections.

Schall v. Martin. 1984. 467 U.S. 253.

Schlossman, Steven L. 1983. "Juvenile Justice: History and Philosophy." Pp. 961–969 in Sanford H. Kadish, ed., *Encyclopedia of Crime and Justice,* Vol. 3. New York: Free Press.

Schultz, J. Lawrence. 1974. "The Cycle of Juvenile Court History." Pp. 239–258 in Sheldon L. Messinger et al., eds., *The Aldine Crime and Justice Annual, 1973*. Chicago: Aldine.

Schutt, Russell K., and Dale Dannefer. 1988. "Detention Decisions in Juvenile Cases: JINS, JDs, and Gender." *Law and Society Review* 22:509–520.

Schwartz, Ira M., Linda Harris, and Laurie Levi. 1988. "The Jailing of Juveniles in Minnesota: A Case Study." *Crime and Delinquency* 34 (April): 133–149.

Sickmund, Melissa, Howard N. Snyder, and Eileen Poe-Yamagata. 1997. *Juvenile Offenders and Victims: 1997 Update on Violence: Statistics Summary*. Washington, D.C.: Office of Juvenile Justice and Delinquency Prevention.

Singer, Simon I. 1996a. "Merging and Emerging Systems of Juvenile and Criminal Justice." *Law and Policy* 18 (1/2):1–15.
1996b. *Recriminalizing Delinquency: Violent Juvenile Crime and Juvenile Justice Reform*. New York: Cambridge University Press.

Snyder, Howard N., and Melissa Sickmund. 1995. *Juvenile Offenders and Victims: A National Report*. Washington, D.C.: Office of Juvenile Justice and Delinquency Prevention.

Soler, Mark. 1988. "Litigation on Behalf of Children in Adult Jails." *Crime and Delinquency* 34 (April): 190–208.

Sosin, Michael, and Rosemary Sarri. 1976. "Due Process—Reality or Myth?" Pp. 176–206 in Rosemary Sarri and Yeheskel Hasenfeld, eds., *Brought to Justice? Juveniles, the Courts, and the Law*. Ann Arbor: University of Michigan, National Assessment of Juvenile Corrections.

Stafford, Mark C. 1995. "Children's Legal Rights in the U.S." *Marriage and Family Review* 21 (3/4): 121–140.

Stanford v. *Kentucky*. 1989. 45 CrL 3203.

Staples, William G. 1987. "Law and Social Control in Juvenile Justice Dispositions." *Journal of Research in Crime and Delinquency* 24 (February): 7–22.

Steinhart, David. 1988. "California Legislature Ends the Jailing of Children: The Story of a Policy Reversal." *Crime and Delinquency* 34 (April): 169–189.

Streib, Victor L. 1987. *The Death Penalty for Juveniles*. Bloomington: Indiana University Press.

Sumner, Helen. 1971. "Locking Them Up." *Crime and Delinquency* 17 (April):168–179.

Swanger, Harry E. 1988. "*Hendrickson v. Griggs*: A Review of the Legal and Policy Implications for Juvenile Justice Policymakers." *Crime and Delinquency* 34 (April):209–227.

Teilmann, Katherine S., and Pierre H. Landry, Jr. 1981. "Gender Bias in Juvenile Justice." *Journal of Research in Crime and Delinquency* 18 (January): 47–80.

Terry, Robert M. 1967. "Discrimination in the Handling of Juvenile Offenders by Social-Control Agencies." *Journal of Research in Crime and Delinquency* 4 (July):218–230.

Thornberry, Terence P. 1973. "Race, Socioeconomic Status and Sentencing in the Juvenile Justice System." *Journal of Criminal Law and Criminology* 64 (March):90–98.
1979. "Sentencing Disparities in the Juvenile Justice System." *Journal of Criminal Law and Criminology* 70 (Summer):164–171.

Tittle, Charles R., and Debra A. Curran. 1988. "Contingencies for Dispositional Disparities in Juvenile Justice." *Social Forces* 67 (September): 23–58.

Torbet, Patricia McFall, Richard Gable, Hunter Hurst IV, Imogene Montgomery, Linda Szymanski, and Douglas Thomas. 1996. *State Responses to Serious and Violent Juvenile Crime*. Washington, D.C.: Office of Juvenile Justice and Delinquency Prevention.

United Nations. 1961. *Second United Nations Congress on the Prevention of Crime and the Treatment of Offenders: Report Prepared by the Secretariat*. New York: United Nations.

U.S. Department of Justice. 1989. *Children in Custody, 1975–85: Census of Public and Private Juve-*

nile Detention, Correctional, and Shelter Facilities, 1975, 1977, 1979, 1983, and 1985. Washington, D.C.: Bureau of Justice Statistics.

U.S. General Accounting Office. 1995. *Juvenile Justice: Minimal Gender Bias Occurred in Processing Noncriminal Juveniles.* Washington, D.C.: U.S. General Accounting Office.

Wakin, Edward. 1975. *Children Without Justice.* New York: National Council of Jewish Women.

Wald, Patricia M. 1976. "Pretrial Detention for Juveniles." Pp. 119–137 in Margaret K. Rosenheim, ed., *Pursuing Justice for the Child.* Chicago: University of Chicago Press.

Wordes, Madeline, Timothy S. Bynum, and Charles J. Corley. 1994. "Locking Up Youth: The Impact of Race on Detention Decisions." *Journal of Research in Crime and Delinquency* 31 (May): 149–165.

Zimring, Franklin E. 1991. "The Treatment of Hard Cases in American Juvenile Justice: In Defense of Discretionary Transfer." *Notre Dame Journal of Law, Ethics, and Public Policy* 5(2):267–280.

REHABILITATION LONG HAS
BEEN A CENTRAL FUNCTION OF
THE JUVENILE JUSTICE SYSTEM.

CHAPTER EIGHTEEN

REHABILITATING DELINQUENTS

As we learned in the previous chapter, by the mid-1970s it had become clear that the juvenile court had not lived up to the ideals expected of it. The same was true of efforts to rehabilitate offenders. Just as the concept of juvenile justice was viewed with disillusionment and cynicism, so was the concept of rehabilitation. To discover how that came about, we will review the development of the rehabilitative philosophy and explore the reasons it was greeted initially with hope and optimism but was viewed later as a bankrupt concept with little redeeming value.

FORERUNNERS OF REHABILITATION

The philosophy of rehabilitation, like that of positivist criminology, was a product of the late 1800s and early 1900s. Only a century earlier, delinquents still were being treated less than humanely.

Retribution

Even though the modern concept of childhood was becoming widely accepted by the late 1700s, **retribution** was still the dominant response to young criminals:

> Nicholas Carter, about fourteen Years of Age, was condemned [hanged] for Robbery. He said, That his Father imployed him in sewing and making of Gloves: But he being Idle, and regardless of his Parents Good Admonitions, ran away from them, and joyned himself to bad Company. . . . Nicholas Carter . . . desired all Young People to take timely warning by his so sudden a Death. (Sanders, 1970:24–25)

Although a few children, like Nicholas, were hanged, most of them received clemency after being sentenced to die (Sanders, 1970:21). In New England in the 1600s, for example, colonial laws stated that children could be put to death for cursing or smiting their parents, treating the scriptures with blasphemy, being stubborn or rebellious, or committing other "notorious" crimes of this sort. In practice, however, punishments usually were less severe. Consider the court's ruling in the case of Mistress How:

> The Court upon consideration of what is testified, ordered that for her swearing she pay ten shillings, and for her cursing speeches and rebellion to her mother, and profane speeches of the scriptures, tending to blasphemy, that she be corrected publicly by whipping, suitable to her years, and if this be not a warning but that she go on in these courses, it will come to a higher censure. (Bremner, 1970, I:38)

Besides whipping, other kinds of corporal punishment also were common:

> William Carter a little Boy, about Ten Years of Age, was Indicted for stealing . . . two Gold Rings . . . , a piece of Coined Gold . . . and . . . Money. . . . It was fully proved, so he was found Guilty. [Sentenced to be burnt in the hand.]. (Sanders, 1970:25–26)

In North Carolina, a young slave, Peter, confessed that he was present when his master was murdered by his brother:

> The Court haveing taken into consideration the youth of the said Peter and considering him under the Influence of his said older Brother Darby, have thought proper to pass his Sentence in the following words to wit. That the said Negro boy Peter be committed to Gaol and there to Remain under a Good Guard, till Tomorrow, and then between the Hours of one and four o'clock he be taken out thence and tied to a Post on the Court House lott and there to have one half of Each of his Ears cut off and be branded on Each Cheek with the letter M and Receive one hundred lashes well laid on his bare back and that the Sheriff See this order Executed. (Sanders, 1970:324)

Finally, because disfigurement, death, and whipping sometimes were viewed as too cruel or as ineffective deterrents, English reformers suggested another kind of punishment:

> The methods now employed to dispose of delinquent children failing either to reform them or relieve society from their presence, it is certainly expedient a new experiment should be tried. . . . Now it appears to us that it would be real humanity towards these unfortunate creatures to subject them to compulsory and perpetual exile from England. . . . Abroad, in New South Wales [Australia], they often become prosperous and useful citizens; but, at home, they seem incapable of resisting the temptations presented by a luxurious and refined community. (Sanders, 1970:137)

This new idea, called *transportation,* was quickly accepted and widely used in England and France. The following is an example of its application to a young English girl:

> Susannah Tyrell, a Girl about ten Years Old, was Indicted for stealing two Gold Rings . . . and 14s. [shillings]. . . . The Evidence was, That she confest, That one Elizabeth Sallowes (now in Newgate) did give her a Key to open the Door. . . . So that upon the whole, she was found guilty to the value of 9s. She was ordered to be transported. (Sanders, 1970:26)

A somewhat similar kind of punishment, which was even older than transportation, involved the removal of children to the "hulks"—abandoned, rotting ships, unfit for service—that were anchored offshore in rivers, bays, and inlets (Sanders, 1970: 70). Sometimes, children served out their sentences alongside adult convicts on hulks, working as tailors, shoemakers, carpenters, and bookbinders. In other cases, they were confined to hulks awaiting transportation to Australia.

The important thing about the use of hulks, along with capital punishment, branding, whipping, disfigurement, and transportation, was that those methods, rather than treatment or imprisonment, were the primary punishments prior to the 1800s. In virtually all Western nations, "prisons were uniformly considered to be merely places of safekeeping, that might serve a deterrent purpose but had no concern for the rehabilitation or reformation of those confined" (Sellin, 1964:xix). Gradually, however, the treatment of offenders was revolutionized.

Restraint

Beginning in the late 1700s, efforts to control crime concentrated increasingly on the notion that lawbreakers, young or old, could be reformed by *restraining* them in prison. Stimulated by the philosophy of the Enlightenment and the belief of classical criminologists that legal punishments should be decreased in severity and graded by the seriousness of criminal acts (see the introduction to Part Three), reformers began to construct prisons as alternatives to the barbaric punishments of the past.

THE PENNSYLVANIA SYSTEM Pennsylvania led the way in 1790 by passing a law that led to one of the most important innovations in penal history: a prison in which convicts could be confined in solitary cells as a method of reforming them (McKelvey, 1936:6). Led by the Quakers, by influential reform societies, and by such as Benjamin Franklin and William Bradford, reformers assumed that by segregating offenders from all corrupting influences and denying them all but the physical necessities of life, they could recognize the errors of their ways and refrain from committing more crimes (Barnes, 1972: 120–131).

The **Pennsylvania system** first was tried in the Walnut Street Jail in Philadelphia, but it soon failed because of overcrowding (Barnes, 1972:129). Undiscouraged, however, reformers passed legislation to construct two new prisons (Barnes, 1972:129–131; Hawkins and Alpert, 1989:39–46). The most famous was the Eastern State Penitentiary, constructed at Cherry Hill, Pennsylvania, in 1829. This prison featured a series of massive stone corridors radiating like the spokes of a wheel from a central rotunda (Pettigrove, 1910). Each of the corridors contained a series of large cells, 8 by 15 feet, with 12-foot ceilings, into which inmates were placed in solitary confinement and left entirely by themselves for the duration of their sentences. Each offender had access to his own small exercise yard, entirely walled off to "prevent any communication between the convicts" (McKelvey, 1936:11).

THE AUBURN (NEW YORK) SYSTEM Leaders in New York were impressed with the Pennsylvania system (Barnes, 1972:132–133). Hence, in 1816, a law was passed permitting construction of a prison at Auburn, New York, to be designed with individual cells (Barnes, 1972:133–134). But whereas the cells at Eastern State Penitentiary in Pennsylvania were large and permitted access to the outside, those in the new Auburn prison were only small cages, 3½ by 7 feet, with 7-foot ceilings and no outside access (McKelvey, 1936:8). The results were disastrous. Locked in their tiny cells, left in complete idleness, and lacking any means for exercise or human contact, many Auburn prisoners became ill or went insane (Barnes, 1972: 134–135). Officials took only two years to conclude that the experiment had failed. The result was the development of an alternative system called the **Auburn system.**

Although inmates in the new Auburn prison were locked up in their cells at night, they were permitted to work together during the day (Barnes, 1972:135; Hawkins and Alpert, 1989:40–41). However, to forestall disobedience and opposition, officials hit upon some new methods of control. They required prisoners to be silent at all times, march in lockstep, keep their eyes downcast, and never face another prisoner (Barnes, 1972:136; Hawkins and Alpert, 1989:42–43; McKelvey, 1936:8). Given these new means of maintaining order and the fact that working prisoners could help to pay for their own keep, Auburn officials were proud of their achievements:

> It is not possible to describe the pleasure which we feel in contemplating this noble institution. . . . We regard it as a model worthy of the world's imitation. . . .
>
> The whole establishment, from the gate to the sewer, is a specimen of neatness. The unremitted industry, the entire subordination and subdued feeling of the convicts, has probably no parallel among an equal number of criminals. In their solitary cells they spend the night, with no other book but the Bible, and at sunrise they proceed . . . in solid columns, with the lock march, to their workshops; thence, in the same order, at the hour of breakfast, to the common hall, where they partake of their wholesome and frugal meal in silence. Not even a whisper is heard. . . . When they have done eating, at the ringing of a little bell, . . . they rise from the table, form the solid columns, and return . . . to the workshops. . . . It is the testimony of many witnesses, that they have passed more than three hundred convicts, without seeing one leave his work, or turn his head to gaze at them. . . . At the close of the day, . . . the work is all laid aside at once, and the convicts return . . . to the solitary cells, where they partake of the frugal meal. . . . After supper, they can, if they choose, read Scripture undisturbed and then reflect in silence on the errors of their lives. (Louis Dwight, the foremost champion of the Auburn System, as quoted by Barnes, 1972:136–137)

It was not mentioned in this glowing statement, however, that, in addition to the requirements of silence, lockstep marching, and downcast eyes, whipping also was used to maintain order and to encourage prisoners to reflect on the errors of their ways (Barnes, 1972:136; Hawkins and Alpert, 1989:43).

Restraint for Juveniles

Institutions designed exclusively for delinquents followed the construction of prisons by several years. Until then, and even after, many juveniles were confined in the Pennsylvania, Auburn, and other prisons. Although **houses of refuge** and asylums, run largely by private groups, had begun to appear about 1825, the first public **reformatories** and training schools were not built until almost 1850:

> The Lyman School for Boys opened in Westborough, Mass., in 1846. Then came the New York State Agricultural and Industrial School in 1849 and the Maine Boys Training Center in 1853. By 1870, Connecticut, Indiana, Maryland, Nevada, New Hampshire, New Jersey, Ohio, and Vermont had also set up separate juvenile training facilities; by 1900, 36 states had done so. (President's Commission on Law Enforcement and Administration of Justice, 1967a:141)

Just as the prison was viewed as humane and progressive, so were those juvenile institutions. At the same time, the treatment of unruly and delinquent children did not suddenly partake of methods that we might consider enlightened or that differed greatly from how adults were treated:

> Many of the juvenile reformatories were . . . , in reality, juvenile prisons, with prison bars, prison cells, prison garb, prison labor, prison punishments, and prison discipline. . . . It was recognized as a legitimate part of the purpose of the institution to inflict upon the child punishment for his wrong-doing. (Hart, 1910:11)

As the 1800s wore on, however, changes were made. Perhaps the most profound change was the increasing preoccupation with the developmental needs of children: "Every child allowed to grow up in ignorance and vice, and so to become a pauper or a criminal, is liable to become in turn the progenitor of generations of criminals" (Platt, 1969:130). To many Americans, it seemed that if their worst fears were to be avoided, all poor, uneducated, and parentless children had to be treated *and* disciplined.

Concerns over children extended to concerns over adults. The line between childhood and adulthood increasingly was becoming blurred as the concept of adolescence began to develop and extend farther into the traditional adult ages. As Rothman (1971:76) suggested, Americans in the 1800s eventually became so sensitive to childhood that "they stripped away the years from adults and made everyone into a child."

REHABILITATION

Following the Civil War, those tendencies were reflected in the recommendations of a remarkable gathering of America's leading penal reformers. Meeting at the Cincinnati Prison Congress of 1870, the reformers concluded that considerable good could be accomplished if criminals were made the "objects of a generous parental care" and "trained to virtue" instead of being left to suffer in prison (Henderson, 1910:40). The implication, of course, was the concept of rehabilitation.

Declaration of Principles

In a series of pronouncements, the reformers enunciated the first philosophy of rehabilitation and then embodied it in a formal **Declaration of Principles.** The following, attributed to Enoch Wines, who also drafted the principles, constitutes a kind of preamble to them:

> A prison governed by force and fear is a prison mismanaged, in which hope and love, the two great spiritual, uplifting, regenerating forces to which mankind must ever look for redemption, are asleep or dead. . . . Why not try the effect of rewards upon the prisoner? Rewards, as truly as punishments, appeal to the inextinguishable principle of self-interest in his breast. (Wines, 1910:12)

The difference between the ideas expressed in that preamble and past punishment philosophies was striking, but Wines was not content to be an idealistic philosopher. His Declaration of Principles not only described rehabilitation in abstract terms but also outlined the specific methods by which it should be accomplished (Henderson, 1910:17, 39–63).

REHABILITATION The primary goal of penology should not be punishment, but **rehabilitation**:

> Whatever differences of opinion may exist among penologists on other questions . . . , there is one point on which there may be . . . almost . . . perfect unanimity, namely, that the moral cure of criminals, adult as well as juvenile, . . . is the best

means of attaining the end in view—the repression and extirpation of crime; . . . hence . . . reformation is the primary object to be aimed at in the administration of penal justice. (Henderson, 1910:17)

TREATMENT OF CRIMINALS, NOT CRIMES The Declaration of Principles opposed the premise of the classical school of criminology that legal punishments should be allocated according to the seriousness of crimes. Instead, rehabilitation should be administered according to the needs of offenders:

> The treatment of criminals by society is for the protection of society. But since such treatment is directed to the criminal rather than to the crime, its great object should be his moral regeneration. Hence the supreme aim of prison discipline is the reformation of criminals, not the infliction of vindictive suffering. (Henderson, 1910:39)

THE INDETERMINATE SENTENCE The practice of giving offenders **determinate** (definite) **sentences,** according to the seriousness of their crimes, should be replaced by a policy of **indeterminate** (indefinite) **sentences**:

> Peremptory sentences ought to be replaced by those of indeterminate length. . . . Reformation is a work of time; and a benevolent regard to the good of the criminal himself, as well as to the protection of society, requires that his sentence be long enough for reformatory processes to take effect. (Henderson, 1910:40–41)

CLASSIFICATION The practice of confining all prisoners together regardless of age, character, or gender should be eliminated. Prisons should be designed to meet the needs of different kinds of prisoners:

> Prisons, as well as prisoners, should be classified or graded so that there shall be prisons for the untried, for the incorrigible and for other degrees of depraved character, as well as separate establishments for women and for criminals of the younger class. (Henderson, 1910:41)

EDUCATION Education is indispensable in rehabilitating offenders:

Education is a vital force in the reformation of fallen men and women. Its tendency is to quicken the intellect, inspire self-respect, excite to higher aims, and afford a healthful substitute for low and vicious amusements. (Henderson, 1910:40)

INDUSTRIAL TRAINING Occupational training is beneficial for practical and personal reasons:

Industrial training should have both a higher development and a greater breadth than has heretofore been, or is now, commonly given to it in our prisons. Work is no less an auxiliary to virtue than it is a means of support. (Henderson, 1910:41)

REWARDS Change is more likely to be produced by rewards than by punishments:

Since hope is a more potent agent than fear, it should be made an ever-present force in the minds of prisoners, by a well-devised and skillfully applied system of rewards for good conduct, industry and attention to learning. Rewards, more than punishments, are essential to every good prison system. (Henderson, 1910:39)

SELF-RESPECT Punishment only degrades; correctional practices should uplift:

The prisoner's self-respect should be cultivated to the utmost, and every effort made to give back to him his manhood. There is no greater mistake in the whole compass of penal discipline than its studied imposition of degradation as a part of punishment. Such imposition destroys every better impulse and aspiration. It crushes the weak, irritates the strong, and indisposes all to submission and reform. It is trampling where we ought to raise, and is therefore as unchristian in principle as it is unwise in policy. (Henderson, 1910: 40–41)

PAROLE Treatment in an institution completes only half the task; offenders require help when they return to the community:

More systematic and comprehensive methods should be adopted to save discharged prisoners, by providing them with work and encouraging

them to redeem their character and regain their lost position in society. . . . And to this end it is desirable that state societies be formed, which shall co-operate with each other in this work. (Henderson, 1910:42)

PREVENTION Prevention of crime is more promising than confinement after committing a crime:

Preventive institutions, such as truant homes, industrial schools, etc., for the reception and treatment of children not yet criminal, but in danger of becoming so, constitute the true field of promise in which to labor for the repression of crime.

It is our conviction that one of the most effective agencies in the repression of crime would be the enactment of laws by which the education of all the children of the state should be made obligatory. Better to force education upon the people than to force them into prison to suffer for crimes. (Henderson, 1910:41–42, 44)

Distinctive Features

This remarkable declaration was characterized by three distinctive features. The first was *optimism*. In contrast to the pessimistic and retributive features of prior penal philosophies, the rehabilitative philosophy reflected a belief that men and women, as well as children, could be reclaimed from evil. That belief was only strengthened by the invention of the juvenile court. By applying the principles of rehabilitation, children could be redeemed, and future offending could be prevented.

The second feature of the rehabilitative philosophy was its focus on the *individual offender*. It was the individual's morals that required regeneration. It was the individual's characteristics for which classification, separate institutions, and indeterminate sentences were needed. It was the individual's educational deficiencies that demanded attention. And it was the individual's character from which other people required protection. Indeed, nothing could be more democratic: Crime and delinquency could be controlled if the individual was treated and given a helping hand.

The third key feature of the declaration was its belief that the *institution* is the most effective means for treating children not yet criminal, as well as for rehabilitating those who are. Throughout the 1800s, there was some (albeit ineffective) opposition to institutional confinement of children. However, the idea prevailed that the best place for meeting the needs of deprived children was in self-sufficient, correctional utopias that provided everything an understanding family and well-organized community could provide—only better:

> In the ordinary family home the [delinquent] child is often at a great disadvantage. . . . The neighborhood may be thoroughly bad. The daily journey to and from school may lead past saloons. . . . The mother may be lazy, slatternly and shiftless. The father may be drunken, vicious, improvident. . . . In the institution, however, we are able to control absolutely the child's environment. We can create ideal sanitary conditions. . . . We can select his school teacher and his Sunday School teacher. We can bring to bear upon him the most helpful and elevating influences. The boy will never play truant, he will never be out with a gang, he will never be late to school. Under these circumstances, why should we not be able to produce satisfactory results? (Hart, 1910:62)

Overall, then, the rehabilitative philosophy was both optimistic and revolutionary. Zebulon R. Brockway (1910:93), who was the first correctional administrator to apply the principles of rehabilitation in a youth reformatory, quoted a distinguished jurist as saying that the principles were "destined to change men's habits of thought concerning crime and the attitude of society toward criminals; to rewrite from end to end every penal code in Christendom; and to modify and ennoble the fundamental law of every state." Brockway (1910:93) added that "it is a change from a plane where feeling sways, to the loftier realm and reign of wisdom." Much of his prophecy came true.

CORRECTIONAL UTOPIAS

The principles of rehabilitation first were applied in a revolutionary new reformatory constructed for

boys and young men, ages 16–30 (Scott, 1910:90). The tendency for Americans in the 1800s to "strip away the years" from adults clearly was evident. Contrary to the idea that children should be punished like adults, the reverse was suggested: Young men were to be treated and disciplined like children.

The Scientific Reformatory

Enoch Wines again led the way. As leader of the New York Prison Association, he gained authorization in 1869 to plan for a new reformatory at Elmira, New York. Construction was completed about 1876, and Zebulon Brockway was chosen as its first superintendent (Brockway, 1910; Scott, 1910:93–98).

Brockway was impressed by the growth of science in the 1800s. In 1877, as a result, he drafted and gained the passage of an "organic" law designed to implement the principles of the Cincinnati Prison Congress: indeterminate sentences; a classification system; a program of treatment, education, physical discipline, and work; and parole (Scott, 1910:94–112). Although the new reformatory resembled a strict military school more than anything else (Hawkins and Alpert, 1989:50–52; Mennel, 1973:102–103), Brockway's (1912:238) general approach had lasting appeal:

> The [Elmira] Reformatory system meets a demand of enlightened public sentiment which favors the idea that young offenders . . . shall be wisely and humanely treated, be supplied with incentives and opportunities to reform, and, as far as possible, the unworthy and determined offenders shall be subjected to lengthened detention . . . and all, when released, be properly supervised until they are established in industry, respectable associations, and good behavior.

Reformatories for Girls

Institutions also were constructed for girls and young women. According to Frederick Wines, female offenders had specific problems that required treatment and training:

> Neglect, brutality on the part of others; . . . disobedience, self-will, laziness, the love of dress, the want of education, poverty, animal appetites and passions cultivated and not held in check; . . . curiosity to see life, social ambition and the

desire for a career; evil associations, the lack . . . of a good home, in general the want of training in the power of self-control. (Barrows, 1910:147)

Given those problems, ideal reformatories for young females were operated in the same general way as Brockway's institution for males:

There may be some difference in minor points, but in each one we find the graded [classification] system, parole upon earning a certain degree of credit, industries that will be useful in the outer world, lighter employment as a means of recreation, physical drill in the gymnasium, with baths and scrupulous neatness of person and domicile, attention to music, . . . good academic schools in most, outdoor work, and recreation of all kinds. . . . Nowhere does the state do more than try to develop a religious and reverential atmosphere, and inculcate the belief that the noblest ideal of pure religion is to keep one's self unspotted from the world. (Barrows, 1910:139)

In principle, then, the new reformatory created by Enoch Wines and Brockway became the prototype for progressive penology throughout the United States.

Industrial and Training Schools

Just as reformatories were built for older youths and young adults, **industrial and training schools** were constructed for younger status offenders and delinquents. New guidelines stressed the importance of locating both types of institutions in rural areas and reaffirmed that they should emulate the characteristics of a well-disciplined family. These schools were widespread by the time the juvenile court was established, except in the South, which had not yet constructed special institutions for juveniles (Bremner, 1970, 1:672; Platt, 1969:61–62). As child saving increased, it became more difficult to distinguish among industrial schools, reformatories, and training schools, and there was evidence of growing problems. As Hart (1910:70) put it:

Juvenile reformatories were known first as houses of refuge; when that term became opprobrious, they were called reform schools; when that term in turn became obnoxious, the name industrial

school was used; [and] when that name became offensive, they were called training schools.

Likewise, it became increasingly difficult to distinguish among types of institutionalized children. Because the purpose of rehabilitation was to treat children, not crimes, there was little need to distinguish among offenders; they all needed help. Furthermore, biological and psychodynamic control theories suggested that serious crimes were inevitable unless the hidden drives and unconscious motives of problem children were identified and treated. Education and job training would do little good unless those obstructions were first eliminated.

THE TREND TOWARD THE COMMUNITY

Despite the construction of new institutions, reformers began to voice opposition to them in the early 1900s. The difficulty with locking children up, said Hastings Hart (1910:62), is "institutionalism":

In a great institution like the New York House of Refuge, with 700 boys, or Girard College, with 1700 boys, or the Catholic Protectory, with 2700 children, the child is lost in the mass. He is one of a multitude. It is almost impossible to give him that personal attention which is essential to the normal development of a child, or to give opportunity for such development. The child lacks initiative; he lacks courage; he lacks power to act for himself. In the institution someone else is doing his thinking for him, someone else is planning his life for him; and when he goes into the world, he goes at a disadvantage.

Hart (1910:12) was voicing a complaint that since has become common. That is, children raised by the state are incapable of free and independent judgment, become accustomed to confinement as a way of life, and are comfortable only in a setting in which all decisions are made for them:

However good an institution may be, however kindly its spirit, however genial its atmosphere, however homelike its cottages, however fatherly and motherly its officers, however admirable its training, it is now generally agreed . . . that institutional life is at the best artificial and unnatural, and that the child ought to be returned at the earliest practicable moment to the more natural environment of the family.

It was such reasoning that led many of the first juvenile court judges to argue that **probation,** and not institutionalization, should be the "cord upon which all the pearls of the juvenile court are strung" (Rothman, 1979:50). Treatment in the community was preferable for most juveniles:

> When we have exhausted the resources of the home, the church, the juvenile court, the probation officer, then we turn to the juvenile reformatory, and ask of it success in dealing with the problem in whose solution all other agencies have failed. (Hart, 1910:11)

Probation

Probation actually had earlier roots than the first juvenile courts (Diana, 1960:189–190). It was used first in Boston in 1841 when a shoemaker, John Augustus, began to provide bail for petty offenders—men, women, and children—and to assist them following their court appearances. After Augustus died, the Boston Children's Aid Society and other volunteers continued his activities. Massachusetts formalized those activities in 1869 by appointing a worker from the Board of State Charities, a private agency, to investigate children's cases, make recommendations to the criminal court, and receive children for placement. In 1878, an additional law was passed permitting the employment of paid probation officers in Boston (United Nations, 1951:29–42). A few other states, as well as Great Britain, legalized probation late in the 1800s, permitting first-time offenders to be released on good conduct (Tappan, 1960: 546). It was the juvenile court movement, however, that truly legitimized probation and gave it its impetus. "By 1933 all states except Wyoming had juvenile probation laws" (Diana, 1960:189). As discussed in the previous chapter, the practice has become so widespread that far more delinquents now are placed on probation than are institutionalized (Torbet et al., 1996).

Parole

Along with probation, parole gradually was added as a rehabilitative tool (Carter and Wilkins, 1970:177–276). Recall that parole was first suggested by the Cincinnati Prison Congress in 1870 and was first used at the Elmira Reformatory by Brockway in about 1880.

Like probation, **parole** has a dual purpose: (1) casework assistance for the offender and (2) protection of the community. Unlike probation, however, parole is a community service that follows, rather than precedes, institutionalization. The idea is that delinquents who have suffered "institutionalism" should not be suddenly released to the community without adult supervision and assistance. Instead, parole should be part of the indeterminate sentence. If delinquents are given help when they leave an institution and can successfully adjust to the community, they will be permitted to remain there. But if they seem unable to cope with the many demands of community life, they will be returned to the institution for further rehabilitation. Hence, following the pattern of other elements of the rehabilitative philosophy, parole was legalized in virtually every state as a part of the juvenile court movement.

JUSTICE REVOLUTIONIZED

All of those developments tended to support of Brockway's belief that the principles of rehabilitation would modify the laws of every state. Their impact was so great that they revolutionized the administration of American justice. Prior to the application of the methods and principles set down in 1870, the fate of an offender, juvenile or adult, was prescribed by law and decided by a judge once his or her guilt was established: imprisonment, hard labor, a fine, or some other punishment. But the rehabilitative revolution diminished judicial power and transferred it elsewhere. In the juvenile court, for example, new laws permitted deferred sentencing until an offender could be studied and recommendations made to a judge. Probation officers and others shared and influenced judges' dispositional decisions. But that was only the beginning.

Once a dispositional decision was made, the court turned an offender over to probation or institutional personnel for imprecisely defined treatment. Responsibility and power were divided, not only among people close to the court but, eventually, throughout the whole correctional system. The adoption of indeterminate sentences and the classification of offenders lodged new power in probation officers and correctional officials. The decisions handed down from those people, in turn, led to construction of diagnostic centers, specialized institutions, reformatories, industrial schools, work farms, probation camps, and cottage programs. All of these facilities were designed to respond to different classes of offenders rather than classes of crimes—first-time offenders, neglected children, hard-core delinquents, as well as males and females.

This resulted in such specialized roles for correctional officials as administration, care and feeding, custody, supervision, casework, education, therapy, and vocational training. Then, following institutionalization, the use of parole further divided power and responsibility, and lodged them in parole boards and parole officers. They, rather than judges or correctional officials, decided when offenders would receive their freedom.

In short, the concept of rehabilitation totally altered the classical system of justice. As a result, delinquents were made to answer for their rehabilitation, not merely to a judge but to a host of decision makers, all of whom were given a role in deciding delinquents' fates and judging their performances. A crucial question, therefore, is this: Did the grand hopes of the justice revolution come true?

DISMAY OVER THE SYSTEM

For more than half of the 20th century, no one seriously challenged the belief that rehabilitation worked. The juvenile justice system operated in relative tranquillity, with only occasional criticisms (Tonry, 1976). But many Americans have become dismayed and cynical in recent decades.

Norman Carlson, former director of the Federal Bureau of Prisons, described the situation in an address to the American Academy of Psychiatry and the Law in 1975. His first step was to disavow the most fundamental premise of rehabilitation—that the causes of delinquency could be identified and treatment successfully administered. "We cannot diagnose criminality . . . , we cannot prescribe a precise treatment and we certainly cannot guarantee a cure" (p. 1). But that was not all. Carlson (1975) also argued that the juvenile justice system could not correct the consequences of such social problems as poverty, neglect, and racism, and therefore, could not save young people from delinquency. "Neither you nor I," he told his audience, "can control unemployment, social inequity, racial discrimination and poverty. Neither the psychiatrists nor the correctional officer can deal with broken families, poor neighborhoods, bad schools and lack of opportunity" (p. 1).

One reason for Carlson's cynicism was the increasing official delinquency rates of the 1960s and 1970s (see Chapter 4). The desirable outcomes predicted by Wines, Brockway, and the founders of the juvenile court had not come to pass. But beyond that, his cynicism was generated by (1) attacks on the concept of rehabilitation itself, (2) the lack of resources for fully implementing the methods of rehabilitation, and (3) theories and findings of the scientific community.

Deficiencies in Concept

Addressing a gathering of social scientists at Harvard University in 1974, Sarri, Vinter, and Kish (1974:1) declared that the juvenile justice system represented "the failure of a nation." That system, they continued, "remains an anachronistic local-government vehicle, overwhelmed with the shortcomings of an entire society." Historically, the care and handling of children had been the responsibility of family, school, and community. Over the years, however, those tasks increasingly had been relinquished to police officers, judges, and correctional officials. The juvenile justice system, as a result, was inundated with clients. It was expected to solve problems that it could not possibly hope to solve.

Those critical remarks seemed to suggest that judges and probation officers, no less than delinquents, had been victims of overdemanding parents and communities. Undeniably, this sometimes had been the case. But the dumping of unwanted children often had been invited by juvenile justice officials. The reformers who wrote the Declaration of Principles in 1870 or who invented the juvenile court in 1899 argued that problem children *should* be turned over to the juvenile court, that treatment *should* be left to experts.

Influential critics like Edwin Lemert (1967:96–97) called for a marked change in philosophy. Rather than assuming that the rehabilitative ideal is a cure-all, he suggested, judges and professionals within the system should leaven their arrogance with humility and should lower their expectations:

> It would be well to delete entirely from such laws [of the land] pious injunctions that "care, custody and discipline of children under the control of the juvenile court shall approximate that which they would receive from their parents," which taken literally becomes meaningless either as ideal or reality. Neither the modern state nor an harassed juvenile court judge is a father; a halfway house is not a home; a reformatory cell is not a teenager's bedroom; a juvenile hall counselor is not a dutch uncle; and a cottage matron is not a mother. (Lemert, 1967:92)

Lemert (1967:96) also suggested that the "treatment of delinquency is . . . much more akin to midwifery than medicine." Judges, probation officers, psychologists, and counselors should recognize that, like midwives, they do not have the knowledge to diagnose ills and prescribe cures. At best, they could only assist the process of maturation and could not be expected to have much impact on its outcome. Hence, the only defensible philosophy for the juvenile justice system is "judicious nonintervention" (p. 96).

Lack of Resources

In rebuttal to Lemert's critical remarks, many judges, correctional officials, members of national commissions, and treatment personnel maintained that correctional problems were due more to a lack of resources than to flaws in the concept of rehabilitation. Indeed, that theme had been a persistent one since juvenile courts became widespread.

In the 1930s, two national commissions—the National Commission on Law Observance and Enforcement (1931:passim) and the White House Conference on Child Health and Protection (1932:22)—noted the lack of support for rehabilitative facilities and programs. Specifically, they cited continued detention of juveniles in jails, poorly paid and unqualified judges, inadequate numbers of probation officers, a lack of psychiatric services, inadequate foster homes and institutional care, and an ineffective parole system. But while those national commissions lamented the lack of rehabilitative tools, their faith in individualized treatment remained unchanged. Thus, their recommendations continued to stress what Tonry (1976:287) described as a "familiar litany": Current problems would be solved if there were more rehabilitation programs and better-paid and better-qualified personnel.

In 1967, the President's Commission on Law Enforcement and Administration of Justice continued to lament the lack of adequate resources (1967b:4–5). The average probation officer, for example, was expected to maintain a caseload of about seventy-five probationers, conduct presentence investigations, maintain extensive paperwork, and carry out other functions as well (pp. 4–5, 140). As a result, there was little time for dealing with the actual problems of juveniles.

The same was true of the nation's training schools. Too many of them were custodial institutions in which children were warehoused and isolated "from the outside world—in an overcrowded, understaffed security institution with little education, little vocational training, little counseling or job placement, or other guidance upon release" (President's Commission on Law Enforcement and Administration of Justice, 1967c:80).

When Sarri, Vinter, and Kish (1974) added up all those problems, they questioned whether American society really liked its children. After all, it offered them minimal provision of their constitutional rights; it cast them aside, stigmatized but unaided; and it denied them other community services once they entered the juvenile justice system.

THE FINDINGS OF SCIENCE

Despite the complaints, many of which were scarcely new, scientific theories and findings possibly had an even more devastating impact. They questioned whether rehabilitation programs had *any* positive effects.

Effects of Institutional Programs

Twentieth-century criminologists added to Hastings Hart's complaint about institutionalism. Most of them questioned the effectiveness of institutionalization, even under optimal conditions.

OPPOSITION TO AUTHORITY Many delinquents had negative attitudes toward authority when they entered institutions. However, the institutionalization made their attitudes worse. Even among people without delinquent histories—patients in mental hospitals, children in orphanages, or soldiers in prisoner-of-war camps—captivity generates an inmate code of resistance to authority (Bartollas, Miller, and Dinitz, 1976:62–69; Clemmer, 1940:109, 152–164; Cressey, 1961:passim; Schrag, 1954; Sykes, 1965:Chap. 5; Sykes and Messinger, 1960:13–19).

Consider the statement of a young criminal who had spent much of his life in juvenile institutions:

> The easiest way to get a bad name in . . . [an institution] is to talk to bulls. That's one of the rules: you don't talk to bulls, and bulls include anyone . . . who doesn't have a number. The best way to get along in the joint is to completely ignore the staff. (Manocchio and Dunn, 1970:38)

Juvenile institutions were viewed as caste systems (Barker and Adams, 1959; Bartollas, Miller, and Dinitz, 1976:Chaps. 11–12), in which inmates and staff were divided into mutually exclusive groups. Inmates "played it cool" and gave an outward appearance of good behavior without ever becoming involved with staff or trying to change (Ohlin and Lawrence, 1959: 7–11).

ISOLATION AND FEAR Researchers also found that institutional life was characterized by personal isolation and fear (Bartollas, Miller, and Dinitz, 1976: Chap. 10; Clemmer, 1940:297–298; Glaser, 1964: Chap. 5). Inmate relationships could not overcome the effects of institutionalization. Even in cottage programs, to say nothing of training schools, inmates

BOOT CAMPS

How effective are boot camps (also known as shock incarceration programs) in reducing recidivism? Boot camps for juveniles have emphasized academic achievement, discipline through physical conditioning, a strong work ethic, and community-based aftercare involving academic and job training and intensive supervision. Many observers have believed that the combination of such "get-tough" and rehabilitative strategies would reduce the likelihood of recidivism. However, in an evaluation of boot camps in Ohio, Colorado, and Alabama, Peters and his associates (1997:31) found that "boot camp participants . . . were . . . no less likely to reoffend after release than [were] their control group counterparts." Indeed, the boot camp recidivists committed new offenses more quickly than did the control group recidivists (Peters et al., 1997:23).

preyed on inmates, resulting in homosexual rape and assault (Polsky, 1962:passim).

Different patterns were found among institutionalized girls. The deprivation of normal relationships resulted in artificial "families" that encouraged girls to adopt family roles as functional substitutes for the normal relationships denied to them by institutionalization (Giallombardo, 1974:passim: Propper, 1981:Chap. 7).

STAFF CONFLICTS Some researchers contended that staff members did not share a belief in the importance of rehabilitative goals (Schrag, 1961:331–342). Treatment staff was at odds with custodial staff, and teachers resented social workers (Bartollas, Miller, and Dinitz, 1976:219–221). Newly hired professionals often added their own ideas to existing programs without any awareness of the problems they created (Weber, 1957). Thus, even the most treatment-oriented institutions apparently were incapable of achieving desirable ends. Although they suppressed offenders, they could do little to rehabilitate them (Goffman, 1961).

RECIDIVISM RATES Such a view appealed to both common sense and scientific theory. For almost 200 years, doubters had argued that if held in captivity, people would not change for the better. Yet some scholars cautioned against excessive overgeneralization. Several studies suggested that group and individual counseling, milieu therapy, and other techniques of this type, particularly in smaller institutions, would improve institutional adjustment. The social distance between inmates and staff would be decreased, and inmates would become more manageable and cooperative (Feld, 1981; Lipton, Martinson, and Wilks, 1975:311–330; Street, 1965).

If that were the case, inmates would be more likely to stay out of trouble after release from institutions. Most studies revealed, however, that even in the more enlightened institutions, recidivism rates were not markedly reduced, if at all (Kassebaum, Ward, and Wilner, 1971:Chaps. 8–10; Lipton, Martinson, and Wilks, 1975:315–316, 528–529).

Effects of Community Treatment

Such findings helped to reinforce the arguments of early child savers that the principles of rehabilitation, if they were to work, must be applied in the community. Those arguments had been so persuasive that by the mid-1960s, almost five times more delinquents were on probation than were institutionalized (President's Commission on Law Enforcement and Administration of Justice, 1967a:1). Spurred by psychodynamic theory, the Child Guidance Movement of the 1940s and 1950s also led to the development of a number of programs for predelinquents—unruly children who had not yet committed delinquent acts, at least serious offenses. Finally, in the 1960s, some intensive community programs were created for serious delinquents who already had failed on probation—delinquents for whom incarceration or-

dinarily would have been the only choice. How successful, then, were those programs?

PROBATION We have seen already that probation often consisted of little more than occasional contact with an overworked probation officer. Some evidence, however, indicated that it was a useful tool. In a summary analysis of fifteen probation studies, Ralph England (1957:674) reported success rates of between 60 and 90 percent. Another summary by Grunhut (1948:309–312) put the success rate at about 75 percent. Furthermore, Scarpitti and Stephenson (1968:369) found that probation was more effective for boys who were less delinquent and who came from fairly stable backgrounds than for those who, ordinarily, would have been institutionalized.

Such findings, however, did not prove that probation rehabilitates, because most of the studies had not been designed to answer a crucial question: If offenders placed on probation had been released without any supervision whatsoever, would they have committed less delinquency? One can answer such a question best by comparing randomly assigned experimental and control groups regarding the effects of alternative programs on delinquents. The experimental group is treated—in this case, assigned to probation—and the control group is not subjected to treatment or is treated in some other fashion. Unfortunately, few probation studies followed such a procedure (Gottfredson and Gottfredson, 1988:180, 190–196), and the results were disappointing in those that did (Adams, 1970:724–728). The California Youth Authority, for example, discontinued use of smaller caseloads when it was found that caseloads of only thirty-six delinquents did not reduce recidivism any better than did caseloads of seventy-two delinquents.

Moreover, there was still the question raised earlier: If offenders placed on probation had been released without any supervision, would they have committed any less delinquency? In one of the few studies to address that question, McEachern and Taylor (1967) found that offenders who were convicted and made wards of the court, but who were not supervised by probation officers, had lower recidivism rates than those who were supervised. The same was true of delinquents handled informally and released at intake without actual conviction.

PREVENTION FOR PREDELINQUENTS Perhaps the best-known study of a prevention effort for predelinquents was the Cambridge–Somerville Youth Study conducted between 1937 and 1945 (McCord, 1990; McCord and McCord, 1959; Powers and Witmer, 1951:6, 8). In that study, 650 boys attending schools in Cambridge and Somerville, Massachusetts, were identified by teacher interviews, psychiatric evaluations, and psychological tests as troublemakers who were likely to become delinquents (Powers and Witmer, 1951:6–7, 45, 53–60). Using a complicated selection procedure, 325 of the boys were placed in an experimental group to receive services, and the remaining 325 were placed in a control group for which nothing was done (pp. vii, 321, Chap. 6).

The experimentals received all of the services that probationers ideally were supposed to receive: individual counseling, family guidance, tutoring, medical treatment, recreational services, and even occasional financial assistance (Powers and Witmer, 1951:100–101, 114–118). This rich array of services, which would make the ordinary juvenile court judge green with envy, was provided to each boy for an average of about five years (p. 322). Contrary to expectations, repeated follow-up studies revealed that, if anything, the experimental program had a negative effect (p. 337). Thirty years after treatment, experimentals had higher rates of crime, disease, and death, and less occupational success and satisfaction (McCord, 1978, 1990:3–5; also see McCord and McCord, 1959).

COMMUNITY ALTERNATIVES TO INSTITUTIONALIZATION Although such results might have been expected to discourage development of still more community alternatives, that was not the case. The desire to get away from institutionalization persisted. Thus, the late 1950s and early 1960s were marked by the development of community programs for serious convicted delinquents—young people who, for the most part, had already failed in probation and seemed headed for institutions.

One of the first of those programs was Highfields (McCorkle, Elias, and Bixby, 1958). Although not a community program in the strict sense, neither was Highfields a traditional institutional program. A group of no more than twenty boys, ages 16 and 17, was sent to live with a small staff but without guards or detailed routines (pp. iii–iv, 42). During the day, the boys worked at a nearby mental hospital, usually as farm laborers (p. 25). In the evening, the total population was broken into two equal groups for meetings (pp. 22–23). Formal rules were scarce (pp. iv, 60–67). Instead, control was exercised informally through the development of a group culture that presumably decreased distance between staff and offenders, and sponsored the latter in more active, reformation roles (Chap. 5). The idea was that people could be helped best when they helped others.

To test the effectiveness of Highfields, its graduates were compared to a group of boys who had been committed to the New Jersey State Reformatory at Annandale (Weeks, 1958:9–10). A lower percentage of Highfields than Annandale boys recidivated—37 versus 53 percent (pp. 42–43). However, the results of the comparison were questionable because the boys were not randomly assigned to the two groups. The Annandale boys tended to be a little older and more experienced in delinquency, and they were poorer (pp. 28–40, 174, 176). As a consequence, the most appropriate conclusion is that Highfields had proved to be neither less nor more successful than institutionalization. In terms of recidivism, at least, it would be difficult to argue that one method was superior to the other.

The findings were important, nonetheless, because they seemed to indicate that Highfields was able to do just as well as total confinement, but at less expense to the state and at less personal cost to the delinquents involved. Delinquents stayed at Highfields only three or four months, as contrasted with many more months at Annandale. Still, they did just as well after release.

Whatever the object of study—the variation of treatment within institutions, probation, parole, preventive or intensive community programming—it had been difficult to prove that one rehabilitative approach was consistently more effective than any other (Robison and Smith, 1971). Moreover, the findings were ironic because they were produced by positivist criminology—the same school of thought that had hoped, like the Cincinnati Prison Congress, to use science to save delinquents and eradicate law-violating behavior.

REVIEWING THE EVIDENCE

In 1966, the New York State Governor's Special Committee on Criminal Offenders financed a survey of correctional research to make sure that some promising leads had not been overlooked (Martinson, 1974:23). Clearly, the commission hoped that, if isolated, some correctional programs might be redesigned and revitalized. Consequently, three criminologists—Douglas Lipton, Robert Martinson, and Judith Wilks—were commissioned to find them.

In pursuit of that task, they gathered and reviewed the results of 231 evaluation studies (Martinson, 1974:24). By 1970, they had completed their work and produced a report that shocked the Governor's Special Committee (p. 23). Rather than identifying successful programs, the report seemed to suggest that there were none. But because the Governor's Special Committee was either disbelieving, defensive, or both, it suppressed the report (p. 23). Indeed, the report might still be unavailable for public scrutiny if not for the fact that it was subpoenaed as evidence for a case before the Bronx Supreme Court. It was thus freed from the controls of the state and published in a large volume entitled *The Effectiveness of Correctional Treatment: A Survey of Treatment Evaluation Studies* (Lipton, Martinson, and Wilks, 1975).

Rehabilitation Is Dead

When this volume was interpreted publicly by Martinson (1974), it was treated as though it were a coroner's report announcing the death of rehabilitation. "With few and isolated exceptions," Martinson (1974:25) concluded, "the rehabilitative efforts that have been reported so far have had no appreciable effect on recidivism." In other words, *nothing works!*

In another era, when optimism rather than pessimism was the order of the day, that conclusion might have gone unnoticed. But the 1970s was not such an era. Instead, reformers used it as a means for

condemning the juvenile justice system and for suggesting that methods other than rehabilitation had to be found for controlling delinquency.

UTILITARIAN PHILOSOPHY One such group of reformers consisted of utilitarian philosophers. They contended that in attempting to rehabilitate delinquents, the juvenile justice system had been excessively lenient, had denied the rights of victims, had eroded discipline and respect for authority, and now threatened to destroy a tenuous social order (Miller, 1974:454–455). Thus, the following reforms were advocated: (1) Abolish the juvenile court (McCarthy, 1977), (2) lower the age of accountability for crime (van den Haag, 1975:173–175), and (3) punish and incapacitate offenders (van den Haag, 1975:Chap. 21; Wilson, 1975:Chap. 8, 1983:Chaps. 7–8).

Because the rehabilitative philosophy had failed, it was futile to attempt to control crime by trying to undo the effects of its causes (van den Haag, 1975: 77–78; Wilson, 1975:Chap. 3). Rather, its purposes should be to ensure that legal punishment is certain and severe and that chronic offenders are incapacitated for long periods of time, perhaps even until age 40, when the "impulse" to commit crimes has diminished considerably (van den Haag, 1975:61, 70, 195, 214–215, 241, Chap. 21; Wilson, 1975:Chap. 8).

LIBERAL PHILOSOPHY Liberal reformers, by contrast, argued that increasing delinquency rates were due to the failures of the juvenile justice system itself. It had overcriminalized the young, labeled and stigmatized them unnecessarily, denied them their civil rights, and not only had failed to rehabilitate them but also had been excessively punitive (National Advisory Commission on Criminal Justice Standards and Goals, 1973a:34–36; 1973b:Chap. 14; President's Commission on Law Enforcement and Administration of Justice, 1967b:7–40). The only defensible philosophy for the juvenile justice system, therefore, was one of "judicious nonintervention" (Lemert, 1967:96): *Leave kids alone wherever possible* (Schur, 1973:155).

JUST DESERTS PHILOSOPHY Finally, there were the just deserts philosophers (Fogel, 1975; Fox, 1974; Gaylin and Rothman, 1976; von Hirsch, 1976). Their philosophy was that because nothing works, the only defensible policy is one that ensures that justice is administered uniformly and that offenders are punished according to the gravity of their offenses. They suggested that our treatment-oriented system of justice has "produced far too many instances of recorded abuse to think fairly that it is much more than simply a vehicle for abuse" (Fox, 1974:3).

Unlike utilitarian philosophers, however, just deserts proponents argued that we should not believe that legal punishments will deter persons from committing crimes. Instead, the state should reduce the length of sentences to the point at which it satisfies our sense of equity, but no more than that: "'warnings' for crimes low on a scale of seriousness, intermittent confinement (weekends or evenings) for more serious offenses, and ... full-time incarceration only for the most serious crimes" (Gaylin and Rothman, 1976:xxxv). In other words, social policy should be concerned "less with the administration of justice and more ... with the *justice of administration*" (Fogel, 1975:xv).

Death Reports Are Premature

The popularity of such conclusions notwithstanding, some scholars felt that the reported death of rehabilitation was premature (a feeling even expressed by Martinson, 1979). In 1977, a special panel of scientists from various disciplines—sociology, psychology, psychiatry, political science, economics, penology, and applied statistics—was convened by the National Academy of Sciences to examine the autopsy report. In light of the widespread belief that correctional treatment was certifiably dead, the conclusions of the panel were striking.

To begin with, the panel observed that although "Lipton, Martinson, and Wilks were reasonably accurate and fair in their appraisal of the rehabilitation literature," they were "overly lenient" in their assessment of the quality of the research on which their conclusion was based (Sechrest, White, and Brown, 1979:5). Hence, the panel did *not* draw the same conclusion as that of the original researchers. Instead, it concluded that research on the effects of treatment programs was so weak that existing studies could not yield reliable knowledge about the effects of rehabilitation (Martin, Sechrest, and Redner, 1981:9).

That did not mean, however, that the panel believed that the patient was alive and well, and that the utility of treatment had been demonstrated. Rather, it reached two general conclusions.

DEATH NEITHER PROVED NOR DISPROVED The panel noted that there may be limited evidence that "some treatments . . . are effective for certain subgroups of offenders" (Sechrest, White, and Brown, 1979:6). Nonetheless, it argued that the best conclusion would be that the utility of treatment methods had been neither proved nor disproved. Furthermore, if blame for the lack of knowledge was to be assigned, the scientific community was responsible for at least some of it:

> In general, techniques have been tested as isolated treatments rather than as complex combinations, which would seem more suited to the task. And even when techniques have been tested in good designs, insufficient attention has been paid to maintaining their integrity, so that often the treatment to be tested was delivered in a substantially weakened form. It is also not clear that all the theoretical power and the individual imagination that could be invoked in the planning of rehabilitative efforts have ever been capitalized on. Thus, the recommendation in this report that has the strongest support is that more and better thinking and research should be invested in efforts to devise programs for offender rehabilitation. (pp. 3–4)

A COMPELLING GOAL The panel was so convinced of the importance of the debate about rehabilitation that it met for an additional two years to "suggest . . . directions for both program development and research" (Martin, Sechrest, and Redner, 1981:viii). An underlying belief was that it would be premature to bury a humane ideal:

> The currently fashionable suggestion that society abandon efforts to find more effective programs to rehabilitate offenders is, we believe, irresponsible and premature. . . . The promise of the "rehabilitative ideal" (Allen, 1959) is so compelling a goal that the strongest possible efforts should

be made to determine whether it can be realized and to seek to realize it. (pp. 17, 22)

Coming from a group of scientists supposedly known for their cold and dispassionate approach to emotional issues, those statements were remarkable. Indeed, the panel rejected

the idea that efforts to facilitate the rehabilitation of criminal offenders . . . should be terminated. . . . This position rests on the assumptions that rehabilitation as a form of behavior change is (1) possible . . . (2) more likely to occur through the adoption of a more systematic approach to the accumulation of knowledge . . . (3) morally and socially desirable; and (4) likely, in the long run, to prove to be the most practical and cost-effective option available to the criminal justice system. (pp. 22–23)

THE CURRENT SITUATION

There have been continued calls during the 1980s and 1990s to rethink the juvenile justice system and to abolish the juvenile court (Ainsworth, 1991; Dawson, 1990; Federle, 1990; Feld, 1990, 1993). Many states have changed their juvenile codes to deemphasize rehabilitation and more strongly emphasize public protection, punishment, justice, deterrence, and accountability (Feld, 1993:245–246; Snyder and Sikmund, 1995:71). The purpose of the 1996 Texas Juvenile Justice Code (Ch. 51.01), for example, was mainly to "provide for the protection of the public and public safety." Consistent with that purpose, the code was first to "promote the concept of punishment for criminal acts" and second to rehabilitate. Although explicitly identifying rehabilitation as a purpose, the code revealed only partial commitment to the rehabilitative philosophy by linking it to accountability: "to provide treatment, training, and rehabilitation that emphasizes the accountability and responsibility of both the parent and the child for the child's conduct." That partial commitment is at odds with judicial interpretations of pre-1960 Texas juvenile justice codes, which stated that the purpose of the juvenile justice system was "not one of punishment, but . . . protection of the child for its own good, . . . not . . . to convict and punish juveniles but to guide and direct them."

Rehabilitation

The debate about rehabilitation also has continued during the 1980s and 1990s (Andrews et al., 1990; Doob and Brodeur, 1989; Gendreau and Ross, 1987; Greenwood and Zimring, 1985; Lab and Whitehead, 1988, 1990; Lipsey, 1992; Palmer, 1983, 1991; Roberts and Camasso, 1991; Shichor, 1992; Whitehead and Lab, 1989); three perspectives dominate. The first is that, whether or not it works, the rehabilitative philosophy should be retained because it is the only guarantee for a humane correctional environment (Cullen and Gilbert, 1982). The second is that "the effectiveness of correctional treatment is dependent upon what is delivered to whom in particular settings" (Andrews et al., 1990:372). Although not all treatment programs work in reducing recidivism, many do. In particular, recidivism is reduced by "treatment that is delivered to high risk cases, that targets criminogenic need, and that is matched with the learning styles of offenders" (Andrews et al., 1990:377). Rehabilitation programs in community settings are more effective in reducing recidivism than those in institutional settings (Andrews et al., 1990:384–386; Lipsey, 1992:122). Moreover, the "more structured and focused treatments (e.g., behavioral, skill-oriented) and multimodal treatments seem to be more effective than the less structured and [less] focused approaches (e.g., counseling)" (Lipsey, 1992:123). The third perspective is contrary to the second. Proponents do not deny that some rehabilitation programs work. They argue, however, that *most* programs do not reduce recidivism and that even the most successful programs produce "mediocre" results at best (Lab and Whitehead, 1990: 408, 414; also see Lab and Whitehead, 1988; Whitehead and Lab, 1989).

The issue is far from resolved. In a recent review of the results of 443 evaluation studies, however, Lipsey (1992:94) reported that in 285 (64 percent), there was a reduction in recidivism. Moreover, the most successful programs showed "effects . . . in the range of 10–20 percentage points reduction in recidivism" (Lipsey, 1992:123). Although such a reduction "may

D.A.R.E.

Drug Abuse Resistance Education (D.A.R.E.), with uniformed police officers teaching antidrug messages in schools, is probably the most popular drug prevention program ever conducted in the United States. "It is administered in about 70 percent of the nation's school districts, reaching 25 million students in 1996, and has been adopted in 44 foreign countries" (Rosenbaum and Hanson, 1998:381). Unfortunately, it appears to be ineffective for most students and actually to increase drug use for some. In a comprehensive study of urban, suburban, and rural students who were surveyed each year from 6th to 12th grades, Rosenbaum and Hanson (1998:401) found that "students who participated in D.A.R.E. were no different from students in the control group [those who did not participate in D.A.R.E.] with regard to their recent and lifetime use of drugs and alcohol." The only exception was suburban students among whom "participation in D.A.R.E. is associated with an increased level of drug use" (Rosenbaum and Hanson, 1998:402). There may be less respect for the police in the suburbs, or suburban students may be less knowledgeable about drugs and more fascinated with drug paraphernalia. Whatever the reason, the overall ineffectiveness of D.A.R.E. is disappointing, and it points to the need to carefully evaluate the results of all efforts to prevent delinquency and rehabilitate delinquents.

not be spectacular, it cannot be said to be . . . negligible (Lipsey, 1992:98).

Prevention

Just as there is recent evidence for the effectiveness of some rehabilitation programs, there is evidence for the effectiveness of some prevention programs for predelinquents (Briscoe, 1997; Sherman et al., 1997, 1998). In a recently completed, comprehensive assessment of prevention programs, Sherman and his colleagues (1998:7) identify several types of programs that work to prevent delinquency. These include (1) home visits to infants ages 0–2 by nurses and other helpers in order to reduce child abuse, (2) preschool and home visits by teachers to children under age 5, (3) family therapy and parent training, (4) antibullying campaigns in schools, and (5) social competency skills curricula in schools, involving stress management, problem solving, and self-control. They also identify several types of programs that don't work. These include (1) Drug Abuse Resistance Education (D.A.R.E.), (2) programs focusing on self-esteem, (3) supervised homework programs in schools, and (4) summer job or subsidized work programs for youths.

SUMMARY AND CONCLUSIONS

Three important issues have been highlighted in this chapter.

The History of Correctional Epochs

Correctional history has been characterized by three revolutionary epochs:

1. *Retribution.* Prior to the 1800s, efforts to control crime were dominated by a philosophy of retribution. Legal punishments were cruel but were justified on the grounds that suffering is fair recompense for criminal acts. Little thought was given to the idea of rehabilitating offenders, young or old.

2. *Restraint.* In the first part of the 1800s, the retributive philosophy gradually was replaced by a philosophy of restraint. Stimulated by the principles of classical criminology, offenders were confined in prisons and reformatories, where

the length of stay was graded according to the seriousness of criminal acts. Reformers anticipated that both inmates and others would thus be deterred from committing crimes.

3. *Rehabilitation.* Throughout the 1800s, people became increasingly sensitive to childhood, not only softening their attitudes toward children but "stripping away the years from adults." Toward the end of the century, therefore, these attitudes were crystalized into a complex philosophy of rehabilitation. By attending to the needs of the individual and implementing scientific programs of diagnosis and treatment, offenders could be rehabilitated and delinquency prevented.

Despite marked differences among these philosophies, each new one did not make a complete break from those preceding it. When prisons and reformatories were built, retributive punishments did not suddenly disappear; they simply changed form. Transportation, burning, branding, and disfigurement were replaced by solitary confinement, silence, the lockstep, and whipping. Although somewhat less severe, those were punishments nevertheless.

Equally obvious was the overlap of restraint and rehabilitation. Rather than suggesting that rehabilitation might be more successful in a different environment, proponents of treatment merely argued that reformatories and training schools should not be eliminated, but made into correctional utopias. It was not until the 1900s that this idea became somewhat diluted.

Nevertheless, elements of all three philosophies remain in our belief system today. And in times of stress, they reappear once again in the juvenile justice system.

From Optimism to Dismay

Each new epoch has begun in a flurry of optimism and ended in a blizzard of criticism and dismay. When retributive punishments became too difficult for humanists to tolerate, the invention of prisons was hailed as a gesture befitting the most noble inclinations of humankind. The same was true of the rehabilitative epoch. Indeed, the idea is still unthinkable that concerted efforts should not be made to reclaim children from evil—that somewhere, under some set of circumstances, dedicated correctional workers can change young offenders and return them to society as healthy and productive citizens.

Yet, in recent years, it has become increasingly unfashionable to think in such hopeful terms. Indeed, research on the effectiveness of correctional treatment has been interpreted as suggesting that the concept of rehabilitation is dead and should be buried. Consequently, recommendations for reform have ranged from the suggestion that children should be left entirely alone to the claim that they be confined in institutions and severely punished for their acts.

What these trends suggest, of course, is that history is repeating itself. Once again, we are in one of those transitional periods in which a philosophy that captured the imagination of the nation has ended in despair. But is this despair warranted? Is it based on fact or popular belief?

Fact Versus Ideology

Undeniably, an impossible burden has been placed on the juvenile justice system. At times, it has been arbitrary and unfair; it cannot, by itself, remedy the effects of poverty and discrimination; and its resources often have been inadequate. But those limitations do not mean that under controlled conditions, delinquents cannot be rehabilitated. Such a conclusion will not stem the tide of events. A new revolution is under way that may change forever the assumptions about and organization of the original system of juvenile justice.

DISCUSSION QUESTIONS

1. What was it about the early juvenile court that made it receptive to the principles of rehabilitation?
2. Which rehabilitative tools, introduced in the 1800s, are still found today in the juvenile justice system?
3. What would you do to make rehabilitation programs more effective in reducing the likelihood of recidivism?

4. What accounts for the popularity of D.A.R.E. programs in the United States and other countries? What is so appealing about this approach to drug prevention?

5. Do you believe the concept of rehabilitation should be buried or resurrected? What should be done with delinquents in the future?

REFERENCES

Adams, Stuart. 1970. "Correctional and Caseload Research." Pp. 721–732 in Norman Johnston, Leonard Savitz, and Marvin E. Wolfgang, eds., *The Sociology of Punishment and Correction,* 2nd ed. New York: Wiley.

Allen, Francis A. 1959. "Criminal Justice, Legal Values and the Rehabilitative Ideal." *Journal of Criminal Law, Criminology and Police Science* 50 (September–October):226–232.

Andrews, D. A., et al. 1990. "Does Correctional Treatment Work?: A Clinically Relevant and Psychologically Informed Meta-Analysis." *Criminology* 28 (August):369–404.

Barker, Gordon H., and W. Thomas Adams. 1959. "The Social Structure of a Correctional Institution." *Journal of Criminal Law, Criminology and Police Science* 49 (January–February):417–422.

Barnes, Harry Elmer. 1972. *The Story of Punishment,* 2nd ed. Montclair, N.J.: Patterson Smith.

Barrows, Isabel C. 1910. "The Reformatory Treatment of Women in the United States." Pp. 129–167 in Charles R. Henderson, ed., *Penal and Reformatory Institutions.* New York: Charities Publication Committee.

Bartollas, Clemens, Stuart J. Miller, and Simon Dinitz. 1976. *Juvenile Victimization: The Institutional Paradox.* New York: Wiley.

Bremner, Robert H., ed. 1970. *Children and Youth in America: A Documentary History.* 3 vols. Cambridge, Mass.: Harvard University Press.

Brockway, Z. R. 1910. "The American Reformatory Prison System." Pp. 88–107 in Charles R. Henderson, ed., *Prison Reform and Criminal Law.* New York: Charities Publication Committee.

1912. *Fifty Years of Prison Service: An Autobiography.* New York: Charities Publication Committee.

Carlson, Norman. 1975. "Giving Up the Medical Model?" *Behavior Today* 6 (November):1.

Carter, Robert M., and Leslie T. Wilkins, eds. 1970. *Probation and Parole: Selected Readings.* New York: Wiley.

Clemmer, Donald. 1940. *The Prison Community.* Boston: Christopher.

Cressey, Donald R., ed. 1961. *The Prison: Studies in Institutional Organization and Change.* New York: Holt, Rinehart & Winston.

Cullen, Francis T., and Karen E. Gilbert. 1982. *Reaffirming Rehabilitation.* Cincinnati: Anderson.

Diana, Lewis. 1960. "What Is Probation?" *Journal of Criminal Law, Criminology and Police Science* 51 (July–August):189–208.

Doob, Anthony N., and Jean-Paul Brodeur. 1989. "Rehabilitating the Debate on Rehabilitation." *Canadian Journal of Criminology* 31 (April): 179–192.

England, Ralph W., Jr. 1957. "What Is Responsible for Satisfactory Probation and Post-Probation Outcome?" *Journal of Criminal Law, Criminology and Police Science* 47 (March–April):667–676.

Feld, Barry C. 1981. "A Comparative Analysis of Organizational Structure and Inmate Subcultures in Institutions for Juvenile Offenders." *Crime and Delinquency* 27 (July):336–363.

Fogel, David. 1975. *We Are the Living Proof: The Justice Model for Corrections.* Cincinnati: Anderson.

Fox, Sanford J. 1974. "The Reform of Juvenile Justice: The Child's Right to Punishment." *Juvenile Justice* 25 (August):2–9.

Gaylin, Willard, and David J. Rothman. 1976. "Introduction." Pp. xxi–xli in Andrew von Hirsch, *Doing Justice: The Choice of Punishments.* New York: Hill & Wang.

Gendreau, Paul, and Robert R. Ross. 1987. "Revivification of Rehabilitation: Evidence from the 1980s." *Justice Quarterly* 4 (September):349–407.

Giallombardo, Rose. 1974. *The Social World of Imprisoned Girls: A Comparative Study of Institutions for Juvenile Delinquents.* New York: Wiley.

Glaser, Daniel. 1964. *The Effectiveness of a Prison and Parole System.* Indianapolis, Ind.: Bobbs-Merrill.

Goffman, Erving. 1961. *Asylums: Essays on the Social Situation of Mental Patients and Other Inmates.* Garden City, N.Y.: Anchor Books.

Gottfredson, Michael R., and Don M. Gottfredson. 1988. *Decision Making in Criminal Justice: Toward the Rational Exercise of Discretion,* 2nd ed. New York: Plenum.

Greenwood, Peter W., and Franklin E. Zimring. 1985. *One More Chance: The Pursuit of Promising Intervention Strategies for Chronic Delinquent Offenders.* Santa Monica, Calif.: Rand.

Grunhut, Max. 1948. *Penal Reform: A Comparative Study.* Oxford: Clarendon Press.

Hart, Hastings. 1910. *Preventive Treatment of Neglected Children.* New York: Russell Sage.

Hawkins, Richard, and Geoffrey P. Alpert. 1989. *American Prison Systems: Punishment and Justice.* Englewood Cliffs, N.J.: Prentice-Hall.

Henderson, Charles R., ed. 1910. *Prison Reform and Criminal Law.* New York: Charities Publication Committee.

Kassebaum, Gene, David Ward, and Daniel Wilner. 1971. *Prison Treatment and Parole Survival: An Empirical Assessment.* New York: Wiley.

Lab, Steven P., and John T. Whitehead. 1988. "An Analysis of Juvenile Correctional Treatment." *Crime and Delinquency* 34 (January):60–83.
1990. "From 'Nothing Works' to 'The Appropriate Works': The Latest Stop on the Search for the Secular Grail." *Criminology* 28 (August):405–417.

Lemert, Edwin M. 1967. "The Juvenile Court—Quest and Realities." Pp. 91–106 in President's Commission on Law Enforcement and Administration of Justice, *Task Force Report: Juvenile Delinquency and Youth Crime.* Washington, D.C.: U.S. Government Printing Office.

Lipton, Douglas, Robert Martinson, and Judith Wilks. 1975. *The Effectiveness of Correctional Treatment: A Survey of Treatment Evaluation Studies.* New York: Praeger.

Manocchio, Anthony J., and Jimmy Dunn. 1970. *The Time Game: Two Views of a Prison.* Beverly Hills, Calif.: Sage.

Martin, Susan E., Lee B. Sechrest, and Robin Redner, eds. 1981. *New Directions in the Rehabilitation of Criminal Offenders.* Washington, D.C.: National Academy of Sciences.

Martinson, Robert. 1974. "What Works? Questions and Answers About Prison Reform." *The Public Interest* 35 (Spring):22–54.
1979. "New Findings, New Views: A Note of Caution Regarding Sentencing Reform." *Hofstra Law Review* 7 (Winter):243–258.

McCarthy, Francis B. 1977. "Should Juvenile Delinquency Be Abolished?" *Crime and Delinquency* 23 (April):196–203.

McCord, Joan. 1978. "A Thirty-Year Follow-up of Treatment Effects." *American Psychologist* 33 (March):284–289.
1990. "Crime in Moral and Social Contexts—The American Society of Criminology, 1989 Presidential Address." *Criminology* 28 (February):1–26.

McCord, Joan, and William McCord. 1959. "A Follow-up Report on the Cambridge–Somerville Youth Study." *Annals of the American Academy of Political and Social Science* 322 (March):89–96.

McCorkle, Lloyd W., Albert Elias, and F. Lovell Bixby. 1958. *The Highfields Story: An Experimental Treatment Project for Youthful Offenders.* New York: Henry Holt.

McEachern, Alexander W., and Edward M. Taylor. 1967. *The Effects of Probation.* Probation Project Report No. 2, Youth Studies Center. Los Angeles: University of Southern California.

McKelvey, Blake. 1936. *American Prisons: A Study in American Social History Prior to 1915.* Chicago: University of Chicago Press.

Mennel, Robert M. 1973. *Thorns and Thistles: Juvenile Delinquents in the United States, 1825–1940.* Hanover, N.H.: University Press of New England.

Miller, Walter B. 1974. "Ideology and Criminal Justice Policy: Some Current Issues." Pp. 453–473 in

Sheldon L. Messinger et al., eds. *The Aldine Crime and Justice Annual, 1973.* Chicago: Aldine.

National Advisory Commission on Criminal Justice Standards and Goals. 1973a. *A National Strategy to Reduce Crime.* Washington, D.C.: U.S. Government Printing Office.
1973b. *Courts.* Washington, D.C.: U.S. Government Printing Office.

National Commission on Law Observance and Enforcement. 1931. *Report on the Child Offender in the Federal System of Justice,* No. 6. Washington, D.C.: U.S. Government Printing Office.

Ohlin, Lloyd E., and William C. Lawrence. 1959. "Social Interaction among Clients as a Treatment Problem." *Social Work* 4 (April):3–13.

Palmer, Ted (Theodore) B. 1983. "The 'Effectiveness' Issue Today: An Overview." *Federal Probation* 47 (June):3–10.

Pettigrove, Frederick G. 1910. "The State Prisons of the United States Under Separate and Congregate Systems." Pp. 27–67 in Charles R. Henderson, ed., *Penal and Reformatory Institutions.* New York: Charities Publication Committee.

Platt, Anthony. 1969. *The Child Savers.* Chicago: University of Chicago Press.
1974. "The Triumph of Benevolence: The Origins of the Juvenile Justice System in the United States." Pp. 356–389 in Richard Quinney, ed., *Criminal Justice in America.* Boston: Little, Brown.

Polsky, Howard W. 1962. *Cottage Six: The Social System of Delinquent Boys in Residential Treatment.* New York: Wiley.

Powers, Edwin, and Helen Witmer. 1951. *An Experiment in the Prevention of Delinquency: The Cambridge–Somerville Youth Study.* New York: Columbia University Press.

President's Commission on Law Enforcement and Administration of Justice. 1967a. *Task Force Report: Corrections.* Washington, D.C.: U.S. Government Printing Office.
1967b. *Task Force Report: Juvenile Delinquency and Youth Crime.* Washington, D.C.: U.S. Government Printing Office.
1967c. *Task Force Report: The Challenge of Crime in a Free Society.* Washington, D.C.: U.S. Government Printing Office.

Propper, Alice M. 1981. *Prison Homosexuality: Myth and Reality.* Lexington, Mass.: Heath.

Robison, James, and Gerald Smith. 1971. "The Effectiveness of Correctional Programs." *Crime and Delinquency* 17 (January):67–80.

Rothman, David J. 1971. *The Discovery of the Asylum.* Boston: Little, Brown.
1979. "The Progressive Legacy: Development of American Attitudes Toward Juvenile Delinquency." Pp. 34–68 in LaMar T. Empey, ed., *Juvenile Justice: The Progressive Legacy and Current Reforms.* Charlottesville: University Press of Virginia.

Sanders, Wiley B., ed. 1970. *Juvenile Offenders for a Thousand Years: Selected Readings from Anglo-Saxon Times to 1900.* Chapel Hill: University of North Carolina Press.

Sarri, Rosemary, Robert D. Vinter, and Rhea Kish. 1974. "Juvenile Justice: Failure of a Nation." Paper presented at the annual meetings of the Directors of Criminal Justice Research Centers. Unpublished. Cambridge, Mass.: Harvard Law School.

Scarpitti, Frank R., and Richard M. Stephenson. 1968. "A Study of Probation Effectiveness." *Journal of Criminal Law, Criminology and Police Science* 59 (September):361–369.

Schrag, Clarence. 1954. "Leadership Among Prison Inmates." *American Sociological Review* 19 (February):37–42.
1961. "Some Foundations for a Theory of Correction." Pp. 309–357 in Donald R. Cressey, ed., *The Prison: Studies in Institutional Organization and Change.* New York: Holt, Rinehart & Winston.

Schur, Edwin M. 1973. *Radical Nonintervention: Rethinking the Delinquency Problem.* Englewood Cliffs, N.J.: Prentice-Hall.

Scott, Joseph F. 1910. "American Reformatories for Male Adults." Pp. 89–120 in Charles R. Henderson, ed., *Penal and Reformatory Institutions.* New York: Charities Publication Committee.

Sechrest, Lee, Susan O. White, and Elizabeth D. Brown, eds. 1979. *The Rehabilitation of Criminal Offenders: Problems and Prospects.* Washington, D.C.: National Academy of Sciences.

Sellin, Thorsten. 1964. "Introduction: Tocqueville and Beaumont and Prison Reform in France." Pp. xv–xl in Gustave de Beaumont and Alexis de Tocqueville, *On the Penitentiary System in the United States and Its Application in France.* Carbondale: Southern Illinois University Press.

Snyder, Howard N., and Melissa Sickmund. 1995. *Juvenile Offenders and Victims: A National Report.* Washington, D.C.: Office of Juvenile Justice and Delinquency Prevention.

Street, David. 1965. "The Inmate Group in Custodial and Treatment Settings." *American Sociological Review* 30 (February):40–55.

Sykes, Gresham M. 1965. *The Society of Captives: A Study of a Maximum Security Prison.* New York: Atheneum Press.

Sykes, Gresham M., and Sheldon L. Messinger. 1960. "The Inmate Social System." Pp. 5–19 in *Theoretical Studies in Social Organization of the Prison.* Social Science Research Council, Pamphlet No. 15.

Tappan, Paul W. 1960. *Crime, Justice and Correction.* New York: McGraw-Hill.

Tonry, Michael H. 1976. "Juvenile Justice and the National Crime Commissions." Pp. 281–298 in Margaret K. Rosenheim, ed., *Pursuing Justice for the Child.* Chicago: University of Chicago Press.

United Nations. 1951. *Probation and Related Measures.* New York: Department of Social Affairs.

van den Haag, Ernest. 1975. *Punishing Criminals: Concerning a Very Old and Painful Question.* New York: Basic Books.

von Hirsch, Andrew. 1976. *Doing Justice: The Choice of Punishments.* New York: Hill & Wang.

Weber, George H. 1957. "Conflicts Between Professional and Non-Professional Personnel in Institutional Delinquency Treatment." *Journal of Criminal Law, Criminology and Police Science* 48 (May–June):26–43.

Weeks, H. Ashley. 1958. *Youthful Offenders at Highfields: An Evaluation of the Short-Term Treatment of Delinquent Boys.* Ann Arbor: University of Michigan Press.

Whitehead, John T., and Steven P. Lab. 1989. "A Meta-Analysis of Juvenile Correctional Treatment." *Journal of Research in Crime and Delinquency* 26 (August):276–295.

White House Conference on Child Health and Protection. 1932. *The Delinquent Child.* New York: Century.

Wilson, James Q. 1975. *Thinking About Crime.* New York: Vintage Books.
1983. *Thinking About Crime,* rev. ed. New York: Vintage Books.

Wines, Federick H. 1910. "Historical Introduction." Pp. 3–38 in Charles R. Henderson, ed., *Prison Reform and Criminal Law.* New York: Charities Publication Committee.

AN INCREASING NUMBER OF BIRTHS TO YOUNG UNMARRIED MOTHERS CORRESPONDS TO CHANGES IN AMERICAN CONCEPTS OF CHILDHOOD AND JUVENILE JUSTICE.

CHAPTER NINETEEN

CONCLUSIONS: CHILDHOOD AND DELINQUENCY

A major premise of this book has been that delinquency and juvenile justice are social constructions that arise out of particular cultural and historical contexts. With that idea in mind, let us review four main elements of our discussion: (1) the changing concept of childhood, (2) the extent and nature of delinquent behavior, (3) the current state of delinquency theory and its relation to juvenile justice, and (4) the policy dilemmas associated with current reforms. By reviewing each of these, our conclusions about current trends may be better informed.

OUR CHANGING CONCEPT OF CHILDHOOD

Our review of childhood and delinquency revealed that in premodern times, children were treated with indifference and often were exploited. With the discovery of childhood, however, Western civilization became increasingly preoccupied with children. During the past century, in particular, major bodies of knowledge and social institutions have been modified and new ones erected, all in the belief that children are qualitatively different from adults and must be carefully safeguarded. Children have therefore become both the most indulged and the most constrained segment of our society (Coleman, 1974:29). The invention of delinquency, the creation of the juvenile court, the drafting of child labor laws, legal requirements regulating the age for leaving school, pediatricians, child psychiatrists, and elementary and secondary school teachers—all reflect our modern construction of childhood. Let us consider some of the ways in which that construction has changed in recent history.

Children's Rights

At the cutting edge of this change is a small group of moralist reformers. Two of the most prominent, Richard Farson (1974) and John Holt (1974), would do away with childhood as we know it. "We are on the threshold of a new consciousness of children's rights," argued Farson (1975), "a dramatically new concept of childhood itself. The fundamental change will be a recognition of the child's right to live with the same guarantee of freedom that adults enjoy, the basic right being that of self-determination." To be liberated, children should be empowered against their parents and other adult oppressors. The only way to protect them is to grant them the same rights as adults, so anything that is legally permissible for grown-ups should be permissible for children.

As one might guess, Farson's argument was greeted with disbelief, and even derision. For example, Franklin Zimring, a legal scholar, commented that "it would be remarkable indeed if the same public policy was appropriate for 6-year-olds and 16-year-olds" (1982:23). It would also be "foolhardy," "preposterous," "simple-minded," and "utopian" (pp. 23–27). It is hard to disagree with Zimring. Yet, many changes during the past several decades suggest that, more than ever, children are treated similarly to adults and often engage in the same behaviors.

POLITICAL SUFFRAGE Until 1920, adult women did not enjoy the right to vote, to say nothing of children.

But in 1944, Georgia lowered the voting age to 18. In 1955, President Eisenhower urged Congress and the states to pass a constitutional amendment establishing 18 as the voting age for the entire country. In 1960, the White House Conference on Children and Youth urged greater participation of young people in political affairs. Finally, in 1971, the Twenty-Sixth Amendment to the Constitution was ratified by the states, granting full suffrage to young people ages 18 and older (Coleman, 1974:42).

FREE SPEECH IN SCHOOL Children traditionally have been denied the right to free speech and expression in school because of their subordinate status and the belief that parents and school officials know what is best for them. During the 1960s and early 1970s, however, a variety of appellate court decisions took a different position (Oberman, 1984:528–529). In *Tinker* v. *Des Moines* (1969), involving students who were protesting the Vietnam War by wearing black armbands in school, the Supreme Court held that children were "persons" under the Constitution, not mere chattel. Thus, they should not be constrained from expressing their opinions, except when it might severely disrupt class work or interfere with the rights of others.[1]

THE RIGHT TO WORK Child labor legislation was originally written to protect children from exploitation in the sweatshops, mines, and factories of the 19th century. During the 20th century, even more restrictive legislation has confined adolescents to low-paying, part-time jobs without any career potential. In 1970, however, delegates to the White House Conference on Children asserted that child labor laws have been too constraining and should be discarded (Coleman, 1974:43). Other opponents of child labor legislation have voiced similar senti-

---

[1]The First Amendment rights of students in public schools, however, are not the same as those for adults in other settings. In *School District* v. *Kuhlmeier* (1988), the Supreme Court distinguished between "educators' ability to silence a student's personal expression that happens to occur on the school premises" (the issue covered in the *Tinker* case) and "educators' authority over school-sponsored . . . activities that students, parents, and members of the public might reasonably perceive to bear the imprimatur of the school." Arguing that the publication of student newspapers involves the latter issue, the Supreme Court held that school officials could exercise "editorial control over . . . content . . . so long as their actions are reasonably related to legitimate pedagogical concerns."

ments, suggesting that "protection from responsibility (in the guise of exclusion from the world of work and too-long exposure to the artificial atmosphere of the classroom) is a deprivation of their [children's] rights" (Coleman, 1974:43; also see Coleman and Husen, 1985:9).

SEXUAL FREEDOM Well into this century, children were expected to remain chaste and were warned about the sinful character of sexual license and the dangers of "masturbation insanity" (Skolnick, 1973: 175). "The sexual secretions, it was taught, must be conserved, lest character and intellect be weakened or destroyed" (Hale, 1971: 465). Today, by contrast, young people are besieged by the media with images and stories about the joys of sex and the rights of all people—young or old—to enjoy it with relatively few restraints. Perhaps as a result of that exposure, adolescents are becoming "sexually active in greater numbers and at younger ages" (Dornbusch, 1989: 251). Billy, Rodgers, and Udry (1984:660–661) reported the following percentages of 12- to 17-year-olds who had had sexual intercourse: black males, 85.4 percent; black females, 43.8 percent; white males, 34.9 percent; and white females, 12.5 percent.

Increased sexual activity among today's youths may be due to the earlier age at which they reach physical maturity (Dornbusch, 1989:237). For example, in 1900, boys did not reach their full growth until about age 23; now they are fully mature at 17 and are capable of reproducing far earlier than that (Gillis, 1974:188). The same is true of girls. Formerly, they did not begin to menstruate until their late teens; now they do so at a much younger age (p. 7). Hence, greater sexual freedoms are reinforced by changing biological drives.

Finally, a series of controversial Supreme Court decisions in the 1970s and early 1980s established several basic principles about a girl's right to have an abortion. In a 1976 decision, *Planned Parenthood of Central Missouri* v. *Danforth,* the Supreme Court held that a state could not give a third party—either a spouse or parents—absolute veto authority over the decision of a girl and her physician to terminate a pregnancy.

A few years later, in *Bellotti* v. *Baird* (1979), the Supreme Court considered a Massachusetts statute that required an unmarried minor to secure the con-

sent of both parents for an abortion. If her parents refused, she could petition a judge to override their decision, but the parents were to be informed of the petition and permitted to present their side of the dispute. Four justices argued that the statute was unconstitutional because, contrary to the ruling in the earlier *Planned Parenthood* case, "the minor's decision to secure an abortion is subject to an absolute third-party veto." Four other justices concluded, in the more influential plurality opinion, that the statute was unconstitutional because it did not provide for an alternative judicial proceeding whereby a minor could show either "(1) that she is mature enough and well enough informed to make her abortion decision, in consultation with her physician, independently of her parents' wishes; or (2) that even if she is not able to make this decision independently, the desired abortion would be in her best interests." This alternative judicial proceeding should be confidential; that is, parents need not be informed.[2]

In *H. L.* v. *Matheson* (1981), the Supreme Court upheld the constitutionality of a Utah statute requiring a physician to notify the parents of an "immature, dependent minor" before an abortion is performed. Parents could not veto their "immature" daughter's decision, but they could counsel her and supply information that might be helpful to the physician performing the abortion. Although it is obvious from this and the earlier cases that the constitutional rights of children are restricted with regard to abortion, the fact that a girl can choose to terminate a pregnancy against the wishes of her parents would have been unthinkable just a generation ago.[3]

FREEDOM WITHOUT RESPONSIBILITY The protected and affluent status of middle- and upper-class youths has afforded them freedoms that were unavailable to the vast majority of adults until very recently:

> Grand tours of foreign countries were once the exclusive prerogative of sons of noblemen; now a broad segment of middle class youth enjoys foreign travel along with the ability to gratify its

---

[2]For an analysis of the *Bellotti* case and its implications, see Mnookin (1985: Chaps. 9–12).
[3]For a full discussion of the changing legal rights of children in the United States, see Stafford (1995).

tastes in clothes, music, and a multitude of forms of entertainment. . . . Young people today are far more cosmopolitan in outlook than their predecessors. (Coleman, 1974:128)

Also, freedoms previously associated with college-age youths—such as unchaperoned vacations with friends—have been rapidly appropriated by adolescents in high school who take trips to California or Florida during spring break. Furthermore, because of the anonymity of urban life, young people are subject to less supervision from adults. It is impossible to quarantine them from *evil* when both biological and social conditions render older methods of control obsolete.

Children's Liberation and Population Structure

Our concept of childhood likely has been affected by profound demographic changes occurring in modern society. In the late 17th century, life expectancy at birth was 32 years in England and 27.5 years in Germany (Gillis, 1974:10). This meant that the ratio of young to old people was extremely high:

> It has been estimated that, in the English village of Stoke-on-Trent in 1701, 49% of the population were under 20 years of age. In Sweden in 1750 the ratio of those persons aged 15–29 years to every 100 persons aged 30 years and over was 63%. In France in 1776 the ratio was 65%; and as late as 1840 it was approximately 77% in England. (Gillis, 1974:11)

Davis (1979:125) reported that young people ages 15–19 made up 10.5 percent of the American population in 1890. However, they made up only 9.3 percent of the population in 1980 and only 7.0 percent in 1996 (Bureau of the Census, 1997: Table 14).

The reason for these changes is twofold: (1) a decrease in the fertility rate and (2) an increase in life expectancy. In 1960, the fertility rate was 118.0 births per 1,000 women ages 15–44 (National Center for Health Statistics, 1989:Table 1-1), but by 1996, it had decreased to 66.7 (Bureau of the Census, 1997: Table 90). Meanwhile, average life expectancy at birth has increased to about 72 years for men and 78

years for women (National Center for Health Statistics, 1990:Table 6-3).

The obvious consequence of both of these trends is a striking change in the age structure of society. Whereas society used to be extremely bottom heavy with young people, it is now growing heavier at the top with older people. For example, between 1950 and 1988, the number of young Americans, ages 10–24, increased by 62 percent. By contrast, the number of older people, ages 65 and over, increased by 147 percent. Even more striking has been the increase in the number of people ages 85 and over—a 400 percent increase, from 578,000 in 1950 to 2.9 million in 1988 (Bureau of the Census, 1965:11; 1990:52). What, then, are some of the implications of these remarkable trends?

THE RIGHTS OF THE ELDERLY One obvious implication has to do with the character of a society with an increasingly older population. Current trends may cause a decline in our protective stance toward the young and a focus instead on older populations (Davis and van den Oever, 1981:4).

> Right now about one in eight Americans is sixty-five or older. That will start changing fast, as the Baby Boom generation marches in unprecedented numbers across the line between work and retirement. According to projections by the Census Bureau, by late in the 2020s one in five Americans will be sixty-five or older. As the proportion of dependent elderly people in the adult population rises, the number of workers supporting [covering health and pension costs for] each of them must fall. And that is exactly what is going to happen. The number of working-age people on hand to support each elderly person will drop by almost half, from almost five in 1990 to about two and a half by 2030 or so. (Rauch, 1989:57)

As a consequence, children may enjoy the right to vote at younger ages, work, and have sex, but they may also be saddled with a great many responsibilities. Rather than being the major recipients of society's largesse, they may have to be the providers of it.

In the short run, the changes will be less dramatic but nonetheless serious. For children to be liberated, they must have jobs. Yet, because of the increasing number of older people, youths are in direct competition with them for employment. "The country is already moving to raise the retirement age" (Rauch, 1989:57). But while this will block the employment or occupational advancement of some teenagers, elderly people are not the only source of competition. Adult women have become an even more potent source.

THE RIGHTS OF WOMEN Whereas 32 percent of men ages 65 and over were in the labor force in 1960 (Bureau of the Census, 1975:Table 559), this figure had decreased to 17 percent by 1996 (Bureau of the Census, 1997:Table 620). This decrease was not accompanied by a large increase in the labor force participation of youths (Bureau of Labor Statistics, 1988:135). Instead, the most sizable increase was among adult women (p. 140). The labor force participation rate for women ages 25–54 increased from about 45 percent in 1960 to about 90 percent in 1996 (Bureau of the Census, 1975:Table 559; 1997:Table 620).

Increasing employment of adult women, like the potential increase of older persons, is obviously a serious obstacle to the fulfillment of the right to work for children. In 1933, when unemployment was high, a spokesperson for the National Child Labor Committee declared that the employment of children had become an economic menace: "Children should be in school and adults should have whatever worthwhile jobs there are" (Coleman, 1974:35). Child advocates notwithstanding, the same sentiment tends to prevail today. In a highly competitive job market, the preference is for supplying adults, not children, with jobs.

As a result, about 35 percent of the nation's unemployed in 1996 were young people, ages 16–24—2.5 million of them (Bureau of the Census, 1997:Table 652). But if unemployment is a problem for young people in general, consider the problems of black youngsters. The unemployment rate in some cities for white juveniles ages 16–19 is 20 to 25 percent, but for black teenagers it is as high as 50 percent (Duster, 1987:310). "More and more black youth, including many who are no longer in school, are obtaining no job experience at all" (Wilson, 1987:143).

What all of this means is that the movement to grant greater freedoms to children is not yet matched by a set of institutional arrangements by which their so-called rights can become a reality. Unless economic and political structures change, the roles and statuses of the young cannot change either (Skolnick, 1979:167). The notion that children should have the same rights as adults is relatively empty unless it is consistent with the means to become self-sufficient.

Alterations in Family Life

Some of the most dramatic changes for children have involved alterations in family life. To begin with, the cost of raising children has grown increasingly onerous. "A middle-class family with two children is likely to spend about $100,000 to rear each child to age eighteen" (Rauch, 1989:56). This makes the cost of raising a large family almost prohibitive, particularly when that cost must compete with the desires of husbands and wives to travel, own their own cars, purchase houses, and so on.

Second, children now interfere not only with the occupational aspirations of fathers but also with those of mothers. Women, as well as men, want to forge their own destinies, and children can be distinct hindrances to doing so. Indeed, that is one reason the fertility rate has decreased so precipitously.

But if the costs of raising children are increasing, what about the impact on children of the changing character of family life? In his analysis of the subject, Davis highlighted the dramatic finding that because of high divorce and separation rates, the likelihood that an American child will remain with both parents throughout childhood has been reduced to about the same level as it was in the preindustrial era. Of course, then, it was high death rates, not divorce and separation, that disrupted families (1979:114). Not only has the divorce rate doubled since 1960 (Bureau of the Census, 1975:Table 96; 1997:Table 152), but the number of births to unmarried women as a percentage of all births has almost quintupled (Bureau of the Census, 1987:Table 87; National Center for Health Statistics, 1989:209). In 1960, only 1 child in 20 was born to an unmarried woman; by 1987, it had reached 1 in 4.

Increases in divorce, separation, and births to unmarried women are strongly related to a rise in female-headed families, among both whites and blacks. In 1970, 8 percent of white families with their own children present in the home were headed by females; for black families, the figure was 31 percent (Bureau of the Census, 1980:Table 4). These figures had increased to 15 percent for whites and 48 percent for blacks by 1988 (Bureau of the Census, 1989a: 4–5). Moreover, the economic factors associated with such trends are profound. In 1988, 38 percent of all white, female-headed families with children lived below the poverty level—an annual income of about $12,000 for a family of four (Bureau of the Census, 1989b:5, 63). Among blacks, the figures are even worse. Fully 56 percent of black, female-headed families with children lived below the poverty line (Bureau of the Census, 1989b:64).

The Schools

For the better part of three centuries, Western nations have placed increasing emphasis on the school as a vital institution for socializing children, second only to the family in importance. Education has been described as the means by which cultural life might be shaped into a new, more moral pattern. As Short pointed out, however, the belief that schools should no longer play an *in loco parentis* role is steadily gaining strength (Short, 1979:185; also see Coleman and Husen, 1985:9). It is argued that children should be allowed to assert their independence not only from familial controls but also from school constraints. As a consequence, we should not be surprised that many of our schools have become unstable sources of training for the young, marked by defiance and violence and by a decrease in educational effectiveness (Coleman and Husen, 1985:30; National Commission on Excellence in Education, 1983).

Citing several studies, Short noted that educational authorities have responded to this state of affairs by absolving themselves of responsibility for turbulence in the schools (1979:184–187). Current difficulties, they argue, are rooted in society as a whole. Given the emphasis on children's liberation and the autonomy of the individual, a reliance on schools for resolution of society's problems has been eschewed.

Conclusion

Although the children's rights movement has indeed altered the status of children, its efforts have been beset with difficulties. These include demographic changes that pit children in direct competition with the elderly and with working women and men; alterations in the character of family life that place many children, especially those from poor families, at risk; and the declining influence of the school as a means for socializing youngsters. These trends suggest dilemmas that may arise or have already arisen from perceiving children as equivalent to adults. Zimring (1979:324–325) has suggested a middle ground between the views of child savers and, alternatively, those who would extend all of the rights and responsibilities of adults to children. Perhaps it would be best to adopt a "learning permit" theory of adolescence. That is, we would recognize the existence of a period of transitional learning during which young people might be ready to exercise responsibility—such as driving a car—but during which we would not hold them entirely responsible if they had an accident (also see Zimring, 1982:89–116). The extension of privilege is a gamble that must be taken to nurture and train children for the adult responsibilities that they are not yet ready for.

DELINQUENT BEHAVIOR TODAY

Let us now review what we have learned about delinquent behavior. Delinquency has always been prevalent throughout the youth population, but delinquency rates rose most precipitously when American society was most unstable—that is, when it was plagued by conflicts over civil rights, urban riots, campus protests, and assassinations. Seeming to reflect the turbulence about them, young people not only continued to commit a disproportionate number of all property crimes but also became more violent. And while delinquency rates have subsequently decreased, or at least leveled off, they have not retreated to their earlier levels. Hence, serious problems remain: Juveniles continue to commit a large number of delinquent acts, and research reveals that chronic and violent offenders are concentrated among poor and minority youngsters.

Research also reveals that the victims of crime are not evenly distributed throughout society. In particular, young people are more likely to be victimized than older persons, young males more than young females, blacks more than whites, poor children more than affluent ones, and residents of central cities more than suburbanites.

In short, those segments of society most likely to suffer from or to commit delinquent behaviors are precisely those for whom many of the problems we described earlier are the greatest—disrupted families, ineffective schools, poverty, and uncertainty about jobs. Consequently, this picture of the delinquency problem literally cries out for explanation and understanding. What, then, is the current state of delinquency theory?

DELINQUENCY THEORY AND CRIMINOLOGY

To answer that question, let us review briefly the history of delinquency theory and criminology. Their parallel developments, particularly in recent years, reveal some striking outcomes.

Positivist Criminology

Until about a century ago, there were few theoretical alternatives to the classical perspective. "Politicians and philosophers . . . routinely assumed that criminals simply choose to be bad and will choose to change their ways if they are punished severely enough" (Cressey, 1978:181–182). Then, along with the growth of science in general, positivist criminology developed (Gottfredson and Hirschi, 1987). Just as scientists in other fields were seeking to establish cause-and-effect relationships in biology, chemistry, and physics, so criminologists began to ask: What causes delinquent behavior? Why do some juveniles, but not others, commit serious crimes?

Such questions were based on the ancient and honorable principle that the control of any problem—whether it is a disease, a natural disaster, or a crime—is gained by first achieving an understanding of its causes and then using that knowledge

to modify or eliminate those causes (Cressey, 1978: 177–178). Indeed, because the classical perspective had failed to address these issues, early theories, with all their limitations, "were at the base of many significant criminal justice innovations . . . , including the juvenile court, the probation system, the parole system, changes in the insanity defense, and changes in the conditions of imprisonment" (pp. 173–174).

Over time, theories of many different types were constructed—including control, cultural deviance, symbolic interactionist, and strain theories. And while many of these theories were inadequate by themselves, they have contributed collectively to the identification of several causes of delinquency. In particular, delinquents appear to lack a stake in conformity: Their attachments to the basic child-rearing institutions—the family and the school—are weak or disrupted; their academic achievement is poor; they are not committed to conventional means for success; and they are inclined to identify with delinquent peers. Consequently, several principles for intervention are implied: to reestablish or reinforce attachments to family and school, provide delinquents with renewed opportunities for education, strengthen their commitment to conventional pursuits, and assimilate them into law-abiding groups.

Labeling Theory

But when efforts to implement these principles were unsuccessful, an alternative perspective—labeling theory—emerged. Rather than stressing the effects of cultural conflict, unstable families and schools, blocked opportunities, and delinquent subcultures, labeling theory suggested that the real cause of serious delinquency is the dramatization of evil. Society and the legal system are at fault. Were it not for discriminatory rules and the effects of labeling and stigmatization, there would be no serious delinquents.

In a strictly scientific sense—indeed, even to leading labeling theorists themselves—this perspective was meant to refocus attention on rule makers and rule enforcers, as well as on rule breakers. The basic concerns of positive criminology, first suggested by Edwin Sutherland, were simply being reasserted; that is, criminology should be devoted to constructing theories that explain the processes of making and enforcing laws, as well as breaking laws, and explaining the interrelations among these processes (Cressey, 1978:175).

But to a new breed of criminologists, the implications of labeling theory meant something quite different. To them, it meant that in the absence of legal processing, there is no crime and there are no criminals. Because the legal system is the source of secondary deviance (serious delinquency), efforts to understand primary deviance (the reasons misbehaving children break the law in the first place) are wasted. Instead, the only role for science, if there is one, is to study the processes by which some people, but not others, are labeled as criminals and subjected to destructive legal controls. Furthermore, social policy should be directed not to measures designed to alter families, schools, and communities or to enhance economic opportunities, but to reforms designed to leave children alone whenever possible—a policy of benign neglect. If status and victimless offenses are decriminalized and if young offenders are diverted from legal processing, delinquency will take care of itself.

Radical Criminology

To radical theorists, that was nonsense. As representatives of yet another offshoot of criminology, the radicals attacked not only the philosophy of benign neglect implied by labeling theory but also the underlying assumptions of positivist criminology. According to radicals, delinquency is endemic to capitalist society—a product of a perpetual class struggle in which capitalist rulers create the social conditions that spawn delinquency and then turn around and prosecute those who are oppressed and exploited by the capitalist system.

In seeking to justify these contentions, radicals did not endear themselves to most other criminologists because of their stinging indictment of positivism. Rather than joining with others in the pursuit of freedom and equality, radicals contended, positivists are the technocratic servants of capitalism—an intellectual elite that, like good capitalists everywhere, bastardizes the pursuit of truth in their own self-interest.

Stated that way, radical theory has had paradoxical effects. On the one hand, the theory has been justifiably criticized as being more ideological than

theoretical. It has been concerned more with promoting social revolution than with formulating and testing propositions to explain the effects of recent changes in advanced capitalist societies—some of the very changes described previously. It also has failed to indicate why, contrary to all the lessons of history, sociology, and anthropology, delinquency can be expected to disappear in a truly socialist society—why such a society could be expected to avoid the disorienting conditions that all advanced societies, capitalist and noncapitalist, are now experiencing. In terms of traditional scientific standards, at least, the theory has been deficient.

On the other hand, the halting efforts of American society to prevent delinquency, to say nothing of the subversion of many legal reforms by juvenile justice officials, have lent indirect support to radical arguments. Instead of mobilizing the political will, economic resources, and innovative ideas necessary to promote adequate familial, educational, and employment opportunities for juveniles, our capitalist society has grown increasingly pessimistic, is cutting back on its support for such programs, and now threatens to resort once again to more punitive measures for controlling the young. Paradoxically, therefore, radical theory comes closer to positivist theories than any other in suggesting why recent reforms have not been effective. Hence, one might argue that, rather than continuing to savagely disparage one another, radicals and positivists should reconcile.

If positivists would only concentrate more on the relationship between political and economic institutions and delinquency, and if radicals would only acknowledge that societies include some institutions besides those that are political and economic, the two might become partners. Indeed, recent radical theories have sought just that union (e.g., Colvin and Pauly, 1983; Hagan, Simpson, and Gillis, 1987). For the most part, however, squabbles between positivists and radicals have cleared the way for neoclassical philosophers—the proponents of just deserts, mechanized justice, legal punishment, and deterrence.

Neoclassical Criminology

As in the past, the activities and interests of these proponents are a remarkable example of the extent to which the intellectual concerns of criminologists reflect changing cultural beliefs. Whereas positivist criminology was born in a time of optimism and sustained by the belief that humankind could be perfected through the pursuit of knowledge, contemporary criminology reflects a belief in the imperfectibility of humans and their social institutions.

Neoclassical philosophy is the prime example of these despairing beliefs. Although its proponents differ somewhat over the solutions they propose, they do agree on one thing: We must discard the esoteric search for knowledge and concentrate on being practical. Their justifications for practicality, however, are not only varied but also inconsistent.

On the one hand, utilitarian philosophers contend that positivist theories are impractical because the causes they identify cannot be addressed by social policy: Child-rearing practices cannot be improved; schools cannot be made more effective; identification with delinquent peers cannot be altered; and the pockets of poverty and demoralization produced by capitalist society cannot be remedied. Yet, after having discredited the relevance of these "causes," utilitarian philosophers identify other causes that they contend are amenable to policy.

Utilitarians tend to believe that people commit crimes either because they are inherently wicked or because they are hedonistic calculators who perceive that legal punishment is not forthcoming. In short, they reject positivist theories not merely because they consider them impractical but also because they have alternative explanations. They subscribe to the hedonistic school of psychology first enunciated by the classical philosophers of the 1700s. Hence, if delinquency is to be prevented and controlled, the certainty and severity of legal punishment must be increased.

Just deserts philosophers, by contrast, have a different reason for stressing the need to be practical. It is not that positivist theories are necessarily wrong. Instead, it is that juvenile justice officials cannot be trusted to exercise the benevolence, love, and charity necessary to ensure that the causes of delinquency are addressed. Like labeling theorists, but for different reasons, just deserts philosophers view authorities as oppressors, not benefactors.

In the interest of minimizing harm, therefore, we must do two things. First, we must divide juveniles into two groups: (1) the misbehaving, but still deserving, kids who commit status, victimless, and petty offenses, and (2) the nondeserving kids who commit serious crimes or are chronic offenders. Then, we must adopt separate policies for each. That is, we must decriminalize the offenses of the deserving youngsters while we do justice for the undeserving—eliminating discretionary concern for individual differences among them, concentrating on protecting their rights, and submitting them to standardized legal punishments.

Finally, rational choice theories unite positivism with utilitarian philosophy by using classical assumptions about human nature to derive scientific theories of delinquency. Expanded deterrence theory, for example, argues that crime is the result of a rational process of maximizing benefits and minimizing costs. But in addition to legal punishments, the costs of delinquency include such things as shame, embarrassment, loss of respect from significant others, and diminished occupational and educational opportunities.

Perhaps the most astonishing consequence of the resurrection of classical philosophy has been its impact on the criminologists' outlook (Bayer, 1981). Until recently, "most criminologists were arguing that repression is neither scientifically nor democratically sound and that therefore the effort to understand the conditions spawning crime and criminals should be enlarged" (Cressey, 1978:181). Now, by contrast, "criminologists, like politicians, are saying that our efforts to change criminals and the society that produces them have been ineffective and that we must therefore retain punishment and abandon the effort to understand criminals and society" (p. 180). What, then, are the implications of these profound changes in criminological and political thought?

POLICY DILEMMAS

There are five issues for which recent changes are very important—those having to do with delinquency prevention, due process for juveniles, the increasing tendency to treat status offenders with benign neglect, the growing enthusiasm for legal punishment, and prospects for the rehabilitative ideal.

Prevention

When we reviewed the implications of positivist theories in Chapter 15, we found that they implied certain principles for the prevention of delinquency:

1. The primary focus of efforts to prevent delinquency should be on establishing a stake in conformity in young people.
2. A stake in conformity is most likely to occur if children are effectively socialized: attached to families and schools, committed to conventional pursuits, provided with opportunities for the assumption of legitimate adult roles, and helped to identify with law-abiding peers.
3. Effective socialization is a product of institutional design and process—a result of the way families, schools, and communities are organized. In short, programs designed to prevent delinquency should be a part of the ongoing, relatively normal processes of the community.

Although these principles have always been attractive in a theoretical sense, they have rarely been tried in any systematic way. Rather than altering the ways schools deal with marginal children, for example, the use of diversion often has increased their flow toward programs controlled by legal officials. And because educational and vocational programs have not linked adolescents with the adult world of work, their effects have been marginal at best. Consequently, it cannot honestly be said that the implications of either positivist or radical theories have been fairly tested. Even more importantly, the increasing competition of young people for scarce jobs and resources, combined with the newfound faith in a classical model of juvenile justice, suggests that the practice of prevention may be rejected not because it is without promise, but because it will not be given a chance to fulfill that promise.

Due Process

The invention of the juvenile court was predicated on three assumptions: (1) Children are qualitatively different from adults; (2) legal intervention in their lives is justified because of their dependent and protected status; and (3) the goal of intervention is rehabilitation, not punishment. As a result, children's rights were defined in terms of protecting them from parental neglect, physical abuse, immorality, and excessive and dangerous work, and ensuring that they attended school to prepare them for adulthood.

In our review of juvenile court practices, however, we found that juvenile justice officials often abused the tremendous powers granted to them. Both status and delinquent offenders were detained, adjudicated, and deprived of liberty without the benefit of specific, written charges against them, access to legal counsel, and the right to confront witnesses.

Coupled with this is the fact that our assumptions about children have also changed: (1) Children are not qualitatively different from adults, at least not so much as we thought; (2) their right to self-determination should prevent legal interference into their lives for behavior that, if exhibited by adults, would not be considered illegal; and (3) they should be granted greater rights, not merely in legal proceedings but also in their dealings with parents, schools, and the political system. Thus, not surprisingly, the advocates of virtually every philosophy have joined in demanding the implementation of due process in all legal proceedings.

Although the need for due process goes without saying, constant vigilance with regard to its use must be exercised. Constitutional safeguards may depend heavily on the capacities of parents to find and employ competent legal counsel; the juvenile court in many states has not been raised to the stature of the adult criminal court; and the resources and personnel necessary to implement formal procedures have not been forthcoming.

Even more importantly, the formalities of due process—written charges, codified procedures, and the presence of prosecutors and defense attorneys—are not designed to solve the problems of youths. Instead, they are designed to ensure fairness and protect the innocent. Thus, to the degree that punishment replaces rehabilitation as the primary goal of juvenile justice, there is always the chance that the mitigating circumstances associated with the commission of a delinquent act will be ignored.

All juveniles are not the same, and their reasons for violating the law differ. That is why, in the *Gault* case, the Supreme Court ruled that "the observance of due process standards, intelligently and not ruthlessly administered, will not compel the States to abandon or displace any of the substantive benefits of the juvenile process" (*In re Gault,* 1967). Yet, the growing faith in rules of evidence, determinate sentencing, legal punishment, and deterrence threatens to eliminate our concern with individual differences. Indeed, this is such a crucial issue that we will discuss it further in our consideration of punishment.

Status Offenders and Benign Neglect

One of the most frequent criticisms of the traditional juvenile court was that status offenders constituted a relatively high percentage of all court referrals. Though this is less the case today, status offenders are still as likely as more serious offenders to be held in detention facilities while awaiting disposition. Such practices might not have offended the sensibilities of reformers had court referral and detention of status offenders proved to be of clear benefit to them, but this has not always been true. In the interests of justice, then, decriminalization has been hailed as a constructive reform.

Like many other outcomes of the children's rights movement, however, decriminalization has done more to highlight undesirable practices than to promote desirable alternatives. We have already seen that declines in the socializing influences of the family and school have not been matched by compensatory changes in other social institutions. Thus, it is significant that decriminalization represents more of the same. Although few would disagree with the assertion that children should be protected from official abuse, it is quite another thing to suggest that they require no controls. What will happen if the juvenile court, along with other child-oriented institutions, loses its capacity to place limits on any behaviors except those that are clearly criminal?

Critics from both ends of the ideological spectrum have raised cries of alarm. Radical theorists Herman Schwendinger and Julia Schwendinger argued that while decriminalization may reduce the harassment of working-class children by the police, it might also do them lasting harm (1979:269–273). "Working-class families have a difficult enough time controlling their children in the face of poor public schools and meager community resources" (p. 271). Hence, if decriminalization is combined with all the

other freedoms advocated by the children's rights movement, it would simply result in another instance of benign neglect, justified by lofty, but class-biased, principles. Although well-to-do parents may have sufficient resources to make legal controls unnecessary, poor parents need the juvenile court as a *backup* institution. Otherwise, their children will continue to suffer from ignorance, poverty, and high rates of illegitimacy and delinquency.

Writing as an advocate of the traditional juvenile court, Polier said much the same thing (1979:233–236). In doing so, she cited a problem with which every police officer, judge, and correctional worker is familiar—namely, that such terms as *incorrigibility* and *truancy* may cover a multitude of problems. Desperate parents often come to legal officials asking for help, not only because their children are truant, stay out late, and get drunk, but also because they are drug users, gang members, prostitutes, or thieves. However, because these children have been referred to the juvenile justice system by their parents, and officials have no firsthand knowledge of any crimes committed, the children usually are designated as status offenders. If, however, all status offenses are decriminalized, officials could not take action, parental wishes notwithstanding. Thus, the problems of status offenders are ignored until, or unless, these youths are apprehended for delinquent offenses. Even then, their personal problems might never be addressed.

Punishment

This brings us to the topic of punishment. To weigh the dilemmas it poses, several issues must be considered.

PUNISHMENT AND FAIRNESS What about the growing movement to hold juveniles fully accountable for their delinquency, without attention to their backgrounds or developmental histories? What about the idea that we should sentence delinquency and not the delinquent? What about the belief that legal punishment will deter persons from committing crimes?

If a juvenile has a decent home life, has attended school, and might be able to find a job, then accountability and legal punishment may make sense. In this case, the youngster is better prepared to make an informed choice among realistic alternatives. But if he or she is illiterate and has no help from external support systems, legal punishment makes less sense, because the youngster is incapable of making informed and reasonable choices. Indeed, that is why for those juveniles whose backgrounds are characterized by deprivation, ignorance, and abuse, an exclusive emphasis on the letter of the law, mechanized justice, and legal punishment may be inappropriate.

Lacking any stake in conformity, such juveniles have little to lose by violating the law. Because delinquency may be the only alternative to continued deprivation and self-degradation, legal punishment serves only to widen the gap between the offender and the rest of society. If accountability is emphasized at the expense of social justice, the most vulnerable juveniles will become the victims of a cruel hoax that, at best, will subject them to a policy of benign neglect if their delinquent behavior is not particularly serious, or that, at worst, will severely punish them if their delinquency is serious—punishments that may have no benefits. One cannot expect responsibility and autonomy from those who have never experienced them and who do not know what they mean.

PESSIMISM In light of these considerations, why not reject the use of legal punishment and concentrate on rehabilitation of offenders? The answer is threefold.

First, as we learned in prior chapters, society has been besieged with reports that attempts at rehabilitation have failed. Because the available evidence indicates that rehabilitation is no more successful than institutionalization in reducing recidivism, we should concentrate on protecting society.

Second, experience tends to support the contention of just deserts philosophers that the actual treatment afforded juveniles has never approached the goals envisioned for it. Correctional bureaucracies have become self-perpetuating organizations that use professionals and professionalism to justify their existence. Under the guise of scientific diagnosis and treatment, these bureaucracies have been little more than repositories for undeserving children. Over the past hundred years, diagnostic labels and treatment procedures have changed markedly; yet, the process

of extrusion, exclusion, and isolation remains the same (Miller, 1979).

Finally, the past twenty-five years or so have been characterized by a growing sense of pessimism. The belief that nothing works is but one symbol of a much wider sense of disillusionment with all of our social institutions. Thus, it is not merely that we lack evidence that rehabilitation can reduce recidivism, but also that we are losing faith in the belief that benevolently motivated intervention will work (Bayer, 1981).

LIMITATIONS OF PUNISHMENT What is remarkable about this pessimism is the extent to which it permits today's reformers to forget the limitations of legal punishment. When we reviewed neoclassical theory, we discovered the problems in assuming that legal punishments deter. Moreover, if incapacitation is employed, it will be at the expense of many young people who would not commit delinquent acts if left free in the community and not institutionalized.

Rehabilitation

One of the most compelling counterarguments to the direction of today's reforms has been made by a small band of persons who insist that the rehabilitative ideal has never really been tried (Cullen and Gilbert, 1982; Glaser, 1979; Martin, Sechrest, and Redner, 1981; Sechrest, White, and Brown, 1979). We do not know whether it works because the intervention principles implied by scientific theory have never been systematically implemented and evaluated. Their application has been primitive; promising approaches have been undermined by methods that are substantially weak and without integrity; sound experimental designs have been rare; and the resources needed to sustain a search for solutions—like that associated with research on cancer or heart disease—have not been available.

Rather than identifying specific target groups, using theory and research to isolate their unique problems, and then devising appropriate programs for them, we employ such "reforms" as decriminalization, diversion, and deinstitutionalization in indiscriminate ways for indiscriminate populations. But a more promising strategy might be to commit resources and set target dates that are more consistent with the difficult problems involved. With regard to rehabilitation, for example, such a strategy could impose the rigors of scientific investigation in a way that is analogous to the efforts that were made a generation ago to learn more about space, when the talents of scientists and engineers were united in a common endeavor. Rather than more technology, communication satellites, and a space industry, however, the goal in this case would be the invention of new social arrangements and methods by which the socialization of young people might be more equitable, less characterized by serious delinquency, and more satisfying to all.

Relative to these tasks, Glaser pointed out that it is not rehabilitation—restoration to some prior state—that most marginal youngsters need most, but habilitation—the opportunity to live in a warm and supportive environment and be prepared for and experience legitimate adult roles for the first time (1979:269). In other words, the task of rehabilitation too often has been approached negatively. Rather than conceiving of rehabilitation programs as devices by which structural as well as individual change is facilitated, we have concentrated on ways by which to control and undo the criminogenic influences that are presumed to inhibit only the individual. This may be why success has been so limited.

CONCLUSIONS AND A LOOK TO THE FUTURE

Although current reforms in juvenile justice are part of a larger social movement to grant greater rights to children, they have many unanticipated limitations. They have done little to rectify the ambiguous position of children in society or to remedy neglect, poverty, and ignorance among youths. And, although reforms have helped to correct some of the worst features of the juvenile court system, they have failed to adequately address the most significant feature of the delinquency problem—the heavy concentration of law-violating behavior among juveniles. It would appear, therefore, that until ways are found to reorganize that crucial phase in the life cycle we call childhood and to give young people a greater stake

in conformity, society will continue to bear the costs of delinquency.

It is very difficult to predict the future, given all the factors that must be considered. However, we can at least speculate about what the future for children may entail. In that connection, a commentary by Philippe Aries (1980) is particularly relevant. Recall that Aries' work on the history of childhood was discussed at length in the first part of this book. In contrast to earlier historical epochs when children were treated with indifference, Western societies during much, if not most, of this century have been "child-oriented" (p. 647). During the 1940s and 1950s, for example, "the child was king and gave every indication of being as desired as he was fawned upon" (p. 648). Aries argued, however, that the "days of the child-king are over" (p. 649). We may be moving into a new epoch "in which the child occupies a smaller place."

Aries pointed mainly to decreasing fertility rates as evidence for his argument (p. 645). However, he noted that such decreases are nothing new; they are part of a long-term trend that began at the end of the 1700s (p. 649). Yet, until recently, low fertility rates were means for ensuring that "children got ahead" (p. 647). Reflecting a child-centeredness, parents had small families to enhance the chances of their children's social mobility. According to Aries, the reason for limiting family size is different today in that it stems from a growing *intolerance* of children (p. 649). Children in today's society are valued not for their own sake, but for what they can offer their parents:

> Couples—and individuals—no longer plan life in terms of the child and his personal future. . . . This does not mean that the child has disappeared from such plans but that he fits into them as one of the various components that make it possible for adults to blossom as individuals. His existence, therefore, is related to plans for a future in which he is no longer the essential variable. (p. 650)

Aries' argument implies that the lives of future generations of children may be very different from those of the past century. In short, we may be witnessing the resurrection, in modern guise, of an ancient concept of childhood. If so, we will have come full circle: Parents will be less involved with their own children, as in ages past; childhood will not be a highly protected phase in the life cycle; and children will be viewed less as having great virtue in their own right and more as providing a means for the fulfillment of adult desires and aspirations.

DISCUSSION QUESTIONS

1. What two factors have altered the age structure of society?
2. What changes have occurred in the last 30–40 years with respect to the rate of labor force participation among women?
3. With respect to the issue of due process, in what ways have our assumptions about children changed over the years?
4. Describe three reasons why policymakers have not rejected the use of legal punishment and concentrated only on rehabilitation.
5. Describe Aries' (1980) arguments about the future of childhood.

REFERENCES

Aries, Philippe. 1980. "Two Successive Motivations for the Declining Birth Rate in the West." *Population and Development Review* 6 (December): 645–650.

Bayer, Ronald. 1981. "Crime, Punishment, and the Decline of Liberal Optimism." *Crime and Delinquency* 27 (April):169–190.

Bellotti v. *Baird.* 1979. 443 U.S. 622, 643–644, 654.

Billy, John O. G., Joseph Lee Rodgers, and Richard J. Udry. 1984. "Adolescent Sexual Behavior and Friendship Choice." *Social Forces* 62 (March): 653–678.

Bureau of the Census. 1965. *Current Population Reports.* Series P-25, no. 310. Washington, D.C.: U.S. Government Printing Office.
1975. *Statistical Abstract of the United States:*
1975. Washington, D.C.: U.S. Government Printing Office.
1980. *Current Population Reports.* Series P-23, no. 107. Washington, D.C.: U.S. Government Printing Office.
1987. *Statistical Abstract of the United States: 1988.* Washington, D.C.: U.S. Government Printing Office.
1989a. *Current Population Reports.* Series P-20, no. 437. Washington, D.C.: U.S. Government Printing Office.
1989b. *Current Population Reports.* Series P-60, no. 166. Washington, D.C.: U.S. Government Printing Office.
1990. *Current Population Reports.* Series P-25, no. 1045. Washington, D.C.: U.S. Government Printing Office.
1997. *Statistical Abstract of the United States: 1997.* Washington, D.C.: U.S. Government Printing Office.

Coleman, James S. 1974. *Youth: Transition to Adulthood.* Chicago: University of Chicago Press.

Coleman, James S., and Torsten Husen. 1985. *Becoming Adult in a Changing Society.* Paris: Organisation for Economic CoOperation and Development.

Colvin, Mark, and John Pauly. 1983. "A Critique of Criminology: Toward an Integrated Structural-Marxist Theory of Delinquency Production." *American Journal of Sociology* 89 (November): 513–551.

Cressey, Donald R. 1978. "Criminological Theory, Social Science, and the Repression of Crime." *Criminology* 16 (August):171–191.

Cullen, Francis T., and Karen E. Gilbert. 1982. *Reaffirming Rehabilitation.* Cincinnati: Anderson.

Davis, Kingsley. 1979. "Demographic Changes and the Future of Childhood." Pp. 113–137 in LaMar T. Empey, ed., *The Future of Childhood and Juvenile Justice.* Charlottesville: University Press of Virginia.

Davis, Kingsley, and Pietronella van den Oever. 1981. "Age Relations and Public Policy in Advanced Industrial Societies." *Population and Development Review* 7 (March):1–18.

Dornbusch, Sanford M. 1989. "The Sociology of Adolescence." Pp. 233–259 in W. Richard Scott and Judith Blake, eds., *Annual Review of Sociology,* Vol. 15. Palo Alto, Calif.: Annual Reviews.

Duster, Troy. 1987. "Crime, Youth Unemployment, and the Black Urban Underclass." *Crime and Delinquency* 33 (April):300–316.

Farson, Richard. 1974. *Birthrights.* New York: Macmillan.
1975. "Busing Violates the Rights of Children." *Los Angeles Times,* January 28, sec. 2, p. 5.

Gillis, John R. 1974. *Youth and History.* New York: Academic Press.

Glaser, Daniel. 1979. "Disillusion with Rehabilitation: Theoretical and Empirical Questions." Pp. 234–276 in LaMar T. Empey, ed., *The Future of Childhood and Juvenile Justice.* Charlottesville: University Press of Virginia.

Gottfredson, Michael R., and Travis Hirschi. 1987. "The Positive Tradition." Pp. 9–22 in Michael R. Gottfredson and Travis Hirschi, eds., *Positive Criminology.* Newbury Park, Calif.: Sage.

H. L. v. *Matheson.* 1981. 450 U.S. 398.

Hagan, John, John Simpson, and A. R. Gillis. 1987. "Class in the Household: A Power-Control Theory of Gender and Delinquency." *American Journal of Sociology* 92 (January):788–816.

Hale, Nathan G., Jr. 1971. *Freud and the Americans: The Beginnings of Psychoanalysis in the United States, 1876–1917.* New York: Oxford University Press.

Hazelwood School District v. *Kuhlmeier.* 1988. 484 U.S. 260, 271, 273 (Preliminary Print).

Holt, John. 1974. *Escape from Childhood.* New York: Dutton.

In re Gault. 1967. 387 U.S. 1, 21.

Martin, Susan E., Lee B. Sechrest, and Robin Redner, eds. 1981. *New Directions in the Rehabilitation of Criminal Offenders.* Washington, D.C.: National Academy of Sciences.

Miller, Jerome G. 1979. "The Revolution in Juvenile Justice: From Rhetoric to Rhetoric." Pp. 66–111

in LaMar T. Empey, ed., *The Future of Childhood and Juvenile Justice.* Charlottesville: University Press of Virginia.

Mnookin, Robert H. 1985. *In the Interest of Children: Advocacy, Law Reform, and Public Policy.* New York: Freeman.

National Center for Health Statistics. 1989. *Vital Statistics of the United States, 1987,* Vol. I. Washington, D.C.: U.S. Government Printing Office. 1990. *Vital Statistics of the United States, 1987,* Vol. II, sec. 6, Life Tables. Washington, D.C.: U.S. Government Printing Office.

National Commission on Excellence in Education. 1983. *A Nation at Risk: The Imperative for Educational Reform.* Washington, D.C.: U.S. Government Printing Office.

Oberman, Caryl Andrea. 1984. "Education Rights." Pp. 515–569 in Robert M. Horowitz and Howard A. Davidson, eds., *Legal Rights of Children.* New York: McGraw-Hill.

Planned Parenthood of Central Missouri v. *Danforth.* 1976. 428 U.S. 52.

Polier, Justine Wise. 1979. "Prescriptions for Reform: Doing What We Set Out to Do?" Pp. 213–244 in LaMar T. Empey, ed., *Juvenile Justice: The Progressive Legacy and Current Reforms.* Charlottesville: University Press of Virginia.

Rauch, Jonathan. 1989. "Kids as Capital." *Atlantic Monthly* 264 (August), pp. 56–61.

Schwendinger, Herman, and Julia Schwendinger. 1979. "Delinquency and Social Reform: A Radical Perspective." Pp. 245–287 in LaMar T. Empey, ed., *Juvenile Justice: The Progressive Legacy and Current Reforms.* Charlottesville: University Press of Virginia.

Sechrest, Lee, Susan O. White, and Elizabeth D. Brown, eds. 1979. *The Rehabilitation of Criminal Offenders: Problems and Prospects.* Washington, D.C.: National Academy of Sciences.

Short, James F., Jr. 1979. "Social Contexts of Child Rights and Delinquency." Pp. 175–210 in LaMar T. Empey, ed., *The Future of Childhood and Juve-*

nile Justice. Charlottesville: University Press of Virginia.

Skolnick, Arlene. 1973. *The Intimate Environment: Exploring Marriage and the Family.* Boston: Little, Brown.
1979. "Children's Rights, Children's Development." Pp. 138–174 in LaMar T. Empey, ed., *The Future of Childhood and Juvenile Justice.* Charlottesville: University Press of Virginia.

Stafford, Mark C. 1995. "Children's Legal Rights in the U.S." *Marriage and Family Review* 21(3/4): 121–140.

Tinker v. *Des Moines Independent Community School District.* 1969. 393 U.S. 503, 511.

Wilson, William J. 1987. *The Truly Disadvantaged: The Inner City, the Underclass, and Public Policy.* Chicago: University of Chicago Press.

Zimring, Franklin E. 1979. "Privilege, Maturity, and Responsibility: Notes on the Evolving Jurisprudence of Adolescence." Pp. 312–335 in LaMar T. Empey, ed., *The Future of Childhood and Juvenile Justice.* Charlottesville: University Press of Virginia.
1982. *The Changing Legal World of Adolescence.* New York: Free Press.

GLOSSARY

A

abandonment Leaving an infant to be cared for by others or to die.

adjudication The legal process, conducted by a judge, during which the court determines whether the allegations against a juvenile are proven or disproven and whether he or she should be defined as delinquent or as dependent or neglected.

adolescence-limited delinquency According to Moffitt, a kind of delinquency limited to the teen years and caused mainly by association with delinquent peers.

American Dream The widely shared dream of achieving a high-status job, social recognition, and all the things that money will buy.

anal stage of development According to Freud, the stage at which an infant gains erotic satisfaction from the evacuation of bowels and bladder (ages 1–3).

apprenticeship The binding of a child to the house of another in order to live, work, and learn a trade.

attachment Ties of affection and respect between children and such key people as parents, teachers, and friends (social control theory—Hirschi).

Auburn System New York prison system (1816) in which criminals were confined in small cells at night and put to work during the day.

B

belief Respect for the law and belief in its moral legitimacy (social control theory—Hirschi).

biological control theory Body of theory suggesting that a biological defect—genetic, chemical, or neurological—reduces the capacity of the individual to control his or her antisocial impulses and thus leads to delinquent behavior.

C

capitalism An economic system in which economic life, particularly ownership and investment in production goods, is carried on under private auspices by means of economic competition and the pursuit of profit.

Chicago Area Project Community program fathered by Clifford Shaw that sought to (1) induce slum dwellers to engage in delinquency prevention; (2) assist them in organizing projects and resources for their children; and (3) foster cooperation among local residents, schools, the police, and the courts.

child Historically, an ambiguous term used to refer to a young person between infancy and maturity who has not reached the legal age of adulthood.

childhood A vaguely defined social position for young people between infancy and adulthood to which a special set of values, beliefs, and roles is attached.

children's rights Rights that grew out of the modern concept of childhood and stressed the needs of children for food, clothing, and shelter; protection from exploitation by adults; secular and moral education; and care and treatment for such problems as delinquency, dependency, and neglect.

classic strain theory Body of theory suggesting that delinquent subcultures develop among lower-class boys because of their anger and frustration over their lack of opportunity or their personal inability to achieve the American Dream through conventional means.

classical deterrence theory Theory suggesting that since people are rational, they will be deterred from committing crimes if they can be certain that lawbreakers will be caught, convicted, and severely punished.

classical school of criminology Eighteenth-century school of thought that (1) criminal, like law-abiding, behavior is the result of rational free choice in the pursuit of personal satisfaction; (2) if society is run on democratic principles, most people will refrain from crime; and (3) crime among noncriminals can be deterred if those who do break the law are justly convicted and punished according to the seriousness of their crimes.

cognitive learning theory Body of psychological theory, associated with Bandura, suggesting that people learn behavior not merely from direct experience, but also from observing the consequences of others' behavior. A central part of the learning is thoughts and images about behavior.

college boy In Cohen's version of classic strain theory, the rare lower-class boy who accepts the challenge of middle-class striving, ruptures his ties with corner-boy society, and goes on to college.

command class In power-control theory, the dominant social class whose members are either employers or supervisors of others.

commitment The extent to which a child is dedicated to living according to the ideal requirements of childhood (social control theory—Hirschi).

confinement The practice of placing delinquent, dependent, or neglected children in orphan asylums, reformatories, or training schools, or adult criminals in jails and prisons.

conflict framework Theoretical framework used by conflict theorists who contend that society is held together, not by an overriding agreement on basic values and rules, but by force and constraint.

conflict subculture According to the Cloward-Ohlin version of classic strain theory, conflict subculture refers to the deviant values and traditions that arise when lower-class juveniles can find neither legitimate nor illegitimate means for success and that are characterized by violent and malicious acts.

consensus framework The theoretical framework suggesting that social integration and stability are made possible by the general agreement of virtually all people on basic values, beliefs, and rules.

contraculture A shared way of life opposed to everything conventional; that is, a malicious, negativistic, delinquent subculture.

control balance theory Integrated theory by Tittle that argues that deviance is a response to an imbalance in the amounts of control to which a person is subject,

relative to the amount of control that he or she can exercise.

control theories Theories that suggest that both law-abiding and delinquent behaviors are products of the ability or inability of people to control their antisocial impulses.

corner boy According to Cohen's version of classic strain theory, the lower-class boy who deals with frustration and failure by disengaging from competition and withdrawing into a community of like-minded peers, that is, corner-boy society.

counsel and release The traditional police practice of warning juveniles about their bad conduct and releasing them to parents rather than referring them to juvenile court for formal processing.

crimes against households Crimes included in the National Crime Victimization Survey in which there is no direct contact between offenders and victims. These are burglary, motor vehicle theft, and theft of other property.

crimes against persons Crimes included in the National Crime Victimization Survey in which there is direct contact between offenders and victims. These are rape/sexual assault, robbery, nonsexual assault, purse snatching, and pocket picking.

criminal offense An act, whether committed by a child or an adult, that is contrary to criminal law.

criminal subculture In general, shared values, customs, and roles that are deviant. More specifically, the Cloward-Ohlin version of classic strain theory that a criminal subculture among juveniles is one that favors success through illegitimate, rather than legitimate, means. Deviant traditions and methods are transmitted from adults to children who are oriented toward a criminal career.

criminal victimization survey Survey of a representative sample of the population to determine the extent to which people have been victims of crime and the types of offenses committed against them.

cultural deviance theory Theory that delinquent behavior is an expression of conformity to cultural or subcultural values that run counter to those of the larger society.

culture The traditional way of life of a people, including their knowledge, beliefs, rules, prejudices, language, and technology.

D

dark figure of crime That proportion (or percent) of all illegal acts that never becomes a part of the official record, a proportion that is thought to be large.

Declaration of Principles A product of the Cincinnati Prison Congress of 1870 stating both the philosophy and the methods of rehabilitation: indeterminate sentence, treatment, education, physical and vocational training, and parole.

decriminalization A reform in the 1970s that suggested children should no longer be labeled as delinquent for committing such status offenses as running away, defying parents, sexual promiscuity, and truancy.

deinstitutionalization A reform in the 1970s that suggested that fewer children should be confined in jails, detention centers, and training schools and instead should be treated in the community.

delinquent boy In Cohen's version of classic strain theory, the term refers to the lower-class boy who rejects both corner-boy and college-boy societies and turns to the standards of the delinquent subculture for a solution to the frustration and anger he feels for his failure in middle-class pursuits.

delinquent children Young people beneath the age of adulthood (18 in most states) who have violated either the criminal law or laws that prohibit status offenses.

delinquent subculture The deviant values, customs, and standards that juvenile groups develop, share, and transmit when they have experienced isolation from the larger culture and have turned to their peers for a solution.

dependent children Children whose parents, through no fault of their own, are unable to care for them.

detention The confinement of a juvenile in a detention center or jail prior to an official hearing, whether the juvenile is charged with violating the law or is merely dependent or neglected.

determinate sentence A predetermined sentence for a specific offense. Set by law, the determinate sentence is used to limit the discretion of a judge in setting an offender's punishment.

determinism The belief that any event or phenomenon, crime included, is caused; it does not just happen.

dialectic An argument that places two contradictory ideas—a thesis and its antithesis—against the other and then seeks to resolve their differences and to reach a new synthesis.

dialectic materialism An argument by Marx that human progress is the result of the rise and fall of contrasting economic systems.

differential association A concept from Sutherland and Cressey's symbolic interactionist theory suggesting that whether an individual commits delinquent acts depends on the groups with which he or she associates. Prosocial groups tend to promote law-abiding behavior; deviant groups motivate and rationalize delinquent behavior.

differential social control theory Integrated theory by Matsueda that is rooted in symbolic interactionism, specifically, the idea that a person's behavior results from the roles he or she develops in social interactions.

disposition That stage of the legal process during which a court determines what should be done with a juvenile adjudged to be delinquent, dependent, and/or neglected.

diversion A practice in which nonserious delinquents are diverted away from processing in juvenile court into another, ideally nonlegal, agency for some form of help.

dramatization of evil A concept of labeling theory suggesting that the reason people become "bad" is that they are defined as "bad." They become what they are labeled as being.

drift A concept of Matza's symbolic interactionist theory, suggesting that many children are committed neither to law-abiding behavior and traditions nor to deviant behavior and traditions; they drift.

drift-neutralization theory A theory formulated by Matza and Sykes suggesting that (1) behavior involves a continuous interaction process; (2) delinquents are committed neither to law-violating nor law-abiding traditions; and (3) delinquents use verbal statements to lessen the impact of, and even justify, law violations.

due process The term used to describe the procedural fairness that is required by the Constitution when legal officials attempt to deprive any citizen of life, liberty, or property. Recent reforms in juvenile justice have granted more of the protections of due process to juveniles, such as notice of their rights, legal counsel, exclusion of hearsay evidence, and greater formality.

E

ego According to Freud, the rational part of a person's personality that permits reasoned choices between primitive drives (id) and the person's conscience (superego).

ethnocentrism The tendency for people to view their way of life as superior to all others.

eugenics A movement devoted to improving the human race through controlled breeding and the killing or confinement of those identified as physically, mentally, or morally unfit.

expanded deterrence theory Variation of classical deterrence theory that people refrain from crime as a result of the perceived costs, but that those costs include more than the perceived certainty and severity of legal punishment. Of central importance are informal punishments, such as embarrassment, loss of respect from friends and family, and diminished educational and occupational chances.

F

Federal Bureau of Investigation The federal police agency that is charged with enforcing federal criminal laws.

G

group therapy A means of treatment used by professionals in a variety of fields—corrections, mental health, alcohol and drug dependency, and child abuse—to solve problems and produce change among group members.

H

Highfields A small residential program in New Jersey, in which daily group meetings and paid work were used to sponsor delinquents in reformation roles, to teach them to make prosocial decisions, and to find alternatives to delinquent behavior.

house of refuge A 19th-century place of confinement for dependent, neglected, and delinquent children in which inmates were separated from hardened criminals and expected to learn proper conduct.

hue and cry Medieval English practice of making a loud clamor when a crime was committed, collecting one's neighbors, and pursuing the criminal.

human nature The attitudes, values, and behaviors that are uniquely human. Classical theorists believed that people are inherently human at birth, while positivists largely contended that, while people are born with the capacity to be human, that capacity must be cultivated through learning in a process of interaction with others.

I

id Term coined by Freud to indicate the primitive and antisocial instincts with which he believed every child is born.

incidence of law violation The number of delinquent acts reportedly committed by an individual, a group, or a complete population.

indenturing contract A contract binding a person to work for another for a specified period of time. An indentured person was a virtual slave for the period of his or her contract.

indeterminate sentence A court sentence of unspecified length, predicated on the belief that since rehabilitation takes time, sentencing should not be for a fixed term.

index offenses The list of eight serious crimes found in the annual *Uniform Crime Reports,* published by the FBI: murder and nonnegligent manslaughter, forcible rape, robbery, aggravated assault, burglary, larceny-theft, motor vehicle theft, and arson.

industrial schools Places of confinement invented in the late 1800s to replace houses of refuge and orphan asylums as places to provide dependent, neglected, and some delinquent children with the benefits of discipline, education, and training.

infanticide The deliberate killing of an infant; a method of controlling family size or getting rid of an unwanted infant during the Middle Ages.

insiders A term used by labeling theorists to describe people lucky enough to avoid being labeled as deviant and who, therefore, tend to remain law-abiding citizens.

intake That stage of the juvenile court process during which an officer of the court determines whether a juvenile should be held in detention or released to his or her parents, should be formally tried or freed with a warning, or should be referred to some other agency.

integrated structural-Marxist theory Theory put forth by Colvin and Pauly that argues that the type of control parents are exposed to at work affects the control strategies used by them at home, which then affects their children's involvement in delinquency.

intelligence quotient (IQ) A test-derived measure of intelligence that indicates how an individual's score compares with others of his or her age.

involvement A concept of social control theory (Hirschi) that indicates the degree to which a child is involved in conventional activities, such as helping at home, studying, taking music lessons, or playing sports.

J

just deserts philosophy A part of neoclassical theory that grants that legal punishment may not deter crime, but nevertheless advocates its use because lawbreakers deserve to be punished.

juvenile court The court that has jurisdiction over people legally defined as children and who are alleged to be criminal offenders or status offenders, or who are dependent or neglected.

juvenile delinquency A changing social construction that includes: (1) a concept of childhood that defines children as different from adults; (2) rules that prescribe appropriate behavior for children; (3) behavior by children that violates rules; (4) explanations of rule-breaking behavior; and (5) legal institutions designed to enforce appropriate behavior by children.

juvenile justice system The legal rules, agencies, and organizations—laws, police, courts, and correctional agencies—responsible for the administration of juvenile justice and delinquency control.

L

labeling theory Body of theory suggesting that delinquent characteristics are not inherent properties of children but rather are properties conferred upon them by others. Children become and remain delinquent because they are labeled as such by families, legal officials, and communities.

law-violating behavior Any behavior that violates the laws defining criminal or delinquent behavior, regardless of whether the violator is caught.

learning theory Body of theory, including cognitive learning theory and operant behavioral theory, that suggests that a behavior will occur or recur if the rewards for the behavior outweigh the punishments.

liberated society A concept in radical theory to describe a society in which exploitation and greed have ended; class differences have been eliminated; individual and group rights are honored; and all sexism, racism, poverty, and crime have ended.

life-course persistent delinquency According to Moffitt, a kind of delinquency (1) committed by a small group of offenders who begin to behave antisocially during early childhood and continue their antisocial behavior through adolescence to adulthood and (2) caused by neuropsychological impairments.

looking-glass self A concept proposed by Cooley suggesting that the "self" is a product of interaction with others. The reactions of others to one's clothes, manners, and behaviors provide a reflection by which one evaluates oneself.

lower-class culture theory A theory (Miller) suggesting that delinquent behavior is the product of an integrated, lower-class culture in which youthful misconduct reflects unique, but widely shared, values among all lower-class people.

M

market society A society in which the economy is governed by the laws of supply and demand in the pursuit of personal economic gain.

Marxian theory A theory suggesting that modern capitalist societies are characterized by a perpetual struggle among the social classes and that the working class is exploited by the ruling class.

middle-class measuring rod The conventional standard for measuring the ability of every person, child or adult, to compete, work hard, and defer gratification in order to succeed.

middle-class subculture theory Body of theory suggesting that delinquency among middle-class children, while not serious because it includes such behaviors as drinking, petty theft, sexual transgressions, and automobile violations, is simply a subcultural variation of the worst features of middle-class, adult values and behaviors.

Mobilization for Youth An ambitious program located on the Lower East Side of New York City that was based on classic strain theory and was designed to improve education, provide jobs, organize the lower-class community, and provide specialized services to children and their families.

modern concept of childhood A Western concept suggesting that because children are not fully mature and are in need of special care, they require years of moral, physical, and intellectual quarantine and education before they can be permitted to become full-fledged adults.

moral crusaders A term used by labeling theorists to refer to influential people, also called "moral entrepreneurs," who create new rules and new agencies to enforce their views of morality.

moral rules Informal, usually nonlegal, rules believed essential to a society's welfare and to which strong feelings are attached.

mutual pledge system An old English system of crime control in which ordinary citizens were pledged by their social superiors to maintain law and order and to be responsible for their own actions and those of their neighbors.

N

National Crime Victimization Survey Conducted by the Bureau of the Census since the early 1970s, it is the most comprehensive victim survey in the United States.

nature versus nurture A phrase used to refer to the argument about whether behavior is determined by heredity (nature) or by culture and environment (nurture).

neglected children Children whose parents fail to provide proper care and guidance for them, although the parents are able to do so.

neoclassical theory A recent body of theory that contends that scientific criminology (positivism), with its belief in rehabilitation, is invalid and that society should return to the principles of classical criminology and should deal with crime by concentrating on the administration of justice and on punishing criminals.

nonindex offenses The less serious crimes listed in the *Uniform Crime Reports,* published by the FBI, including for juveniles, such offenses as running away, vandalism, drinking, drug abuse, nonaggravated assault, and disorderly conduct.

O

obey class A term derived from power-control theory that is used to indicate a subservient social class made up of workers who are under the supervision of someone else.

official delinquency The number and kinds of delinquent acts reported by police, courts, and other legal agencies. In contrast to law-violating behavior, which

may not be officially recorded, official delinquency is known and has been made a matter of record.

operant behavioral theory Body of psychological theory, associated with Skinner, suggesting that people learn the consequences of behavior from direct experience and that behavior will be repeated to the extent that the rewards for the behavior outweigh the punishments.

oral stage of development According to Freud, the developmental stage during which an infant is preoccupied with the mouth as the principal source of gratification, represented by such behaviors as sucking, swallowing, and kissing (before age 1).

outsiders A concept from labeling theory to indicate people who have become permanent pariahs after having been officially labeled as deviant.

P

parens patriae An English tradition, expressed in Latin and adopted in America, granting the power to the juvenile court to assume the role of parents in those cases where the care, custody, and discipline of children are at stake.

parole Supervised release of offenders, following confinement, permitting them to serve part of their sentences in the community providing they do not violate specific conditions.

Pennsylvania system A penal system created by the state of Pennsylvania in 1790 in which convicted felons were placed in solitary confinement—in cells where they saw no one else but an occasional guard or minister—for the duration of their sentences, as a method of reforming them.

phallic stage of development According to Freud, a stage of development during which a child's preoccupation is with his or her genitals, masturbation, and sexual play (ages 3–6).

pillory An instrument of punishment in colonial America in which offenders were held standing up, in the public square, with their head and hands locked in a large wooden frame.

placing out The 19th-century practice of sending dependent, neglected, and delinquent children from larger eastern cities to live with and work for midwestern farm families.

positive school of criminology An approach developed by theorists in the 1800s and 1900s contending that (1) lawbreaking is caused by personal or social forces over which the lawbreaker may not have rational control, (2) science should work to document those causes, and (3) lawbreaking can be controlled if lawbreakers are rehabilitated and the causes of their lawbreaking eliminated.

power-control theory Recent theory that, first, the social classes should be renamed "command" and "obey" classes and, second, that in the command class, the delinquency of males will exceed that of females, while in the obey class, the delinquency of the two genders will be approximately equal.

President's Committee on Juvenile Delinquency and Youth Crime A committee formed in 1961 by President John Kennedy to encourage communities to become more involved in trying to prevent delinquency by providing greater opportunities for lower class youths.

prevalence of law violation The proportion (or percentage) of young people that report having committed one or more delinquent acts.

preventive incapacitation The practice of banning, exiling, or confining chronic or suspected offenders, even though they already may have served sentences for their prior offenses and have not been convicted of new ones.

primary deviance A concept from labeling theory pertaining to the deviant behavior of a person who has neither been identified nor punished by anyone in authority.

probation A sentence whereby an adjudicated offender is released into the community in lieu of confinement, but must remain under the supervision of a probation officer and abide by special conditions imposed by the court.

property crimes The four crimes of the eight index crimes listed by the FBI in its *Uniform Crime Reports* that involve offenses against property rather than violent acts: burglary, larceny-theft, motor vehicle theft, and arson. In the National Crime Victimization Survey, the property crimes are burglary, motor vehicle theft, and theft of other property.

Provo Experiment An evaluated, experimental program for serious delinquents who, in lieu of institutionalization, lived at home, attended school, or were employed, and attended daily group meetings in which members analyzed problems, made decisions, and exercised controls.

psychodynamic control theory Theory that locates the sources of conformist or delinquent behavior in a person's psychological development and makeup and implies that delinquent behavior is due to the inability of the person to control his or her antisocial impulses.

R

radical theory Body of theory suggesting that delinquency is the product of a class struggle in which the ruling segments of society define what is delinquent behavior, create social conditions that make delinquents out of working-class people, and then devise legal machinery to control those people.

rational choice theory Neoclassical theory that argues that the principles of classical criminology can be used to construct scientific theories to explain delinquent behavior.

reaction formation Term used to describe the exaggerated, abnormal reaction by an individual against some highly desired, but psychologically repressed, objective, person, or thing. The individual appears to reject something he or she desperately wants.

recidivism The tendency among offenders to commit additional delinquent acts—to repeat offending.

reformatory Late 19th-century and 20th-century place of confinement in which young lawbreakers were to be classified according to need and then given a stern, but enlightened, regimen of education, physical training, and work.

rehabilitation A concept formulated in the Cincinnati Prison Congress of 1870 suggesting that, instead of punishment, counseling, education, training, parole, and other methods should be used to reform lawbreakers.

reintegrative shaming Reactions to deviance that (1) express strong disapproval of the deviant act and (2) attempt to reintegrate offenders back into the community of law-abiding citizens.

restorative justice Just deserts perspective that argues that true justice is achieved only when there is a concern with justice for both victims of crime and offenders.

restraint Term used to describe the belief that confinement in a prison or reformatory is the best method for reforming offenders.

retreatist subculture A term used by Cloward and Ohlin to describe the deviant values and traditions that arise among some juveniles in response to their failures in conventional pursuits, but that also favor retreat from the competitive struggle by turning to drug use.

retribution A key concept of classical and neoclassical theories suggesting that punishment vindicates the social order, is fair payment for a criminal act, and demonstrates the solemn condemnation of crime by members of the community.

retroflexive reformation A concept or process suggested by symbolic interactionist theory (Cressey) that suggests that if delinquents are engaged in trying to change other delinquents, they will be more likely to change themselves.

revised strain theory Theory recently formulated by Agnew that proposes that delinquency is caused not only by blocked opportunities to achieve the American Dream (which is the focus of classic strain theory), but also by blocked opportunities to achieve other goals, removal of positively valued stimuli (e.g., the death of a parent), and the presentation of aversive stimuli (e.g., parental abuse).

routine activities theory Rational choice theory that assumes a ready supply of motivated offenders and focuses instead on the ways in which routine daily activities affect the extent and distribution of opportunities for crime.

S

secondary deviance A concept from labeling theory indicating that a long process of labeling causes labeled persons to begin to accept definitions of themselves as deviant, and as a result they begin to behave accordingly. They become what they are labeled as being.

self-control theory Theory formulated by Gottfredson and Hirschi that crime and delinquency are due to low self-control and opportunities to violate the law.

self-reported law violation Illegal acts that usually are unknown to legal officials and are reported by respondents to social scientists studying unofficial delinquent behavior.

Silverlake Experiment An evaluated community experiment in Los Angeles in which serious delinquents lived in an ordinary home, attended a local high school, and analyzed problems and made decisions (including decisions regarding their release) in daily group meetings.

social bond A concept from social control theory (Hirschi) stressing the importance of a child's sensitivity and ties to others as barriers to delinquency. The social bond is composed of four elements: attachment, commitment, involvement, and belief.

social control theory Theory formulated by Hirschi that assumes that human nature is inherently antisocial and that the social order is characterized by consensus, but also suggests that one's bond to society rather than one's biological or psychological makeup makes the difference between conformist and delinquent behavior.

social disorganization A social condition characterized by value conflict, a high degree of social mobility, and absence of a shared sense of community.

socialization The process by which a child acquires the values, beliefs, attitudes, behaviors, and skills that are considered desirable by his or her parents and other people.

social learning theory Theory by Akers that delinquency is learned, just as law-abiding behavior is learned, in a process of differential reinforcement and imitation.

social order The totality of social relationships in any society and the values, rules, and social structures by which they are maintained.

social stratification A condition in which people are differentiated from one another in terms of wealth, power, and prestige and eventually are grouped with like persons into different social classes or strata.

sociology Behavioral science concerned with developing reliable knowledge about human social relations and the institutions, social structures, and interaction patterns that organize those relations.

stake in conformity A condition in which a young person feels that he or she has more to lose than to gain by committing a delinquent act and risking arrest.

status offense An act that violates the laws governing appropriate behavior for children and is illegal only for them.

stigmatization Reactions to deviance that (1) express strong disapproval of the deviant act and (2) involve little or no effort to forgive offenders or affirm the basic goodness of their character.

stocks An instrument of punishment, brought from Europe to America, in which the offender was held sitting down in the public square with his or her head and hands locked in a large wooden frame.

strain theory Theories that suggest that law violators are moral people who have violated the law because they have experienced stresses or strains that make it difficult for them to conform to the law.

subculture The values, norms, and practices that set any subgroup apart from the values, norms, and practices of the larger society of which the subgroup is a part.

subterranean traditions A concept from drift-neutralization theory suggesting that American culture is comprised of deviant beliefs that contribute to the formation of a delinquent subculture.

superego Freudian term used to indicate a person's conscience, the moral inhibitor of one's inborn, antisocial impulses.

swaddling Medieval practice in Europe and other societies in which an infant is deprived of movement by wrapping it in long, narrow strips of cloth.

symbolic interactionist theory A body of theory from sociology and psychology (Sutherland and Cressey, Mead, Cooley, Matza) that suggests that both the individual and his or her culture are flexible and constantly changing. One's interaction in a variety of small groups not only introduces new ways of seeing oneself, but produces new ideas and behaviors for the group.

T

techniques of neutralization Term introduced by Sykes and Matza to describe verbal statements used to disavow the implications of, if not justify, the commission of a crime.

theoretical integration Technique that involves combining the postulates of two or more theories to create a new theory.

theory competition Process in which theory development proceeds by using scientific tests to compare the predictive power of theories. The acceptability of a theory depends on how well it fares in such tests.

theory of differential association A symbolic interactionist theory formulated by Sutherland and Cressey that hypothesizes that (1) human nature is flexible and

changing; (2) a constantly changing social order provides both deviant and conformist guides for behavior; and (3) delinquent, no less than conformist, behavior is learned in a process of interaction and reinforcement from differential association in small, intimate groups.

U

Uniform Crime Reports Reports, compiled and published by the FBI, that provide annual estimates of crime and delinquency in the United States, based on arrest rates. Those reports provide data gathered from thousands of law enforcement agencies.

utilitarian philosophy The part of neoclassical theory that contends that legal punishment deters people from lawbreaking and protects society.

V

violent crimes The four crimes of the eight index crimes listed by the FBI in its *Uniform Crime Reports* that involve violence: murder and nonnegligent manslaughter, forcible rape, robbery, and aggravated assault. In the National Crime Victimization Survey, the violent crimes are rape/sexual assault, robbery, and nonsexual assault.

W

War on Poverty National effort conceived in the 1960s by the administration of John Kennedy and implemented by the Lyndon Johnson administration after Kennedy was assassinated. A federal program designed to prevent delinquency and other social problems by providing the poor with legitimate opportunities for success.

watch and ward People in ancient England who were expected to protect the community against fire during the night, guard the city gates against intruders, and arrest criminals between sunset and daybreak.

wet-nursing The care and suckling of infants, usually by poor women who are hired by wealthy women to care for their babies.

INDEX